Sticking It to the Man

CONTRIBUTORS

Scott Adlerberg

Steve Aldous

Eric Beaumont

Danae Bosler

Michael Bronski

Brian Coffey

David James Foster

Michael A. Gonzales

Molly Grattan

Brian Greene

Woody Haut

Alley Hector

Emory Holmes II

Maitland McDonagh

Iain McIntyre

Bill Mohr

Andrew Nette

Kinohi Nishikawa

Bill Osgerby

Jenny Pausacker

Gary Phillips

J. Kingston Pierce

Susie Thomas

Nicolas Tredell

Linda S. Watts

David Whish-Wilson

Sticking It to the Man

Revolution and Counterculture in Pulp and Popular Fiction, 1950 to 1980

Edited by **Andrew Nette** and **Iain McIntyre**

Sticking It to the Man: Revolution and Counterculture in Pulp and Popular Fiction, 1950 to 1980
Edited by Iain McIntyre and Andrew Nette

ISBN: 978–1–62963–524–8
Library of Congress Control Number: 2018949081

Cover by John Yates / www.stealworks.com
Interior design by briandesign

10 9 8 7 6 5 4 3 2 1

PM Press
PO Box 23912
Oakland, CA 94623
www.pmpress.org

Printed in the USA.

Contents

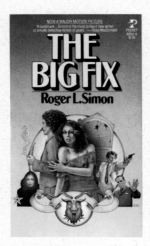

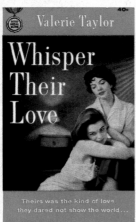

The Big Fix (Pocket, 1978)
Whisper Their Love (Gold Medal, 1957)
The Heart In Exile (Four Square, 1953)
Insurrection (Belmont, 1970)

A Total Assault on the Culture?

Pulp and Popular Fiction during the Long Sixties

As has been widely celebrated, derided, and mythologized, the 1960s was a time of significant social and political change across the world. Decolonization, second-wave feminism, mass opposition to conscription and the Vietnam War, Black Power, wildcat strikes, campus ferment, lesbian and gay liberation, a flood of "hip and groovy" consumer items, and the radical countercultural group the White Panthers' infamous call (channeling poet and social activist Ed Sanders) for "a Total Assault on the Culture by any means necessary, including rock 'n' roll, dope and fucking in the streets"—all of these swirled together in a surge of radical and rebellious ideas and practices challenging everyday life and existing structures. In some cases it transformed them, while in others it merely retooled them for continued exploitation and new forms of ennui. Given that many of the key social and political trends associated with the era extended back into the previous decade and didn't fully unfold until the mid-1970s, some have come to label this extended period the "long sixties."

Inspired by, and part of, these revolutionary times were a host of wild and challenging novels. While many of these became intrinsic to the ferment and zeitgeist of the period, potboilers by the likes of Jacqueline Susann, Harold Robbins, and Arthur Hailey continued to dominate sales, with only the occasional breakthrough of left-field works from Rita Mae Brown, Kurt Vonnegut, Alex Haley, and Gore Vidal. For every novel and novelist who became iconic, hundreds have been forgotten and whole genres written off.

This collection brings a number of overlooked, entertaining, and revealing texts and writers from 1950 to 1980 back into the light. It also explores how popular culture in the form of fiction dealt with and portrayed the radicalism and social shifts of the era. Unable to cover the entire world, we concentrate on the United States, Australia, and the UK, three countries which all had homegrown publishing industries dealing in mass-market paperbacks and original paperback titles. Although this collection considers books dealing

with dystopian and utopian near-future scenarios, the sheer volume of New Wave and other experimentation among science fiction will be covered in our next book, *Dangerous Visions and New Worlds: Radical Science Fiction, 1960 to 1985.*

Sticking It to the Man's contributors mainly focus on novels that were aimed at a mass audience, written in an accessible style, or in genres that were then highly popular. Much of this output could be labeled "pulp" and was written quickly by dozens of little-known authors eager for their next advance and for whom mainstream publishing success remained elusive. Some of the books were penned by scribes who were successful in making it from the margins into the bestseller lists. Some of have become accepted and analyzed in academic and "highbrow" literary circles long after their original publication. Some aimed for and received such recognition upon release. Many remain undeservedly obscure.

The long sixties was not just a time of social and political upheaval but also took in the heyday of the paperback novel. During the mid to late 1940s this format displaced pulp magazines as the primary fictional and printed form of mass entertainment. By the 1950s, novels increasingly made their debut as paperbacks, and because paperback publishers put out more titles and often paid better rates than their more highbrow competitors, this allowed a growing number of authors to make it into print, if not sustain a comfortable living. Even with television making increasing inroads, novels remained hugely popular. By the 1970s medium-to-large publishers could still expect the majority of their successful releases to sell in the tens of thousands or more. Alongside these major firms, smaller outfits eked out reasonable profits through the production of pornography and genre fiction. Much of their output represented pale imitations of the books their bigger rivals were producing, but some of it was superior due to their propensity to take a chance on something different or unusual. This fiction, particularly in the fields of crime, erotica, thrillers, and

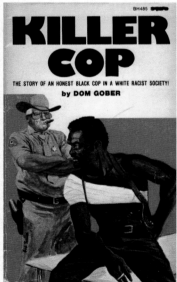

Bronson Blind Rage
(Manor Books, 1975)
Killer Cop (Holloway
House, 1975)

romance, retained the approach of the 1930s magazine-based pulp: quickly written and produced for cheap thrills with a focus on action, titillation, and the sensational, and little expectation or view to posterity.

The thousands of novels produced from the 1950s to 1980 that deal with social change remain fascinating for a number of reasons. On a historical, cultural, and sociological level they give the modern reader an insight into how political and social transformations and challenges were portrayed and understood by authors, publishers, and readers. Many, probably the majority, of the authors responsible for these novels had little if any connection to the movements or communities depicted in their fiction. In many cases, their portrayals were negative and inaccurate, filled with salacious, hyperbolic, and sometimes reactionary observations and material befitting the sensational nature of the publishers they worked for. Nonetheless, these writers dealt with issues and communities few others in popular culture would touch, at the very least giving readers a sense that alternatives existed. This was particularly so up until the early 1960s when the culturally conformist and, in the case of the United States, McCarthyist atmosphere of the 1950s was beginning to be challenged. And even the books that are made up of the most reprehensible rubbish still provide an insight into the social mores, fears, and mind-sets of earlier times.

These novels not only reflected their times but also shaped them, providing new opportunities to air and explore progressive ideas or, alternatively, to ridicule and oppose them. The challenges posed in much of the fiction covered in this book increased as the years rolled on and the ranks of working novelists were swelled by active participants of the long sixties' political and cultural ferment. Pulp, erotica, and mass market fiction publishers' incessant appetite and need for new work to meet consumer demand had long provided outsiders a chance to break into writing and, within the editorial confines of the time and particular firms, spaces within which to expound alternative views. New opportunities arose for women, people of color, LGBTQI writers, former convicts, leftists, and others to get their work into print. Often this was via firms owned and operated by conservative, older white men trying to increase sales by sourcing work that would connect them with rapidly changing audience tastes. Sometimes it was via new entrepreneurs or movement-based and -influenced presses, such as Australia's left-nationalist Gold Star and the U.S. lesbian feminist Daughters Inc., who sought to defy the mainstream and print works that could find no other home. The examinations of popular fiction contained here provide insights into the lives and work of a range of writers, the industries within which they labored, and the changes all were experiencing.

This book makes no pretense at being a definitive history of the period it covers. Rather it presents a variety of mass-market fiction snapshots of the assault on culture mounted in U.S., UK, and Australian society in the 1960s, and the reaction from other parts to this, with all the omissions such an overview by definition presents. Present are the civil rights movement and the growth of Black Power across all three countries, as well as the white backlash against it. There is the rise of the New Left and its offshoots, the anarchists and Maoists, Weatherman and the Angry Brigade, antiwar protesters and draft resisters, and Yippies blending "smash the state" rhetoric with the mirthful and cultural approach of the hippies to court media attention and "turn on the kids." Although female writers, especially women of color, had far less opportunity than their male counterparts to get their experiences published, this era saw the beginning of second-wave feminism and its concept that "the personal is political," which feminists wielded to fight dismissals of their issues as something to be sorted out "after the revolution." There are the growing demands of gays and lesbians for equality, tolerance, and liberation, both pre- and post-Stonewall.

These books offer portrayals of the maelstrom of militants, activists, protesters, and everyday people who consciously threw themselves into movements and causes or got caught up in them; those who, inspired by urban revolts and disillusioned with their inability to stop the Vietnam War and gain equality, called for revolution; and those who stayed in the struggle or dropped back into apolitical workaday lives and interrupted careers, got involved with cults and New Age spirituality, wiped themselves out with drugs and booze, or entered what was called the "long march through institutions" via unions, universities, and government. Many novels offer wild, cartoonish takes on the lives and times of such people, while others successfully portrayed and catered to communities previously ignored by the publishing industry. Some did both.

Also present is the fictional counter or backlash to these radical movements, characters who hail from

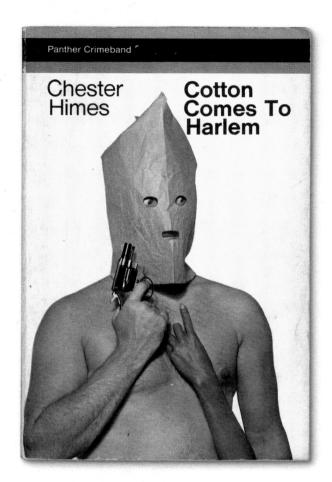

Cotton Comes to Harlem (Panther, 1967)
The Queer Frenzy (Tuxedo Books, 1962)

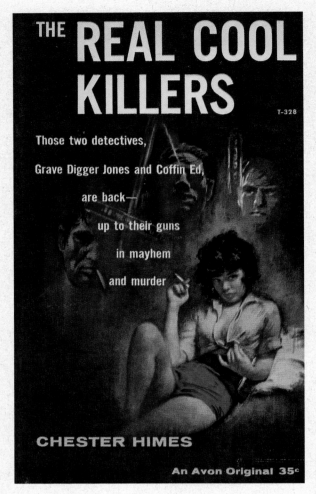

the intelligence services and law enforcement, those Vietnam veterans and disillusioned, often unhinged cops and members of the public who turned to vigilantism in the numerous lurid and over the top paperback men's adventure titles of the 1970s. All of them not only reflect the times but also popular fiction's insatiable demand for new material and plot lines.

Most importantly, the majority of the books covered within are entertaining. Some thrillingly so due to their fast-paced, action-packed, and unpredictable plots, chilling insights and heart wrenching pathos. Others are arresting and hilarious for all the wrong reasons. While some are only worthy of an amusing paragraph (our writers have read these all the way through to spare you the pain and effort), many are fascinating curios. This is despite, or more often because of, their blunderingly bad dialogue, woefully inaccurate "hep" patter, erratic plotting, and lack of continuity.

And then of course, there are the covers, of which we've included more than 350. Due to their lowbrow nature, few of these books were ever reviewed in major newspapers or magazines, instead relying on their lurid, eye-catching titles, images, and bylines to draw consumers passing through newsstands, chemists, barbers, supermarkets, and second-tier bookstores. And as with the stories they housed, the style and genius, or alternatively the pure awfulness, of these jackets unsurprisingly cuts through to the present.

Iain McIntyre and Andrew Nette

The Real Cool Killers (Avon, 1959)
Death Squad (Manor Books, 1975)

Survival Mode

The Crime Fiction of Chester Himes

Chester Himes became a crime fiction writer almost by accident. The creator of the Harlem Detective series, the man who gave us Coffin Ed Johnson and Grave Digger Jones, as tough and furious a pair of cops as you'll find, wrote his thrillers grudgingly at first and until middle age showed no inclination to write genre fiction.

He'd published his first book, *If He Hollers Let Him Go* (1945), when he was thirty-six years old. By then, he'd experienced ejection from Ohio State University—for a prank he'd pulled—and imprisonment for armed robbery. Arrested in Ohio in 1928, given a sentence of twenty to twenty-five years, he wound up doing seven and a half years behind bars, and it was in jail that he started writing fiction. He was still incarcerated when his short stories began appearing in prestigious magazines such as *Esquire*. After his parole, Himes embarked on novels, and his first five were social realist works focused on race relations. One, *Cast the First Stone* (1952), later published in unabridged form as *Yesterday Will Make You Cry* (1998), told a stark tale about prison. Writing these novels, Himes achieved modest success, but in the meantime he needed to support himself. Transplanted to Los Angeles, he was able to find work in Hollywood. But what started out well quickly turned sour, as Himes described in *Dear Chester, Dear John: Letters between Chester Himes and John A. Williams* (2008):

> I met the head of the reading department, I suppose they call it, you know, where they have people read the novels and write a one-page synopsis, which is all the producers read; they don't have time to read a book. So I was tried out by the young man who was head of this department at Warner Brothers. . . . Anyway, he offered me the job, and I was going to take it. I wrote a synopsis for *The Magic Bow*, a well-known book about Paganini, and submitted it. He said it was a good job and that they would employ me. And then— this is what *he* said: he was walking across the

lot one day and he ran into Jack Warner and told him, "I have a new man, Mr. Warner, and I think he's going to work out very well indeed." Warner said, "That's fine, boy," and so forth. "Who is he?" And he said, "He's a young black man." And Warner said, "I don't want no niggers on this lot."

Himes persisted, moving to New York City, taking different jobs, but by the early 1950s he had become convinced that sustaining oneself as a black writer in the United States was impossible, due to both a lack of money and respect from the literary establishment for writers of color. In 1953, like Richard Wright and James Baldwin before him, he left the United States and settled in Paris. Here he continued to have middling sales, but unlike in his native country, he was well respected among the literati. He would have regular café get-togethers with Wright, cartoonist Ollie Harrington, and others. But it was a meeting in 1956 that changed his writing life and ultimately led to the glowing reputation he has today.

In reaction to Himes's comments about his financial difficulties, French publisher Marcel Duhamel suggested that he write a crime novel. Duhamel had founded Editions Gallimard's Série noire line of crime fiction paperbacks, and in so doing had brought Raymond Chandler, Horace McCoy, and a good deal of American hard-boiled fiction to France. He knew Himes's work and had translated *If He Hollers Let Him Go* into French. But Himes saw himself as a literary writer, not one to demean himself by writing a thriller, and reacted with skepticism to the proposal. He said he had no idea how to write that type of book. He couldn't do it. Unfazed, Duhamel offered him a decent advance and wrote to him with advice that has since become famous:

> Get an idea. Start with action, somebody does something—a man reaches out a hand and opens a door, light shines in his eyes, a body lies on the floor, he turns, looks up and down

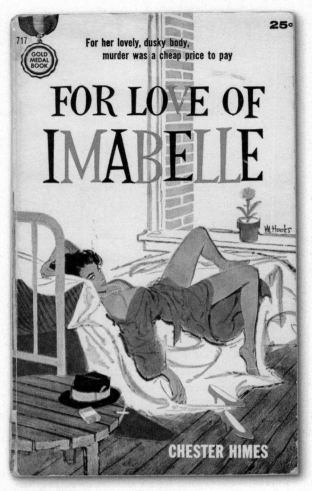

For Love of Imabelle
(Gold Medal, 1957)
For Love of Imabelle
(Dell, 1971)

the hall. . . . Always action in detail. Make pictures. Like motion pictures. Always the scenes are visible. No stream of consciousness at all. We don't give a damn who's thinking what—only what they're doing. Always doing something. From one scene to another.

After a false start or two, Himes produced *For the Love of Imabelle* (1957), later retitled *A Rage in Harlem*, the book that introduces Coffin Ed and Grave Digger Jones. In 1958 the book won the Grand Prix de la literature policière, the first time a non-French author won the award, and Himes's career as a crime novelist was launched.

In terms of style, Duhamel had recommended he use Hammett and Chandler as models. Himes seems not to have loved Chandler as a writer—in his talks with John A. Williams, he refers to "some of Raymond Chandler's crap out there"—but he did admire Hammett and also William Faulkner. The sense of absurdity in Faulkner, and how Faulkner mixed that absurdity with violence, struck a chord with Himes. For his second crime novel, *Il pleut des coups durs* (1959), published in English as *The Real Cool Killers*, he reread Faulkner's *Sanctuary* (1931) to immerse his mind in precisely that sort of overheated violence. And this time Coffin Ed and Grave Digger Jones were central characters in the story; he only added them to *A Rage in Harlem* when well into the book, at Duhamel's behest. The approach for Himes was now set, and though he'd never intended to, he found himself churning out what he'd once considered potboilers. He preferred to call his Harlem thrillers "domestic" novels rather than detective or crime or mystery novels, but whatever their label, over a fifteen-year span, he wrote ten of them, nine featuring Coffin Ed and Grave Digger. The one book they don't appear in is *Run Man Run* (1960), which centers on the actions of a white policeman. Harlem is a world unto itself in these works, and if Himes began writing them with the feeling that the thriller form was beneath him, he ended up reshaping the crime novel to meet his artistic and socially engaged needs.

From their first appearance, Grave Digger and Ed occupied an unusual position. Himes may have studied Hammett and Chandler and their hard-boiled ilk, but he rejected the model so common to the genre of the lone-wolf, self-employed investigator who reports only to his client. Grave Digger and Ed work in tandem, and scenes involving one without the other are rare. Himes may have felt he could not create a black equivalent to Sam Spade or Philip Marlowe, men who, though outsiders, have societal permission to move through different circles, moneyed and unsavory, all the while questioning people, busting heads, and solving mysteries. As blacks, Grave Digger and Ed don't have this privilege. They'd never get the calls for work from wealthy men like General Sternwood in *The Big Sleep* (1939). They need some form of state authority to sanction their crime investigations, so they have to be cops. But that means they are part of an organization and answer to superiors. These superiors are all white; in fact, from the little we see of other black cops in the books, it almost seems as if Grave Digger and Ed are the only black police officers in New York City. To put it bluntly, these two ace detectives are black cops working in the largest black section of New York, policing primarily blacks, but they serve a white power structure.

Through their skill, toughness, and obvious effectiveness, they've gained the respect of their superiors. In several books we see them talking to their main commander, Lieutenant Anderson, without deference. They relate to him, and to their peers in general, cop to cop. White or black, they all have a job to do, and it's a hard job, full of stress and danger. But at the same time, Coffin Ed and Grave Digger do see the racism around them. They recognize and comprehend the injustices and obstacles the power structure they work for has foisted on the world they inhabit. In a nutshell, Grave Digger and Ed bob and weave and work and sweat in a world filled with contradictions. They have job obligations that often conflict with their personal sympathies. They negotiate racial thickets Spade and Marlowe could not imagine. For most of the series, they perform a kind of social/professional balancing act, and it's fascinating to go through their books and see how they deal with these tensions.

To begin with, they brook no nonsense from anyone they police. Himes paints a picture of Harlem as unruly and frenetic, brimming with energy both creative and destructive, and it's telling that in the midst of this whirlwind, Grave Digger and Ed frequently try to get people to stand in straight lines. When they're introduced in *A Rage in Harlem*, the pair are outside a theater doing precisely this, and they enact a military type ritual we'll see them do in book after book.

If He Hollers Let Him Go (Ace, 1959)
If He Hollers Let Him Go (Signet, 1950)
If He Hollers Let Him Go (Signet, 1971)

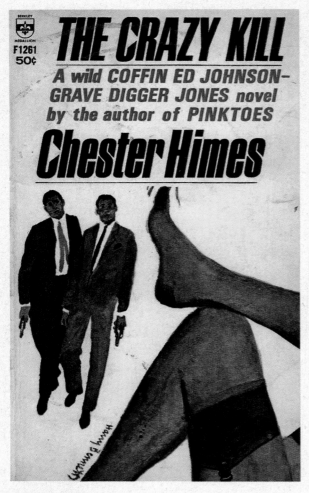

Whenever anyone moved out of line, Grave Digger would shout "Straighten up!" and Coffin Ed would echo "Count off!" If the offender didn't straighten up the line immediately, one of the detectives would shoot into the air. The couples in the queue would close together as though pressed between two concrete walls. Folks in Harlem believed that Grave Digger Jones and Coffin Ed Johnson would shoot a man stone dead for not standing straight in a line.

Clearly Digger and Ed represent the forces of order fighting against an ever-threatening chaos. But whose order are they defending? Who benefits by this order being maintained? In the first two books in the series, these questions are only slightly addressed, but we are made to see how Grave Digger and Ed view and battle the criminal activity around them. They understand that they can't keep the Harlem streets "clean," but they know their world intimately and want to keep it livable for the law-abiding. Since "colored folks didn't respect colored cops," they have to be harsh, and they prioritize whom they crack down on. For their own ends, they tolerate and work with "the established underworld catering to the essential needs of the people—gamekeepers, madams, streetwalkers, numbers writers, numbers bankers. But they are rough on purse snatchers, muggers, burglars, con men, and all strangers working on any racket." Religious con men particularly irk them, like Reverend Short in *The Crazy Kill* (whose "visions" are enhanced by the laudanum he takes), and as the books progress into the sixties, Ed and Digger encounter drug trafficking and fight against it with ferocity.

What's startling, especially by today's sensibilities, is just how violent the pair can get when doing their jobs. Grave Digger and Ed engage in police brutality, but at the time Himes was writing, their righteous violence, on the side of the law, was something new in black characters. Their violence, it must be said, is conducted against other blacks. It would have been interesting to see how Himes would have written a scene where the partners strike a white suspect as they strike black ones, but that doesn't happen. Himes himself may have realized that he'd be pushing credibility beyond the breaking point had he written a scene like that. But when it comes to the black Harlem residents, Grave Digger and Ed are equal-opportunity enforcers; they will hit women as readily as they hit men. In

The Crazy Kill (Berkley Medallion, 1966)
The Crazy Kill (Avon, 1959)

A Rage in Harlem, when Grave Digger comes across Imabelle sitting in the police precinct after other cops have taken her in, he recognizes her as the woman involved in the incident that got his partner's face splashed with acid. Losing it, he slaps her. He does it "with such savage violence it spun her out of her chair." Not done with her, he then drags her in cuffs to the whorehouse where the men he's pursuing have holed up, and he uses her as bait to draw the suspects out. When he says she'd better cooperate or he'll use her as a shield against the men's bullets, she believes him, and so do we.

Neither eases up in *The Crazy Kill*. In one scene, Grave Digger and Ed neck chop a suspect to stun him, then handcuff his ankles and handcuff his hands behind his back. With him constrained in this position, they hang him upside down from the top of a door "by his handcuffed ankles, so that the top part of the door split his legs down to the crotch." Both of them proceed to stick their heels into his armpits, pressing down slowly, and sure enough, the man answers the questions they're asking. One can only imagine how the exact same scene would read if two white cops were doing this to a black guy, but somehow when reading this one is not outraged at Grave Digger and Ed's behavior, and there's nothing in Himes's tone that indicates that one should be outraged. As readers, we're meant to be on their side, and already Himes is creating a portrait of them as men caught between disparate forces.

Just after the murder that sets *The Crazy Kill's* plot in motion, we are treated to a scene showing what they have to swallow. Grave Digger and Ed arrive at the crime scene along with their white cop colleagues, and in true Digger and Johnson style, they bark their "Straighten up…Count off" orders. It's not like Harlem folk love hearing that; one guy says, "Now we've got those damned Wild West gunmen here to mess up everything." But it's the smarmy attitude of the white cops that stands out here, and we get a look at the irritation that racial quips beget in the pair.

The sergeant said, winking at a white cop, "Herd 'em into the store, Jones, you and Johnson. You fellows know how to handle 'em."

Grave Digger gave him a hard look. "They all look alike to us, Commissioner—white, blue, black, and merino." Then turning to the crowd he shouted, "Inside, cousins."

By the time Grave Digger and Ed reach their sixth book, *The Heat's On* (published in France in 1961 and in the United States in 1966), they actually are brought up on disciplinary charges. The book's plot revolves around a heroin shipment that both the cops and a group of criminals are pursuing, though the plot itself is at once fractured and elliptical. By now, through a series of novels ever more purposely chaotic, Himes has all but dispensed with the linear, orderly plot one gets in conventional crime fiction. He gives us a book that always seems about to explode into chaos. There are lots of characters, a violence level that's a touch surreal, and a narrative structure that jumps around in time. The reader hangs on to every plot point he grasps, afraid to lose the story's thread, fearful that incoherence will set in. Of course, in Himes's skillful hands, incoherence never sets in, and the reader sees events through Digger and Ed's eyes because they too, amid the shoot-outs and murders and car chases and exploding houses, are trying to piece together what is going on. It's a kind of authorial magic Himes works— he puts you in the shoes of his implacable pair and makes them seem like the sane ones in a world gone completely mad—and it's a magic present from the novel's first chapter, when Ed and Digger arrive on a scene involving a black dwarf, a black albino giant, white firefighters, and white cops.

Out in the street, the firefighters and cops are in a charged confrontation with the dwarf and albino. Grave Digger and Ed come driving up. At once they size up the situation, which the white law enforcement was unable to do. Coffin Ed manages to catch hold of the dwarf, and Grave Digger punches him in the stomach. No questions asked, no hesitation. The dwarf winds up vomiting up "half-chewed packets of paper" that Grave Digger collects with his handkerchief. These, we'll find out, contain heroin, but the scene has only gotten started. The dwarf faints but the firemen continue to prod the huge albino, who seems like a gentle halfwit. Insistent on knowing why the albino rang the fire alarm that drew out his men, the fire captain begins to rough him up. Coffin Ed and Grave Digger try to intervene, saying that the albino is answering his questions. Things escalate to the point where the fire captain hits the giant "in the back with the flat of his ax" and a white cop, taking out his revolver, warns Digger, "Keep out of this." Coffin Ed and Grave Digger draw their guns. Violence among NYPD cops and firemen, black against white, nearly results, as Himes

The Heat's On (Panther, 1968)
Chester Himes, author image from the back cover of 1959 Ace
edition, *If He Hollers Let Him Go*

again underlines the torturous position the partners inhabit. Without any mercy they've taken down a criminal they viewed as destructive to their world, while trying to shield from racist authorities someone not deserving of nasty treatment. The scene still has not concluded, though. When the albino, pounding his way through a bunch of firefighters, makes a desperate run for it, Grave Digger and Ed draw apart to let him through. But will the other cops simply let him escape? Fat chance, and Himes knows it:

> Automatically, as though the target were irresistible, a cop drew a bead with his service revolver. At the same instant, as though part of the same motion sprung from another source, Coffin Ed knocked his arm up with the long nickel-plated barrel of his own revolver. The cop's pistol went off. The giant seemed to fly from the roof of the prowl car and crashed into the foliage of the park.
>
> For a moment everyone was sobered by the sound of the shot and the sight of the giant crashing to earth. All were gripped by the single thought—the cop had shot him. Reactions varied; but all were held in momentary silence.
>
> Then Coffin Ed said to the cop who had fired the shot, "You can't kill a man for putting in a false fire alarm."
>
> The cop had only intended to wing him, but Coffin Ed's rebuke infuriated him.

This exchange has an eerie prescience for people in the U.S. today who have seen or heard of many incidents where something minor—selling bootleg cigarettes, running from a traffic stop, resisting a random search and frisk—has led to the shooting of an unarmed black male, and only because of Coffin Ed's action does the albino not take a bullet. The albino gets away, but not before we see how these white police view their two black colleagues. While two uniformed cops restrain the angry one, stopping the hostilities, the angry one says, "These two black bastards are crazy."

It turns out that the punch Grave Digger gave the dwarf ruptured his spleen and killed him, and since both he and Coffin Ed were involved, both face charges of "unwarranted brutality." The scene that ensues has an ironic edge, as the two black cops defend their actions to a white commissioner, other white police officials, and a white assistant DA. Coffin Ed and Grave Digger explain how the business of drug dealing works in Harlem. When they are reminded that they are primarily peace officers, their duty being to keep the peace and let the courts punish offenders, Coffin Ed asks, "Peace at what price?" and Grave Digger adds, "You think you can have a peaceful city letting criminals run loose?"

In the United States, no conservative law and order politician (read white politician) would put it any differently. The criminals he'd have in mind are urban blacks. But Himes frames the exchange so that it's hard to disagree with his blunt pair. Unlike the assistant DA, who says they killed a man "suspected of a minor crime," they see nothing minor about drug peddling, and Grave Digger goes on a verbal rampage describing the scourge of drugs in his precinct. Heroin "has murdered more people than Hitler" he says, and there should be no going easy on anyone involved, including the street-level peddlers. They're the ones who get people hooked, Digger yells, but the assistant DA says that Digger and Ed should be indicted. He claims that the public is indignant over all the police brutality in Harlem, and it's decided, for the time being, that the two will be suspended. The meeting over, Grave Digger and Ed are left standing with their friend among the bunch, Lieutenant Anderson. Their boss assures them nothing will come of the indictment threat and says, "It's just the newspaper pressure. . . . The papers are on one of their periodic humanitarian kicks."

As usual, what comes back is a sharp response:

"Yeah, humanitarian," Grave Digger said bitterly. "It's all right to kill a few colored people for trying to get their children an education, but don't hurt a mother-raping white punk for selling dope."

Lieutenant Anderson winced. As accustomed as he was to these two colored detectives' racial connotations, that one hurt.

★

Other cops and the residents of Harlem may call Grave Digger and Ed crazy, but readers know that the partners are crazy like foxes. At the end of *The Heat's On*, Coffin Ed has a few drinks at a bar with his wife and Lieutenant Anderson, and in a rare, emotion-revealing moment Coffin Ed talks about the thought process behind his and Digger's policing:

What hurts me most about this business is the attitude of the public toward cops like me and Digger. Folks just don't want to believe that what

we're trying to do is make a decent peaceful city for people to live in, and we're going about it the best way we know how. People think we enjoy being tough, shooting people, and knocking them in the head.

No insanity here, but what if you do have a cop with mental problems whose underlying intentions are malicious? And what if that cop is white and his victims are black? What kind of recourse do black people have if a trusted representative of the power structure is a malevolent force? These are questions asked in the one Harlem thriller Himes wrote that doesn't feature Grave Digger and Ed, his 1966 book *Run Man Run*.

The book's plot is straightforward but terrifying. Off-duty detective Matt Walker gets drunk one night and can't remember where in midtown Manhattan he parked his car. In the predawn hours, he comes upon a black hotel porter at work, getting the hotel restaurant ready for the day. He tells the man about his car, and the porter, while friendly, is lightly mocking of him. "Haw-haw-haw! Here he is, a detective like Sherlock Holmes, pride of the New York City police force, and you've gone and got so full of holiday cheer you've let some punk steal your car."

As Stephen Soitos points out in *The Blues Detective: A Study of African American Detective Fiction* (1996), Himes's reference here to Sherlock Holmes is hardly accidental. Himes is setting a tone that serves to undercut what a reader expects from a detective novel. Instead of a figure bringing reason and order and the presumption of safety, Matt Walker becomes the novel's murderer. He shoots the chatty porter for no other reason than he's drunk and frustrated and racist (he shoots him because he can), and right afterward, he kills another porter who comes across the murder scene. A third worker there, also a witness, manages to escape with a bullet wound, and the rest of the novel switches back and forth between the limited third-person perspectives of Walker and the survivor, hunter and hunted. The survivor, Jimmy, is a college-educated black man, intelligent and articulate, and when questioned by police about what happened, he never expresses any doubt about who shot him. He never deviates from his story. But such is the way of the world that when a person accuses a cop of coldblooded murder, let alone a black accusing a white, the odds are long that they will be believed. In *Run Man Run*, it's not

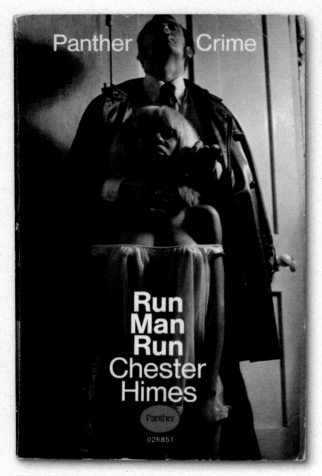

only the police brass that mistrust Jimmy's story; his own girlfriend voices incredulity.

Run Man Run is less stylized and hectic than the Grave Digger and Ed books. While those are chock-full of outrageous characters, their foibles and quirks described hyperbolically, *Run Man Run* has a tone more consistent with sober realist fiction. This tone fits because Himes is not trying for laughs in this book. He aims for straight-up menace and suspense and the social critiques he supplies come in undisguised form. Though he's the murderer, Walker has enough clout in the police force to get the double homicide case assigned to him, and he uses his privilege and power to taint evidence and attack Jimmy's credibility. He even seeks out and seduces Jimmy's black girlfriend, eliciting information from her while in her bed. It doesn't take long for Jimmy to realize he will have to rely on himself to extricate himself from his predicament, and he has cutting words for those who put his fear down to paranoia. When his girlfriend says that the newspapers are "saying that maybe you've got a persecution complex," Jimmy makes the argument that one person's persecution complex is another's survival mechanism:

> Goddamn right! Anytime a Negro accuses a white man of injuring him in any way, the first thing they say is he's got a persecution complex. He's blaming it on the power structure. Bullshit! I suppose it was a persecution complex that got old Luke and Fat Sam shot full of holes.

Only in Harlem does he find a feeling of safety, a refuge, and this is something that strikes a Himes reader as amusing. Through the Grave Digger and Ed books, Harlem has been a place that is wild and dangerous. Yet it's not these for Jimmy:

> There in the heart of the Negro community he was lulled into a sense of absolute security. He was surrounded by black people who talked his language and thought his thoughts; he was served by black people in businesses catering to black people; he was presented with the literature of black people. Black was a big word in Harlem. No wonder so many Negro people desired their own neighborhood, he thought. They felt safe; there was safety in numbers.
>
> The idea of a white maniac hunting him down to kill him seemed as remote as yesterday's

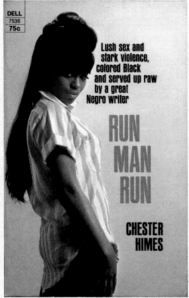

Run, Man, Run (Panther, 1969)
Run, Man, Run (Dell, 1969)

dream. If he had seen Walker at the moment he would have walked up to him and knocked out his teeth.

It was a funny thing, he thought. He'd told the truth about the murders to a number of people. He'd told his girl; he'd told the D.A.; he'd told the lawyer. . . . And none of them believed him. But he could walk up to any colored man in sight on that corner and tell him, and the man would believe him implicitly.

At his wit's end, Jimmy buys a handgun through illicit channels. Though uncomfortable with the weapon, he feels he must arm himself. His decision builds the novel's suspense, and the wider implication of his purchase is clear: because black people can't rely on the lawful authorities to protect them, they have to take matters into their own hands in regard to self-defense. Sometimes, unfortunately, it's kill or be killed. In the context of the civil rights movements of the 1960s, Himes seems to be aligning himself more with Malcolm X–type thinking (hit back when hit) than that of Martin Luther King (peaceful resistance at all costs). Jimmy has no criminal record and no zeal for violence—he is, in essence, a cerebral individual—but white authority doesn't distinguish between a "ghetto" black and an intellectual black. At bottom, for the power structure, black is black. You can be a black person who routinely flouts the law or, like Jimmy, a black person who has played by the so-called rules. In the end, no matter where you come from or what you have done, if a white power figure has it in for you, your very life could become endangered.

This unsparing view, unleavened by humor in *Run Man Run*, carries over to the penultimate (and last completed) Grave Digger and Ed book, *Blind Man with a Pistol* (1969). Here we have a novel that shows Himes getting, if anything, more radical and anguished with age. Where *The Heat's On* has a plot that barely hangs together, *Blind Man with a Pistol* takes narrative chaos further. A white man apparently trolling for homosexual sex is murdered, and Grave Digger and Coffin Ed get the case. Their investigation leads them nowhere. Simultaneously, various factions vie for political dominance in Harlem. Marcus Mackenzie, "pure in heart" but not very bright, aided in his efforts by a white Swedish woman, wants the blacks to rise and has an integrated group of white and black marchers behind him. Doctor Moore extols black power and yells his

political views from street corners while running a brothel and trying to raise funds from Harlem residents. Prophet Ham runs The Temple of Black Jesus and urges his flock to do violence. "I ain't a race leader," he says. "That's the trouble with you so-called Negroes. You're always looking for a race leader. The only place to race whitey is on the cinder track. . . . I'm a soldier. . . . We got to fight, not race."

Himes jumps around from scene to scene, character to character, more than ever. He does not connect the dots, and no pretense is made at creating a comprehensible story. Even chronology is hazy: it's a challenge to determine when events are happening in relation to other events. The Harlem he delineated that was semilawless but colorful, overflowing with humor and eccentric creativity, has transformed into something else. In *Blind Man with a Pistol* nearly everyone seems angry and bitter and unfulfilled. Violence is rampant. The novel has an almost absurdist feel, and Grave Digger and Ed, once so potent, seem powerless. When the three competing political movements all stage marches on Nat Turner Day, July 15, honoring the Virginia slave who led a massive slave rebellion in 1831, they run into each other and start clashing. Racial tensions and racial hatred explode; a riot erupts. In the midst of this are Ed and Grave Digger, and how far they have come from being the enforcers who commanded respect and fear in their district:

> They had got to their own feet . . . and had begun fistfighting their opponents, back to back. Their long holstered pistols were exposed, but they had orders not to draw them. They couldn't have drawn them anyway, in the rain of fists showering over them. . . .
>
> "One . . ." Grave Digger panted.
>
> After an interval Coffin Ed echoed, "Two . . ."
>
> Instead of saying "three," they covered their heads with their hands and broke for the sidewalk, ploughing through a hail of fists. But once through, having gained the sidewalk in front of the jewelry store, no one tried to follow. Their opponents seemed satisfied with them out of the way . . .

The pair who used to count off like drill sergeants to make others get in line can't even finish counting to three themselves. In their impotence, all they can do is stand by and watch as the violence spreads and looting breaks out. Men and women pillage the stores they

Blind Man With A Pistol
Chester Himes

'The greatest find in American crime fiction since Raymond Chandler' THE OBSERVER

Panther

586 03507 9

Blind Man with a Pistol (Panther, 1969) The retitled edition of *Blind Man with a Pistol, Hot Day, Hot Night* (Signet, 1975)

pass every day. Harlem has become a self-destructive place feeding on itself, destroying itself, and the true societal powers outside Harlem that the various Black Power leaders have been ranting about go untouched.

The novel's final pages concentrate on the bleak and absurd. Realizing that they're aging, Grave Digger and Ed analyze the youth around them and find that young people are naive and idealistic. While the partners' generation grew up in the Depression and fought in World War II "under hypocrites against hypocrites," as Grave Digger puts it, never believing the lies of white people, the new generation believes the propaganda saying that equality is coming. They have genuine expectations. But equality hasn't yet come and doesn't seem to be coming anytime soon, so young people feel betrayed. As Ed says, that's why riots erupt.

In their relations with Captain Anderson, white but once something of a friend, Coffin Ed and Grave Digger have grown distant, partly because their superior officer has steered them away from suspects and clues that might help them solve their case. It's never made clear why Anderson has done this, but it seems as if he has ties to corrupt people behind the scenes, politicians or crime figures, or both. When he sends them one morning to a bookstore to check out the Black Muslims, Coffin Ed snarls, "If somebody was to shit on the street, you white folks would send for the Black Muslims." Anderson, upset, says that "Once upon a time you guys were cops—and maybe friends: now you're black racists."

Not quite, but Grave Digger and Ed do have more political conversations in *Blind Man with a Pistol* than in any of the previous books. Could a reason for this be the futility they've experienced this time around? Unable to solve their murder case, the two vent their frustrations near the novel's end by shooting rats in a tenement building. "Hey! Hey! Rat!" Coffin Ed calls to one, "like a toreador trying to get the attention of his bull." To see the duo that had been so feared and impactful in earlier novels reduced to blasting vermin with their long-barreled, police-issued guns is a mordant commentary for sure, but *Blind Man with a Pistol* saves its most corrosive scene for its grand finale.

A white man taunts and slaps a blind black man in a subway car. The blind man thinks it was a black man who hit him until the white man uses language that tells the blind man he is white. The black man takes out a .45 caliber pistol. He fires it, shattering a window. All hell breaks loose in the subway car and a black woman shrieks, "BLIND MAN WITH A PISTOL!" What ensues is a vision of indiscriminate violence and total communication breakdown, a scene of terror and the ridiculous mixed. Cops, witnesses, the subway passengers, and the blind man himself do a bloody dance where no one is in sync with anyone else. Lieutenant Anderson calls in Grave Digger and Ed to quell yet another riot, and the conversation they have about the situation ends the novel:

> "Can you men stop the riot?" he demanded.
>   "It's out of hand, boss," Grave Digger said.
>   "All right. I'll call for reinforcements. What started it?"
>   "A blind man with a pistol."
>   "What's that?"
>   "You heard me, boss."
>   "That don't make any sense."
>   "Sure don't."

It's a world where a misunderstanding has set off a bloodbath, where the blind terrorize the misinformed. And the people who represent order, who try to keep the lid on the powder keg, can see that they make no difference. This is the book Himes published in 1969, reflecting what he saw in the U.S. then, and it's instructive to remember that it's a mere decade after he wrote *A Rage in Harlem*. He had come a long way from that first crime novel, both in how his themes had darkened and how he'd stopped using anything resembling traditional detective fiction architecture. But where would Himes go from here?

There's a fascinating exchange about halfway through *Blind Man with a Pistol* that leads directly to Himes's final (and unfinished) Grave Digger and Ed book, *Plan B*. Sitting at a lunch counter in Harlem, the two discuss Malcolm X:

> "You know one thing, Digger. He was safe as long as he kept hating the white folks—they wouldn't have hurt him, probably made him rich; it wasn't until he began including them in the human race they killed him. That ought to tell you something."
>   "It does. It tells me white people don't want to be included in a human race with black people. Before they'll be included they'll give 'em the

whole human race. But it don't tell me who you mean by they."
>   "*They*, man, *they*. They'll kill you and me too if we ever stop being colored cops."

Digger and Ed seem to have reached the conclusion that integration, when all is said and done, will never happen. And their progression from controlled anger in the service of the law to utter disillusion with American society as a whole matches the thinking of their creator. *Plan B* is the work of a man who seems to believe that racial justice through peaceful means is a pipe dream and that only violent revolution by blacks against whites will change the established order. Himes said as much in a 1970 interview with John A. Williams, telling his fellow novelist that "in any form of uprising, the major objective is to kill as many people as you can, by whatever means you can kill them, because the very fact of killing them and killing them in sufficient numbers is supposed to help you gain your objectives." *Plan B* is his novel about this revolution and its possible consequences.

The most violent of his books, *Plan B* has a loose plot that follows the doings of one Tomsson Black, a black man of humble origins. Through a series of unlikely events, he becomes a wealthy revolutionary masquerading as a black businessman. Rich white people befriend and financially support him during his rise to respectability, and he uses their money to buy huge stocks of weapons that he funnels to blacks for his uprising. The novel alternates between historical chapters tracing Tomsson's background and contemporary chapters in Harlem where the revolution breaks out. Grave Digger and Coffin Ed come into it when they respond to what seems like an ordinary killing in Harlem among junkies. At the apartment where a heroin addict killed a woman friend of his, they find a high-powered rifle that was mysteriously sent to the man along with an incendiary note. The note promises that "FREEDOM IS NEAR!!!!" and tells the weapon's recipient to learn how to use the gun, wait for instructions, and not inform the police. *Plan B* is part thriller, part satire, part political screed. As blacks perpetuate random and horrific violence against whites and whites retaliate thunderously against blacks, Himes peppers his narrative with acid observations:

> It was then, as both escape and therapy that he [Tomsson Black] had begun moving in the circles

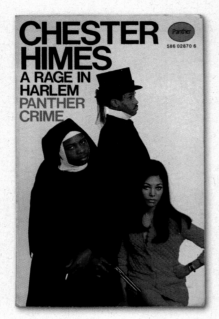

A Rage in Harlem
(Panther, 1969)
Plan B (University
Press of
Mississippi, 1993)

of Northern white liberals who needed the presence of a black face to prove their liberalism.

And there were some whites who went about crying publicly ... touching blacks on the street as if to express their suffering through contact, and sobbingly confessing their sorrow and begging the blacks' forgiveness. There were a few extremists who even bent over and offered their asses for blacks to kick, but blacks weren't sure whether they were meant to kick them or kiss them, so in their traditional manner, they cautiously avoided making any decision at all.

The citizens of other nations in the world found it difficult to reconcile this excessive display of guilt by America's white community with its traditional treatment of blacks. What the citizens of the world didn't understand was that American whites are a traditionally masochistic people, and their sense of guilt toward their blacks is an integral part of the national character.

There's an over-the-top quality to this novel, an apocalyptic tone. Himes pours on the violence and depicts the carnage with gusto. Blacks massacre white men, women, and children. Whites talk about bringing back slavery and castrating black males. They enlist big-game hunters to go on "The Black Hunt." Blood flows in the streets. Blacks are unintimidated and continue killing whites. It's as if Himes is indulging in a fantasy long held and until now somewhat suppressed: the ultimate revenge of American blacks against American whites for the legacy of racism and injustice. No nonviolent method of protest has achieved racial equality, so the only option left is violence. At the very least, even with whites striking back, using a tank to level a Harlem house, lynching a man at a concert in Central Park, violence offers black people consolation; they have the satisfaction of seeing white people in constant fear. The disorder spread through the secret machinations of Tomsson Black provides for a catharsis no sit-in or march can create.

Or does it? Is that catharsis false, leading nowhere? For all Himes's expressed belief in the necessity of armed insurrection, *Plan B* betrays an ambivalence in him. For starters, the insurrection he lays out, whatever Tomsson Black's original plans for it, deteriorates fast into haphazard violence. People given weapons to use, with virtually no one to guide them, without an overarching plan among them, run amuck. Blacks are no different than whites in this aspect. Near the end of the novel, Tomsson confesses that he should have anticipated this. The uprising he envisioned has spun out of his control. Blacks committing their murderous acts against whites has resulted in the United States becoming a field of pandemonium. How this will end even Tomsson Black can't predict, but he feels that he must keep distributing guns and "let maniacal, unorganized, and uncontrolled blacks massacre enough whites to make a dent in the white man's hypocrisy."

As I mentioned, Himes never finished *Plan B*. One wonders whether Himes stopped working on it because he'd written himself into a cul-de-sac. How do you end such a book? Reconciliation after all the violence would seem implausible, so what do you do instead? Have the whites exterminate the blacks? The blacks wipe out the whites? Does Himes really think mayhem like this will lead to racial equality, or is he saying that uncoordinated violence doesn't work and will never help blacks attain their goals? Maybe Himes is suggesting that whatever blacks do, they have to get their numbers in order before they mount any serious offensives against the white power machine. It's not violence itself that Himes seems to frown on, but violence that squanders opportunity and becomes misdirected. Considered in this light, *Plan B* reads as an extension of the ideas explored in *Blind Man with a Pistol*—only in the later book Himes is willing to cut loose entirely and get didactic.

Plan B was both Himes's last Harlem detective novel and his last novel overall. It's his most nightmarish work, and we are left with nothing comforting or hopeful at the end. To cap it off, he goes where only a handful of detective story series writers have gone and kills off his popular protagonists. The storm of racial violence that has become the United States sweeps up and engulfs both Digger and Ed. That Digger, over an ideological disagreement, shoots Ed through the head comes as a shock to the reader, and this shock is accentuated when Tomsson Black kills Digger because "he knew too much." Himes proves uncompromising to the end, and reader expectations be damned. You may close *Plan B* feeling pissed off and anxious (because Himes killed Grave Digger and Ed, because of the book's lack of closure), but after a minute's reflection you think that Himes wouldn't be a bit displeased if he knew he left you feeling troubled. All he did in book after book was probe and examine worlds of trouble, and, as entertaining as he can be, he doesn't play. Laughs come with stings, pleasures with pain. It's the way of the world, the way of Chester Himes.

Scott Adlerberg

Fictions about Pulp

Gay Pulp in the Years before Stonewall

Pulp novels: everyone knows the covers. With their garish colors, their cartoonish mock-heroic studs, and tempting titles such as *The Butt Boy*, *Dirt Road Cousins*, *Three on a Broomstick*, and *Up Your Pleasure*, they're old-time gay male iconography for a new, younger generation of homosexuals. They are artifacts from the past that have acquired new, ironic meanings for our time and now grace refrigerator magnets, postcards, and address books. But these book covers—and the novels they luridly trumpeted—are more than camp remnants or a curious slice of gay life past. They are an integral aspect of gay male culture and gay history that is as vital as—indeed inseparable from—our fight for legal equality and personal freedom. They are the records—albeit fictional ones, often seen through the peculiar lenses of their times—of how gay men lived, thought, desired, loved, and survived. Even with their exaggeration, high-queen dramatics, silly (even naive) eroticism, and sometimes internalized homophobia, they give us a glimpse of what it meant to be gay in the tumultuous years before Stonewall.

By the 1950s the publishing industry in the United States had reached a new level of production. The printing and distribution of cheaply produced and cheaply priced paperback novels, which had begun full force in the 1930s, was at a new high. Their eye-catching, provocative covers created and defined a new artistic and marketing genre. Screaming damsels in distress represented a favorite motif, as did risqué clothing for both women and men. While mystery, crime, romance, and action stories benefitted enormously from these graphic designs, authors from Shakespeare to Aldous Huxley to Edna Ferber also found a new readership.

This new advance in the publishing world, particularly in the late 1940s and the 1950s also included a huge number of original novels focusing on illegal or taboo sex—adultery, prostitution, rape, interracial relationships, lesbianism, male homosexuality—topics that were, in the words of the jacket-copy writers, "controversial," "explosive," "shocking," and ready to "reveal the sordid truth in a way you have never read before."

Often these books traded on current social obsessions and "headline news"—juvenile delinquency, motorcycle gangs, wife swapping, teen drug use, college scandals, mob racketeering, suburban malaise, and the erotic dangers of psychoanalysis. Collectively they represent, beneath a veneer of enticing exploitation, a compendium of the not-so-hidden preoccupations and fears of the tempestuous and socially unstable postwar years.

A prominent and best-selling subgenre of these exploitation paperback originals dealt with male and female homosexuality. With jacket copy that spoke in easily decipherable code about "the world of twilight lovers, the love society forbids," and "the hidden shame of . . . secret love," these books promised to expose the "hidden world of the third sex."

While there were still many ways that books with sexual material could be marginalized—primarily through church-sponsored national pressure and watchdog groups such as the National Organization for Decent Literature and Citizens for Decent Literature—one of the major thresholds in the public dissemination of gay-themed books was a series of court cases that essentially broke down the major legal barriers for the publication of explicitly sexual materials. While these largely concerned reputable publishing houses, their effect on smaller publishers was enormous. Established publishers such as the Paris-based Olympia Press and Grove Press in New York, both of whom had mounted attacks on censorship and customs laws, were now freer to publish work, usually of high literary quality.

In 1959 a California state judge declared that Allen Ginsberg's *Howl* was not obscene and that San Francisco's City Lights bookstore was not in violation of the law for selling a copy of it. That same year, the U.S. Supreme Court reversed a New York court's decision to suppress a non–sexually explicit French film version of D.H. Lawrence's *Lady Chatterley's Lover* because the First Amendment precluded the government from banning the advocacy of "immoral ideas." Later that

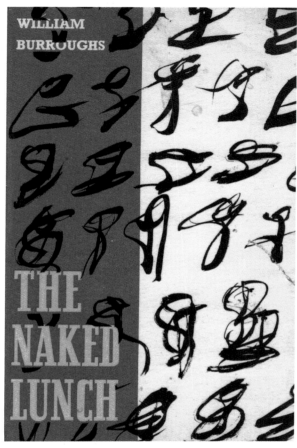

The Naked Lunch (Olympia Press, 1959)

year, the U.S. Postal Service lost a suit they brought to the U.S. District Court for the Southern District of New York against Grove Press's publication and use of mail to transport the first paperback American edition of Lawrence's book. The court claimed that the book, because of its literary merit, was not obscene, and the case was so clear-cut that it was the last time the post office attempted such suits.

In 1964, the U.S. Supreme Court ruled after a series of differing state court decisions that Henry Miller's 1934 novel *Tropic of Cancer*, published by Grove, was not obscene, and instituted the concept of a national standard for judging obscenity that would do away with publishers having to fight censorship on a state-by-state or city-by-city basis. In 1966, the Supreme Court ruled that John Cleland's 1749 *Fanny Hill: The Memoirs of a Woman of Pleasure*, published by George Putnam and Sons, was not obscene because it was not utterly without redeeming social value. The protracted trial of Grove Press's 1962 publication of William Burroughs's

Naked Lunch in Boston ended in 1966 and was the last major case limiting censorship in the United States.

The immediate effect of these judicial decisions was startling and allowed a new group of erotic publishers to begin operation. Well financed and connected to extensive and reliable distribution networks these new companies published hundreds of titles every month, which became readily available in a variety of venues. The majority of these titles were heterosexual in content, and books that featured lesbian content were aimed explicitly at the heterosexual male reader. But within this new publishing framework there were publishers and separate lines within the larger houses whose books were aimed at gay male audiences including Brandon House, Greenleaf Classics, Regency Books, Pendulum Books, French Line, Award Books, and others. What's more, the majority of these books were written by gay men for a gay male readership eager to buy anything with homosexual context. While not technically pulps, these books were a visceral and visible marker of personal as well as group identity. Because they reached a far greater number of men than those who had read or even been aware of the earlier literary novels, they played a large role in expanding gay men's experience of community, and in reassuring men who desired sex with other men that they were not alone.

It is a commonplace belief that in the 1950s and '60s homosexuality was a taboo topic, that it was never spoken about or was discussed only in hushed tones. This is completely untrue: as these books attest, homosexuality was very much in the public consciousness. If anything, it was more integrated into popular culture than it would be in the late '60s and early '70s. This is not to say that the public discourse about homosexuality in the '50s was more enlightened or tolerant—although many of these writings are surprising for their frankness and level of acceptance—but it was understood and discussed in very different ways.

While the homophile movements of the 1950s placed homosexuality in a broader (reformist) political context, it was the later gay liberation movement's political and social advances that transformed U.S. (and world) culture and made life immeasurably better for lesbians and gay men. But this movement also created a deep rupture in how homosexuality was conceptualized and represented in mainstream culture. Certainly homosexuality was profoundly stigmatized and pathologized during the 1950s, a situation that often created enormous hardships in the

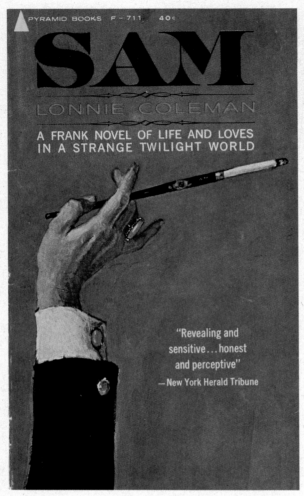

Sam (Pyramid Books, 1960)

When I began assembling the entries for my 2003 anthology *Pulp Friction*, which included extracts from eighteen books and a guide to gay novels from 1949 to 1969, I was repeatedly pushed to reconsider my original preconceptions about the material. Each of these reconsiderations led me to rethink how I and other scholars of gay history and culture have viewed the position and situation of homosexuality in the two decades before Stonewall. Historians such as Allan Berube, Lillian Faderman, Jonathan Katz, George Chauncey, Elizabeth Lapovsky Kennedy, and Madeline Davis have explored the rich complexity of interactions between myriad forms of homosexuality and what is generally considered to be "mainstream culture" in the U.S. This was certainly true of the process I underwent in putting together the materials for *Pulp Friction*.

One of the most startling reversals in my thinking was the realization that it is a mistake to think of all gay fiction written after the war up to the Stonewall riots as a separate literary category. I would argue instead that the very concept of "gay fiction" is probably most usefully understood as a post-Stonewall invention, one that serves a specific political function. There were many postwar novels that explicitly featured gay male characters. These were novels published by respected publishing houses that regularly received critical attention from mainstream critics. Some of them were written by men who were gay, with varying degrees of openness, and some were not. While they were obviously read by gay people, they were never labeled as "gay novels" or marginalized with accusations of special pleading. Certainly there were publishers that marketed their novels to a more distinctly homosexual readership, but even these novels were advertised and reviewed in conventional, mainstream newspapers and magazines.

The second major preconception that I had was that the majority of novels published before Stonewall had tragic endings. This is one of the most deeply inscribed myths and images of the last three decades—the long-suffering, usually self-hating hero or heroine of a gay novel or film doomed to die at their own hands, thus enacting the inevitable, implicitly deserved fate of all homosexuals. This has been investigated by critical studies such as Roger Austin's *Playing the Game: The Homosexual Novel in America* (1977) and Vito Russo's *The Celluloid Closet: Homosexuality in the Movies* (1981), as well as endless offhand references to the phenomenon in popular fiction and nonfiction. But in fact,

lives of gay men and lesbians. Yet as much as the gay liberation movement presented an agenda of freedom, it also redefined homosexuality in such a manner as to set it decisively apart the dominant culture. Before the modern gay rights movement, homosexuality—lacking a clear and decisive political character—was generally conceptualized as part of the continuum of human sexuality. Thus, while homosexuality was often imagined to be "unnatural" or "sick," its position on a continuum of human sexual behavior meant that it was understood as a deviant sexuality, not a radically different one. In this context, homosexuality was not the opposite of heterosexuality but rather a perverse deflection from it. This conceptualization of sexuality easily allowed for an alternative understanding of homosexuality that viewed same-sex desire as no more than a variant of human sexual desire and behavior.

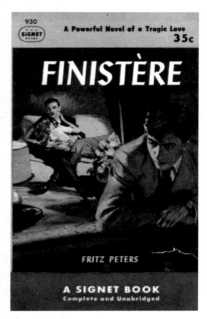

The Bitterweed Path (Brown Watson, 1966)

Never the Same Again (Pyramid, 1958)

Finistère (Signet, 1952)

there are many pre-Stonewall novels that ended, if not completely happily, at least with an optimism, understanding, or degree of self-knowledge. Even novels that did end badly were not necessarily promoting homophobic sentiments or themes.

Take for instance, Fritz Peters's exquisite 1951 *Finistère*, a book that has repeatedly been classified as a "tragic" gay novel. Here, Matthew, a sixteen-year-old American schoolboy, has an affair with Michel, a young male teacher at his French school. Matthew drowns himself in the book's final pages, but it's clear that his suicide results from the attitudes of his uncaring and self-involved parents, his stepfather's harassment, and his lover's temporary unkindness. The novel is about many things—the clash of American and French mores, a young man's coming of age, the subtle but deadly dynamics of dysfunctional families, the unbearable pressures of conforming to acceptable standards of maleness—but more than anything it is a novel about how intolerance and ignorance can destroy a young life. In his perceptive *Saturday Review* critique of the novel, Gore Vidal suggested that the "great theme" of Finistère was "the corruption and murder of innocence."

My third preconception about pulp novels concerned sex. I was completely startled by how much sex there was even in the earlier novels of the postwar period. While none of it is anatomically explicit or graphic, the sexual references, the indications of erotic

interest, the importance of sex to the characters' lives, and the sexualization of the male body are equal to—and in some cases greater than—the sexual content in comparable heterosexual novels of the period.

This is particularly astonishing in the novels from mainstream publishers in the late 1940s and the 1950s. The reader has full access to the erotic imagination of the main character in Stuart Engstrand's 1947 *The Sling and the Arrow* as he negotiates his overt sexual fantasies of sailors and his own tendencies to transvestitism and transgenderism. There are scenes in Thomas Hal Phillip's 1948 *The Bitterweed Path* in which the main character goes to bed with both his best friend and his best friend's father, as the author stops just short of describing—but certainly leads us to imagine—what happens next. The pivotal scene in Lonnie Coleman's 1959 *Sam* is set in a gay bathhouse, and there's no doubt about what's happening as the newly boyfriendless Sam attempts to lose himself in mindless sex (but ends up finding the perfect lover instead). Much of what happens in these novels is completely at odds with the popular belief that pre-Stonewall literary homosexual activity was nonexistent, invisible, or desperately fumbling due to overwhelming repression.

The question arises, how had I and so many others formed these preconceived ideas in the first place? What had created the myth that there were no books about homosexuality before Stonewall or the contradictory

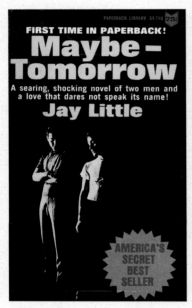

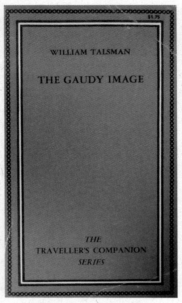

Maybe—Tomorrow (Paperback Library, 1965)

The Gaudy Image (Olympia Press, 1966)

Sheeper (Grove Press, 1966)

idea that all of the pre-Stonewall novels about homosexuality had tragic endings? A great deal of this was, I contend, due to the need to believe that the Stonewall Riots and the gay liberation movement were a decisive break from the past and a radical new beginning. This attitude was apparent in the dismissive attitude that many gay liberationists took toward the older homophile groups such as Mattachine, SIR, and Daughters of Bilitis and their publications. Indeed, one of the great projects of gay liberation was to create a new gay culture that would replace the oppressed homosexual culture of the past and that would salve the wounds that homosexuals had hitherto endured. There was no doubt in the minds of gay liberationists that the progenitor of antigay hatred was what Christopher Isherwood labeled "the heterosexual dictatorship," but that did not prevent a similar—and at times even more forceful and ferocious—attack on pre-Stonewall gay culture as well.

Like most of the social movements of the 1960s—the antiwar movement, the music and drug counterculture, hippies and Yippies, environmentalism, black power, radical and separatist feminism—gay liberation was a youth movement whose sense of history was defined mostly by a rejection of the past. Not surprisingly, some earlier gay writers, such as Allen Ginsberg and the other Beat poets—who carried their antiestablishment 1950s political agenda to the antiwar and

counterculture movements—were accepted as post-Stonewall literature. After witnessing the Stonewall riots. Ginsberg was said to have commented to a friend that "the fags have lost that wounded look." But with few exceptions, the liberationist rejection of the gay culture of the 1950s and '60s was decisive. It was, in many ways, a frightened response to the pain and the suffering that visibly stalked gay life in the decades before Stonewall.

While pulp novels functioned as validation for gay male sexual desires, they performed other functions as well. Without denying the enjoyment, sexual or otherwise that came from reading them, these books also functioned pedagogically. Hidden within their plots and their characters' lives were maps, hints, and clues that told gay men how they might live their lives. Because so many of the novels that dealt with homosexuality were written by gay men and drawn, at least to some degree, from their own experience they are filled with insights into how gay men of this period lived. This is not to say that their intent was documentary, but they provided glimpses into a half-hidden gay world that was not accessible to most readers of the day. Reading through these books, we see how gay men dressed, what their homes looked like, where they lived, and how they spoke. Most of this knowledge is filtered through the lens of art and storytelling—bounded also by the pressures of the marketplace and the censors—but it was useful information for those who needed to know.

And what exactly might gay readers learn from these books? Sometimes it was just a matter of learning where gay men tended to live. In book after book—from Michael de Forrest's 1949 *The Gay Year* to Lonnie Coleman's 1959 *Sam*—we are treated to scenes set in apartments in Greenwich Village. The decor and the furnishings of the rooms are described, as are the characters' clothing and colloquial speech. We learn what the inside of a gay bar and a gay bathhouse look like, and how people behave in them. In Jay Little's 1952 *Maybe—Tomorrow* and William Talsman's 1958 *The Gaudy Image* we see gay life in the French Quarter of New Orleans. It is true that the former work is drenched in earnest, literal descriptions while the latter is rather fanciful—as though Jean Genet were rewriting a Tennessee Williams short story—but both leave vivid impressions. In Gerald Tesch's 1956 *Never the Same Again*, we see what it's like to live in a small town, and in "Spur Piece" from James Barr's 1951 collection *Derricks* we get what life is like for rural gay men in the Midwest. Even a book like Irving Rosenthal's *Sheeper* (1967)—an out-of-control, junked-out speed-rap on gay life in the Beat scene with characters based on Allen Ginsberg, Herbert Huncke, and filmmaker Jack Smith—gives us a vivid image of a specific gay time and place. In the more sexually explicit books, such as Richard Amory's *Song of the Loon* (1966), gay male readers could learn about (while being turned on by) the specifics of gay male sex.

The importance of these novels as educational, self-help, how-to manuals cannot be overestimated. No one was brought up to be gay, and hardly anyone (even today) comes from a "gay family." Having sexual desires is one thing, but finding people with whom to act upon them is another, and finding a community is yet another: a step that's as liberating as it is fraught with peril and confusion. These books were the maps and the signposts, the etiquette manuals, and the foreign phrase books for gay men entering the invisible world of homosexuality. The fanciful language of pulp covers was not altogether wrong: homosexual culture was a shadow world, whose presence was becoming increasingly prominent, but whose inner workings and interior life were only barely visible at this time. These books often present this with a through-the-looking-glass effect: even as many of their characters are finding their way through the emotional

Song of the Loon (Greenleaf, 1966)

and psychological labyrinths of coming out and discovering what being gay might be like, so the readers of these books are often engaged in a similar process.

As important as the social function of these books was, it is vital not to lose sight of them as literature, as well. First and foremost, they are works of imagination, written primarily by gay men who were committed to the hard reality of committing to paper the passions and longings of same-sex desire. They may vary in form and tone, and certainly their literary quality ranges from very high to idiosyncratically low, but each of them exhibits a rebellious, radical urge that injects the possibility of same-sex eroticism into a world that's both fascinated by and fearful of it.

Michael Bronski

To Sir, with Love
Race and the Unreal City of the Colonial Imagination

Edward Ricardo Braithwaite's autobiographical 1959 novel *To Sir, with Love*, which is based on his experience as a black teacher in a tough East End secondary modern school, offers a remarkable insight into the politics of class and race in postwar London. Sidney Poitier came to London to star in the film version of the novel in 1967, and later appeared in a sequel, based in Chicago, which was made for television in 1996 (*To Sir, with Love II*, directed by Peter Bogdanovich). Yet, surprisingly, the novel itself has been largely overlooked.

When the narrator of *To Sir, with Love* arrives in London in 1948 he is struck by the disparity between his expectations and the reality:

> I had read references to it in both classical and contemporary writings and was eager to know the London of Chaucer and Erasmus and the Sorores Minories. I had dreamed of walking along the cobbled Street of the Cable Makers to the echoes of Chancellor and the brothers Willoughby. I wanted to look on the reach of the Thames at Blackwall from which Captain John Smith had sailed aboard the good ship Susan Lawrence to found an English colony in Virginia.

The narrator has clearly also read Conrad's *Heart of Darkness* (1902), and London does indeed turn out to be a city of "brooding gloom." Those who haven't had the elite education that Braithwaite received, first at Queen's College, British Guyana, then at City University in New York and, after he was demobbed, at Cambridge, maybe grateful that they can turn to Wikipedia for explanations of the more obscure references in this passage.

London as the "unreal city," to quote T.S. Eliot, of the colonial imagination pervades postwar English fiction. If Braithwaite's is the most erudite version of this trope, the most ecstatically literary is to be found in *Beer in the Snooker Club* (1964) by the Egyptian novelist Waguih Ghali:

> I wanted to live. I read and read … and I wanted to live. I wanted to have affairs with countesses and to fall in love with a barmaid and to be a gigolo and to be a political leader and to win at Monte Carlo and to be down-and-out in London and to be an artist and to be elegant and also to be in rags.

Perhaps the most lyrical exponent of the dream city and the devastating encounter with its "actualities" is found in Sam Selvon's *The Lonely Londoners* (1956), where the "boys" from the West Indies are at first thrilled to be "coasting a lime" by the Serpentine and rendezvousing under the clock at Charing Cross but sooner or later find themselves despondent at the round of "eat, sleep, work, hustle pussy" and at being repeatedly turned down for jobs and housing and pointed at in the street. As Galahad lies in his basement room licking his wounds after one humiliating encounter he wonders: "Lord, what is it we people do in this world that we have to suffer so?"

By the time Hanif Kureishi looked back on the postwar experience of migration in the chapter about Karim's father's journey from British India to England in *The Buddha of Suburbia* (1990), the disenchantment was distant enough to be treated with irony:

> London, the Old Kent Road, was a freezing shock. … Dad had never seen the English in poverty, as roadsweepers, dustmen, shopkeepers and barmen. He'd never seen an Englishman stuffing bread into his mouth with his fingers, and no one had told him that the English didn't wash regularly because the water was so cold. … And when Dad tried to discuss Byron in local pubs no one warned him that not every Englishman could read or that they didn't necessarily want tutoring by an Indian on the poetry of a pervert and a madman.

As he deftly reverses the colonial gaze, Haroon is "amazed and heartened" by how unimpressive the metropolitan center turns out to be.

Interestingly, Braithwaite's novel spoke directly to Hanif Kureishi as a young man. In his collection of essays *The Word and the Bomb* (2005) Kureishi describes his search for the British equivalents of the great African American writers James Baldwin, Richard Wright, and Ralph Ellison. Although he enjoyed Forster, Greene, and Waugh, they did not explore the "profound and permanent alterations to British life that had begun with the Empire and had now, as it were, come home":

> Living in the London suburbs with an Indian father and English mother, I wanted to read works set in England, works that might help make sense of my own situation. Racism was real to me; the Empire was not. I liked Colin MacInnes and E.R. Braithwaite, whose *To Sir, with Love* so moved me when I read it under the desk at school.

No writer of the 1950s and '60s, not even V.S. Naipaul, the laureate of disenchantment, plumbs the depths of colonial aspiration and metropolitan disappointment quite as devastatingly as E.R. Braithwaite. Through the novel we learn that during his years as a pilot in the Royal Air Force he had never encountered racial prejudice, but after the war he is turned down for a job for which he is eminently qualified simply because he is black. Despite having risked his life for the ideal of the British Way of Life he is seen as an alien. After his rejection, he steps out of the "grand, imposing building" in Mayfair: "disappointment and resentment were a solid bitter rising lump inside me; I hurried into the nearest public lavatory and was violently sick." Remembering the joyous celebrations on each Royal visit to British Guiana, he concludes: "Yes, it is wonderful to be British—until one comes to Britain."

And so, without any sense of vocation, as he candidly admits, he becomes a teacher in an East End school because that is the best job he can get. It's a dark and gloomy building located in a rubbish-strewn bomb-wrecked area, which he compares unfavorably with his light and cool schoolhouse in sunny Georgetown. Life around Cable Street turns out to be hard, and not just for the narrator. At first he is rather snobbishly shocked by working-class East Enders whom he sees as "peasants," a term that Albert Angelo also uses about his East End pupils in B.S. Johnson's eponymous novel (1964). Braithwaite resists seeing the children as victims despite their damp, impoverished

To Sir, with Love (Bodley Head, 1959)
To Sir, with Love (Four Square, 1966)
Poster for 1967 film adaption of *To Sir, with Love*

E R Braithwaite
To Sir, with Love (Four
Square, 1967)

and overcrowded conditions at home: "hungry or filled, naked or clothed, they were white, and as far as I was concerned, that fact alone made the only difference between the haves and have-nots." But by the end of the school year Braithwaite has had an education in class and has come to "love them, these brutal, disarming bastards."

The climax of the novel occurs after the death of the mother of one of his pupils. Braithwaite arranges for the class to send a wreath to the family, but none of the children will deliver it because they can't be seen going to a "coloured person's home." The children are friendly to Seales, "who was born among them, grew up among them, played with them" but they cannot break the social taboo, which seems primarily to be about miscegenation:

> A coloured boy with a white mother, a West Indian boy with an English mother. Always the same. Never an English boy with a Negro or West Indian father. No, that would be placing the emphasis on his Englishness, his identification with them.

The narrator is bitterly disappointed in his students and thinks that he has been wasting his time (a common complaint among teachers!) but is overjoyed to discover that his tolerance and patient goodwill have paid off: his pupils, looking washed and smart, attend the funeral—proof of the efficacy of his pedagogy and a triumph for humanity. It's a pity, as Bruce King says, that "Braithwaite seems too insistent on proclaiming his abilities, attractiveness, intelligence, judgement, and unassertiveness." But given the pervasive prejudice he encounters, it is hardly surprising that he

should sometimes cast himself as the hero of his own story especially since, unlike "the boys" in Selvon's *The Lonely Londoners*, Braithwaite has no one he can run to when he is insulted on the bus or on the tube. He lives with a kindly white couple, whom he calls "Mom" and "Dad," but beyond that has no community. As Caryl Phillips says in his introduction to the 2005 Vintage edition of the novel, "We do feel sympathy for this somewhat isolated, patrician man who attempts now to make a community out of the pupils in his charge and his fellow teachers in the staffroom."

Perhaps the most striking aspect of the novel is not the narrator's occasional self-congratulation but his quietism. When one of the boys attacks the bullying sports teacher for his sadistic treatment of a fellow pupil, Braithwaite insists that the boy must apologize to the "master." The class is shocked by what they consider to be this double injustice, but Braithwaite counsels against rebellion:

> "I've been pushed around, Seales," I said quietly, "in a way I cannot explain to you. I've been pushed around until I began to hate people so much that I wanted to hurt them, really hurt them. I know how it feels, believe me, and one thing I've learned, Seales, is to try always to be a bit bigger than the people who hurt me."

Although the speech is given in front of the whole class, it is directed particularly at Seales, the mixed-race boy, even though he is not the culprit. It is as if Braithwaite fears that Seales, above all, is the one who will need to learn the lesson of self-discipline or risk being provoked into reaching "for a knife or a gun" and finding himself in deep trouble.

In another scene the mother of one of the girls in the class comes in to complain about her daughter's bad behavior. The girl, Pamela, confides in her teacher: she is upset about the men who call on her widowed mother and in particular about something that happened that she cannot bring herself to mention. Again Braithwaite warns against rebellion and insists that Pamela should be an obedient and courteous daughter. Braithwaite's message to the children seems to be: the world will do its dirty job; there's no use kicking against the pricks; try to maintain your dignity; that's the best you can hope for.

At several points in the novel Braithwaite is publicly humiliated. On the bus an Englishwoman refuses to sit next to him. He guesses that she is secretly enjoying

Publicity image from the 1967 film adaption of *To Sir, with Love*

herself: "What a smooth, elegant, superior bitch!" he thinks to himself, but he says nothing. On the tube, taking his pupils to the Victoria and Albert Museum, two elderly, well-dressed women start "muttering darkly about 'shameless young girls and these black men'" until one of the pupils, Pamela, shouts at them: "He is our teacher, do you mind?" Again, Braithwaite himself is silent and so maintains his dignity.

Braithwaite's stoicism infuriates his white English girlfriend. When they go to an expensive restaurant in Chelsea, the waiter keeps them waiting for a very long time and then deliberately spills his soup. Gillian insists on storming out, but Braithwaite, we assume, would have remained at the table in a dignified way—or would have sucked it up.

At the end of the novel Braithwaite spells out his philosophy:

> I made it clear that…coloured people in England were gradually working for their own salvation, realising that it was not enough for them to complain about injustices done to them, or rely on interested parties to agitate on their behalf. They were working to show their worth, integrity and dignity in spite of the forces opposed to them.

To Sir, with Love is mainly remembered today because of the 1967 film version starring Sidney Poitier, which turned Braithwaite's particular and surprising story into a generic version of the 1955 movie *Blackboard Jungle*, with a wailing theme tune sung by Lulu. The film, although a travesty, was a commercial success. In an interview for Radio 4 with Burt Caesar in (2007) Braithwaite admitted to ambivalent feelings about the film although its commercial success

guaranteed that the novel would never sink into oblivion.

A major strand of *To Sir, with Love* concerns the love affair between Ricky and Gillian, but you wouldn't know it from watching the 1967 movie. Poitier may have been one of the biggest box office draws of his day (*Guess Who's Coming to Dinner* and *In the Heat of the Night* came out in the same year) but he was not considered worthy to win the heart of the English rose on screen.

We only have to think of the critical reception of Ira Aldridge in the nineteenth century and Paul Robeson in the twentieth century when playing *Othello* to understand why this was so. A novel can persuade readers through its voice, but on stage or in the cinema, as Braithwaite knew all too well, people tend to see "only the skin" and not the person inside it.

In the novel Ricky and Gillian strike up a friendship in the staffroom which gradually develops into a romance. The main obstacle seems to be his worry about the effect of a racist society on her: "How long would our happy association survive the malignity of stares which were deliberately intended to make the woman feel unclean, as if she had abjectly degraded not merely herself but all womanhood?" Meanwhile, she wants him to stand up to racists whether on the tube or in the restaurant. Once they decide to marry, they have to overcome her father's unwillingness to grant his consent. The father objects: "You might have children; what happens to them? They'll belong nowhere, and nobody will want them." When racists were not complaining that black men were "taking our women," they pretended to be concerned for the mixed-race children who, they argued, would not know who they were. Braithwaite assures Gillian's father that their children "will belong to us and we will want them." But he also prefaces this article of faith by saying, "If Gillian and I marry." Since *To Sir, with Love* is a fictionalized autobiography, it would be very interesting to know whether Braithwaite got his girl in the end and what happened then.

As for the accuracy of *To Sir, with Love*, it has been argued that Braithwaite got it all wrong. In his 2013 self-published memoir, *An East End Story*, Alfred Gardner recalls being a pupil in Braithwaite's classroom: he "was a tall, humourless disciplinarian" who "struck fear into us by favouring corporal punishment." He added, "I saw him on more than one occasion strike a child," even though the headmaster had prohibited

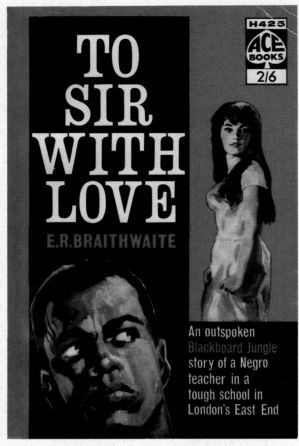

To Sir, with Love (Ace, 1961)

had a girlfriend or two on first coming to London, "he sincerely hoped he achieved no special notoriety as a boudoir athlete." In the novel, Braithwaite suggests that one of the girls, Pamela, has a crush on her teacher. Gillian warns him to be very careful indeed never to be alone with Pamela. Reading Gardner's memoir makes one realize how easily Braithwaite could have been falsely smeared and ended up in a very different story—like Tom Robinson's in *To Kill a Mockingbird* (1960).

Although Gardner's portrait of Braithwaite is uncomplimentary, his account of the children's hero worship of their headmaster does seem to be reliable. *To Sir, with Love*'s Greendale Secondary School was based on St. George-in-the-East Secondary Modern on Cable Street, whose head was the charismatic and innovative educationalist Alex Bloom (called Alex Florian in the novel). This survivor of the Holocaust who died in 1955 was a passionate advocate of a radical, democratic schooling that was neither competitive nor authoritarian and which encouraged both the individual's development and commitment to the wider community. Braithwaite is initially shocked by the school's ethos: the children "are encouraged to speak up for themselves," even if what they say is "alarming or embarrassing"; and there is no corporal punishment or "any other form of punishment." Pupils write weekly reviews of their lessons, participate in School Council meetings and help decide on their own curriculum. Much to his surprise, Braithwaite discovers that this libertarian education does not lead to chaos or violence in the classroom; quite the opposite. He is gradually won over by the head teacher's philosophy: listen to the children, let the children dance (to their own music during the lunch hour), and teach them how to learn from their mistakes instead of punishing them.

St. George's school sounds like the Summerhill of the East End, and Alex Bloom's work is greatly admired by academics such as Michael Fielding at the University of London's Institute of Education. *To Sir, with Love* still has a lot to teach us about class and race in London in the 1950s, and about the education system then—as now.

Susie Thomas

such forms of punishment. It may have been the case that Braithwaite's own strict education in the colonial school system made him appear a bit of a stickler to some of his pupils, but the discrepancy between Gardner's account of "mutual resentment" between the kids and their teacher and the novel's representation of a developing love and respect comes as a shock.

The novel ends with Braithwaite being given a leaving present and card addressed "To Sir, with Love," while Gardner asserts that the children hated him so much that they cheered when he left the school. Gardner goes on: "There was also a rumour that some of the older girls sometimes felt uncomfortable around him." At this point, one may begin to question Gardner's version of events: this insinuation seems to tap into fears of the black man's superior sexuality that were rampant in postwar discourse about why Britain should stay white. Braithwaite seems to have been very conscious of this fear and did his best to reassure his readers (quite amusingly) that although he had

The Odd Girls' Journey out of the Shadows

Lesbi-Pulp Novels

The Stonewall riots of June 1969 marked the public debut of the modern American gay liberation movement and the decade that followed saw much gay and lesbian political action. With it, new discourses regarding sexuality emerged. But rather than marking a decisive break, the foundations of this movement were already extant. Both inside and outside of gay and lesbian subcultures, levels of acceptability and visibility fluctuated throughout the twentieth century according to time and place. Significantly, groups were forming, different language being used, and nonpathological images produced before the 1970s. In the 1950s and '60s, part of this transition was happening on the racks of neighborhood drugstores and in the corners of lesbians' bookshelves.

Lesbian pulp novels emerged out of a thriving mass-market paperback industry controlled by a culture little invested in promoting a positive image of lesbians. Female authors working in this genre, however, possessed both the desire and freedom to create such images. Regardless of the intended audience or the emphasis on profit-making stereotypes, these novels provided a forum for lesbian understandings to emerge in a way that was at once nonthreatening and conforming, while at the same time possessed of radical implications. That is, while the women writing these novels were still overseen by mainstream publishers and male audiences, they were given the space to make decisions about the social meaning of lesbians that differed from those produced by hostile, heterosexual institutions.

An understanding of lesbian pulp novels must first consider the history and conventions of the paperback. Slowly emerging in Europe and North America since the late 1800s, such mass-market novels began to gain a significant following in the 1940s. These books were often driven by exaggerated plots, a sense of fantasy and, in the case of the lesbian paperback, voyeurism and titillation.

Portability was an important issue, and standard sizes were often used, with the term "pocket book" coming into general use along with the designation "pulp novel." Because working-class people were considered a target market these books were available in a wide array of places including newsstands and drugstores.

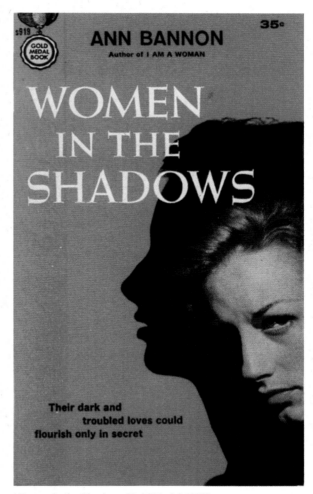

Woman in the Shadows (Gold Medal, 1959)

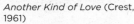

Another Kind of Love (Crest, 1961)

Amanda (Belmont, 1965)

The Other Side of Desire (Paperback Library, 1965)

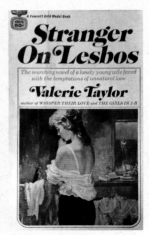

Stranger on Lesbos (Gold Medal, 1960)

Valerie Taylor, a popular lesbi-pulp author of the time, included the presence of the paperback itself in the text of *Journey to Fulfillment* (1964):

> The girls wandered around looking at costume jewelry, nail polish and eyeliner, paperback books on the racks. They would buy something they didn't really want, she knew, to justify wasting their time this way. The place was full of people buying things for something to do.

In some ways this appears to be simply a mirror, a way for the audience to see themselves within the text in a concrete way, but Taylor also compares her genre to the other cheap things young women felt compelled to buy. The girls have nothing better to do, no better options, which, in a way also tells us something about the representations of lesbians at the time. That is to say that there were not better representations of lesbians, of themselves, in the literature of their everyday lives. In this passage Taylor subtly asserts the importance of the existence of the paperback novel, which can be extended to the lesbian paperback, while at the same time pointing out its inadequacies. This makes sense as *Journey to Fulfillment* was published in 1964, right on the tail end of the lesbi-pulp craze and prior to the beginning of a new political movement.

Because the drugstore was an integral part of readers' lives, often situated right across from church and school, such items were within easy reach. Part of what made these novels desirable was their salacious covers, some of which Thomas Bonn, editor of *Under Cover: An Illustrated History of Mass Market Paperbacks*, recalls literally featured "a keyhole or window to peek through." According to Bonn one of the first books to use this idea, in the form of a knothole was *God's Little Acre* (1946), which "promised forbidden insights into Southern comforts [with the voyeurism of the knothole] credited with stimulating much of the sales."

This sales tactic points to the intense voyeuristic quality of pulp paperbacks in general, something which especially applied to lesbi-pulp novels. Perhaps more importantly, the voyeurism promised by the keyhole was delivered on. Though a book could be found in a common context it was constituted as the "other" because the characters within belonged to sexual categories that were not normative. Yet, according to pulp scholar Yvonne Keller, because "the lesbians depicted were still women—[this] meant, to more men than Hugh Hefner, that they were still sexually available to men and, moreover, nonthreatening to depict."

Because women were viewed as always accessible to men in society, their possible sexual transgression could be seen as easily controllable, a lure rather than a threat like male homosexuality. More often than not, feminine women adorned the cover to entice the masculine reader, that is, the pleasure seeker. He (which turned out to also be she) actively looked upon the woman on the cover—familiar, attractive, inviting—who turned out to be completely unfamiliar. But because the reader had already been invited to look, he continued to watch. The portrayals of sexual acts between two women were moments that a man could thus experience in a fictional, nonthreatening way.

Female characters might be feminine, which fit well with the idea of straight male desire, but often one of the partners was a butch woman. In this way gender roles and heterosexuality appeared familiar to the male reader and reinforced by butch/femme. In some ways he might even identify with the butch. But identification was not the only goal. He could desire the butch as well and so keep his sexuality in the realm of the heteronormative while desiring a masculine body. Although the focus of his lust was still female, the action he gazed upon was homosexual. Scholar Michele Barale uses Ann Bannon's lesbi-pulp novel *Beebo Brinker* (1962) to illustrate this point:

> I want to suggest that among the pleasures—and dangers—offered the heterosexual male reader of this novel is the opportunity to engage in non-heterosexual imaginings. Moreover, it is the opportunity to encounter them not as the distant observer of other folks' rituals of romance, but as a participant. To put it simply, *Beebo Brinker* invites the straight male reader to leave his homosexual panic behind. It shows him how folks who might look straight—folks like himself, for instance—do indeed have dreams and desires of a gayer sort. It invites him to come out of the cold and take part in Close Encounters of the Queer Kind.

This freedom to move in and out of the queer world, though targeted at heterosexual males, could also be accessed by women. This created not only a new lesbian discourse but also made it possible to view sexuality as fluid and complex. Sexuality was constructed as a continuum and not a binary system, even in a culture that valued the binary. The difference between identification with, and desire for, was blurred.

The "straight" woman too could be invited into the sexual transgression party. She might be intrigued and titillated by the idea of sexual and gender play, and could see herself readily in the positions many of the books' characters found themselves in. That is, assuming the characters were straight, only to discover their lesbianism through a seduction. In a seduction, then, the woman was not wholly responsible for her homosexual actions/yearnings but coerced. So too could the book function as a seducer of women. For the woman reader, then, the characters and their actions were accessible and applicable to their own lives; the distinction between themselves, whom they saw as heterosexual, and the characters, seen as homosexual, was not so clear.

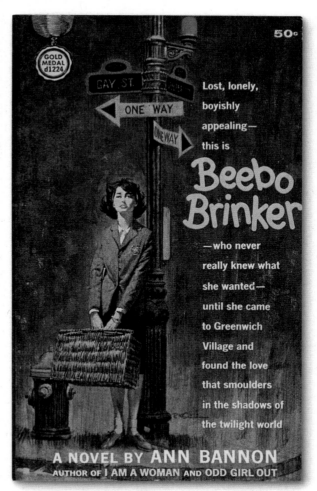

Beebo Brinker (Gold Medal, 1962)

Clearly, the ability to purchase a novel at any local drugstore was a more accessible way for heterosexual, semiheterosexual, or presumed heterosexual women to learn about and experience homosexual life than entering actual lesbian gathering places, especially if they did not happen to live near New York or San Francisco. Yet in an unpublished 1983 article, Joan Nestle asserts: "These books were often hidden away on the pulp racks of the more sleazy drugstores. To pick the books out, carry them to the counter and face the other shoppers and the cashier was often tantamount to a coming out declaration." Many of the buyers of these novels, like Nestle, were lesbian women leading lesbian lives. They recognized these texts as powerful and visible, despite multiple problems regarding background, voyeurism, and basic inaccuracies. This recognition paved the way for the beginnings of a distinctly lesbian discourse.

While women authors wanted to create a positive image of lesbians for both their lesbian readership and the general populace, and were wary of including too much gratuitous sex, publishers pushed for it, viewing their audience as heterosexual men interested only in the titillation factor. In a 1959 article in the early lesbian activist magazine *The Ladder*, writer Lora Sela (pseudonym for Carol Hales) talked about the compromises she made with her publisher: "I agreed to give him overt sex scenes *if* he would allow me to get my own propaganda over—to gain understanding and tolerance for Lesbians with the readers of these books."

But to dismiss sexual content is to disregard not only significant moments within lesbi-pulp novels but also the role they played in creating a literary lesbian language. Gender scholar Gabriele Griffin asserts that, although certain passages "could come from any romantic pulp writing," in these novels "the assertion of lesbian sexual desire and the need to have it fulfilled is made over and over again in ways designed to support the validity of these desires, their urgency and power" and "the joy and sexual release women find in having sex with each other is repeatedly emphasized."

So, while certain novels were criticized for containing too much sex, the sex included in the female-authored pulps had a positive meaning. Clear examples of this can be found in Ann Bannon's Beebo Brinker series. In *Odd Girl Out* (1957) core characters Laura and Beth meet in college and have an affair. Beth then falls in love with Charlie—a college boy. Laura tries to get Beth to leave him but they remain together and Laura leaves college alone.

The sequel *I Am a Woman* (1959) opens with Laura after she has left school and gotten a job in a NYC doctor's office. She befriends Jack Mann, who is gay, and visits her first gay bar where she meets and goes home with Beebo Brinker. She continues to see her but also has a crush on her straight roommate Marcie. After a bad visit from her father (who attempts to seduce her), Laura disappears for a couple of days before returning to the arms of Beebo.

Women in the Shadows (1959) is Bannon's darkest novel and includes a faked rape, dog murder, Beebo's slide into alcoholism and a tortured affair between Laura and a black woman who pretends she is of Indian background. In the end Laura and Jack get married, and she gets artificially inseminated.

In *Journey to a Woman* (1960), Beth is married to Charlie and has two children. After an affair with a woman named Vega, she leaves Charlie to search for Laura. Before finding her, she has a liaison with Nina, a lesbian pulp author. When Beth finally locates Laura, who is married with a daughter to Jack, the pair make love but soon realize it is over for them. Vega goes to Beth's hotel and shoots herself. Charlie bails Beth out of jail, wanting her to return but she refuses. Beebo and Beth then fall in love.

The last book to be published, *Beebo Brinker*, is actually the first in the series chronologically and begins with Jack meeting Beebo. Beebo gets involved with a woman, Paula, for the first time before meeting Venus Bogardus, a famous movie star. After moving to California with her, she is forced to go back to New York when rumors begin to spread about the relationship. Beebo returns to the open arms of Paula.

The series has many sex scenes that are joyous and positive. In *Odd Girl Out* Laura's first lesbian encounter speaks of "shock[s] of intense pleasure, as she heard her faraway voice groan in ecstasy and held Beth so tightly it seemed they must somehow melt together ... when finally the furious desire abated a little it was only to gather strength for a fresh explosion."

Her encounter with Beebo is equally intense: "Her own body responded with violent spasms—joyous, crazy, deep as her soul ... She felt like a column of fire, all heat and light, impossibly sensual, impossibly sexual. She was all feeling, warm and melting, strong and sweet."

The language Bannon uses to describe these encounters speaks of pleasure and does not refer to lesbian lovemaking as dirty in any way. Because sexual pleasure was not necessarily something that the acceptable heterosexual woman of the 1950s enjoyed, portraying lesbians as enjoying sex potentially made them seem promiscuous and oversexed. But if women of any sexual orientation are allowed to enjoy sex, then these scenes can be viewed as celebratory. The power of sexual portrayal may have worked against the desire of women authors to depict lesbians positively by the standards of the 1950s, but it worked for positive representation in other ways.

The way sex is treated in these books in quantity and explicitness lies between male-targeted pornography and female-targeted romance. Feminist scholar Suzanna Danuta Walters asserts:

> For it is not only that [female-authored] novels tend to be less explicit sexually than

Whisper Their Love (Neville Spearman, 1959)
Odd Girl Out (Gold Medal, 1960)
Unlike Others (Midwood, 1963)

male-authored ones, but that the construction of sexuality and sexual preference itself is constituted differently from both the male version of this genre as well as from the dominant culture. . . . The description of the female pornographic genre of the Harlequin as desexualized and decontextualized ("waiting and yearning") could not be more at odds with the "sex in context" style of the Bannon books.

Because lesbi-pulp novels situated themselves between the narratives associated with males and those associated with females, but directly mirrored neither extreme, it spoke in a new language. This language, though feminine, did not hold to the framework of traditionally feminine genres. It built a new structure that housed a new feminine discourse, that of the lesbian.

In contrast to earlier texts, such as the famous 1928 "lesbian" novel *The Well of Loneliness*, Ann Bannon's Beebo Brinker identified the main character clearly as a butch lesbian. Activist scholar Diane Hamer argues that the name Stephen in the novel "is unambiguously intended to designate the masculine gender," whereas Beebo's name "bears no pre-given assumptions of gender; it is a name that could belong to a boy or a girl."

The characters too make choices about naming lesbianism. This can be seen specifically in the butch positioning herself as neither traditional woman nor man. This image of masculine woman/gender transgressor was already prevalent. What the characters in Bannon's books articulated was the desirability of such a being. While Beebo eventually loses her famous love interest, Venus Bogardus, due to the star's inability to live as a lesbian in her career, it is still clear that Venus prefers Beebo to her husband and all the other relationships with men she has had. Venus and other feminine lesbian characters throughout the series do not desire a man even as they lust after a masculine woman because, as Taylor points out, "Beebo's lovers make it quite clear that their desire for her is precisely as a butch or masculine *woman*, not as a poor imitation of a man."

Butch, then, in the context of lesbi-pulp novels of the 1950s is quite different from earlier representations of the mannish lesbian. Beebo has the desire to wear the clothes associated with men, to perform the actions associated with men, to *perform* as a man, but not to be one. The representations of butch vs. femme in the bar culture (reflected in the novels) were not only prevalent but also an essential part of performing working-class lesbianism in the 1950s. It was problematic and not always inclusive. It was framed by heterosexual norms of gender representation, but it was not heterosexual. It paved the way for further distancing from the original heterosexual signifiers.

By 1964 Valerie Taylor was also discussing role playing within her narratives. In a scene from *Journey to Fulfillment*, Peg, an experienced college girl, comes on to Erika, a younger girl who is new to America:

Peg asked abruptly, "Are you butch?"

"Please?"

"Are you the active one? You look more like a boy than a girl."

"Oh, I would like to be a boy! Then I could have a nice girlfriend who is beautiful here." She flashed a suddenly mischievous smile, putting her palms against her chest.

Peg laughed. "I'm kiki. I can be either, depending on who I'm with. Comes in handy sometimes."

In this scene Peg, is not only aware of butch/femme roles but is ready to step in and out of them as she sees fit. While this scene is not set in bar culture, she seems to attach no stigma to the word "kiki," which acted as both signifier of a lesbian community—slang that was created out of gay culture—but also as a transgression of certain role-playing aspects of lesbian culture that found their roots in heterosexual relations. This new term creates a place to deviate from what (arguably) became lesbian norms but does not negate role playing in doing so. Peg, here, feels comfortable in not conforming to butch or femme, yet she gives Erika the freedom to identify as one or the other if she wishes. The ambiguity behind Erika's desire to be a boy, however, creates a space for the beginnings of questioning gender and sexuality separately, critiquing roles (specifically butch/femme), and bringing those critiques into everyday practice—all of which were vital to emergent lesbian discourse.

While butch/femme plays a large part in Ann Bannon's Beebo Brinker series, there are important shifts in the stations of certain characters. Bannon has archetypes but actively subverts them. In *Odd Girl Out*, Laura most definitely thinks of herself as a girl and is frightened to think she would have to act mannish to be a lesbian. "She looked back at herself, hugging her bosom to comfort herself, and she thought, 'I don't want to be a boy. I don't want to be like them. I'm a *girl*. I *am* a girl. That's what I want to be.'"

Interviewed by feminist magazine *Off Our Backs* in 1983, Bannon made it clear that she had crafted Beebo to be the perfect butch of her dreams:

I think there is some mystique about Beebo. And I suppose it's partly because I wrote her as a love object that people see her that way. But I look back and see not only how narrowly I cast her in that diesel dyke mode, but how much of that role playing I depict. . . . She was part of my own personal, private fantasy world before I ever wrote anything.

Laura and Beebo are the two characters most focused on in Bannon's novels, and they seem to represent fairly rigid models of butch and femme. Other characters' may not be easily categorized in terms of quintessential butch and femme identities, however. Beth, with whom Laura had her first relationship in college, reacts to Laura in a somewhat butch manner, although they are more equal in manner of dress and in their eventual lovemaking. But Beth asks for a kiss, tells Laura to be her date, persuades her to sleep in the same bed alone with her, and eventually seduces her in an ambivalent sort of way.

Even without these flimsy sorts of butch markers, one may consider Beth, as Laura's opposite, to be a butch. But Beth, at the end of the series in *Journey to a Woman*, ends up with Beebo after realizing she has no future with Laura, thereby positioning herself as femme. And in *Beebo Brinker*, Beebo has a relationship with a femme named Paula who has just broken up with a woman identified only by her plaid pajamas. Throughout the novel the assumption is that this woman was butch, though "plaid pajamas" turns out to have been one of Beebo's own love interests and therefore a femme, and very feminine in her own gender performance.

So, while Bannon mirrored butch/femme culture as both an exaggerated fantasy and the reality of lesbian norms, she also transgressed the norms she, herself, helped set up. In doing so she aided in creating a lesbian culture derived from heterosexual norms, while also initiating a further lesbian culture framed around nontraditional role playing and no role playing. Without necessarily realizing the implications in such contradictions and ambiguities concerning roles and

Edge of Twilight (Crest, 1959)

Similarly, Val, a character in Paula Christian's 1959 lesbi-pulp *Edge of Twilight*, says after a sexual encounter with another woman, "There's a name for what we're doing now." She specifically points out that the action she is taking part in can be named, yet she does not state that name. In doing so, she can be seen as refusing to use a label set up for her by heterosexual institutions, without yet having created her own name. Nevertheless, by identifying the action she makes room for herself and others to later name such actions. Toni, the woman she falls in love with, then articulates her naming of the lesbian, telling Val, "We're 'gay,' or Lesbians, or homosexuals, and sometimes 'twilight people,' but not 'queers'!" While Val may be conscious that she does not want to identify using terminology she has not created, Toni actually puts forth names she prefers to identify as.

Significant internal struggles mark the lesbian pulp novel of the 1950s and early 1960s as a place of transition. The cultural roles these novels played were as varied as the roles of the characters within them: quite rigid in some ways yet flexible in others. New visibility and representations of lesbians, made by and for lesbians, were publicly available to the middle and working classes as relatively commonplace items. This is not to say that there was not still risk involved in purchasing an openly lesbian text or a stake in claiming that text as your own (as a writer or buyer), but rather that this investment made room for individuals to first identify as members of a group, thereby uniting people and their ideas in community. Within such communities, change began. But aside from the group identification it gave, the lesbian paperback was also an important tool for the individual. It was a piece of accessible literature that suggested not only that there were other lesbians out there but that, although a lesbian life may be difficult one, it could also be a happy and sexually fulfilling one. It made the idea of living as a lesbian *possible* where it had not even been imaginable before.

Alley Hector

identification, Bannon allowed for a more progressive representation of the lesbian. Older writings had pathologized lesbians, and elements of pathology can be found in Bannon's texts as well, but she also negates this concept. According to Hamer, Bannon's writing has a more radical emphasis: "This is Bannon's refusal to settle on *any* definitive cause of lesbianism. If at moments she appears to condone dominant explanations, at others she reworks them entirely, or drops them altogether." There is power in this ambivalence. And it helped move the uncelebrated, cheaply produced pulp paperback novel into the radical era via the "personal is political" concept of the 1970s. This occurred by, as Hamer argues, "allow[ing] lesbian characters to speak their own identities in a way that challenges the presumption of a dominant heterosexual culture to define lesbianism."

City of Night, John Rechy (Grove Press, 1963)

In a review on the website of the gay literature magazine *Chelsea Station*, Eric Andrews-Katz describes *City of Night* as "one of those novels that made Gay Literature history." The autobiographical book was a mainstream publishing sensation when it first appeared. On the fiftieth anniversary of its debut, Charles Casillo wrote in the *Los Angeles Review of Books*: "What grabbed the attention of the general reading public in 1963 was the story of a gay, male prostitute—obviously modeled on Rechy himself—on a journey of self-discovery and acceptance in a society that was not ready to accept him."

It is also interesting to speculate about *City of Night*'s role in encouraging the growth of the explicitly gay male novel. In her 2001 book, *Queer Pulp: Perverted Passions from the Golden Age of the Paperback*, Susan Stryker writes that gay-themed paperbacks started to appear about the same time as lesbian pulp and paperback fiction in the early 1950s, but in much smaller numbers. Lesbian-themed paperbacks—such as those written by Marijane Meaker and Ann Weldy, writing under the pseudonyms Vin Packer and Ann Bannon, respectively—flourished because they also appealed to and were marketed for the salacious entertainment of males. A similar mass market for gay-themed literature took far longer to appear. This was, according to Stryker, partly due to gay men having better access to the then more prestigious path of hardcover publication and, hence, not having to rely on the paperback market. But it was also because of the need to package gay content in a more respectable manner to avoid possible prosecution for peddling pornography. *City of Night* appears to have been a direct catalyst for what Stryker describes as the growth of gay male paperbacks the year after it was published. These would go onto became even more numerous, as well as more openly pornographic, by the late 1960s.

City of Night opens with the never named narrator leaving for life the small, rural Texas town of his birth. He quickly falls into work as a hustler, first in New York's Times Square, then in Chicago, Los Angeles, San Francisco, and, finally, during Mardi Gras in New Orleans. In a prose style that veers between dreamy and sharp social realist observation, he describes a world of pool halls, movie theaters, dingy bars, greasy-spoon diners, and cheap apartments, inhabited by

City of Night (Grove Press, 1963)

City of Night (Panther, 1968)

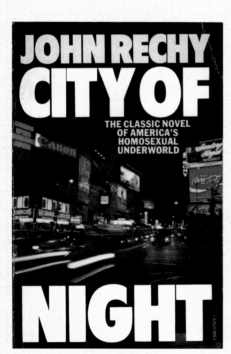

City of Night (Grenada, 1980)

As the weather had changed, from hurricane warnings to cool, I had stood along 42nd Street and Bryant Park, waiting to be picked up, and with the changing season I felt a change within me too: a frantic lonesomeness that sometimes took me, paradoxically, to the height of elation, then flung me into depression. The figure of my mother standing by the kitchen door crying, watching me leave, hovered ghostlike over me, but in the absence of that overwhelming tearing love—away from it if only physically—I felt a violent craving for something indefinable.

Throughout those weeks, on 42nd Street, the park, the movie houses, I had learned to sift the different types that haunted those places: The queens swished by in superficial gayety—giggling males acting like teenage girls; eyeing the youngmen coquettishly: but seldom offering more than a place to stay for the night. And I could spot the scores easily—the men who paid other men sexmoney, anywhere from $5.00—usually more—but sometimes even less (for some, meals and drinks and a place to stay): the amount determined by the time of day, the day of the week, the place of execution of the sex scene (their apartment, a rented room, a public toilet); their franticness, your franticness; their manner of dress, indicating affluence or otherwise; the competition on the street—the other youngmen stationed along the block like tattered guards for that defeated army, which, somehow, life had spewed out, rejected.

I found that you cant always tell a score by his age or appearance. There are the young and goodlooking ones—the ones about whom you wonder why they prefer to pay someone (who will most likely at least not indicate desiring them back) where there exists—much, much vaster than the hustling world—the world of unpaid, mutually desiring males—the easy pickups. . . . But most often the scores are near middle-aged or older men. And they are mostly uneffeminate. And so you learn to identify them by their method of approaching you (a means of identification that becomes instinctively surer and easier as you hang around longer. They will make one of the standard oriented remarks; they will offer a cigarette, a cup of coffee, a drink in a bar: anything to give them time in which to decide whether to trust you during those interludes in which there is always a suggestion of violence (although, for some, I would learn later, this is one of the proclaimed appeals—that steady hint of violence): time in which to find out if you'll fit their particular sex fantasy.

drag queens, butch and femme homosexuals, fairies, and studs.

Rechy breaks up these descriptive passages—what surely must have been among the earliest and most detailed depictions of gay street life in the U.S.—with the narrator's encounters with the citizens of this world: an over-the-top black drag queen called Miss Destiny; a man called "Mom," who enjoyed picking up men to take home and looking after them as if they were children, for money; a married man who is secretly gay; and a dying old man called "the professor," who just wants to tell him his life story. The narrator interacts with these people as friends, mentors, rivals, and, sometimes, lovers.

It is a fairly brutal world, for the most part, stripped to its basics of sex, money, status, and appearance. Many of the gay male characters are alienated and lonely. More than a few are self-loathing, not so much due to the rejection of straight society, which is largely absent from this book, but the dismissal of members of the same world. Rechy also delves into the insecurity of those worried about aging and losing their looks and, hence, their desirability.

Despite its almost forensic analysis of the craft of street hustling and the hustler's code, there is virtually no explicit sex in *City of Night*. And while the narrator never holds a day job for long before returning to the street, he is portrayed as having a vexed relationship with his trade. At times, Rechy makes hustling seem almost narcotic. At others, the narrator loathes the scene and only wants to be alone.

The one commonality shared by the characters in Rechy's book is the ever-present threat of raids from the "bulls," as the police are referred to.

> Life is lived on the brink of panic on the streets, intensifying the immediate experience . . . and panic is generated by the threat of the vice-squad (plainclothesmen sitting in the known heads licking their lips; sometimes roaming the streets, even offering you money before they bust you): by the cop car driving along the streets—a slowly moving hearse. Like a gang looking for a rumble from a rival gang, cops hunt this area, personally vindictive.

City of Night reputedly started life as a letter written about Rechy's life as a hustler in New Orleans, and the author was still doing sex work in Los Angeles when it was published. Of the book's success, Rechy said in a January 2015 interview: "The implied desirability of the narrator aroused envy in some males. Some of the worst reviews I have gotten were written by gay men who wrote about hustlers, from the point of view of the buyer. I wrote from the point of view of the hustler." The author has gone on to have a prestigious literary career, which includes penning ten books of fiction and nonfiction as well as teaching writing at universities.

Andrew Nette

The Cool, the Square, and the Tough

The Archetypes of Black Male Characters in Mystery and Crime Novels

The late Edgar Award–winning white mystery writer John D. Ball created the erudite, straight-laced, dedicated black plainclothes detective Virgil Tibbs. In Ball's groundbreaking 1965 book *In the Heat of the Night*, Pasadena plainclothes detective Tibbs finds himself in Wells, a small southern town somewhere in the Carolinas. The youngish African American is between trains on his way back home after visiting his mother somewhere else in the south. He will soon find himself investigating a crime in this small southern town. The novel begins from the viewpoint of Sam Wood, a white deputy who has just found an out-of-town conductor named Mantoli murdered and dumped in the roadway.

On the search for a suspect, Wood spots Tibbs waiting in the colored section of the train station at 3:00 am, and as this Brooks-Brothers-suit-wearing "black boy" is a likely suspect, arrests him, and hauls him off to jail. Tibbs goes along docilely.

> "And what do you do in Pasadena, California, that makes you money like that?" [Bill Gillespie, the new sheriff, a transported white Texan, asked Tibbs. Wood had confiscated Tibbs' wallet, and the two lawmen just knew no black man could come by the tens, twenties and fifties in it legitimately.]
>
> The prisoner took the barest moment before he replied.
>
> "I'm a police officer," he said.

Ball's Tibbs was specifically nonthreatening yet subversive in the ways an educated black man can be. This archetype has an antecedent in black writer Hughes Allison's Joe Hill (apparently his name was not a nod to white radical labor organizer Joe Hill, who was executed on trumped-up charges by the bosses in Utah in 1915), a hardworking and insightful black homicide detective on who appeared in one short story, "Corollary," in the July 1948 issue of *Ellery Queen Mystery Magazine*.

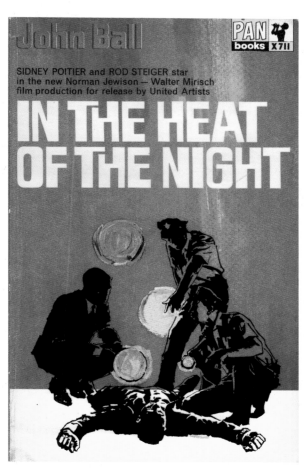

In the Heat of the Night (Pan, 1967)

Tibbs, unlike the larger, huskier Hill, is described as about fire feet nine, one hundred and fifty pounds, though all of it is taut muscle, and he doesn't have the big butt Wood is used to seeing on black men. Further, "Sam saw his face lacked the broad nose and thick, heavy lips that characterized so many southern laborers. His nose was almost like a white man's and the line of his mouth was straight and disciplined. If he had been a little lighter, Sam would have seen white blood in him, but his skin was too black for that."

We first encounter Tibbs reading a paperback by James B. Conant, *On Understanding Science*. As the investigation progresses, Tibbs refers to the deputy by his first name, considering him an equal (though Tibbs is clearly superior in his knowledge and application of police science). In further novels such as *The Cool Cottontail* (1966), where Tibbs investigates a murder in a California nudist camp, and *Five Pieces of Jade* (1972), he is the detached professional examining the clues and assembling the data that will lead him to the guilty.

Tibbs is, in the best 1960s-era liberal sense of the word, a credit to his race, as the omniscient narrator reminds us. He is a man acutely aware that he must excel not only in his police work—in the first book he does a quasi-autopsy of the body—but in his moral probity too. To the point of being corny, the Tibbs books present him as the honorable standard bearer. In both *Five Pieces of Jade* (1972) and *The Eyes of Buddha* (1976), Tibbs prefers to call himself a Negro, considering it a dignified word. Tibbs was a square. There is irony in the books, but Ball always points out the sardonic humor rather than letting the readers derive it for themselves. Though given the Asian subtext of three of Tibbs's novels, including a relationship he has with a half-black, half-Japanese woman, Tibbs is ahead of the curve in modeling relations in the emerging multicultural Los Angeles. He's presented as having virtually no flaws. Though he does have moments of self-doubt, he experiences no lapses of judgment that the reader might identify with, and thus rally to his side as he struggles to overcome such weaknesses in the pursuit of his cases.

Unlike the nefarious reputation of the Los Angeles Police Department just over the city line, there's little hint of racism or corruption within the ranks of the more bucolically portrayed Pasadena PD. It seems unlikely that Tibbs might someday come into conflict with his bosses over a questionable shooting or deadly choke hold of a black suspect. It is only in his journeys beyond the confines of a city best known for the Rose Bowl and as baseball player Jackie Robinson's birthplace that Tibbs must navigate the sharper edges of American society.

How different is the crime-solving creation of another late white writer, Ernest Tidyman, black private eye John Shaft, who premiered in the eponymously titled novel in 1971. The name alone suggests a certain attitude paired with sexual innuendo. The words on the cover of the paperback edition say it all: "Shaft has no prejudice, he'll kill anyone—black or white." And Shaft doesn't operate out of some genteel town with rolling ivy-covered hills, he works out of an office near Times Square and has a pad in the Village, in one of the most dangerous and alive cities in the world, New York.

In a teletype staccato style reminiscent of Mickey Spillane, the originator of the crypto-fascist red-hunting 1950s PI Mike Hammer, Tidyman sets the tone of the Shaft mysteries from jump:

> Shaft felt warm, loose, in step as he turned east at Thirty-ninth Street for the truncated block between Seventh Avenue and Broadway. It had been a long walk from her place in the far West Twenties. Long and good. The city was still fresh that early. Even the exhaust fans of the coffee shops along the way were blowing fresh smells, bacon, egg and toasted-bagel smells, into the fact of the gray spring morning. He had been digging it all the way. Digging it, walking fast and thinking mostly about the girl. She was crazy. Freaky beautiful. Crazy. They went out to dinner and she was wearing a tangerine wig and a long purple coat that looked like a blanket on a Central Park plug pulling one of those creaky carriages. It was the mood she was in and he had become a part of it. He never got back to his apartment. She wanted a night like that.

Shaft does not have to leave his northern city to find racism, conflict, or threats to his life in some southern backwater town. He can walk out the door and into trouble. Tibbs represents the striver, the man of humble origins who through dint of hard work and perseverance becomes a professional, and who will rise to the middle class having gained the respect of his white peers through example.

Shaft said, in effect, "Fuck that." He was a private investigator in the tradition of Raymond Chandler's prototype Philip Marlowe or Dashiell Hammett's Continental Op, men who rejected the convention of regularized law enforcement work. And in a modern sense, Shaft could not operate among the contradictions that formal police work would invariably lead to, butting up against the institutional racism of a big city police department and the structures that stood behind it. Shaft confronted racism head on, not obliquely as Tibbs would. Shaft is part of the canon of detective protagonists who know the distinction between what the powers-that-be deem to be lawlessness and what the people—the working folks, the down-trodden—understand as justice. And he knew that sometimes situations had to be arranged to achieve the latter.

There was an international spin to the careers of both Tibbs and Shaft too. They would become involved in cases taking them outside the United States. Thus settings wherein the concept of being the double outsider—black and a cop out of his jurisdiction or a PI, the "other" seeking information in alien territory—were explored. The internationalist theme in black mystery fiction was first explored by John E. Bruce, a black writer and follower of Marcus Garvey, in *Black Sleuth*, a serialized thriller-mystery written from 1907 to 1909. In this ahead-of-its time tale, African private eye Sadipe Okukenu works for the International Detective Agency and is on the trail of a stolen diamond. In the course of events, he journeys from England, to America, and then to Africa, and ruminates on the state of race relations on these various continents. It's worth noting too that it was a black woman, Pauline Hopkins, who several years before Bruce, wrote *Hagar's Daughter* (1901–2), which is now recognized as the first detective story written by an African American with black characters.

Another international traveler was Alexander Scott, "Scotty," the black CIA agent of the *I Spy* TV series (1965–1968) and novels based on the series, written by Walter Wager under the pseudonym John Tiger, with titles like *Superkill* and *Wipeout*, both published in 1967. Scott and his white fellow agent Kelly Robinson pose as an amateur "tennis bum" and his trainer to travel all over the Asian and European theaters of the 1960s Cold War. Like Scott was of the methodical, earnest school, though Cosby eventually hipped the character up on the TV show. It was assumed that the women involved in their cases, no matter their race unless they were black, would be falling all over Robinson.

In the Virgil Tibbs series, the international theme emerged in the final novel, *Singapore* (1986), in which Tibbs solves a crime and deepens a relationship with an African woman he had encountered in a previous novel. And in *Good-bye, Mr. Shaft* (1973), the roughneck detective goes to London to safeguard an African diplomat's children. Back home, Shaft's New York is a patchwork of various ethnic neighborhoods he interacts with positively and negatively in the course of his

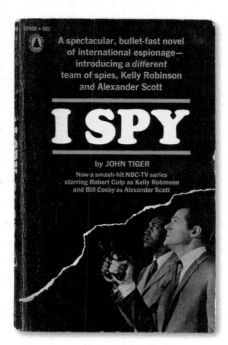

I Spy (Popular Library, 1965) *The Cool Cottontail* (Pan, 1967)

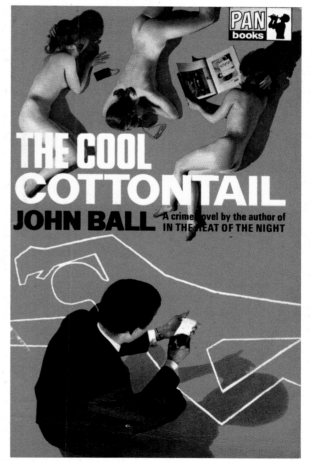

investigations in his books, a portrayal of the city in the '70s.

The New York of black writer Chester Himes's Coffin Ed Johnson and Grave Digger Jones books, written in the late 1950s through late 1960s, is essentially black and white. The two are detectives assigned to the NYPD's Harlem precinct, they work mostly at night, and both men feel very protective of their Harlem, though neither actually lives there. To them, Harlem is a black homestead surrounded by a hostile white world that is generally presented without nuance. What happens outside of Harlem bears little on the thinking of Coffin Ed or Grave Digger Jones, unless a particular case should happen to lead them to other parts of the city. As to what occurs inside Harlem—which Himes wrote about from Paris—is the underlying motivation to their work. Moving about as they do in their rumpled dark suits, pork pie and snap brim hats, and dark sedan, they are truly men in black. And as Himes chronicles their travails, there is always a satiric gallows humor to the plots, as Grave Digger and Coffin Ed chase around after fanciful hoodlums in bizarre situations.

There's Deke O'Hara, an ersatz Marcus Garvey bilking the hardworking people of Harlem with his back-to-Africa scam; there's the country-bred femme fatale Imabelle manipulating men to retrieve stolen gold ore; and there's the preacher who falls out of a window, lands in a bread basket, and then is murdered. These are some of the members of the cast of the absurdist plays that the humorless and at times brutal Coffin Ed and the slightly more idealistic Grave Digger find themselves populating.

> The reason the sergeant couldn't get Grave Digger Jones and Coffin Ed Johnson is that they were in the back room of Mammy Louise's pork store eating hot "chicken feetsy." ... Their beat-up black hats hung above their overcoats on nails in the outside wall. Sweat beaded on their skulls underneath their short-cropped, kinky hair and streamed down their dark, intent faces. Coffin Ed's hair was peppered with gray. He had a crescent-shaped scar on the right-side top of his skull, where Grave Digger had hit him with his pistol barrel, the time he had gone berserk after being blinded by acid thrown into his face. That had been more than three years ago, and the acid scars had been covered by skin grafted from

his thigh. But the new skin was a shade or so lighter than his natural face skin and it had been grafted on in pieces. The result was that Coffin Ed's face looked as though it had been made up in Hollywood for the role of the Frankenstein monster. Grave Digger's rough lumpy face could have belonged to any number of hard, Harlem characters.

The absurdist nature of their lives and cases becomes more pronounced with each book. By the time of *Blind Man with a Pistol* (1969), Himes is little interested in the complexities of plotting the mystery. Rather, the book is a reflection of race relations and his characters' (and apparently Himes's own) growing cynicism about the likelihood of change.

In the duo's last outing, *Plan B* (published posthumously in 1993), Himes was advocating or at least exploring the notion of black armed insurrection, when presumably Plan A, advocating for equality within the system had failed. The two partners have an ideological split, and Grave Digger is fired, while Coffin Ed is removed from the field. In the end, both men die. Like Tibbs, they maintained the bourgeois apparatus of law and order, if only nominally, but like Shaft were, as Frankie Y. Bailey posits in her book *Out of the Woodpile*, heirs to the bad-man mantle of black folklore.

How fitting it is, given *Plan B's* existentialist treatment of racial themes, that his characters should follow Himes, an "appreciator" of the ultimate irony, racism, to the grave. But the bad black man, the antihero protagonist, did not die in black mystery and crime fiction.

In Larry "Daddy Cool" Jackson, former pimp, thief, and drug addict Donald Goines took portions of a hard life he knew and lived, incorporating those experiences into his tough, hard-boiled crime novels. He was the black writer who wrote of the underground black life with an unfettered pulp style to which the National Association for the Advancement of Colored People (NAACP) would never bestow an Image Award, as they had Tidyman for the Shaft books.

In the 1974 book named after the main character, *Daddy Cool*, the antihero is a middle-aged black hit man who specializes in murders for hire using handmade knives. In a sardonic twist of 1970s-era efforts by African Americans to move solidly into the middle class by initiative, Jackson has done it through amoral means. He has a comfortable home, a loving wife who accepts his frequent unexplained business trips, and like many an uptight white suburban Brahman, a wayward teenaged daughter.

But his daughter wasn't experimenting with drugs or burning her bra in feminist rebellion; she was coming under the sway of a pimp named Ronald. Goines, doing time, again, at Jackson Penitentiary, had been inspired to write after reading the works of Robert a.k.a. "Iceberg Slim" Beck, also a former pimp. He gave his main character one redeeming quality: he loved his daughter. And it's this love that is his flaw. For this sense of sacrifice will eventually march Daddy Cool willingly to his doom.

For many years a writer known only in the inner cities of America, Goines was shot and killed in his home at the age of thirty-seven in 1974. His books—which included *Never Die Alone* (1974), *Whoreson* (written in prison and published in 1972), *Black Gangster* (1972), and *Eldorado Red* (1974)—were all published as paperback originals by Holloway House, a white-owned Los Angeles publisher that directed its publications toward black audiences.

The firm was also the home of such terse and urgent fare as the books of the late Beck, the hustler from whom Tracy Morrow, a.k.a. rapper Ice-T, derived his stage moniker. Holloway—whose books in those days you could find in black bookstores, ghetto markets, and an occasional newsstand—was the storehouse of a sometimes unpolished but nonetheless black pop literature that spoke to many young African Americans looking for adventures with someone who looked like them. Someone who would take it to the Man.

Holloway House published three other black anti-hero series that were paralleled in the white world in such series as Donald Westlake's (writing as Richard Stark) professional thief and killer Parker, Don Pendleton's the Executioner, and Lawrence Block's Keller, a caring hit man. Goines produced four books featuring a quasi–black nationalist crime lord called Kenyatta. Roosevelt Mallory wrote about black hit man, Radcliff, who willingly and often took on white gangsters. And the late Joe Nazel, who was also an editor at *Players*, wrote more than fifty books in various genres for the House. Among his books was a series about Henry West, the Iceman, a socially conscious hit man/vigilante who disposed of dope peddlers, wise guys, and racist cops.

"I wrote the Iceman books (nine), my black cop series featuring James Rhodes, and the Spider series

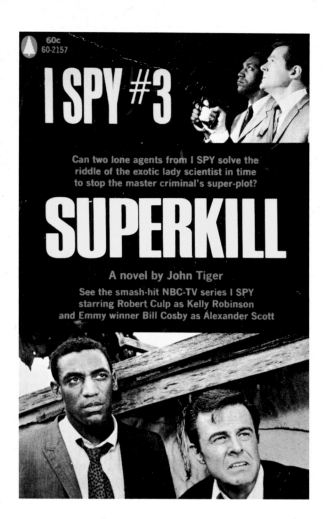

I Spy Superkill (Popular Library, 1967)
Blind Man with A Pistol (William Morrow, 1969)

featuring an investigative reporter because I was an avid reader. I read everything from the Hardy Boys to Ellery Queen," Nazel said. "But there were no black heroes in those stories. In Iceman, I wanted to do something exciting like James Bond, generate something for the African American audience to identify with and cheer about."

Nazel's terse prose and deft handling of plot and characters helped set the Holloway House style that was imitated by mainstream publishers looking to tap the black urban market back then. Notably Popular Library's late 1960s and early 1970s series featuring black troubleshooter Richard Spade a.k.a. "Superspade." Written by the pseudonymous black writer B.B. Johnson, Spade was a somewhat hip urban Doc Savage in that he was a former pro football player, head of a black studies department at a private college on the edge of Santa Barbara, taught martial arts, and assisted with the football team. He also had a secret power: a pheromone he secreted when aroused. He called it his musk, and the smell would drive a woman mad with desire—for him, of course.

Another white writer, Kenn Davis gave us another black PI, the cerebral Carver Bascombe (created by Davis and John Stanley) for Fawcett, a kind of amalgam of Shaft and Tibbs. Kevin Burton Smith noted in an article in 2000, "Beyond Shaft: Black Private Eyes in Fiction," for the online journal *January*:

> Bascombe's a young Vietnam vet with a military police background, who's now an ambitious, art-loving private eye and part-time student working his way through law school in San Francisco. Bascombe's passion comes in handy, because his cases invariably involve the arts somehow, be it opera, drama, literature, art photography, ballet, painting or poetry.

The prolific Marc Olden wrote a series of paperback martial-arts adventure novels about Robert Sand, the Black Samurai, in the 1970s for Signet. There was also a low-budget, chop-and-slice filmic effort starring Jim Kelly as Sand.

Black adventure characters go back as far as the pulp era of the 1930s and '40s, and in 1939 there came on the scene a somewhat minor-league righter of wrongs, Richard Henry Benson, the Avenger. He ran an operation of like-minded comrades-in-arms called Justice, Inc. Under the house name of Kenneth Robeson, Paul Ernst wrote these tales of thunder and lightning. What

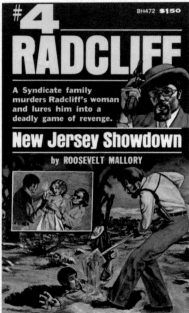

I Spy: Death-Twist (Popular Library, 1968)
Radcliff #4 New Jersey Showdown (Holloway House, 1976)

STICKING IT TO THE MAN

set him apart from a score of others was that two of the Avenger's operatives were a black husband-and-wife crime-fighting team, Josh and Rosabel Newton.

Sometimes for camouflage in plain sight, Josh in particular acted "coonish" in the vein of Stepin Fetchit [a black actor famous for playing the stereotypical slow-witted, lazy black man in films]:

> "They's shos good," the colored man added.
>
> He didn't have to talk like that. Joshua Elijah Newton was an honor graduate from a famous college. He could talk as excellent English as any professor, and he did when among friends. But when with strangers or in public places, Josh talked and acted as people expect Negroes to talk and act. It was good protective coloration.

As white pulp protagonists were masters of disguises, the disguise for Josh and Rosabel was like that of Ralph Ellison's Rinehart, an Invisible Man in broad daylight. This business of using less formal diction to conform to racist expectations, thus to be able to better observe and learn clues, is something that Walter Mosley's revisionist protagonist Easy Rawlins also admits to doing.

Then there's Hawk, a man who utilizes ebonics mixed with a laconic delivery. He is a close cousin to several of Nazel's and Goines's characters. The bad-ass enforcer is a friend and frequent partner of Robert Parker's PI, Spenser.

> Hawk nodded. He was slouched in the driver's seat, his eyes half shut, at rest. He was perfectly capable of staying still for hours, and feeling rested, and missing nothing.
>
> "Something will develop," Hawk said.
> "Because we're here." I said.
> "Un huh."
> "They won't be able to tolerate us sitting here," I said.
> Hawk grinned.
> "We an affront to their dignity," he said.
> "So they'll finally have to do something."
> "Un huh."
> "Sort of like bait," I said.
> "Exactly," Hawk said.
> "What a dandy plan!"
> "You got a better idea?" Hawk said.
> "No."
> "Me either."

The current wave of people of color as both writers and characters in mystery and crime writing expands the purview of a genre many still derogate as lowbrow writing. And as its practitioners have increased in diversity, many are coming to the field as readers who had not before, discovering stories that deal with issues of racism, class, power, and wealth, along with healthy doses of love, avarice, and the ambiguities of human nature.

That's crazy, baby . . . crazy.

Gary Phillips

Resilience and Representation

Representations of Aboriginal Australians in Pulp and Popular Fiction

It was Karl Marx who suggested that those who don't represent themselves will inevitably suffer the representations of others. This has certainly been the case for Australia's First Nations peoples, although the situation appears to be slowly changing. Because Indigenous writing is a relatively recent phenomenon, albeit largely co-opted into more literary forms of expression, the body of pulp writing that relates to Aboriginal Australia is necessarily a small one. Many texts that might ordinarily be described as pulp, in terms of theme and aesthetic, as they relate to Aboriginal Australia, have been released under literary imprints, which necessitates looking beyond pulp publishers and imprints.

The history of Australian colonization and the specific stereotypes relating to indigeneity can be clearly ascertained not only in the minimal textual production of a "black pulp" literature but also in the specific absences. In the U.S., for example, Indigenous peoples were often represented in pulp texts as a fierce enemy, but one at least worthy of being represented as a significant force in opposition to the inevitable forces of a manifest destiny, thereby amplifying the "heroism" of the invader. Yet this has rarely been the case in Australian frontier writing, where the "Western," as it relates to the Australian story of dispossession, never really took hold. This has a lot to do with the differences in social structure and population of Aboriginal Australia, where people generally lived in smaller clan groups rather than in large tribal "armies," as commonly represented in the American Western genre. This meant that where open conflict broke out between Europeans and Aborigines, the warfare was "guerrilla," and the overwhelming force of arms of the invaders and the smaller population groups of the invaded meant that the matter was usually quickly decided (with exceptions such as in Tasmania, the Kimberleys, and Northern Queensland). In this context, it was not the "battles" between the two groups that were significant in terms of representation, or the representations of rugged frontier masculinity, but rather the silence.

The massacres that occurred all over Australia were dirty secrets it was thought best to conceal or deny. Because of this, and despite the presence of some significant resistance leaders across Australia, the Aboriginal warrior was rarely romanticized, aestheticized, fetishized, or even given due respect.

In effect, the rapid subjugation of Australia's Indigenous population and the effectiveness of successive government policies in terms of institutionalizing the dispossession, cultural damage and removal from country and removal of children, meant that the most persistent narrative from the late nineteenth century to the mid-twentieth century related to Aboriginal peoples inevitable "dying out," based on the misunderstood Darwinian theory survival of the fittest and corresponding extinction of the least fit. Aboriginal people effectively became fringe dwellers in their own land, surviving on the margins of the national consciousness; including the literary consciousness. Unlike in the United States, there was no eroticization in Australia of the Aboriginal male body analogous to the "Mandingo" narratives of American pulp, or reification of Aboriginal resistance leaders or particular "tribes," as in the tropes of the American Western.

It was the resilience of Aboriginal people in the face of a general culture of antipathy and apathy that explains the anger of extant novels written about Aboriginal Australia that may be considered pulp. Similarly, due to the higher rates of incarceration of Aboriginal Australians, it's hardly surprising that the majority of these texts reference the broader features of social crime as acceptable; that is, crime can be justified in the context of acts of rebelliousness and resistance amid the struggle to survive. Many of the most forceful texts belonging to this subgenre of pulp crime—that is, fiction that seeks to explain the mind of "the delinquent" as a legitimate response to ineluctable social forces and particularly racial oppression—have been produced by non-Indigenous writers. In this sense, this brand of Aboriginal pulp is where issues of authenticity and Indigeneity have perhaps intersected most forcefully, as shall be discussed.

Perhaps the best-known and earliest example of this is Arthur Upfield's Bony series of twenty-nine crime novels, published between 1929 and 1966. The novels featured the "half-caste"—a colonial term for people of mixed Indigenous and non-Indigenous descent, which has taken on a pejorative overtone—protagonist Napoleon Bonaparte. These were best sellers in Australia and abroad and many are still in print. Upfield was an Englishman who arrived in Australia in 1911 and served with the Australian Imperial Force at Gallipoli during World War I. He spent the best part of the following decades in the Australian bush, where most of the Bony series takes place. He became particularly well-known when working in Western Australia, after describing in his novel *The Sands of Windee* (1931) how to commit the perfect murder, by destroying all traces of a human body. One of the men who'd worked alongside Upfield in the bush, Snowy Rowles, took this information to heart and is said to have committed three murders using the method, before he was caught and hanged. The murder trial received great publicity, and the Bony novels reached a broader audience.

The character of Bony soon became Australia's best-loved fictional detective, an anomaly perhaps in the context of the majority of Aboriginal lives, but a character whose agency was importantly a product of his mixed-race status as a man "of two tribes." In other words, Bony's ability to "code-shift" and his knowledge of the outback gave him an advantage over the whites in the novels. Upfield has subsequently been criticized for the simple fact that while Bony is himself a sympathetic character, the broader representations of Aboriginality are inevitably cast through the political lens of the period. Postcolonial understandings of the inappropriateness of unmediated European representations of Aboriginal life have meant that his novels have fallen out of favor in Australia and have been criticized in particular by Australia's best-known Aboriginal crime writer, Philip McLaren. Despite this, the Bony novels are still very popular outside Australia, where the pulp-looking Pan Books paperback editions in particular made them widely available.

When Colin Johnson's novel *Wild Cat Falling* was released in 1965, it was touted as the first Australian novel written by an Aboriginal person. Kath Walker's (Oodgeroo Noonuccal's) volume of poetry *We Are Going* (1954), the first poetry collection written by an

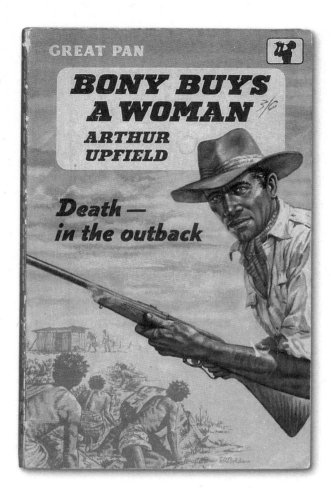

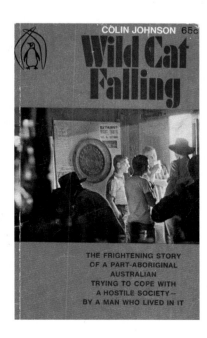

Boney Buys a Woman (Pan, 1959)
Wild Cat Falling (Penguin, 1966)

Long Live Sandawara (Hyland House, 1992)

the life a teenage Nyungar [Aboriginal person from Western Australia's southwest] in Perth's streets. The story opens with the release of the unnamed narrator from Fremantle Prison. His attitude is reflexively antiauthoritarian, as a clear product of the government policies relating to the assimilation of lighter-skinned Aboriginal people in Western Australia, one of the "stolen generation" resulting from policies that made all Aboriginal people wards of the state. The narrator hits the streets but doesn't expect to be free for too long. As Stephen Muecke suggests in the book's introduction, "This character is not self-motivated—things just happen to him. This is a novel more—on the surface—about *indifference* than moral direction, and that indifference lies both in the "empty" character and in the structure of the social world that produces the indifference." Black men with "bad" attitudes can expect to be incarcerated, in other words. It is the subject matter of the countless pulp novels of the period aiming to articulate the mindset of a delinquent youth with the usual complexes of resentments and a larger than usual chip on the shoulder. What sets this novel apart is not the writing, which employs the usual American jargon associated with the hepcat beatnik, or the sometimes awkward existential philosophizing, or the apt and ironic readings of social class in sixties Perth. Rather it is distinguished by its ending, in which the narrator, having committed a serious crime, returns to his true country and embraces his Indigenous family, long denied.

The complexity of the rebellious youth and the dawning of a political or cultural consciousness is perhaps better explored in Johnson's follow-up novel *Long Live Sandawara* (1979). This employs more playfully and expertly the lurid language of the pulp form, in the context of a group of young people endeavoring to both survive and enjoin "revolution," collected around a leader based upon the Kimberley warrior Jandamarra. This character's instincts are sound, but he finds the complications of modern life derail and in some cases cast into farcical relief the idea of a modern Aboriginal rebellion. *Wild Cat Falling* ends in violence and inevitable white retribution, the narrator having shot a policeman, although he feels no remorse, stating that "all policemen deserve to die."

Frank Clune's 1959 pulp biography *Jimmy Governor* works the same terrain but in a more sustained fashion. Governor's story became well-known in Australia after Thomas Keneally's *The Chant of Jimmie Blacksmith*

Aboriginal person, had been released a few years previously, and quickly became a best seller. The readership was there, in other words, although Johnson's life was very different from that of Oodgeroo Noonacal, who was a prominent activist at the time of *We Are Going*. Johnson, now known as Mudrooroo Narogin or Mudrooroo Nyungah, was twenty-seven at the time of *Wild Cat Falling*'s release, and it was the novel's critical success that spurred a subsequent career as one of Australia's leading Indigenous writers and academics. Many of his works were placed on school and university course reading lists, and he was a prominent and outspoken commentator on Indigenous issues. This prominence and outspokenness led to controversy, however, when he attacked another Aboriginal writer in print, and his indigeneity was subsequently questioned by those he'd claimed kinship with.

Regardless of the controversy surrounding its author, *Wild Cat Falling* provided a fierce picture of

(1972) and its 1978 film adaptation, although Keneally has since stated that he regretted writing the novel from the POV of an Indigenous character. Interestingly, it's one of the main points of Clune's biography that Jimmy Governor did not like to regard himself as Indigenous, with his pale skin and red hair, but rather as a "half-caste." His eventual violent rampage stemmed from his efforts to assimilate having been thwarted by a culture that only saw him as black, but in keeping with the widespread beliefs of his era, Governor's murderousness was attributed solely to "natural flaws" of his Aboriginal ancestry.

Clune's book, on the surface of it, is a condemnation of this cultural bias against a hardworking man, married to a white woman, and the institutional racism and injustice that kept black Australians "in their place." A product of its time, however, Clune's Horwitz biography, while nominally sympathetic, contains sensationalist renderings of the crimes and lines that effectively reproduce the racism that he's apparently proscribing, such as the claim that "Joe [Jimmy's younger brother] was neither as intelligent, nor as well-educated as Jimmy. He was a throw-back to the aboriginal side, rather than to the white." Regardless, the book charts the inception of Governor's series of twelve murders, the realization of the futility of his trying to fit in, and his decision to hit back and become a "bushranger" (a term for Australian nineteenth-century outlaws), although this ambition was never realized. The crimes so horrified New South Wales that at one point there were thousands of armed men hunting him. Despite this, he and his brother eluded capture for two months before being caught, with Joe shot dead and Jimmy hanged in Sydney.

One other novel whose writing, characterization, and overt ideological purpose as a celebration of pulp energy was Diana Fuller's novelization of the 1977 movie *Journey among Women*. The film was a box-office success in Australia, allegedly because of its risqué subject matter depicting open lesbian relationships with full nudity. The novel of the same name that was published in the same year extends this representation, employing on the cover a picture of a naked Aboriginal woman wielding an adze. The novel follows the same plot and contains the same characters, exploring the brutal treatment of convict women in the early days of Australian settlement, in the context of the generally subservient role women of the period were expected to play. One such woman, Elizabeth Harrington, the

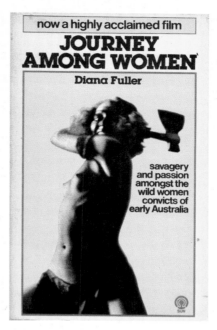

Journey among Women (Sun Books, 1977)
The Running Man (Horwitz, 1967)

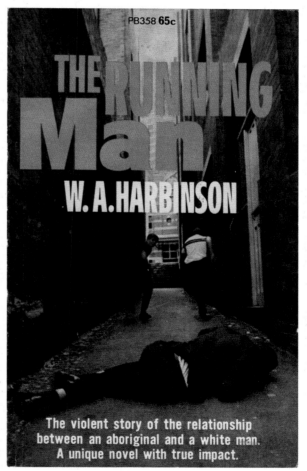

daughter of the brutish judge-advocate, helps several convict women to escape and follows them out into the bush, where a utopia of sorts is soon established. The white women are aided by a young Aboriginal woman, who teaches them how to survive, as well as the importance of ritual and respect for the land.

As a revisionist feminist exploitation tract, *Journey among Women* depicts each of the convict women's refusal to bend to the wills of their male masters and characterizes the young Aboriginal woman as a paragon of feminine fierceness, tenderness, and resourcefulness, an indicator of the way the white escapees hope their colony might evolve. For daring to be different, they are hunted by the patriarchy, and the language of the text becomes more and more extreme and obvious in its depictions of masculine brutishness and ignorance, set against the democratic feminine virtues of quietude, humor, caring, and sharing, as expressed in their camp. When Elizabeth Harrington's fiancé, the dashing Captain McEwan, approaches their camp toward the novel's end, she is forced to choose between living as a free woman and returning to life under a man's rule.

Another book/film combination that incorporated the idea of white people lost in the bush being aided by an Aboriginal helper was the novel *Walkabout* by James Vance Marshall (1959) and its 1971 adaptation of the same name by Nicolas Roeg. The film is far better known than its source novel, and in it the incident that begets the children's marooning in the harsh outback is more dramatic, involving the suicide of the father after shooting at his own children (in the novel it's a plane crash). In the same vein as *Journey among Women*, Marshall's text also positions its white characters as removed from the natural world, to an extent that they are helpless, "Coddled in babyhood, psychoanalysed in childhood, nourished on pre-digested patent foods, provided with continuous push-button entertainment, the basic realities of life were something that they'd never had to face." Although the writing of *Walkabout* is less lurid or overtly ideological, the function of the novel's Aboriginal character is the same—that is, as a vehicle to bring the narrative's white characters closer to a fuller realization of the fragility of life, of their survival, and of the power of the land and of the joys to be had living the simple life. The cost of this representation of Aboriginals as guides in both novels is found in their idealization and romanticization, however well meaning.

Walkabout (Penguin, 1959)
The Day of the Dog (Pan, 1981)
Jimmy Governor (Horwitz, 1970)

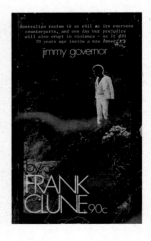

Archie Weller's 1981 novel *The Day of the Dog*, which won the Australian Vogel Literary Award of that year, contains themes and characters which share much with pulp novels that have traditionally centered upon troubled youth. Much like *Wild Cat Falling* before it, the plot focuses upon a protagonist newly released from jail. Doug Dooligan is also of a mixed-race background, and his mother too has tried her best to assimilate into white society, although this too has been largely thwarted. Her husband, after failing on the land, has become an alcoholic, and after her eldest son is killed in Vietnam, the responsibility of being the good son is too much for Dougie.

In many respects the novel works against stereotypes, both racist and romantic, as the chaos and culture of desperation and poverty, of fighting, drinking, theft, and domestic violence, constantly derail his and his mother's attempts to walk the line. Doug just wants to fit in, but family is family, and if his family is anarchic and don't always have his best interests at heart, then so be it. He finds love and a job, but the call of the street and of his friends is too great. He too is lured into a scheme that ends violently and tragically, but unlike in *Wild Cat Falling*, there is little or no absolution or solace in culture. The cadences of Nyungar street slang, and the descriptions and the rituals of urban poverty and hopelessness, leavened only by the brief comforts of intoxication and tenderness, are all authentically if ferociously rendered. Leaving aside the fact that Weller's indigeneity has also been questioned, and despite the book's literary plaudits and publisher, *Day of the Dog* is perhaps the best example of the Australian pulp genre that pertains to troubled youth, albeit in this case specifically looking at Indigenous subjects.

W.A. Harbinson's 1970 pulp novel *The Running Man* falls between the publication of Colin Johnson's *Wild Cat Falling* and Weller's *Day of the Dog*. Harbinson (b. 1941) is an Irishman who migrated to Australia and served time in the Royal Australian Airforce. After the publication of *The Running Man* and having returned to Britain, he went on to become a successful novelist, writing primarily science fiction and war novels. The cover of the 1970 U.S. edition of the novel is highly disingenuous, showing a picture of a black man in naked communion with a redheaded woman who gazes at him longingly. The caption beside the picture reads: "A raw, gritty novel of today's most taboo subject." In fact, the hinted-at miscegenation between black and white plays very little part in what is an excellently written account of yet another troubled youth, Andy, a white kid on the run from a boring life in Perth and headed for the bright lights of Kings Cross, Sydney. Here he finds a room in a lodging house run by an Indigenous man ("He was black, cool … corrupt. … His name was Collins"), bought by the proceeds of crime. Collins is certainly an intriguing character in the pantheon of white writing about Aboriginal subjects. Utterly unsentimental, entirely ruthless, and very much a loner, Collins has decided to survive by preying on the weaknesses and appetites of whites on the skids. He is alternately cruel and generous to the inhabitants of the rooming house, but most of all he despises weakness and seeks to destroy those who are weak, in the belief that in the context of being an Aboriginal man in a racist society, to display any weakness of his own would be fatal to himself.

Collins befriends Andy but is unflinchingly honest about his actions and the reasons for them. Despite his ruthlessness, he is something of a charismatic character, a creature of the street that knows the rules of the street, and therefore is best placed to survive where others falter and die. When he is the subject of a racist attack, he defends himself with his knife, killing a white man, but he is unremorseful, and Andy can understand why. In this way Collins is a singular figure in black pulp writing in Australia. Neither romanticized, politicized, nor in any way ideological, he is yet the novel's best-drawn and most sympathetic character. He is articulate and canny and resourceful, and underneath the ruthlessness there is vulnerability and clarity. The novel ends with Collins barricaded inside his rooming house while on the street coppers with rifles await. It's a clear recapitulation of the heroic swagman story of "Waltzing Matilda" fame, central to the Australian mythos, translated to the situation of a tough young black male in a stand-off where he knows he'll be killed while incarcerated, becoming another black death in custody if he surrenders. His choice is no choice at all, in accordance with the logic of survival that has defined his life thus far. He chooses death by cop, instead of handing himself in, a decision that even the coppers who kill him are forced to respect. *The Running Man* is a one-off, which is a pity, as reading the novel leads to the inevitable conclusion that a distinctive and controlled voice like Harbinson's when applied to pulp subjects would have been a boon to Australian writing in the longer term.

Dick Peters's 1973 *Operation Concrete Butterfly*, on the other hand, takes the genuine concerns of Aboriginal Australians and buries them in a narrative that, while entertaining in its fashion, marginalizes its Aboriginal characters further by way of subtle devices that foreground instead the hypermasculinity and aesthetic sexualization of an African American lead character, by way of a fictional mashup of the softcore "slavery porn" and blaxploitation narratives produced in Britain and the U.S. during the period. *Operation Concrete Butterfly* pits the tall, black, and sexually potent Elmore Glover and his gang consisting of three Aboriginal people, a Maori, and a revolutionary Vietnamese male against the local coppers during the hijacking of the opening ceremony of the Sydney Opera House, complete with a cast of real-life dignitaries such as then prime minister Gough Whitlam, then union leader and later prime minister Bob Hawke, and Queen Elizabeth II.

Written in a breathless, stoner hippie style, the novel pays lip service to the concerns of black liberation movements around the world, including Australia (Glover is a Black Panther on the run), while running a main narrative consisting of Glover and a stunning white woman circling one another before the inevitable coupling. The softcore porn, comic violence, and revolutionary fervor is a strange concoction, but not without its charms. One of its themes, if that's the correct word, is that of sexual desire undermining political consciousness, in that the falling apart of the hijack plot is due in each case to the characters' lust distracting them from the main game. In particular, the representation of the two Aboriginal lovers, Jomo Rose and JoJo Ebony, who never become more than ciphers, falls apart because of Jomo's jealousy over JoJo's lusting for the more virile "authentic black" American, with tragic results. By this reading, *Operation Concrete Butterfly* can be read as a lurid and anarchic celebration and critique of the libidinous energies at the heart of ideological thinking, if nothing else.

In the intervening years since the publication of operation *Concrete Butterfly*, *Day of the Dog*, and *Wild Cat Falling*, several Indigenous writers have turned to the crime genre as a corrective to the usual positioning of Aboriginal characters as criminal and victim, producing more nuanced and authentic representations of Aboriginal subjectivities as expressions of an enduring resilience.

David Whish-Wilson

Operation Concrete Butterfly (Arkon, 1973)

Black Lightning, Dymphna Cusack (Readers Books Club, 1964)

Black Lightning opens with a glamorous Sydney socialite and television lifestyle personality, Tempe Caxton, recovering in hospital after a failed suicide attempt. Keith, her dashing journalist lover, has left her to marry the daughter of the media mogul who owns the newspaper he has taken over editorship of. Her television career is over after she is dumped for a younger woman. And her son, Christopher, who she and her ex-husband press-ganged into accepting conscripted national service in the army, has been killed in Malaya, a casualty of the long-running effort by Britain and its Commonwealth and Malaysian allies to defeat communist insurgents in the country.

"Left childless and barren," she reads her late son's diary, which leaves her in no doubt just how much he despised her and how shallow and narcissistic he believed her to be. The diary passages, told from Christopher's point of view, also reveal his growing attraction, and eventual marriage to a young half-Aboriginal woman, Zanny, who lives with her Swedish former whaler father, Aboriginal mother, and large family on a stretch of deserted beach in northern New South Wales, near the army base where he is undertaking basic training. Tempe had disapproved of her son's marriage to Zanny, which resulted in a granddaughter she has never met, an attitude she bitterly regrets.

When Zanny's family reach out to Tempe, she travels to meet them. She is shocked to discover that Zanny is dead, from an illness related to the shock of Christopher's death, and that the family have plans of their own. They want to use her public profile to fight their threatened eviction by real-estate developers, who in league with the local town's corrupt council want to build a resort on the beach. Tempe agrees to help and is quickly radicalized by the horrific racism that the family and other members of the local Aboriginal community are subjected to.

Read through a contemporary lens, the story of a white woman who is unremarkable except for her media profile and who comes to the aid of an Aboriginal family has a somewhat paternalistic feel. But Cusack pulls no punches in depicting the lack of even the most basic human rights enjoyed by Aboriginal people prior to the civil and land rights campaigns of the late 1960s and '70s, and the brutal state control they were subjected to. The book was influenced by Cusack's friendship with members of the Aboriginal

Black Lightning (Pan, 1964)

civil rights movement pushing for the ultimately successful vote in Australia's 1967 referendum. Technically, this only concerned amendments that would allow the federal government to count Indigenous people in the census as well as pass laws concerning them, which had previously been the prerogative of individual states. However, support for constitutional change encapsulated rising progressive feeling and fueled Indigenous claims for self-determination that came to include demands that non-Indigenous Australians act as allies rather than leaders within the antiracist and land rights movements. That so much of what Cusack writes about could be so easily set today only makes the novel more forceful.

Cusack is best known as the coauthor of *Come in Spinner* (1951), the title a slang term for the call given to signal that all bets are placed and the coin is ready to be tossed in a once-popular Australian gambling game called "two up." The story of three women in wartime Sydney, it was a best seller but also hugely controversial due its portrayal of issues such as abortion, prostitution, and vice in 1940s Sydney, and the book was not published in full until 1987.

Much of Cusack's work was dismissed as romance or "women's fiction." As a British *Sunday Times* review quoted on the back cover of the 1964 Pan version of *Black Lightning*, put it: "THREE QUARTERS TOP CLASS LADIES FICTION—ONE QUARTER HIGHLY DISTURBING." But this label obscured the fact that her books dealt with deeply radical themes.

She tackled racism in an earlier book, *The Sun in Exile* (1955), and the continuing threat of Nazism in *Heatwave in Berlin* (1961). A dedicated antiwar activist, her 1955 play *Pacific Islands*, dealt with the arms race. The 1969 novel *The Half-Burnt Tree* was a well ahead of its time in its depiction of a Vietnam veteran, wounded by napalm, and his difficulties upon returning home. The plot of *The Sun Is Not Enough* (1967, reprinted by Gold Star Publications in 1972) looked at the Ustasha, an ultranationalist Croatian fascist organization active in Australia in the 1960s and '70s, which carried out bombings against Yugoslavian government and tourist offices in Australia and had secret training camps in the country.

Cusack's novels were not only published overseas but were very successful in the Eastern bloc. She battled poor health all her life and was only diagnosed in 1980 with multiple sclerosis. She died a year later.

Andrew Nette

Come in Spinner (Pan, 1960)
The Half-Burnt Tree
(Heinemann, 1969)

Paul pulled away from him. "If she's going to be of any use to us she's got to hear them sooner or later and I think sooner's best. No good her thinking she's only got to lift a lily-white hand for the magic to work. There isn't any magic for Aborigines and that's the truth."

He reached for the demijohn of hop-beer and poured himself another mugful. "The law says we've got a right to drink in a pub, but what happened when I go into a pub in Wallaba? The pub-keeper said to me: 'Out of here, black fella.' Another white tripped me as I was going out the door. Me that fought in the war.

"What rights have we got? None. They've taken our land from us. They've taken our names. I don't know the songs of my people, and I speak the white man's language." He pointed a finger at Tempe. "You've got an Aboriginal granddaughter—but did you know that the Constitution of the Commonwealth doesn't even mention Aborigines as people to be legislated for as people of any other race are legislated in this country? Do you know we're not even counted in the census?"

Ferment in Fiction

British Novels and Radical Movements, 1965–75

The 1960s and '70s were a time of literary, cultural, social, and political ferment in England. Although Kenneth Allsop had titled his 1958 book on the 1950s *The Angry Decade*, it seems, in longer retrospect, a docile decade, with austerity giving way to affluence but structures of deference staying largely in place. In literary terms, the early 1950s had been dominated by "the Movement," which paradoxically combined rebellion with conformity: its leading figures—the novelists and poets Kingsley Amis, Philip Larkin, and John Wain—rebelled against modernist experimentation as variously represented by Joyce, Woolf, Eliot, and Pound but conformed to more traditional literary modes in their work and eschewed anything more than vague and occasional political references.

In 1956, the "Angry Young Men" emerged, a media-amplified cultural phenomenon primarily represented by two very different works that appeared within a month of each other in that year: John Osborne's play *Look Back in Anger*, first performed in May that year, and Colin Wilson's exploration of existential crises, *The Outsider*, published in the same month. Neither of these works, however, demonstrated or advocated literary and aesthetic innovation or political activism. Osborne's Jimmy Porter complained that "there aren't any good, brave causes left" but had no faith that old ones could be revived or new ones revealed. Wilson's various Outsiders saw politics as superficial compared to the quest for spiritual intensity. Alan Sillitoe's *Saturday Night and Sunday Morning* (1958) was the most rebellious novel of the "angry decade"; but its working-class antihero, Arthur Seaton, rejected both trade union activism and upward mobility, staying in his class of origin and enjoying relative affluence without aspiring to move into the middle class.

The 1960s, however, ushered in seismic social and political changes. On October 15, 1964, the Labour Party won the general election, ending thirteen years of Conservative government. British pop music, embodied above all in the Beatles, broke away from imitating American pop music to gain a distinctive identity of its own. In its issue of April 15, 1966, *Time* magazine identified Swinging London as the epicenter of a fashion and lifestyle earthquake. Sexual constraints started to loosen as a bill that gained royal assent on July 27, 1967, decriminalized homosexual acts in private between men over twenty-one, and the permissive society burgeoned. Political protest grew, particularly against American involvement in Vietnam, and occupations took place at British universities, especially the London School of Economics and the new University of Essex. Experiments in living in communes rather than in families and couples developed. And in 1970–71, the Angry Brigade, a British guerrilla group with some similarities to the Weather Underground, carried out a series of bombings whose targets included, on January 12, 1971, the house of the then home secretary, Robert Carr, at a time when Carr and his wife and thirteen-year-old daughter were inside.

The relationship between these events and the development of the English novel in this period was by no means straightforward; but in fiction, as in other areas of cultural life and social behavior, there was a new climate of exploration, experimentation, innovation and sometimes aggression. We explore here nine novels from the 1960s and '70s that engage, with varying degrees of directness, with key aspects of the political tumults of the time. All of these were offered as "serious" novels rather than genre or pulp fiction, at a time when the division between "serious" and popular fiction was, in the UK, still fairly firmly in place. Yet none of them has achieved canonical literary status in the sense of being extensively discussed in studies of, or courses on, the fiction of the period. Along with their intrinsic merit, that is another good reason why they deserve attention.

Alan Sillitoe: The William Posters Trilogy, 1965–74

Among the new writers who became famous in the 1950s, Alan Sillitoe had the least formal education and the greatest claim to the status of an authentically

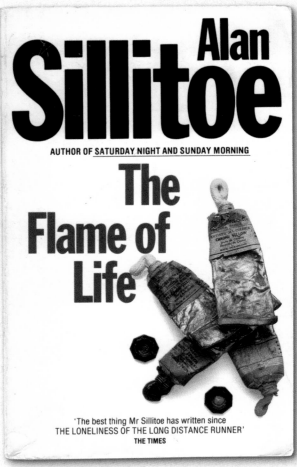

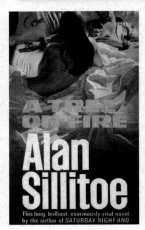
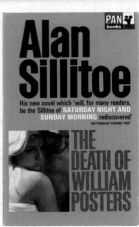

Flame of Life (Grafton, 1986)
A Tree on Fire (Pan, 1969)
Death of William Posters (Pan, 1967)

working-class writer, although he himself vigorously repudiated the label. Born on March 4, 1928, in the city of Nottingham in the English East Midlands, he was the second of five children of Christopher Archibald and Sabina Sillitoe; his father was feckless, illiterate, often unemployed and sometimes violent. He left school in 1942, at the age of fourteen, to work for Raleigh Bicycles and other local factories. In 1947, he was sent as an RAF wireless operator to Malaya, still then a British protectorate where conflict loomed between the Malayan National Liberation Army and British troops. When he returned to England in 1948 for demobilization, he was diagnosed with tuberculosis and, after nearly ten months in hospital, was discharged from the RAF with a small disability pension. He began a relationship with the Jewish American poet Ruth Fainlight, whom he would marry in 1959. They went to live in France and then Majorca until his debut novel, *Saturday Night and Sunday Morning* (1958), made him famous and prosperous. He followed this up with the short-story collection *The Loneliness of the Long-Distance Runner* (1960), whose title tale is the vivid vernacular narrative of Colin Smith, petty crook, Borstal boy, and intransigent rebel. Both *Saturday Night* and *Loneliness* became classic British New Wave films.

In the later 1960s and the early 1970s, Sillitoe produced the William Posters trilogy, consisting of *The Death of William Posters* (1965); *A Tree on Fire* (1967) and *The Flame of Life* (1974). These are hybrid mixed-genre works that combine realist, picaresque, fabulatory, melodramatic, existential-quest, expressionist and adventure elements. The William Posters of the trilogy's title is an archly formal version of "Bill Posters," the figure of urban folklore engendered by the inscription aimed at deterring illegal bill-posting on buildings and hoardings: "Bill Posters will be prosecuted." Bill Posters is the man who is endlessly persecuted and pursued, for no specified crime, but who always eludes his hunters. "Everywhere he was threatened with prosecution. . . . The whole country, it seemed, was after him. . . . But the great and marvellous thing was that they never got him!" But to the trilogy's main protagonist, Frank Dawley, Bill is a symbol of servility, with "the typical mentality of the workman-underdog, the put-upon dreg whose spiritual attributes he had been soaked and bombarded with all through his school, home and working life." Frank wants to reject this symbol, to bring about the death of William Posters, at least in himself.

At the start of the trilogy, Frank has thrown up the job in a Nottingham factory he has held for twelve years (with a break for compulsory National Service) and left his wife and two children. *The Death of William Posters* takes him to Lincolnshire and London and then out of England to Spain, Majorca, Tangier, and the Moroccan/Algerian border. In his factory days, Frank was a keen trade unionist, "a bit of a troublemaker" who once brought the whole shop out on strike against the management, and forced it to back down, when it used its favorite technique of targeting the colored workers in its attempt to reduce work rates. But his rebellion now is individualist and idiosyncratic—for example, when he mounts a verbal assault, in classic Sillitoe style, on his mistress's estranged husband, who seems to him to embody the manipulative class enemy:

> Your cock crow's hoarse and false, mate, full of maggots, you miseducated boatfaced bastard eating food and wearing clothes you never earned or advertised on the telly. You speak calm but you boil like an empty kettle, the moon in your mouth and the sun up your arse. You're starry-eyed and cloudy at the brain except when it comes to doing the sort of job that will keep you like it forever. The world's top heavy with you and your sort who wank people's brains off every night with telly advertisements that make them happy at carrying slugs like you on their backs, but I'd like to see you do a real day's work, if you could, if anybody'd be crazy enough to set you on.

In London, Frank goes to the private view of the paintings of Albert Handley, an artist in his early forties who lives in a ramshackle Lincolnshire house with his seven children and who is, after years of poverty, on the verge of a huge success. At the private view he encounters Myra Bassingfield, who comes from a prosperous Jewish family in Hampstead and has a first-class degree from the London School of Economics and a private income of £500 a year (equivalent to about £10,500 today). She is quietly dissatisfied with her life and marriage to George, a surveyor and lecturer, and is drawn to the idea of the working classes, which primes her for a relationship with Frank:

> Myra . . . thanked God for the voting Labour masses that still seemed to inhabit the north:

cloth-capped, hardworking, generous and bruto, or was that the impression she got from reading a book (or was it books?) called *Hurry on Jim* by Kingsley Wain that started by someone with eighteen pints and fifteen whiskies in him falling downstairs on his way to the top.

In this passage Sillitoe comically scrambles references to writers (himself included) who were labeled "Angry Young Men" in the 1950s, often against their will. Myra mixes up the titles and authors of John Wain's *Hurry on Down* (1953), Kingsley Amis's *Lucky Jim* (1954), and John Braine's *Room at the Top* (1957) and creates an even more crapulent version of the spectacular opening scene of Sillitoe's own *Saturday Night*, in which Arthur Seaton drinks seven gins and eleven pints of beer and tumbles down a flight of pub stairs.

Frank sets off abroad with Myra, who is now pregnant. In Morocco, Shelley Jones, a tall young American who studied history at the University of Chicago, worked on Madison Avenue, and is now a committed revolutionary roaming the globe in quest of causes, asks Frank to accompany him on a mission to deliver guns and printed matter such as maps and guerrilla manuals in Arabic to the Front de Libération Nationale, fighting for Algerian independence against French colonial rule. Frank agrees and they set off with Myra's consent, leaving her to give birth alone. Near the Algerian border, after a gunfight that leaves six French foot soldiers and one Moroccan dead, Shelley wants to return to Tangier, but Frank insists on pressing on and makes it clear he will shoot Shelley, if necessary, to get his way. Shelley yields, and the novel ends as they drive into the desert. "Frank felt that the desert was the only place where he would find something. People might say he'd had everything: job, wife, children. What more was there? He wanted to go into the desert to find out."

The second William Posters novel, *A Tree on Fire*, is set around 1960. Its major theme, embodied in Frank and Albert Handley, is the attempt to achieve existential authenticity—to become, in a sense, "a tree . . . on fire," a recurrent motif in the text—while also maintaining some kind of communal relationship. Frank seeks this as he faces danger and death in the desert helping the FLN fight for Algerian independence against French troops. Handley seeks it by trying to retain his integrity as a painter and live an energetic family life while fighting off the pressures of success.

On a more mundane, materialistic level, Mandy, one of Handley's daughters, seeks an identity for herself through the red Mini car that she urges her father to buy her—a symbol of the consumer society that, by the early 1960s, was assimilating the existential intensities and austerities of the immediate postwar era—and, more profoundly, through marriage and motherhood. When Frank returns to England, he joins a kind of community, a mixture of family and commune, based at Myra's house and financed by the interest on her invested share of her father's will and the proceeds of Handley's paintings. *Tree* ends with Cuthbert, the Handleys' eldest son, proposing a toast to all the community's members and Frank raising his glass, but only to his private vision of "many weeks, even years of invigorating chaos ahead, of great ideas, and great work."

Seven years passed before the last volume of the trilogy, *The Flame of Life*, appeared. In his "author's note" to this novel, Sillitoe says he began it in August 1967 and finished it in January 1974 and attributes the delay both to the pressure of other writing and to the plot and form of *Flame* being less "absolutely clear in my mind than they subsequently became." A further likely reason for the delay was the change in Sillitoe's own political position as he came under attack from a radical Left that ranked him, in the words of one flysheet, among the "Traitors to the English Working Class" and as he became more firmly committed to the defense of Israel against what he saw as unjustified and anti-Semitic criticism.

Flame focuses on the travails of the community that emerged toward the end of *Tree*. Although *Flame* is loosely set in the early 1960s—as chapter 47 concludes, "the radio was playing a song by that new group called The Beatles"—some of its elements are more redolent of the later years of the decade, particularly the experiment in communal living on which its action centers. Communal life is not calm: its monthly meetings are fraught with (sometimes comic) difficulties and highlight tensions and differences, not least over gender issues—for example, the extent to which men should share in household domestic tasks.

The "William Posters" motif explicitly recurs in *Flame* in the shape of a ginger-haired eighteen-year-old youth who drifts into the community and gives his name as Dean W. Posters—W. standing for William, "Billy" for short. In an echo of Frank's earlier rebellion, Dean has thrown up the job threading bobbins in a

Nottingham lace factory that he held for two years and is on his way from Nottingham to London, with some vague notion of hitchhiking to Turkey or India, supporting himself by peddling hash.

Dean's father, who was unemployed in the 1930s, turned to theft, and went on the run during World War II, used to joke about Bill Posters being prosecuted and called his son after him to carry on the name. Yet his son prefers the name Dean, affirming, "I'm not Bill bloody Posters. If I go on the run it's at my own fair speed." But he is nonetheless a kind of 1960s hippie version of Sillitoe's symbol of working-class servitude, though he is another of the slightly anachronistic elements of *Flame* that seem to belong to the later rather than the earlier 1960s. Dean stays with the community for a while, attracted by the "lotus-ease of this slack mob" and by Handley's much older wife Enid.

After various vicissitudes, the community breaks up (Dean and Enid go abroad together) and in the last paragraphs of the novel Frank reflects uneasily on the relationship between his current condition, as the successful writer of a book based on his Algerian experiences and happy family man, and his revolutionary aspirations. In a shift marked by the respective titles of the second and third volumes, the "flame of life" has replaced the "tree on fire" as the leading metaphor of the trilogy. Frank thinks of

The fire of life, in which the flame was often invisible, nonexistent. How could one live without this flame? You didn't have to see it to believe it was there. If it was in your heart you could see it spring up in all different places. As long as it stayed in your heart your revolutionary principles were not at variance with the way you lived.

The reader is left to judge whether Frank has sold out.

Each volume of the trilogy aroused variegated review responses. In the *Times* (May 13, 1965), the anonymous reviewer of *Posters* felt that "the real trouble [was] Frank himself," who made only a "superficial . . . impact on the reader," just as the figure of William Posters, "a symbol of modern enslavement," made only a superficial "imprint on the book." In the *Times Literary Supplement* (May 13, 1965), Anthony Cronin acknowledged the "grim reality" of "the initial dilemma" posed in the novel—"What should an intelligent, imaginative man do who does not want to go on working in a factory for the rest of his life?"—but felt that, unfortunately, "this problem ha[d] been factitiously solved before we start," that "though the hero talks a great deal, his discussion of it and his motives are confused, sometimes silly and often contradictory," and that "it certainly cannot be said that the subsequent fable throws any light of lifelike reality on the problem at all."

In the *Times Literary Supplement* (November 9, 1967), the anonymous reviewer of *Tree* felt the novel failed to integrate the narratives of Frank and Handley; the contrast between them "quickly becomes ludicrous" and while Frank's "adventures" with the FLN were "solidly presented," the figure of John, Handley's brother, was "as near as the book can get to a link between Handley the painter and Dawley the revolutionary." Julian Jebb, in the *Times* (November 11, 1967), judged *Tree* "a major failure" with "none of the painful, reserved passion" of *Loneliness* or "the tenderness or emotional accuracy" of the short story collection *The Ragman's Daughter* (1964) and the first volume in the trilogy. Instead it displayed "a great deal of rant, melodrama, overheated prose and moral generalization."

In the journal *Contemporary Literature* (Summer 1970), however, the American academic Frederick P.W. McDowell was more sympathetic to *Tree*. In contrast to Jebb, he judged it an improvement on *Posters* and felt the completed trilogy "promises to be an achievement of importance" because its second volume had "passed beyond the arbitrary and contrived situations" that may have seemed a flaw in the first. In *Tree*, Frank Dawley "has now become an authentic projection of the contemporary consciousness" with "scruples which command our respect" and "has evolved from his earlier quixotic temper to a new seriousness." In his essay "Myths of Identity" (1976), James W. Lee found that the "question of Frank Dawley's identity" in both *Posters* and *Life* was "one of Sillitoe's most interesting explorations of the question of authentic being as opposed to the dead, automatic life." Lee sees Sillitoe as "much less concerned with establishing a blueprint for conflict than with seeing how certain people create a revolution within themselves."

In the *Times* (November 21, 1974), the novelist Susan Hill judged the third volume of the trilogy, *Flame*, Sillitoe's best work since *Loneliness*, praising its dexterous and sensitive interweaving of "some complex philosophical and political concepts with the activities and relationships of a large cast of varied characters."

But in the *Times Literary Supplement* (November 29, 1974), Russell Davies complained that "even as the 300th page approaches, it is still difficult to tell the characters apart, to lend or withdraw moral support as the focus shifts, chapter by chapter."

Since these early reviews and essays, the three William Posters novels have attracted little critical analysis, but fruitful interpretation might start by taking the features Davies deprecates not as flaws but as formal innovations springing from Sillitoe's engagements with the complexities Susan Hill registers. The trilogy is, in its way, a remarkable and bold attempt to grapple with questions of individual and communal identity and commitment in the tumults and crosscurrents of the 1960s and '70s. But its leading characters, Frank and Albert, are not affiliated to any institutions other than their families; in contrast, the next three novels we consider focus on characters who are, to differing extents, linked with or part of an institution that was a prominent site of protest in the period: the university.

Simon Raven: *Places Where They Sing*, 1970

Simon Raven's most direct engagement with radical university agitation of the 1960s and '70s was in his novel *Places Where They Sing*, the sixth novel of his ten-volume Alms for Oblivion series. Raven was born in 1927 into a prosperous family—his father lived on the proceeds of his own father's hosiery business—and in 1941 he won a scholarship to Charterhouse, a leading English public school. After National Service in the Parachute Regiment, when he was stationed in Bangalore in India, he went up to King's College, Cambridge, where he read Classics and gambled, incurred debts and pursued heterosexual and homosexual liaisons. He gained a 2:1 degree and a studentship from Kings to pursue research, but a diversion occurred when, in 1951, he married an undergraduate student whom he had got pregnant. Their son was born in 1952. But he disliked the demands of married life. On receiving a telegram from his wife that said "Wife and baby starving. Send money soonest," he replied, "Sorry no money. Suggest eat baby," confirming his reputation as a cad. He was divorced in 1957. His research failed to make headway and he enlisted in the King's Own Shropshire Light Infantry but his discharge was discreetly engineered three years later after he had incurred debts he could not meet—an offense that could have led to a court-martial if he had stayed

Places Where They Sing (Panther, 1979)

in the army. For the rest of his life he became a full-time writer, prolific and self-disciplined in his work though prone to personal debauches until ill health constrained him.

The Alms for Oblivion series is an idiosyncratic chronicle of the intrigue, corruption, and chicaneries of British upper-middle-class life in the postwar era from Raven's viewpoint as an "inside outsider"—a lover of institutions who could never fully conform to them, a reactionary who was never wholly respectable. *Places Where They Sing* focuses on student agitation in one of its most privileged enclaves, Cambridge, and Raven's fictional Lancaster College has several features that make it resemble his own college, King's. The plot of the novel turns on the debate within the college on the best way to spend a £250,000 surplus (equivalent to about £4 million today) that has been raised through the sale of land. Radical students, notably Hugh Balliston and Hetta Frith, and progressive Fellows, such as the social scientist Lord Beyfus, seize on the issue to provoke disruption. For example, Beyfus proposes that the money be used to build two large student hostels on the college's sacred lawns and that their inhabitants, in order to encourage a communal, egalitarian ethos, will not have servants but take turns with cooking and cleaning duties and will not eat in Hall but in "the Student Co-operative Cafeteria." The dispute mounts into a climax that exemplifies one of Raven's specialties in his fiction: the account of the disruption of a public event. In this instance, a brass band and a cavalcade of student rebels invade a madrigal concert in the sacrosanct space of the college chapel and almost destroy the precious east window.

Places Where They Sing garnered little praise. For example, the reviewer in the *Times Literary Supplement* (February 26, 1970), observed that the "pattern is well-wrought but only as a collage of odd juxtapositions which jar and startle." Raven's portrayal of the student rebels and their allies allows them a certain manipulative skill and energy but slips too easily into overly hostile caricature. The novel does succeed, however, in symbolizing the perceived threat to aesthetic values—englassed, so to speak, in the east window of the college chapel—which student revolt could seem to pose. In this perspective, such revolt not only endangered the social system but the survival of beauty. For a novel more sympathetic to student revolt—though by no means uncritically so—we can turn to David Caute's *The Occupation.*

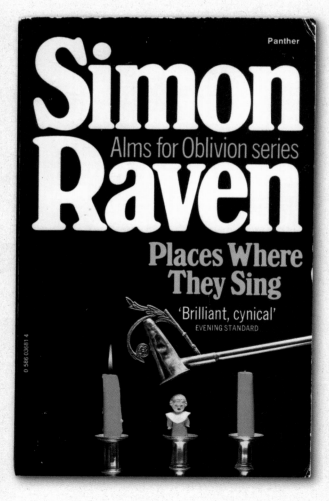

Simon Raven

Panther

Alms for Oblivion series

Places Where They Sing

'Brilliant, cynical'
EVENING STANDARD

0 586 03681 4

David Caute: *The Occupation*, 1971

The Occupation, David Caute's fourth novel, is not auto-biographical in any simple sense, but it draws on key elements of its author's polychromatic life. Born in Alexandria, the son of an army dentist who died when his son was eleven, Caute's formation might have been expected to produce a reactionary like Simon Raven, yet he has always stood on the Left, though skeptical of the motivations for commitment. He went to an English public school whose military associations are announced in its name, Wellington, the victor of the Battle of Waterloo in 1815. He then did compulsory National Service in the British Army in Ghana on the eve of independence, an experience that fed into his first novel, *At Fever Pitch* (1959). After the army, he read history at Wadham College, Oxford and *At Fever Pitch* was published while he was still an undergraduate, sharing the window of Blackwell's bookshop with a translation of a celebrated Russian novel—Boris Pasternak's *Doctor Zhivago*—and winning the prestigious James Tait Black Memorial Prize. Caute got a degree in history and won a Prize Fellowship at All Souls, a student-free college whose fellows included, then as now, many people of influence in British political and cultural fields. He went on to publish a second novel, *Comrade Jacob* (1961), and nonfiction works such as *Communism and the French Intellectuals, 1914–1960* (1964).

At this stage, Caute might have seemed made for life; but things then took a different turn. He supported a reform movement within All Souls to persuade it to use some of its ample revenues to finance a scheme to admit graduate students. When this was rejected, he resigned his fellowship in 1965 and published an essay in *Encounter*, "Crisis in All Souls" (March 1966), which made public a dispute that had unfolded within the confidentiality of the college walls. He then taught at Brunel University in the UK and at some American universities in the heyday of student protest. It was from this turbulent period of his life that the Confrontation trilogy emerged.

The Occupation (1971) forms one leg of this trilogy, and its others are a play, *The Demonstration* (first performed 1969), and a critical and theoretical work, *The Illusion* (1971). The main theme of *The Occupation* is the confrontation between the Old Left in the shape of an English academic, Steven Bright, and the New Left, in the shape of militant American students opposing the Vietnam War and antiblack racism who condemn what

The Occupation (André Deutsch, 1971)

they see as the Old Left's passivity and hesitation. The English/American aspect means that *The Occupation* also has what Henry James would have called a transatlantic theme, but in reverse: not the encounter of an American with Europe but of an Englishman with America. *The Occupation* is an expressionist and metafictional work in which the characters that invade Bright's New York office are aspects of his own tortured consciousness and in which we are recurrently reminded that we are reading a novel, a fiction. Bright has to confront the militants' accusations and his own painful relationship with one of his students, the sister of one of the leading militants, Max Brown, and the daughter of an émigré German and former self-confessed Nazi. Her own name, Eva Brown, mirrors that of Hitler's mistress (and, in his last hours, wife).

The final chapter of the novel portrays Bright returning to England and to his alma mater, Oxford, to find the city in the grip of revolution, with one exception, the student-free college of which he, like Caute himself, was once a Fellow—All Souls. Once he enters, he finds the usual tranquility prevails and he ends up in the library, finding a copy of his own book, *The Illusion*, and reading it with pleasure, his political impotence confirmed.

The Occupation received some hostile reviews. In the *Times* (July 22, 1971), Dennis Potter found its illusion-breaking devices "so crude" and "contrived" as to be "almost embarrassing"; D.A.N. Jones in the *Listener* (July 22, 1971) felt it offered "repellent confessions in an atmosphere of contrived unreality." By contrast, C.P. Snow in *The Malcontents* offered a realist treatment of a group of student activists.

C.P. Snow: *The Malcontents*, 1972

The Malcontents was C.P. Snow's first published novel after he completed his eleven-book Strangers and Brothers series (1940–70). It is set in an unidentified provincial town that shares some of its street names with Snow's native city of Leicester in the English East Midlands. Snow, the second of four brothers, was born there on October 15, 1905, to William Edward and Ada Sophia Snow. His father was a shoe factory clerk and an Associate, and then Fellow, of the Royal College of Organists who gave music lessons and played the organ at local churches. Charles Percy went to Alderman Newton's school in Leicester, stayed on for two years as a laboratory assistant, and then took an external London University BSc and MSc at Leicester, Leicestershire and Rutland University College (later Leicester University). He moved on to Christ's College, Cambridge, completed his doctorate on the infrared spectra of diatomic molecules in two years, and was elected a Fellow of Christ's in December 1930. It was an extraordinary rise from an unprivileged background that might otherwise have led to a life of provincial obscurity.

Snow's first novel, *Death under Sail* (1932), launched him on what he saw as his true vocation: writing. After working in the Ministry of Labour from 1940 to 1944, recruiting scientists and technicians for vital war duties, he became in the postwar era well-known as a novelist and a controversial commentator who promulgated the idea of a division between "the Two Cultures," one humanistic, one scientific. As Baron Snow, he served from 1964 to 1966 as a junior minister of technology in Harold Wilson's Labour government.

The Malcontents focuses on "the core," as they call themselves: a group of young radicals—five men and two women—from different social and educational backgrounds but apparently united by their political commitments. Stephen Freer, nearly twenty-two, is doing research in astrophysics at Cambridge and spends his vacation in the town at his parents' house in the cathedral precincts. He is the only child of Thomas Freer, a prosperous solicitor and cathedral registrar. Mark Robinson, six months younger than Stephen and the son of a wealthy local hosiery manufacturer, is reading history at Cambridge. Neil St. John, aged twenty, is a sociology student at the local University and, despite his aristocratic surname, the son of an Irish Catholic docker in Bootle. Bernard Kelshall, also twenty and a top-flight economics student at the local University, is the only child of German-Jewish parents who came to England as refugees from Nazi Germany in the 1930s, changing their name from Kornfeld. His father is a technician at the town's Infirmary. Tess Boltwood, the Bishop's daughter, is also studying at the local University. She is in love with Stephen. Emma Knott, aged twenty-two, a student at St Hugh's College, Oxford, is the daughter of a well-off local surgeon. Lance Forrester, the son of a property developer, failed to get into Oxford and is now flunking his English literature examinations at the local university. He is the only "core" member who is into smoking marijuana and taking LSD—a point that is significant for the plot of the novel but also perhaps indicates Snow's desire to encompass the narcotic as well as the political and erotic aspects of the youth culture of the time.

The Malcontents (Penguin, 1975)

The action of *The Malcontents* runs from the evening of Saturday January 10, to the evening of Saturday January 17, 1970. Before the action starts, the core has uncovered an indirect connection between an influential Conservative MP and Shadow Cabinet member with interests in apartheid South Africa and a terraced street in the town in which rooms for West Indians are "being rack-rented as they might have been in a nineteenth-century slum." The core plans to make this connection public, using their contacts with other radical student groups and sympathetic media elements. But the group has compromised its idealism by engaging in morally and legally dubious behavior in order to obtain their information, and the MP has allies in the security services who are concerned about a possible illegal conspiracy to defame a public figure and who are covertly monitoring the core.

On January 10, 1970, the core is plunged into crisis when its members learn that their plan is known to the authorities and that they risk prosecution. The crisis redoubles when they quickly realize that one of their number is an informer—the authorities could not have obtained so much information in any other way. The crisis culminates in an urgent meeting on Tuesday evening at Lance's expensive fifth-floor flat in a converted Regency house. The core, while knowing there is a traitor in its midst, decides to implement its contingency plan, which entails publicizing the connection between the MP and the rack-rented rooms as quickly as possible, before the authorities can silence it. The core members then have a party which is wilder than usual due to the strain they are under; Lance persuades Emma to take some LSD and even Bernard, usually a nondrinker, sips a glass of beer. But the evening ends in disaster: Bernard walks out of an open window and falls five floors to his death.

Bernard's demise kills the contingency plan. Mark, Stephen and Tess learn that the authorities will not proceed with any conspiracy charges but that the police will arrest Lance and Neil for drug offenses. They also discover the identity of the informer. Stephen and Tess speculate that LSD may have sparked Bernard's lethal leap, but the postmortem report on drug traces in Bernard's body is inconclusive. Stephen and Tess do learn, however, that Bernard's drink was spiked—though not by their first suspect, Lance.

At the end of *The Malcontents*, Stephen has decided to testify on behalf of Neil but not of Lance, and has proposed to Tess, who has eagerly accepted. Neil has resolved to pursue "Marxist politics on the shop floor" by finding work in a Liverpool factory and becoming a shop steward. And Mark has decided to leave Cambridge and to find a job in a hospital "somewhere among the really poor," perhaps in Calcutta. By January 17, 1970, the core, which eight days before had seemed to be bonded in a common cause, has disintegrated.

Snow himself, in his 1983 interviews with John Halperin, described *The Malcontents* as an attempt "to break quite new ground" and move away from writing about "elderly" and "responsible" people as he had done in the later volumes of Strangers and Brothers. But he did not think it had worked. A notably balanced and perceptive appraisal of the book's strengths and weaknesses was offered by a budding twenty-one-year-old writer Martin Amis, then yet to publish his first novel, *The Rachel Papers* (1973). In his *Observer* review of *The Malcontents*, later collected in *The War against Cliché* (2001), Amis argued that Snow's knowledge of young people and his characterization were sketchy but that he did manage "to locate and examine a suggestive assortment of motives and dialectic" and he admired Snow's "tolerance and honesty, and his eloquence when writing about the possibilities of doing good and the difficulties of behaving well." B.S. Johnson, however, in *Christie Malry's Own Double-Entry*, would portray a malcontent who was concerned not with doing good or behaving well but with balancing the books of himself and society.

B.S. Johnson: *Christie Malry's Own Double-Entry*, 1973

Christie Malry's Own Double-Entry was B.S. Johnson's last completed novel. Johnson was born in London in 1933, the only child of Stanley and Emily Johnson. His father worked as a stock keeper for the SPCK (Society for Promoting Christian Knowledge) bookshop in Westminster, although Johnson himself, in his adult life, was aggressively anti-Christian. The separation from his parents that wartime evacuation entailed was profoundly painful. He failed the eleven-plus and thus attended a secondary modern rather than grammar school, which he left at fourteen to go to a commercial school where he learned shorthand, typing, commerce, and bookkeeping—this last skill would be significant in relation to *Christie Malry*. He then worked as an accounts clerk at a bank, a building firm, a bakery, and an oil company. In contrast to Sillitoe and Caute, he did not do National Service; the RAF rejected him due to

a perforated eardrum. At the age of twenty-three, he entered King's College, London, to read for a degree in English, and he graduated in 1959. He then worked mainly as a supply teacher in London until the publication of his first novel, *Travelling People* (1963). This was well received and launched him on his career as a novelist. Its variety of styles and narrative techniques already suggested, however, that he would not rest content with traditional realism.

In the decade between the appearance of *Travelling People* and his suicide in 1973, Johnson produced six novels that broke the boundaries of conventional fiction in a range of ways. *Christie Malry* is a mixture of a hard-edged black comedy and a case study of a "criminal-terrorist" mentality. On leaving school, Christie gets a job in a bank, then becomes an invoice clerk with Tapper's, a manufacturer of cakes and sweets. He takes a correspondence course in accountancy and then develops his "great idea": to apply the double-entry bookkeeping system to his own life and to balance every debit he incurs from society—a slight, an insult, a rebuff—with a corresponding credit. He begins modestly; feeling that an office building has constrained his freedom of movement, he scratches its stone facing; irked by his supervisor at Tapper's, he conceals a complaining letter. But his activities escalate until he becomes a solo "terrorist" organization, a "cell of one. In that way, he could not be betrayed." He thus avoids the fate that befalls the "core" in *The Malcontents*.

In mainland Britain in the 1970s, terrorism—as defined by the government, mainstream media, police, and security services—had two main sources: the Provisional IRA, whose attacks were often lethal, and the Angry Brigade, which has been called, on the cover of Gordon Carr's book on the subject, "Britain's first urban guerrilla group" and which planted small bombs in strategic places, though no one was killed or seriously injured. Christie, in his cell of one, eschews membership of any political group. When he overhears a group of revolutionaries talking about launching an attack on London's clubs and defoliating the capital's squares and green spaces, he grimaces and passes on, "for these were but children." The revolutionaries are presented satirically, as bungling, ineffectual dreamers who, in contrast to Christie, are unlikely to translate talk into action. Nonetheless, one of their remarks—that "socialism has never been given a chance in this country"—has stayed in Christie's mind and he enters

Debit Aggravation			Credit Recompense		
June 1	Balance brought forward	106 61	June 2	Torn Poster	0 50
June 2	General diminution of Christie's life caused by advertising	30 00	June 2	Streetlamp glass	0 30
			June 2	Aldwych theatre	3 81
June 8	Wagner's savage workload	7 00	June 5	... club removed	0 01
June 9	General Wagner...	6 30	June 6	Rubber stamp pad removed	0 02
June 30	General exploitation by Tappers for month	200 00	June 7	General removal of small items of stationery	0 06
			June 13	Cabinet minister call hoax	0 70
			June 21	Hythe House and the little Vermifuge	110 10
			June 30	Balance owing Christie carried forward to next reckoning	257 91
		373 41			373 41

Christie Malry's Own Double-Entry (Collins, 1973)

it into his debit account twenty days before putting cyanide into a reservoir and thus killing 20,479 West Londoners—a far larger death toll than any crazed lone gunman could rack up, though minuscule compared to those of tyrannical perpetrators of state terrorism such as Hitler and Stalin. There is an implication here that revolutionary aspirations may provide the pretext for psychotic exterminations, but it would be wrong to draw an explicit moral of such a kind from this disturbingly ambivalent book.

A further implication that runs through the whole novel is that Christie, despite his large-scale slaughter, is not wholly distinct from the society he attacks. He employs one of the methods that contributed to the growth of the mercantile, capitalist West—the double-entry bookkeeping system, an image of reason and calculation—and he reveals the dark side of instrumental rationality, of utilitarian quantification. Christie is, in his way, a small businessman who thinks big, an individualist entrepreneur determined to balance the books but retain his own advantage. But his plan to succeed where the Gunpowder Plotters of 1605 failed and dynamite the Houses of Parliament is thwarted when he is diagnosed with advanced terminal cancer and dies. Thus a kind of poetic justice prevails. But his whole life is conducted in barely mitigated isolation; it would be Johnson's friend Alan Burns who would aim to portray collective terrorist activity.

Alan Burns: *The Angry Brigade: A Documentary Novel*, 1973

Alan Burns, like B.S. Johnson, was an innovative novelist who boldly challenged the limits of conventional British fiction in the 1960s and '70s. Born on December 29, 1929, to middle-class parents, he went to Merchant Taylors' School. He did National Service in the Royal Army Education Corps from 1949 to 1951, though as he was stationed on Salisbury Plain, this did not take him to distant regions of the British Empire, in contrast to Sillitoe, Raven, and Caute. After studying law at Middle Temple, he was called to the Bar in 1956, and practiced as a barrister in London until 1959. He then spent a year at the London School of Economics doing postgraduate research and worked for the following three years, checking copy for libel and copyright infringement, for the company owned by the tycoon Baron Beaverbrook that published two right-wing popular newspapers, the *Daily Express* and the *Sunday Express*. John Calder published Burns's first novel, *Buster*, in

The Angry Brigade (Quartet Books Allison & Busby, 1973)

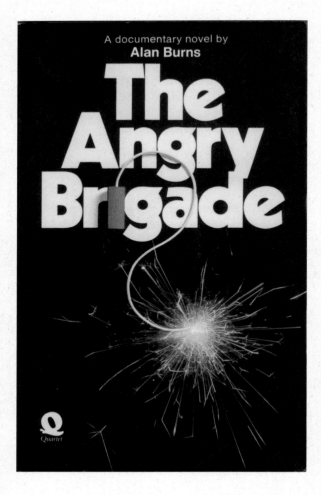

A documentary novel by
Alan Burns

The Angry Brigade

Q
Quartet

1961 and paid him an allowance that enabled him to give up his legal job and write full time. He went on to produce seven more novels, and *The Angry Brigade* was the fifth of these.

The Angry Brigade is subtitled *A Documentary Novel* and can at first seem exactly that. At the outset, it cites a supposed press report that poses the question of who was responsible for a recent spate of bombings in England, at least three of which have been claimed by the Angry Brigade as its work. It quotes a Special Branch officer as saying, however, that the Angry Brigade is "a myth" because "there is no one organization" with this name; it is "a many-headed hydra" of independent, autonomous groups. In an introduction, "A.B.," whom we take to be Alan Burns, confirms the accuracy of this press report and explains that the book is based on notes and tape-recordings of interviews with members of "two activist communes": two women, Jean and Suzanne, and four men, Barry, Dave, Ivor and Mehta (no surnames are supplied). This introduction gives the impression of documentary veracity and there is nothing in the main body of the book to contradict this. Yet apparently Burns acknowledged in a letter that *The Angry Brigade* offers not fact but "the fiction of a journalistic *coup*—real interviews with real member of the Brigade." In preparing the book Burns did conduct tape-recorded interviews, mostly with friends, but these were on topics unconnected with the Angry Brigade. He then adapted the transcriptions of the interviews to the subject matter of the book— for example, a friend's description of a series of visits to the dentist was the basis of an account of going to intimidating meetings of an Angry Brigade faction.

The Angry Brigade is divided into six sections whose headings summarize the trajectory the book traces: RADICALIZE, ORGANIZE, FRATERNIZE, MOBILIZE, REVOLUTIONIZE, TERRORIZE. Whereas *Christie Malry* focused on a determinedly isolated figure, a "cell of one," *The Angry Brigade* is concerned with attempted collective action and draws out the internal divisions, the policy and personality differences and the gender politics of small, committed groups—in this way resembling *The Malcontents* and anticipating Doris Lessing's *The Good Terrorist* (1985). As in *Christie Malry*, there is an escalation in *The Angry Brigade* from relatively harmless to homicidal activities: handing out political pamphlets gives way to the occupation of the Ministry of Housing, the bombing of the Post Office Tower restaurant kills a waitress, and the blowing up of a wall near a railway line blinds a child. The novel ends with Suzanne and Ivor lying under two metal beds for protection after three of their *plastique* bombs have fallen from a shelf and exploded. These explosions and casualties are invented but by means of them Burns envisages the possible consequences of the practice of planting bombs even if they are, supposedly, carefully targeted. (For example, the bombs at Robert Carr's house could have killed or maimed not only Carr himself but his wife, his thirteen-year-old daughter, and the policeman guarding the property). *The Angry Brigade* provides a compelling imaginative projection of the potentially high cost of violent dissent for both its victims and perpetrators. In this respect, it resembles Joseph Conrad's *The Secret Agent* (1907).

Burns himself recalls that the considerable review coverage of *The Angry Brigade* "generally [saw it] as an attack on the 'real' Brigade, satirizing them, depicting their petty squabbles, and so on." But he had in fact written the novel to protest against and offset "the demonizing of the members of the Angry Brigade in the press and other media" and had regarded the portrayal of their negative aspects as elements of his "intended subtle characterization of people I did not see as simple heroes and heroines, but with whom I had many sympathies."

One issue that *The Angry Brigade* deals with is race, through the figure of Mehta, the son of a prosperous Indian who comes to England and encounters racial prejudice and abuse. But this issue is not central to the novel and there is little sense of any activism organized around issues of racial discrimination. Such activism is among the key topics, however, of Samuel Selvon's *Moses Ascending*—though the novel is written from the viewpoint of an older West Indian who is well aware of racial prejudice but averse to such activism.

Samuel Selvon: *Moses Ascending*, 1975

Moses Ascending was Samuel Selvon's ninth novel. Born in 1923 in San Fernando, Trinidad, to an Indian father and a half-Indian mother, Selvon went to Naparimo College in his early teens and became a Royal Naval Reserve wireless operator in World War II. After the war, he spent five years as a journalist for the *Trinidad Guardian*, then moved to London in 1950. His best-known novel is his third, *The Lonely Londoners* (1956), which evokes the experiences of a range of West Indian immigrants in the capital through a skillfully constructed language that employs elements of

Moses Ascending (Heinemann, 1984)

Caribbean vernacular. Selvon moved to Canada in 1978 and intended to return there after an illness but died in Trinidad in 1994. One reason for his departure from England may have been the uneasy response to *Moses Ascending*.

In *Moses Ascending*, the West Indian Moses Aloeta, who featured as a kind of welfare officer for new immigrants in *The Lonely Londoners*, buys a house in Shepherd's Bush and is able, for the first time in his London life, to ascend from the basements in which he has always lived to the attic. Moses becomes a landlord and takes on as a factotum a young white immigrant from the Midlands, Bob, whom he calls his Man Friday (one of the recurring references to Defoe's *Robinson Crusoe* in the novel). Moses starts to write his memoirs, in a lively mixture of West Indian, Standard, and literary English. But his literary progress is interrupted by two pressing concerns that literally invade his house: black militancy and illegal Asian immigration. His friend Sir Galahad has become an advocate of Black Power:

> When Black Power come into vogue Galahad was one of the first to rally to the colours—I mean colour, of course. An American visitor from the Deep South indoctrinate him, and he became a rabid disciple, calling everybody Brother and Sister and advising them to change their names from Churchill or ffoulkes-Sutherland to Obozee or Fadghewi or some other African names what I can't spell. He form up a Party in Ladbroke Grove and start to fight oppression and all the other ills that beset black people.

Moses, however, does not want to get engaged in politics or any other form of collective activity. He is annoyed at "how people want you to become involve, whether you want to or not." His account of "BP," an American militant visiting London, is satirical, rather like Dickens's portrayal of the trade union activist Slackbridge in *Hard Times* (1854). BP works his audience up to a paroxysm of violent feeling—"kill all the whites and burn down the City of London"—and solicits donations before police with Alsatian dogs aggressively break up the meeting. BP later absconds with the local Black Panther Party's funds of about £500 (equivalent to around £4,700 today).

In his introduction to the 2007 Penguin edition of *Moses Ascending*, the novelist Hari Kunzru, criticizes what he sees as the book's stereotypical, populist, and uninformed representations of its West Indian and Asian characters and contends these "contributed to Selvon's critical eclipse, and put *Moses Ascending* beyond the pale for a generation of critics whose work on "postcolonial" literature was part of a wider anti-racist politics." But the disillusion *Moses Ascending* evokes did correspond to a more general mood of the mid-1970s when radical political agitation in the UK was subsiding. In retrospect, a large blue arrow points from this time toward Thatcherland and the release of a right-wing dynamism that forced the British Left to stay in the pits or trail in its slipstream. British fiction would also find its own dynamism in the 1980s in response to, and reaction against, the changes of that decade. The adventurous and accomplished fiction of this era overshadowed the novels of the 1960s and '70s that engaged, in their different ways, with political radicalism and often with artistic innovation; but their probings into possibility, at a time of relative openness and uncertainty, remain enjoyable, alive, and potentially valuable in the constraints and conflicts of the twenty-first century.

Nicolas Tredell

Betty Collins and the Australian Industrial Novel

Classic novels that rightly deserve widespread recognition slip into obscurity for any number of reasons, political or otherwise. Betty Collins's 1966 book *The Copper Crucible*, a fictionalized account of a worker uprising in the famous mining town of Mt. Isa, Queensland during the early 1960s, is a case in point.

It is an industrial novel told from the perspective of the workers, a rarity among Australian texts. The book opens with Julie moving to Mt. Isa with her young son to be with her Greek husband, Nick. Mt. Isa in inland northern Queensland is a famous landmark in Australian industrial history; one of the most productive single mines in the world it served as a stronghold of unionism for Australia's oldest union, the Australian Workers Union (AWU). Nick is a union delegate and soon loses his job with the giant mining company there. Blacklisted, he struggles to find steady work in the town.

Along with a handful of men, Nick continues his work as an industrial agitator, and Julie is drawn in to help organize the women in the town in support of a strike over wages. As the strike heats up, Nick and Julie's marriage slowly breaks down because of cultural differences and expectations about women's role in married life.

The story is far from exclusively about Julie and Nick. It deals with a number of key men and women—union leaders and their wives, based on real-life players—that organized the strikes in Mt. Isa. The dispute drags in the industrial tribunal, state branches of left and right-wing unions and then the state Labor government in Queensland.

Layered behind this already complex story is a dispute over control of the all-powerful, conservative union, the AWU, as local activists in Mt. Isa, who also happen to be members of the Communist Party of Australia, try to agitate for more militant action. Both the conservative unions and the state Labor government, based down in Brisbane, over a thousand miles away from the Mt. Isa coalface, seem content to side with the mining company.

Betty Collins, 1972

In her preface to the 1996 reprint of the novel, Collins wrote of her own experience in Mt. Isa:

> I had come to a place where the working class politics of the time were inherent in the very geography, and daily impinged upon our lives. . . . While this is a novel, with the freedom of fictionalised history, I hope it will serve to remind us that reforms and improvements have always had to be won by those who preceded us, often against all odds, just as we in 1957 were successors of those whose only supply base was the Company Store, and who began their life in the Isa in tin shacks and tents on rough and shaly ground. To them I dedicate this book.

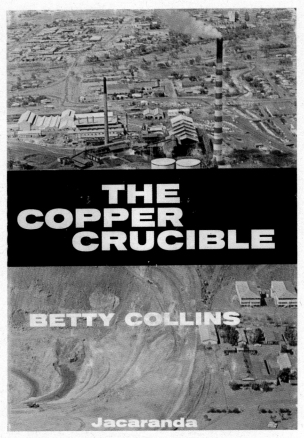

The Copper Crucible (Jacaranda Press, 1966)
The Copper Crucible (University of Queensland Press, 1996)
Bobbin Up (Australasian Book Society, 1959)

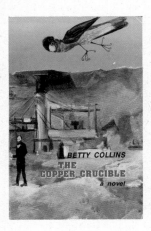
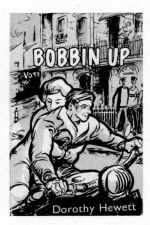

The Copper Crucible deals with unionism, communism, gender, race, and multiculturalism head on. It manages to be both a passionate call to arms for unionists and, at the same time, an utterly realistic representation of working life in the hot and gritty Mt. Isa.

That it slipped into obscurity is perhaps unsurprising. It's a text that spoke keenly in favor of communism and worker-led unionism. It criticized Queensland's powerful, conservative unions and Labor governments alike, not to mention a then giant of the Australian corporate landscape, the Mt. Isa Mines Company.

The censorship that occurred I will discuss later, but it's worth noting that Collins wrote an article specifically about it for the autumn 1969 edition of the Australian Communist Party–affiliated journal *The Realist*, titled "Precensorship and the Industrial Novel." She also discussed censorship through letters and interviews with the editor of the 1996 edition of *The Copper Crucible*, Dr. Ian Syson. Collins has noted that the mainstream newspaper, *The Australian*, blacklisted her from any work with them for many years, probably at the behest of Mt. Isa Mines.

Because it was heavily edited and censored when first published, the original version of *The Copper Crucible* reads to some critics as disjointed. Reviewers at the time spotted this, and it seems not all realized it was due to censorship. Frank Stevens wrote in *The Australian* in April 1966 that Collins "has not fully exploited her craft," while Tom Healy in *The Age* wrote two months later that the story was "as competent as far as it goes, which was not far enough."

Some critics might argue the novel was too didactic in nature, as is often said of political novels. It was also deemed a little too realistic in subject matter making it unpopular with the scholarly, literary canon types, and the editor had cut many of the domestic scenes about the women's lives. This is often the treatment that women working-class writers in Australian get. Syson writing on Betty Collins in *Hecate* (vol. 15, 1989) said:

> The politics underlying [the] marginalisation of working class writers . . . rarely manifest as cases of overt political discrimination. In many streams of critical practice—in both academia and reviewing—these works are more often devalued on aesthetic grounds. Aspects ranging from subject matter to literary style are raised as points of criticism.

The Copper Crucible was not obscure to begin with. It was broadly supported in the union movement and the launch in Sydney was held at the Teacher's Federation hall, and the liquor trades union provided the alcohol. Jack Edgerton, head of the Queensland Trades and Labour Council, delivered the main speech. Collins toured Queensland doing radio and TV interviews, including getting a very warm reception in Mt. Isa from the locals, particularly women.

The mainstream press reviewed it, mostly favorably, and all copies sold out in about six weeks. The international mining union bought twenty-one copies and gave them to each mining town in Canada, meaning it reached the audience Collins intended it for. It was also translated and published in the Soviet Union soon after publication in Australia.

A deeply political novel, *The Copper Crucible* follows in the tradition of a handful of other industrial novels written by Australian women writers, such as Dorothy Hewett's *Bobbin Up* (1959) and Jean Devanny's *Sugar Heaven* (1936). Interested readers should also consider tracking down Mena Calthorpe's *The Dyehouse* (1964).

Technically similar to Collins's novel, these other books also provide personal accounts of real-life strikes and worker uprisings. For example, Hewett's book deals with the women workers at a Sydney textile factory in the 1950s. Over sixteen chapters, readers meet a number of the women who slave away in hot and dangerous conditions at the factory. The women do not go on strike until the final scene, but as we have gotten to know the characters so intimately, we fully comprehend the enormity of their decision. *Sugar Heaven* tells the story of Eileen, who has a political awakening while supporting her husband in the Silkwood (again in Queensland) sugar cane strikes in the 1930s.

Collins—who in later life preferred to be referred to as Liz rather than Betty—was born in Melbourne in 1921. Her November 11, 2006, obituary in the *Sydney Morning Herald*, written by her daughter Mahni Dugan, notes that Collins's mother was an international opera singer and her father a Broken Hill Proprietary executive, making her own life "a hard act to follow." This also demonstrates that Collins did not exactly start out working-class.

Her grandfather on her mother's side, Randolph Bedford, had a significant impact on her life. He was a

The Dyehouse (Seven Seasons Books, 1964)

writer and member of the Queensland Parliament, but most relevant, a miner, land owner, and pioneer of the minefields in 1920s Mt. Isa. The back-page biography of Collins in her first edition (1966) of *The Copper Crucible* notes: "Her grandfather was one of the miners who agreed not to sell out to Mount Isa Mines—and did."

Collins was involved with the Realist Writers Group, an organization of Australian writers interested in telling local stories about working people, first in Melbourne in 1949, and in later years she became its national president. Realist Writers Groups were being established in many cities across Australia, usually closely affiliated to the Community Party but also as a backlash against the rigid and theoretical writings of Communist newspapers. Her friends included notable Australian authors Frank Hardy (*Power without Glory*, 1950) and Dymphna Cusack (*Come in Spinner* with Florence James, 1951), among others. She had also been an active member of the Communist Party since her twenties, which was not uncommon for realist writers of the period. Her obituary notes that she worked for General Douglas MacArthur in his Brisbane headquarters during World War II but, after the war, ran campaigns against nuclear weapons and organized peace marches.

In 1957, Collins spent a year in Mt. Isa, having moved there with her Greek Cypriot husband, Jimmy Anastassiou. There, she became president of the Women's Committee of the Mt. Isa Industrial Council, the organization representing the different unions operating in the town.

She wrote a short story about her time there called "The Handkerchief." On her return to Sydney from Mt. Isa, at a Realist Writers Group workshop meeting, she was encouraged to develop the short story into a full-length novel. It took five redrafts before it was published in 1966 as *The Copper Crucible*.

Collins was married and divorced three times, and she raised her three children predominantly as a single mother. She wrote about this experience in her second novel, *The Second Step* (1972), in which the main character must fight to keep her children, juggle full-time work with childrearing, and struggle to find homes for them during the 1960s housing crisis in Sydney. What is striking is how this second novel, written only a few years after her first, could be so different.

Those readers looking for a follow-up industrial novel that again passionately advocates for collective action will be a little disappointed. Instead, *The Second*

The Second Step (Australasian Book Society, 1972)

Step is a bleak novel about the painful disconnect between a mother and her daughters, set against the 1960s Sydney backdrop of dramatic social upheaval. Unlike *The Copper Crucible*, this book never made it to Russia for publication among the Communist nations, as it dealt openly with drug use and sexual freedom for women. It reads as a bitterly truthful account of a poor working mother who, in one of the most poignant scenes, is abandoned by her daughters to live with their wealthier father in Melbourne. The title refers to the moment when offspring sever ties with their mother.

The process of getting *The Copper Crucible* to publication is a story in and of itself. Firstly, Collins was a full-time worker and single mother. One of the greatest challenges in accurate representation of workers' lives is the question of who will tell these stories. Who has the language skills, the significant time required, and even the necessary equipment, and who has experienced the working class such that it can be accurately told?

Collins wrote at night after a day's work and putting her children to bed. She drew heavily on her own experience in Mt. Isa but also collected stories from her uncle (another Bedford who worked in Mt. Isa) and union leaders, who provided the bulk of the industrial detail. The novel went through five redrafts before Brian Clouston at Jacaranda Press accepted it for publication. It takes an enormous amount of commitment and dedication to get a book through to publication, especially so for those of the working class. But Collins was determined to contribute to the debate and the story of Mt. Isa as, after she left, industrial disputes continued in the town.

Second, it was a risky time to be writing radical literature in Australia. Collins understood the challenges involved in writing this sort of novel so soon after famous but contested events. She was taking on a powerful enemy in the mining company giant.

Her friend and fellow Realist Writers Group colleague Frank Hardy had previously been sued for his novel *Power without Glory*, based on the notorious Melbourne figure, John Wren. In a book full of well-known truths, Wren tried to sue Hardy for criminal libel on the seemingly minor implication (compared with theft, murder, and other crimes) that Wren's wife had an affair. It was Wren's wife, Ellen, who filed the libel case that was ultimately unsuccessful.

As a result, Jacaranda's solicitor had a very real fear and scoured the drafts of *The Copper Crucible* for even the most minor possible libel issues, concerned that Mt. Isa Mines might try to find a similar, third-party figure to take up their case. As Collins wrote in 1969, "The greater the truth, the greater the libel"—no doubt referring to Hardy's work.

The impact this fear of libel had on the final version of *The Copper Crucible* was huge: twenty-five thousand words were cut, truly an enormous figure for a book of about 150 pages. The 1996 reissue would be 50 pages longer. The cutting was the outcome of legal requirements but also some harsh editing, which saw the removal of some of the finer details in the women characters' lives.

While there was some negotiation back and forth between editor and author, Collins says, as a result, her book was "emasculated." Jacaranda also had some trouble in finding a printer and binder willing to touch the work, and more edits were made to accommodate the publishing company. Thus the final product published was a shy imitation of the original intent.

Finally, in her article for *The Realist*, Collins noted there are two types of censorship, one imposed on the author by editors and lawyers and the other self-inflicted by writers limiting themselves during the writing process. It seems Collins recognized this and sought to reduce the book's impact as she named her fictional town "Mt. Irene." This is a common technique used by writers to provide distance from the material they might be working on if it feels too emotionally close to home. Collins described it as a "puny stratagem . . . but it did enable me to write without fear, the whole of the truth as I could see it." How much Collins might have censored herself despite this we will never know, but it strikes the reader, even today, as nothing short of a brutally honest account.

This brutal honestly was also a personal risk for Collins. Her novel dealt with deeply personal aspects of women lives, including affairs, divorce, and domestic violence. Among her radical group of Communist allies and union activists, these home truths might not have been well received in their day.

It is possible to glean from her obituary, and also through letters and interviews with Syson (now a lecturer at Victoria University in Melbourne), that Collins drifted away from her roots in unionism, communism, and even realist writing in the later stages of her life. She left the Party in 1968, focusing instead on Zen Buddhism.

From the mid-1970s onward, Collins—by her own admission—gave up fiction writing and instead worked as a book reviewer and as a secretary in the Sydney University's English Department, where she was the department's most published writer. She wrote nonfiction works on topics related to religion and altered states of consciousness such as *Joy and the Age of Aquarius* (Liz Enterprises and Austwan, 1983) and *The Alexander Conspiracy: A New Perspective on History, Religion and Values* (Vordon Phoenix, 1998). Interestingly, her obituary written by her daughter focuses more on the later nonfiction works, mentioning *The Copper Crucible* only once in parentheses. Finally, Collins worked as a personal growth astrologer.

It was in Collins's later years, in 1989, that *The Copper Crucible* again got some of the attention it deserved. Syson (then at the University of Queensland) resurrected the book and through a substantial editing process with Collins, brought it back to its original intended form. It was then republished in 1996 by University of Queensland Press with a new introduction by Syson and an author's note from Collins. Reading both versions, it's apparent the amount of work the reprint went through: whole chapters, segments, and sentences have been restored and repositioned in the updated version.

The book first caught Syson's attention as he was born and raised in Mt. Isa. As an honors student, he had spent some time trying to track down the book, an account of which he gives in his November 1989 article for the feminist journal *Hecate*, "In Search of Betty Collins":

> The parochial curiosity that determined my search for the Copper Crucible quickly made way for the recognition that here was a writer who was worthy of further investigation. Her balancing of such issues as class, gender, sexuality, ethnicity and race in a way that did not reduce social conflict to a simplistic "us and them" situation, and the power of the representation of the working class struggle, suggested that her other writings deserved investigation.

Without his efforts to arrange republication and the latest edition of the book, *The Copper Crucible* might not have made it into this century, and at very least it would not have made it into this keen reader's hands.

Collins died in 2006, but her legacy will hopefully live on in the hundreds, nay thousands, of women writers or unionists or activists who have read and love her work because it tells their story. She was undoubtedly brave and a maverick to have written about something so truthfully and so close to home; to have taken on the "wrath of the [conservative] institution," as Collins herself said; and to have challenged gendered norms within cultures.

She remains an inspiration for young writers who care about social justice and are inclined to activism, and who believe that writing, particularly fiction, does serve a purpose beyond simply aesthetic pleasure or entertainment. Novels can teach us about our radical past that is suppressed by mainstream media and conservative state structures, and those same novels can inspire us to participate in current social justice causes.

In 1969, Collins wrote in *The Realist*:

> Australia needs more industrial novels. To the potential writers of them, I say go ahead. Call your place "Mt Irene" or some such pseudonym if this makes the task easier, but when the day comes that it is given its real name and comes out in spite of libel laws and precensorship, know that there is a public waiting—the mass reached through radio and television, the organised thousands in trade unions who need your skill.

With declining union membership and consolidated, conservative media on the rise in Australia, Collins's words of wisdom still ring true today, more than ever.

Danae Bosler
(With thanks to Dr. Ian Syson)

Hog Butcher, Ronald L. Fair (Harcourt, Brace & World, 1966)

"It used to be a writer's town and it's always been a fighter's town," novelist Nelson Algren described the Windy City in his celebrated 1951 essay *Chicago: City on the Make*. Of course, often times in that booming metropolis one was forced to be both—especially if that writer was a black person trying to make their way out of the chaotic South Side slums and other segregated spaces. To be fair, Chicago has produced more than a few successful African American writers, in both the literary and sales sense—including Richard Wright, Gwendolyn Brooks, Lorraine Hansberry, and Willard Motley—but it has always had a corrupt and racist foundation that brought out the fighter in even the gentlest of souls.

While novelist Ronald L. Fair may not as well known as his textual contemporaries, he was another wonderful writer who emerged from that hard city fighting every step of the way as he embarked on the revolutionary road of creating literature on his own terms. Before stepping away from publishing books to pursue the life of a born-again sculptor living as an expat in Europe, he wrote four novels and won several major literary awards including the Guggenheim Fellowship. Fair's 1963 debut was the slim *Many Thousand Gone: An American Fable*. A dark satire in more ways than one, the novel depicts a fictional community, Jacobs County, Mississippi, that has neglected to tell their local black population that slavery is over. Taking place in the late 1950s (though it was hardly *Happy Days*) the book is a brutal study of racism that also manages to be as funny as a surreal Richard Pryor sketch told by his own Mississippi-born character, Mudbone.

After a few of the slaves, most notably Jacobs County elders Granny Jacobs and Preacher Harris (the only black person in town who could read) discover that there exists a free world beyond their plantations, they became fixated on getting their families to the Negro Promised Land they believe Chicago to be. When a copy of the black-owned/Chicago-based *Ebony* magazine is mailed to the town, word gets out that there was a place where they could live as nicely as white people and keep a few dollars in their pockets. Certainly, as documented in the migration series paintings of Jacob Lawrence and the masterful 2010 nonfiction tome *The Warmth of Other Suns* by Isabel Wilkerson, for many Negro southerners the move to Chicago was the big gold dream. For many "colored" people seeking to escape the strange-fruit lynch mobs, crazy Jim Crow

Hog Butcher (Harcourt, Brace & World, 1966)

A novel about courage
By Ronald L. Fair

Formerly published as Hog Butcher

Now an AMERICAN INTERNATIONAL Release

Cornbread, Earle and Me (Bantam, 1975) Poster for the 1975 film adaption of *Hog Butcher, Cornbread, Earl and Me*

laws, and other extreme prejudices they were forced to face daily, whatever hardships and sacrifices they had to endure to change their lives for the better was worth it.

When Fair decided to satirize slavery, it could have gone all wrong, but as *Negro World* (owned by *Ebony*'s parent company Johnson Publications) observed in 1965: "It is a measure of Mr. Fair's artistry that the pain and fury behind the laughter is always finely felt." Yet, while the golden streets of Chicago and other northern wonderlands (Pittsburgh, Detroit, New York) served as the perfect strivers' fantasy, the reality of those harsh, cold cities was quite different than expected: shabby tenements, and later housing projects, replaced the plantations and the laws of justice still weren't balanced. Fair, whose own parents made the trek from Mississippi, was born and raised in Chicago and knew very well the levels of racial inequality that were prevalent in housing, schooling, banking, salaries paid, and the policing of black communities.

These heavy subjects are tackled in Fair's powerful and naturalistic second novel *Hog Butcher* (1966). This told the story of a college-bound Chicago high school basketball champion named Nathaniel Hamilton, known to everyone in his hood as Cornbread, who is gunned down by two policemen as he is running home in the rain holding an orange soda. The policemen, an interracial duo of blue boys, claim they thought Cornbread was a burglar they had been pursuing minutes before. After a small riot breaks out minutes after Cornbread is slain, the mayor's office uses this as a justification to bring in a task force of "twelve officers, all over six feet, cruising slowly down the block on motorcycles. They were so big the motorcycles looked like children's toys under them, to occupy the neighborhood like a military force."

The only witness to the senseless crime is a ten-year-old kid, Wilford Robinson, who along with his buddy Earl had idolized every cool move Cornbread made on the battlegrounds of the basketball court. The goal of everyone—civic leaders, the welfare agency and violent cops, one who beats up Wilford's mother—is to make the boy be quiet. As the state builds their web of lies, the truth becomes the scariest enemy.

Published in 1966, forty-eight years before teenager Laquan McDonald was shot seventeen times on those same Chicago streets, *Hog Butcher* was inspired by Fair's day job as a court reporter, which he worked from 1955 to 1967. According to *New Day in Babylon:*

The Black Power Movement and American Culture by William L. Van Deburg, in 1965 Fair was in the middle of writing a novel populated by mostly white characters when he had an epiphany that he would be betraying his people. "Furious with himself, Fair tore the manuscript into tiny pieces, lit a match and watched it burn."

In *The Contemporary African American Novel: Its Folk Roots and Modern Literary Branches* (2005), Bernard W. Bell wrote that Fair borrowed the term "hog butcher" from Carl Sandburg's 1914 poem "Chicago" ("Hog Butcher for the World, Tool Maker, Stacker of Wheat, Player with Railroads and the Nation's Freight Handler; Stormy, husky, brawling, City of the Big Shoulders…") but also believed that "the white Chicago system is the hog butcher that cuts out the souls of blacks."

In 1975, during the height of the blaxploitation movement in American movies, *Hog Butcher* was adapted by screenwriter Leonard Lamensdorf and director Joseph Manduke. Released under the title *Cornbread, Earl and Me*, the picture was an American International Picture release that starred a thirteen-year-old Laurence Fishburne in his film debut as Wilford. While the adaption, considered a classic in some quarters, told the story from Wilford's point of view, Fair used the third-person omniscient that showed readers how Cornbread's murder affected each side from the sellout black cop and the frightened grocery store owner to the uncaring Deputy Coroner and the knight in shining armor lawyer Benjamin Blackwell, who works for Cornbread's family.

Four years before the film was released, Fair was encouraged by writer Chester Himes to flee the racism of Chicago in 1971 and lived in various European countries before finally settling in Finland in 1972.

Although Fair never claimed that *Hog Butcher* was based on a specific case, more than fifty years after its initial publication the searing novel serves as a reminder that American police brutality in the black community was not something that began in the age of cell phone cameras, police dashcam footage and surveillance monitors. Indeed, what happened to Michael Brown in Ferguson, Missouri, to Eric Garner in Staten Island, and to Freddie Gray in Baltimore has been going on for years. As *Negro Digest* editor Hoyt W. Fuller wrote in its October 1966 issue, "Hog Butcher is… a sharp portrayal of a diseased city." That the picture might fit any American city is merely coincidental.

Michael Gonzales

Wilford saw a flash of lightning and heard a tremendous roar of thunder as the policemen jumped from the squad car and drew their revolvers. Then he heard four rapid explosions of man-made thunder and saw four flashes of angry, murderous thunder and Cornbread's body convulsing violently with each bullet that pried its way into his back before he crumbled, lifeless, heavily to the ground, the pop bottle flying into the air and smashing into hundreds of little pieces of glass that reflected no light at all on this gray day.

Young, Hip, and Angry

Pulp Fiction and Campus Revolt

University campuses are microcosms of the societies in which they occur, yet are also places of knowledge and learning, where "truth" is produced. Further, they are also places that encourage debate (or at least should). But what knowledge is counted as legitimate is far from settled, and university politics often spill beyond the confines of the campus. This was particularly evident in the 1960s and '70s New Left as student politics became increasingly synonymous with radicalism in general and campuses served as a launch pad for a host of campaigns. Developments related to the Cold War politics and McCarthyism of the 1950s; the anti–Vietnam War, peace, and civil rights movements of the 1960s (including the Paris spring of 1968); the late 1960s revolutionary anti-imperialism of the Weather Underground; and the infamous Baader-Meinhof gang in Germany during the 1970s all saw student milieus become intricately entwined in revolutionary and progressive social movements.

Pulps are a perfect vehicle for stories of campus politics, protest, and revolt, with some of this diversity illustrated in the following: *The Sit-In* by George B. Anderson (1970); *Getting Straight* by Ken Kolb (1968); Richard Allen's *Demo* (1971); *The Demonstrator* (1970) by Elizabeth and Don Campbell; *Campus Rebels* by John Post (1966); Ellery Queen's *Campus Murders*, published in 1969 and written by Gil Brewer; and Richard Deming's *Spy-In* (1969).

★

Campus revolutionaries don't come more radical (or pitiful) than twenty-three-year-old Kenneth Milburn, the central figure in George B. Anderson's *The Sit-In*. Milburn is a graduate student at Midwest State University (working toward a master's degree in sociology) and the organizer of a sit-in of the university administration building. But Milburn is no "champagne socialist," and this sit-in is far from your ordinary, run-of-the-mill student union hijinks. As the front covers puts it: "He was young, hip, angry—and he was a killer."

Surprisingly for a campus revolt novel, the action largely takes place in a middle-class suburban home rather than on campus, although the reasons for this are evident from the beginning: Kenneth Milburn is seeking refuge after shooting and killing a police officer attempting to break up student protests associated with the sit-in. In order to hide out, Milburn weasels his way into a middle-class suburban house and takes its occupants, the Martin family, hostage. What keeps the reader involved are the consequences arising from the killing of the police officer, and the uncovering of why Milburn came to shoot.

Much of the action takes place as exchanges between Milburn and young housewife, mother, and university graduate Jean Martin. While Jean's university days were only eight years earlier, she clearly lives in a different world to Milburn as "she didn't understand the current campus revolts, and they made her feel old." Jean's revulsion toward Milburn is evident from their first encounter:

> She was instantly repelled. "Beatnik" was the first word that entered her mind as she looked at the face largely concealed by a heavy unkempt black beard. Long, straight, greasy black hair hung to his shoulders. Jean knew that "beatnik" was a tired label, applied inaccurately as often as that other catch-all tag "hippie." She supposed her caller was a Young Radical or Activist.

Importantly, though, this isn't a story of the generation gap, with Milburn instead viewing Jean Martin as a well-heeled middle-class WASP: "It's ingrained, isn't it. You never fought for anything you believed in did you?"

Nominally, Milburn's politics are directed against the Establishment, as evident in this exchange with Angus Martin, Jean's husband, who Milburn also takes hostage:

> "Did you ever have any military service?"
> "Yeah."

"Did you enjoy it?"

"No," Angus answered, "but it was my duty, and I didn't try to duck it."

"Your duty to who?"

"To my country," Angus answered.

"To the Establishment," Milburn corrected.

"I said to my country, and that's what I meant. Sure the government makes mistakes—but I feel lucky to be living here instead of somewhere else."

"The military has taken over the government," Milburn said. "Call what we have a democracy or whatever you like, but we're living under a military regime. The military controls everything"

"I suppose," Angus said, "you think everything's going to be just jim-dandy in Cuba"

The remainder of the story details Milburn's increasingly desperate attempt to escape, and as the tension rises, the "real" sources of Milburn's anger become apparent. In doing so, the point is made that not all "Young Radicals" are bad, as evident from the lyrics of a song sung by a hippie couple that cross paths with Milburn and the Martins:

It's not enough to sit and wait
Until the world is free of hate
Put down the hawks and be a dove
To make a new world full of love

A different (and more lighthearted) vision of campus revolt is explored in *Getting Straight*. Ken Kolb's book follows the exploits of Harry, who according to the front cover is the "bastard king of campus revolutionaries" as he grapples with love, lust, and the travails of getting by while being true to himself. The action centers on Harry's experience as a post graduate student who loves English (but dislikes teaching and the hypocrisy of university leadership); is uncertain about his affections toward his girlfriend Jan; struggles with the discipline of regular nine-to-five work; and deals with crises arising from troublesome friendships. For example, due to experimentation with various mind-expanding drugs, one friend, Nick, becomes unhinged and "sees god," which creates all sorts of problems, including that Harry has to manage Nick to ensure that Harry isn't reported to university authorities for an academic misdemeanor (Nick did a simple

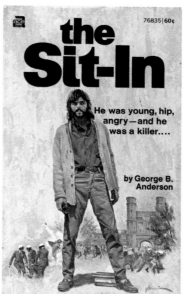

The Sit-In (Ace, 1970)

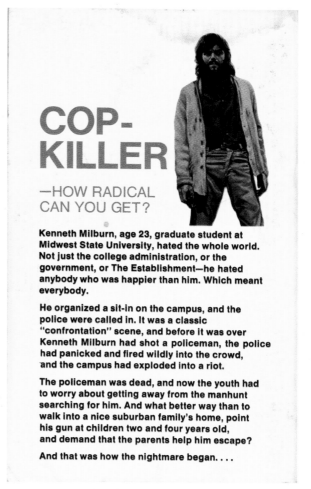

COP-KILLER
—HOW RADICAL CAN YOU GET?

Kenneth Milburn, age 23, graduate student at Midwest State University, hated the whole world. Not just the college administration, or the government, or The Establishment—he hated anybody who was happier than him. Which meant everybody.

He organized a sit-in on the campus, and the police were called in. It was a classic "confrontation" scene, and before it was over Kenneth Milburn had shot a policeman, the police had panicked and fired wildly into the crowd, and the campus had exploded into a riot.

The policeman was dead, and now the youth had to worry about getting away from the manhunt searching for him. And what better way than to walk into a nice suburban family's home, point his gun at children two and four years old, and demand that the parents help him escape?

And that was how the nightmare began. . . .

test for Harry so he could go to work). Nick's circumstances and its associated implications are explained in this exchange between Harry, his friend Jake, and psychologist Miss Summers:

"What would you say is the root cause of his difficulty?"

"Those three caps of acid he swallowed."

"I beg your pardon?"

"LSD, baby. You know, the Long Swift Drive into the groovy void." . . .

"I didn't know LSD was involved. How does that affect the situation?"

"His psychosis may be temporary—but it's just as real and fully as dangerous. He'll be more unpredictable than a patient with the usual messiah complex."

The story culminates in a chaotic week in which Harry tries to cope with demonstrating his academic bona fides (to a panel of mostly unsympathetic professors) while managing the unhinged Nick, coping with a relationship meltdown, and dealing with numerous crises that threaten to derail a weeklong marketing expo at the store where he works. (Harry has a key role in hosting a store promotion.)

While Harry is apparently something of a campus revolutionary, throughout this tale, his politics are personal rather than collective and organized. First, when confronted by senior members of faculty with the need to sign a loyalty oath affirming his opposition to communism, Harry reveals the absurdity of being obligated to sign such a document: "I'm saying it would take a very dumb subversive to make a public issue over signing this piece of paper. So dumb in fact, he'd be harmless." In doing so, Harry reveals the compromised position of some university elites: instead of requiring he sign such an oath, they should be defending freedom of expression. Second, Harry's left-leaning politics prevent him from succumbing to the charms of "all the way with LBJ"–supporting Miss Janice Rohl: "Couldn't he forget a few thousand Vietnamese for the sake of a wee bite on that alabaster neck?"

While its treatment of political foment is limited, what provides *Getting Straight* with enduring interest is that it is written by well-known Hollywood screenwriter, Ken Kolb, and was made into a movie. If not actually autobiographical, then *Getting Straight* is at least informed by Kolb's experience as a student at the University of California (there is a disclaimer to this

Getting Straight
(Bantam, 1968)
Demo (New English
Library, 1970)

effect). Apparently Kolb graduated with honors from the University of California and then went on to obtain a master's degree and teaching certificate. Trivia buffs will be interested to know that Kolb studied English and was a member of the Mu Chapter of the Theta Chi fraternity at the University of California, Berkeley.

A movie version was released in 1970 starring the high-profile actors Elliot Gould as Harry and Candice Bergen as girlfriend Jan. Movie trivia buffs may also be delighted to know that Harrison Ford makes an appearance in the movie, as Harry's friend Jake. While Kolb is better known as a screenwriter, he did write other novels, including *The Couch Trip* (1970), which also became a 1988 movie of the same name, starring Dan Aykroyd and Walter Matthau.

★

Demo by cult UK-based author Richard Allen (whose real name was James Moffatt) is different to his usual pulp offerings for New English Library. In place of skinheads, mods, and punks, the subjects of his better-known youthsploitation books for NEL, the subcultural focus in *Demo* is student unrest. As the back cover puts it: "FROM LONDON TO LOS ANGELES, FROM BERLIN TO PARIS, STUDENT RIOTS ARE BECOMING MORE MILITANT, MORE PROFICIENT. THE THREAT OF A YOUNG PEOPLE'S GLOBAL UPRISING GROWS MORE REAL EVERY DAY."

The back cover also claims *Demo* is a "MASTERFULLY RESEARCHED NOVEL" with added legitimacy provided by way of a hard-hitting foreword by the author: "No sane individual would refute youth's right to protest," yet "demonstration is an ugly word," with the reason for this being "professional demonstrators, militants and debased power-seekers" who seek to "infiltrate and control aspects of community life."

The focus of the plot is efforts to prevent an undercover Soviet "agent provocateur" from igniting foment among youth around the world: clearly campus rebellion is not confined to the United States. The globe-trotting agent uses many guises to inveigle his way into student politics: in London he is Julius Gold; in Los Angeles Stanley Edmond; and in Paris he is M'sieur Armand Pettu, a man who believes that "student power is disruptive" and who does whatever is required to ignite student revolt: "Students are not producers nor do people have sympathy when we simply stay away from classes to make our protest. Therefore, students are forced to take remedial action; to incite workers and others so that their voices can be heard."

Other themes in *Demo* concern imperialism, empire, and racism. One conservative character exclaims:

I'm an "EMPIRE" enthusiast and that excludes those of coloured blood. Whilst I readily admit to having a prejudice I still decline to go whole hog and condemn every black nation seeking its future apart from the Commonwealth, or Colonialism. I believe in every man being equal, but some being less capable of governing themselves than others.

and further,

The Canadian [Colonel Brett Hart] did not erect colour bars against black men. He simply could not comprehend the changes this loss of empire had brought. Nor could he assimilate self-governing black nations with his old-fashioned British justice is best notions.

The action takes places in various exotic locations, such as the Cochon, a subterranean Left Bank bar in Paris, or an apartment in LA, home for the beautiful Syl:

It was furnished in modern style with little attention to décor. Some of the walls were outrageously hued, the paintings hug at crazy angles a complete mixture of old masters and neurotic moderns. Underwear littered the deep pile carpet seeming to shout that the owner was confused, muddled, frustrated, without volition.

But no matter the location, what is at stake is not merely students letting off some steam by gaining concessions from the campus authorities. No. What is at stake is freedom and the future of democracy, as Colonel Hart explains: "I engaged in espionage because I knew where my duty lay—because I honestly believe in freedom under duly elected government. Not mob rule." Hart's effort to thwart revolution and "mob rule" is through assembling a ragtag alliance of ex-military colleagues and their young adult children:

This is a problem for young people to face. I propose we call ourselves Network Forty as that was the era in which we found companionship. Our children are Network Seventy—their age of insanity.... I suggest we bring the children here a week from today and ask if they will be guided by us.

What follows is a series of missions by members of Network Seventy in locations around the globe. Colonel Hart's twenty-three-year-old son Tim makes contact with radical activists in LA (where he also gets to make out with the beautiful Syl). Later on, in Paris, Network Seventy member Nanette Aubin goes undercover, figuratively and literally, in order to get close to the mysterious M'sieur Pettu:

> From the swollen river the sound of drumming drops increased in volume; heard above the traffic's growling.
>
> "If we could get a taxi" the girl suggested.
>
> "And where would we go together?"
>
> She shrugged. "Your apartment. Mine. It makes no difference."
>
> "Whatever gave you the notion I want to accompany you?"
>
> She snuggled against his side as rain cascaded down from the overladen branches. "You're not married, and you're not meeting a mistress, so why not me?"

Finally, given James Moffatt's Canadian heritage, the various references to Canada included in *Demo* add extra interest. Julius Gold travels under a Canadian passport, and Brett Hart's love of Canada is valorized:

> Your father, Tim, had more guts than a regiment of the line. He didn't try to defend his birthplace. He just wanted his subordinates to understand that he thought quite differently from us. And, whether or not you agree, Canadians are not misplaced Britishers. Nor are they American. They have a nationality of their own; a definite thinking process that touches on old links, new frontiers while keeping a separate, positive path.

★

Another novel dealing with "professional demonstrators" is *The Demonstrator*, coauthored by Australian couple Elizabeth and Don Campbell. *The Demonstrator* is a politically and emotionally charged novel focusing on political unrest in the lead-up to an international security conference involving Southeast Asian nations, which is to be held in Australia.

Like the nefarious Stanley Edmonds in *Demo*, Stephen Slater is an influential "professional demonstrator":

> Thao said, "Are you worried about the demonstrator?"
>
> "He's started riots and sit-ins all over Australia" Sarah said. "The students look on him as some sort of high priest. He was drafted for the army but he burned his draft card at the Cenotaph in Martin Place [a high-profile landmark in Sydney], and actually asked the place to arrest him."
>
> "Your sacred Anzac statue?"
>
> "Yes, sort of."
>
> "And defied the government? He would not be a soldier?"
>
> "He doesn't believe in violence."

But unlike Edmonds, Slater receives a relatively sympathetic hearing and is engaged in a more "wholesome" approach to political agitation:

> She nodded. "The one in the centre is a professional demonstrator." Seven of the girls were crowding Steven in a tightly formed circle, laughing as they changed position under his direction. Then, quite suddenly, they fanned out shoulder to shoulder and walked slowly through the terminal. Thao laughed and the delegates stared incredulously. One large scarlet letter was fixed on each prominent bosom. The girls were of uniform height and excellently equipped to display the easily readable message.
>
> Make love not war.

This "acceptable" face of protest is reinforced later in a testy exchange between Steven Slater and government liaison officer (and graduate of the Australian National University in Canberra), Miss Sarah Wainwright:

> She ignored the question. "What do you demonstrate for?"
>
> "I don't demonstrate. I organise other people to do it for me. You'd be astonished how many demonstrations bomb out. I'd like to get some system into them."
>
> "Like a mercenary?"
>
> "That's right. Demonstration is a young art. It's civilised revolution."

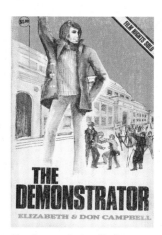

The Demonstrator (Dalton, 1970)

Campus Rebels (All Star Books, 1966)

The Campus Murders (Lancer Books, 1969)

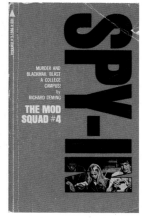

Spy-In (Pyramid, 1969)

But *The Demonstrator* concerns not only peace and security in the Asia-Pacific but also peace and security within the Slater family:

> Steven Slater is absolutely opposed to the concept of war, but his father, Osgood Slater is the Minister for Defence in the Australian Government. Years of confrontation between father and son reaches a dramatic climax when the Minister invites a large number of Asian countries to join in a defence treaty.

As the opposing efforts of Steven Slater and his father continue to collide, the tension surrounding the international conference increases as it draws closer. Yet the father-son conflict threatens to be overtaken by the intervention of far more sinister interests.

Beyond its being an enjoyable story of student rebellion and the generation gap with a hint of romance, another reason why *The Demonstrator* is of continuing interest is that it was made into a full-length feature film in 1971, which Australia's National Film and Sound Archives considers having played a role in highlighting the need for a viable commercial Australian film industry. Students from the Australian National University appeared as extras, and the launch was attended by high-profile politicians, including one who later became prime minister.

If ever there is a book that deserves to be called pulp, then it would be difficult to go beyond *Campus Rebels* by John Post. The setting is a university where, as the front cover puts it, "THE STUDENTS WANTED TO MAKE

LOVE NOT WAR," and the plot revolves around honeypot agents conspiring to enlist students to their cause: not a traditional political cause but the cause of freethinking (interpreted as "free loving").

What follows is a tale of the seductions of nineteen-year-old Ralph, who is some sort of an intellectual leader around the campus and is threatening to burn his draft card, and eighteen-year-old Jody, who will inherit a large fortune once she turns twenty-one. Within the blink of an eye Ralph's beard is gone, he's wearing perfume and women's lingerie and going by the name Darling, and then shortly after that he's getting it on with the much older Karl. For Jody, she is introduced to lesbianism via freethinkers Helga and Monica and ends up at a cocktail bar The Lagoon, which is frequented by people of diverse sexualities. From there, the action shifts to a raucous free-love party, designed to further "the cause." Part of the "charm" of *Campus Rebels*, if that is the correct word, is that the production is low-rent: about 45 of the 160 pages are blank; there are a number of spelling mistakes, and some sentences are repeated. All in all, it was well worth the 95-cent price tag on the cover.

More mainstream treatments of campus rebellion are provided in *The Campus Murders*, written by well-known pulp author Gil Brewer as part of the Ellery Queen series, and *Spy-In* by Richard Deming, which appeared as number four in the Mod Squad series of books. Gil Brewer's contribution centers on the disappearance from a West Coast college of a female student, Laura Thornton. As the daughter of a rambunctious candidate for the state governorship, she's no ordinary student. This leads the current state governor to send troubleshooter Mike McCall to Tisquanto State College to sort things out. But given the campus unrest, this may not be a straightforward missing-person case.

> Along with reports of widespread dormitory sex, the spreading use of LSD, marijuana, amphetamines, barbiturates, and other drugs. . . . There was outspoken defiance of the Establishment, threats against the administrative authority, a minor revolt of some of the younger faculty, and at least one medium sized campus riot that had hospitalized ten students and one of Pearson's [the local policy commissioner] officers.

Along the way McCall gains the assistance, and affection, of the "pretty as sin" dean's assistant, Miss Katherine Cohon:

> "Frightening, it was directed. Like a movie scene. Who's behind things like this on campus? Outsiders?" [asks McCall]
>
> "Et tu," she asked scornfully. "Next thing I know you'll be looking under my skirt for Communists. No Mike, not outsiders. There's a small group of militant student leaders who are—or claim to be—true revolutionaries. They're the ones who direct these attacks."

McCall's investigations take him to a number of student hangouts, including the basement apartment of the "snake-tight Levi" wearing Perry Eastman:

> McCall opened the door and stepped into the cavern like place, shadow filled from candles that burned everywhere . . . posters covered the walls: a heady incense filled the room, but it did not entirely blot out the acrid odor of marijuana. The incense was curling lazily from a brass Indian urn on the mantelpiece, at least five sticks worth. The pixilated Bach was coming out of a cheap record player.

★

Richard Deming, another well-known pulp author, who also ghost authored for the Ellery Queen series, had a panache for TV novelizations. Of interest here is *Spy-In*, number four in the Mod Squad series, in which, according to the back cover: "The crime-busting teen trio swings into undercover action to discover Mafia violence, deception and sudden death on a campus blazing with unrest and crime."

Throughout *Spy-In* the focus is an investigation into a gambling scheme that rewards students for influencing the outcomes of athletic events. The Mod Squad—Lincoln Hayes (an African American youth from the ghetto), Peter Cochrane (the only child of well-heeled Beverly Hills parents), and Julie Barnes (who'd grown up in San Francisco without parental support)—encounter the full spectrum of campus politics as part of their investigation.

> "You're not interested in reform," Pete said. . . . "You simply want to shut this college down."
>
> "That's not true," Trotter denied hotly.
>
> "The ultimate aim of the SDS isn't anarchy?" Pete demanded.
>
> "Our goal is to tear down the present corrupt Establishment and rebuild American society from scratch," Trotter said. "Maybe you call that anarchy, but I call it a search for true democracy. We don't have any in our present society."
>
> "There's plenty wrong with our society," Pete conceded. "But what's wrong with trying to mend it from within, instead of flushing the good parts down the drain along with the bad?"
>
> "It's beyond mending. The powers that be are too firmly entrenched, and there aren't any good parts. The only solution is to uproot the whole system and start over."

What is evident from these novels is a strong focus on aspects of left-wing politics, although coverage of ecological politics and the women's movement seems to have attracted relatively limited attention. Further, university campuses have changed so much since these novels of rebellion were written, that equivalent pulps today would more likely focus on right-wing politics, although the results are unlikely to be as enjoyable.

Brian Coffey

The Player

Iceberg Slim and the Allure of the Street

It is rare for the pulp author to enjoy any celebrity beyond having his name displayed on book covers. They have legions of fans, to be sure, but most of them just want the next story; the person is of secondary interest. Iceberg Slim, however, was no ordinary author. In the late 1960s and early 1970s Slim gained notoriety for writing pulp novels about the ghetto underworld. Though retired from hustling by the time he began his literary career, Slim drew from firsthand experience to structure and fill in the details of each story. The result was some of the most daring and controversial pulp fiction of the era. That he had a vexed relationship with the social and cultural movements of the day was not lost on him. But Slim kept writing, for he understood that his books spoke to the political situation of black people in a different register.

Iceberg Slim was born Robert Lee Moppins Jr. on August 4, 1918, to Mary Brown and Robert Moppins. Originally from Nashville, Tennessee, the Moppinses had moved to Chicago in the Great Migration. Like millions of other African Americans, they had left the South of Jim Crow segregation in the hope of starting a better life in the North. That dream was quickly abandoned, however, when Robert Sr. deserted the family to pursue his own pleasures. Struggling to raise Junior on her own, in 1922 Mary married a respectable businessman, Henry Upshaw, and moved to Rockford, Illinois; there a young Robert enjoyed a measure of stability. But the allure of the street proved too powerful even for Mary to resist. In 1931 an inveterate hustler walked into her beauty shop and swept her off her feet. Mary packed up her son and left her husband to follow him to Milwaukee. The loss of Henry, a genuine father figure, deeply affected Robert. The hustler barely lasted a year, and with Robert's mother occupied at work it was only a matter of time before he took to the streets on his own.

In Milwaukee Robert began to hang out with older black men. These hustlers introduced him to "The Game": the art of taking advantage of others as way to make one's living. Robert started out with small cons

Pimp (Holloway House, 1967)

but quickly learned that the big money came from pimping. From Milwaukee to Chicago, he mastered the psychological manipulation required to exploit women's sexual labor in the informal economy. In the process, he shed his square-world name and went by two monikers: first Slim Lancaster and then Cavanaugh Slim. Over the next two decades, Robert harnessed a formidable "stable" of prostitutes, became a serious cocaine addict, and did several stints in prison for his illegal activities.

The years veered wildly between boom and bust. By the early 1960s, he had predictably lost it all. After a final stint in jail, Robert reconciled with his long-suffering mother, who had relocated to Los Angeles with her late husband Ural Beck. He took her married name as a gesture of forgiveness. And so it was as Robert Beck—now a middle-aged, door-to-door exterminator—that he approached the independent publisher Holloway House with dreams of becoming a writer. He brought in a manuscript based on his criminal past that would become the underground classic *Pimp: The Story of My Life* (1967).

Beck came to Holloway House at just the right time. The Watts Riots had made international headlines in 1965, drawing attention to the problems blacks faced in urban areas outside the South. Joblessness, police brutality, residential segregation—this was Jim Crow by another name. For its part, Los Angeles–based Holloway House was looking for writers who could address racial unrest from the perspective of the black community. The company had been the book-publishing arm of two men's pinup magazines, *Adam* and *Knight*, since 1961. Their fare was risqué but not envelope-pushing—cheesecake stuff. It was also lily-white. Beck was who Holloway House was looking for. Though the story he presented to the editors was set mainly in the interwar years, it gave voice to the quality of dispossession that many blacks still felt in the 1960s. Moreover, because it was a postmigration narrative set in the greater Midwest, *Pimp* zoomed in on urban black discontent in a way that conventional civil rights discourse had some difficulty addressing. Beck, in other words, had penned a story that was very much of the moment, a book forged from the fires of Watts.

Pimp was published under the pen name Iceberg Slim in March 1967. Although Beck had gone by other monikers on the street, he embraced the fiction of Iceberg as a strategy of building his literary mythos. Not coincidentally, the book's climax is the scene in which he earns the nickname. Known around town as Young Blood (or Blood for short) because he is a hungry, up-and-coming pimp, the narrator is sitting at a bar with his mentor Glass Top when a gunshot rings out. Everyone scrambles for cover except Blood, who remains in his seat, nonplussed by all the commotion. Blood is unfazed, we learn, because he is actually high on cocaine. The others do not know that, however, so his stone-cold demeanor comes across as impressive, death-defying. As they are walking out of the bar, an amazed Glass Top announces: "Kid, you were cold in there, icy; icy, like an iceberg. Kid, I got it. You're getting to be a good young pimp. All good pimps got monickers. I'm gonna hang one on you." Thus the naming of Iceberg Slim coincides with the narrator's coming into his own as a fearless hustler and pimp. How he pulled off the illusion matters less than the fact that he looked the part. It is a perfectly timed plot point.

That this episode was entirely made up suggests that, although Slim insisted on the veracity of his recollection, the book was an occasion to portray himself as larger than life. Who could blame the hustler for not continuing the hustle? *Pimp* was an exercise in myth-making, a way for Slim to rewrite his life according to the script of his choosing. Odie Hawkins, another Holloway House author from Chicago, once revealed, "I knew Iceberg Slim. I had a funny kind of relationship with him. I knew him as a boy. He was not a major league pimp—no, no, no. That's a correction that needs to be made." But Slim did not want his life story to be fact-checked. *Pimp* was a new way of recollecting his past.

Still, the fact that his debut effort was autobiographical fiction did not mean that Slim was uninterested in telling the truth. The book is an episodic coming-of-age story in which a young black man, Bobby, rejects the path of middle-class security in favor of the fast life of the streets. Based on his own resentment toward his mother, Mary Moppins, Slim figures Bobby's steady descent into the underworld as a reaction against not having a stable father figure at home. "The slide was greased," the narrator remarks early on of his choosing a life of crime. While Mama struggles to provide for her son, Bobby enters into a fraternity of black hustlers and pimps. As the narrative progresses, he learns from successive mentors (all of whom have evocative nicknames) both the practical elements of criminal activity and the psychology of control that yokes women's sexual exploitation to a man's inner strength and personal development. From Party Time, Bobby learns how to con prospective "johns," or clients, out of their money by dressing up as a black girl and tempting them with an illusory tryst. From Weeping Shorty, he learns the pimping fundamentals and how to amass his own stable. Finally, from Sweet Jones, he learns the most important lesson of all: "A good pimp could cut his swipe [penis] off and still pimp his ass off. Pimping ain't no sex game. It's a skull game." The pimp achieves such complete self-possession that the exploited willingly submit to its aura of control. Not coincidentally, this is the lesson the narrator learns just before he is rechristened Iceberg.

Why would *Pimp* have struck a chord with black readers in 1967? Because Slim, drawing on his own experiences, created a fantasy world where black men were on top and where the purpose of the Game was to retain that spot. Sweet Jones, again, provided the relevant counsel:

> Believe me, Slim, a pimp is really a whore who's reversed the game on whores. Slim, be as sweet as the scratch. Don't be no sweeter. Always stick a whore for a bundle before you sex her. A whore ain't nothing but a trick to a pimp. Don't let 'em "Georgia" [take advantage of] you. Always get your money in front just like a whore.

Given the precariousness of life in the black ghetto, a pimp was only ever one step away from becoming a whore. His prostitutes would ruin him if they had the chance, so he had to play with steely determination. Defending his position was coextensive with defining his manhood: either use or be used. Who had time for lofty ideals anymore? The Game reigned supreme.

Slim's cynicism was fitting for the year in which the civil rights struggle gave way to strident militancy. After another summer of major urban rioting, the feeling in 1967 was that integration was mere lip service compared to street-level truths. Toward the end of the year, Slim revisited the theme in another full-length book, the novel *Trick Baby*. Propping up his own mythos, Slim incorporates Iceberg into the frame narrative, where in jail he encounters a man "who could have been Errol Flynn's twin." When this handsome fellow reveals himself to be a "White Negro," Iceberg sits back and listens to his story. The reader learns that, like Bobby, John Patrick O'Brien Jr. grows up without a father on the South Side of Chicago. Unlike Bobby, Johnny is half-white, the son of a black woman and a touring white jazz musician whose name he bears. In his early years, other children presume Johnny is the product of a prostitute-john liaison (hence "trick baby"). Even though his parents had been married, the stigma sticks like glue. The children tease Johnny mercilessly, making him feel like an outcast in the black community. Once again Slim poses the question, How will this fatherless son survive?

At the brink of despair, Johnny meets Blue Howard, a respected hustler in the neighborhood. Seeing how

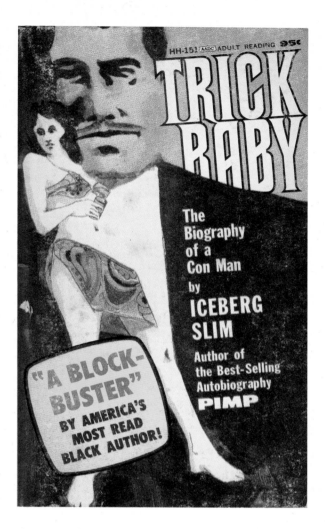

Trick Baby (Holloway House, 1967)

out of sorts he is, Blue takes Johnny in and nurses him back to health. As a fatherly bond emerges with Johnny, Blue decides to give him the nickname White Folks. More important, he gives him a clear purpose in life: pass for white to play the con. This is the direction he has been looking for all along. From Blue, Folks learns not to be ashamed by his whiteness but to use it to his advantage. He tricks his intended targets, or "marks," into thinking they can trust him because of the way he looks. Once he gains their confidence, Blue comes in as the false mark they will fleece. When all is said and done, the duo can claim to have pilfered a nice sum of money and to have done so at the expense of some racist who deserved it. Paradoxically, it is by passing for white—a way of bonding with Blue—that Folks finally feels connected to his blackness. "Inside," Blue says, "you feel and think black like me."

Compared to *Pimp*, *Trick Baby* is a light diversion. The former's exploitation of women is alleviated somewhat by the latter's pursuit of the purest con, one where the mark does all the (racist) work of setting himself up to lose. In a general sense, though, the books tell two sides of the same story. At root, Iceberg and Folks learn from older black hustlers how to play the Game from within the conditions of their own oppression. Neither tells a story of uplift. This is even true of *Trick Baby*, where toward the end Blue admits that he initially took Folks in because he wanted to use him in his schemes. His was an altruism of opportunity. Yet it is precisely such pessimism of the spirit that Slim was trying to capture in his writing. If, in the end, you could trust no one, then you had to learn how to trust only in yourself. Iceberg and Folks walk away with that lesson in their pockets.

As 1967 turned into 1968, *Pimp* and *Trick Baby* became underground best sellers. Slim had struck a nerve with black readers, many of whom could relate to the inner-city characters and setting of the narratives. He also had a way with words that made it seem as if he was telling a story at the barbershop. With a flair for the vernacular, Slim was like a street-corner raconteur coming in for a trim. By all accounts, the books actually did find their way into barbershops, as well as bars, pool halls, and other spaces of black men's congregation. The books' standard paperback format made them easy to trade among friends and acquaintances. Finally, and perhaps most importantly, readers could delight in these characters' winning at the Game, even if for a time, as a fantasied victory

for black people everywhere. Slim had combined the badman of folklore with the con man of city life to a degree that no other author had achieved up to that point. Chester Himes and Malcolm X came close, but it was Slim who truly captured the ethos of the urban black outlaw in fiction.

Slim followed up on his early success with a third book, the novel *Mama Black Widow* (1969). Arguably the darkest work he ever penned, it is an anomaly in Slim's oeuvre for focusing on what he perceived to be the extreme effects of black masculine dispossession. *Mama Black Widow* relates the story of Otis Tilson, a black "transvestite" who struggles to free himself from the influence of his overbearing mother, Sedalia. The Tilson family had moved from Meridian, Mississippi, to Chicago in the hope of finding the Promised Land up north. What they found, instead, is a discriminatory system that chews up black masculinity and spits it out. Papa's God-fearing, wage-earning life in the South is completely, irrevocably undone by joblessness and despair in the city. Stepping into the patriarchal role is Mama, who begins working as a domestic to make ends meet.

Once this gender-role shift transpires, the Tilsons, as a family unit, are doomed. Mama starts going out with a local minister, not caring to hide her indiscretions from Papa, who is forced to stand by in "slaw jaw shock and awful anguish." When he dares to make a final, desperate move on Mama, she deals the fatal blow to his manhood: "Niggah, git you paws offen me. Ah ain't gappin' mah laigs fer you. Uh man foots th bills fer whuts his'n. Mabbe yu is uh drunkard and mabbe you uh tramp. You sumpthin, but for sho you ain't no man." Papa is vanquished.

Mama is no less forgiving of her wayward children. Cruel and uncompromising, her physical and emotional abuse results in the deaths of two daughters and one son being locked away for life. Otis is the only Tilson who lives to tell. Yet his particular burden, as it were, is to try to survive as a "niggerized and deballed" black man. Mama's wielding of phallic power turns Otis inside out, instituting in his psyche a "freakish bitch" named Sally who likes to dress in drag and have sex with men. In Slim's imagination, this is a decidedly unnatural position, a travesty of stunted black masculinity. He drives home the point in a horrifying scene. At a house party, Otis throws caution to the wind and goes to bed with an ugly stranger nicknamed Lovee. The man's huge stature, "gorilla face," and "fat

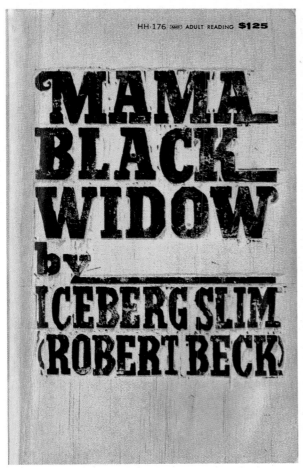

Mama Black Widow (Holloway House, 1969)

BIOGRAPHY

"Iceberg Slim" — a pseudonym he was forced to use — is Robert Beck, and Robert Beck's power is in his pen. He has written, in MAMA BLACK WIDOW, a chronicle of Negro ghetto life which should be recognized as the most vivid and important ever published.

Beck's premise is that hatred is as destructive to those who hate as it is to those who are hated. His life on Chicago's Southside lends ample authority to his writing.

Other books by Robert Beck are PIMP and TRICK BABY.

lips" all fail to warn Otis of his potential monstrosity. Lovee turns out to be a hustler. He steals Otis's money, beats him to a pulp, and then viciously rapes him. The brutality of the attack—"horrible rending pain exploded through the raw core of my being like I had been halved by an axe"—drives home for Otis, and the reader, how utterly debased his condition is.

On the face of it, there is no mistaking Sally, Otis's alter ego, for Young Blood or White Folks. She embodies the emasculation from which young men in the black ghetto are trying to escape. Yet, insofar as Otis too grows up fatherless on the South Side, Sally is inextricably linked to Slim's other protagonists. Specifically, she symbolizes the ever-present threat of what could happen if they allowed themselves to slip up. To be sure, this message is homophobic and misogynist in the extreme. Structural racism in the North is displaced onto two intertwined figures: a libidinous, self-serving matriarch and a pathetic, cross-dressing boy. But Slim

did not write *Mama Black Widow* to make friends, of course. He tapped into the masculinist ethos of pulp to deliver an indictment of the postmigration experience. He was practically unique in imagining the breakdown of the black family as a kind of urban Gothic. Slim gained even more fans after the book was published.

Not everyone was pleased with his rising star. One of Slim's earliest critics was the Black Arts editor, poet, and theorist Larry Neal. In his 1969 poetry collection *Black Boogaloo (Notes on Black Liberation)*, Neal dedicated "Brother Pimp" to the memory of Iceberg Slim. The poem illuminates how the pimp lives by the false consciousness of the Game. According to Neal, his is an illusory masculinity:

> you just as bad as the honky,
> only you dress better motherfucker,
> only you drive your cadillac better mother-
> fuck-er.

The Naked Soul of Iceberg Slim (Holloway House, 1971)

And further:

> you and your brother pimps kill each other
> for the right to destroy our women.
> would-be heroes. would be black men.

Neal's biting wordplay cuts to the core of the pimp's allure: his self-possession. He effectively emasculates the pimp, pointing out that his power is the effect of so much smoke and mirrors. Neal concludes the poem, though, with something like a gesture toward reconciliation. He encourages the pimp to change his ways and "pimp for the revolution" rather than for himself. If he is able to channel his talent and ambition into serving the collective good, then, Neal reckons, the pimp might be worth saving.

Slim's response to the nationalist critique of his persona was deferential; he did not want to be seen as opposed to the revolution. But Slim also understood this was a prime opportunity to burnish his reputation in the black community. He could sell even more books if he played his cards right. To that end, in 1971 Holloway House published *The Naked Soul of Iceberg Slim*, a collection of essays and shorter pieces that bore some resemblance to Black Panther Party leader Eldridge Cleaver's *Soul on Ice* (1968). Slim signals his intentions at the very beginning of the book:

> I dedicate this book to the heroic memory of Malcolm X, Jack Johnson, Melvin X, Jonathan Jackson; to Huey P. Newton, Bobby Seale, Ericka Huggins, George Jackson, Angela Davis; and to all street niggers and strugglers in and out of the joints.

It is a striking declaration of faith. By linking past and present black revolutionaries to those lowest down, Slim repurposes "street niggers and strugglers" for political use. In this tacit response to Larry Neal, he affirms the Black Panther Party's own stated wish to convert the "brothers on the block" to black revolution.

Naked Soul is an interesting mishmash of memoir, political commentary, pop psychology, and epistolary exchanges. Slim outlines his theory that "pimps require the secretly buried fuel of Mother hatred to stoke their fiery vendetta of cruelty and merciless exploitation against whores primarily and ultimately all women." Like his Black Power contemporaries, he skewers the "boob black bourgeoisie" for producing "the kind of nigger robot who strives and hungers for the approval and favor of his enemies." In a moment of introspection, he confesses that his boyhood admiration for "the flash and dazzle of well-heeled pimps cruising the poverty-mauled slums in gaudy cars" led him down a path of ruin. And he even recounts visiting the local southern California chapter of the Black Panther Party, where he finds (to his approval) that "the Panther youngsters were blind to my negative glamour and, in fact, expressed a polite disdain for my former profession and its phony flash of big cars, jewelry and clothes."

But arguably the most intriguing chapter is a letter Slim writes to his estranged father, Robert Moppins, Sr. He makes his resentment known, blaming his father for "causing the vital vine of black family stability and strength to be poisoned." But Slim also seeks a means of reconciliation. He finds it in the ongoing revolution in the streets:

> Papa, if you are still in this mortal coil I know that you, like me and millions of other black men of all ages, have gained wonderful new ball power from the courage and daring exploits of the Black Panthers in this Eden of genocide. It is tragic that too many black fathers have always lacked something their children could be proud of and remember.

And then:

> Papa, we older black men must guard against condemning and hating the young rejuvenators of our balls for despising us and blaming us for letting them be born into this hellish society—one we at least could have risked our lives to demolish. Perhaps our black heroes of revolt would be less bitter towards old niggers if they could understand that they owe their very existence as revolutionaries to all those disenchanted black men who, since slavery, have probed and challenged America's oppressive power structure.

In this rhetorical performance of dizzying complexity, Slim first lends a sympathetic ear to his father's struggles. He is able to do so because the revolution has shown up his own deficiencies as a man. From there it is only one step to identifying completely with his father and turning the question back on the Black Panthers. Yes, they—"disenchanted black men"—were wrong, but did they not subvert the power structure all the same? A subtle vindication of his own past is embedded in his effort to reconnect with this father.

As Holloway House probably had planned all along, *Naked Soul* catapulted Slim into the lucrative college lecture circuit, turning him into a minor literary celebrity. He now appeared at the same institutions where the Panthers and other revolutionary groups were making passionate appeals to students. Set up as rap sessions rather than formal talks, Slim's events elicited coverage from the black press and mainstream media alike. He spoke with young people on the state of the Black Power movement and on why they should reject the path he had taken. Much of what he said echoed the main points of the book. But many came out just to see the bad boy of black letters in person. *Pimp*'s sales went up along with *Naked Soul*'s, and for all intents and purposes Slim played up, even romanticized, his past in these appearances. "The Psychology of the Pimp," the title of his 1975 interview with the magazine *The Black Collegian*, proved the point.

At the same time that he was enjoying his greatest success, Slim's relationship with Holloway House began to sour. Facts about his contract and royalty arrangements remain sketchy, but legal proceedings filed against the company reveal that Slim thought he was being cheated. He never believed Holloway House's sales figures and thus always felt he was being underpaid. This alone was a major sticking point, but Slim's frustration was not just about money. In 1972 Universal optioned the film rights to *Trick Baby*. The blaxploitation boom was going strong, and Holloway House wanted a piece of the action generated by the likes of Melvin Van Peebles's *Sweet Sweetback's Baadasssss Song* (1971) and Gordon Parks Jr.'s *Super Fly* (1972). The movie version of *Trick Baby* came out in December 1972, and to Slim's great dismay it was a dud. The issue was not simply that the script, on which Slim had not been consulted, was a shadow of the source material. It was also that, for the titular role, the producers had cast Kiel Martin, a white television actor with no background in black culture. His performance as White Folks was belabored and stiff, and it was unbelievable that this character could have grown up in the black ghetto. And though the dialogue was already bad, with Martin's delivery, it sounded exactly like what it was: a white man trying to talk jive. The movie sputtered, and Holloway House would not venture another adaptation until the 2000s.

In the face of these difficulties, Slim rode his infamy for a while, even dropping *Reflections*, an album of toasts (ribald poems from oral tradition), in

1976. But he would not publish with Holloway House again until the following year, when two novels came out in quick succession. The first, *Long White Con*, is a sequel to *Trick Baby*. It follows White Folks's exploits after he has decided to permanently pass for white. Iceberg returns to the frame narrative, but the veneer of meeting up with his old acquaintance wears thin almost immediately. When Folks gives him a preview of what he has to relate, Iceberg exclaims, "What a follow-up novel to TRICK BABY that story would make!" It is as if the author is writing ad copy for Holloway House. The story does not fare much better. Folks relocates to Canada, where he teams up with the Vicksburg Kid to play a bizarre con, the "Unsuspecting Virgin Game," on investors. The con itself does not require Folks to play off his marks' racism, nor does it ask him to reflect on his mixed-race ancestry. Because Folks no longer feels the pull of his blackness, socially or culturally, the story reads like a straightforward caper. It is a far cry from the interracial tension that made *Trick Baby* stand out.

Iceberg Slim's *Death Wish: A Story of the Mafia* also came out in 1977, but it is perhaps his least-read book. It ended up being a mere blip in the Mafia craze that had followed the publication of Mario Puzo's *The Godfather* in 1969. To its credit, the novel is set in Chicago to great effect, returning us to the streets Slim knew so well. Moreover, *Death Wish* advances a gripping premise—one that pits the Italian Mafia against a black underground organization called the Warriors. From one angle, the book delivers a titanic clash between equally matched criminal underworlds. In truth, though, the execution of this cross-racial crime narrative is no better than blaxploitation's awkward Mafia aesthetic, codified in films like *Hell Up in Harlem* (1973) and *Black Belt Jones* (1974). The broad ethnic characterizations are cringe-worthy, and there is little to distinguish the narrative's structure from any number of *Godfather* copycats that were on the market at the time. This was Slim's second strike in the calendar year.

By that time, it was clear that the peak of Slim's literary celebrity had well and truly passed. Donald Goines, his pulp protégé, was now the big thing at Holloway House. His direct, flat-footed style and action-packed storylines seemed better suited to the pulp format anyway. And while *Pimp* was still a best seller, new readers seemed to fall for the burnished image of Slim rather than for the man himself. His public appearances waned in direct proportion to how

Death Wish (Holloway House, 1977)
Airtight Willie and Me (Holloway House, 1979)

STICKING IT TO THE MAN

familiar he became in readers' minds. In a way, Slim's body had become redundant to his mythos.

Slim published a collection of short stories, *Airtight Willie and Me*, in 1979. These had been published previously in *Players*, the all-black pinup magazine that was run by Holloway House's owners. It seemed the more Slim tried to prolong his literary career the more embedded he became in the company's operations. The four stories in the collection are breezy and unremarkable, but there is one part of the book that sticks in the mind. At the very beginning Slim writes:

> This volume is dedicated to time. It gives us memories, fine wine and wrinkles. But the only thing worse than getting old is not getting old. So here's to time, dear reader, yours and mine. May you have many more wrinkles, a lot of fine wine and memories to last two lifetimes.

A dedication to his own advancing age, this statement says a lot about Slim's situation at the close of the decade. Although he might have appreciated being a man of experience, the moroseness of his words betrayed a tinge of regret that he no longer was a man of his time.

Slim stepped away from the limelight after the release of *Airtight Willie*. Fed up with the way Holloway House had treated him, and perhaps acutely aware that he could never equal the success of his early works, Slim refused to publish anything else with the company. He lived out the rest of his days in a small apartment in South Central Los Angeles, where he could recall better times in solitude.

Slim died from complications related to diabetes on April 30, 1992. The day before his passing, another round of mass civil unrest consumed Los Angeles. Four police officers had just been acquitted of criminal charges related to the beating of Rodney King. Frustration over the verdicts boiled over onto the streets, and for six days rioters burned parts of Los Angeles's poorest neighborhoods to the ground. Looting was rampant. In addition to thousands of injuries and arrests, there were over fifty fatalities. Despair over this state of affairs was as widespread as it had been in 1965. It was like Watts all over again.

It is no coincidence that Slim's streetwise persona influenced the very musical subgenre—gangsta rap—that was the soundtrack to the Los Angeles riots. In life and in death, Slim expressed black people's belief that the system would never change. When it came right

down to it, The Game was rigged—there was no escape from the black ghetto. Slim's most famous fan, Tracy Marrow, brought this cynical outlook on life to bear on his musical artistry. He paid homage to his hero by taking up the rap moniker Ice-T. If Slim's writing had found an audience among the disaffected in the wake of civil rights, Ice-T's gangsta rap appealed to the same in the wake of a decade of self-proclaimed Reaganite prosperity. In both cases, Iceberg Slim and Ice-T were keen to point out that the state's promises were never kept and that an era's lofty ideals were leveraged against the grim realities of the dispossessed.

Kinohi Nishikawa

Canadian Carnage

Quebecois Separatism through the Lens of Men's Adventure Novels

When the protagonists of American men's adventure and spy thrillers ventured out of their homeland during the 1960s and '70s it was generally to party down in exotic locales while battling fantastical super-villains and agents. Sometimes playing a lone hand, often working for communist Russia and China, these adversaries were soon supplemented with a new brand of evildoer. As the level and scope of anticolonial struggles increased—and along with them the attendant use of what has come to be known as asymmetrical warfare—so did the entrance of "terrorist" villains.

Often used interchangeably as cookie-cutter bombers and skyjackers—only distinguishable by their accents and a few phrasebook derived foreign language exclamations—the world's many and varied guerrilla movements provided hack writers with topical material and new locations. Textbook bad guys were usually drawn from the ranks of high-profile movements like the Palestinian Liberation Organization (PLO) and Irish Republican Army (IRA), but residing in the lower ranks of pulp's revolutionary foot soldiers were Canada's Quebecois nationalists. The half dozen novels dealing with the province not only number among them some of the most bizarre novels of the era but also provide insights into the genre as a whole.

Quebecois nationalist sentiment has existed within Canada since rival British colonialists consolidated their hold on First Nations territory in the 1760s. The descendants of the French settlers who opposed this have formed a distinct community ever since, leading to various armed rebellions and attempts to turn the province of Quebec into an autonomous state. Inspired by the Algerian revolution and in the context of what became known as the Quiet Revolution—a period of intensified secularization, industrial modernization, economic reform, and social struggle in the province—support for secession mounted from the early

1960s onward. Militants associated with the Front de Libération du Québec (FLQ) began to carry out bombings in 1963 against military, economic, and symbolic targets. Occurring alongside, but largely separate to widespread strikes and upheaval among workers, such bombings, and the robberies required to fund them, intensified to the point where hundreds of armed actions had been carried out by 1970.

Unsurprisingly dozens of Canadian novels, ranging from experimental novels-within-novels to alternate realities and adventure actioners, have been inspired by the events of the period. Possibly the first installment of an American thriller series to reference what was occurring was *Tanner's Tiger* in 1968. The fifth of eight novels in the Evan Tanner series by crime stalwart Lawrence Block, the Canadian connection seems to have been largely inspired by Montreal's hosting of the World Fair in 1967. Expo '67, as it was locally known, packed in more than fifty million visitors over six months. Among its various construction projects was the construction of the artificial Notre Dame Island in the Saint Lawrence River. One of the various controversies to hit the event was a month-long transportation strike, the picketing of the opening day by anti–Vietnam War protesters, and French president De Gaulle's rapid exit following a speech on the steps of Montreal City Hall in which he exclaimed "Vive Montréal . . . Vive le Québec . . . Vive le Québec Libre!" The FLQ made threats against the event, which were never carried out, but it was anti-Castro militants who took action in planting a small bomb in the Cuba Pavilion.

Tanner is far from your typical spy. For a start he literally never sleeps, "having lost the habit forever when a shard of North Korean shrapnel performed random brain surgery and knocked out something called the sleep center." While he officially collects a disability pension he unofficially engages in a range of adventures, including carrying out missions for an unnamed U.S. agency. But his relationship to the

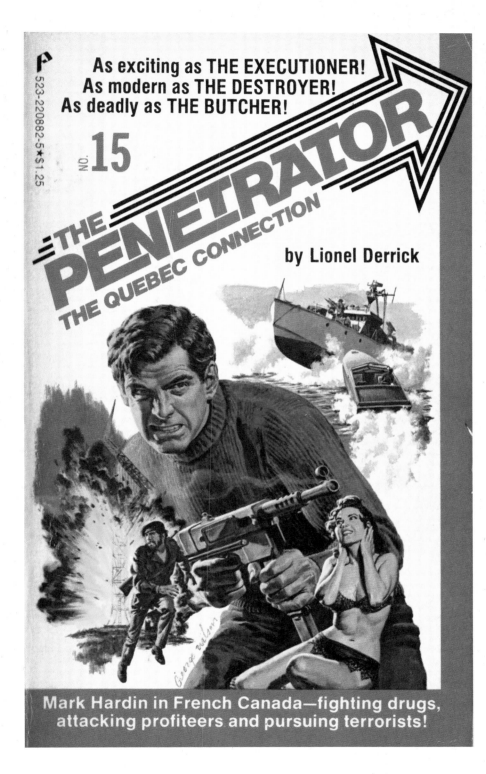

As exciting as THE EXECUTIONER!
As modern as THE DESTROYER!
As deadly as THE BUTCHER!

NO. 15

THE PENETRATOR

THE QUEBEC CONNECTION

by Lionel Derrick

523-220882-5★$1.25

Mark Hardin in French Canada—fighting drugs, attacking profiteers and pursuing terrorists!

TANNER'S TIGER

Tanner knew you always grabbed a purring tiger right where it counts—by the tail.

By LAWRENCE BLOCK

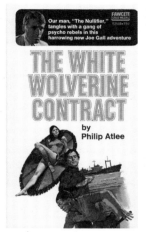

Our man, "The Nullifier," tangles with a gang of psycho rebels in this harrowing new Joe Gall adventure

THE WHITE WOLVERINE CONTRACT

by Philip Atlee

No. 24   CORGI

Mack Bolan is The EXECUTIONER

CANADIAN CRISIS

Trouble between the USA and Canada — stirred up by the Mafia

DON PENDLETON

The Quebec Connection (Pinnacle, 1976)
Tanner's Tiger (Gold Medal, 1968)
The White Wolverine Contract (Fawcett, 1971)
Canadian Crisis (Corgi, 1977)

government, like everything else in his life, is far from straightforward:

> The Chief thinks I'm one of his men. Maybe I am. It's hard to say. He once sprang me from a CIA dungeon somewhere in darkest Washington and since then he has made contact time to time to hand me assignments. I'd rather he didn't do this, but the man is convinced I'm one of his most reliable operatives, and I've never been able to figure out a way to change his mind. Besides there's something to be said for the connection—as it stands. I'm under fairly constant surveillance by the CIA, which is sure I am some kind of secret agent, never mind whose, and by the FBI, which is positive I am six kinds of subversive. With all of the consequent wiretapping and mail-snooping going on, it's vaguely reassuring to have at least one government factotum who thinks, right or wrong, that I'm on his side.

All this interest from the authorities largely stems from another of Tanner's quirks, his membership of "marginal movements" from the Irish Republican Brotherhood to the Flat Earth Society. He expresses his ardent support for these early on in the novel, declaring: "One either identifies with little ragged bands of political extremists or considers them to be madmen; one either embraces lost causes or deplores them."

Tanner is not only marked out by his diverse political allegiances but also his personal relationships. If they weren't raised in orphanages then most spies, vigilantes and other men's adventure protagonists have lost any connections to family and significant others via attacks by the Mafia, muggers or other evildoers. In Tanner's case he is an unofficial foster parent to a young girl named Minna, the sole surviving heir to the Lithuanian throne who he rescued by stealing an experimental vertical-lift jet fighter from a Soviet base.

Ostensibly Tanner is taking Minna on a trip to the World's Fair, but in actuality he's on a mission to investigate strange goings on at the Cuban pavilion. Getting into Canada immediately proves difficult however due to our hero's membership of the obscure separatist organization Le Mouvement National de Québec. Forced to sneak across the border, with the aid of a hapless Polish nationalist, the pair make it to Expo '67 whereupon Minna promptly disappears. Escaping an attempt to deport him, Tanner engages in a number of escapades including stealing a Mountie's horse,

hooking up with the aforementioned separatists and getting righteously stoned with a bunch of draft-dodging hippies. Conspiracies within conspiracies abound as Tanner rushes to solve the mystery of the disappearing tourists, save Minna, and prevent a plot involving the Queen of England turning from kidnap to murder and martyrdom.

Despite a somewhat throwaway resolution regarding the Cuban carry-on, *Tanner's Tiger* is an enjoyable read that lightly satirizes pretty much everyone and everything its hero encounters, including himself and his genre. That Block was able to do so without becoming painful, hokey, or boring is a tribute to his skills, ones that have served him well over a five-decade career and dozens of novels.

Most of the men's adventure novels dealing with Quebecois nationalism appeared after 1970s "October Crisis." Following a period of concerted pressure from Canadian authorities FLQ members took Paul Cross, the British trade commissioner in Montreal, hostage on October 5. In return for his freedom they demanded the government publish their manifesto as well as free twenty-three prisoners associated with the organization and supply them with $500,000 and a plane to Cuba. Perceiving that the government was stalling, a separate guerrilla cell captured Minister of Labour Pierre Laporte on October 10.

This second kidnapping triggered the invocation of draconian powers associated with Canada's War Measures Act for the first time in the nation's peacetime history. The FLQ was banned, troops sent into Ottawa and Montreal, mass raids carried out and more than 450 people detained without charge. Asked in a TV interview how far how he would go in defense of the state, Prime Minister Trudeau infamously replied, "Just watch me." La Porte's kidnappers responded by executing their hostage, an action for which two of their number would later receive life sentences. The cell detaining Cross were located in December and negotiated passage for themselves and family members to Cuba in exchange for his release.

The next American action writer to tackle Quebec was Philip Atlee (real name James Atlee Phillips). Starting out as a publicist for showman Billy Rose in 1939, he later switched to a career writing short stories for popular magazines such as *Colliers*, *Argosy*, and the *Saturday Evening Post* while serving in the air force during World War II. By the 1960s he was financing a life of regular travel by penning the Contract espionage series for Fawcett Gold Medal. Wherever Atlee visited his protagonist Joe Gall—a Korean War veteran who pays for an opulent lifestyle in the Ozarks by working as a counterespionage agent on contract for an unnamed U.S. government agency—was sure to go.

Canada was no exception, with the twelfth and thirteenth installments set in that country. The first of these, 1971's *The Canadian Bomber Contract* sees Gall, a.k.a. "The Nullifier," on the trail of a truckload of TNT smuggled across the border by an operative linked to Weathermen exiles and Quebecois separatists. In this case the latter are members of a FLQ spinoff known as the Union for the Armed Liberation of Quebec. Unusually for such a regionally focused group they include members from Iraq, Iran, Algeria, France, and Britain. The multinational nature of the organization seems to have been a thought bubble Atlee didn't bother to pursue because we only encounter a few evildoers, all of whom are of North American extraction, in the novel.

Most of the action revolves around Gall tracking an American hippie known as "the Mohawk" for the fact that his "head was shaved except a long center lock on the top of his cranium." Hiding in plain sight the flamboyant, panhandling dropout is far from the dope he appears to be and fairly soon Gall finds himself the target of car-bombing. This is hardly surprising as according to Gall:

> Before this trip to Canada it had always seemed to me that Manila was the most violent city in the world. . . . Montreal, Canada, after only a few weeks was rapidly revising that estimate. In this beautiful island city with its imaginative architecture and lovely parks, sudden death, maimings, bombings and stabbings seemed endemic, like religion or sports enthusiasm in other large cities.

Amid such carnage Gall manages to fit in the requisite trip to an ice hockey match and visits to the various "Man and His World" exhibition centers the original Expo '67's sites had been turned into. As the protagonist stalks, and frequently loses, his quarry, we are treated to various titbits regarding local soft drinks, food, and other details. Atlee regularly packed (or, depending on your point of view, padded out) his stories with such local color.

Eventually Gall figures out that a festival on the Canadian border, which the Mohawk is performing

at with a folk-rock group, is really being used as a cover for . . . a plot to blow to up the American side of Niagara Falls! Exactly how this would fail to damage the Canadian section, and who might seek to gain from such an act of environmental vandalism, is unclear but Gall suggests to his employer:

> Several candidates for the honour of making us look bad. The FLQ, the separatist movement in Quebec Province, might like to demonstrate they can blow up something bigger than buildings. Our own dodgers and deserters in Canada might like the shaming effect, Uncle Sam with a pisspot trickle, while the Canadian Horseshoe Falls get bigger.

Other than the insertion of some massive Chinook military helicopters and chaos associated with a police strike, referencing real events from 1969, this is about as wild as the novel gets. Gall utters a few profanities and beds the requisite number of local women, but by men's adventure standards he's pretty subdued. While Atlee's writing is clipped and taut, he fails to turn in anything other than an adequate effort on this occasion.

The author clearly decided to make the most of his Canadian trip because in the next installment in the series, *The White Wolverine Contract* (1971) we find Gall out west in British Columbia. Here he finds yet more of those "hippie-lemmings" cluttering the streets of Vancouver. Soon they're forced to squat in the abandoned Jericho military barracks after being evicted from the "downtown arsenal where they slept until noon without segregation of the sexes, and openly turned on night and day with speed, hash, pot and cocaine." Despite his distaste for the local authorities' policies vis-à-vis "the indolent hippie beast," Gall is otherwise having a fine time drinking Canadian Club and checking out the region.

During the late 1960s tens of thousands of young American men did indeed head to Canada in order to avoid service in the military and Vietnam War. American draft resisters and military deserters were not subject to deportation, received support from local left-wing and religious organizations in gaining legal status and were generally welcomed by the authorities and wider population. Communities soon formed amid existing alternative enclaves in cities such as Montreal, Vancouver, and Toronto.

Given that exile in Canada had become a viable option for men of draft age their existence was regularly commented upon in American novels set in that country. Unlike Tanner, Gall clearly has little time for hippies or subversives, but Atlee does engineer a falling out between the spy and his agency on the basis of his belief that his employers should be lobbying for an amnesty to be granted to the many "draft dodgers" holed up in Canada. It is unclear whether this was an attempt to make the character less predictable or the result of personal conviction on the part of Atlee, but the position sits oddly with the rest of the character's statements. Either way its inclusion, and Tanner's less surprising description of resisters as "brave souls," reflects the growing American weariness regarding Vietnam and an increasing shift in attitudes that would eventually see objectors legally able to return to the United States in 1977.

In *The White Wolverine Contract* the spy-for-hire's holiday and banishment from the agency soon come to an abrupt an end after the assassination of local politician. The need to counter a convoluted and confusing disinformation conspiracy, involving enemy agents promoting the idea that British Columbia secede from Canada and join the United States in order to stoke anti-American feeling and thereby push the nation closer to China, sees Gall hurriedly rehired. Overall the novel is another slight effort with very little reference to Quebecois separatism beyond it providing inspiration to the Red agents planning a wave of anti-American bombings as well as a few references to the way in which authorities were using the War Measures Act beyond its initial anti-FLQ remit.

Things went quietly for Quebec, U.S. action hero wise, for the next few years. In 1974's *Canadian Kill* Joseph Nazel's pimp turned multimillionaire Harry Highland, a.k.a. Iceman, travels from his Las Vegas stronghold/casino/brothel to Northern Quebec for a skiing holiday. Before you know it the hero, goofy side-kick Christmas Tree, and a few of the many "gorgeous women devoted to Iceman and the style of living he had shown them" find themselves crash-landing after their plane is shot out of sky. The ghetto schooled crew of stone-cold, ass-kicking black killers soon find themselves up against white supremacists in the form of the Next Dimension of Man. This outfit are apparently "a thousand times worse than Hitler" and responsible for "murder, treason and rioting throughout the world," but they don't seem to be active in local politics and there's nary a nationalist of the Quebecois kind to be found.

The next big event which drew interest from a variety of crime, pulp, and thriller writers was the 1976 Montreal Olympics. Among them was Don Pendleton, who having dabbled in magazine and novel writing for some years, began his Executioner series in 1969. The stunning success of its Vietnam veteran turned vigilante Mack Bolan has led to over two hundred million book sales and spawned a host of imitators. Unlike the many other tough guys wielding big guns and insatiable vendettas, the thirty-seven novels written by Pendleton up until 1980, after which ghost writers have produced more than nine hundred more, saw Bolan pretty keep his laser-eyed focus on the Mafia at all times. When asked why this was so, Pendleton explained, on his personal website, "My biggest job throughout writing the series was to keep faith with Bolan—that what he is doing is right. I wanted an enemy beyond redemption—an enemy that all civilized procedures had failed to put down. The Mafia was ready-made. They embodied all the evils of mankind."

Typically, Bolan's motives are highly personal since he blames mob loan sharks for the series of events that led his sister into prostitution and caused a subsequent murder-suicide spree in which their father killed her along with all but one of the family in shame and despair. This monstrous act of debt-fueled domestic violence could have sent the sniper on a mission against Capitalism and the Patriarchy, but in keeping with the author's conservative streak, and society's false consciousness, the Executioner obsesses on a single evil, the Mafia, instead.

Throughout the series Bolan methodically traipses from city to city shooting, blowing up, and eviscerating mob outfits one by one. Having already taken advantage of the local color provided by Miami, Las Vegas, New Jersey and more than a dozen other stateside burgs, installment no. 24 in the series, 1976's *Canadian Crisis*, sends Bolan on a rare trip (at this point) outside of the U.S.

In the midst of slaughtering a Mafia crew in Buffalo, New York, the Executioner rescues an undercover Canadian operative, Andre Chebleu. With the Bolan's one-man war knocking them hither and thither, the gangsters have decided to make Montreal the new center of their crime empire. In reality, Quebec's guerrilla outbreak had been well and truly quelled by this point, but in Bolan's world the province is headed into failed state territory due to "a national convulsion

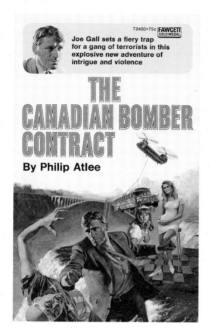

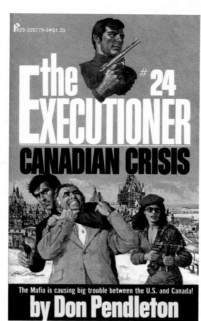

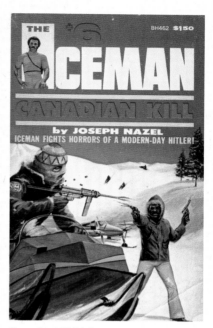

The Canadian Bomber Contract
(Fawcett, 1971)

Canadian Crisis (Pinnacle, 1976)

Canadian Kill (Holloway House, 1974)

being fed by separatist politics, economic woes, fierce nationalism, the open spirit of rebellion." All of which makes it easy pickings for the world's premier crime network, who "beneath the cauldron are building a bonfire." Teaming up with Chebleu, the Executioner soon heads north in his heavily armed, high-tech, tricked-out motor home, a.k.a. "The Warwagon."

Following some cross-border carnage at Niagara Falls, Bolan infiltrates the "long whispered about, meticulously planned, super event of the criminal world, an international underground congress" of the world's premier Capos. While, as already mentioned, the hero's main goal is to exterminate mobsters, he's none too keen on the nationalists and student troublemakers who are targeting the Games and giving his opponents cover. Unusually for the series, he dabbles in some romance with a young revolutionary, the surprisingly non-Francophone sounding Betsy Gordon, while remaining dismissive of what he deems a petty war in relation to his. Although "he had not come to Canada to save her from herself," he winds up meddling in matters only to discover, "the final answer, as always, is death." Not his or Betsy's, of course, as the book ends happily ever after with the couple on a fishing trip, presumably using the Executioner's Warwagon RV and super-optic surveillance fishing rod for the purposes they were originally intended.

Canadian Crisis was a fairly unremarkable addition to the Executioner canon, something that could not be said for another book released by Pinnacle in the same year, *The Quebec Connection*. Turned out rapidly by authors desperately seeking new angles, and no doubt bored out of their brains, men's adventure novels could head into some pretty wacky territory, but number 15 in the Penetrator series was particularly out there.

Penned by Chet Cunningham, under the series pseudonym Lionel Derrick, it all starts ordinarily enough. The Penetrator, a.k.a. Mark Hardin is a "warrior without a uniform or rank pledged to fight anyone on either side of the law who seeks to destroy the American way of life. The most watched, yet unseen person in the nation" turns his attention, and that of his two-man support crew holed up in an underground bunker, to Canada after a Quebecois militant group carry their war over the border, blowing up banks and a radio transmitter.

In previous novels, Hardin had defeated black militants in New York and Weatherpeople-style white radicals in Kansas, so at first blush dealing with the 23 May Liberation Front's attempt to force the U.S. to withdraw its support for Canadian unity seems like everyday work. But information on the group proves sketchy. Going undercover as a liberal priest he is soon forced to casually dispatch a few junkie street punks, leaving his trademark arrowheads behind as a calling sign.

In the world of 1970s vigilante novels, muggers, rapists, and other lowlifes were constantly lurking down alleyways and on street corners, just waiting to mess with the wrong man before being dealt gunslinger style justice updated to include martial-arts moves and silencers. Although the crime rate was nothing like the hype had it, said hype in the mainstream media and popular culture sold well, tapping into the insecurities of a section of the white working and middle classes hit by economic downturn on one side and diminishing social privilege and certainty on the other. And, as with Pendleton's Mafia, violent criminals were a convenient target whose stomping had widespread appeal.

As a crossover with the spy genre, the likes of the Penetrator generally dealt with higher-order bad guys. The appearance of small fry in this novel was likely padding, but the otherwise pointless digression allows the author to play to his audience's prejudices in musing on the need to "take the well-meaning, the do-gooders and the would-be utopian planners away from the fantasies of their ivory tower dream worlds and bring them face to face with the brutal reality of crime in the streets." Such sentiments were already tired clichés by the mid-1970s but would be repeated ad infinitum in the decades to come fueling a punitive social turn that would lead America to top the world in prison population with close to 3 percent of its population under correctional control. Meanwhile the fearmongering regarding worsening crime and the ever-harder measures needed to combat it played, and plays, ever on.

Having done his bit regarding crime in the streets, Hardin gets back on the job. As it turns out the separatists' military actions are only a fraction of their evil-doing as they're also peddling the latest party drug, a synthetic powder called Ziff. According to 23 May lieutenant Richard L'Blanc, Ziff is a "different kind of high. Not like heroin, acid . . . anything else. But it's unreal. Weird, but real nice. No hangover from it nothing, and you can't get hooked."

Riffing on the "LSD causes chromosomal damage" canard, still popular in the seventies, a single whiff of ziff not only gets the user off their face but, via the inclusion of the Soviet developed chemical agent G-174, changes their DNA to cause dwarfism in any children they might later have. Following the trail to France, Hardin eventually uncovers, in a twist as offensive as it is bizarre, the real band of revolutionaries behind the revolutionaries. No, it's not the Russians, Chinese, Cubans, or their com-symp useful idiots, but a cabal of short statured people determined to increase their numbers in a plot to achieve world domination within a generation. There's an environmental twist to the conspiracy since, as the leader of the Little Men expounds, the sudden shift in the population's size will also solve a host of issues related to overcrowding including, "Huge buildings that deplete the resources of the nation to build them. Not enough food for billions of mouths. Polluted air, fouled oceans and too rapid a consumption of energy and dwindling reserves of fossil fuels. G-174 eliminates all these problems. It reduces things to their proper proportions . . . starting with people."

Just when you can't think it can get any more ridiculous the climax finds Hardin fencing a trio of short statured people . . . atop the Eiffel Tower . . . on Bastille Day! As with so many of these novels the protagonist's super-skills nullify any surprise regarding the outcome. What the book lacks in tension, it makes up in gore as Cunningham/Derrick graphically describes the way in which Hardin's rapier "succeeds in what evolution and the surgeon's knife had failed to do before" in removing his foe's appendix. Glowing depictions of assailants smashing to the ground and being impaled on spikes also feature.

Having already destroyed the remaining supplies of G-174 the Penetrator flies off into the sunset to await future battles with zombified killer orphans and giant Nicaraguan killer ants. A relative lightweight in popularity and longevity compared to the Executioner, he would return for another thirty-eight installments, eventually selling around five million copies. As for Quebecois nationalism, the twin effects of state repression and public revulsion at the murder of La Porte in 1970 saw the FLQ collapse, but support for separatism in the province remained strong. Although two referenda have since rejected an exit from the Canadian state, the pro-sovereignty Parti Quebecois first took parliamentary power in the province in 1976, and reformists have remained a political force ever since.

Iain McIntyre

Cold Fire Burning

The Nathan Heard Interviews

When I finished reading Nathan C. Heard's novel *Howard Street* (1968) for the first time in the 1990s, I felt that I'd been living under a cultural rock for too long. I'd read Richard Wright, Ralph Ellison, Malcolm X, and other great black male "individualist" writers. I'd read about Howard Beach, Tawana Brawley, Crown Heights and other incidents of racist violence and listened to the warnings coming from Brixton, Brooklyn, Compton, Houston, and Kingston. I'd dug black culture from closer than the microscope can get. But—Caucasian boy that I was—I never had the role of outsider forced upon me.

In 1992, while I was working for Milwaukee's Harry W. Schwartz Bookshops, Los Angeles's Amok Books reissued *Howard Street*. When I read the book it was a cultural revelation, and I dedicated the next few months to learning about the life of the author, a high school dropout who spent eight years in prison during the 1960s, wrote his first novel on a borrowed typewriter, and shortly thereafter became a college lecturer, all without a high school degree. Ten years later, I would become a jail librarian. To this day I work with incarcerated people, and Nathan C. Heard is the main reason.

The following is an edited collection of interviews conducted during June and July of 1993 with Heard—author of the beautiful, desperate street tales *Howard Street*, *To Reach a Dream* (1971), *A Cold Fire Burning* (1974), *When Shadows Fall* (1977), and *House of Slammers* (1983). Nathan's acidic, sophisticated wit, mixed with his gentle laugh, could be disarming, especially when you'd seen nothing but the intimidating photos on the man's book jackets: wearing tight, flashy threads in various eras, never without a menacing pair of shades, he looked like someone who just beat up the entire 1975 Pittsburgh Steelers defensive line. But his words—recorded eleven years before his death in 2004—came softly, deliberately, and precisely.

Author Nathan Heard, 1974

Where and when did you learn the most important elements of writing, the elements that shaped your style the most?

Well, while I was doing this nine to thirteen years in the state prison in New Jersey.

Did you have access to a lot of literature in your incarceration?

Yeah, only limited by what kind. When a guy goes to prison, especially being from my neighborhood, there's no shock of privation, of being lost. It's almost like going to homecoming, because everybody in the neighborhood's there already. So one of the things they do—because of the first few days you have to spend in quarantine—is start sending you all sorts of reading materials, usually sexual escapist stuff. And I got familiar with that. I just started reading to pass the time, mainly.

Did you read before you were in prison?

No. Before I went to prison, I had read two books in my life, *The Babe Ruth Story* and *The Lou Gehrig Story*, because I wanted to be a ballplayer. Those were the only two books I'd ever read voluntarily.

What was the most important book—or were there several important books—that made you decide that you wanted to write or that you could write?

Well, it was the lack of important books that made me decide. There was a guy in Fresno, California, named Sanford Aday. And he had a book publishing venture out there. And I had read somewhere that he paid a $2,000 advance for a manuscript. And I said, "Hell, if I'm sitting up in jail for thirteen years and I didn't steal $200, let me try this, make some money this way." [Laughs.] And I proceeded to write the same kind of junk I had been reading, you know, just copycat stuff, stuff that used to belong only on Forty-Second Street, but it's now all over.

Was [adult book publisher and gay activist] Sanford Aday an acquaintance of yours?

No. And it was ironic, because when I got out of prison and got a teaching position, it was in Fresno! [Laughs.]

What role did he play in your formation? You were just inspired by the fact that he would pay $2,000 advances?

That's it, totally. Another thing that this brings up: I had done all this reading, but it wasn't all that critical. It was just eclectic. And to pick these things out of thin air, you know, you had to have something. I was, I guess, kind of writing my way out of a hole.

Upon its publication by Dial, *Howard Street*—a flavorful, morally powerful but prosaically pure and non-judgmental portrait of a stretch of black homes, clubs, and hangouts in Heard's hometown, Newark—was a knockout success with readers and critics. The book sold over half a million copies. Nikki Giovanni called it "a masterpiece" in *Negro Digest*. Claude Brown likened Heard to Richard Wright and William Faulkner. If you've read *Howard Street*, you know the story to be such a heart-stopping one and the author's style so hard and refined that you might be prompted by Mr. Brown's comparison to check out this Faulkner cat. Even the doubting and the envious, like the *New*

***York Times*'s Alan Cheuse, acknowledged the blunt wisdom of Heard's tale. I was knocked out by the passionate, meticulous characterizations and the amazing linguistic transitions from crude, evocative street slang to elegant, descriptive narration.**

It's a very dramatic thing, to raise yourself to the literary level that you did for *Howard Street*.

The only thing that I believe was behind the creative instinct back then was that there were no televisions or radios or furloughs to distract you. Had they had television in the cells when I was in prison, I probably never would have been a writer. I'd have been like most of those guys there now, living from television show to television show—in my case, *The Lucy Show* or something like that, you know. [Laughs.]

You mention, with some sarcasm, television and movies as "privileges" in *House of Slammers*.

Yeah. Well, that's because they're really not privileges at all. They're self-destructive. Because, you know, they're like giant pacifiers that you suck on.

How did you change over from writing what you've described as the "sexual escapist" stuff?

I started reading about writers and writing, and it got serious. Suddenly I began to understand some of the thought processes, or the results of the thought processes, that some of these creative people went through. And what I literally had to do was get tired of that portion of my life, like an alcoholic or something. You get tired of that portion of your life, so you try to change it. 'Cause my thing was sports and standing around in the yard singing doo-wop songs, you know, waiting for the moment when I'd get out. When I stopped looking for that moment to get out and started looking for those shorter moments in time, then I could make use of myself in my cell.

But the real thing came—I think what you have in mind—when it surprised me to be able to understand what some of our most progressive thinkers were saying. You know, things were no longer surprising to me. I guess it's a sort of osmosis that creeps in if you do a lot of reading, because I read well over two thousand books while I was in there.

Was prison your closest contact with the Nation of Islam?

Yeah, I guess so. On a daily basis, yes.

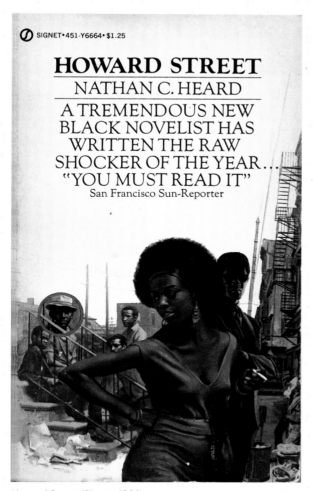

Howard Street (Signet, 1968)

Did you ever have an audience with Elijah Muhammad?
No. And the Muslims I knew were just inmates like me, mainly.

Were they as articulate as your character Mustafa in *House of Slammers*?
Yes, see, because they were the prime dispensers of knowledge at the time, like with books and stuff. They were trying to educate everybody, but to a cause rather than to a purpose. The purpose was what it did to guys like me. It made me think. The cause was . . . it hooked guys into it and made them start looking for mother-ships in the air.

So they were effective in gaining converts in prison.
Yeah, but if you got entangled in that web . . . you know, that's a different story. I was never convinced of that or any other religion—luckily, as far as I'm concerned.

But the Muslims sure answered more legal and psycho-logical questions than anybody else did. It was hard for guys growing up around violence to see a solution to violence in any other terms but violence.

Were the Muslims your primary sources of literature?
No, no, because I had grown up with those guys. I knew 'em before they changed their names to the Arabic. [Laughs.]

Were you able to plunder the prison libraries? Did you have friends on the outside who supplied you?
No, you bought your own books, or in my case you traded. My reading habits changed, because I stopped reading that Forty-Second Street pulp stuff and started getting into an idea. And then I started playing music and listening to jazz, which I had only a cursory knowl-edge of before, and it took me. And that connected me

to wanting to know aspects of black history. Then there was the voice of Malcolm X all in the back of that, you know, shouting and challenging you in a way that you hadn't been challenged before.

I assume Malcolm X influenced your writing.

I was listening to him and cheering him when we thought we were putting these white people in their place. He represented strong black manhood, while the other guys, the civil righters, seemed kind of shameful to a lot of guys, you know, street-level guys.

What do you feel the role of the Nation of Islam is today in uplifting people?

I don't assign roles to people, right? 'Cause I don't believe them, you know. I don't believe anything. I've got no faith, but I've got all the hope in the world.

An interesting distinction.

I have no faith in religion, in any manner, except in your own personal demeanor. It will never help you do anything because it makes you satisfied. This is why these coalitions of middle-class blacks always come together and are continually bombarding you with dumb ideas like, "Well, here we've got a neighborhood full of poverty. But if we can help just one, our mission won't be in vain." To me, that's a blatant lie. If your mission is to save thousands or hundreds, and you only save one, you're a damn failure. Your mission is a failure! They gave us the impression that "One can teach one," and that would be all right. But the point is, you'll never catch up to their extending lie, their lie of extending yourself. It is not enough to be satisfied to save one! That doesn't mean that you shouldn't "teach one," but it does not address the problem. The problem is how to get these people into some sort of cohesive force, not to be satisfied with some gains, and then to satisfy the other people by saying, "Well, we got one. Let's keep going." You'll never catch up.

I want to get clear how much time you served in prison. You mentioned the sentence was nine to thirteen.

Yeah. I served six, and then I got out and was on parole, when, in the next eleven months, I was locked up again. [Laughs.]

Okay, so you served a total of . . .

Eight years.

Were you published before the release of _Howard Street_?

Oh, no, no. _Howard Street_ was the first real good manuscript I came up with. And that lay in my closet for years because I didn't know what I had. I had two other novels before, that I had finished before _Howard Street_, and never submitted any of them. The second novel out, _To Reach a Dream_, was ultimately the first novel that I wrote, really.

Who was it who let you know that _Howard Street_ was good?

Well, my mother [Gladys Johnson, née Pruitt] took it. Right after I got in jail, got in trouble again. She took it to a lawyer [Joel Steinberg of East Orange] and asked him to read it, 'cause she couldn't understand why—if I had all this talent for singing, for playing drums, for writing—I went around stickin' up people with a gun. This lawyer read the manuscript that my mother pushed on him, and he went directly to Paul Reynolds's agency in New York and got me an agent, because they had a saleable product, you know. That was in 1968. The book came out in November, a month before I did.

Would you prefer not to talk about what landed you in jail?

I was the local tough guy, stickup, a thug—just not as acutely painless or without hurt, like the crime these new kids are creating, you know? Without any feeling.

In reading _Howard Street_, I'm struck by the moral force that your writing carries in some classically immoral scenarios. There's a sense that you're able to pull yourself completely away from the street and look at it from a purely moral perspective.

Well, I had to. That happened in prison. That's when writing really became interesting to me. I was reading about writers and reading about writing, and absorbing all of this, even if it was by osmosis. It changed my habits in jail, so that I didn't feel the same. There was no more fun in talking about which girls you're gonna get when you get out, or all that gang stuff, or singing those doo-wop songs. All of that changed because I started to hear, I guess, a different challenge with the writing, even though I didn't know it.

It seems that you know a very eclectic selection of people that may have turned you on to different ways

House of Slammers (Macmillan, 1983)

of thinking than the average person who might find himself in that situation.

No, I was turned on by a lot of guys after I started getting interested in reading and writing. My influences during that time were James Baldwin, Norman Mailer—lot of Norman Mailer—and Richard Wright. And then I was turned on to Chester Himes; then a whole network of books was passing through, you know. I read a hell of a lot of books before I came out at eight years, but I still didn't have anything practical. You know, I could write, but so what? I didn't know it, and nobody had ever told me it. And so I wrote the manuscript *Howard Street* as a challenge, because, you know, I said, "I can write stuff better than this."

How did it make you feel when the reviews came in? You must have had an inkling that you could write better than most of those clowns out there.

Yeah, well, I got a whole lot of interest, and I'm glad, but I can only attribute it to a sort of innocence. Had I been trying to write with, say, a message or a singular or tunnel-vision message, I probably would never have succeeded.

With *Howard Street*, speaking purely in terms of sales, you enjoyed a success that few writers have. Do you have any outstanding memories of that? Half a million people bought the book, and you must have been sort of a household name.

Yeah, for a while there. And it was a wrong turn to get so involved. I lost sight of what was really going on around me. The book got me noticed, but all the attention that stemmed from it made me less sensitive to a lot of people. So my literary friends are a very small circle. I've spent most of my time in bars and jails, and so I feel comfortable where I'm at, and I really don't miss those literature collectives. I know and like Amiri Baraka, I know and like Claude Brown, I knew and liked John O. Killens, and the same with Jimmy Baldwin. I'd see him once or twice, maybe, in a couple of years.

***Howard Street* strikes me as a powerful statement about, on one hand, the true nature of a person's soul and, in a cultural sense, black soul. In a way, it's also about the death of soul. You see all these young people's lives being wasted.**

Well, you see what that generation has brought forth here, in the kids we have today: killers without mercy, remorseless killers. And what's much more amazing than that is that the hardness with which they talk about it seems to surprise so many people. I don't know why people are surprised. You got these so-called skills that the civil rights era took us through, and we got cities full of mayors, black mayors, black councilmen, and all that, and sometimes senators. Yet the condition is worse. That's because there were too many of us, myself included, who didn't do anything or didn't prepare the Ice-Ts of the world for the structured living that we wanted. And so, now that they've turned callous and hard, we're surprised. I mean, dummies can't raise anything but dummies!

It seems that, since *Howard Street*, each novel you've written has become increasingly more idealistic.
Yeah, because I was trying to address problems and prepare solutions rather than write. I never knew *Howard Street* was going to get published, you know, so it was just something I did. There was no pressure to perform. There was no pressure to duplicate that experience or that time. And more importantly, there was no real pressure to direct it, until I saw that black leaders were losing the audience to the advent of technology, mainly TV, from *Sesame Street* on. I mean, what teacher standing in front of a classroom could compare to these electronic whizzes and sounds and loudness that stimulate these kids today? You start to lose, automatically, what you've built.

We were supposed to get skills in those days and bring 'em back to this community and, in a way, free ourselves. But they came back as mayors, they came back as city councilmen and state officials, and they didn't change a damned thing. They jumped into the mainstream bourgeois waters—and never brought those skills back home. [Laughs.] We forgot our passion. We forgot a whole lot of things. We would make excuses for the failures that we had in the black community, teaching kids values or forgetting to tell them that they were worth anything. Damn, I'm having a problem here! I don't want this to seem like it's an insult to us, but in fact what we did to the generation of teens now was to harm them.

Yet your writing doesn't carry with it the bitterness of even, say, James Baldwin.
Yeah.

Sometimes I think your writing is not always as burning as that in *Howard Street*.

To Reach a Dream (Signet, 1972)

Right! Well, along the line somewhere, I guess maybe I was trying to live up to other expectations. You get didactic, you know. And you get so you're not writing, you're trying to teach. I think that sort of derived from all those damned black poets in the '60s who disappeared, you know. [Laughs.] To get back to Malcolm for a minute—I had my biggest joy when Malcolm was debating some black intellectual on TV. The guy had made some remark about his schooling or his degrees, and Malcolm looked at the guy and said, "Do you know what they call . . ."

". . . a black man with a PhD?"
Uh-huh. The guy said, "What?" Malcolm said, "A nigger." [Laughs.] That was Malcolm's comeback. And we felt that. Because we felt that, no matter what we did, we were never going to be good enough in this society. You know, like our music. We knew we had

beautiful people in music and jazz and every sphere who couldn't make it in terms of crossing over, reaching that wider audience.

To Reach a Dream, Heard's second novel for Dial, released in 1972, is a refinement of his first real manuscript. The story of a young, grade-B player named Bart's fast and furious descent from naiveté into murderous con artistry, played out against the background of ostensibly twisted but essentially simple sexual/economic relationships (one with an older woman, the other with her daughter). To Reach a Dream failed to duplicate the commercial success of Howard Street but retained its gripping edge. Lean, economically written, and truly horrifying, the novel reads even more like Shakespeare than does its groundbreaking predecessor.

For me, the most disturbing aspect of To Reach a Dream is that the characters Bart and Qurell [the daughter] went to an evil means to secure a good end—their love. What was the inspiration for that story?
Just watching guys who were living that sort of life—not so much being companions but being recipients of a sort of meal ticket. That's a very common thing, even now. You find a lot of women who take care of men.

I want to talk about your depiction of the pimp-whore relationship in Howard Street. There are parallels with the husband-wife relationship, or the boyfriend-girlfriend relationship. Are they that different? Aren't there still questions of ownership?
Well, there is difference in that the law of the pimp-hustler thing that was between those two [Lonnie "Hip" Ritchwood, a young, ruthless hustler, and Gypsy Pearl, a beautiful, deluded prostitute] was just a mutual agreement based on both of their weaknesses. His need for drugs fed into her need to mother him in some way. He wasn't a real pimp, he was a street hustlin' pimp, and it could have been any girl. The formal pimp thing, you know, the "gentleman of leisure" kind of pimp thing, were guys who were like peacocks. They strolled around being proud, saying, "Look what my woman bought me. Look what the bitch did for me." His whole life process is not to make any damned thing but to show that he has this something. It's sort of like the need in To Reach a Dream, where the guy gains

everything that he wanted. But what good is it if he can't go around, show it to his friends?

I think one of the most interesting things about To Reach a Dream is how the narrative weaves in and out of the hipster jargon.
Yeah, dialogue can change according to the person. One day I can answer the phone and you'll never know that I'm black. Most white critics make the mistake of not giving more than one voice to these characters—they're just black or white, you know? And all the dialogue is one way. But I write about people who say things differently. They have been living in the same neighborhood for years, but they come up with different words. And so, to me, that makes the dialogue live, because it's always of the people.

"Proper English," discussed briefly in House of Slammers, is an amusing question, especially when Mustafa, the Muslim, asks Beans if it makes him feel more black when he uses incorrect grammar. House of Slammers seems very much the most autobiographical of the books, although knowing very little about you, maybe that's presumptuous.
No, I don't think that it's presumptuous of you. And I don't think it's a big deal. As long as you're getting the things I want you to feel, it doesn't matter. What I try to hear is the person's character that I try to build. I try to make them real in my mind, and some of them talk in different voices, you know. That turns out to be a legitimate feeling, which a lot of critics don't understand, because they're so used to these characters speaking in one voice, usually down-south talk, you know.

I managed to rent Gordon's War [a fairly intelligent vigilante film made in 1973 starring Paul Winfield, in which Heard has a brief cameo as Big Pink, a dangerous mack who wears a long, pink leather trench coat and wields a mean two-by-four].
Oh, my goodness! [Laughs.]

Were you paid properly for your role?
I was paid minimum salary.

Have you acted in any other films?
No, and I didn't want to.

You did not enjoy the experience?
No.

Let's talk about the academic world briefly. Where did you teach?

Fresno State College [teaching creative writing] and three years at Livingston College here at Rutgers [teaching writing and black literature as an assistant professor].

What have you been doing since?

Well, *Howard Street* was very good to me. I lived off that for ten years. You know, royalties and the options that people had bought. It's been optioned about three or four times for a movie, but for some reason it never pans out.

Since *House of Slammers*, you've been able to subsist on profits from *Howard Street*?

Yeah, just about. And of course I had jobs in between. During the CETA Administration [a federally financed public service employment program defunded under Reagan], I worked for the mayor of Newark, Kenneth Gibson.

Having spent time in the academic world, what is your opinion of where their heads are at?

Well, I found out one thing when I went there. When I first started there, having only gone through the tenth grade myself, I had a tremendous amount of respect for people who had official status as educators and so forth. But I think what had the greatest impact was finding out that they don't have that many smart people in college, you know. Before that, I grew up thinking that anybody who went to college was smart.

The Nathan Heard book about which no two people seem to agree is *A Cold Fire Burning* (Simon & Schuster, 1974). It's a sexually explicit satire of ignorance in all walks of life and is more ambitious and realistic than Spike Lee's 1991 film *Jungle Fever* in that its black male and white female couple come into their relationship with equal helpings of prejudice and minimal stereotypical qualities. Neither of the two black women I've lent the book to have finished it. One, who enjoyed Heard's other novels, found the story "boring." The other, who had never read Heard's work, was astonished and appalled by the book's sexually explicit nature. Of all of his novels, *A Cold Fire Burning* still strikes me as best lending itself to a filmed adaptation. Not as bloody or linguistically charged as Heard's

other novels, it's a quiet and wise little fucked-up love story.

How do you feel about *A Cold Fire Burning* now?

Well, that was almost like a political statement, all predicated on the fact that this guy—though he loved his woman and cared about her—couldn't really be with her. He couldn't ejaculate unless she was in a degraded position—mainly, you know, fellatio. And only that could satisfy him. I was speaking out of a certain relationship at that point, because "things" just weren't going away, and I saw a lot of stuff happening that I thought was wrong. And there didn't seem to be anybody really stopping it. This was going into the depths of the Reagan era. When I think of all that black people suffered during those whole twelve years . . .

***A Cold Fire Burning* was actually written during the Nixon era. Was the Reagan era any different from that?**

No, I mean, it looked like a natural progression to me, to most of us. During the Nixon administration, I really got popular. And there were no complaints. So that was probably due to the malaise that came over me. Plus, I wanted to make a statement on certain things. Relationships could be achieved; everything didn't have to do with race.

The satire on the so-called political revolutionaries is some of your most biting.

Yeah. You know, here's a guy who has to learn that your commitment to your race does not come through the end of your penis.

Heard's fourth novel, *When Shadows Fall*, was published in 1977 by the short-lived, Chicago-based Playboy Press. If it weren't so precisely evocative of the impotent rock music scene preceding punk rock and rap, and the drug culture which continues to blunt rock's so-called cutting edge, it would read just like a western. For his story of Joe Billy White, a coke-snorting, bell-bottomed jean-wearing, "up-and-coming" white rhythm-and-blues cliché reminiscent of Eric Clapton, Rick Derringer, or perhaps Roy Buchanan, Heard trims all the fat from the fast, dirty, and rather senseless story of personal corruption, corporate corruption, musical corruption, police corruption, and more corruption. It would be funny if it weren't utterly truthful.

A Cold Fire Burning (Amok, 1995)
A Cold Fire Burning (Simon and Schuster, 1974)

It seems as if you almost approached *When Shadows Fall* like an experiment.

It was. You're very perceptive.

Were you commissioned to write that book?

It wasn't by commission, but it was for quick money.

Do you have any interesting inside thoughts on that book?

No, not very many.

[Laughs.] I notice it's your only book to include significant white characters.

Yeah, well, I changed Joe Billy on purpose. He was a black saxophone player, and I changed him to the white guitar player.

***House of Slammers*—in particular, its final scene—is a heartening indication that Heard's skills remained sharp. As with *Howard Street* fifteen years earlier, Heard lifts the reader's emotions and finally lets them down hard. When the four prison strike leaders [protagonist Beans, Nation of Islam member Mustafa, Joe Valli, and Wally Allen] walk out into the courtyard with the shadow of death over them, the tragedy is just as pure and profound as when young Jimmy Johnson loses his shoot-out with the cops in *Howard Street*.**

In *Howard Street* you have Franchot. In *To Reach a Dream*, there's Bart. You have the unnamed narrator in *A Cold Fire Burning*. You have Joe Billy White and Haines the cop in *When Shadows Fall*, and Beans in *House of Slammers*. Of all your protagonists, are there any that you identify most closely with?

Oh, probably with Beans.

I did notice that some of the things that occurred to Beans seem to parallel a few of the things that I know about your life. Did you undergo a similar crisis of where you stood?

On that rage and anger?

Yeah.

Yeah, I had to live through that, because, you know, I was one of those guys who didn't believe in that Martin Luther King philosophy. "You hit me, I'm gonna hit you back," you know, that was the school that I and most of my friends came from. And we were

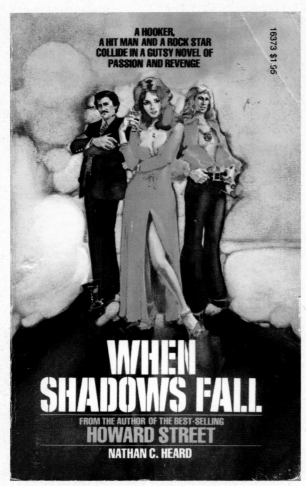

When Shadows Fall (Playboy Press, 1977)

influenced by the Panthers, and especially Malcolm X, Elijah Muhammad, and a few others. So that was an inner rage that was building up.

What influenced us was the intellectual challenge these guys presented. Malcolm was saying things that we hardly said among ourselves, you know? I mean, some of the most dynamic things he said challenged us as we were going through this sort of training process from half-ape to half-man. [Laughs.] Malcolm did influence us. The Panthers showed us that there was a methodology that we could get around. But there were no delusions, at least for me, that they would solve anything that wouldn't be solved on a personal level first. I mean, the Panthers had a methodology and that's all. Malcolm had a soul because, in the depth of all this here—prison and the feeling sorry for yourself—here was one guy who stood up and said, like the guy in [the

1976 film] *Network*, "I'm mad as hell, and I ain't gonna take it anymore."

Did you ever have to make a decision like Beans did, to take the risk of leading a worthy but potentially dangerous mission?
Yeah, I made that decision, except I dramatized it and made him get shot. I lost my chance at parole for what I did.

You led a strike in prison?
Yeah.

How much longer did you spend in prison as a result?
Probably two years. I hadn't gone up for parole yet, so I can't factually say.

Was this at Trenton?
Rahway. The next sentence happened at Trenton. *Howard Street* had been published, and I was so popular that they put me out of jail four months early. [Laughs.]

I'm intrigued by Beans's ability to speak to the prison psychologist in a sort of psychologist's language.
Yeah, on equal terms.

Exactly. And everyone in prison, down to the Nazi scumbag, is able to talk to him.
Yeah, well, that was a lot of me too. We had to talk to some Nazi guy, had to get him to see that, you know, "Your best interest's with us now."

Eric Beaumont

The Soul Brothers and Sister Lou, Kristin Hunter

(Charles Scribner's Sons, 1968)

When the soul vocal group that fourteen-year-old Louretta Hawkins forms with her neighborhood friends gets its big break, it comes with both unexpected costs and rewards in Kristin Hunter's coming-of-age novel.

Hunter subtly shades her portrait of life in the poverty trap of an unnamed northern ghetto: while the younger generation suffers the racism and brutality of a corrupt police force and talks of revolution in the streets, their parents live in mortal fear of change, acknowledging that things are bad but worried about upsetting the status quo.

Trapped between these competing ideas is Lou's oldest brother, William, who has become the family breadwinner with his steady job at the post office after their father abandoned the family. While he dreams of marrying his girlfriend, a local teacher, and going into the printing business, those plans have been put on permanent hold to support his mother, siblings, and new niece.

Louretta urges her brother to do something for himself and rent a vacant storefront for a print shop. Louretta has ulterior motives: after her brother signs the lease, she suggests that the back room could be used as a clubhouse and rehearsal space for the neighborhood kids so they can do their vocalizing off the street corners and away from the heavy-handed local cops.

Straight-arrow William insists upon adult supervision, but soon Louretta is granted a place in the Hawks, the block's social club-cum-doo-wop group. Neither Louretta nor William know what to make of the new kid on the block, Phil Satterthwaite, nicknamed Fess for his intellectual bent. A transplant from Boston, Fess has arrived in town with both dangerous new political ideas and a suitcase full of new kinds of records: soul music.

Fess has no use for Mr. Lucitanno, the square, white high school music teacher that is brought in to supervise the enterprise, and no patience for harmonizing the Irving Berlin chords that he primly plunks out on the piano.

More successful is the efforts of Blind Eddie Bell, a legendary blues guitarist that the group digs out of obscurity. More than capable of verbally sparing with Fess, Blind Eddie convinces the group that there is a

The Soul Brothers and Sister Lou (Avon, 1968)

The Landlord
(Avon, 1969)
The Landlord
(Avon, 1977)

direct lineage from the blues to soul and becomes their mentor (handily providing the eager group a history lesson on black contributions to arts in the process). Fess also convinces William to print a weekly bulletin for the neighborhood to provide news and act as a political action tool for the residents. (Hunter herself worked as a teenage reporter for the politically progressive *Pittsburgh Courier*.)

But when the Hawks throw a fundraising dance at the clubhouse for the venture, it's busted up by the police in search of weapons. Jethro, the group's tenor, is shot by a jumpy rookie cop.

The shooting radicalizes Louretta. Rejecting her mother and brother's advice to lie low until the incident blows over, she starts speaking out against the day-to-day indignities she is subjected to as a young black woman. While her family and teachers are appalled by what they see as newfound cynicism coming from a "good girl," Fess is intrigued by Louretta's new political consciousness. She agrees to go with Fess to meeting of a Nation of Islam–like group, but she is skeptical about the group's prescribed roles for women: "Women have a place in this movement, but they can't be leaders. Not in a war."

When Louretta walks out, Fess stops just short of sexually assaulting her, presumably due to frustration and his emasculated male ego. While Louretta manages to forgive him, she learns more and more that there are no easy answers, especially after her mother reveals the truth about why her father left the family: unable to find employment but not qualifying for welfare because the family was "intact," he left hoping that it would force his wife to accept welfare as a single mother and provide some stability for his family.

When Jethro dies of his wounds, Fess is eager to make a martyr of him, but the violence directed toward the police force bleeds into the community, and Louretta is the one who steps in and puts down a potential riot. In the aftermath, the Hawks are discovered after a public performance at Jethro's memorial and are offered a record contract, while William, heartened by his sister's bravery, reopens his print shop.

A coda picks up six months later, after the Hawks (now called the Soul Brothers and Sister Lou) have a hit record. But fame and fortune are a mixed blessing: one member has already left the group, taking his earnings to pursue his real passion, a career as a chef. Now wealthy, Fess has traded in his radical politics for capitalism, more interested in his investments than writing

new lyrics. Blind Eddie meanwhile has invested back in the community, building the Hawks' old clubhouse into a proper community center.

Louretta finds that with a professional career comes professional obligations: the music that was once her greatest pleasure in life has become work, and she spends more time reviewing her accounting than she does singing. Becoming the higher earner also causes conflict with her new boyfriend, and she wonders if she is perpetuating the same old resentments in the black community. And finally, she admits that there is no guarantee that the Soul Brothers will be anything more than a one-hit wonder. While a trust has been established for her college education, for Louretta the future seems more uncertain than ever.

Hunter's writing was ahead of its time: decades before "intersectionality" would become a buzzword, Hunter frankly examined the intense (and sometimes contradictory) emotions concerning race, class, color, and sex in her best-known novels, including *God Bless the Child* (1964) and *The Landlord* (1966).

More than a decade later Hunter would pen a sequel, *Lou in the Limelight* (1981), which finds the remaining members of the group struggling to find success amid the excesses of the showbiz world without compromising their artistic gifts. While it at last grants Lou a happy ending, it has not had the staying power of the original and remains out of print.

Molly Grattan

He beamed his idiotic smile at her. "We don't want any teachers," Louretta said. "They just teach us a lot of lies and confuse us, anyway. Let the building stay closed. I've decided the clubhouse wasn't such a good idea."

"Oh, no, Louretta!" he cried. "It was a wonderful idea!"

"When you don't know what you're doing," she said, trying to teach him what she had learned, "it's better to leave things alone."

"Just because you had a little trouble at the start doesn't mean you should abandon your whole idea."

A little trouble? Louretta laughed again at this. "Sorry, Mr. Lucitanno," she said, "I got to go now."

"What's your hurry?"

"Go to go round up some blood donors for Jethro."

"What type of blood does he need?"

Louretta gave him a long, insulting look. "Any type but white."

The teacher blushed deeply under his olive skin, but he did not give up. "I'll go to the hospital as soon as I leave school," he said quietly. "You're not doing your friend any favor with your attitude, Louretta. Blood is just blood. It's all red, and if you were sick as he is, you'd know it. I think Jethro will welcome my blood as much as anyone else's."

"Suit yourself," she said with a shrug, and walked out coolly, leaving Mr. Lucitanno frowning at his desk. If he were a woman, she was sure, he would have been crying. It served him right. Why did white people always think that they deserved extra gratitude when they offered to help you?

Blowback

Late 1960s and '70s Pulp and Popular Fiction about the Vietnam War

The conflict in Vietnam cast a long shadow over pulp and popular fiction in the late 1960s and the 1970s. Vietnam veterans were hunted by small-town redneck police in David Morrell's 1972 novel, *First Blood*, dealt drugs in Vern E. Smith's *The Jones Men*, and staged an abortive bank heist in *Dog Day Afternoon*, both published in 1974. In the Lone Wolf series, New York ex-cop and Vietnam veteran Burt Wulff mounted a fourteen-book battle from 1973 to 1975 against the drug dealing criminal organization, "the network," in which he treated the streets of America's major cities as an extension of jungles of Southeast Asia.

Vietnam was the training ground for many of the characters that populated men's adventure and crime pulp in the 1970s. These included Remo Williams, a.k.a. "The Destroyer"; Mark Hardin, a.k.a. "The Penetrator"; Mack Bolan in Don Pendleton's long-running series, The Executioner; Joseph Greene's suave trouble shooting PI, Superspade; and Joe Nazel's Harlem native Henry Highland West, referred to as "The Iceman." Johnny Rocetti used his skills acquired as a Green Beret in Vietnam to take on the Mafia in Frank Scarpetta's blood-drenched Marksman series. Jim Rainey, the central character in the Soldier of Fortune series, learned his craft working for the American government's "Phoenix Group" in Vietnam, no doubt a fictional take on the real-life CIA-directed covert assassination program, the Phoenix Program. And the Mind Masters series by John F. Rossman and Ian Ross depicted a character called Britte St. Vincent, a top-secret U.S. government agent whose special psychic powers were activated by the horrors he experienced in Vietnam. More broadly, Vietnam's traumatic impact on American society would become a cypher through which pulp and popular fiction namechecked cultural fragmentation, growing disillusionment with the American dream, dishonest and unaccountable government and corporations, and the power of the military-industrial complex.

But while Vietnam equipped numerous fictional characters with the skills to combat the Mafia, terrorists or various other threats, few books in the late 1960s and '70s focused on the war and its consequences as anything more than a background or reason for why a character was as confused/damaged/homicidal as they were. Removing reportage and autobiographies, fewer still were actually set in Vietnam. Given the lengthy U.S. involvement in the war—the first major deployment of combat troops took place in May 1965—and pulp's time-proven ability to riff off the latest prominent issues or newspaper headlines, we can only speculate as to why writers and publishers were loath to sensationalize the conflict with the enthusiasm they did with everything else. Was it a case of self-censorship? Or was the conflict simply too close to the bone, given the deep divisions over the war in West that grew as the conflict dragged on?

More likely, the answer involves sales or, more to the point, the lack of them generated by stories that focused on Vietnam. Vietnam stories "were absolute poison," recalls Mario Puzo in an interview in the 2012 book *Weasels Ripped My Flesh! Two-Fisted Stories from Men's Adventure Magazines of the 1950s, '60s & '70s*. Puzo, who penned numerous war and crime stories for men's magazines in addition to his more famous work such as his 1969 novel *The Godfather*, says: "They [readers] hated it [Vietnam]. Also, we weren't the heroes. Just like the Korean War—we used to call that The No Fun War. World War II was The Fun War. And you could get some mileage out of the Civil War and World War I. World War II was a Bonanza. But Korea and Vietnam were losers."

A similar dynamic appeared to have been at play in film. Among the first films to directly tackle the war was *The Green Berets* (1968), a jingoistic and bombastic war film developed by John Wayne with the express intent of influencing U.S. public opinion in favor of the war. In the years that followed, few mainstream films expressly dealt with the Vietnam War until the release of Michael Cimino's *The Deer Hunter* in 1978 and Francis Ford Coppola's *Apocalypse Now* in 1979.

Two early pulp books that break with the reluctance to examine America's Vietnam War experience in detail are Con Sellers's *Where Have All the Soldiers Gone?* (1969) and *The Man Who Won the Medal of Honor* by Len Giovannitti, published in 1973.

The main character in *Where Have All the Soldiers Gone?* is antiwar activist Lee Boyd, who decides that he will have more impact by joining the marines and exposing what is going on from the inside. The book opens with him in Vietnam, dealing with the hostile intentions of the enemy and his hard-charging, right-wing, college-student-hating, career-soldier superior, Sergeant Garrick. Boyd's efforts to stay alive are interspersed with passages in which he reminisces about his life back in San Francisco, "the City," as he refers to it, and his girlfriend, Lisa, who he fears is drifting apart from him. "She was getting mixed in with the other wild, swinging chicks in Monterey and the City and points around and between."

Boyd tells anyone who will listen about the antiwar movement and how wonderful life is in San Francisco:

> ... the creatively intellectual atmosphere of Haight-Ashbury where everyone used the mind-expanding, senses expanding stuff, and found themselves reveling in the new knowledge, the new and strong importance of putting together a society completely apart from the phony values of the present one. It was bathing in the sounds from the different folk-rock groups as color wheels spun lazy. ... It was swaying together, holding hands with the everywhere flowers and chanting Hell no, we won't go, answering the thickbeard speaker who thundered all these irrefutable truths from the platform. ... What else was it? *Freedom*, man—real freedom for the first time anywhere. ... It was freedom to listen to Ginsberg and block the induction center and tell the fuzz to kiss off, and what the hell could they *do* about it.

Though it had been a big deal in the States when he announced he was joining up, Boyd's plan to spill the beans on what is going in Vietnam—the misuse of authority, the unauthorized deaths of civilians, the poverty of the locals—is frustrated because the media are no longer interested. He has been forgotten. His fellow American soldiers either couldn't care less or consider him an oddity. Most just want to do their tour, survive and get back home. He is particularly

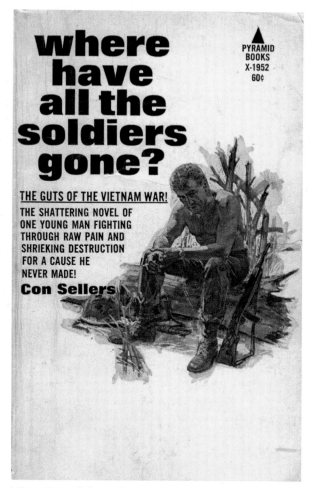

Where Have All the Soldiers Gone? (Pyramid, 1969)

disheartened that the increasingly radicalized black marines don't consider him a fellow revolutionary. To them, he's just whitey and a weirdo. "You think Charlie and me are the same color? You think Charlie hasn't got a word that means nigger in his language?" a black soldier asks him, possibly riffing on and upending Muhammad Ali's iconic statement, "I ain't got no quarrel with them Vietcong. No Vietcong ever called me nigger."

Boyd witnesses numerous atrocities by American forces, including a young Vietnamese girl killed by a fragmentation grenade thrown by Garrick and a village shot up by a psychopathic marine called Whiney, in retaliation for a bomb attack on the local village bar frequented by off-duty Americans. Boyd protests these acts to the military authorities higher up, but they do nothing. His only respite is a local prostitute, Mai. A "small fury, miniature tigress" in bed, she is a thinly drawn character who, when she does speak, communicates only in broken English.

The author's agenda becomes clear about halfway through *Where Have All the Soldiers Gone?*. Realizing he is a good medic, Boyd starts to take pride in his work. This eases tensions with Garrick, who in turn reveals himself to the young marine as a self-made scholar who can discuss the relative nature of poverty and why America is at war. He gets Boyd to slowly change his antiwar views and becomes something of a father figure to him. Parallel with this, Sellers ups the ante in terms of the horrific acts committed by the Viet Cong on American soldiers. There are graphic punji stick injuries, and the Americans discover a dead member of their platoon skinned alive by the enemy. Boyd's final metamorphosis occurs when Garrick is killed trying to rescue a wounded marine. When journalists eventually find him and ask him for the low down about what is happening in Vietnam, he refuses to talk to them. Then he applies for a transfer to become a fighting marine.

This none too latent Pax Americana aside, this book is well written and deserves kudos for at least attempting to tackle the war itself directly. That Sellers was no peacenik is evident from the brief biography in a February 3, 1992, obituary in the *Lewiston Tribune*. He served seventeen years in the army, was wounded twice as an infantryman during World War II, and was decorated with Silver and Bronze stars and a Purple Heart. He served as an army combat correspondent in Korea but was supposedly discharged in 1956 for alcoholism. He turned to writing stories for men's pulp magazines and wrote some 230 novels under ninety-four names, everything from science fiction to spy novels, westerns, movie tie-ins, and smut.

The Man Who Won the Medal of Honor is a far more radical take on the in-country experience of American troops in Vietnam. The author, Len Giovannitti, was another World War II veteran, serving in the Army Air Corps as a navigator. His *New York Times* obituary states that on his fiftieth mission, his plane was shot down in Austria, and he was held prisoner for a year. He told of this experience in his first novel, *The Prisoners of Combine D* (1957). He was also an award-winning television writer and filmmaker who made hard-hitting stories about social issues such as the energy crisis, racial tension, and juvenile delinquency. His Vietnam novel begins with the protagonist, eighteen-year-old private David Glass, recounting the

events that saw him mistakenly awarded the Medal of Honor, America's most prestigious military decoration, while waiting in jail on death row. As the pull quote on the front cover says, "I AM A MEDAL OF HONOR RECIPIENT. I HAVE NEVER KILLED A SINGLE ENEMY SOLDIER. ON THE OTHER HAND, I HAVE KILLED A NUMBER OF AMERICAN SOLDIERS."

An orphan who joined the army to escape the institution he grew up in, Glass shows little aptitude for military life except for being an excellent marksman. Stationed in central Vietnam in the summer of 1968, his first encounter with "Charlie," the most common slang term for the Vietnamese, is a young boy who the marines discover on a routine sweep of a village, and who his tough, uncompromising commander, Sergeant Stone, is convinced is a spy. After pumping the boy for whatever information he has, Stone slits his throat. Glass reports him, but in much the same way as Boyd is ignored in Sellers's book, the military command is unconcerned by what is obviously just one more civilian death among so many. They also view Glass's attempts to bypass the chain of command as a threat to military harmony and discipline. At this point, Glass resolves "not to kill any Vietnamese except to save my own life."

He takes a further step when he kills a marine he suspects has murdered a Vietnamese civilian on a night patrol. Transferred to the role of a door gunner on a chopper in the Mekong Delta, his vigilante-style actions culminate on a routine reconnaissance mission with a ruthless George Patton–style Brigadier General George Rusty Gunn. Gunn shoots three "gooks" working in a field with a machine gun out of frustration because they have not encountered the enemy. "You know something?" Gunn tells Glass, "Killing gooks gives me a hard on." At which point Glass pushes Gunn and the colonel accompanying him out of the helicopter. The deaths are covered up by the military.

Glass completes his tour of duty and, through some sort of accident, is awarded the Medal of Honor. He wants to turn the awards ceremony into an antiwar protest, but instead it becomes a fumbling and uncertain attempted assassination of the president. The book concludes with the possibility that Glass is insane, although whether he was always like this or was made this way by his experiences in Vietnam is unclear.

The Man Who Won the Medal of Honor is full of passages detailing the horror and futility of the war, particularly the more often than not one-sided, high-tech

"I am a Medal of Honor recipient. I have never killed a single enemy soldier. On the other hand, I have killed a number of American soldiers."

The Man Who Won The Medal Of Honor
A Novel by Len Giovannitti

carnage inflicted on the Vietnamese. There is so much killing that Glass's acts of vigilante justice can easily be concealed amid the chaos. Also writ large is the farcical nature of Washington's strategy of trying to win the hearts and minds of the Vietnamese while destroying their country. Interestingly, it must also be one of the first novels to deal with the practice of "fragging." As military morale collapsed, soldiers increasingly moved from refusing orders to deliberately wounding or killing those who issued them, as well as other unpopular combatants, often through the use of fragmentation grenades. Estimates of the number of incidents vary, with some putting them as high as one thousand attacks and at least fifty-seven deaths. Giovannitti also namechecks a number of other key aspects associated with America's Vietnam experience: drug use, the racial divide between black and white troops, the total alienation of the Americans from the Vietnamese, the division between those who revel in the war and those whose only aim, in Glass's words, is to get through "a nightmare that measured 365 days—and when it ended we would go home and resume our lives as if it had never happened."

At least one critic branded the book as sensationalist and criticized the character of Glass for "committing the same crimes with the same rationalizations that the army used to explain its actions in this mess: killing is OK as long as you're on the right side, wherever that happens to be." Another take on *The Man Who Won the Medal of Honor* is that it speaks to the radical energy of the times, when a small but significant section of the U.S. population not only openly disagreed with America's mission in Vietnam but supported the enemy.

The book can also be viewed as a meditation on the trauma of war, a reading that similarly applies to the much-better-known text, Tim O'Brien's 1978 novel, *Going after Cacciato*. Labeled by the author, himself a Vietnam veteran, a "peace novel" rather than an antiwar book, it won the National Book Award. It has been dealt with extensively elsewhere, so I will not devote too much space to it here. It tells of the events that ensue after a soldier called Cacciato goes AWOL from his unit in Vietnam and seven soldiers led by Paul Berlin go after him, tracking him to France and through Asia. Cacciato, a Forrest Gump–type character, leaves evidence of his passing along the way, such as equipment and bits of a map. The book has an almost magical realist quality, interspersed with combat and

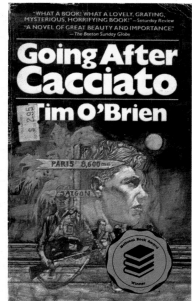

"WHAT A BOOK! WHAT A LOVELY, GRATING, MYSTERIOUS, HORRIFYING BOOK!" —Saturday Review
"A NOVEL OF GREAT BEAUTY AND IMPORTANCE." —The Boston Sunday Globe

Going After Cacciato
Tim O'Brien

PARIS 8,600
SAIGON

The Man Who Won the Medal of Honor (Popular Library, 1973)
Going after Cacciato (Dell, 1978)

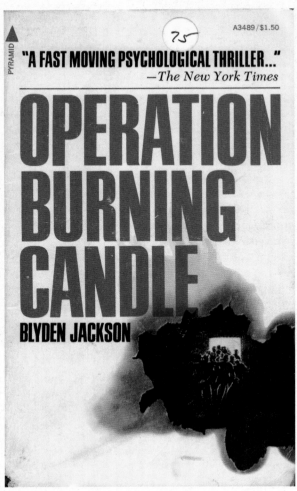

Operation Burning Candle (Pyramid, 1974)

Berlin's thoughts on Vietnam, suggesting that the entire story might be a fantasy, Berlin's mechanism for coping with the horror of the war.

Plots by militant black liberation groups to destroy major infrastructure or assassinate political figures so as to inspire black insurrection were a common preoccupation of late 1960s and early 1970s pulp fiction. *Operation Burning Candle* (1974), written by black academic and writer Blyden Jackson, takes this trope and infuses it with a Vietnam War plotline. Disillusioned by the Nixon presidency and having watched every major black leader who offered hope get killed or jailed, black psychology student Aaron Rogers enlists to fight in Vietnam. The move is a cover for his plan to put together a group of black men, all Green Berets like him who have cut their teeth working covert special ops behind enemy lines, and who have each passed the

initiation ceremony of fragging a white officer. They switch identities with soldiers killed in action, return to the U.S. and congregate in New York, where, as part of a much larger force, they aim to put into effect Operation Burning Candle. Mass transit shutdowns and power blackouts across Manhattan are intended as a prelude to assassinating the most trenchant racists in the U.S. Senate at the upcoming Democratic National Convention in Madison Square Garden.

The story shifts between multiple points of view in addition to that of Rogers: members of Rogers's family in Harlem, including his broken, alcoholic, but still politically radical father, none of whom know Rogers is alive; virulently racist southern "Dixiecrat" Senator Josiah Brace, who is trying to sabotage the nomination of a liberal candidate at the convention so he can take the top slot himself; and Dan Roberts, a police officer and Korean War vet who is investigating the disappearance of an undercover police operative planted in a street gang known as the Black Warriors, killed by Rogers as a potentially weak link in his plan. Roberts connects the death to a series of well-organized bank robberies that, unbeknownst to him, are being staged to fund Operation Burning Candle. The idea of planting police agents in black organizations is a direct reference to the FBI's infamous COINTELPRO operations, aimed at infiltrating, spying on, disrupting, and ultimately breaking up organizations viewed by the authorities as subversive. These included antiwar and civil rights groups and the Black Power movement. Roberts is a racist, who considers Harlem enemy territory. "You've been in the streets of Harlem day and night for the last three years," a senior policeman tells him at one point. "You read the papers—Chicago, Detroit, Newark, Cleveland. There's another kind of war shaping up, Dan. It's *that* war that we mustn't let happen." Each of those cities experienced major race riots and ghetto uprisings between 1964 and 1967.

Operation Burning Candle is a well written, compelling thriller, in which Rogers's attempts to bring his plan to fruition run parallel with the dawning awareness on the part of the police that something major is going down, their efforts to discover what it is and prevent it. The story is also a sophisticated political statement that feels alarmingly relevant today. Particularly interesting are the passages elaborating on Rogers's plan, his contention that only through "cleansing violence" can the cycle of black oppression and its dehumanizing impact on white America be broken. As part of this, the novel specially mentions the influence on Rogers of the work of Frantz Fanon and Malcolm X about the use of targeted violence to galvanize the black people into action. In one key scene, when the insurrectionaries seize a radio station, Rogers makes a lengthy broadcast about the group's aims.

> "Brothers and sisters." Aaron went on, more urgently now, "this weekend, in the next 72 hours, brothers and sisters, we are going to find that unity! Our unity as black people, as brothers and sisters. . . . We are going to end four centuries of separation from each other. We shall no longer be alone, dying, crying, by ourselves, unable to reach out to each other—unable to touch the black hand so close to our own, outstretched in anguish! An end to that, brothers and sisters! In the next 72 hours! We are going to establish our own humanity and force them to act as humans too!"

He asks everyone who supports the uprising to put a lighted candle in their window "so that we know your home is our home." Not only do candles proliferate but mass spontaneous rallies break out across the country. Toward the end of the book, thousands of black Americans watch guerrillas assassinate twelve senators live on prime-time television, shouting joyfully, "They're killing the honkies!"

The one blind spot of *Operation Burning Candle*'s otherwise sharp politics are the scenes set in Vietnam. While Jackson depicts the racism in the U.S. military, Rogers and his men seem largely uncritical of the destruction of which they are a part of in Southeast Asia. They formulate their plan in "Soulville," a slum in Saigon where black GIs go on R&R, largely off limits to whites, where they sleep with local women, impoverished by the war, and bond in a gun battle against racist military police.

Another key trope about the Vietnam War explored by pulp and popular fiction in the early 1970, was the returned soldier, damaged, sometimes irrevocably, by experience of the war, who has difficulty readjusting to a country that had changed while he had been overseas. One example is Newton Thornburg's excellent 1976 noir novel *Cutter and Bone*, about an embittered Vietnam veteran who becomes so obsessed with the possibility that his gigolo friend Bone has witnessed a murder that he tries to find the culprit. Another fictional examination is the 1979 novel *Coming Home* by

Coming Home (Dell, 1971)

George Davis, who joined the U.S. Air Force in 1961 and flew numerous missions in Vietnam. This is not to be confused with Hal Ashby's 1978 movie in which a woman (Jane Fonda) whose husband (Bruce Dern) is in Vietnam falls into a relationship with a veteran (Jon Voight) crippled in the war.

One of the hardest-hitting takes on the domestic blowback of the war is Robert Stone's *Dog Soldiers*. First published in hardback by Houghton Mifflin in 1974, it enjoyed a double life as a paperback, as the cover for the 1976 version by downmarket UK publisher Star Books demonstrates. The book was also made into the underappreciated 1978 film *Who'll Stop the Rain*.

John Converse is a freelance journalist covering the conflict in Vietnam. The reasons why he chose to go are unclear. "He hopes something worthwhile might emerge from such an expedition, there might be a book or a play." But Stone hints the journey is just as much about a search for meaning and an escape from his life in the States, including a child and an unhappy union with his wife, Marge. In Saigon he finds writing work and falls in with a crowd of "dope people." Politically liberal, he quickly grows weary with the war, spending most of his time stoned and hanging out in the bars on Saigon's Tu Do Street. After eighteen months in country and "for all the discoveries, it had become apparent that there would be no book, no play. It seemed necessary that there be something." That something is a drug deal.

The decision to import three kilograms of heroin is motivated by money but also disgust about America's actions in the war. The final straw is "the Great Elephant Zap of the previous year," when U.S. Army Command decided elephants "were enemy agents because the NVA used them to carry things, and there had ensued a scene worthy of the Ramayana," in which helicopters are sent to hunt elephants all over the south. Whether this occurred in real life or not is unclear, but as Converse tells it, the move produced "a feeling that there were no limits. And as for dope, Converse thought, and addicts—if the world is going to contain elephants pursued by flying men, people are just naturally going to want to get high."

Converse enlists an old friend, Hicks, a Nietzsche-reading, paranoid former marine now working as a merchant sailor, to traffic the dope to America and bring it to his wife in Berkeley. Overcoming his concerns about the "bad karma" associated with the deal, Hicks smuggles the drugs to the U.S. and brings them to Marge only to discover that corrupt drug enforcement agents have got wind of the deal and are waiting for him. Escaping with Marge, they dump her child with a relative and try and sell the drugs while evading the narcs.

Marge, whom Hicks is soon sleeping with, is an extremely unreliable partner as loneliness and ennui have led her to develop an addiction to the opiate Dilaudid. Meanwhile, Converse returns home to finds his wife and kid gone, and in their place is Antheil, the head narc, who threatens to turn over the journalist to the various illegal interests his heroin deal has threatened unless he helps track Marge and Hicks down.

One of the many strengths of *Dog Soldiers* is its depiction of the American civilians who flooded into South Vietnam during the war, an aspect of the conflict rarely explored in fiction, certainly not as early as 1974. Stone told the author of *Vietnam, We've All Been There: Interviews with American Writers* (1992) that he drew on

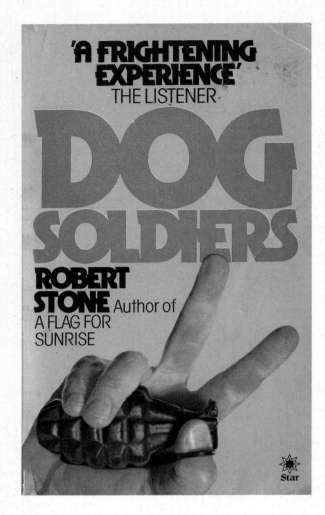

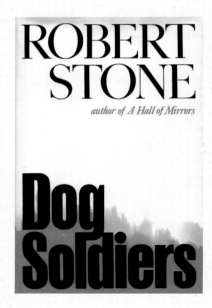

Dog Soldiers
(Star, 1976)
Dog Soldiers
(Houghton
Mifflin, 1974)

his own experience as a correspondent in Saigon in the early 1970s for *Dog Soldiers*.

> Nineteen seventy-one was probably the baroque period of Saigon. You could run into anybody on the streets of Saigon. There was a whole anti-war contingent of people. Saigon was just full of Americans and Europeans of any possible description. It was a real carnival. There were lots of people with marginal accreditations: stringers from quasi papers, people with forged accreditation letters that they had written for themselves. A lot of people were dealing dope. There were a lot of marginal people around, a lot of people only nominally press. There were reporters who allegedly dealt with the black market. There certainly were such reporters who dabbled in gold or cinnamon or dope.

While the Vietnam section of the novel is over after a hundred pages, the shockwaves of the war infuse everything that follows. Particularly evocative is Stone's portrayal of the conclusion of the Summer of Love, and the self-interest, paranoia, and disillusionment that followed. This shift was described by Stone as "the time of the dying dream of the sixties in California and also the dying dream of the Great Society—all sorts of bills were coming up due for payment in the early seventies." This is illustrated in *Dog Soldiers* through journey undertaken by Hicks and Marge, during which they encounter various refugees from the sixties, including a drug-dealing Hollywood moviemaker and middle-class swingers interested in turning on, before ending up at a semi-abandoned commune in the middle of the desert for the final showdown with Atheil.

While the exact bureaucratic affiliation of Antheil and his men is never directly revealed, their vulture-like pursuit of Converse's hapless drug deal personifies another major aspect of the domestic and international blowback from the Indochina conflict, America's involvement in drug trafficking. Alfred McCoy's seminal 1972 book *The Politics of Heroin in South East Asia* was the first authoritative work to document Washington's direct complicity in the drug trade, particularly during America's "secret war" in Laos. There the CIA used its covert airline, Air America, to transport opium cultivated by anticommunist Hmong tribesmen in return for their loyalty against the communist Pathet Lao, with the organization in turn ploughing profits from the drug trade back into

the conflict. McCoy also revealed that the United States was, at best, turning a blind eye to the processing of opium into heroin in jungle laboratories in Thailand. The supply of cheap drugs was one of the facts linked to the poor morale of American troops in the later stages of the war, with some estimating that as many as 15 percent of enlisted U.S. troops were heroin users.

The United Kingdom did not officially become involved in Vietnam, although British troops did provide some training early on to South Vietnamese forces and its special forces were active in a covert role. Australia had been unofficially involved, sending military equipment and advisors to South Vietnam since the early 1960s. This become official when the first Australian ground troops were dispatched in April 1965. Long-serving conservative prime minister Robert Menzies saw the war as part of a broader Communist push into Asia, which, if unchecked, could threaten Australia. Public sentiment was broadly in favor of Australia's involvement until around 1969, when organized opposition to the conflict and the conscription of young men to fight in it became a mass movement. Australia's military participation in Vietnam ended in January 1973, when the newly elected reformist Labor government pulled Australian troops out. Approximately sixty thousand Australian troops served in Vietnam, of whom over five hundred were killed and three thousand wounded.

Australian pulp publishers displayed the same reticence to tackle Vietnam as those in the United States. They focused the bulk of their war titles on often-lurid tales of Australian heroism and suffering during World War II, restricting their Vietnam related offerings to the occasional medical romance or spy thriller. That said, several popular novels on the war by Australian authors appeared in the 1960s and early 1970s, including John Rowe's *Count Your Dead* (1968), *Wake in Fright* author Kenneth Cook's *The Wine God's Anger* (1968), and Rhys Pollard's *The Cream Machine* (1972).

Rowe, whose military service included a stint in Vietnam, wrote his novel while serving in Washington with the Defense Intelligence Agency. His account of the fortunes of an American officer who finds himself politically at odds with a combat officer about the U.S. involvement in the war, while broadly antiwar, is more about the American experience in Vietnam than that of Australians. The almost impossible to procure book *The Wine God's Anger* concerns an army volunteer who becomes disillusioned with the fight against

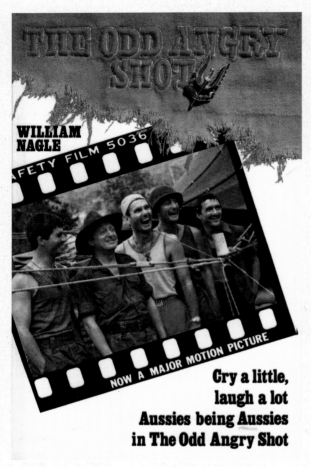

Cry a little,
laugh a lot
Aussies being Aussies
in The Odd Angry Shot

The Odd Angry Shot (Angus and Robertson, 1979)

an antiwar book in the sense that it depicts the futility of the conflict and the alienation of the men who went to Vietnam fight it. The soldiers, including the narrator, start off as believers, keen to do their duty and fight communism: "My rifle feels good as it rests on my lap, oiled and shiny. Twenty-eight rounds of keep Australia free from sin and yellow bastards." But this sentiment quickly fades in the face of dangerous but largely pointless patrols interspersed by large periods of boredom. At times, the book tries to affect a *Catch-22* vibe, but this is undermined by its sullen tone and a depiction of Australian "mateship" that often tips over into racism and sexism, the latter focused on the women the troops have left behind who fail to remain loyal. The book evinces little sympathy for those protesting the war back home, who are depicted as having sold out the troops.

Three other Australian takes on Vietnam from the late 1960s and the 1970s worthy of brief mention are Wal Watkins's *Prisoners in Paradise*, first published in 1968 and rereleased with a racy cover in 1972 by Gold Star Publications, and two crime tales, *The Unforgiven* (1978) and *Death by Demonstration* (1970).

Nelson, the main character in *Prisoners in Paradise*, is a sickly schoolteacher involved in the antiwar movement, who is advised by his doctor to give up his political activities because they are bad for his health. His best years behind him and with a disintegrating marriage to a cheating wife, he packs in his Australian life and heads to Bangkok on a voyage of self-discovery. There he falls in love with a young Thai girl, Nan, who claims she is not a prostitute but sleeps with him in return for being kept. Nelson gradually discovers both sides of the escalating conflict in nearby Vietnam have an interest in Nan. The Americans, in the form of a calculating U.S. Army intelligence officer, Murchison, believe Nan is the mistress of the leader of Thai communists who are linked to the Viet Cong. The Viet Cong meanwhile want her for the intelligence she may have gathered during a sexual liaison she had with a visiting senior figure in the South Vietnamese government. Nelson hatches a plan to get the two of them to safety in Malaya but can't shake the suspicion that the communists are potentially using him as a dupe.

While *Prisoners of Paradise* comes across a bit like a cut-price *The Quiet American*, it nonetheless touches on one of the major impacts of Australian involvement in Vietnam: the way it opened up the up the country's until then parochial culture to greater influence from

communism and deserts to Bangkok, where virtually the entire book is set. *The Cream Machine* covers similar ground to *Where Have All the Soldiers Gone?* in its depiction of a reluctant draftee sent to fight in Vietnam, who slowly comes to appreciate the talents and dedication of the Australian army soldier.

The most famous novel about Australia's Vietnam experience is William Nagle's *The Odd Angry Shot* (1975), made into a movie of the same name in 1979. Nagle joined the army after he left school, trained as a cook and was deployed to Saigon with the Special Air Service (SAS) in 1966. He was later transferred on disciplinary grounds to the infantry in Australia and was discharged at his own request in 1968. He supposedly wrote the first draft of *The Odd Angry Shot* in one sitting, working around the clock for six days. The story of a group of SAS troops, from their departure to Vietnam to their time in "the scrub" and concluding with their unceremonious return home, *The Odd Angry Shot* is

Asia. Watkins also shoehorns in observations about politics and the war via the discussions that take place between the expatriates who congregate in the Bangkok hotel where Nelson is staying. Like the expat denizens of Saigon in *Dog Soldiers*, this group live a precarious, hand-to-mouth existence. The only thing they have in common is the creeping awareness that whatever way the Vietnam War goes, they are witnessing the end of Western superiority in Asia.

No detail is available about C.J. Cairncross, the author of *The Unforgiven*. The novel opens with two men sitting in a car across the street from a gun store, one of them having flashbacks to his time as a soldier in Vietnam. A bomb goes off in the shop and the men steal a number of high-powered weapons. A gun battle ensues between the men and the cops, in which a police officer is injured. One of several bombs that have gone off around Sydney, a criminal informant or "phiz" tells police officer Edward Frazer that they are the work of a couple of professionals from Melbourne: "the Yugos or Arabs or one of that lot." But further investigation reveals that the stolen guns were part of a consignment for a mysterious gun collector, the high-powered, right-wing businessman/industrialist Carl Hackett. Frazer becomes convinced the bombings have something to do with Hackett's son, Michael. An anti–Vietnam War protester and conscientious objector at university, Michael was strongarmed by his father into joining the army and going to Vietnam, where he had a complete breakdown and was discharged as medically unfit. He spent time in hospital in Australia before leaving for Canada. Intersecting with the bombing investigation is the discovery of the body of a young female sex worker in a dingy hotel room in Sydney's vice district, Kings Cross. One of the cops who discover the body, formerly a military police officer in Vietnam, believes the murder has similarities to one that took place in Saigon during the war.

As the story develops it becomes clear Hackett's son is indeed back in Sydney and has teamed up with another Vietnam veteran, Arch Morley—who may have something to do with the murders—wants revenge on his father. Although *The Unforgiven* is an average crime novel, it must rank among the first popular Australian novels to fictionalize what was at the time the unnamed and unexplored issue of post-traumatic stress disorder affecting soldiers returning from Vietnam. Some would come to argue this was a particularly pronounced problem for Vietnam vets

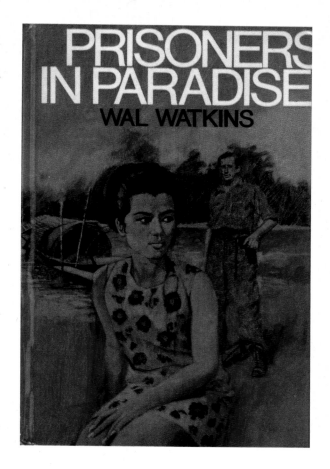

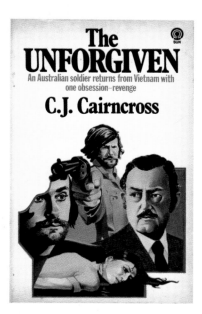

Prisoners in Paradise (Robert Hale, 1968)
The Unforgiven (Sun Books, 1978)

due to factors such as the guerrilla nature of the war, which resulted in a lack of definition about where the conflict started and ended, the use of defoliants, controversy about the war back home, the young age of those who fought—the average age of Australian servicemen in Vietnam was twenty—and the war being widely viewed as a defeat. As Cairncross writes at one point about Michael and his partner, they "were part of a world that no longer existed, a world where the sun shone and people laughed and fell in love and had babies. That world had been murdered in Asia. Michael had seen it die."

Death by Demonstration was the last novel of Sydney crime writer Patricia Carlon, a recluse who, it was discovered only after her death, had been profoundly deaf since the age of eleven. *Death by Demonstration* sees private detective Jefferson Shield drawn into investigating the murder of a young female protestor, Robyn Calder, at an anticonscription demonstration in Sydney. The police and the university where the demonstrators are studying want to pin the killing on the protest's organizers. A middle-aged, middle-class white man and veteran of World War II, Shields is no fan of the young, modish antiwar students whose world he has to penetrate in order to uncover the true story behind the woman's death.

The organizers appear to have made every effort to ensure the demonstration in question was peaceful. But contradicting their story, a photograph surfaces that shows Robyn acting aggressively and brandishing what appears to be an iron bar. One avenue of Shields's investigation is the so-called Thought Club, a left-wing organization run by a couple of arrogant Saul Alinsky–style professional demonstrators, who help organize radical protests in return for money. There is also some speculation that the demonstration and others like it could be being used as cover by criminals for various robberies occurring in their vicinity at the same time.

Death by Demonstration has a strange, almost featureless setting, probably because all of Carlon's books were published in the UK, so she may have been keen not to burden British readers with too much Sydney detail. The book does work in depicting what must have been the alarm many experienced at the upsurge in militant youth protest against Vietnam, part of much broader social change sweeping Australian as the country entered the 1970s. Where the book falls down is Carlon's reliance on slabs of exposition, which comes off as preachy and bogs the story down, as well

The 2001 Soho Press rerelease of Patricia Carlon's 1971 novel, *Death by Demonstration*

as the injection of the author's only thinly veiled political bias against those protesting the war.

In the late 1970s and the '80s, men's adventure pulp characters would travel back to Vietnam on missions to eliminate evil drug lords or, as in the case of Stephen Mertz's Stone M.I.A. Hunter series, to locate and rescue U.S. servicemen allegedly left behind after the war to languish in various communist hell hole prisons. The one perspective that would not be dealt with in any of the pulp and popular fiction from the late 1960s to the early '80s was that of the Vietnamese, both North and South, combatants and civilians. It would not be until much later for Western audiences that "Charlie" would acquire a face and get to write their own story.

Andrew Nette

STICKING IT TO THE MAN

A Black Sinclair Lewis

The Novels of Robert Deane Pharr

"When I first started writing my desire was to be called 'a black Sinclair Lewis.'"

That's what Robert Deane Pharr told interviewers John O'Brien and Raman K. Singh, as published in the journal *Negro American Literature Forum* in 1974. At that point Pharr, then fifty-eight, had published two novels. And if writing like Sinclair Lewis means authoring daring works that take an unblinkingly critical look at the social atmosphere at a place in time, he had more than achieved his goal. But Pharr's milieu was something very different from Lewis's. While Lewis wrote about the likes of white, middle-American social conformists like George Babbitt, Pharr's penetrating gaze focused on black people and their actions and surroundings.

Very little is known about Pharr's life. He was born in 1916 in Richmond, Virginia, and was a college graduate who mostly worked as a waiter. He seems to have lived in some of the rough-and-tumble inner-city environments, in Harlem and other places, where his novels take place. It is that duality of being an educated man who led a hand-to-mouth life amid squalor that gives his writing its signature.

It was while he was employed as a waiter that Pharr, through some friends who were studying at Columbia University, got a professor at that school to read his novel *The Book of Numbers*. The prof was impressed and played a role in the book's eventual publication by Doubleday in 1969. The novel was lauded by the *New York Times* and other outlets, and Pharr was now a middle-aged man with a promising literary career ahead of him.

Unlike his other novels, all of which are set close to the time in which they were written, *The Book of Numbers* takes place during the Great Depression. It involves two drifting waiters, Dave Greene and Blueboy Harris, who move to an unnamed city in Virginia in 1935 and set up a numbers racket in a section of the town only referred to as "the Ward." Greene, twenty-three at the outset of the story, is a seemingly lazy but deceptively crafty and ambitious young man. Harris,

Robert Deane Pharr from back cover of the 1978 edition, *Giveaway Brown*

who's old enough to be Greene's father, is the more charismatic of the two. Their personalities complement each other, and as a racketeering team running an illegal lottery game among their black neighbors in the Ward, they become wildly successful, at least initially.

Roughly two years after he and Harris start up their numbers gaming racket, Greene, who is the novel's real focus, finds himself at a crossroads. He is now a big-time player around the Ward, a money man with a bottomless cash flow, a fleet of cars, etc. But where is he to go, socially? All the well-to-do black people Greene encounters after earning his illegal fortune either try to use him in some way or consider themselves to be above somebody who made his money the way he has.

Meanwhile, many of Greene's current neighbors have picked up the lottery bug. Several of them get so caught up in playing numbers that they are driven to extreme acts such as suicide and murder, so now Greene has all of that on his conscience.

Some of Greene's difficulties as a wealthy racketeer are summed up in conversations he has with his present girlfriend, Kelly Simms. Simms is a black college student who's in love with Greene, but she tells him she will only date him until she's finished with school. After she graduates from college, she will want nothing to do with a numbers banker. At one point they have this discussion:

> "I am asking a young Negro male, a member of an underprivileged minority, a man twenty-six years of age who is well on his way to becoming a millionaire before his thirtieth birthday, I am asking that enterprising young man if he has any ambitions at all?"
>
> "I am sick and tired of this crap," David said tightly. "Every bastard and his brother thinks me, my brain, and money is something that belongs to him personal like. And I am goddamn sick and tired of it. You hear me? As of this minute, my only ambition is for niggers to leave my private affairs alone. You hear me? Left-goddamn-alone."

Throughout the lengthy novel, which is told by an omniscient narrator, Pharr uses his characters to explore the condition of black people's experiences in America at the time. Blueboy Harris and a varied group of other black men, some of them educated professionals, often gather at a particular table a local eatery/drinking hole, and discuss "the race problem," as they call it. The different characters each have their own take on the plight of their ilk, but perhaps the strongest statement of all comes from Dave Greene, to his girlfriend Kelly, as he explains to her his rationale for not trying to make his money through legal means:

> "I can't buy a franchise to sell a damn thing in this Ward. You think I can sit down and write a check and be the owner of an automobile agency? You think the manufacturer of electrical appliances will give me a franchise? You think I can get a Coke concession? . . . When the day comes that I can open a retail store selling gas ranges, or radios and stuff, or anything else a darky really needs in his home I'll be ready to invest every

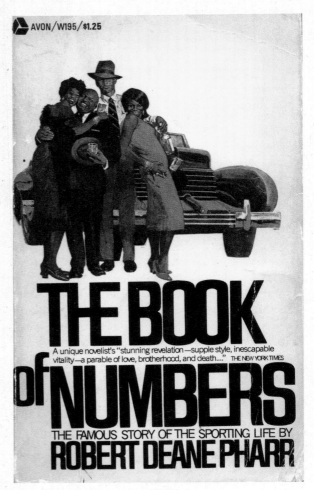

The Book of Numbers (Avon, 1970)

penny I got. But right now you niggers ain't ready. I am, but you're not. And me and my bank is gonna stay ready."

Pharr felt a combination of disappointment and sympathy about these characters he created. He told O'Brien and Singh, "Well, I have a group of black men who stumble across a way to make a million dollars. And not a single one ever did anything for black people." But later in the discussion he states, "In order for there to be wealth in that novel, there had to be law breaking. As long as black people could not break out of the economic ghetto into a world of free enterprise, they had to commit crime. The American dream tells us that we're free to get what everyone else has. And in the ghetto we see that crime pays and pays very well."

Overall, *The Book of Numbers* is a powerful novel and Pharr's most memorable literary work. It suffers from too many diversions from the main plot, many of them tediously long, but on balance this is a book that belongs in the top tier of black pulp.

If readers found the content of *The Book of Numbers* shocking in its unbridled portrayal of hardened inner-city characters, Pharr only tested their sensibilities more with his 1971 follow-up, *S.R.O.* Lengthy, like its predecessor, *S.R.O.* is a sprawling, unhinged saga involving the denizens of a decrepit single room occupancy hotel in Harlem in the mid-1960s. Most of the people who live in, or hang around, the down-and-out rooming house are alcoholics or heroin addicts, and some who occupy it are people who will go any way sexually to suit a given moment's craving or to get them some fleeting gain over another person. Everybody in and around the dumpy residence hotel is in a constant state of trying to get over. Few have gainful employment, and most collect welfare or do street work such as selling drugs or the use of their bodies. The whole of the book reads like a William S. Burroughs novel if Burroughs had written about inner-city black characters, and it has the feel of a Velvet Underground song, with its intense view of the dark side of a city and its people.

The novel is narrated for the most part by a character named Sid Bailey, a forty-two-year-old guy who has a college education and thoughts of being a writer. He comes to the Logan in a damaged state, having recently come out the bad end of an emotionally harmful divorce. Bailey is set apart from most of the people in the Logan, in a couple of ways. For one, he works (at the beginning of the story, anyway) as a waiter. Two, he does not use heroin, although he is a raging alcoholic. Three, he only goes for women. Women are a big part of the story. Sid becomes involved with several of the Logan's female regulars over the course of the tale, and it's his interactions with, and reflections on, these women that in large part drive the story. Unrequited love, sex both with and without emotional attachment, people using each other for what they need at the moment with no long-term concerns about their relations—these are some of the things that happen between Sid and his many girlfriends.

Something else that propels *S.R.O.* is just the way all the different characters relate to Sid. As he is something of a straight man surrounded by offbeat characters, a lot of the others characters' personality essentials come out in how they interact with the narrator. Whether it's the effeminate, philosophical guru who is

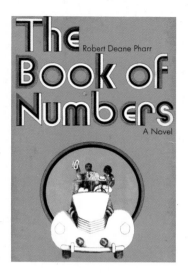

The Book of Numbers (Doubleday, 1969) *S.R.O.* (Old School Books, 1998)

the social leader of the Logan's crowd and who always wants to preach to Sid; or the blind and volatile man who hates or is indifferent to most others but takes Sid under his wing; or all the women who either love Sid, use him, or just like to have him around for emotional security (and money), he is the magnet that draws all the others to him.

In the 1974 interview quoted previously, Pharr stated that *S.R.O.* is an autobiographical novel and that he had lived in such a hotel at some point in his life. Allowing the reader see Pharr in the character of Sid Bailey, at one point Bailey starts to write in the midst of all the mayhem surrounding him at the Logan, and what he's working on is clearly *The Book of Numbers*. Bailey has this to say about writing, during the stretch of the tale when he is attempting to pen this book:

> Writing can fill all the lonely wells and desolate pits in your soul. You become a god, granting to this character life, this one death, that one riches, another cancer. You cure or condemn. And your characters all belong to you.

There is plenty of curing and condemnation done to the various characters in *S.R.O.*, and all of them are uniquely Robert Deane Pharr creations. It's a fascinating story and a book that should be read by anyone interested in black pulp, or just a novel about hardened inner-city characters. It would have been an even better book if Pharr had been more economical. There's a lot of repetition, and after a while the characters and all their doings become monotonous. Its five hundred plus pages could have easily been reduced to less than three hundred, without any of the story's key parts going missing. Still, it's a landmark novel by an important, underread black writer.

In his next book, 1975's *The Soul Murder Case*, Pharr narrowed his scope. The novel is several hundred pages shorter than the two that preceded it. It also has far fewer characters than the others, so that it's more *Notes from the Underground* and less *The Brothers Karamazov*.

The Soul Murder Case is told in the first person, just like *S.R.O.* This is interesting, considering that in the 1974 interview, Pharr stated, "I can't read anything in the first person. If a novel starts out in the first person, I just put it down." He added that he had originally meant *S.R.O.* to be told in the third person but made the switch at his publisher's request, so perhaps he was given the same directive for this newer novel.

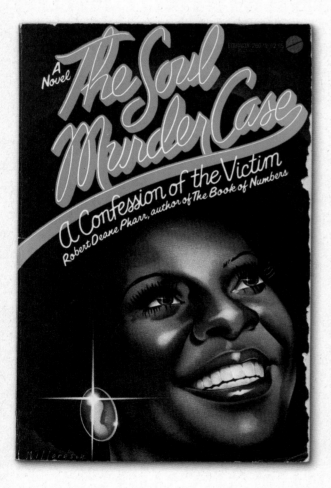

In any event, the narrator of *The Soul Murder Case* is a man named Bobbie Dee. Dee is a much different kind of cat than *S.R.O.*'s Sid Bailey. Where Bailey is a ne'er-do-well waiter who has distant dreams of being a published playwright or author, Dee has achieved major success in his life. He was once a big name in show business, both as a singer and film actor. But he was also a junkie then, and when he got busted while shooting up with a group of people during a stopover on one of his concert tours, he was sent to prison for a few years. Dee was never able to resurrect his performing career after that, and instead he later became a literary agent based in New York.

The main plotline of the brief novel centers on a character named Candace Brown and her relations with Dee. Dee once rescued Brown after she'd been brutally assaulted by a neighbor when she was a teenager, when they were both living in a rural part of Virginia. Fast forward to the present and Brown is a grown woman who is a blues singer. She has written a batch of fierce poetry, and she calls on Dee and tells him she wants him to get her explosive poems (all about black people's experiences in the present day) printed up, in two hundred copies. She says she doesn't care who he gets to make the copies and doesn't want to see or know about the book once it's prepared. Brown is determined to get her poems in print, yet her indifference to what happens to them afterward leads Dee to suspect that she believes she's about to die, either by a planned suicide or a murder she knows she's about to become victim to. All of this has thrown Dee's life into a whirlwind.

That's a promising setup for a novel. And there are some positive things to say about Pharr's execution in penning the book. He uses Dee's voice to project a whole manifesto of philosophical thoughts on race relations in America, drug addiction, love and lust, and more, just as he did in his two previous novels, through different characters and settings. And, in Pharr fashion, he doesn't hold back in uttering words that some would find shocking and that others might find bravely truthful. But where he came up short in *The Soul Murder Case* is that far too much of the text is made up of those musings from Dee. Pharr created a fascinating character and situation via Brown and her poems, yet he spent very little time writing about her or any of the interesting side characters he brought in. Instead, he had Dee go on an unrelenting series of lengthy rants, with his thoughts on life and its people,

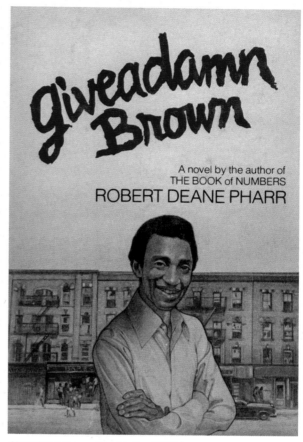

Giveadamn Brown (Doubleday, 1978)

to the point that there's almost no story and one may wonder how the book could even be considered a novel. Had Pharr done more with the fertile premise of this tale, *The Soul Murder Case* could have been an excellent story. But he didn't, and in the end it's a tough read and the least effective of his four books.

Still, there are some interesting reflections from Dee, such as this one on the state of black cinema:

> Black movies are a brand new way of life. A new life! And I'm going to be the midwife—dig it? You realize that the market is already demanding a new black movie every week? You realize that the white money that produces black movies has not woke up to the fact that rewriting *Shaft* every week is going to bankrupt them instead of making them more money?
>
> And the reasons all black movies are just another *Shaft* or *Super Fly* is because the white boys are writing the scenarios. But there is going

to be a revolution, a great awakening. The movie-makers are going to suddenly discover that there have been black literary geniuses from way back.

The last part of that statement from Dee is interesting in light of the fact that in the 1974 interview Pharr stated, when discussing his mind-set while authoring *The Book of Numbers*, "Looking back, I can't think of any black writer I wished to be compared to because what they were writing about I simply wasn't interested in."

Pharr's final novel, 1978's *Giveadamn Brown*, is his most easily readable. It contains the best of two Pharr worlds, in covering a whole scene of inner-city life, just as his first two novels did, while being compact and approachable like *The Soul Murder Case*. The book is just over two hundred pages and never becomes a labor to read à la *The Book of Numbers* and *S.R.O.*, and it contains the storytelling aspect that was missing from *The Soul Murder Case*. Robert Deane Pharr was never going to write a novel and not use some of its pages to spout off his theories on black Americans' condition, but in this book he kept the lecturing to a minimum and developed a compelling plot and well-drawn characters.

The titular character is a twenty-six-year-old do-nothing dude named Lawrence Brown, who was given the nickname "Giveadamn" when he told a Florida judge that he didn't give a damn what kind of punishment the judge handed to him for a drunk and disorderly charge. The story, which is told in the third person, begins when Giveadamn moves to Harlem and comes under the wing of a man he initially believes is his Uncle Harry, a feared, powerful man who's a big-time player in the Harlem drug-dealing scene. That scene gets shaken up when another heavy dealer is killed by police after trying to make a power play against them. The death leaves a huge segment of the underground market open, and Harry and the other big players now have to make moves to see who will seize control of the dead man's corner of the empire. Along the way, Giveadamn learns that Harry is actually his father rather than his uncle. And when Harry becomes victim to an arranged car explosion and is left in a comatose state, this puts the blasé Giveadamn in the position of having to lead Harry's racket at a time when a major drug war is about to erupt.

Giveadamn Brown has the feel of a blaxploitation film, with character names like Doll Baby, Deep Freeze, Foxy, and Studs. These people are an assortment of junkies, drug-dealing bosses and their minions, hookers, and the like. As in all of Pharr's novels, the characters are hardened black people who talk in edgy, streetwise ways. Pharr uses a female character—Giveadamn's main love interest—to voice words about the state of inner-city black women at the time:

> A ghetto chick used to have three choices. Now she got four, with college. But when these kids first started making it, there was only three. They could get knocked up by the dude they loved and get their asses put on welfare. They could be a junkie 'ho'. Or they could go downtown and get a job.
>
> Those that go downtown are roughly divided into two parts. . . . Some go down there to pick fights with the whiteys all day long. The others go down there to get their asses felt.

Writing in the *New Yorker* in 1978, book reviewer Susan Lardner had this to say about *Giveadamn Brown*: "The plot is too contrived to be convincing, but the tough, emotion-laden dialogue and the scores of scarred lives the author describes ring absolutely true."

Robert Deane Pharr died in 1992. The splash he made with his debut novel didn't bring him literary fame or riches. But then savagely honest novels about heroin addicts living in residence hotels in Harlem and inner-city drug wars were never likely to become popular blockbusters. Pharr knew by 1974 that to a great extent the words in his books were destined to fall on mostly deaf ears. He told his interviewers, "The public does not like the unvarnished truth about anything. America is not ready to stand and look at itself."

It's time the public stands and takes a second look at the work of Robert Deane Pharr.

Brian Greene

Author's Note: In some places where Pharr's writing is referenced, there is mention of a 1973 novel titled *The Welfare Bitch*. I have not been able to find evidence that this book actually exists, and it is never mentioned in the 1974 interview.

The Presidential Plot, **Stanley Johnson** (Paperback Library, 1969)

Equal parts conspiracy thriller and space science fiction, *The Presidential Plot* draws on different strands of the late-sixties Zeitgeist to spin an outlandish counterfactual narrative about how the CIA helped bring an end to the Vietnam War.

You wouldn't know it from the cover, but the protagonist of *The Presidential Plot* is Hersch Feldman, a thirty-two-year-old political operative who rises through the ranks of the DC power structure to become the president's right-hand man. (His official title is special assistant to the president for ideas.) Feldman's boss is Ellsworth Barnes, a liberal hawk facing a tough reelection campaign in 1968. The problem for the president is simple: the American public views him as out of step with the times. Barnes's rhetoric is "cornpone," his demeanor "quaint." He may be fit to lead, but President Barnes comes across as ineffectual and lame. Feldman's most pressing task, then, is to give the president a makeover suited for the television age—one that can carry the day with America's culturally ascendant youth.

This is where the book's cover comes into play. At the party's nominating convention in Miami, the biggest news is expected to be who Barnes will select as his vice presidential running mate. Manufacturing the drama surrounding the decision, the president gathers all the candidates in the convention hotel, hoping to keep reporters both intrigued and guessing. Between a senator from Missouri, the governor of California, the mayor of New York City, and the secretaries of state and of defense—not to mention the current vice president—Barnes has his pick of establishment candidates. But the television crews aren't trained on the hotel—they're following a flotilla of sailboats in which the firebrand populist Panther Jones, "architect of Black Power," has made his own announcement on a huge banner: "Panther Jones Peace Party Candidate for President."

Feldman recognizes Jones's appeal long before the convention. The activist commands a mass following that includes students, ethnic minorities, and, most important, everyone who has grown weary of American interventionism into far-flung conflicts around the world. Indeed, more than any other aspect of his politics, Jones's strong antiwar message unites radicals, liberals, and hardnosed realists under the umbrella of peace. A composite of Martin Luther

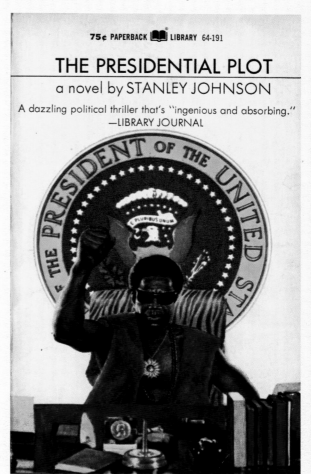

The Presidential Plot (Paperback Library, 1969)

King humanism and Huey Newton militancy, Jones, in a rally in front of the United Nations building, is egged on by his followers one minute with the chant, "Kill, Panther, kill!," only to be hailed another minute with the plea, "Sing, Panther, sing!," to which he obligingly responds by belting out "a li'l peace 'n freedom song." It is Feldman's field report on Panther Jones that President Barnes consults before making his pick for a running mate.

Needless to say, Barnes finds in Jones the perfect antidote to his perceived failings. Hip, progressive, and righteous, Jones, after some cajoling by Barnes and wrangling by the Secret Service, is brought on to the ticket as the party's vice presidential candidate. The announcement sends shockwaves throughout the convention and across the country. But the unlikely pairing proves to be a success. Ellsworth Barnes wins a second term thanks to his strategic coalition, engineered by the mild-mannered Feldman and symbolized by vice president Jones.

When the novel picks up the story with Barnes and Jones in the White House, we find the former continuing his unpopular, hawkish policies while the latter languishes in political limbo, co-opted as he is by the system. This is the point at which the real "presidential plot" kicks into gear. Feldman is approached by Willard Burns, director of the CIA, with an audacious proposal: help the agency stage a coup against Barnes so that America can finally extricate itself from the quagmire in Indochina. Feldman risks being charged with treason if he goes along with the plan. Nonetheless, he finds the opportunity irresistible, in no small part because his lover, the buxom Zenobia Russell, happens to be Burns's assistant. With Barnes's warmongering still on full display, Feldman decides to helm "Operation Topsoil."

The first part of the operation is to get the goods on Barnes's closest allies. An audacious break-in at the FBI's headquarters yields compromising information on key members of the president's cabinet. The secretaries of transportation and of the interior, as well as the attorney general, are caught using their respective offices for personal gain, while the secretary of the treasury is identified as regularly experimenting with hallucinogenic drugs—this is the sixties, after all. All four men are discreetly informed that they are to do the bidding of their blackmailer upon hearing the following sentence: "Even if the snake goes through the bamboo tube, it will come out crooked."

The second part of Topsoil is even more far out. Feldman consults with Dr. Weiner, a former advisor from his days at Princeton. Dr. Weiner describes in alarming detail what would happen if astronauts unwittingly brought contaminants (viruses, toxins, and the like) back with them from their lunar mission. He flatly states that anyone exposed to such contaminants would need to be quarantined for an indefinite period of time. This conclusion sends Feldman's head spinning. A NASA mission is just about to return to earth from the moon; if he can maneuver Barnes into a contamination scare, then he would need to be quarantined, leaving the door open for Jones to take over as commander in chief.

And so it plays out. Taking up Feldman's suggestion that he bask in the media spotlight, Barnes travels to Guam, where the astronauts have landed. There the CIA stages a contamination scare, eventuating in one astronaut's death and forcing the president to be quarantined. Over the next month or so, scientists and politicos alike play a waiting game, content to leave Barnes in his proverbial cage while tests are being run. It's all quite inconclusive, as the scientists can't figure out what caused the contamination. Little do they know that forces more powerful than they are invested in keeping Barnes right where he is.

The only person who's innocent of all this plotting is Panther Jones. He's loath to assume power, but he also recognizes the power vacuum left by Barnes's involuntary incarceration. Citing the (in reality, recently passed) Twenty-Fifth Amendment to the U.S. Constitution, which outlines the procedures for presidential succession, Jones calls the Cabinet to meet and determine whether he should assume the presidency (thereby concluding that Barnes is irrevocably indisposed). For all his adherence to procedure, Jones delivers an impassioned speech in which he declines to vote for himself. Rather than pursue naked ambition, he simply wants to "have ol' Ellsworth back," even if the tests remain inconclusive. The Cabinet looks likely to concur with this assessment until Feldman steps in and reads out loud a telegram supposedly sent from Soviet leadership. Its message: "Even if the snake goes through the bamboo tube, it will come out crooked." The blackmailed politicians reverse course and vote for Jones to become the next president of the United States.

Legitimated by his peers and still very popular with the American public, Panther Jones emerges out of the cabinet meeting a natural leader. In short order he extricates the U.S. military from Vietnam and restores the country's moral standing among Western democracies. While this geopolitical realignment is going on, the mild-mannered Feldman is content knowing he helped the CIA engineer a rather improbable revolution—a revolution of peace.

Surprisingly, this dovish novel was not written by a hippie or New Age spiritualist. Stanley Johnson was a British author and environmental activist who would later become a Conservative member of the European Parliament for Wight & Hampshire East (1979–84). He is also the father of former London mayor and current prime minister Boris Johnson. The original title of Johnson's book, when it was published in the UK in 1968, was *Panther Jones for President*. This British background to the story might help explain why *The Presidential Plot* is unusually hopeful in its outlook on American foreign policy. While the country in 1968 was in fact riven by mass protest, racial conflict, and a deeply partisan political and generational divide, Johnson could imagine a fantastical America whose geopolitical standing in the Cold War was not just salvaged but redeemed by a peace-loving Black Panther.

Kinohi Nishikawa

"My friends," Panther began softly, caressingly, "my friends, is there any one here—any soul-brother among you—who doesn't know my name, what I'm called? So you all know it, do you?" And the crowd shouted its assent. "Then say it, friends and soul-brothers, say it!"

And the crowd cried, "Panther, Panther!"

"That's right, cats. That's right. I'm the greatest panther in the jungle." And Mr. Jones jumped lithely onto the highest step of the podium. "I lead the people out of the great white wilderness, I feed them, I give them bread and manna together with the blessed Elijah Mohammed!"

"Amen, Amen," they cried. Panther held out his arms as though to bless the multitude. The sea of banners and upturned faces swayed beneath him.

"Black brothers, all my brothers," he cried. "We have come here to protest, to voice our indignity, to offer up our complaints. Today, you protest the war. But when you go back to your homes, in Chicago or Cleveland, Washington or up in Harlem, you can protest the peace as well. For this war in Vietnam, this lousy filthy war"—and here his voice reached almost a scream—"is but a symptom of all the rottenness that afflicts this country."

Hersch watched, fascinated. He had seldom seen such magnetism, such control. The civil rights movement had merged with the peace movement, or else the peace movement had merged with civil rights. But whichever way it was didn't matter. It suddenly came to him that this was a force of immense power; a force he should try to reach. The idea had, he realized, been at the back of his mind for weeks. But Panther Jones somehow had made it real.

Adolescent Homosexuality

A Novel Problem

Along with separate clothes, separate music, and a separate language, there has long been a separate literature for adolescents. It kicked off in the 1950s with a series of romantic novels, described by John Rowe Townsend as "not so much about first love as about first dating." At the same time, J.D. Salinger's *Catcher in the Rye* (1951), originally published as an adult novel, was becoming a cult among teenagers for its contemporary language, its adolescent angst, and its taboo subjects—sex, booze, and acne. Gradually the problems facing fictional teenage girls accelerated from "Who will take me to the prom?" to "How will I cope with my parents' divorce?," while simultaneously the colloquial Salinger style started to infiltrate the adolescent novel. A genre was born: the adolescent problem novel.

Authors ran riot in their search for problems. There was a standard set of problems that cropped up in book after book—parental repression, divorce, drugs, pregnancy, relationships, and alienation. Race, class, physical disability, and weight came in for their fair share of attention, while more inventive authors devoted books to the problems such as falling in love with one's stepfather. And by 1980 a handful of books had tackled the problem of homosexuality.

There were two drastic limitations inherent in the adolescent problem novel, though some books did manage to escape them. The first limitation was that, by labeling a social issue a *problem*, the author established a standard of normality in advance, without even having to explain what normality was. For example, labeling homosexuality a problem preempted any questioning about sexuality in the novel. The second limitation was that problems imply solutions, and the solutions in the adolescent problem novel were usually the problem in reverse or the problem done away with. If the problem was being overweight, the solution was losing weight; if the problem was drugs, the solution was to stop taking drugs; if the problem was homosexuality, the solution was to stop being homosexual. The result of these limitations is that it takes some detective work to figure out the actual values being expressed in the adolescent problem novels on homosexuality.

There were a number of adolescent problem novels with homosexual minor characters, but I've chosen to deal only with those books whose main characters are homosexual or have homosexual feelings. I've also limited this survey to books where the homosexuality is acknowledged to some degree, though the acknowledgement often takes the form of accusations that are then denied—that is, I don't include books about latent homosexuality or intense friendships between boys or girls. So the following books are concerned with the choice to be or not to be homosexual and with what the different authors saw as the causes and consequences of that choice. I want to start by giving an account of the individual books, first on male homosexuality and then on lesbianism, and then go on to draw some general conclusions.

Not unexpectedly, the first novel that seriously raised the issue of homosexuality within the adolescent problem novel was about male homosexuality. John Donovan's *I'll Get There. It Better Be Worth the Trip.* (1969) concerns Davy's worry and confusion over his sexual feelings for his friend Altschuler. The action in the book is more minimal than that of the "first date" novels: Davy and Altschuler kiss once, then drink whisky and fall asleep together, after which Davy goes through an agony of renunciation. A number of themes are raised which recur throughout the survey. Davy, the main character, is not really homosexual, just confused by his grandmother's death, his parents' separation, his mother's alcoholism, and his father's inability to relate to him. He is saved from his brush with homosexuality by a violent coincidence—the death of his beloved dog, while he is talking to his father about Altschuler. On the other hand, Altschuler goes on being positive about his feelings for Davy. He is sensitive, charismatic, and foreign, traits that come to identify the "real" homosexuals in these books. Donovan has much in common with the later authors in this survey: the quality that is all his own is a cautious approach to the issue of homosexuality, which leaves some episodes totally obscure. *I'll Get There...* opened the discussion of homosexuality in adolescent literature but that was about all it did.

Three years later, Lynn Hall produced a book which stands in almost total contrast to Donovan's. *Sticks and Stones* (1972) describes Tom's growing friendship with the young novelist Ward Alexander, and his growing isolation following the spread of small-town gossip about the friendship. Hall shows us the details of Tom and Ward's friendship—what they do, what they talk about, what shifts in their feelings take place. At the same time, she makes very clear the personal hurts and failings that motivate the gossipers, viewing them with compassion but not softening her account of their destructive effect on Tom. Both homosexual feelings and homosexual oppression are pictured with a complexity and absence of melodrama that are to remain unusual within the survey.

When Ward admits to Tom that he is in fact homosexual, Tom's isolation and unhappiness cause him to reject Ward, which makes him unhappier still. Melodrama erupts for a moment when Tom, taunted by his chief tormentor, crashes his car and kills his passenger, but Hill's tone of calm good sense is resumed as Tom, convalescing, realizes that he has let the gossipers get to him and decides to continue his friendship with Ward. The ending is positive, to a degree, but inevitably one asks, "If Tom is now free from public opinion, and his relationship with Ward is so good, why shouldn't they be lovers as well as friends?"

Lynn Hall asked the same question herself. In response to a letter from U.S. activist group the Gay Task Force, she wrote:

> I had begun writing the book to show the destructive potential of gossip, but by the time I got well into it, I'm afraid I lost sight of that theme. I wanted Ward and Tom to love each other, to live happily ever after, and that was the way I ended it. But the publishers would not let me do it. In their words, this was showing a homosexual relationship as a possible happy ending, and this might be dangerous to young people teetering on the brink. One editor wanted me to kill Tom in a car accident. At least I held out for a friendship at the end, one which might or might not develop into something more, depending on the reader's imagination.

I'll Get There. It Better Be Worth the Trip. (Dell, 1969)
Sticks and Stones (Dell, 1972)

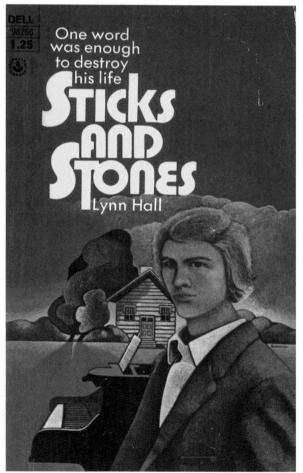

So, if authors hadn't internalized the appropriate values, those values were imposed on them. Hall's ambiguous ending remains one of the best of the era, but it is clearly less affirmative than her original ending and continues the association of homosexuality and sudden death. Hall's limitations are shown by her serious use of the phrase "happily ever after" and her idealization of Ward, another sensitive, charismatic homosexual, but one could reasonably be indignant at being deprived of an intelligently written homosexual romance.

Isabelle Holland's *The Man without a Face* (1973) firmly restored homosexuality to its problem status. Charles's mother, who has married several times, alternately smothers and rejects him. His step-sister Gloria is jealous of him, and Charles feels as if he is "drowning in women." He is coached for his escape to a boys' boarding school by Justin, a mysterious recluse injured in an accident where his boy passenger was killed; and during the coaching Justin becomes identified in Charles's mind with his father. The obtrusive sub-Freudian pointers function for Holland as "reasons" for Charles's homosexual feelings for Justin, but paradoxically they also allow her to say that Charles is not really homosexual, just nudged in that direction by his environment.

The book is melodramatic and heavy-handed to a degree impossible to capture in a brief summary. Charles is the narrator and while he is supposed to be confused, he is also supposed to be accurate about the people around him, so we are asked to believe that Gloria is a harpy, that their mother marries as a "hobby," and that Justin is a reincarnation of Mr. Rochester. Holland is a dealer in stereotypes: the one positive thing that can be said about the book is that she does allow Charles and Justin to sleep together, and this is largely negated by the fact that she proceeds to kill Justin off by a heart attack, to make sure it doesn't happen again. Her attempted liberalism is a veneer over a strong intolerance, manifested both in the Freudian explanations and the arbitrary death of Justin. And once again, the main character is not a real homosexual; the real homosexual is "different" (artistic, sensitive, charismatic, *and* older), and the relationship is ended by a violent coincidence.

Sandra Scoppettone's *Trying Hard to Hear You* (1974) returned to relationships between peers. The narrator, Camilla, talks about how she and her friends react when they discover that her boyfriend Phil and

The Man without a Face (Bantam, 1977)
Trying Hard to Hear You (Bantam, 1976)

her friend Jeff are lovers. Where Lynn Hall presented gossip as subtle and pervasive, Scoppettone goes for the sensational public response—an attempted tarring and feathering of the two boys and a "test of manhood" for Phil where he crashes his car and kills himself and the girl involved. This overstatement of the case distances the book from most readers' experience, while the forces of reason are represented by theoretical pronouncements about the normality of homosexuality from some handy experts, which seems quite remote from the destruction and death in the narrative.

Scoppettone is making a gallant try for ideological soundness, but her theory is not integrated into her plot. By choosing Camilla as narrator, she cuts us off from seeing Jeff and Phil's relationship in progress, and despite her insistence on the normality and potential good of homosexuality, she also equips Jeff with the standard possessive mother and distant father, negating the question of choice in advance. The formula remains unchanged. And the style, veering between melodrama and cute chattiness, keeps the issues determinedly simple.

Eleanor Spence's *A Candle for St. Antony* (1977) is another homosexual romance, but Spence internalized what was imposed on Lynn Hall. Australian Justin and Austrian Rudi progress from the regulation hate at first sight, through an ever-closer friendship, to an idyllic school holiday in Vienna, where Rudi makes a declaration of love and suggests that they stay abroad. But an envious classmate accuses Rudi of being homosexual, and when Justin admits he will return to Australia, Rudi runs away. It is a story of ill-fated love, although the ill fate is in fact only Rudi's arbitrary and unexplained insistence that they must stay in Vienna.

The book is further complicated by Spence's insistence, via Rudi, that "It wasn't *like* that." Spence clearly feels she is doing her characters a favor by denying the label "homosexual" to all this love, closeness, and sensuality between two boys, but it is impossible to work out from the book what her own definition of homosexuality would be. Presumably she was basing some kind of case on the fact that Rudi and Justin are talking about love, rather than sex, although one doubts that she would deny the heterosexuality of a character on the same grounds.

Foreign, poor, hardworking, gifted, sensitive, "angular and sardonic," with a "sudden radiant smile," Rudi is the most extreme example in this survey of the homosexual as superior being—just as removed from

everyday life by his superiority as he might be by any inferiority. Clearly, ordinary Justin could not have been charmed from the path of heterosexuality by anything less, and we can hardly blame him for failing to live up to these high standards and for returning to Australia and Rudi's pretty sister. Spence offers a pleasant romance and shows a liberal concern about the ways in which Rudi and Justin are oppressed by their schoolmates' sneers, but her willful refusal to recognize that she is writing about a homosexual relationship turns her liberal concern into the regulation dictatorship.

The only book about male homosexuality to break the basic pattern established in *I'll Get There*... during the 1970s was David Rees's *In the Tent* (1979). Stranded on a camping holiday, Tim, Aaron, John, and Ray draw closer to each other, and in consequence Tim's homosexuality becomes acknowledged and accepted by the group. While his beloved Aaron makes it clear that he is heterosexual, Tim ends up sleeping with Ray, although they decide not to fall in love. After they are rescued, Ray decides to come out to his parents, and the two boys go to a gay bar and are impressed by its ordinariness.

The events of this book are much closer to the general run of coming out stories than are the car crashes and tarrings and featherings of the previous books. Unfortunately, Rees chose to parallel Tim's story with flashes of a Royalist boy in the English Civil War who has Roundhead sympathies. Besides being obscurely written, the historical scenes add nothing to our understanding of Tim's situation. To my mind, they represent nothing more than an attempt to make the homosexual material respectable. And while Tim's much-stressed refusal to fall in love with Ray may be ideologically sound, his hopeless crush on Aaron thereby comes across as more exciting, and the book ends on a gray note, leaving us to wonder whether Tim is a victim of fear of success.

Like Scoppettone, Rees is trying hard, but the early accounts of Tim's tormented (and somewhat too clearly expressed) musings on homosexuality are presented with more power than his eventual acceptance, which consequently seems more like a letdown than liberation. Nonetheless, Rees's novel rejects the stereotypes of the real homosexual and the not really homosexual; it doesn't solve the problem of homosexuality by a violent crisis, usually involving death; and it presents Tim and Ray as arriving at the decision to identify as homosexual by different paths, thus dispelling the

Freudianisms. The only one of the earlier stereotypes perpetuated by Rees is the link between homosexuality and foreignness: Ray is Spanish-English and in consequence is sexually freer than Tim, although he is also shown as more closeted.

The statement that emerges from these novels as a group is a reasonably familiar one for the era, though with some unusual emphases. The compelling attraction of homosexuality is presented with particular force through Altschuler, Ward, Justin, and Rudi, all gifted, charismatic, and real homosexuals. Having created this attractive picture, the authors then turn and combat it with the threat of ostracism, but in the end they are forced to introduce unlikely and melodramatic catastrophes to bring the relationships to an arbitrary halt. Once the relationship is halted, the main character is generally presented with the "going through a phase" theory, by a handy adult or by strong implication. The process is completely illogical. None of the standard arguments then offered in everyday life appear here—"You'll be lonely," "The gay world is shallow and brittle," "You can't have children," "You'll be an outsider." Instead, and for the purposes of propaganda more effectively, the attraction of homosexuality is admitted, and then countered by a bland assumption that *of course* it can't continue.

This assumption carries over to the series of novels about lesbianism, which begins with a trio of novels that only recognize lesbianism as emotional, not as sexual. Madeleine L'Engle's *Prelude*, published as an adult novel in 1945 and republished as an adolescent novel in 1968, predated *I'll Get There...* but the lesbianism in L'Engle's book passed without comment. The book traces the development of a young pianist, Katherine, who becomes deeply involved with another girl, Sarah, when she is sent to boarding school after her mother's death. One evening Katherine cries out her misery about her mother on Sarah's shoulder, and when they are discovered, the conservative forces in the school work to break up the friendship.

The intense feelings between the two girls make it hard to believe, as L'Engle asks us to, that Sarah gives in at once to the headmistress's demands, and that Katherine accepts this with relative calm. We are offered the red herring of identifying with Katherine's indignation against a conservative world, to stop us from going into the implications of Katherine's and Sarah's feelings for each other. L'Engle's spare objective style in fact outlines the familiar Freudian progression.

Sarah consoles Katherine for the loss of her mother and Justin, the piano teacher, consoles her for the loss of Sarah. At the end of the book, in what is to become a familiar image, Katherine sits at a window and watches Sarah walking away. She has successfully passed through a phase.

Alice Rogers, of Alice Bach's *They'll Never Make a Movie Starring Me* (1973), is more aware that what she feels is lesbianism, although the word itself is never used. Indeed the whole novel is taken up with her endless worrying about her feelings for Wendy, an older student at her new boarding school. Still, the novel has a strangely unfocused quality: Wendy is very sketchily drawn, her extreme conventionality being her only defining feature, and Bach gives no sensual dimension to Alice's response to Wendy, which makes her obsession hard to understand and creates a very claustrophobic atmosphere. Finally, when Wendy drops Alice because she has been involved in a few minor rule-breakings, Alice becomes disillusioned with her and, coincidentally landing a double date with a friend, decides that her phase is over. The novel ends with Alice saying her farewells to Wendy, although this time we don't have the image of Wendy walking away.

Winifred Madison in *Bird on the Wing* (1974), rather than relying on the phase theory, uses the same evasion tactic as Eleanor Spence, allowing herself to describe a passionate romance between two people of the same sex by denying that this is homosexuality. Her heroine Elizabeth runs away from home and meets the foreign, gifted, charismatic weaver Maija. She becomes Maija's apprentice and they live an idyllic life together, full of mutual expressions of warmth and commitment. When Elizabeth meets Eric, who wants her to go away with him, Maija blanches but heroically allows it, whereupon, of course, Elizabeth no longer wants to. Eric calls them dykes and Maija replies, with the same grand lack of argument as Spence's Rudi, "You're all wrong."

Although the two women are tearfully reunited, within pages Maija has been attacked and killed by muggers, Madison's agents summoned to rescue her from the inevitable dilemma. There is no question within the novel that Eric, or any man, is superior to Maija, but equally there is no question that Elizabeth and Maija can admit a sexual dimension into a relationship that is otherwise far more compelling than their interludes with men. So enjoyment of the romance has a kickback: once the word "dyke" has been

A Candle for Saint Antony (Oxford University Press, 1977)
They'll Never Make a Movie Starring Me (Dell, 1973)
Hey, Dollface (Hamish Hamilton, 1979)
Happy Endings Are All Alike (Dell, 1979)

uttered, Maija has to die. It is some compensation that Elizabeth finishes Maija's last weaving and, though she returns home, will obviously become a weaver herself. But once again we have a strong denial by the author of strongly presented lesbian feelings.

Rosa Guy's *Ruby* (1976) broke the problem-novel mold. It was not about lesbianism, but about the relationship between Ruby and Daphne, which is to say that Guy was not primarily concerned with social attitudes toward homosexuality, as were all the other authors in this survey, but with lesbian feelings, and between two specific individuals. Ruby, mainly preoccupied by the desire to love and be needed, finds no outlet for her feelings with her autocratic West Indian father Calvin or her cool sister Phyllisia. So she throws herself into her relationship with Daphne, a strong-minded and impetuous young woman who is determined that her options won't be limited by the fact that she is black. Their sexual attraction is strongly presented, though the book is as much about the clash and interaction between their views of the world.

Ruby is a powerfully written and complex book, head and shoulders above any other in the survey, and consequently Ruby, Daphne, and their relationship are made far more real and vivid. We see their relationship in a number of different stages: first love, a period of separation, reunion, and an attempt to work on their differences. Finally Daphne ends it, because Ruby's refusal to defy Calvin's prohibitions has put Daphne into situations that compromise her need for dignity. Guy doesn't ignore the question of social hostility toward lesbians but she also makes it clear that the only thing that can end the relationship is a decision by Ruby or Daphne themselves.

The *Interracial Books for Children Bulletin* criticized Guy for presenting Daphne as "masculine" and a real lesbian, and Ruby as "feminine" and therefore basically straight. These stereotypes seem to me to be imposed by the criticism, rather than created by Guy, but Ruby's sudden turning to an ex-boyfriend at the end of the book is still disturbing. Certainly, Ruby is presented as someone who needs love so urgently that it deprives her of Daphne's firm consistency; and certainly we can't judge books solely on the grounds of where their characters rate on the Kinsey scale in the final chapter. But Ruby's feelings for Daphne follow her feelings for her father in a diagrammatic fashion that is not in evidence anywhere else in the book. Her initial feelings for Daphne are accelerated, though not

created, by her father's rejection of her, and she turns to her old boyfriend Orlando after getting a renewed sense of Calvin's love when he stops her from killing herself after Daphne's rejection. So the book is marred to some degree by the imposition of oversimplified psychological theorizing.

Deborah Hautzig's *Hey, Dollface* (1978), in contrast to *Ruby*, is a typical adolescent problem novel. The book is about Val's struggle to name her feelings for her friend Chloe, whom she likes and laughs with but also fantasizes about touching. Val's mother says she knows happy homosexuals, and her teacher says that homosexual feelings are normal, but neither is quite prepared to say that homosexuality is natural. Then, when Val accidentally touches Chloe's breast while comforting her about her father's death, the two girls at first withdraw from each other, then talk about the situation together.

Chloe is the stereotypic unconventional "zany" throughout the book but in their final talk she unconditionally rejects the possibility that she and Val could have a sexual relationship. Because neither Chloe nor Val is very strongly characterized, it is impossible to say categorically that the denial is out of character for Chloe but it certainly is surprising—although it is also part of a pattern in these books that the heroine's beloved will let the heroine down. Val herself is prepared to accept her feelings for Chloe but not the label "lesbian." So, though the book has an air of honest endeavor, it ends in as much confusion as it began. It ends with Val at a window watching Chloe walk away, as *Ruby* ended with Ruby's memory of Daphne walking away.

Sandra Scoppettone's *Happy Endings Are All Alike* (1978) was the first of the adolescent novels about lesbianism to end without a farewell. Superficially, the book was a gay liberation dream. Jaret and Peggy are involved in a sexual and loving relationship as the book opens. Jaret is courageous in defense of the rightness of her feelings, while Peggy's remaining doubts add the necessary conflict. Their family and friends make honest attempts to understand, and Jaret uncompromisingly pushes them toward further understanding. Both Jaret and Scoppettone in her authorial comments are strong on ideology—but as a result the book hovers uneasily on a borderline between fiction and a political pamphlet. Scoppettone uses the same one-dimensional characters, melodramatic events, and rampant rhetoric to show that homosexuality is a free and valid choice, as Isabelle Holland did to show that homosexuality was a phase. Scoppettone's readers didn't get a chance to see the complexities of their everyday life mirrored in statements like: "It didn't matter that they felt right about their love; *Claire represented society* and her constant put-downs had an undermining effect" (my italics).

It is also strange that, in a book that was clearly aiming to give a positive view of lesbianism, the most passionately written section should be the one where Jaret is raped by a boy who resents her freedom and her lesbianism. The rape appears to have no long-term consequences—Jaret insists on prosecuting; Peggy is scared away by the publicity but comes back eventually—but we are left with the sobering impression that the more you stand out against society, the harder you will get hit. In the context of feeling compelled to describe the rape of her strong confident lesbian, Scoppettone's vehement ideological statements start to look more like whistling in the dark than they did at first. Still, at least she was whistling . . .

Apart from *Bird on the Wing*, which follows the charisma and catastrophe pattern of the male homosexual novels, the lesbian novels gave a very different view of homosexuality. This time the main characters are the real lesbians, constantly betrayed by the women they love—even Peggy lets Jaret down on a number of occasions, although their relationship is at least still workable by the end of the novel. The message, heavily influenced by Radclyffe Hall's *The Well of Loneliness*, was that lesbians were doomed to loneliness because "ordinary women" will never match the quality of their feelings—hence the recurring image of the other woman walking away or being farewelled by the main character. The only escape from isolation was to accept the phase theory, Scoppettone's book being the only exception.

By 1980 there was still no novel for adolescents that was completely comfortable about homosexuality. Only *In the Tent* and *Happy Endings Are All Alike* showed the homosexual relationship still existing at the end of the novel, and they covertly accepted homosexuality as a problem, in Rees's stress on Tim's unfulfilled love for Aaron and Scoppettone's concentration on Jaret's rape. Only *Sticks and Stones* and *Ruby* showed strong, complex, and attractive homosexual relationships that rose above social disapproval, and they both ended with a cop-out. And the other novels were remarkable for their palmed cards and loaded

dice. There were no logical reasons why all the boys should be checked by melodramatic accidents, or why all the girls should fall in love with girls who let them down; nor did these literary incidents prove anything about homosexuality itself, except that their authors are prepared to go all out to sabotage it.

The propaganda of these books was very aptly pitched at adolescents questioning their sexuality. To show homosexuality as totally unattractive would have invited disbelief, so the authors first offered the charismatic beloveds of the male homosexual books and the powerful feelings of the lesbian novels, before using coincidence or letdowns to say, "However, it's not possible," and rounding off the exercise with the spurious consolation, "It's only a phase." The vagueness and illogicality surrounding the failure of the homosexual relationship was in itself an effective propaganda tactic, carrying with it a sense of inevitability and fatalism. Indeed, too much logic about homosexuality would have implied that it was also possible to talk logically about heterosexuality—a concept never even raised in these books, where the opposite to "homosexual" was "normal."

Jenny Pausacker

Author's note: This article was originally published in *Gay Information* (no. 6, Winter 1981). I'd been reading all the American Young Adult novels with LGBQ main characters that I could find, and I had a lot of criticisms of them, which I sorted out by writing them down. These days I'd place more emphasis on the writers' courage in taking on a taboo subject, but at the time I was clearly summoning my own courage: my biographical note at the end of the original article said, "Jenny Pausacker reads, writes and teaches children's literature and really ought to get around to writing an adolescent novel about lesbians," as indeed I did.

Sons of Darkness, Sons of Light, John A. Williams
(Eyre & Spottiswoode, 1970)

Sons of Darkness, Sons of Light (Penguin, 1973)

According to Jerry H. Bryant in *Victims and Heroes: Racial Violence in the African American Novel*, (1997) "It was virtually impossible for any African American novelist writing in the years between 1967 and 1977 to ignore the well-publicized proclamations of first the Black Power advocates and then the cultural nationalists." John A. Williams's *Sons of Darkness, Sons of Light*, which first appeared in 1969, is one such literary attempt to deal with the Black Power movement and the issues it threw up.

Gene Browning is a former university political science lecturer now working at a New York–based nongovernmental organization, Institute of Racial Justice (IRJ). Like many civil rights activists post the April 1968 assassination of Martin Luther King,

Browning feels ground down by the pervasive and seemingly unassailable extent of white racism.

The latest example involves a case of white policeman charged with the shooting death of a sixteen-year-old African American boy. The killing, and the sure knowledge that the assailant Carrigan will escape punishment for the crime, rob Browning of any last remaining vestiges of faith in mainstream methods of trying to improve the situation of African Americans, such as peaceful demonstrations, using courts, and voter registration. "You could work in a famous and vigorous civil rights organization in charge of the college programs as the number two man," thinks Browning. "You could work with all your heart and what was left of your soul, but you also had to know, finally, that none of that was going to do any good."

Browning's solution is to pay an old Sicilian, referred to as "the Don," $1,500 to have Carrigan killed. Browning hopes to alert black America to the futility of legal struggles against racism and to serve notice on white America that it is no longer acceptable to murder blacks with impunity. He also hopes it will head off the sort of unorganized ghetto revolts in which, he believes, only blacks suffer.

The Don farms the job out to a shadowy Zionist called Itzhak Hod. A Russian Jew whose family fled the Warsaw Ghetto for Palestine, Hod killed Arabs for the new Jewish state and then hunted Nazis. He wants to return to Israel with his young bride-to-be and needs the money.

The book is told from multiple points of view, mainly that of Browning but also those of the Don and Hod, which gives Williams a vehicle to examine the latter two men's experiences of political violence. Browning develops a strange friendship with the Don who had to flee his home country as a boy and whose own experiences of prejudice at the hands of white America makes him sympathetic to the situation of African Americans.

The book also explores the perspectives of two black revolutionaries, Trotman and Greene, who, unknown to Browning and unrelated to anything he has set in motion, are part of revolutionary cell that intends to mark the upcoming Labor Day weekend holiday by blowing up a number of bridges and tunnels connecting Manhattan and holding the island to ransom.

Among their demands to the U.S. government are the immediate resignation of every senator and congressman from any state in which African Americans do not have full enfranchisement, the allocation of land to every black family that needs it, the withdrawal of U.S. forces from the war in Vietnam, and U.S. disinvestment from South Africa, Mozambique, Angola, and Rhodesia.

Williams also gives us a brief glimpse into the inner thoughts of Carrigan. The policeman is an aging racist who believes that "behind the so-called 'Negro Revolution' lay the spectre of communism." He has a long history of excessive force violations and is dissatisfied with his career and his wife, who he is cheating on with a single woman he met at a crime scene in Manhattan. Carrigan is suspended as a result of the shooting, but he's completely confident he'll walk away from any murder charge. "Every man on the force would turn in his badge if he were found guilty, and City Hall knew it," he thinks at one point. "The suspension was just to make it look good."

Hod kills Carrigan as the cop leaves his mistress's apartment. The resulting police investigation identifies Greene as the main suspect. Meanwhile, gangs of off-duty cops and "white toughs" start to invade black sections of major cities across the country. The black citizens resist, which only makes the whites come in greater numbers, leading to fiercer resistance and open warfare in some neighborhoods such as Harlem. Black snipers invade white neighborhoods and kill police. The death tolls on both sides mount.

Sons of Darkness, Sons of Light ends with Browning listening to the reports of mounting violence, including news of the destruction of bridges and tunnels to Manhattan and the announcement of Greene's demands, on a radio at the beachside house where he and his wife and two daughters are spending the Labor Day weekend.

In contrast to Trotman and Greene, hardcore black revolutionaries committed to overthrowing the U.S. government, Browne's politics are less well defined. He arrives at the decision to pay to have Carrigan killed with trepidation and out of sheer desperation that nothing else seems to work. Otherwise his views are moderate. A member of New York's rising black middle class, in some respects he looks down on the very people he so passionately wants to help, an attitude skewered by his eldest daughter, Nora: "Daddy, you're always talking about brothers and sisters and

Greene was remembering back to the time of the first sit-ins in 1960, remembering meetings in middle-class black apartments, with people shuffling back and forth to the telephones to talk to the students down South; he was remembering the Freedom Rides and the burned-out buses, the beatings; remembering the Martin King marches, the SNCC voter registration drives in the Deep South, and the plunging fear and disintegration that had come after the murders of Goodman, Chaney and Schwerner [three young civil rights workers abducted and murdered by members of the White Knights of the Ku Klux Klan in Mississippi in June 1964]. Remembering all the years, the false starts, the false hopes, all the waiting, all the killing, and now it was 1973, and game-time was over. It had to be over.

you know darn well that half these brothers and sisters you're talking about, you wouldn't even let in our home."

He is also deeply uncomfortable about the fact Nora is sexually active and her boyfriend is white. Earlier in the book, his boss at the IRJ assigns him the job of traveling around the country to get money off wealthy black sympathizers. These include a Las Vegas showman and movie star, Gary Drake. Drake gives Browning a companion for the night, a groupie, Maya, who he sleeps with. This doesn't make Browning any more sensitive to his own wife when she cheats on him later in the book.

The author of *Sons of Darkness, Sons of Light* was born in Jackson, Mississippi, but raised in Syracuse, New York, where he was schooled with white children. According to Bryant, "He made the mistake early on of thinking they all had the same relationship to America and to each other." He soon discovered this was not the case. "One of Williams's main convictions is that African Americans must, in order to survive, acknowledge the full truth of their place in the white scheme of things, and understand with absolute clarity the true nature of white prejudice." Williams went to university after serving in the navy in World War II and onto a literary career that included twelve novels and a number of nonfiction titles.

Williams achieved a measure of international recognition with his 1967 book, *The Man Who Cried I Am*. The main protagonist, a black writer, Max Reddick, uncovers a plot by Western nations to prevent Africa from taking charge of its own destiny and, in particular, the profits of its abundant natural resources. The American arm of this alliance forms a sinister plan, code-named the "King Alfred Plan," that calls for law enforcement officials to imprison the leaders of all prominent black organizations and for their possible extermination in high-volume, potentially nuclear-powered, incinerators.

Reddick makes a political decision to make the plan public before being killed, ironically by two black CIA agents. He made the decision, despite realizing it will cause a civil war, because, similar to Browning, he feels blacks have exhausted every avenue of potential change and have no option left but violence.

Some in the black community have cited the King Alfred Plan as fact. According to journalist Herb Boyd, to promote his book Williams photocopied excerpts dealing with the plan and left them on subway seats in New York City, leading many readers to believe the plan was real. Poet and musician Gil Scott-Heron recorded a song titled "The King Alfred Plan" for his 1972 album *Free Will* that warned of the plan. Jim Jones, leader of the People's Temple cult, discussed the plan in detail in various recorded speeches in the U.S. and the Jonestown settlement in Guyana, treating it as legitimate, and references to it can be found on the internet, including so-called portions of the plan.

Andrew Nette

Sons of Darkness, Sons of Light (Eyre & Spottiswoode, 1970)

"Up Against the Wall, Motherfucker!"
The Yippie Literaries

CAN A NICE, LIBERAL, MIDDLE-CLASS GIRL FROM QUEENS FIND HAPPINESS IN THE AGITATION, PROCLAMATION, CONFRONTATION, DENOTATION AND LIBERATION OF A STONE-FREAK REVOLUTIONARY WORLD?

That's the tough question posed on the dust jacket to the first edition of *Trashing*, Ann Fettamen's tale of a young woman who becomes immersed in New York's wild and weird countercultural scene of the late 1960s. Originally published in hardback by Straight Arrow Books in 1970, *Trashing* chronicles the adventures of heroine Ann as she falls for Danny—a hip, young mover-and-shaker in the local underground—and becomes immersed in the way-out world of hippie activism and radical mischief. As the dust jacket enthuses:

> The scenario runs from our heroine's first LSD trip and hippy wedding in Central Park to rape, orgy, stealing, and street-fighting: the pranks from Halloween smoke-ins to bombings! In short, folks it's what you've been dying to know: the genuine first-hand stuff on what's going on backstage in the underground—funny, sexy, tough, candid all told in an unadorned up-front style . . . but with the immediacy and sensation of today's revolutionary anti-culture as never so shockingly revealed.

And to guarantee the tale was bursting with no-holds-barred disclosures from a clued-up insider, the dust jacket proudly boasted that "Ann Fettamen" was actually "the carefully-guarded pseudonym of a well-known Yippie troublemaker."

The author was, indeed, "a well-known Yippie troublemaker." "Ann Fettamen" was a pen name used by the writer and political activist Anita Hoffman who, with her husband—the countercultural icon Abbie Hoffman—established the Youth International Party, or "Yippies" in 1967. The Yippies emerged among the kaleidoscope of factions, protest movements, and radical sects that proliferated in America during the late 1960s and early '70s. New York's Lower East side, in particular,

was a hothouse for a plethora of anarchist-inflected groups who eschewed the strategies of the old-school Left in favor of antiauthoritarianism, direct action, and the use of theatrical pranks as political weapons that could ridicule and undermine the status quo. An early entry was Up Against the Wall Motherfucker (sometimes known as simply "The Motherfuckers"), a group spawned in 1966 from a fusion of a Dada-influenced art group called Black Mask with elements of the anti–Vietnam War movement. Their name taken from a poem by Amiri Baraka, Up Against the Wall Motherfucker were trailblazers of New York's countercultural underground, fermenting protest and deliberately courting confrontation. The Yippies were cut from the same colorful cloth, scorning traditional politics as a "brain disease" and promoting hippie culture as a way of turning on and transforming conventional society.

Formed by Abbie and Anita Hoffman, along with Jerry Rubin, Nancy Kurshan, and Paul Krassner, the Yippies were pioneers of mass media manipulation and were adept at using politically themed pranks to enthrall the press and TV. In 1967, for instance an antiwar demonstration saw the Yippies organize a "mass exorcism" of the Pentagon. The same year saw Abbie Hoffman, together with a band of Yippie funsters, infiltrate a tour of the New York Stock Exchange and throw fistfuls of dollar bills from the visitors' gallery onto the trading floor, sending stockbrokers scurrying to grab the money. In 1968, the Yippies nominated a 145-pound pig, "Pigasus the Immortal," as a candidate for president, and in 1969 Abbie Hoffman and Jerry Rubin made a mockery of the "Chicago Eight" conspiracy trial. Accused with fellow radical leaders of inciting a riot at the 1968 Democratic National Convention in Chicago, Hoffman and Rubin used the proceedings as a platform for Yippie antics. At one stage the pair arrived at court dressed in judicial robes and, on being told to remove them, the duo cheerfully complied—only to reveal Chicago police uniforms underneath.

The Yippies used a battery of media ventures to spread the word of revolt. In 1971, for example, Abbie

Hoffman and Al Bell launched the first newsletter for communications hackers, *The Youth International Party Line* (YIPL); while Dana Beal founded a Yippie newspaper, the *Yipster Times,* in New York in 1972. Abbie Hoffman and Jerry Rubin also became popular public speakers, instigating militant hijinks wherever they appeared. Their literary output too was prolific. In 1968, for instance, Hoffman's *Revolution for the Hell of It* was a collection of essays on the state of the hippie scene and the antiwar movement, while 1969's *Woodstock Nation* was his account of that year's Woodstock Music and Arts Festival. And in 1971's *Steal This Book*, Hoffman provided budding radicals with illicit tips on how to live outside, and fight against, America's "Pig Empire." Rejected by thirty publishers, *Steal This Book* sold more than a quarter of a million copies after Hoffman resorted to setting up his own publishing company.

Rubin also made his literary mark. The flamboyant provocateur laid out his antiestablishment agenda in 1970's *DO IT! Scenarios of the Revolution,* with an introduction by Black Panther leader Eldridge Cleaver. And in 1971's *We Are Everywhere*, written while locked up in Cook County Jail, Rubin gave his account of the Chicago Eight trial, together with his views on a spectrum of simmering revolutionary groups.

But, along with the political tracts and the seditious musings, several countercultural scenesters also penned a small canon of pulp-esque fiction which, like Anita Hoffman's *Trashing*, is testimony not only to the radical aspirations of the period but also to the imagination and creativity of the 1960s underground.

★

The countercultural turbulence of the late 1960s and early 1970s engendered a welter of juicy pulps that cashed in on the radical groove. "Factual" accounts like Burton Wolfe's *The Hippies* (1968), for instance, offered the uninitiated "a hard but sympathetic look at the Hippie scene and a (duly spiced up) profile of the widespread psychosis induced by mind-blowing drugs." The Age of Aquarius also inspired a collection of seedy fiction that tempted readers with paperback fantasies of sex and drugs among the Flower Children. Joseph Mathewson's *The Love Tribe* (1968), for example, concocted a tale of freak-outs and love-ins set in New York's East Village, where the "drop-outs from an adult world . . . blow their minds on acid and meth . . . always live in revolt—and sometimes die by violence."

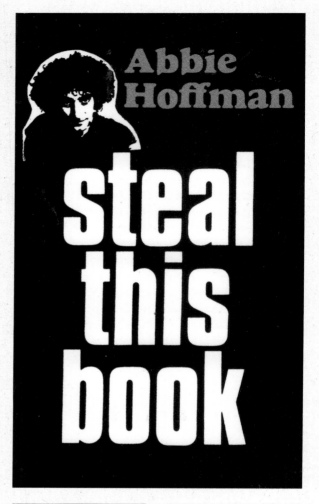

Steal This Book (Pirate Editions, 1971)
The Love Tribe (Signet, 1968)
The Hippies (Signet, 1968)

And *Psychedelic Sex* (1968), credited to Ralph Benton, enticed readers with a vision of countercultural carnality run amok ("Attila was a sex crazed demi-God who showed no mercy to his female sex slaves"). Dominated by wildly imagined exercises in exploitation, the genre contained little produced by anyone intimately aquatinted with the scene. An exception was Marge Piercy's *Dance the Eagle to Sleep* (1970).

Piercy would later find fame as an award-winning poet and writer, with novels including best sellers like *Woman on the Edge of Time* (1976), *Braided Lives* (1982), and *Gone to Soldiers* (1988) as well as a critically acclaimed memoir, *Sleeping with Cats* (2002). But during the late 1960s Piercy was a committed activist in many of the progressive political battles of the day, serving as an organizer in Students for a Democratic Society (SDS) and leading protests against the Vietnam War. She was also a key player in the burgeoning feminist movement, and her widely circulated essay "The Grand Coolie Damn" sent out shockwaves with its angry exposé of the American Left's endemic sexism. *Dance the Eagle to Sleep*, Piercy's second novel, drew on her experiences among the hippies and radicals of the Lower East Side and, although the narrative is set in a dystopian America of the near future, it stands as an intriguing "period piece" that chronicles the ideals, myths, and conflicts of the late 1960s radical scene.

Dance the Eagle to Sleep is set in a magnified, more intense version of the Nixon era. It is a world of surveillance, suppression, and social conditioning, where the state conscripts young people at nineteen and channels them into lives of compliance and conformity. But amid the suffocating system of oppression bubbles a rebellious youth revolt, and the book follows the lives of four young insurgents—Shawn, Corey, Billy, and Joanna—as they challenge the authoritarian government and struggle to build a visionary new society.

Shawn is the eighteen-year-old frontman for The Coming Thing, a trendy rock band who wow teen audiences with their hugely commercial, and unintentionally hilarious, hits and lyrics ("My front gets cold, I might come down with flu / Don't want no electric blanket, all I want is bed!"). Shawn is at the top of his game but has become jaded with being one of the "organ-grinder's monkeys." Disillusioned, he winds up living rough in New York, but has a rude awakening when the police knock him around. Looking for greater fulfilment, the disaffected celebrity drops out, resolving to play nothing but free festivals for "the kids."

After one of his concerts is brutally trashed by the cops, he hooks up with the other young protagonists.

Foremost is Corey, a Native American dope dealer. A born leader and a veteran of defiant high school occupations, he is angry at his people's history of being tricked and exploited by the white man. Billy, meanwhile, is a twitchy, bespectacled scholar who has racked up science prizes by the cupboardful but is intoxicated by the thrill of revolt. And lanky, redheaded Joanna is a runaway from an army family who "survives on pot and sex" until she finds a sense of purpose with the rebellion.

Setting up a commune in the Lower East Side, the group begin organizing a nationwide movement of dissidents, known as "the Indians," with the aim of creating "a new nation of the young and the free." The commune is an ideal of the 1960s hippie scene. A daily council allows members to voice their thoughts and opinions, and share in peyote-fueled consciousness raising; while a raunchy update of the traditional Native American Ghost Dance serves as an avenue for "a better understanding of decisions," a way the group can "dance out any ruptures or quarrels, and another way of being together, of expressing the tribe and each other":

> A girl was spinning in trance, spinning, spinning till she fell and lay on the floor, and another girl squatted to take care of her and eventually to lead her to resume a place in the outer circle. Sometimes after they had danced, people would dress again, but often they did not—especially if they had painted their bodies with care. The music pounded on. Bodies expressed the music's rhythms and their own.

Sex is also free and easy. And, despite Piercy's polished prose, there is a distinctly pulpy feel to the steamy sex scenes that punctuate the storyline:

> Then more shameless than before, she bent and unzipped his pants and took his penis into her mouth. Slowly he swelled into her mouth. Then stirring himself gently, he undressed her and laid her on her back, knelt between her thighs and pushed himself . . . into her. Then moaning he gathered her up against him and began, and in a moment she began writhing and calling out.

Despite these distractions the group still find time to organize and recruit. Above all, it's the young

generation that the Indians see as society's salvation. As Shawn, the group's arch-sloganeer explains:

> We have to start over. We have to start while there are still human people left. Kids have a chance. We aren't mortgaged yet. We have to get all the kids out who are still alive and keep them alive. People who still have eyes will pick up on the way to live. The others can go on trying to make their crazy machine work on each other. But the young won't go into their system to be ground to hamburger any more, and gradually it will slow down and come to a halt. And people will walk away and learn to live again.

The elevation of youth as an untainted force that can transform a corrupt and authoritarian society is clearly analogous with sixties radical rhetoric. The counterculture's romantic take on "back-to-the-land" authenticity is also mirrored by the Indians' decision to relocate to a communal farm in New Jersey. But while they settle into a life of bucolic self-sufficiency, the group continue agitating for revolt. Clashes over strategy, however, soon surface. No doubt drawing on her own experience with SDS, the author paints a vivid picture of the movement's struggles to maintain coherence and solidarity, together with the schisms between those who seek to opt out of the system and those set on a more confrontational path.

Other frictions also parallel those faced by the sixties counterculture. Commercial co-option threatens to leach militant energy, the radicals despairing over "kids who thought they were Indians tricked out in costumes from the local Bizarre Bazaar of their town's fattest department store." The Indians also heap scorn on a group of affluent hippies who embrace only the hedonism of an alternative lifestyle. They are, the author observes, "the children of abundance turning plastic plenty into waste" who lack meaningful commitment to change. And Piercy's own critique of the chauvinism and gender inequalities in the counterculture also surfaces:

> Whatever the rhetoric, in tribe after tribe women mostly ended up running the kitchen, taking care of housework and babies, running the mimeograph machine, serving as bodies in demonstrations they had not planned or directed, serving as runners carrying messages or equipment of whose purpose they were often

Dance the Eagle to Sleep (Coronet, 1970)
Dance the Eagle to Sleep (Doubleday, 1970)
Dance the Eagle to Sleep (Fawcett, 1971)

kept ignorant, doing all the tedious daily tasks that made tribal life possible.

The mounting political tensions of the late 1960s are also reflected in the sense of foreboding that pervades *Dance the Eagle to Sleep*. By 1969 the revolutionary hopes of 1968 were ebbing. As the optimism of Woodstock gave way to the despair of Altamont, movements for progressive change faced greater repression and violence, and they began responding in kind. In 1970—the year Piercy's novel was published—the Vietnam War escalated as President Nixon rolled U.S. forces into Cambodia. At home, meanwhile, the Ohio National Guard opened fire on unarmed college students protesting against the war, killing four and wounding nine. And in the same year the Weather Underground Organization (a splinter group from SDS) issued a "Declaration of a State of War" against the U.S. government, launching a bombing campaign against federal buildings and banks. Taking these events as inspiration, Piercy's novel magnifies them a hundredfold.

As the influence of the Indians grows, the state crackdown becomes more violent and vindictive, provoking an angry call-to-arms from the radicals' leaders: "Call out the high schools! Call out the tribes! Into the streets and onto the housetops. This is our city. The streets belong to the people. Let's take them!"

Mass protests through the streets of Lower Manhattan explode into violent confrontation. Echoing the police riot that tore through Chicago's Grant Park during the 1968 Democratic Convention, the cops are indiscriminate: ". . . arresting any kid who looked to them like a demonstrator—or a kid. Any long-hair. Pulling them off the streets and working them over in the cars and beating them in relays in the station houses."

Fighting back, the Indians trade in bricks and bottles for Molotov cocktails, rifles, and shotguns. As civil war erupts throughout the Lower East Side, machine guns and mortars are brought in for more serious support, together with half-tracks and armored trucks bought (somewhat improbably) from surplus stores. Days of house-to-house fighting follow, but the Indians' situation is hopeless. As the government brings in artillery and tanks, the uprising is mercilessly crushed, and the heroic Indians are blown to pieces by withering shellfire. Despite concluding with a sense of world-weary defeat, however, *Dance the Eagle to Sleep*

still leaves readers a kernel of hope. Hiding out in the Catskill Mountains, remnants of the Indians live off the land, evading the security forces' dragnet. And the birth of a baby among the routed rebels gives hope for the future. A small promise of new possibilities, new beginnings.

★

Piercy's *Dance the Eagle to Sleep* drew inspiration from the rise, fragmentation, and fall of SDS. But other countercultural insiders found influence in the wider timbre of the times. The growing social and political paranoia of the late 1960s and early '70s, for example, is brilliantly captured in Warren Dearden's 1971 novel, *A Free Country*. Described in his book's blurb as "an itinerant utopian communard" who had been successively "a beatnik, hippie and freak" but had suffered brief lapses into employment as "a taxicab driver, dope peddler and smuggler," Dearden served time in jail for dealing dope and became a lead figure in the prison activist scene. In *A Free Country* Dearden cooks up a fast-paced narrative that crystalizes the period's spiraling sense of conspiracy, mistrust and cynicism.

The book's protagonist, Doug Leaf, is a twenty-two-year-old, long-haired draft-dodger who—perhaps in an echo of Dearden's own life—has "not only turned his back on his hardworking honest family and its society but has become a hippie, a dope-pusher, a bum and a petty criminal." The novel kicks off with Leaf as a laid-back, streetwise dope-dealer hustling a living in Boston. He is feeling quietly smug (and pleasantly stoned), having just scored five kilos of prime marijuana. But fate deals him a bum hand when his attaché case gets mixed up with another that is identical. Returning home, the luckless pusher is astonished when he opens the case to see not his beloved dope, but $75,000 in bundles of cash and a mysterious spool of audio tape. Evidence in a plot to assassinate an unnamed politician, Leaf's discovery makes him the unwitting target of the conspirators and the novel follows his exploits as he takes off across America, trying to stay one jump ahead of the assassins.

A Free Country is an urban paranoid thriller that encapsulates tropes that became common in the early 1970s. In Hollywood, for example, the same sense of paranoia and distrust ran through movies like Francis Ford Coppola's *The Conversation* (1974), Alan Pakula's *The Parallax View* (1974), and Sydney Pollack's *Three Days of the Condor* (1975). But in tracing Doug Leaf's dope-fueled flight across America, the book also echoes the late-1960s vogue for countercultural road movies such as *Easy Rider* (1969) and *Vanishing Point* (1971). With the conspirators at his heels, Leaf hightails it out of Boston, heading for New York. Plans to lie low in the East Village, however, are short-lived. Realizing his pursuers are onto him, Leaf hitches a ride to San Francisco with three stoner hippies aboard a panel truck painted in psychedelic swirls. As the pursuit continues, Leaf jumps ship in Ohio. Taking to the byways, he hitches to Cincinnati and there ensues an incident-filled odyssey as Leaf treks from Indianapolis to Dallas, St. Louis, San Francisco, and finally arrives in Berkeley where he hides out with his childhood pal—and fellow drug-dealer—Gerhard.

With prose that is terse and punchy, and told in the laconic first person, *A Free Country* evokes the heritage of hard-boiled noir. But it also masterfully captures the mood of the early '70s. Of course, there's sex and drugs aplenty, and Dearden (clearly something of an aficionado) readily guides readers through the latest recreational pharmaceuticals, with quick explanations and the occasional footnote. More than this, though, the novel expertly depicts a time when the sun has set on the Summer of Love and the flower children have been left wilting on the compost heap. Downbeat and disillusioned, *A Free Country* delivers a redolent portrait of the hippie scene turned sour and seedy:

> Up four dingy flights on Avenue C, I found Alan and three chicks listening to Ravi Shankar records in a squalid two-room apartment. I was admitted . . . by a fat chick in a tent dress. She led me through a filthy, smelly kitchen into the other room. Three mattresses occupied most of the floorspace; what was not covered by a mattress was heaped with miscellaneous baggage. A couple of posters had been stuck in an abortive attempt to brighten cracked and peeling walls. The only window, a narrow slit covered completely by loose-woven burlap, admitted little light. That was groovy . . . I didn't want to see too well anyway.

The book's title, however, has a neat double meaning. Certainly, irony is writ large. The country claiming to be a crucible of freedom is actually a font of violence and repression. But like the road movies it emulates, Dearden's novel also hints that the land beset with conflict and corruption still retains its roots

ATILLA WAS A SEX CRAZED DEMI-GOD WHO SHOWED NO MERCY TO HIS FEMALE SEX SLAVES . . . HE RAPED AND PILLAGED THEIR BODIES TO SATISFY THE SEXUAL CRAVINGS OF HIS HENCHMEN
by RALPH BENTON

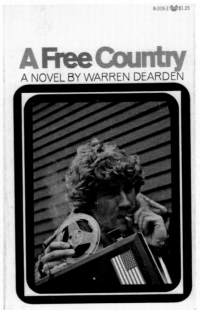

Psychedelic Sex (Viceroy Books, 1968)
A Free Country (Grove Press, 1971)

STICKING IT TO THE MAN

in traditions of liberty. The narrative of movement and space always points toward open choices, tantalizing possibilities, and a wealth of potentials. And while Leaf's transcontinental road trip begins in the bleak backstreets of Boston, it ends in the bliss of the Golden State as the hero beds down in Gerhard's well-appointed (sex and drugs-wise, at least) West Coast pad.

Nevertheless, for most of the novel Leaf is a fugitive, ducking and diving and constantly looking over his shoulder. Indeed, at the core of the book are feelings of distrust and paranoia that mirror the atmosphere of the period. As he lies low in a greasy diner, Leaf flicks through a recent newspaper, noting the stories of the day—U.S. losses in Vietnam, political assassinations, escalating tensions in the Middle East—all clearly resonating with the reality of America at the time. The assassination of JFK in 1963, followed by that of Malcolm X in 1965, heralded a shift of national mood into an era of mistrust and skepticism. And with the assassinations of Martin Luther King and Bobby Kennedy in 1968, suspicions of political conspiracies became pervasive. The plot of *A Free Country*, then, is a clear reflection of the book's historical context.

The novel's reference to an incriminating audio tape also seems an interesting allusion to contemporary events, though the Watergate scandal and revelations about the White House taping system would not break until 1973, two years *after* the book's publication. In a sense, then, Dearden's story seems eerily prescient. That said, by 1971 government conspiracies and official cover-ups were already well established in the headlines. That year, for example, Daniel Ellsberg leaked the Pentagon Papers to the *New York Times*, revealing that the U.S. had secretly escalated the Vietnam War by bombing Cambodia and Laos and that President Johnson's administration had systematically lied, not only to the public but also to Congress, about the course of the war. In comparison, the conspiracy concocted in Dearden's novel looks relatively routine.

Like Piercy's *Dance the Eagle to Sleep*, Dearden's *A Free Country* also seems to end in retreat. Finally run to ground at Gerhard's apartment, Leaf cuts a deal with his pursuers. Despite being stark naked and held at gunpoint, our hero retains his levelheaded cool and agrees to hand over the tape providing he keeps half the cash. An audacious bid, but it pays off, and Leaf walks away with the dough. Nevertheless, the valiant rebel seems to have thrown in the towel. Using the windfall to buy a farm and settle down with his girlfriend, Leaf seems to have lost his swagger and looks set to end his days lying low. Yet things do not quite end there. Like Piercy's *Dance the Eagle to Sleep* (again), *A Free Country* ultimately leaves the audience with a grain of defiant hope and, in a neat plot twist in the book's final pages, Leaf confides in readers that he is actually "set to piss some people off" by blowing the whole conspiracy wide open.

In contrast to the melancholic feel of Piercy and Dearden's novels, Ed Sanders's *Shards of God* (1970) gives an emphatically triumphal spin on '60s hippiedom. Poet, singer, writer, and activist, Sanders is a luminary of the American counterculture. His first notable poem—"Poem from Jail"—was written on prison toilet paper after Sanders was locked up for a pacifist protest against the launch of nuclear submarines in 1961. In 1962 he founded the (irregularly) mimeographed avant-garde literary journal *Fuck You: A Magazine of the Arts* under the slogan "Total Assault on the Culture" and two years later opened the Peace Eye Bookstore, which became a hub of the Lower East Side's burgeoning bohemia. In 1964 Sanders began his long-running stint as frontman of irreverent rock band the Fugs, with whom he led chants of "Out, Demons, Out!" at the Yippies' exorcism of the Pentagon in 1967. Often at the center of the Yippies' provocative capers, Sanders was an integral member of the group, and their style and attitude are writ large in the pages of *Shards of God*.

Published in 1970 and subtitled "A Novel of Yippies," *Shards of God* is an outrageously over-the-top take on the battles between the Yippies and the institutions of America power. Intentionally wild and fragmented, the storyline (such as it is) chronicles a series of fantastic and absurd conflicts between the government and Abbie Hoffman and Jerry Rubin, who aim to replace the "total vomit that rules the nations of the west" with a new, magical "Aeon of community."

The book begins in summer 1967 with "The Great Pentagon Hunching Contest," which pits Hoffman against a Pentagon-designed android in a contest of sexual endurance. After six hours of hot competition (Hoffman servicing a long line of volunteers from women's air corps) the android malfunctions; but the military top brass disallow Hoffman's victory and renege on their agreement to share intelligence on the "Council of Eye Forms," a cosmic leadership instructing the Yippies (the council's membership comprising various icons of the time, Buddha: Ra, Jesus, Che Guevara, Karl Marx, and Malcolm X). The narrative then switches to Rubin's apartment for a Yippie initiation ceremony. The occasion sees Sanders playfully rework the group as an arcane religious cult with its own sacrament and rituals dedicated to "a workable government of freedom and sharing." Sanders's impish enthusiasm for libertine excess also slips into gear; the event developing into an orgiastic whirl of sex and dope that culminates with a young neophyte pressed into sexual service for a 1,500-pound bull:

> "Faster, pretty bull, faster," she panted, "faster, faster." One will not say that the bull culminated in haste, but rather the eagerness of the event created a situation whereby after ten minutes of heinie-flash, a muffled explosion, like a hand grenade exploding inside a tank in a war movie, occurred and jets of semen spilled back out of the nooky on all sides of the dick. The girl came also and fell into an immediate coma of paradise.

After an interlude aboard a flying saucer (communing with emissaries from the Council of Forms), Rubin and Hoffman return to earth and lead planning for protests at Chicago's 1968 Democratic Convention. Tactics include computerized tapping of "electric information . . . from the war-machine, from the CIA, from the FBI, from banks" and a plan to sabotage the "Hate Computer" located at the University of Chicago and serving the interests of the "oil people."

The "storyline" then jumps to a trio of chapters where Sanders describes a "Psychedelic Concentration Camp" set up to deal with possible "dope dope-fiend commie youth invasions." But the brutality of the camp's goons is no match for the resolute Yippies. Summoning up the spirit of Che Guevara, Rubin takes instruction from the guerrilla leader on strategy for the Chicago protests, and the book's closing chapters rework the Convention debacle into a fantasy of countercultural revolt. The city's population are swallowed up in clouds of LSD while the "Great Battle of the Hilton" sees the alien "Sauceroids" help the Yippies storm to victory over the "oinkos," their victory celebrated by an extraterrestrial trip to Zagreus-90 for a colossal orgy.

Interviewed in 1999, Sanders was dismissive of *Shards of God*. Describing the book as "a failure," the author explained, "I'd never written a novel before, and

as a whole it isn't constructed that well. It just didn't live up to what I intended." Nevertheless, the book is still a revealing document of its time. Intentionally outrageous, fantastic and absurd, its pages are peppered with in-group jokes, namechecks, and mutual admiration. The book also reflects the sense of nostalgia for a mythical "lost" America that was a common theme in the '60s counterculture. Describing *Shards* as a "magic rite to make us proud once more of America and a hymn of salvation through smut," Sanders elevates the Yippies as the guardians of American traditions of freedom and independence, valiantly struggling against a malign and corrupt establishment.

The author also deliberately plays with textual form. Sanders not only has a modernist love of linguistic wordplay and invention, he also artfully blends the sublime and the vulgar. Graduating from New York University in 1964 with a degree in Greek, Sanders has a command of classical sources, and *Shards* is modeled as a countercultural epic. The book is replete with classical allusions. Abbie Hoffman, for example, chants Pindar's first Olympian Ode before entering the hunching contest. Hoffman and Jerry Rubin's sexual athleticism is compared to the brave actions of men such as Odysseus and Achilles. Indeed, the recurring references to Homer are used to suggest that Hoffman and Rubin are, like Odysseus and Achilles, far greater than ordinary mortals. Not simply brave men, they are "shards of god"—the god in question being the Egyptian sun god Ra, who installed kings and heroes on earth to act as his successors. But the classical themes are integrated with the Yippies' enthusiasm for the mass media, and *Shards* features a mosaic of elements culled from 1960s popular culture, from contemporary icons such as Merle Haggard and Cassius Clay to sci-fi flying saucers and pornographic fantasies.

Indeed, sexual exploits loom large in *Shards of God*. The book endlessly extols its heroes' sexual stamina, while orgies and sexual excess infuse its pages. The fascination reflects attitudes, prevalent within the counterculture, that sexual freedom not only offers possibilities of sensual pleasure, but that the loss of sexual inhibitions also carries with it an oppositional stance toward conventional culture and "straight" society. Always a champion of free expression and liberated sexuality, Sanders was himself a dedicated "erotic provocateur," and the "politics of ecstasy" are ever-present in *Shards*. The author, for example, explains how "Yippie grew in the oasis of smut, genitals, and dope,"

Shards of God
a novel
of the Yippies
by Ed Sanders

Shards of God (Grove Press, 1970)

and that the group "esteemed above all . . . communal sex, and the wheatfield-in-the-wind beauty of the mobfuck." Modern-day readers, however, may struggle with the novel's sexual politics. Certainly, *Shards* is brazen in its enthusiasm for sexual outrage, but female protagonists are conspicuously absent, and Sanders's women are invariably configured as "sex slaves" (albeit apparently willing ones). Rather than a font of sexual subversion, then, the book might now be seen as testament to the rich vein of macho chauvinism that ran through the counterculture.

The book's view of events is also manifestly partial. No mention is made, for instance, of the arrest of the Chicago Eight, of the disputes between Hoffman and Rubin, or of Sanders's own disputes with the Yippie leaders. To be fair, the book does not pose as an objective document of historical record. Instead, it is a utopian fantasy of how things *should* have been. As the introduction to *Shards* announces, what follows is "a tale of triumph; the intimate story of a successful caper." A rapt homage to the '60s counterculture and its heroes, the novel is an epic chronicle of Yippie success memorialized in the great tradition of Homer, Herodotus, Pindar, and Horace.

Compared to the optimism and comic tone of *Shards of God*, however, Sanders's next literary outing was altogether darker. Published in 1971, *The Family: The Story of Charles Manson's Dune Buggy Attack Battalion* was his delve into Manson's murderous cult and their weird, paranoid take on the hippie dream. The first authoritative telling of the saga, the book was a product of Sanders's fascination with Manson and the Family, whose scene seemed to be a grotesque mirror of his own utopian ethic of free love, free expression, and passion for the transgressive joke.

Sanders's research occupied a year and a half of his life. He attended the Manson group's murder trial, spent time at the Spahn Movie Ranch (The Family's desert hangout) and amassed thousands of pages of data. And, with his impeccable underground credentials, he easily accessed Manson's social circle to produce a compelling chronicle of the lead-up and aftermath to 1969's Tate-LaBianca slayings. The book's style, however, is a stark contrast to the embroidered exuberance of *Shards of God*. Instead, much of the account reads like a police report:

> Tex ordered Sadie to kill Voityck Frykowski. . . .
> Sadie stabbed blindly, one, two, three, four times,

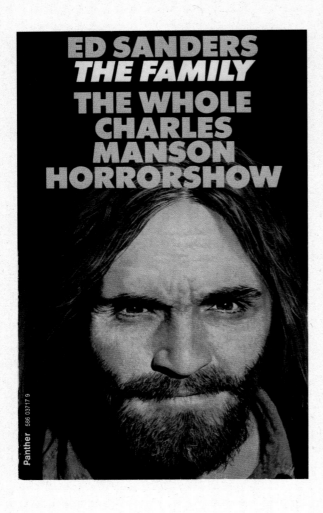

parallel down the front of his left leg. He turned toward the front hall as if to flee. She managed to stab him once in the back but the knife hit bone. Then she stabbed him deeply in the right back lung. The skin surface widths of the wounds were three quarter inch, the same as the width of her Buck knife.

The terse prose is clean and unfussy, as if they want "just the facts, ma'am." Nevertheless, Sanders also throws in regular sardonic gestures that seem to subvert the intent of the main narrative voice. He comes up with hip, hyphenated expressions like "bunch-punching" and "hell-creep," and sometimes adds a jarring note of adolescent sarcasm to especially lurid revelations by ending the paragraph with a brief "far out" or "oo-ee-oo." But the underlying theme of *The Family* is Sanders's concern to understand how the hippie dream could turn into a nightmare. A mordant flipside to *Shards of God*, the book represents the despondent comedown that followed the soaring highs of the counterculture. As Sanders reflects, the age of "new togetherness" had not simply been a story of peace and love. There had always been vicious predators who had cloaked themselves in the counter-cultural groove to stalk a vulnerable prey: "The flower movement was like a valley of thousands of plump white rabbits surrounded by wounded coyotes. Sure, the 'leaders' were tough, some of them geniuses and great poets. But the acid-dropping middle-class children from Des Moines were rabbits."

The Family was written as the rhythms of the 1960s were fading. It was a time when John Lennon announced that "the dream is over" and Bob Dylan sang of the "day of the locusts." But such maudlin sentiments hardly reflect the spirit of energetic, imaginative and (often) harebrained rebellion that was at the heart of groups like the Yippies. In literary terms it was an attitude probably best encapsulated in *Trashing*, Anita Hoffman's tale of a young woman's journey into the underground world of 1960s radicalism.

Anita Hoffman had been central to the Yippie scene from its beginnings. The term "Yippie" had originally been coined by Paul Krassner on New Year's Eve 1967 as a name that could, as he later recalled, signify "an organic coalition of psychedelic hippies and political activists." But it was Hoffman who fleshed out the idea. She liked the name but thought something more formal would prompt the "strait-laced" media to take

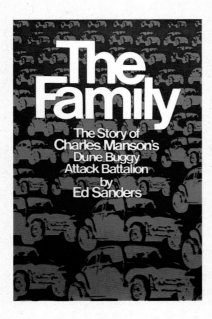

The Family
(Panther, 1974)
The Family (E.P. Dutton, 1970)

the group more seriously. She came up with "Youth International Party"—a tag that seemed to embody the ethos of the movement but also made for a neat play on words. She also helped plan and execute some of the Yippies' most memorable stunts. With fellow activists she had exorcised the Pentagon in 1967 and had thrown money onto the Wall Street trading floor amid the Yippies' invasion of the stock exchange. And in 1970, with husband Abbie and Grace Slick and Paul Kantner of the Jefferson Airplane, she had tried to infiltrate a Nixon tea party at the White House and dose the punch bowl with LSD. It was experiences like these that fed into *Trashed*, Hoffman's semi-autobiographical novel.

The book begins with Ann, a young ingénue, arriving in New York and working as a volunteer for the antiwar movement. She is swept off her feet by Danny, a hip politico ("He seemed so graceful and lithe with his tight jeans and open shirt.... There was a scar on his left cheek near the ear. Had he got it on some march in the South?"), and, as romance blossoms, Ann is initiated into a new life of racy experience by her more worldly beau: "Naive as I was, I knew it was marijuana when Danny took out some cigarette papers and began to roll the tobacco-like substance into very thin cigarettes. He said they we called joints, lit one and passed it to me." Ann moves in with Danny and the pair is soon married—their "flower power" wedding in Central Park a clear echo of the Hoffmans' own marriage, pictured in *Time* magazine in 1967. Ann's "final rite of passage into the new consciousness" is to drop acid listening to a Ravi Shankar LP (what else?) and, with Danny she finds a happy niche in the hippie enclave that had taken root around Gem Spa, St. Mark's Place, and Second Avenue:

> The most magical quality of the Lower East Side was the sense of unity felt by all the long-hairs who walked its streets.... Smoke-Ins, free concerts, benefits, street theater, Be-Ins, all sorts of public happenings were how we expressed ourselves to the outside world, how we celebrated the fact that we were a people. Theater was all around us. The Lower East Side was at that time probably the biggest circus in the world. And it was all free.

Like Hoffman, Ann also helps stage political pranks and zany acts of guerrilla theater. With Danny and his pals she totes water pistols to hold up a bus of elderly tourists; on the anniversary of the Hiroshima bombing,

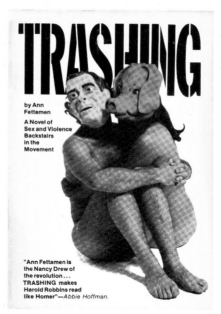

Trashing (Straight Arrow, 1970)
Trashing (Belmont Tower, 1972)

they dye the city's fountains a bloody red; they mail out four thousand joints randomly to the citizens of New York; and they glue the keyholes of hundreds of doors on Wall Street, pasting up signs that read "Closed Because of Business." And, like Hoffman, Ann relishes the adrenalin rush of angry protests and street battles with the cops:

> Running in the streets! I loved it. It was the closest I'd ever come to flying. . . . I guess the adrenalin made you high, like natural speed. There was always the knowledge that you could split from the group and escape down a side street, if it became necessary. It was like a kid's game, only real. Cowboys and Indians. Cops and Robbers. Pigs and Yippies.

Related in the first person, the book's spartan style harks back to the clipped prose of the hard-boiled pulps. Indeed, in the way it plays with genre and style, the novel might be considered a literary equivalent to the theatrics of the Yippies' playful stunts. Hoffman's pseudonym, Ann Fettamen, is a jokey drug reference and, more generally, the book goads conservative sensibilities by filching from the pulps' traditional enthusiasm for the shocking and the outré. Incidents of sex, drugs, and violence are sprinkled through the plot. A particularly nasty scene, for example, sees Ann gang-raped by a trio of grimy bikers, while a hash-fueled orgy gives a countercultural twist to the pulps' penchant for salacious license:

> The smell of lotus incense was strong and pleasant. . . . Then suddenly I felt something placed over my face and fastened at the back. I was wearing a mask. Simultaneously I felt something soft and wet slip into my crotch from behind. The fleshy lips of my vagina were immediately coated with a cool almost peppermint-feeling lotion. My thighs parted involuntarily and I quivered. . . . I could make out other nude figures. All with masks. But what masks! There was Neil Armstrong, here Richard Nixon, there Jackie Onassis. . . . I was sitting near Henry Kissinger. He cupped my breast briefly, then circled the nipple with his finger. I kissed the side of his neck. His hand moved down the inside of my left thigh. Then he pushed my legs apart, sitting comfortably between them as he sucked my left nipple.

Like the other books, *Trashing* also captures the growing mood of conflict and confrontation that hung over the end of the '60s. "The Pig Empire seemed to be encroaching more and more on our lives," Ann observes as the drug busts and police violence intensify. But just as the cops seem set to deliver a crushing blow to the counterculture, the underground's computer wizard hits on a scheme to crash Wall Street's financial systems, bringing the whole establishment tumbling to the ground. Rather than ending on a note of disheartened resignation, then, the book's conclusion points toward a resistance that is unbroken and unbowed. And this sense of enduring defiance is what makes *Trashed* the consummate Yippie novel. With the scheme in place and set to blow, Ann, Danny, and their cohorts make off for Canada. The future seems unwritten. Everything is up for grabs, and the young revolutionaries' voices swell and fill the air:

> We are the forces of chaos and anarchy
> Everything they say we are we are
> And we are very
> Proud of ourselves . . .
> Up against the wall
> Up against the wall motherfucker!

Bill Osgerby

Fifty Shades of Gay

An Introduction to the Gay Adult Pulp of the 1970s

What possible interest could decades-old adult novels have for citizens of the brave new pornutopia, in which suburban housewives make mainstream blockbusters of the *Fifty Shades of Grey* novels, and images that would have made the sybarites of Pompeii blush are never more than a few keystrokes away?

The short answer is: more than you might think. Granted, back in the 1970s adult novels, gay and straight alike, knew their place, which was underneath newsstand counters, in drugstores, sex shops, and bus depot bookracks, under the bed, or stashed at the back of the closet. Operating on the far fringes of the book business, adult-oriented publishers catered to a niche audience unfettered by the constraints of mainstream morality and didn't hesitate to make the leap from hard-R to XXX within the parameters of what had always sold for them: genre fiction with more sex than non-porn imprints dared to deliver—as raunchy as possible within the limits of what seemed unlikely to invite prosecution, which was a moving target when gay thrillers such as *Night of the Sadist* (1971) and *Man Eater* (undated, ca. 1970), the focus of this chapter, were published.

Dismissive stereotypes of vintage gay erotica—which for much of the twentieth century meant most works dealing with same-sex desire—are rooted in novels of the 1940s and '50s that were hobbled by the evasive language of "questing mouths," "sensitive portions," and "heated longing." These novels were kept in rigid narrative check by the far-from-baseless fear that publishing books about homosexuals who were no more marginalized, tormented, or doomed to lives of squalor and degradation than anyone else, whose desires overflowed the boundaries of bourgeois propriety, was the fastest way to draw down the wrath of contemporary Comstocks.

But the overlapping cultural revolutions of the 1960s wrought rapid changes, and as early as 1966 an unambitious and not particularly distinguished novel like John Dexter's *The Self Lover*, while still written to the conventions of fierce cravings and sweeping

shudders, could end with its protagonist—a sexually confused college graduate with years of (underwhelming) heterosexual experience under his belt—in the arms of a handsome, well-adjusted, and 100 percent manly war hero who loves the hell out of him.

There's no consensus as to exactly when the golden age of gay erotica began and ended, but by my reckoning it's roughly 1969–82, when adults-only novels struck a harmonious balance between sexual explicitness and solid narrative. Sexually graphic science fiction stories took place in richly imagined societies and addressed such then hot-button issues as segregation and the politics of sexual repression, which in Larry Townsend's hugely entertaining 2069 trilogy (1969–70) fuel a deep-space exploration program that runs on rum, sodomy, and the lash, minus the rum and the lash. Richard Amory's revisionist Westerns *Song of the Loon* (1966), *The Song of Aaron* (1967) and *Listen, the Loon Sings . . .* (1968) take place in a world where the wildest frontier is manly love between saddle-sore cowboys and Native Americans.

Horror novels like Sonny Barker's *Vampire's Kiss* (1970) and Davy S.'s *Gay Vampire* (1967)—a raunchy riff on the homoerotic subtext of the then-popular supernatural soap opera *Dark Shadows*—associated vampirism with empowering sensuality and counterculture cool rather than wickedness and damnation, well before Anne Rice's *Interview with the Vampire* (1976) made such ideas mainstream. Historical adventures—one of many specialties of the versatile Peter Tuesday Hughes, whose novels include *Seventeen69* (1970), *Garden of Cruel Delights*, and *The Master of Monfortin* (both 1977), offered period pomp, social maneuvering, and swordplay (in both senses of the term) among gentlemen who prefer each other's company to that of fluttering ladies.

Perhaps hoping to counter the perception that their books were both shameful and shameless, many adult publishers slyly added prefaces that situated their output within the realm of transgressive and activist literature. Surrey House congratulated its writers

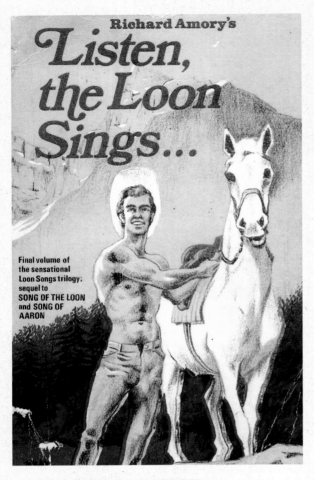

Richard Amory's
Listen, the Loon Sings...

Final volume of the sensational Loon Songs trilogy; sequel to SONG OF THE LOON and SONG OF AARON

My Purple Winter

BY CARL CORLEY

THE FINEST IN ADULT READING!

Listen, the Loon Sings (Greenleaf Classics, 1968)
My Purple Winter (French Line, 1966)

for addressing—however lewdly—such controversial issues as homosexuality in the military, prison sex, and intergenerational relationships. Spartacus Books lauded the richness of "the homophile erotic heritage... from the pure, idealized passions of the ancient Greeks to the dizzying sensuality of Michelangelo and the bizarre underground of cruelty that belongs to Jean Genet," while Blueboy Library simply declared, "The love of Man for Man is as old as Man himself."

And though I doubt that Dwight D. Eisenhower envisioned excerpts from his unequivocal 1953 defense of free speech—"People who hold unpopular ideas . . . have a right to have them, a right to record them and a right to have them in places where they are accessible to others"—in proximity to such terms as "throbbing cock," French Line appropriated his words with cheeky and not-entirely-disingenuous glee.

By 1968, adults-only gay books were letting it all hang out. Hacks just hacked out dirtier variations on a theme: ecstatic escapades during which no one ever gags, sweats, gets sore, or bleeds, and simultaneous orgasms that falleth like the gentle rain from heaven. But writers who had first turned to porn because they wanted to explore gay men's lives in full seized the opportunity to parse the power of sex in all its awkward, compulsive, poignant, tender, raunchy, complicated, rhapsodic, rollicking, intimate, spiteful, funny, degrading, messy, and nerve-tingling particulars—a subject mainstream publishers continued to treat with an extreme caution that favored established literary authors who knew better than to frighten the horses.

And while it's true that the bulk of vintage adult paperbacks amount to little more than the sum of their exotic couplings, most pulp westerns and hard-boiled crime thrillers weren't *Shane* or *The Maltese Falcon*. As the bracingly clear-eyed science fiction writer Theodore Sturgeon once succinctly observed, 90 percent of everything is crap. But the 10 percent—the cream of the gay adults-only crop—includes both serious coming-of-age/coming-out novels like Curt MacLean's two-volume *Teenage '69 Memoirs* (1972), Carl Corley's *A Fool's Advice* (1967) and George Kiva's *Hot Asset!* (1974) and briskly entertaining, often slyly subversive genre tales teeming with queer spies, gangsters, tycoons, cops, gladiators, jocks, marines, and, yes, cowboys, long before *Brokeback Mountain* made homos on the range the stuff of popular discourse.

They're as ripe for rediscovery as the crime novels of Dorothy B. Hughes, Jim Thompson, Charles Williams,

David Goodis, and Raymond Chandler, which were equally marginalized when they were first published—largely ignored or disparaged as sordid distractions for coarse sensibilities.

Dick Jones's *Man Eater* and Paul Laurie's *Night of the Sadist* are both unabashedly dirty. No dirtier than Henry Miller's *Tropic of Cancer* (1934), Genet's *Our Lady of the Flowers* (1943), or anything written by eighteenth-century libertine Donatien Alphonse François, the Marquis de Sade (including, of course, *The 120 Days of Sodom*), but far more so than today's gauzily smutty "mommy porn" (has there ever been a more libido-freezing term?). But while the plots of *Night of the Sadist* and *Man Eater* hew closely to genre conventions, they're also inextricably informed by concerns specific to their era and their intended audience. Both stories are driven by the notion that sexuality and sexual behavior are two separate things—the former innate and natural, the latter explicitly shaped by and in opposition to mainstream cultural and historical forces, which in this context include Vietnam-era political disillusionment, lingering post-civil-rights-movement racism, police corruption, and harshly normative conventions that dictated the way men should act.

Both also explore the challenges of forging a viable gay life in a generally hostile straight world, and their protagonists embody diametrically opposed ways of coping with entrenched homophobia that fostered both a powerful us-against-them mentality and encouraged self-segregation and divisive "right way to be gay" rhetoric that set gay men against each other along lifestyle lines.

Some four decades and a series of massive reconfigurations of the American cultural landscape later, those same issues are still being hashed out in real life and fiction—the overt subject of playwright Michael Perlman's much-lauded *From White Plains* (2013) may be the poisonous aftermath of homophobic high school bullying, but the *New York Times* review made note of the play's attention to "complex sociopolitical issues" like the relative merits of "assimilation versus resistance to cultural norms and biases."

Night of the Sadist unfolds in a self-made gay ghetto where contact with the straight world is minimal and generally demeaning—why would a gay man want to deal with, say, police officers whose default attitude is that "guys like [them]" are "sort of ask[ing]" to be robbed, beaten, and murdered just by virtue of being guys like them? And it intensifies the insularity by taking place within the gay S&M community, which in 1970 was as unfamiliar to most gay men as life in any gay community was to most straight ones.

Man Eater's main character, by contrast, straddles gay and straight communities successfully, if not always comfortably. He makes short work of the homophobic bully he encounters in the army, but as a civilian he's forced to tolerate corrosive verbal abuse from a colleague who equates "faggots" with child molesters, zoophiles, and sexual predators. How little things change. The capper is that both men work for the United Nations Crime Control Commission (more correctly the Commission on Crime Prevention and Control and, since 1992, the Commission on Crime Prevention and Criminal Justice), which—at least in Jones's telling—classifies violence against homosexuals as a form of genocide while tolerating queer-baiting within its own ranks. *Man Eater* also leaps over decades of "glad to be gay" cheerleading, diving headlong into the thorny complexities of radical gay-identity politics.

All things considered, all of this is some heavy freight for a pair of dirty books to haul, but *Man Eater* and *Night of the Sadist* aren't unique. The notion that the personal is political went mainstream during the '70s, and lurking behind suggestive covers and such lewdly winking titles as *Gusher Comin'* (1977) by William Maltese as Chad Stuart, *Tailpipe Trucker* (1975) by G.E. Davies as Clay Caldwell, and Peter Tuesday Hughes's *Come with Me . . .* (1969) lie solid novels whose sexual escapades—from suburban experimentation to adventuring by long-haul truckers and offshore oil rig workers to naive American nirvana-seekers drowning in drug-fueled, Euro-hippie decadence—are inextricably intertwined with specific times and places.

Like most pulp fiction, gay adult novels were written quickly—flat work-for-hire fees that rarely exceeded three figures discouraged writers from revising and polishing their work and rewarded quantity over quality—and edited indifferently at best. At worst, first-draft copy seems to have gone straight to print, rife with typos and inconsistencies like *Night of the Sadist*'s variable spelling of a featured character's name: "Johnathon" in some chapters and the equally unconventional "Jonathon" in others.

Man Eater comes with a back-cover warning that IT'S A BIZARRE TALE, UNUSUAL IN THIS KIND OF LITERATURE, and fair enough: I daresay buyers expecting a titillating one-handed read got an ugly surprise when they discovered just how literal the title is. Diverse though gay smut of the '60s and '70s was, it rarely strayed into such ardor-chilling territory as *Man Eater*'s globetrotting tour of genital mutilation, serial murder, cannibalism, and death by razor-studded dildo (a device reinvented in Val McDermid's mainstream 1994 thriller *The Torment of Others*).

Man Eater is also a bold rethinking of the relationship between popular genre writing and pornography; you could, were you so inclined, position it today as a postmodern exercise in undermining masculine stereotypes while charting the dissolution of a mind held together by routine and strict internal rules designed to keep chaos at bay.

Its protagonist and first-person narrator, Amsterdam-based Vietnam War veteran Jake Gold, is a genre stereotype, a variation on the tough, relentless, and deeply damaged noir antiheroes who, driven by the knowledge that the world is fundamentally cruel, unfair, and tough on the weak, the incautious, and the just plain unlucky, try to right what wrongs they can by any means necessary. What he isn't is a gay stereotype, which in the 1960s and early '70s still meant effeminate, bitchy, high-strung, self-hating, artsy, and inconsequential.

Jake dodged a bullet of the war crimes variety because the UNCCC was recruiting gay agents so aggressively that his military training trumped the warning signs that his experiences in country—notably the bloody death of his lover, Dave—left him on shaky psychological ground. Suffice to say that setting Jake on the bestial serial killer dubbed "Man Eater," who's using a set of razor-sharp, surgical-steel teeth that predate those of both Thomas Harris's *Red Dragon* (1981) and the James Bond villain Jaws (of 1977's *The Spy Who Loved Me*) to gnaw a bloody swath through Europe's velvet underground—a landscape no less surreal than the American frontier of Spaghetti Westerns—does nothing good for Jake's state of mind.

In a genre lousy with haunted protagonists, Jake Gold's self-loathing is epic and unrelenting, without being entirely disconnected from reality. He hates himself for having breezed past the landmine that reduced Dave to shreds of bloody meat, for looking down on flamboyant "super faggots" even though he used to be one, for not even trying to track down the troubled younger brother Dave dearly loved for fear of seeing Dave's face in his, for invariably leading with

A Fool's Advice (French Line, 1967) *Jesse: Man of the Streets* (French Line, 1968)

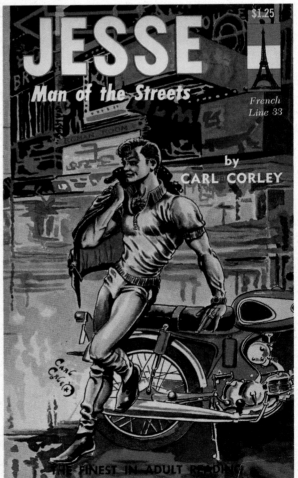

the wrong head, and for somehow putting everyone whose path he crosses on death's radar.

But Jake doesn't hate himself for being queer, no small exception at a time when gay men often internalized the ugly stereotypes that reduced them to unnatural, sinful perverts destined for lives of shame and aching loneliness. And Jake's sympathy for the Man Eater's victims—pricey hustlers whose pitifully violated corpses are "surrounded by the thick odor of blood and cum that told of an orgy of lust and death"—is not only fundamentally decent but rooted in moral principle, perhaps the only one Jake has never compromised: Your right to explore the outer limits of experience—sexual or otherwise—stops at the other guy's right to say, "No, thanks."

Self-evident though that may appear now, when the admonition "no means no" is familiar (if not always honored) from college campuses to corporate boardrooms, it was no such thing in 1970, when in many quarters not nailing every warm body within reach was "uptight," and being uptight implied complicity with the racist, sexist, status-quo-upholding establishment, not to mention general uncoolness.

Nor was it obvious in 1978, when Greta Rideout made legal history by challenging the notion that a husband couldn't rape his wife, no matter what the state of their union. Nor, for that matter, in the mid-1990s, when the "Antioch Rules"—a set of guidelines intended to familiarize hormonal college students with the finer points of consent and negotiating boundaries within the context of general agreement (starting with, failure to say no is not the same as saying yes)—were caricatured as impulse-killing "sexual correctness" conceived by castrating feminists hell-bent on repressing the urgency of male desire.

Which brings us back to the trysexual Jake, whose voracious and flexible appetites are neither inhibited by his scruples nor, at least to his way of thinking, incompatible with his aching need to love and be loved in return. Even when Jake is playing the field, he instinctively plays by the Antioch rules in all but name. Witness this exchange with Charles, the man he's just picked up at the wildest [gay] club in London, during which they establish the rules of engagement:

> "I really don't know just what to do," [said Charles]. "I mean, I don't even know what you like. What if I can't make you happy? It would be so horrid if we couldn't get along."

"Look," I told him, "Why don't you tell me what your scene is—what you enjoy doing—and then we can take it from there?"

"No, no," he said. "You are my guest and we will do what you enjoy. Please, tell me what you like and that is what we will do . . ."

"Most anything that doesn't hurt," I said, "is fine with me. I like oral and anal, as mutual as possible. I think you'll find me game for anything that's fun."

Granted, "most anything that doesn't hurt" is a low bar, but it's to Jake's credit that when, having been shown an exceptionally good time by his accommodating host, he discovers that Charles's scene is thoroughly not his idea of fun, he lives up to the fair-is-fair code and does his part. Unfortunately, Jake's enlightened ethical outlook and self-acceptance in the face of entrenched societal bigotry are at odds with the demands of his job. Zipless screwing is one thing, but using sexual intimacy as a shortcut into people's heads and then either putting them on the Man Eater short list or tossing them aside like used tissues makes Jake feel like scum. Jake's ability to function requires keeping a circle of hell's worth of personal demons behind locked psychological doors, and stalking the Man Eater rips every one of them off its hinges.

Dick Jones, whoever he may have been, writes with more panache than buyers of adults-only pulps had any reason to expect. He has a way with sex-as-a-weapon imagery, from carnal switchblades to billy clubs to land mines to Prussian Krupp cannons (at a Berlin orgy, of course) and mortar shells, and can write a hell of a dream sequence. He puts Jake through the wringer of a fever dream whose psychosexual luridness begins with the funeral of a man-sized penis and concludes with a swarm of cannibal vaginas, complete with fangs and clitoral tongues, gathering beneath an endless blood-red sky. And Jones can be darkly funny, as in this snippy little dig at his own publisher, Gay Way, slipped into Jake's contemptuous assessment of "gay is the only way" rhetoric predicated on the belief that the "gay way" is competitive promiscuity and embracing the can-you-top-this contortions of extreme smut: "If I got laid half as much as the characters in some novels I've read, I'd be long dead of friction burns," he sneers after sampling a much-lauded pornographic novel rife with twincest, bestiality, and more. "Someday people will get smart and there will be some books that treat being gay as just one aspect of being human rather than a sexual road race."

Progressive thinking notwithstanding, in practice Jake gets laid like a carpet by a gallery of porn-fiction stereotypes en route to *Man Eater*'s mind-bending climax. They include a virile matador, a brace of kinky aristocrats, a Nazi-fetishist couple, a studly movie star, and a pair of dewy Danish hustlers, lawless identical twins so sweetly accommodating and impressively acrobatic that their charms are undiminished by the accompanying price tag. Ever the pragmatist (except for occasional fantasies about settling down and living an ordinary life that are oddly poignant for being so profoundly antithetical to his nature, which even he knows)—Jake reasons that paying for any old roll in the hay shows "a lack of style," but opening your wallet for a world-class fantasy come to life is just common sense. After all, the odds of strolling into and picking up a matched set of sweet, guilelessly wanton beauties happy to give it away are slim to none.

Man Eater stands out in other respects as well, including the attention to detail manifest in its use of contemporary military slang and shout-outs to real museums, restaurants, and clubs, including Madrid's Botín, Whiskey Jazz, and the Prado, where Jake spends an afternoon wallowing in the obliterating darkness of Goya's *Saturn Devouring His Son*. There's also the unsettling vividness with which the novel depicts Jake's struggle to function under high-pressure/low-control conditions while in the grip of posttraumatic stress disorder—which didn't even have a proper name when *Man Eater* was written; World War I–era terms like "combat fatigue" and "shell shock" were still in common use—and its subtle evocation of Jake's alienation from his own flesh, which always seems to be doing things of its own volition while he watches with detached curiosity.

That Jake never realizes the connection between a bit of easily overlooked backstory and the case that tears his mind apart is a disquieting denial of genre expectations. But the throwaway revelation on *Man Eater*'s penultimate page is Jones's eleventh-hour bitch slap to thriller conventions, one that yanks the rug out from under the novel's apparently tidy conclusion. Had Jones been a *New York Times Magazine* editor like Gerald Walker, his book might have been accorded the same attention paid to Walker's equally lurid and considerably less sophisticated *Cruising* (1970). But he wasn't . . . or if he was, he kept it to himself, and more's the pity.

Night of the Sadist, set in an unnamed West Coast that strongly suggests San Francisco, also comes with an editorial caveat emptor, albeit one pitched like a carny come-on: IS IT A MYSTERY WITH A SEX TWIST OR A SEX STORY WITH A MYSTERY TWIST? WHO CARES? IT IS AN ENTERTAINING EROTIC NOVEL BY A PROLIFIC AND PROFICIENT WRITER.

I'm on the side of mystery with a sex twist. Granted, the sex story is more viscerally convincing than the mystery, but structurally *Night of the Sadist* resembles nothing so much as a drawing-room puzzler in the Agatha Christie tradition. Unfolding in an insular community rife with hidden alliances and rivalries, the novel features one victim—Bob Maxon, a prolific writer of gay erotic novels—and five suspects, all hustlers who were with him on the night he died, plus an official investigation that's going nowhere fast. In traditional cozy whodunits, the stumbling block is generally a fiendishly clever killer who's always one step ahead of the police rather than institutional apathy rooted in casual prejudice—is it any surprise that some porno-penning queer who hung around with hustlers got himself killed?

Fortunately, the late Mr. Maxon has a champion in his brother, Tom, a tabloid journalist turned amateur sleuth who doesn't like the official attitude one bit and launches his own inquiry with unofficial help from two men, each with his own personal and professional agenda.

Cris, short for Crispus, Taylor was once Bob's lover and, as a gay African American cop, has seen the "just another dead homo/junkie/Negro" syndrome consign plenty of investigations to "a lick and a promise" status. He's in vice, not homicide, but has access to departmental files and is willing to invest his free time in finding Bob's murderer. Rudolph Birndl, a.k.a. "Raunchy Rudy, the Prurient Prussian," was Bob's publisher and pimps all five suspects on the side; he liked Bob, but he'd also like the big sales bump that some splashy news coverage could give Bob's back catalogue—even if it means that one of his boys winds up in prison.

Night of the Sadist is deeply indebted to the gay porn subgenre that revolves around the twilight world of male prostitutes, from John Rechy's grim, exposé-style *City of Night* (1963) to the cheeky series of erotic gay novels Samuel Steward wrote under the pseudonym of Phil Andros from 1966 to 1991. And Rudy's rent boys cover the something-for-everyone waterfront: cross-dressing swish Allan/Elaine, prodigiously

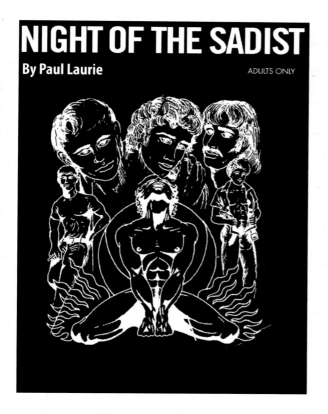

NIGHT OF THE SADIST
By Paul Laurie

ADULTS ONLY

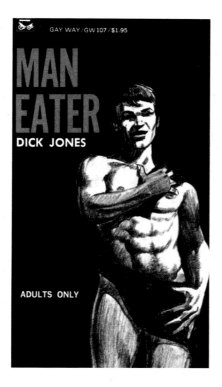

GAY WAY / GW 107 / $1.95

MAN EATER
DICK JONES

ADULTS ONLY

*Night of the
Sadist* (120
Days Books,
2012 reprint)
Man Eater
(Gay Way,
1970)

endowed Johnathon, chubby little masochist Ron;
butch-yet-soulful Gerry, and self-hating urban cowboy
Tex. Like Jones, Laurie exploits the fact that hustlers
are a pornographer's best friend, the go-to guys when
you need to keep the dirty bits coming at regular
intervals because sex is what they do: The very word
"pornography" derives from the Greek *pornographia*—
"writing about prostitutes."

But Laurie imbues each with a measure of indi-
viduality: a glimpse of the diminished fairytale dreams
that underlie disgraced, aging rich twink Allan's nel-
lie-go-lightly persona; perpetual bottom Ron's delight
at getting a chance to top; Tex's corrosive inability
to admit that he's not gay for pay, just plain old gay;
Johnathon's bitter resignation to being treated as a
life-support system for his circus cock; and Gerry's
wounded, restless discontent with the life he drifted
into and can't muster the resolve to leave.

Tom Maxon is Laurie's stance in action; when he's
not looking for clues in the manuscript of Bob's last
novel—an ambitious exploration of madness purchased by a respectable East Coast publishing house
shortly before his death—Tom is fraternizing with
the suspects, trying to see behind their façades in the
hope of glimpsing the seething rage that drove one to
murder a man who spent his last hours treating them
to a lavish night on the town, a thank-you for their willingness to share thoughts, memories, and feelings that
no john's money could have bought. And while Tom
subscribes to the Jake Gold between-the-sheets school
of investigation, he's blessedly free of Jake's tangle of
conflicting desires: Tom actually manages to have
some relatively uncomplicated fun as he screws his
way to the truth about his brother's murder.

Like Jones, Laurie didn't shy away from a bit of
barbed fun at the expense of the hand that fed him.
Rudy is clearly modeled on Roland Boudreault, a
San Francisco–based, French-Canadian porn mogul
nicknamed "the Dirty Old Frenchman." Boudreault
owned Le Salon, a successful chain of erotic shops,
and published hundreds of adult novels under the
Gay Parisian Press and Frenchy's Gay Line imprints,
including *Night of the Sadist*. Like Rudy, Boudreault
was portly—"short, fat [and] greasy," in Steward's vivid
but less-than-generous assessment—and notoriously
stingy, even by the standards of an industry whose
bottom line was predicated on exploiting writers.

"Bob never had any money," Tom retorts when Cris
says his murder is being investigated as a robbery gone

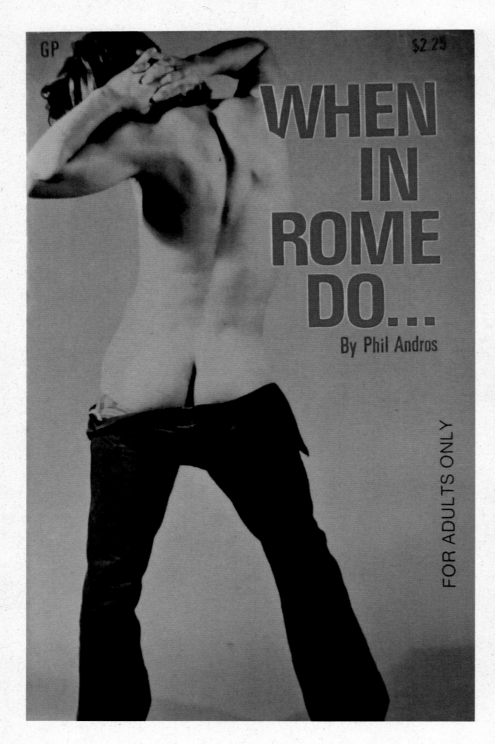

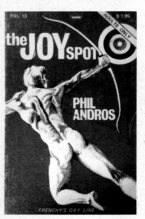

When in Rome (Gay Parisian Press, 1971)
My Brother the Hustler (Gay Parisian Press, 1970)
The Greek Way (Adonis Classics, 1975)
The Joy Spot (Frenchy's Gay Line, 1969)

bad. "He wrote those pocket books. He was paid maybe $500.00–$700.00 apiece."

Either Boudreault had a sense of humor or, more likely, never read the books he published. Not only did that exchange make it into *Night of the Sadist* intact, but a year later he published another Laurie novel, the heist thriller *Come Killer Come*. *Night of the Sadist* is, to put it kindly, a less polished piece of writing than *Man Eater*. The best one can say of Laurie's prose is that it's serviceable. But the novel is a window onto an America all but unimaginable some four decades later, one in which homosexuals are so marginalized—even in a city that has two thriving gay districts, plus a third in an adjacent suburb—that the police are less hostile than indifferent to crimes against them. It also explicitly equates the goals of the civil rights movement and gay activism, touches on the complex dynamics of inter-racial attraction through Tom's brief fling with Cris, and serves as a cheerful little primer on recreational S&M etiquette.

Pedantic digressions into the life and philosophy of the Marquis de Sade aside, *Night of the Sadist* is a quick and breezy read punctuated by a handful of startlingly straightforward glimpses into life in a "tight little gay community" that's both a refuge and gilded cage. Its insularity inflects everything from the progress of the burgeoning romance between Gerry and Tom, who have fallen in love while investigating Bob's murder, to the inevitable awkwardness of advanced sexual choreography, the rituals of postcoital cleanup, and the oddly touching precision brought to bear on Tom's frequent visits to the nameless local liquor store for Scotch, mixers, ice, and barware.

Night of the Sadist is also an eye-opening reminder that not so very long ago everyone smoked everywhere, there was no stigma attached to drinking all night and then driving yourself home (where—at least in the por-nographic imagination—getting it up for one more go was de rigueur) and gay men who used condoms were doing sex wrong.

If the pleasant surprise of gay pulps is what good reads they can be, the bad one is discovering how dif-ficult it is to tease out the real identities of their writers. A handful used their own names, notably the still-underrated Corley, whose novels draw deeply on his own experiences growing up in the poor, semirural Mississippi of the 1920s and '30s, and Prix de Flore winner Bruce Benderson, whose adults-only *Kyle* (undated, ca. 1975), a slippery investigation of desire,

celebrity, and mutable identity, is every bit the equal of his first mainstream literary novel, 1994's *User*. But most didn't, and for every novelist who later stood up and claimed his alter ego(s), hundreds more remain in their closets or have taken their secret identities to the grave. AIDS burned through their generation like napalm.

When I came to republish *Man Eater* and *Night of the Sadist* in 2012 my first objective was to bring these forgotten novels out of the shadows and put them in the hands of twenty-first-century readers unencum-bered by the biases of earlier generations. But I'd also hoped to draw out Paul Laurie and Dick Jones, assum-ing they were still alive. My efforts to find them remain unsuccessful, stymied by a perfect storm of pseudo-nyms, copyright registrations by long-defunct publish-ers, and, I suspect, the authors' own conviction that having written smutty books is nothing to be proud of.

I'd welcome the chance to persuade them that the effort they invested in transcending the utilitarian parameters of adult books was not wasted. The books they produced are both good pulp fiction and texts that bear witness to history, more readable now than they were at a time when gay and straight lives rarely met, except at the intersection of practiced secrecy and overwhelming obliviousness.

Maitland McDonagh

Emotions Doesn't Change Facts

Remembering Joseph Hansen

In the late 1970s, a Hollywood film studio queried Joseph Hansen about optioning his popular series of detective novels, each featuring an out-of-the-closet insurance company investigator named Dave Brandstetter. The usual lunch ensued. "We'll want to make a few changes, of course," the studio suits informed Hansen. Their primary imposition: "Brandstetter's not gay."

In sharing this story with me one afternoon at his house on Cullen Street in Los Angeles, Hansen chuckled and broke off his account. He did not elaborate on his response to the executives because he didn't have to. I knew what to expect of him as a pathbreaking author with contumacious integrity. As a young poet and small press editor with production facilities at Beyond Baroque in Venice, California, I got such glimpses into his life during discussions of his short-story collection, *The Dog and Other Stories* (1979), as well as his first volume of poetry, *One Foot in the Boat* (1977), both of which I published. I got to know him and his writing during the recalibration of his manuscripts into book form and came to understand how his devotion to writing was different from that of many other writers. Redressing inequities was not an option for Joseph Hansen; instead, the politics of being an author in the welter of midcentury homophobia meant that an extraordinary steadfastness was necessary to hold to the course he had set for himself.

That a film company wanted to neuter the first out-of-the-closet detective hero would not have ripped any of Hansen's illusions apart. In his introduction to *Bohannon's Country* (1993), a collection of short stories, he recounts that *Ellery Queen's Mystery Magazine* turned down a story in 1973 that featured Dave Brandstetter as its protagonist. According to Hansen, *EQMM* editor Fred Dannay explicitly justified his decision to reject the story "Surf" because subscribers "were not ready for homosexuality," even as nonnormative inclinations, let alone as part of the ordinary scheme of social life. Fifteen years later, *EQMM* relinquished this editorial policy and in June 1989 published Hansen's story, "Molly's Aim," which featured a gay second

character named Hugh Henderson. This particular publication gave Hansen immense satisfaction:

> I was pleased, because it meant I'd broken down a literary barrier against me and my kind. All my writing life, one of my aims has been to make my readers stand in the shoes of strangers and know what it's like to be someone else— someone perhaps very different from themselves, someone they may heretofore even have hated or feared.

Hansen was not the first to showcase a gay detective. George Baxt (1923–2003) created the first in 1966: Pharaoh Love, the gay (and black) protagonist of *A Queer Kind of Death*. As the social aftershocks of the 1970s grew ever more complicated, however, it was Hansen's detective who proved to be a far more sympathetic and engaging hero. One reason is that Hansen is careful not to misrepresent his subject matter. As he told editor Leland Hickman, in an interview for the last issue of *Bachy* magazine in 1981:

> Not to fake anything. That's the morality of craft. If you have a predisposition to be sentimental, then you have to recognize that as a weakness that will make you a bad writer, and get rid of it every time it crops up. You have to be a hard person when you sit down at the typewriter—not cynical, but clear-sighted, determined to tell the truth. When I'm writing, I insist to myself that things must go down on paper as they are. I do my damnest not to misrepresent the smallest thing, if I can help it.

As Hansen did not want to "misrepresent the smallest thing," he also did not want to exaggerate. If the straight world's fantasy of homosexual life is still dominated by excessive images of erotic gratification, Hansen's writing pushes back and rectifies that error while simultaneously affirming the tactile bond of human companionship. In helping a heterosexual reader comprehend what might still be regarded as an exotic subculture, Hansen is careful not to preach, even obliquely. Instead, he is illustrative. He shows the naive straight world that being gay is no more homogenizing than any other social category. Anthony P. Cohen pointed out years ago that communities are determined by a boundary line, and that those outside of any demarcated sphere perceive those inside the boundary line as all alike. All liberals "know" what Tea Party activists are like. All corporate CEOs "know" what Greenpeace activists are like. Only when one crosses that boundary line does one begin to comprehend the diversity and heterogeneity of any community. For any reader wishing to take that step, Hansen's Brandstetter novels are a superb guide.

★

In *Embracing a Gay Identity* (1993), Wilfrid R. Koponen observes:

> The hard-boiled detective novel, for instance, was originally largely homophobic. Yet Joseph Hansen has written a noteworthy series of frankly gay novels within that genre . . . Surprisingly, Hansen has won high praise from William Buckley's conservative news magazine *National Review*, which has consistently ridiculed gay people, gay rights activists, and the gay rights movement. It said of the sixth Dave Brandstetter mystery, "There's no one more promising on the detective story scene today, and *Gravedigger* [1982] is Hansen's best book yet."

Likewise, on the front cover of a paperback edition of *The Man Everybody Was Afraid Of* (1978), a banner that angles up from the bottom left-hand corner reads "SELECTED AS ONE OF TEN 'BEST BOOKS' OF THE YEAR IN THE CRIME CATEGORY BY THE NEW YORK TIMES BOOK REVIEW." But despite this level of praise from mainstream media outlets, Hansen's breakthrough required redoubled commitment midway through Brandstetter's pursuit of legitimacy: his regular publisher turned down the manuscript of *The Man Everybody Was Afraid Of*. According to Hansen (in his interview with Hickman), a dozen publishers, in fact, turned it down:

> That was a long, scary summer. I thought I was washed up as a writer, and didn't know what else I would do at my age to earn a living. But that novel did very well, much better than the earlier Brandstetter books. Ironically, the plot

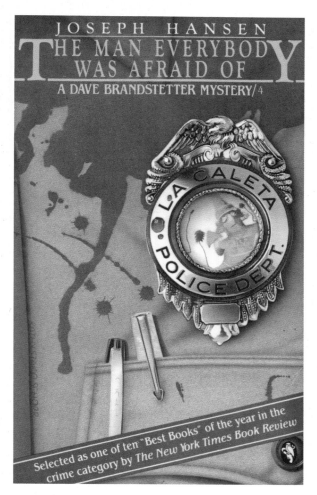

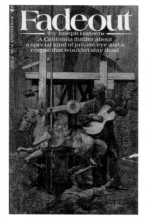

The Man Everybody Was Afraid Of (Owl Books, 1981)
Fadeout (Bantam, 1971)
The Man Everybody Was Afraid Of (Faber & Faber, 1978)

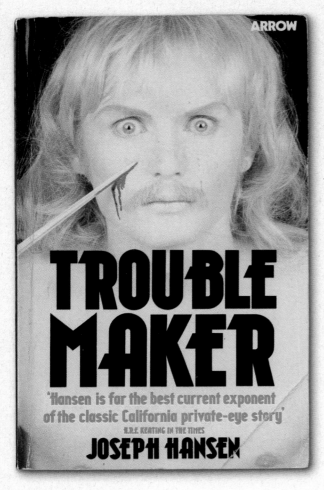

Trouble Maker (Arrow, 1979)
Skinflick (Henry Holt, 1980)
Troublemaker (Grafton, 1986)

was praised everywhere. And the book got me a lot of new goodies…publication in Japan, which hadn't happened to me before.

It may seem hard to believe that with such a solid track record Hansen would have had such problems getting his latest book published, but the problem was almost flagrantly in view. The liaison in *Afraid Of* between Dave Brandstetter and Cecil Harris, a young black man, would have been off-putting to the mainstream publishing establishment. Elsewhere within the same homophobic culture in the late 1970s, Glenn Burke, the African American baseball player who was the first professional ballplayer to come out as gay during his career and who popularized the now-ubiquitous "high-five" gesture, was driven out of the major leagues by antigay prejudice. Jackie Robinson had broken the racial barrier thirty years earlier, but being gay was another matter. In fact, the first mainstream film in which a white gay male had an ongoing relationship with an African American lover was *Philadelphia* (1993). The second? Now consider the sexual and racial lines that Hansen was already crossing in novels like *Afraid Of* and *Gravedigger* (1982).

Halfway through *Gravedigger,* the quest Dave had been on—for definite proof of an insured person's death—appears settled, and Dave and Cecil (his now long-term lover) are set to have an evening to themselves. No sooner have they headed up the staircase than Cecil remembers that there is a message on the answering machine. Within five minutes, Dave realizes the case he's working on needs immediate, renewed attention:

> [Dave] lifted down the sheepskin jacket from a big brass hook beside the door. He called, "I have to go out. See you for breakfast."
>
> "What!" The bedframe jounced. Heels thumped the loft planks. Cecil scowled down at him over the railing. He was naked, the firelight glancing off his blackness. "You going out? You leaving this?" He showed Dave what he meant. "What am I supposed to do with it here all by myself all night long?"
>
> "You can bring it with you." Dave shrugged into the coat. "If you don't mind missing your sleep."
>
> "Sleep would not be what I missed." Cecil vanished from view. "Wait for me. I'll be right there."

In the 1960s, when Hansen first began to sketch out the character of Dave Brandstetter, homosexuality was still classified as a disease. Hansen's stories are a fictional extension of the work done by psychologist Evelyn Hooker—who in 1957 argued against this classification—and help give a local habitation and a name to the kind of normative categorization that Hooker helped to establish. Novelists cannot produce stories worth rereading for their literary value if they focus on social commentary alone, yet one of the remarkable aspects of Hansen's literary career is the degree to which he managed both. In doing so, he makes it possible for readers to understand the intellectual arguments underpinning scientific experiments in the field of personal psychology and social formation. In probing the layered emulsions of Brandstetter's travails as a widowed gay man—having lost his longtime lover to cancer and trying to find a way to recuperate in a hostile society—Hansen demonstrated, long before the battle for gay marriage, that relationships between homosexuals who love each other are as complicated in their enduring intimacy as heterosexual commitments. Hansen's fiction enables his readers, both gay and straight, to encounter the internal dialectic of a social movement.

His accomplishment involved a tortuous journey. Hansen's boyhood was cinched by the Great Depression, and he never went further than high school. It was only in his early forties, in fact, that he began to earn even a modest living from his writing. Even so, by the early 1990s, Dave Brandstetter's investigations of insurance fraud cases had reached a readership in the hundreds of thousands in a total of twelve novels.

★

Beyond Hansen's courage to break through longstanding social mores is the question of whether the writing deserves revisiting.

In *Early Graves* (1987), Cecil confronts Dave Brandstetter in an almost accusatory tone of voice:

> "Did anybody ever tell you, you have ice water in your veins?"
>
> "Several people." Dave blew away smoke, groped for and found the ash tray in the blue dash. "On several occasions. Always when they knew I was right and they were wrong. Emotions doesn't change facts. And they hated believing that."

Pausing to savor Hansen's writing, we see that it would be an error to limit appreciation of his work to his trailblazing alone. Even in casual conversation, Hansen enfolds characterization of imagined people with supple, subtle syntax. The ending of that paragraph reads one way, but in its full unfolding ripples out like this: "Always when they knew I was right and they were wrong (and always) they hated believing that emotions doesn't change facts."

The fact that the spoken thought triggers one of the most acidic emotions only underscores the intransigence of facts under the brunt of inner, obdurate turmoil. One should note that "emotions" is treated like a collective noun and therefore takes the singular verb. Brandstetter is not a grammar sleuth who corrects others' speech, but he holds himself to an admirable standard; this conversation reveals the expectations that the character has for himself in negotiating the boundary between the straight world and the gay world.

Thanks to felicitously deft language like this, Hansen deserves to be remembered as one of the score of writers who changed the status of the detective novel in the field of serious literature. Until Ross Macdonald, Joseph Hansen, and P.D. James held their writing to the same standards of well-crafted sentences that are worth reading and rereading for the pleasure of their rhythmic intrigue, the mystery genre remained this outlier of literature on which only a handful of masterful writers (such as Raymond Chandler) resided. At a crucial stage in the post-Chandler development of the genre, Hansen was among those who made readers pay attention to the story told by the writing itself.

But if Hansen's work ended up alongside that of Chandler and Macdonald, it was not for lack of artistic ambition. He knew very well that "mysteries ghettoize you" as a writer; nevertheless, the formal requirements invigorated his ability to probe human frailty. Perhaps Hansen's passion for poetry was even part of his underlying attraction to the detective genre. "In its restrictions, the detective novel is closer to a poem than to a novel (with its "long, loosely structured" form)," he said in the interview with Hickman, "The music of Mozart, Bach, Hayden, is wonderful, held tight inside restrictive formats. But so is Mahler's *Symphony Number Three* wonderful." I linger on this aspect because to compare Hansen's writing only with other authors who produced memorable work in his primary genre is to fall prey to an easy error. Substantial authors allow us to see the cross-pollination that occurs between genres, and Hansen's prose recoils and imbricates itself with American poets in ways that need further consideration by literary critics. I would argue, in fact, that Hansen's literary project, including his control of tone and diction, owes more to poets such as Robert Frost and E.A. Robinson than to other detective novelists. Indeed, the most relevant books to set alongside Joseph Hansen's *Gravedigger* are Robert Frost's *North of Boston* (1914) and Sherwood Anderson's *Winesburg, Ohio* (1919).

One of my favorite examples of Hansen's ability to make a conventional situation memorable is his short story "Legacy," which was first published in 1965 in *One*, the pioneering gay magazine founded by Don Slater in Los Angeles. Midway through the story, country doctor Arthur Mohr gets a phone call in the middle of the night to help deliver a baby at a poor ranch. The weather is not cooperating, and his vehicular vision is hindered by his haste:

> In front of him loomed a battered pickup truck, not a light showing, no one inside it. Its front wheels were mired in the shoulder gumbo. Its sharp, shovel-shaped rear end half across the blacktop. He tramped the brake pedal, geared down, wrenched the wheel. No good. Not at this speed. Not in the rain. The stalled pickup rushed at him. *No*, he thought, *this can't be happening to me*. Then he thought, *Robie*.
>
> Then he no longer thought.

In many ways, there is no better method for learning how to write than to sit at one's desk and type up a story one admires. I had the fortune of publishing one of Hansen's collections outside of the mystery genre, *The Dog and Other Stories* (1979), in which the story "Legacy" was republished. As a young, aspiring publisher back in the days when typesetting machines had no disc memory, I learned from "Legacy" what *economy* meant in regard to writing. Few one-sentence paragraphs such as the one above have modeled how to render the culmination of a scene with connotative poignancy. The lead-up is on the mark: "No, this can't be happening to me" is followed by his final affirmation. In this scene, as in all his writing, accuracy and the refusal to be emotionally indulgent are crucial matters of artistic integrity.

Death Claims (Quercus, 1973)
Gravedigger (Grafton, 1985)
Death Claims (Holt, Rinehart and Winston, 1980)

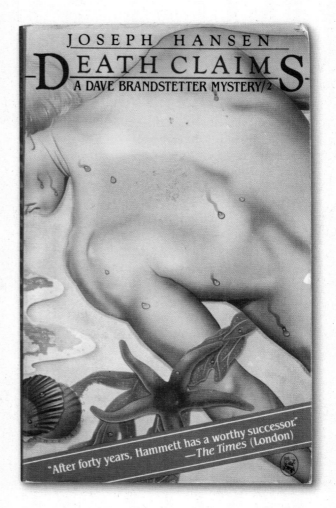

In citing Hansen's kinship with poets, I am also providing a way to address his underrecognized contributions to certain poetic movements, especially in Los Angeles. Of all the writers who contributed to the LA poetry renaissance in the second half of the twentieth century, Joseph Hansen probably gave the most and got the least in return. Most significantly, Hansen was one of the co-founders of the Beyond Baroque poetry workshop, a free and open-to-the-public gathering that has met on Wednesday evenings in Venice for forty-five years. Along with John Harris, Hansen established an accessible public workshop with serious standards of literary excellence. Hansen winning a National Endowment for the Arts Creative Writing Fellowship for his fiction a couple of years after starting the workshop only reinforced his stature as the workshop's standard bearer. And thanks in part to his commitment to helping others become better writers, the Beyond Baroque workshop's alumni include such poets as Wanda Coleman, Leland Hickman, Harry Northup, and Exene Cervenka, as well as noteworthy novelists Jim Krusoe and Kate Braverman.

Without his encouragement, I wonder where Leland Hickman would have found support for his long poem "Tiresias," which was the success upon which Hickman launched his editorial career. Almost no writer associated with or influenced by the Language writing movement realizes that Hickman's journey—which culminated with ten issues of the landmark literary magazine *Temblor*—began in a storefront workshop headed up by Joseph Hansen. As I recount in *Holdouts: The Los Angeles Poetry Renaissance, 1948–1992* (2011), Hansen's enthusiastic endorsement of Leland Hickman's poem was one of the pivotal moments of Los Angeles poetry's maturation in the 1970s.

Surely no other major mystery writer has played such an important role in the maturation of another literary genre in a major American city. Then again, few mystery writers were also poets as accomplished as Hansen. *One Foot in the Boat* compiled poems written between the early 1950s and the 1970s, but I would rather call attention to his best published poem, which remains uncollected. "The Dark/The Diary" is an account of the final illness of his spouse. Written in syllabics and hewing to an exact scheme of seven as a formal reiteration (seven syllables per line, seven lines per stanza, seven stanzas per part, seven parts to the whole poem), this poem is a profoundly tender, hauntingly unsentimental look at nursing a lifetime

One Foot in the Boat

Joseph Hansen

Joseph Hansen on the cover of *One Foot in the Boat*, his poetry collection, released by Momentum Press in 1977 (photo by Fay Godwin)

companion through the harrowing passage out of this life. It was published in an issue of *Zyzzyva* in the mid-1990s and deserves reprinting in any anthology that would claim to present the best American poetry of the past half century. One of Hansen's nondetective novels, *Job's Year* (1985), takes on a similar subject in a month-by-month account of a life's final year. In both "The Dark/The Diary" and *Job's Year*, one gets a sense that rather than just having one foot of his own in the boat of Charon, Hansen is helping his life's companion to step into that boat with both feet still in motion.

While working on this article, I went through several boxes of my personal archives and serendipitously found a flyer from a poetry reading twenty years ago: Joseph Hansen and FrancEyE (a.k.a. Frances Dean Smith) read together as a benefit for the Church in Ocean Park in Santa Monica on Sunday, August 25, 1996. The flyer took note that "FrancEyE's poems disappeared thirty-three years ago due to carelessness and a disordered life. Joseph Hansen's poems were buried in the '94 Northridge Earthquake." How much got buried in that earthquake is hard to determine. It is my understanding that Hansen's literary papers are in the possession of the Huntington Library, and that they remain uncatalogued a decade after arriving in San Marino. At some point, these papers need to become available to researchers. While literary critics have a significant amount of his prose to work with, no anthology of the Los Angeles literary canon will be complete until Hansen's poetry seizes its rightful place among its pages.

It was as a poet, in fact, that Hansen announced his retirement. Two days before the events of 9/11, a sonnet showed up in my email account at the University of California, San Diego:

SHUTTING UP SHOP
Lately, you realize it's all behind you,
You've said it all, there's nothing left to say,
The words you chose, the ideas that defined you
Were uttered long ago and far away.
Yes, a few strangers listened for a minute,
Some of them smiled and nodded, even spoke,

Seconded what you said, and the truth in it,
Lauded your words and what they could evoke.
But they had jobs to go to, lovers, cities
To bomb, children to feed, and words are never
In short supply among us, ironies, pities
Abound, and mouths to speak the words forever.

And then you're old and come to realize
Words are not half as eloquent as sighs.
—Joe Hansen
September 9, 2001

In this overly modest Prospero-like farewell, Hansen forgets his own character's stern reminder: "Emotions doesn't change facts." In this case, the fact is that although Hansen is not remembered to the extent that he deserves, those who treasure his writing should not sigh. His works are mentioned in histories on LGBT literature, detective fiction anthologies, and books such as David Fine's *Imagining Los Angeles: A City in Fiction* (2000). Of course, those mentions tend to be about Dave Brandstetter and fail to address Hansen's poetry, other prose, and even Hank Bohannon, his other detective. It is true that Brandstetter may be the first point of entry for many new readers of Hansen's

work, but any exploration of his writing shouldn't end there. The one thing I regret most in writing this brief piece is that I have not addressed the nondetective novels in the way they deserve. It is not just that such coming-of-age novels as *Living Upstairs* (1993) and *Jack of Hearts* (1996) are equally well written. These bildungsromans enable readers to imagine the vistas of Los Angeles that are described in documentary detail in books such as Daniel Hurewitz's *Bohemian Los Angeles and the Making of Modern Politics* (2007). Hansen's fictionalized accounts of his youth are every bit as engaging and empowering as the best of the Brandstetter series. In his interview with Hickman, he observed "that satisfactory relationships between human beings are so rare as to be nonexistent." One source of satisfaction remains in full force, however: the relationship between a reader and a writer that the reader can trust. Hansen's trust in us is well founded, as long as we make ourselves as vulnerable and honest as he did in his writing.

Bill Mohr

Black Is Beautiful

The Superspade Novels of Joseph Perkins Greene

Joseph Perkins Greene wasn't the most obvious person to concoct a series of pulp action novels. Yet his protagonist Richard Abraham Spade—a.k.a. "Superspade," professional football player turned troubleshooter—briefly rivaled Ernest Tidyman's better-known fictional private eye, John Shaft, as the baddest, blackest, and most beautiful crime solver of the 1970s.

Born in Spokane, Washington, in April 1915, Greene was an African American composer/lyricist who associated early in his career with songwriter Hoagy Carmichael, developed songs for Nat King Cole, and is said to have "discovered" jazz and pop vocalist Ernie Andrews, whose biggest hit, "Soothe Me" (1945), was a Greene creation. Greene rose to prominence during the 1940s and '50s, working with orchestra leader Stan Kenton and such familiar Kenton singers as June Christy and Chris Connor. Along with composer/arranger Pete Rugolo, Greene helped make Kenton's band one of the most popular in the nation. Several members of the Kenton Orchestra would form the genesis of what came to be known as West Coast jazz. Among Greene's most recognizable songs is "Across the Alley from the Alamo" ("Across the alley from the Alamo / lived a pinto pony and a Navajo / who sang a sort of Indian 'Hi-de-ho' / to the people passin' by"), a jazz standard—performed famously by the Mills Brothers—that was also adopted into the western swing songbook, thanks to bandleader Bob Wills.

Interviewed by *Texas Monthly* magazine in 1984, Greene—who, during his lifetime, never once visited San Antonio's historic Alamo Mission, the target of a notorious Mexican Army attack in 1836—recollected how "Across the Alley from the Alamo" was born during a dream he had way back in 1946. "I was lying in bed with a broken arm," said the lyricist. "About two o'clock in the morning I suddenly woke up—you know how you will be half asleep, half awake—then all of a sudden, like a miracle, I saw a picture of this Indian in front of the Alamo. I woke up my wife. I could still write with my right hand, so I started writing the melody,

Joe Greene (left) with Eddie Beal and Stan Kenton (*Jet* magazine, May 15, 1952)

and my wife wrote the lyrics as I told them to her. I finished the song in twenty minutes."

Of course, that ostensibly cheery melody about a Navajo wanderer and his faithful steed who are run over one day by a speeding locomotive is not the only Greene tune that might still strike a chord with modern listeners. The Internet Movie Database provides this short wrap-up of his musical career:

Songwriter ("Across the Alley from the Alamo," "And Her Tears Flowed Like Wine"), composer, author, producer and conductor, educated in high school and in private music study. He was a singer over KFRC in San Francisco, and later produced records for RCA Victor, Liberty and Vee Jay. His credits include conducting, scoring and writing work for television and films. Joining ASCAP in 1946, his other popular-song compositions include "Don't Let the Sun Catch You Crying," "All About Ronnie," "Make Me a Present of You," "Soothe Me," "A Ting A Ling," "Chicken Road," "Softly," "Dusky January," "Let Your Love Walk In," "Tender Touch," and "Annabelle."

Greene's work has been incorporated into a wide variety of movie soundtracks. Lauren Bacall performed part of his 1944 song "And Her Tears Flowed Like Wine" in Humphrey Bogart's 1946 picture *The Big Sleep*. And "Outa-Space" (1972), the funky-as-all-get-out

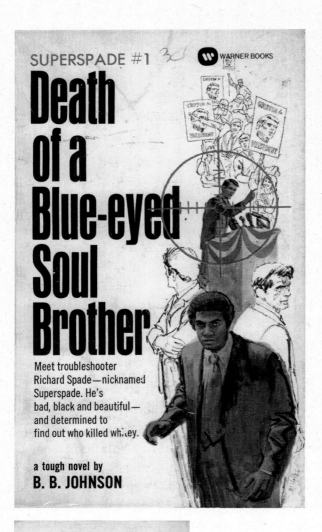

SUPERSPADE #1

WARNER BOOKS

Death of a Blue-eyed Soul Brother

Meet troubleshooter
Richard Spade—nicknamed
Superspade. He's
bad, black and beautiful—
and determined to
find out who killed whitey.

a tough novel by
B. B. JOHNSON

UP AGAINST THE WALL!

Richard Abraham Spade was finished with pro football—but the action in his life was just beginning.

Spade took on a job with a small college as a lecturer and part-time coach, in search of the quiet life. But no such luck.

His best friend, a dedicated politician, was assassinated and Spade was in the middle of a deadly blitz of bullets, broads and burning revolution—scrambling to save his beautiful black skin from being sliced up and served cold!

"B. B. JOHNSON" is the pseudonym for one of Hollywood's most talented and creative black personalities.

U.K. 75p
Printed in U.S.A.

Death of a Blue-Eyed Soul Brother (Warner Books, 1970)
Back cover of UK edition of *Death of a Blue-Eyed Soul Brother*, with shot of supposed author

instrumental piece Greene wrote with musician Billy Preston, featured not only in the 1999 film *Muppets from Space*, but in 2013's *The Look of Love*, a biopic focusing on British publisher/strip club owner Paul Raymond.

So how did this music maker wind up penning action novels? Associated Press Hollywood correspondent Bob Thomas explained the shift in an article syndicated in Ohio's *Toledo Blade* newspaper on May 17, 1970:

> Orphaned at 14, Greene [said he] "earned all the education I got." One of the ways he earned it was to peel 100 pounds of potatoes every morning before going to school.
>
> Greene displayed musical talent early, sang and played in local bands, then drifted south to San Francisco to become a radio singer.
>
> "I made band arrangements in bed and sold them to orchestras," Greene said. "My biggest break came when Stan Kenton recorded one of my songs, 'And Her Tears Flowed Like Wine.' Following that I had 'Across the Alley from the Alamo,' which sold 4 million records by Kenton, the Mills Brothers, Woody Herman, and others."
>
> Greene established himself as a song writer, record producer, and composer of musical scores.
>
> This prompted Paperback Library to commission the Superspade series, which are bylined "B.B. Johnson"—"in case I get tired of writing the books and they hire someone else."

Greene already had a business association with Paperback Library, a publisher that during the 1960s and '70s marketed the work of authors (from M.E. Chaber and Ed Lacy to Harlan Ellison, A.E. Van Vogt, and Wilkie Collins) in a wide variety of genres. Before adopting the B.B. Johnson alias and launching Richard Spade's six-book career, he had written at least one other novel for the same imprint under his own name: *House of Pleasure*, originally released in 1965. An "adult novel" (that fact gratuitously emphasized by the mostly nude blondes fronting its early editions), it exposed the "amorous adventures" of one Francesca Lundeen, a "bold, beautiful and accomplished brothel keeper (as skilled with her wit as she was with her feminine charms)," who catered to a deep-pocketed and powerful clientele in northern California. The 1968 Paperback Library version adds this plot synopsis: "THE DELIGHTS

SHE OFFERED FOR SALE MADE HER THE MOST POPULAR MADAM IN SAN FRANCISCO. DESIRED BY MANY MEN, FRANCESCA WANTED ONLY ONE—THE ONE MAN SHE COULD NEVER HAVE!"

It's unclear whether it was Greene's idea to produce a series of novels about sexy, strapping Richard Spade or the project was brought to him by Paperback Library editors. Whichever was the case, Greene took to the assignment with abundant energy at a time when, as he told the AP's Thomas, "Negroes need to have their own heroes."

Remember, when Greene sat down at his typewriter to bat out the Superspade books, it was the late '60s, an era that witnessed tremendous social and political change in the United States, including advancements made specifically by African Americans. Hard-won civil rights legislation enacted during the presidency of Democrat Lyndon B. Johnson had finally outlawed official discrimination (in the workplace, schools, and elsewhere) against people based on their race, color, religion, sex, or national origin. The Voting Rights Act of 1965 forbade racial inequities at the ballot box, and three years later the Civil Rights Act made it a federal crime to refuse or interfere with the sale or rental of properties based on a person's ethnic, religious, or birthplace heritage. It was also during the late 1960s and early '70s when the Black Power movement gained attention, endorsing racial pride among Americans of African descent and promoting political goals and institutions that were relevant to black communities.

Richard Spade was obviously proud of being African American, but he was no revolutionary. His attitudes reflected those of his creator, who was a moderate when it came to the so-called race situation. "He realizes that progress is not a one-way street," Greene said of Spade. "He knows that with increased respect comes increased responsibility." Although Spade bore the surname of Dashiell Hammett's most celebrated sleuth, he was not a traditional detective but rather a multilingual academic who was respected by blacks and whites alike, and whose cases often found him at odds with black militants.

We're first introduced to Richard A. Spade in *Death of a Blue-Eyed Soul Brother*, published in March 1970, a month before the U.S. release of Tidyman's *Shaft*. Reared in Los Angeles, the son of a Pullman railroad car porter, Spade is now a thirty-three-year-old black studies lecturer at fictional Greene College in Santa

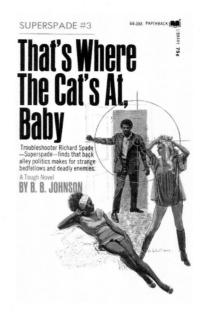

That's Where the Cat's At, Baby (Paperback Library, 1970)
Black Is Beautiful (Paperback Library, 1970)

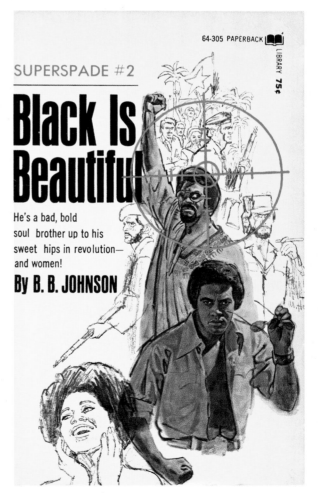

Barbara, a "very conservative, very nervous" Pacific coastal town located some ninety-five miles northwest of LA. On top of his lecturing responsibilities, Spade is hard at work on a master's degree in political science and coaches Greene's football team on a part-time basis. His credentials for the coach's position are unquestioned. Spade had achieved a "fair stature as an offensive tackle playing football" for the University of California–Los Angeles (UCLA) and in the process earned both All-American status and the nickname Superspade (or Super Spade, as it sometimes appears). He was subsequently a first-round draft pick by the San Francisco Forty-Niners, but his charge toward pro football celebrity was sidetracked by a soured relationship with a striking art studies major that led him into a two-year tour of duty in the Vietnam War. After returning to the States bearing a Silver Star and a Purple Heart, and forty-three pounds lighter than he'd left, he dove right back into football, only to have his career with the Forty-Niners ended two traumatic years later when, during a game against the hated LA Rams, Spade sustained serious injuries to his face as well as his torso.

There proves to be an upside to that physical damage, though. For when the plastic-surgery bandages are removed after six weeks, Spade finds that he isn't himself. He's considerably better, the spitting image of Hollywood star Gary Grant "but a bit darker." What's more, his body chemistry has been altered in the most unpredictable fashion, so that his sweat glands now excrete a musk with an aphrodisiac quality irresistible to the opposite sex. Even before Greene's hero can check himself out of the hospital, he is set upon by his "Scandinavian doll" of a nurse, who can't strip her scrubs off fast enough to satisfy her desire. "Thank you, you goddamn Rams!" Spade blurts out after this lustful encounter, the first in a redundant succession of trysts he'll weather before *Death of a Blue-Eyed Soul Brother* concludes.

While such a turn might seem like nothing more than the height of male fantasy, keep in mind that Greene was composing his tale near the start of the modern "sexual revolution," when a growing abundance of young adults were determined to celebrate casual intercourse as a quotidian element of life, rather than as something shocking—a physical act that deserved to be hidden, condemned, or repressed. Spade's steamy couplings reflected a cultural shift, even as they surely titillated any young male readers

who managed to get their mitts on the Superspade stories.

The plot of this initial Richard Spade yarn—promoted, as were all the Superspade books, as "A TOUGH NOVEL BY B.B. JOHNSON"—is rather less stimulating. Set in 1968, it finds the former football "hardnose" (and current judo/karate student) taking time out from his teaching job to serve as bodyguard for a rising U.S. presidential contender, Senator Wayne Griffin of Massachusetts. "Born with a platinum spoon in his mouth," and now a forty-two-year-old widower with seven children, Griffin is cut very obviously from the Robert F. Kennedy pattern: a wealthy but compassionate Democrat who voices the fervent optimism of a political reformer, with the threats on his life to prove it, both from radical right-wingers and other crazies opposed to any changes this liberal aspirant might hope to incite. Spade is tasked with keeping Griffin alive while he struggles to secure his party's nomination (and in the meantime disposes of a stack of *billets-doux* that might prove more than a bit embarrassing to the candidate). The senator is a conspicuous target due to his willingness to meet and work with minority leaders in Los Angeles, and his avid opposition to the stubborn residue of American bigotry. "Racism must be uprooted," he tells Spade. "Intelligent legislation and education must hasten the process." So when Griffin is gunned down in MacArthur Park, near downtown LA, police and pundits are not taken completely by surprise. Then again, they don't know what Spade knows, having seen it with his own eyes but kept it to himself: that the shooter was apparently a black man.

Greene seems torn here between penning a crime novel with political elements and composing a softcore porn tale, rampant with over-the-top sex scenes. Flip to one part of *Blue-Eyed Soul Brother* and you might find Spade enthusiastically bedding a buxom beauty or two (most of whom seem inclined to call our hero Dick, with coy significance). Cut to another and you'll come across a thoughtful analysis of President Johnson's declining political fortunes or a history lesson about Hiram Rhodes Revels, the first African American elected to the U.S. Senate (in 1870).

The five succeeding Superspade novels, all released over a two-year span, suffer from similar dichotomies of purpose. *Black Is Beautiful* (1970) has Spade tangling with "renegade brothers," none of whom can be completely trusted. In *That's Where the Cat's At, Baby* (1970), he steers clear of bullets while trying to help

SUPERSPADE #4

64-343   PAPERBACK LIBRARY   75¢

Mother Of The Year

Troubleshooter
Richard Spade—
Superspade—
has his afro
singed trying to
save a soul
sister on thin ice!

a tough novel
by
B. B. JOHNSON

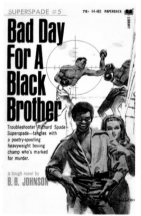

SUPERSPADE #5   75¢   64-482   PAPERBACK LIBRARY

Bad Day For A Black Brother

Troubleshooter Richard Spade—
Superspade—tangles with
a poetry-spouting
heavyweight boxing
champ who's marked
for murder.

a tough novel by
B. B. JOHNSON

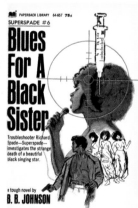

PAPERBACK LIBRARY   64-457   75¢
SUPERSPADE #6

Blues For A Black Sister

Troubleshooter Richard
Spade—Superspade—
investigates the strange
death of a beautiful
black singing star.

a tough novel by
B. B. JOHNSON

a young political opportunist win reelection as the mayor of a conspicuously corrupt town. *Mother of the Year* (1970) puts Spade to work protecting a comely African American beauty queen, Pussy Willow, from belligerent black feminists after she gives the names of only white folks in answer to a question about the ten greatest Americans of all time. *Bad Day for a Black Brother* (1970) sees him coming to the aid of a world heavyweight champion whose antiwar opinions and reproofs of America's political system have made him enemies among both blacks and whites. And in *Blues for a Black Sister* (1971), Spade investigates the fate of a black recording star, who has died suspiciously from a drug overdose.

These paperback novels looked great in their original versions, fronted with paintings by Mitchell Hooks, whose art was also prominent on works by Ross Macdonald, Eric Ambler, Christopher Isherwood, Jack Kerouac, and others. Yet their discordant mix of thrills and lasciviousness left most critics cold.

Still, as Bob Thomas explained in his long-ago AP profile, Greene's Superspade novels drew interest from the Hollywood film industry. At least for a while. Producer Saul David (*Fantastic Voyage*, *Our Man Flint*) was said to have been planning a James Bond–like movie franchise based on the Richard Spade stories, with major assistance to be lent by Greene himself, but nothing seems to have come of that partnership. Steve Aldous, in *The World of Shaft*, his 2015 study of Ernest Tidyman and the John Shaft character, mentions that Tidyman's filmmaking cohorts considered but rejected a proposal from Greene for a sequel to the 1971 motion picture *Shaft*. (The sequel made instead was 1972's *Shaft's Big Score!*)

Joe Greene, whose authorship of the Superspade novels had not been prominently publicized (a note on the books said only that B.B. Johnson was "THE PSEUDO-NYM FOR ONE OF HOLLYWOOD'S MOST TALENTED AND CREATIVE BLACK PERSONALITIES"), perished of kidney failure in June 1986, at age seventy-one. While his obituaries heralded his musical successes, the majority failed to mention that he'd been an author at all.

J. Kingston Pierce

Mother of the Year (Paperback Library, 1970)
Bad Day for a Black Brother (Paperback Library, 1970)
Blues for a Black Sister (Paperback Library, 1971)

What Men Fear

An Interview with M.F. Beal

Author M.F. Beal was born in New York City on September 6, 1937. She attended Cornell University and Barnard College, earning her BA in 1960, and then the University of Oregon, where she received an MFA in 1970. Beal has a long history of political activism, mostly focused on women's issues. For her literary work, she has received numerous accolades, including the Prince Prize for dramatic literature, awarded in 1960, and the Atlantic Grant, conferred in 1975.

Beal released three books in the 1970s. The first, *Amazon One* (1975), was a fictional account of the experiences of the Weather Underground, focusing on four radical women. The book earned critical acclaim. Atlantic Grant prize reviewers praised the manner in which Beal "exposes the political reasoning, the private sensibilities, the anger and fear of a group of radical activists convinced that America is the enemy and violence their salvation."

The second, *Safe House: A Casebook Study of Revolutionary Feminism in the 1970s* (1976), combined cultural criticism, political analysis, and reportage. "What Men Fear," a politically charged essay about the gendered implications of literal and figurative violence, made up 32 of the book's 154 pages. Beal devoted the rest of the volume to the subject of the Symbionese Liberation Army (SLA), a self-described "revolutionary" organization most notorious for kidnapping, on February 4, 1974, newspaper heiress Patricia Campbell Hearst. *Safe House* is not Hearst's story, however, but rather Beal's attempt to reconstruct the final days of six members of the SLA who died in a police raid in Los Angeles on May 16, 1974. *Safe House* also includes an SLA chronology and excerpts from the organization's communiqués.

Beal's third and last published volume, *Angel Dance: A Thriller*, marked a return to fiction. In it, Beal explored detective writing, playing with the form and formulae of the genre. Chiefly, Beal inverts the convention of having male detectives and female victims. Maria Katerina Lorca Guerrera Alcazar (a.k.a. Kat Guerrera), the central figure in the story, is a radical, journalist, bodyguard, and amateur sleuth who finds herself entangled in intrigues surrounding Angel Stone, a prominent feminist educator and author.

Initial reactions to the novel were not terribly positive—even among reviewers in feminist periodicals such as *Ms.* and *off our backs*. Terri Poppe, writing in the latter, led with the line: "This is not a book I would urge you to read." It may be that reviewers were unsure how to respond to fiction that operated so differently from either traditional novels or genre fiction. Scholar Kathleen Gregory Klein described the challenge posed by *Angel Dance*: "Is this a feminist, political, revolutionary novel which organizes itself around the familiar story of mystery or is it a mystery novel which adopts the look of the times for its authenticity and immediacy?" Whatever the book's early reception, scholars have increasingly described *Angel Dance* as a pathbreaking work, especially as it helped establish the genre of female detective fiction and even lesbian detective fiction.

In the following interview from 2010 Beal discusses her life as an author and advocate. She identifies some of her literary influences and describes how she became a writer. Finally, Beal comments on her works and their critical reception, explaining why she stopped publishing but continues writing.

How did you start writing?

Reading a lot when I was a little girl. . . . I'm an only child and had no playmates to speak of, and I just fell into a lot of good writing when I was young. I remember submitting my first manuscript to [teen magazine] *Seventeen*. They had a young writers' contest, and I wrote a horribly lurid, melodramatic thing and sent it off to them. It wasn't accepted. At age thirteen, I guess I wasn't mature enough to make it convincing. I did get a

M.F. Beal, author image from 1974 Little, Brown edition of *Amazon One*, Michael Kidd

very nice rejection note that said, "Keep on trying, this is good stuff," so I cherished that to my bosom.

By the time I got into high school, I was showing a talent for writing and I was encouraged by a very nice guy, named Schroeder... [laughs] *Mr.* Schroeder. Also by another teacher, whose name escapes me entirely.

Did you grow up in Ithaca?

I was born in New York and lived in White Plains during the war, and then after the war, we went to Germany. My father was in the military. He was trying to put together collective bargaining, a system so the workers could communicate with the bosses. The analysis was that this had sparked the Nazis, the suppression of unionists... so the idea was to figure out a way to avoid this in the future, and collective bargaining is what they came up with. So we were over there for quite a while and we lived in France, as well. We came back to Ithaca, where he got his PhD.

And then I got to Barnard [College], and [poet and novelist] George P. Elliott was one of my teachers. He

thought I was a solid B, which is okay. Then, at Cornell, I took a year off, and I just had one class that year, with [author] "Phil" [James] McConkey. It was in that class that those of us who came to be known, in very small literary circles, as the Cornell writers [assembled]: [Thomas] Pynchon, [Richard] Fariña, David Shetzline (my future spouse), and I were in that class, and then there was another guy, David Seidlin. He writes TV scripts now. We were all in that class.

That's quite a group.

Yeah. In retrospect, it was like that Princeton class, the famous class that included F. Scott Fitzgerald and all that group. It just happens now and then, I guess.

So you started with short fiction and worked your way toward longer fiction later on?

I started with the thirteen-page format, which was very popular with magazine editors at the time. It's a real short story. I worked my way up to twenty pages or so, and then I said to myself, "This is silly. I'm being superficial here if I just do this slice-of-life, followed by the *satori* moment," the epiphany, and I thought I'd like to try something a little bigger. Also, I was older. I was in my thirties and I was in this area of California—and that place was jumping back in the late '60s and '70s, and then I came up here [to Oregon] in '70. I came back and finished a master of fine arts at U of O [University of Oregon].

So when did you start your MFA studies? I know you finished in 1970.

I started in spring of '69, and I just plowed through. I had to get a job. My former spouse David was quite ill at the time. It was either that or go on welfare. I decided that the stigma at the time of being on welfare was not good for my kids. I would have been very happy to draw checks from the state and stay home and take care of my family, but I knew from bitter experience how welfare kids were stigmatized by teachers as being not entirely okay. I thought, "I've got a BA, might as well get an MFA." I went through there pretty damn fast.

One of my professors who gave me an "A" for a paper I did on Conrad, he wanted me to expand it into a PhD thesis. He was shocked when I told him I was going to pull up stakes. I sent out seventy-two letters and got three or four replies, and I took the one [job] that was the closest. Started working at wage-slave wages for California State University at Fresno and was able to support my family for eight years, until my former spouse decided he wasn't happy with the thing. I said, "Well, I don't want to teach, either." So I quit, and he got a divorce.

What was your experience with teaching like?
It was wonderful. I enjoyed being paid for something I enjoyed doing, and the students were delightful. I did it well, and therefore I enjoyed doing it. And I got three books written out of it.

How did you get started on *Amazon One*?
By then, I had met all these people who were doing stuff. The thing about the Weathermen, the Weathermen never hurt anyone physically. They destroyed the symbols of the state. They were upper-class children of lawyers, etc. What they were doing—by a socialist, it would be considered what Mao described as leftist adventurism. Trying to make a revolution without the masses just doesn't work, as we're finding in Iraq and as we found in Vietnam. The North Vietnamese had a mass movement, and the South didn't. So the North creamed the South, and us in the bargain.

So, I could see the nobility of the effort, and the sincere attempt on the part of children of privilege to maybe atone a little—assuage them of their guilt. They were going to put themselves into danger, but they weren't going to go and actually fight a war. They were for the most part 4-F [deemed unfit for military service] or they weren't eligible as women. Seventy percent of the Weathermen in 1970 were women. I knew the character of these highly educated young women who were in the movement. There were some working-class people involved, as well. I wanted to portray that. Whites were doing things—they were doing things like putting bombs in buildings. Once again, it was a case of wanting to say something. I knew that all the notice that would be taken of them would be "Oh God, these bad kids."

And they still get characterized that way.
Yeah. That's the fault of [Robert Jay] Lifton, that psychologist. He wrote an article for the *Atlantic Monthly* [as well as a 1970 book *History and Human Survival: Essays on the Young and Old, Survivors and the Dead, Peace and War, and on Contemporary Psychohistory*]. They wanted me to respond to it, but I said, "No, I'm not going up against a psychiatrist." The gist of his argument was that all of these people were in rebellion

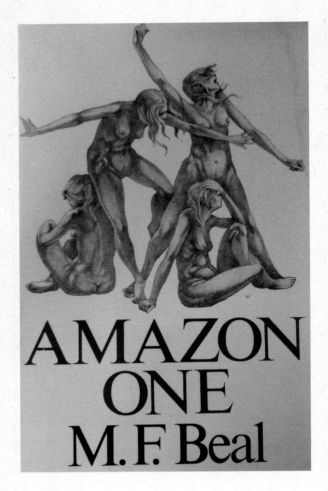

Amazon One (Little, Brown, 1974)

against their fathers, that basically all this was an adolescent revolt against the father. Well, if your father's out there killing people, maybe you ought to have an adolescent rebellion.

Or a lifelong one! So you came to know some people and wanted to tell the human side of the story.
I wanted these people to be human, to be humanized—so they're not just the evil, bad seed, the Lillian Hellman [author of the Broadway drama *The Children's Hour*] thing. People have motivations. They may not act logically, but they act out of motives. The action can be deplorable, but the motive can be very good.

They were trying to make a splash to get noticed. They wanted the authorities—the [U.S. Secretary of Defense Robert] McNamaras and whatnot—to realize that they had a student revolt on their hands, an actual rebellion, similar to what the Women Against the Czar did. The women who were involved in the conspiracy to blow up the czar [in Russia in 1881]. They too were educated women. They had been educated in Switzerland and were upper-class. They just decided to take the matter into their own hands.

I don't know why this is so difficult for men to understand. They understand that if they get between a bear and its cub, the mother bear will attack them. Why can't they see that human females also have instinctual feelings about protecting and nurturing? Don't attack unless you are ready to be attacked back. I see a great deal of that. And it didn't have anything to do with rebellion against the father.

I vowed early in my career that I was not going to write domestic novels. Everybody was appalled. "What? Foreign revolution? Unsuitable!" [laughter]

What motivated you to write *Safe House* as nonfiction?
Safe House was the product of sitting in on the [Patricia] Hearst trial and knowing, once again, being in a place where I literally knew these people—not well and not all of them, but they were out and around Berkeley. I knew what they were reading, and I used the internal texts. The communiqués they put out—they delivered them to Pacifica [Radio], and I would listen to the tapes. You could tell from what they were talking about what they'd been reading.

After the book came out, I was approached by a very slimy little character, who I subsequently realized was FBI. He was just one of those mole type guys, and he was just super-interested in my views on communism.

And I said to him, "I don't know about communism, but it seems like the Russians have a pretty good deal there after millennia of serfdom. What I'm opposed to is totalitarianism; I don't care what form it takes." "Oh, my." Subsequently, after the book had come out, he offered to take me into the witness protection program, resettle me, if I would rat on my obvious friends in the SLA. Well, I had nothing to rat that I hadn't put into the book. I said, "There it is." I referenced it very carefully, you know—index, the whole *schmear*. "You want to read that stuff, go read it. It's there."

The reason I used a nonfiction approach was that I did have the information at my fingertips, and since everybody was dead or in prison, it wasn't the same as writing about live Weathermen. Once again, it was the memory of what the cops did to the Black Panthers in Chicago and Oakland, and now here they are doing it in a ghetto in Los Angeles, Compton.

I went [to the site of the Compton massacre] with some friends. They had a plaque painted on the wall of the house that was next to it, that was still standing. The plaque said, "Here lie seven SLA dead at the hands of the police who came with . . ." (and then describing all the weaponry they had). [The incineration] was an incredibly precision job. The police just took out that one house in a neighborhood where the houses were maybe ten feet apart. Everyone was watching. Everybody in the neighborhood was watching. I thought to myself, if this is the new fascistic way of dealing with dissidents . . . Obviously, these people were severely dissident, but don't they get a trial?

I figured that if they've decided that they should just burn people out for various reasons, I had better get it down on paper, and that was why I undertook [the project]. It was a pretty grim task, I'll tell you, not only the writing and collating of it but also working with all the . . . The whole group of us [Beal, the SLA, and their supporters] working together, boy oh boy oh boy.

I thought, "Well, maybe this will end it. Maybe they'll see that burning people out is not the way to go." But then they burned out the Waco folks, the Branch Davidians.

Was that the only contact you had with the FBI?
Oh, no. There would always be two of them, a Mutt and a Jeff. They would always be terribly polite, but they would ask questions like: "How can you harbor a draft evader? How can you do this? How can you do

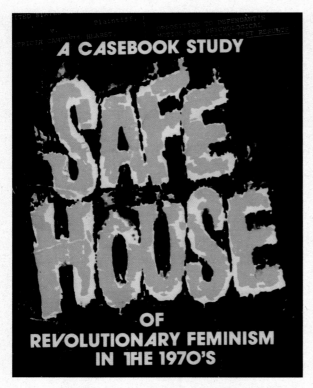

A CASEBOOK STUDY

SAFE HOUSE

OF REVOLUTIONARY FEMINISM IN THE 1970'S

Safe House (Northwest Matrix, 1976)
Safe House back cover
Patty Hearst on the cover of the April 29, 1974, edition of Newsweek

that? You seem like such a well-educated, law-abiding person." You call them "draft dodgers"; I call them "conscientious objectors." I get them lawyers.

One of my neighbors, who was also involved in sheltering fugitives, finally got annoyed. She sent in for her Freedom of Information Act material, and when it came she said, "Oh, Mary, there's about twenty pages on you folks." She was living in our place at the time. She showed them to me, and they were a howl. It would say, "Agent (blanked out) and Agent (blanked out) visited the Shetzline Seal Rock ranch." Now, this is a little, old derelict farm, but I loved the sound of it. Here we are, we're rich ranchers! "And talked about (blanked out the rest of the page)." And it went on like that page after page after page. "Shetzline admitted (blank)." That kind of stuff, you know...

Then, when [in 1978 San Francisco mayor George] Moscone was shot [along with openly gay district supervisor Harvey Milk], we had no idea—and that damn [Dan] White guy, who turned out to have done it, an ex-cop. I thought, "Oh my God, they're starting to wipe out public figures now." So, I said *hasta luego* to California. When they start shooting mayors, I get out. I had met Moscone, and he was a thoroughly nice man. I worked on his campaign. Well, it turned out that that guy [Dan White] wigged out on a Twinkie. That was his excuse.

So, you had a lot of visits from agents, even though the records are more blanks than words . . .
It was always the same thing. "How can you bring yourself . . ." I wouldn't have been as polite as [then spouse] David [Shetzline] was, but he was in the army, and I think he was aware of the power they had in a way that I wasn't.

Besides the slimy agent, what was the response you got to *Safe House*?
Well, I wanted Charlotte Mills, my editor and publisher, to do a press run of four thousand. I said, "This book is going to go to libraries." And she got cold feet, so she wound up doing a print run of one thousand. She put out a flier to libraries—college and university libraries—and that edition of one thousand was gone in two months, and she came to me and said, "Mary, I wish I'd gone for four thousand, but I just didn't realize that it would be this saleable." Oh, well.

It was reviewed in—I don't know whether that magazine is still around—there was a feminist magazine in the '70s, I don't remember the name of it. They just hated it. Oh God—"We can't get into this stuff. We're too busy forming a peaceful movement. This just rakes stuff up and makes us seem like we're a bunch of horrible radicals, and we're not." Oh, you know, the ordinary women stuff. I get so annoyed with some of those people I want to kick them in the . . .

I was quite struck by the piece, "What Men Fear," in which you provided a feminist analysis of the political uses of literature, drawing parallels between the suppression of women writers and the efforts to subdue the SLA.
"What Men Fear"? Yes. They don't like it. That continues to be true. Strong women are a real threat.

That was quite a find. I have often tried to convey some things in teaching, and I've used pieces such as Tillie Olsen's "Silences in Literature" and Joanna Russ's *How to Suppress Women's Writing* to do it, and [in your work I had] a newfound favorite. These seem to me all powerful statements.
Well, any little bit helps. I know my first widely anthologized story—I guess it is the most widely anthologized—is "Survival," the story of the woman whose son is killed in Vietnam. That appeared in a '60s anthology collection and was very widely read in soc[iology] classes. This was before I had written any novels, and it got me started with name recognition. It's always good to have your stuff out in front of students.

What inspired you to write *Angel Dance* as a thriller?
Amazon One, while carefully crafted and all that, was a "small market" book, they call it "small quality" in the book business, and I thought maybe if I place some of these people who are, after all, doing very thrilling things, in the context of a classical thriller.

So, *Angel Dance* has all the classic elements of a thriller. It's got a beautiful heroine who's being pursued by numerous people, it's got kinky sex, it's got lesbian sex, it's got a long lost son who turns out to be the murder victim, drugs, etc.

You've spoken about how you intended to open up a market of new readers by writing it as a thriller. Had you been reading a lot of thrillers and detective fiction?
I don't particularly care for thrillers if they're really the pursuer-with-the-knife type. I can't read Mary Higgins [Clark] because she tends to put her heroines into horrible situations . . . and I've had enough of that in my own life. But I very much enjoy detective stories of the English cozy, where everybody gathers in a stately old home and they proceed to kill the guy who owns it, and you have to figure how who did it—whodunit.

I enjoyed reading Erle Stanley Gardner as a kid. I loved the fact that he wrote so many thrillers. I had a neighbor who had every single one. She got them through some book club. Mabel Sealey. She was a retired English professor at Cornell, and she would loan them to me one at a time. I worked my way through the entire collection. And Agatha Christie. [Her mysteries] have excellent plot and characterizations, although Erle Stanley Gardner is not much in the way of characterizations. . . . And then I went through Raymond Chandler and Dashiell Hammett. But frankly, no one was doing women as heroines in thrillers and detective fiction at that time.

That's true. I've seen *Angel Dance* mentioned several times as a pathbreaking piece.
That was deliberate on my part. I made the victim a male, because so often the victims were female in those days. I roughed her up a little, and then she got her symbolic revenge at the end. I wanted to do a circular plot, you know, where at the end you're brought back to the beginning with the [reprised question] "What did George say to you that night at the Downstairs?" And I really do enjoy my final line there: "Not bad for a welter-weight blond." [laughter]

I was teaching at Fresno State at the time, and I wanted to write the detective as a Hispanic American. She's got a Spanish father and a Cuban mother—because I wanted to just put the whole Cuba thing out there, how people literally had to flee Cuba under Batista. They were the earlier wave of union activists and what-not that he was cracking down on. That was her mother, one of those women, and her father suffered under Franco. Here were a couple of people who had to flee their homelands because of dictatorships, and they give birth to this American child, and she's a leftist.

She's not a Chicana. I don't know why they made her a Chicana on the back-cover blurb—probably because they don't know the difference. Chicanas [are of Mexican descent]. She came from New York City.

There is something in the character of Chicana women that I liked very much, that sense of "I don't need a man; I can do this myself." Now, this is not universally so, but the Chicanas I knew at Fresno State who took my classes, they were interested in building on what they could do as a woman. One of my students was a cofounder of the Teatro de Aztlán, which turned into the theater troupe that went around and did radical skits for Cesar Chavez when he was organizing the United Farm Workers.

Chavez was in Fresno at the time, and I knew him. He was a wonderful person, and it was at that time [1973] that the cops shot the young woman who was on a picket line and let her bleed to death behind the police line. They wouldn't call an ambulance. I had a student who was shot, and the cops let him bleed to death. So I wanted to get something of that sense of purpose that I saw. They were very committed to the cause, *la causa*.

How did you come to meet Chavez?

I was teaching, and I was at a faculty party one night, and he was there telling faculty members what was going on in the union. We developed a friendship. He would come to Fresno State every year and give us a speech, and I would join him and we would walk on the picket line. [You] get a lot of talking done on a picket line.

How did the second edition of the book come to happen?

Daughters Inc. put out the first edition. [Crossing Press reissued it in 1990.] They were trying to put together a library of contemporary women writers of the non-domestic type

Do you continue to write?

Since I stopped publishing out of sheer disgust with the publishing world, I've led an entire different life. We started the first women's shelter in Oregon in Newport. We formed an organization called the Women's Resource Center of Lincoln County and started a shelter. That was back in '75, when we started. We had lots of battered women and children sheltered in our place. We called it a safe house, and it was so unpopular with the local men that they cancelled funding for us. We had a small amount of funding to rent a house, etc. And instead [they] devoted the money to the animal shelter; the rationale given was that they had more complaints about [mistreatment of] animals than they did about women being beaten. So, it was uphill, but we also started a Women Against Rape in

this county and just generally raised hell, to the point where it's no longer fashionable to beat your wife. It's done, but you don't brag about it the way you did when this whole thing started out.

And so that's the second life I had after I left teaching and quit publishing. . . . I got into women's issues very heavily, in a leadership way, 'cause I had the credentials. So that's what happened to the rest of my life, in case anybody's wondering. People say to me, "Well, what happened?" Well, all of a sudden it seemed more important to me to pick up the bleeding out of the street and shelter them than to write about it. Although I do write about it, I quit focusing solely on the writing. I gave up on publishing. My old friends in publishing just vanished. And the people that I didn't like in publishing, they hung on, and I just said, "No, I'm not going to do this."

It's not hard for me to imagine disgust with the publishing world.

Yes. It was never particularly nice, but there used to be a gentlemanly façade, and now it's just, "How come there's not more of this, that, and the next thing?"

You have to write to a formula now. The character of Kat, Katerina Guerrera—people say to me "Well, why don't you make a series out of it?" Well, no. I did it once for the fun of doing it—in the genre—[not] to tie myself to a genre and keep pumping out Kat Guerrera stories.

And so people have picked up on threads of what I did. They've turned it into these female detectives, but they're not true to the genre, because the true detective works alone. If you go back to [Raymond] Chandler and [Dashiell] Hammett, their guys worked alone. That was the whole point. "But down these mean streets a man must go who is not himself mean, who is neither tarnished nor afraid." You know that line from Chandler.

Right—the solitary one . . .

And somehow, the writers of the lady detective stories feel they have to have a guy, they have to have their [female] detectives involved with a cop or somebody with the skills they might need if they get in over their heads. . . . I can't read that stuff. They may as well be writing bodice-rippers. They've turned it into—well, not even Dickens did that much injury. He wrote serials, but he wrote them in a literary way.

They try to make this lady detective thing conventional . . . And what I was trying to do was to make it radical. They want to please people. I didn't give a

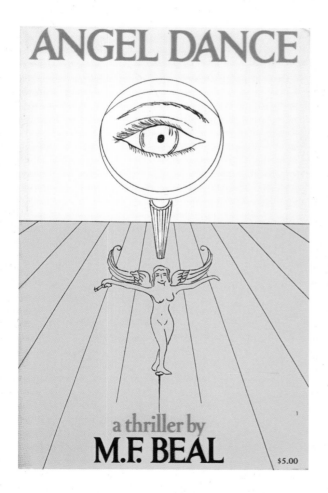

ANGEL DANCE

a thriller by
M.F. BEAL

$5.00

damn whether I pleased people. I knew they wanted certain things, and so I gave it to them in the interest of getting them to experience a new perspective, but I didn't try to make it conventional—where the woman is the conventional, domestic-type woman; she's got a boyfriend, she's got kids—in other words, she's got a life. The detective does not have a life, the true detective. The true detective is his detection. That's all you know about him. You don't know anything about [Philip] Marlowe or [Sam] Spade.

It's part of the mystique.

Yep. Also, in the classic detective story, while the detective was getting bopped on the head now and then and shot at, there was no true mayhem. He didn't get shot, he got shot at. He didn't wind up in the hospital. He got bopped and he had a knot on his head. Now this was unrealistic, but it was the form, basically. An invincible spirit is what it suggests, and I really wanted to capture that.

I know you said earlier that you roughed her up a little bit, but you did more than that.

Yeah, but I didn't leave her permanently maimed. She had a very appropriate response, which is she went out and she bought a gun. Now, I think that she would have been better off taking a refresher martial arts course. But at the time I wrote that, martial arts—karate—was just starting in this country. I knew a guy who was in the Olympic tests for karate and he was my son's age, and that's where I learned it. But there were virtually no dojos, no instruction studios open at that time. That all happened after Vietnam. Guys started coming back and doing that. A lot of stuff that seems very commonplace now was quite new at that time.

I wanted to be realistic. Also, as I mentioned before, I didn't want to have women as victims. I'm so sick and tired of women as victims.

But you turned the tables.

Right. Yup. The guys are the ones who have to moderate their behavior, not the women.

Are you working on anything now?

I'm working on a cookbook with my grandson. He picked the title: *100 Years of Succulent Seafood Cooking on the Oregon Coast.* We're going to do seafood recipes. I may as well turn my forty-two years of living on the coast into something or other.

[Some years ago] my stepmother wanted me to write children's stories. She just was extremely distressed when *Amazon One* was published. It just was so damn *unfeminine*, it made her nervous! "Mary, you're such a good writer. Why don't you write a story for children?" But I just couldn't do it. I think I can show my gentler side with a cookbook, though. I don't think I actually need to descend into children's books to show that I'm multifaceted.

The funny thing is the more naive reader thinks that I did the things I write about. They meet me, and I'm this old lady. I'm not obviously wearing a gun, and I have a fairly feminine appearance. I don't look like a typical stereotyped lesbian. For one thing, I'm not lesbian. I'm bisexual.

So they think you're your own characters somehow.
Yeah. Another thing, they think because I write about people who are involved in illegal acts, that I am espousing them. Well, to quote Florence Kennedy, the black activist lawyer [who died in 2000], "Honey, women got as much right to be violent as we got to shit." Florence Kennedy—she had a wonderful cackle. My editor called her up after *Safe House* went out for pre-reviews and said, "We're getting criticism on *Safe House* because the women are so violent."

So, I don't condemn [illegal acts of violence]. If women are acting in this way, I want to write about it, because I want to say to the world, "Look, folks, women are not merely staying home."

My aunt Helen [Beal] Woodward wrote a book about historical women who did so-called masculine things. Say, a woman who was a surgeon during the Civil War, and the one who was a spy, and the Pankhursts [suffragettes Emmeline and Sylvia] and so forth. She called it *The Bold Women* (1953), because that was the characteristic of all those women—their boldness. I'd like to see a whole lot more encouragement of boldness in girls.

I hate it when young women get the message, which is often consciously given by their female relatives, that if you're smart, [you] won't get a man. Well, we know what that is.

So you say you still write, even though you've given up on the publishers?
I just finished a seventy-page story. It's completely unpublishable. Who the hell will publish a seventy-page story? The only way it could possibly be published would be within a collection of my stories, but I think it's one of my better pieces. It's very tight. I have two novels sitting in a drawer. They're completely finished. I just lack any ambition to send them around . . . and I've got probably about a half dozen unpublished short stories.

I incorporated as much [communalism] as I could in my writings. All of my writings are about communal groups. When you think about it, all revolutionary activity takes place en masse.

I tried to shift the focus a little. There's probably one spokesman or one male who's more prominent, but the women are the movers. They're the ones who keep the whole thing going. And also, in many respects they're the ones who give guys a poke. If you're going to talk about it, you won't do it. If you're going to do it, don't talk about it.

The idea that men are coming up with the motivating issues and that women just sort of fall in behind is ridiculous once you've read Emma Goldman or Rosa Luxemburg. Although I myself am very fond of Prince Peter Kropotkin. He was a communalist; he believed in people living in communal environments. But Luxemburg and Goldman were actually: "Let's smash the state. Let's get rid of dictators. Capitalism stinks, it's got to be gotten rid of."

A great strength of your work is its engagement: keenly observing the world and remarking people's choices.
David Hajdu said a nice thing. He said that he had encountered *Angel Dance* for the first time when he was working on his book *Positively Fourth Street* (1996), about Bob Dylan. He read it, and he said "It took me back to those days. It was very evocative of that time period."

That is something I wanted to do in my writing. I wanted to evoke a period when it was actually happening. I write about the present. It's tough writing about the present. You just have to be real careful with what facets of the present you write about. You have to give as full a picture as possible.

Linda Watts

Shafted

On Ernest R. Tidyman and the Makings of *Shaft*

By all accounts, 1971 was a great year for former news-paperman–turned–pulp novelist Ernest R. Tidyman. Along with the paperback release of his hard-boiled debut *Shaft*, the Cleveland, Ohio, native cowrote the film version for MGM as well as the screenplay for *The French Connection*. The year before, *French Connection* producer Philip D'Antoni and director William Friedkin read *Shaft* in galley form and were impressed with Tidyman's gritty gumshoe story. "I was shocked when he walked into my office, because I was expecting a black person, because *Shaft* was about African Americans," D'Antoni recalls in the 2001 documentary *Making the Connection: The Untold Stories*. "Not only was he white, but a very WASP-y person from Ohio."

At the time, Tidyman was a forty-two-year-old former *New York Times* reporter who began his career as a teenaged journalist for the Cleveland *Plain Dealer*. After Tidyman's stint at the *Times*, he started thinking about writing *Shaft*. "The idea came out of my aware-ness of both social and literary situations in a changing city," Tidyman told a writer in 1973. "There are winners, survivors and losers in the New York scheme of things. It was time for a black winner, whether he was a private detective or an obstetrician."

Three years after the assassination of Martin Luther King, "the black private dick that's a sex machine to all the chicks," as soulful composer Isaac Hayes described him in the Oscar-winning "Theme from *Shaft*," became a cinematic symbol of Black Power and a mainstream household name. The seminal film also helped birth the 1970s blaxploita-tion film movement that includes *Super Fly* (1972) and *The Mack* (1973). The same night Hayes accepted the Academy Award for best song, Tidyman also won a gold statue for *The French Connection* screenplay. Yet, in Shaft's forty-year history as a movie icon, most fans of the film know little about Tidyman's pulp fiction series. Between 1971 and 1975, Tidyman wrote seven Shaft novels, including *Shaft among the Jews* (1972) and *Shaft Has a Ball* (1973).

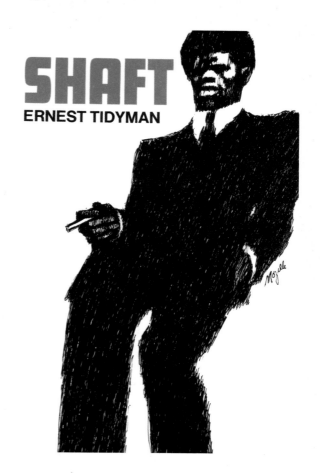

Shaft (Macmillan, 1970)

Tidyman's fourth wife and widow Chris Clark, a former blue-eyed Motown soul singer and screenwriter who was nominated for an Oscar for cowriting the screenplay to the 1972 film, *Lady Sings the Blues*, describes her late husband as "a big grizzly bear who scared people when he was angry." Tidyman dropped out of school at thirteen. His police reporter father forced him to get a job at the paper. "My father was an off-campus journalism professor to hundreds of guys who went through the *Plain Dealer* process," Tidyman once said.

"It was the other reporters who shaped him as a writer and a reader," Clark says from her California home. "He was able to bring both street experience and literary knowledge to his material. Ernest often said, 'Words are a licensed weapon and I never pull them out on people who aren't good adversaries.'"

In Joe Eszterhas's amusing 2004 autobiography *Hollywood Animal*, the infamous screenwriter of *Basic Instinct* (1992) and *Showgirls* (1995) shares a few *Plain Dealer* newsroom stories about Tidyman. "Before I got to Hollywood, when I was a very young newspaperman in Cleveland, I kept hearing from the older reporters about a legendary former reporter who'd wanted to be a Hollywood screenwriter," Eszterhas writes. "He was a legendary drinker and gambler—legendary, too, because he'd been fired from the newspaper for stealing a wristwatch from a jewelry store where he'd gone to cover a holdup."

In a phone conversation, Clark describes her late husband: "Larger than life, he was about six feet one and a big guy. We met on a blind date after talking on the phone a few times. I was thirty-six and he was in his early fifties. When he proposed to me, I had never been married and, after his having three wives, I couldn't understand why he wanted to get married again. He was a complex man who was full of rage and civility, but he also played violin beautifully."

John Shaft, in contrast to his creator, was a Harlem born former foster child and street tough who kept an office in (then) seedy Times Square and knew militant leaders by their first names. While Tidyman's character is one of the most popular black detectives in crime fiction, he wasn't the first. In 1932, Harlem Renaissance author Rudolph Fisher wrote the earliest "Negro" detective novel *The Conjure Man Dies* (1932). Since then, many other books have featured African American detectives including Chester Himes's *A Rage in Harlem* (1957) featuring NYPD detectives Coffin Ed

Johnson and Grave Digger Jones, John Ball's gentlemanly Virgil Tibbs of *In the Heat of the Night* (1965) and, more recently, James Sallis's brilliant Lew Griffin series.

Los Angeles mystery writer Gary Phillips, who created black private eye Ivan Monk, felt the spirit of Shaft hovering over his shoulder while writing his own series, beginning with *Violent Spring* in 1994. "Certainly, I wanted some of Tidyman's toughness in my guy," Phillips says. "Though I was, hopefully, careful not to take it to the extremes of where Tidyman could take his action and violence.

"In a certain way, Shaft was a brother's answer to Spillane's Mike Hammer," Phillips continues. "The novels speak to a time and [its] sensibilities from the sexual loosening [of morals] then, the Black power movement, Vietnam, to our disillusionment as a country with our institutions given the five o'clock shadow of Nixon hangs over those books."

When the movie *Shaft* was released by MGM in the summer of 1971, it was instantly successful and helped save the studio from financial ruin. Directed by *Life* photographer Gordon Parks, who hired screenwriter John D.F. Black to rewrite Tidyman's initial script, the title role played with vigor and swagger by macho model-turned-actor Richard Roundtree. "Tidyman wasn't happy with the film, because he felt the character had been politicized," says frequent NPR commentator and author Jimi Izrael, who wrote his graduate thesis on *Shaft*. "His feelings were that he had written *Shaft* as a detective novel, not a Black Power tome."

Clark, who called out director Gordon Parks in a 1991 *LA Times* article for failing to mention her late husband in his autobiography *Voices in the Mirror* (1991), agreed. "Ernest felt the movies had made Shaft into a comic book character," she says. "Ernest couldn't understand why the filmmakers felt a need to change him. He was especially disappointed with the last one (*Shaft in Africa*, 1973)." Still, Tidyman's unhappiness didn't stop him from penning the successful sequel, both the novel and screenplay for *Shaft's Big Score!* in 1972.

"I think the critics have overrated the movie *Shaft*," says British writer and editor Maxim Jakubowski. In 1997, Jakubowski served as coeditor of a line of book reissues for the Bloomsbury Film Classics series. "Although there wasn't a big demand for Tidyman's work, I included *Shaft* in the series, because for so long the movie overshadowed the book. It was a natural one to do."

The mob wanted
Harlem back.
They got Shaft...
up to here.

SHAFT's his name. SHAFT's his game.

MUSIC BY
ISAAC HAYES
Album available on
ENTERPRISE RECORDS
in Association with
MGM RECORDS

METRO-GOLDWYN-MAYER Presents "SHAFT" A STIRLING SILLIPHANT-ROGER LEWIS PRODUCTION Starring RICHARD
ROUNDTREE · Co-Starring MOSES GUNN · Screenplay by ERNEST TIDYMAN and JOHN D. F. BLACK · Based upon the novel
by ERNEST TIDYMAN · Music by ISAAC HAYES · Produced by JOEL FREEMAN · Directed by GORDON PARKS MGM
R ⓡ METROCOLOR

SEE YOUR NEWSPAPER FOR LOCAL THEATRE LISTINGS

Poster for the 1971 movie adaption of Ernest Tidyman's *Shaft*

Novelist Nelson George, who described Shaft as one of "the only black superheroes we knew" in his 2009 autobiography *City Kid*, is a fan of Tidyman's work. "Richard Roundtree was charming on screen, but the Shaft in Tidyman's novel is a richer character in many ways," George says. "In the book, the character is meaner. We find out his backstory as an orphan and Vietnam vet. None of that is even mentioned in the film."

In 1975, Tidyman penned *The Last Shaft*, the book where he put to death his creation. Shockingly, Tidyman chose to have a random mugger murder Shaft in the last paragraph. "What is this bullshit?" are his last words. "Ernest prided himself as a craftsman who had a great ear for dialogue," explains Chris Clark. "He was juggling a lot of projects and characters and he felt the quality of the Shaft books was slipping. That's why he decided to kill off the character."

But while the novels of Dashiell Hammett and Raymond Chandler receive spiffy reissues and beautiful Library of America editions, the Shaft books have languished out of print for years. (The original novel was finally republished in paperback in 2016.) "Although [Tidyman] was not on a par with Hammett and Chandler, he wasn't far behind," says Woody Haut,

author of *Heartbreak and Vine: The Fate of Hardboiled Writers in Hollywood* (2002). "While I wouldn't rate Tidyman as a noir innovator, he was an authentic tough-guy writer whose work, at its best, is a cross between Chester Himes and Mickey Spillane. His protagonists on the page and screen retain a sense of ethics and some vestige of a political consciousness, while maintaining ties with the criminal world, often blurring the distinction between the two."

Although other contemporary novelists of the period had no problem appearing on talk shows drunk or pitching brews in beer commercials, Tidyman, according to Chris Clark, "Had no interest in selling himself; he'd rather write than promote something he'd already completed."

In 1984, at the age of fifty-six, Ernest Tidyman died in Westminster Hospital in London of a perforated ulcer and complications. Decades later, with the exception of the first book, the Shaft series is still out of print. According to *The Best American Mystery Stories* series editor and Mysterious Bookshop owner Otto Penzler, it is not surprising. "For big publishers to keep books in print, they have to sell about two hundred copies a week, 10,000 books a year," Penzler explains. "You have to realize, those Shaft novels never had such a big print-run in the first place. Unfortunately, a lot of people don't even know Ernest Tidyman's name."

Michael A. Gonzales

Ernest Tidyman's *Shaft*

In 1968, the civil rights movement had been making significant headway in America and one of its leaders, Martin Luther King Jr., was invited to Memphis to speak in support of a workers' strike. On April 4—a day after delivering his "I've Been to the Mountaintop" sermon—King was assassinated. A series of riots followed in major cities across the United States. Chicago, Baltimore, and Washington, DC, in particular witnessed large-scale violence and destruction. Three days later, two members of the Black Panthers were shot by Oakland police in an exchange of fire, seventeen-year-old Bobby Hutton was killed, and Eldridge Cleaver was wounded. The Civil Rights Act was rushed into law by President Lyndon Johnson on April 11, 1968, prohibiting discrimination concerning the sale, rental, and financing of housing based on race, religion, national origin. On August 5 three more Panthers were killed in a gun battle with police at a gas station in Los Angeles, and on October 5 a further Panther was killed in another gun battle. Also in October 1968, Olympic gold medalist winners, Tommie Smith and John Carlos, wore human rights badges and each raised a black-gloved salute on the podium.

Social unrest among black Americans had ascended to a new level and was being demonstrated on the world stage.

Ernest Tidyman, a respected and experienced white newspaper journalist throughout the 1950s and '60s, had gone freelance two years earlier. A man of principle, who had worked as an editor in a number of departments at the *New York Times* since 1960, Tidyman resigned his position when he was transferred full-time to the Women's Department without consultation. Upon leaving the paper he began writing for pulp magazines such as *Confidential*, *Whisper*, *Stag*, and *Men's World*. The pay was low, so he had decided to try his hand at writing a novel that would tap into the cultural metamorphosis. His first attempt, *Flower Power* (1969), which capitalized on the hippie movement, had flopped. Tidyman was close to being broke. His agent Ronald Hobbs, who was also the only

Ernest Tidyman with the Oscar he received for his screenplay for *The French Connection* (1971)

black agent in New York, began scouring the publishing houses for new opportunities.

Alan Rinzler, mystery editor at Macmillan, was tired of the conventional approach to the genre and looking for something fresh. Earlier in the decade Rinzler, who was also white, had been involved in fundraising and ghost writing for the Student Nonviolent Coordinating Committee in New York. He also edited, promoted, and published works highlighting the plight of black America—including Claude Brown's *Manchild in the Promised Land* (1965), which detailed the struggles of growing up in Harlem. These books helped inspire the equal rights movement for African Americans. Rinzler was looking to create a black detective hero and he contacted Hobbs to see if he knew a sympathetic writer. Hobbs suggested Tidyman and arranged a meeting. Rinzler, surprised to see that Tidyman was white, was initially reluctant but allowed Tidyman to work up a seven-page character and story outline and then some sample chapters. Legend has it, and Tidyman tells this story himself in subsequent interviews, that Tidyman had no name for his black detective hero and made it up on the spot when quizzed by Rinzler after looking out through Rinzler's office window and seeing a "Fire Shaft Way" sign on the side of a building opposite.

In his outline Tidyman laid down the character background for John Shaft. He was brought up in the streets of Harlem having been orphaned at four years old. By the time he was twelve he had lived with seven sets of foster parents who were funded by the Welfare Department. By fifteen he had become a warlord in a Harlem street gang. It was during a gang fight he was beaten with a bicycle chain that left him with scars on his hands and face as he tried to protect himself. He joined the army aged nineteen rather than serve a prison sentence and fought in Vietnam. Discharged aged twenty-two, having been shot by a young Vietnamese soldier, he studied law at the City College of New York supported by the GI Bill. By now Shaft was a hardened six-foot-tall man and studying was not his thing, so he dropped out of college. In the books, Tidyman would go into a bit more detail about Shaft's time in the army, during which he boxed as a light heavyweight, and about his apprenticeship at the Pinkerton Detective Agency before branching out as a lone operating private investigator—the first black PI in New York. Tidyman's outline had very effectively captured the essence of John Shaft and would form the basis for the first book and the series of novels that followed.

While Rinzler was impressed with the writing in Tidyman's sample chapters he felt the opening of the story to be too soft. He suggested a show of violence to emphasize the hero's no-nonsense approach to solving problems. Following up on Rinzler's suggestion Tidyman rewrote the early pages to include a fight in which the detective hero ends up throwing a hood out of his office window. Pleased with the rewrite Rinzler offered Tidyman an advance of $3,500 to complete the book and a royalty agreement raising from 10 to 15 percent after ten thousand sales. Tidyman signed the contract on October 18, 1968, and John Shaft was born.

★

Ernest Tidyman worked on *Shaft* while continuing with his magazine work. He would dictate passages in the car as he drove to and from work. Secretaries at the publishing house would later transcribe the work. The nature of the way Tidyman balanced his magazine work with writing the novel meant it would take until July 3, 1969, to complete his first draft, just over a month later than the initially agreed deadline.

Once the final manuscript had been approved, Tidyman circulated galley copies among the movie studios, seeing the potential in his creation for a screen adaptation. One interested reader was producer Phil D'Antoni, who was impressed by Tidyman's use of dialogue and his knowledge of New York City. D'Antoni recommended Tidyman to William Friedkin to write a screenplay based on Robin Moore's nonfiction book *The French Connection*, which would be released on October 7, 1971, earning Tidyman an Academy Award for his adaptation.

Meanwhile, *Shaft* itself was picked up by MGM's new head, Jim Aubrey, who due to the studio's financial difficulties was looking to produce lower-budget movies. *Shaft* seemed perfect for his new vision. A deal was signed in April 1970, the same month as the novel's publication. Tidyman formed Shaft Productions, with initial producers Roger Lewis and Stirling Silliphant acting as equal partners. The studio assigned renowned photographer Gordon Parks as director, but production responsibilities were later passed on to Joel Freeman, at the suggestion of Parks, when Lewis moved to Warner Brothers.

The novel *Shaft* was finally published by Macmillan on April 27, 1970. Tidyman introduces John Shaft in his opening paragraph as he takes in the sounds and smells of a waking Manhattan while walking from his girlfriend's apartment to his office:

> Shaft felt warm, loose, in step as he turned east at Thirty-ninth Street for the truncated block between Seventh Avenue and Broadway. It had been a long walk from her place in the far West Twenties. Long and good. The city was still fresh that early. Even the exhaust fans of the coffee shops along the way were blowing fresh smells, bacon, egg and toasted-bagel smells, into the fact of the gray spring morning. He had been digging it all the way. Digging it, walking fast and thinking mostly about the girl. She was crazy. Freaky beautiful. Crazy. They went out to dinner and she

Shaft (Bantam, 1971)
Shaft (Corgi, 1972)
Shaft (Bantam, 1971)

was wearing a tangerine wig and a long purple coat that looked like a blanket on a Central Park plug pulling one of those creaky carriages. It was the mood she was in and he had become a part of it. He never got back to his apartment. She wanted a night like that. They had it and, then, about 7:30, she handed him a glass of cardboard-container orange juice and began pushing him out of the apartment. It was their night, but the maid's day.

In *Shaft*, the private detective is hired by Harlem crime lord and racketeer Knocks Persons to find his missing rebellious nineteen-year-old daughter, Beatrice. The case propels Shaft into the middle of a turf war between Persons's Harlem set-up and the Mafia. Meanwhile NYPD lieutenant Vic Anderozzi is hearing the noises but can't make any coherent sense of what he is hearing. Anderozzi wants to use Shaft to fill in the blanks for him. When Anderozzi gets Shaft off a possible manslaughter charge when one of Persons's hoodlums is thrown out of his third-floor office window out into Times Square, Shaft reluctantly agrees. Shaft visits an old friend from his teenage street days in Harlem, Ben Buford, who now runs a group of black militant activists. Shaft is looking for information that might help him locate Beatrice. But when Buford's men are killed by a Mafia hit on their headquarters, Shaft realizes Persons has played him as an unwitting finger man. Persons explains to an angry Shaft and Buford that the Mafia are looking to reclaim the heroin trade they lost to him in Spanish Harlem and have kidnapped his daughter in order to force a trade. With Buford wanting revenge for his dead comrades and Persons wanting his daughter back, Persons and Buford pool resources to help Shaft and a daring rescue is planned.

Shaft is an old-school detective story told with modern twists built around its black hero and references to the political agenda of black Americans. John Shaft is cut from similar cloth as Mickey Spillane's Mike Hammer and Raymond Chandler's Philip Marlowe. Shaft adopts Hammer's two-fisted approach to detection and Marlowe's cynical attitude to authority. The plot is built around a simple tale of kidnapping and gang warfare. But in his novel Tidyman has created a character who holds the reader's attention because he is no superman hero. John Shaft's self-confidence and arrogance serve to mask his inadequacies. He is a loner who rejects his past and goes his own way. He is taunted for operating in the white man's world by both Persons and Buford, but he bites back hard at Persons's preying on the weakness of the poor in Harlem and Buford's filling them with false promises. He is beaten and shot and suffers for it. His resilience leads to him fighting back twice as hard and coming out on top.

The John Shaft of the novels is a more rounded character than would eventually appear on screen. We learn more about his orphaned childhood and his unsettled life with various foster parents, about his involvement with street gangs and street crime as a teenager, and about his service in Vietnam. These events have served to create an angry, self-motivated man who trusts no one and acts on his own instinct. Many black Americans would identify with this attitude.

Tidyman also introduces us to a small cast of supporting characters who would inhabit Shaft's world in six further books. Lt. Vic Anderozzi is Shaft's police contact. Shaft and Anderozzi have a mutual respect and a kind of friendship that neither will admit to. Shaft's only real friends though are Marvin and Helen Green. Marvin is his accountant and Helen, his wife, acts like Shaft's sister in her concern for his welfare. They are the closest thing Shaft has to a family. Rollie Nickerson is a part-time actor but also bartender at Shaft's Greenwich Village local, the No Name Bar. Shaft also has an answering service employed by the "We Never Sleep So You Can Answering Service" and a Polish cleaner for his Village apartment, Mrs. Klonsky. Knocks Persons (renamed Bumpy Jonas in the movie adaptation, in reference to real-life racketeer Bumpy Johnson) and political activist Ben Buford would both also appear in later books.

Shaft is ultimately a tough, hard-boiled detective thriller which uses the black political issues of the day as a backdrop to the main story. The movie adaptation would play up the ethnic elements via John D.F. Black's reworking of Tidyman's initial script. Director Gordon Parks cast unknown male model Richard Roundtree in the title role, dressed him in a leather coat, gave him a moustache (Shaft was clean-shaven in the books), and put him on the bleak winter streets of midtown Manhattan backed by Isaac Hayes's funky score, and a cultural icon was born. The resultant movie became a smash hit across the world and was a major inspiration for the so-called blaxploitation genre of movies that emerged in the early to mid 1970s. A deal was also struck between Tidyman and MGM for options to adapt future Shaft novels. Tidyman now had his cash cow and he planned to milk it dry.

★

Ernest Tidyman had already written a screenplay for a sequel to *Shaft*, which MGM had initially accepted on May 28, 1971—before the film was even released. The story was based on a *New York Times* article Tidyman had read back in 1968 about the mysterious deaths of three diamond merchants. In the article executive secretary Arnold J. Lubin spoke on behalf of New York's Diamond Dealers Club expressing fear of "Syndicate" involvement. The story inspired Tidyman to create a plot concerning an Israeli fugitive and his formula for the production of synthetic gems. MGM wanted to look at other options.

Having rejected a screenplay proposal from B. B. Johnson (pseudonym of Joe Greene, writer of the Superspade books), Tidyman's partners at Shaft Productions had developed their own story for the sequel in which Shaft would have an adventure in the Caribbean. Having gained approval from MGM, Lewis developed a screenplay entitled "The Big Bamboo" and along with Silliphant sought Tidyman's approval to proceed. Tidyman however had commenced work on adapting his original sequel proposal into a follow-up novel—*Shaft among the Jews*. Tidyman had also submitted a new original story for the film sequel in which Shaft seeks out the killer of an old friend while infringing on a gangland turf war for control of Queens. The script was developed between October and December 1971 under the working title *Gang Bang* and was initially to be set in Chicago. Once Gordon Parks had persuaded the execs at MGM that shooting in the New York winter would not be expensive, having had a similar experience in shooting *Shaft*, the production was relocated to the Big Apple and retitled *Shaft's Big Score!* Production took place in early 1972, and Tidyman would adapt his screenplay into a novel, which was due to be published in May 1972, but was delayed due to a disagreement over royalties.

Meanwhile, *Shaft among the Jews* was published in hardback in the U.S. by Dial on June 29, 1972, three weeks after the release of the movie sequel. For the book, Tidyman had taken his original eight-page movie outline and fleshed it out with additional characters.

Shaft is hired by a group of Jewish diamond merchants to investigate events causing the destabilization of their business. We are introduced to Morris Blackburn (renamed from the Ian Fleming–like Mr. Sparkles in Tidyman's initial outline), an ambitious trader in financial difficulties. Blackburn uses his right-hand man, David Alexander, to source new stock illegally then kill his suppliers. Blackburn is later visited by Avril Herzel, an old friend of his father, who claims to have developed a formula for manufacturing synthetic diamonds and wants his formula to be a gift to the world. Blackburn's seizes the opportunity for the old man to teach him his methods, then secretly plots to kill Herzel and use the formula for personal profit. Meanwhile, Herzel, having left his homeland with the formula, is also being sought by the Israeli Secret Service. A team of agents led by Ben Fischer arrive in New York following Herzel's daughter, Cara, who is also searching for her father. When Shaft goes undercover at Blackburn's store and Cara turns up looking for her father the various parties come together explosively. *Shaft among the Jews* may well be the best of Tidyman's series. Tidyman himself believed he had improved on the first book—something he noted in a letter to a former colleague at the *New York Times* in which he also outlined his plans to take the series to seven books in total. The characters are colorful, the action fast and furious, and we see a more considerate side to Shaft that we would rarely see again.

As in the original book, Tidyman's style tended toward long and descriptive passages including character introspection and surreal metaphors. The book also takes in more character perspectives, leading to a feeling of a larger ensemble piece. The cast of characters are well drawn from the greed and ambition of Blackburn to the professionalism, single-mindedness, and ruthlessness of Ben Fischer. Tidyman uses a gay character for the first time in the series in David Alexander, who is portrayed as Blackburn's selfish and vicious assistant. Cara Herzel is a vulnerable girl out of her depth but determined to find her father. Cara's vulnerability brings out Shaft's protective instincts and he genuinely falls for her, something acknowledged in the book's finale.

Of the support cast, Lt. Vic Anderozzi returns, and indeed this book contains some of the best Shaft/Anderozzi exchanges, most notably around two separate instances of Shaft being detained. Also back is Rollie Nickerson, who is almost permanently high on drugs. Shaft has a new girlfriend in the snobbish Amy Taylor-Davis who, to Shaft's disgust, has redecorated his office in transparent plastic and garish colors.

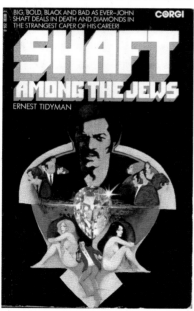

Shaft among the Jews (Bantam, 1973)
Shaft among the Jews (Corgi, 1973)

There is also the opportunistic Willie J. Scott, who teams up with Shaft in a nighttime search through Blackburn's offices, which ends in a gun battle with Fischer's agents.

Future books in the series would become more formulaic, mirroring many of the men's adventure pulp novels of the time, by trading on Shaft's vicious sense of justice.

★

The disagreement with MGM and his partners in Shaft Productions over royalties for the novelization of *Shaft's Big Score!* was finally resolved after some prickly negotiations. The book was published in paperback by Bantam on August 7, 1972, just six weeks after the hardback publication of *Shaft among the Jews*.

In *Shaft's Big Score!*, Shaft receives a call for help from an old army buddy, Cal Asby, who now runs a funeral and insurance business in Queens. On Shaft's late-night arrival at Asby's business office a bomb is detonated killing Asby. While protecting Asby's widow, Arna, Shaft looks to investigate why Asby was hit. Meanwhile, Asby's business partner, Albert J. Kelly, is looking to settle a gambling debt with gangster Gus Mascola using money he and Asby had earned from a numbers racket. But the money, which Mascola wants to use to fund his expanding criminal empire and Asby had instead intended to go to a children's foundation, is missing, and Kelly is desperately trying to locate it. Mascola is also in competition with Harlem crime lord Knocks Persons for control the numbers scene in Queens. Both are part of a fragile citywide syndicate run by the crippled Arthur Sharrett, who has his own interests. The missing loot is the key, and it's up to Shaft to find it before Kelly and Mascola.

Tidyman returned to an earlier draft of his screenplay, which included additional characters not seen in the final film—notably the crippled mob boss Arthur Sharrett and his daughter Gail. The movie took Sharrett's sophistication and added it to Mascola's character, which created a major difference to how Mascola was portrayed in the book as a violent and lecherous thug with little of the class he aspired to on screen. On screen, Gail's character is mixed with that of Rita Towne, Kelly's mistress, so it is Rita in the movie who drives Shaft to the cemetery for the final showdown. Arna Asby is Cal's wife in the book but his sister in the movie. Bollin becomes a captain in the film to remove the need for the Captain Samson character.

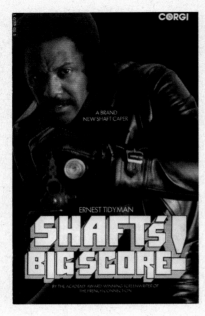

Shaft's Big Score!
(Corgi, 1973)
Shaft's Big Score
(Bantam, 1972)

Tidyman also shortens the chase finale from that seen on screen, restricting it to the cars and abandoning the helicopter chase of Shaft through the Brooklyn docks. He retains the name Knocks Persons to keep continuity with his first novel—Moses Gunn would reprise his role as Bumpy Jonas in the movie. Otherwise the book and film follow similar paths.

Tidyman's novelization is actually a more satisfying telling of the story than would be seen on screen due to the broader scope and richer supporting characters the author uses. But where the book suffers in comparison to both *Shaft* and *Shaft among the Jews* is in its lack of development of Shaft's character. Here he is merely responding to events via wisecracks or tough action—a role we would increasingly see Shaft take over the remainder of the series. We still manage to get inside Shaft's psyche via Tidyman's insightful prose, but again, as in *Shaft among the Jews*, he is less central to the plot than in *Shaft*. The book also echoes some of the themes explored in *Shaft*, pitting gangster against gangster in a turf war and reusing the Knocks Persons character.

Shaft's Big Score! was a box-office hit, and it seemed the franchise had a strong future. Like the James Bond films of the 1960s, Shaft had inspired many imitators. But Tidyman's cooling relationship with his partners in Shaft Productions meant that this would be the last of the books linked to the films. The author would look toward other interests in film production and writing but continue to develop the remaining contracted Shaft books with other writers.

Despite his increasing disenchantment with the big-screen treatment of his creation, Tidyman was keen to maximize his future earnings potential by continuing his series of books as planned. He still had a deal with MGM for options on his Shaft novels, but it was also now obvious they wanted to go their own way with the character. Tidyman therefore began to explore other possibilities for marketing Shaft. In late 1972 he developed the idea of a daily newspaper comic strip. Initial tests were done with artist David Russell (later a highly successful movie storyboard artist), but they could not agree to the terms. Ultimately Tidyman turned to experienced comic book artist Don Rico, who had worked for Marvel. Test panels were circulated to the big newspapers in New York and LA throughout 1973, but they failed to attract interest.

The success of the films *Shaft* and *The French Connection* had also significantly increased demand for Tidyman's services. As a result, he set up Ernest Tidyman Productions and began to spread his time across a number of developing film projects, in both the U.S. and Europe. The increasing workload encouraged Tidyman to hire writers to help out.

Tidyman had sketched out story ideas for four further Shaft books, which he wanted to produce in quick succession so they would fall within the timeframe of the options agreement with MGM. He recruited two writers to help develop the manuscripts, Robert Turner and Phillip Rock. Turner was a vastly experienced writer of pulp fiction who made contributions to many of the pulp magazines of the 1940s and '50s, such as *Black Mask*, *Dime Detective Magazine*, and *Dime Mystery Magazine*. Rock had worked initially as a screenwriter (notably 1967's *The Extraordinary Seaman*) and later became a writer for hire to work major films into novelizations including an adaptation of Clint Eastwood's iconic 1971 film, *Dirty Harry*. Tidyman had also previously used Rock on the novelization of his own script for Eastwood's western *High Plains Drifter*.

Robert Turner took up the first assignment, based on an outline Tidyman had written entitled "The Gang's All Here, Shaft." Tidyman had developed his storyline from an idea used for the plot in the test panels for the proposed comic strip. The idea was built around Ben Buford, the black revolutionary introduced in *Shaft*, being framed for a heist. Turner worked Tidyman's story into a manuscript, deliberately keeping it light, thereby leaving room for Tidyman to fill out and put his own stamp on the piece. He submitted his final pages in August 1972. Tidyman heavily edited Turner's work and shaped it into what became *Shaft Has a Ball*, which Bantam published in paperback in April 1973.

Shaft is asked by Captain Vic Anderozzi to look into claims by a female informant that political extremist Ben Buford is planning a heist. When the informant turns up dead in Shaft's apartment, Shaft takes a personal interest in the case and looks to track down his childhood friend. Meanwhile he has also been hired to bodyguard Senator Albert Congdon Stovall, a high-flying black politician, who is staying at the hotel where the heist is being planned by a five-man team led by Neal Wickman. While Wickman is on board purely for the loot, one of his team, Saul Yancey, is looking to frame Buford in retaliation for him losing his business—Buford had dissuaded local residents against using Yancey's store after he had refused to support Buford's cause. The hotel is also hosting a gay convention and while Shaft is chasing down leads on Buford, Stovall is badly beaten by a rough-trade thug, hired by the gang. Shaft is now looking for the gang that ordered the assault on Stovall and the one looking to frame Buford, not realizing they are one and the same.

Shaft Has a Ball is one of the weakest of the Shaft books. With Tidyman working on other projects, frequently traveling between the States and Europe, there was little room for collaboration with Turner. As a result, the book lacks cohesion and feels rushed. It starts promisingly as Tidyman seems keen to reestablish his version of Shaft (as opposed to the Richard Roundtree image held by the public) by going over his background history via an interview with journalist Winifred Guiterrez, who later disappears from the story abruptly. The book starts well, and there is some humorous interplay between Shaft and Anderozzi in a bar as the plot is set up. Then the two plot threads of Shaft's bodyguard assignment and the planned heist are clumsily linked through some eccentric story development. With the exception of Stovall, the characters are less well drawn than in the first three books and their motivations are sketchy. Wickman lacks the presence of the villains seen in the earlier books, and his gang of misfits are largely incompetent. There is also the involvement of two Mafia hit men, which leads to the shoot-out finale at a cottage in Yonkers. The wrap-up is also very brief, leaving the reader unsatisfied in the story's resolution, with character story arcs left open. Despite some flashes of inspired and witty writing from Tidyman, the series was beginning to resemble the production line approach of other men's adventure pulp novels of the time.

★

As Robert Turner was completing his manuscript for *Shaft Has a Ball*, Phillip Rock had started work on *Good-bye, Mr. Shaft*. Tidyman's story outline saw Shaft move to a location outside of New York, in this instance London, for the first time (emulating the direction taken by the filmmakers for *Shaft in Africa*). Tidyman had seen the limitations for story ideas by continually using NYC locations. Both he and Rock had lived for long periods in London and this seemed the ideal location for Shaft to spread his wings.

Rock took three months over the manuscript and completed his writing on December 22, 1972, with Tidyman's final edit delivered on January 29, 1973. The title *Good-bye, Mr. Shaft* was a nod toward James Hilton's 1934 novel, *Goodbye, Mr. Chips*, acknowledging the Stovall boys' attending an English public school during their stay. The story centers on a kidnapping plot led by a consortium who are aiming to prevent Senator Stovall (returning from *Shaft Has a Ball*) from becoming the first black vice president. Shaft is hired to bodyguard Stovall's two young sons who are moved to London in order to reduce the risk of them being snatched. Once in London Shaft comes up against a Notting Hill razor gang and assorted London villains. He also establishes a contact in Scotland Yard through Inspector Roger Wilkins and takes on a martial arts class at the public school the boys temporarily attend. He dallies with an air hostess, a teacher from the school, and a duchess. It is during the latter assignation that the boys are kidnapped and Shaft feels Stovall's wrath leading to his determined efforts to track them down.

Dial published *Good-bye, Mr. Shaft* in hardback in December 1973. It is something of a return to form after the disappointing and underdeveloped *Shaft Has a Ball*. Shaft is shown to be more fallible here than in the previous book and his failings lead to the facilitation of the eventual kidnapping of the Stovall boys. His rebuke from Stovall, something Shaft would normally respond to with a verbal assault of his own, instead left him humble and determined to correct his mistake.

> "Better stay clear, Shaft. I . . . I won't risk my boys' lives. Stay out of it."
>
> "I'll be cool . . ."
>
> "You won't do anything, period!" A cold, angry voice. A voice filled with pain—and disappointment. The click of the phone sounded final. Good-bye, Shaft, and thanks for nothing.
>
> *You let them down. If you'd been with them this wouldn't have happened.*

While Tidyman and Rock can be rightly accused of adopting clichéd characteristics and names for their London villains (Tinker Bell, Corky Tompkins, etc.), there is a depth to the characters that transcends the genre conventions. Shaft somehow feels at home in Swinging London, taking on the gangs and wooing the women. Even Shaft's relationship with Wilkins mirrors that he has with Anderozzi back in Manhattan.

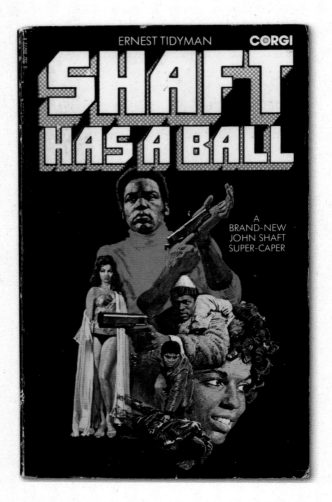

An example of how the books had started to descend into the standard action genre is in the treatment of Shaft by the police when he kills T.J. Kelly, who had been hired to stop Shaft going to London. In *Shaft*, when Shaft throws one of Knocks Persons's hoods out of the window, there is a real threat he could go to jail, or at least be tried. Here Anderozzi writes it off as a public service. Shaft was effectively given license to act as he pleased. This reduced the tension between Shaft and the authorities that was a powerful element in the first two books.

Another element is in the depiction of the female characters as little more than sexual cyphers. This contrasts with the charming vulnerability of Cara Herzel in *Shaft among the Jews*. In *Goodbye* Shaft's main love interest, Dr. Indra Richardson, is given some interesting background around her Indian roots, but once Shaft has had his way, she disappears from the story. The women are seen as disposable sex objects rather than fully formed characters.

The rushed schedule Tidyman had created for the books meant some continuity slips crept in. Notable was that Stovall had children, having been described as a bachelor in *Shaft Has a Ball*. This is explained by the death of his wife in an accident and the boys being raised by her sister. More telling is the mistake with Stovall's name. For example, the character Albert Congdon Stovall in *Shaft Has a Ball* became Creighton Stovall in *Good-bye, Mr. Shaft*. That said, the book has a tight plot with well-drawn villains and some real motivation for Shaft. We see the softer side of his character for the first time since the second book, notably in how he grows fond of the Stovall boys as the story progresses.

Good-bye, Mr. Shaft would be the first Shaft book not to be published in paperback in the U.S.—Bantam had passed, moving on to the paperback-only *Shaft's Carnival of Killers* instead. In the UK, where Corgi had paperback rights the book was published in September 1976, having previously seen a hardback publication through Weidenfeld & Nicolson in June 1974.

Tidyman was keen to progress the Shaft series at a rapid pace and he employed Turner to move on to the next book, *Shaft's Carnival of Killers*, at the same time Rock had started work on *Good-bye, Mr. Shaft*. This time Shaft is taken to Jamaica and becomes embroiled in a plot to assassinate the prime minister. Working alongside the Jamaican police chief, Alex Ashton—who just happens to be a friend of Captain Vic Anderozzi—Shaft

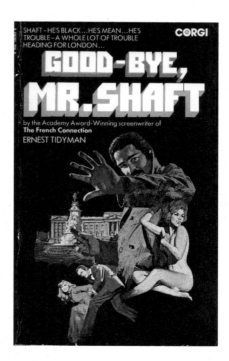

Good-bye, Mr. Shaft (Dial Press, 1973)
Good-bye, Mr. Shaft (Corgi, 1976)

looks to discover who is behind the plot. Suspects range from a jilted mistress, to political factions and even the police themselves. There are scenes of explosive and violent action, with a hunchback dwarf proving to be one memorable villain. It has all the elements of a James Bond thriller without the sophistication. The story was developed from a screenplay Tidyman had originally written in 1971 entitled *A Carnival of Killers* with a ubiquitous private detective hero. There were two otherwise almost identical versions of the screenplay—one featuring Shaft and another a private eye named Francis Clifford. Tidyman had originally intended the screenplay to be considered for a *Shaft* sequel when a Jamaica location was being considered but was open to using the story with a different hero.

Turner struggled with the writing due to an illness in late 1972 and he frequently missed deadlines for portions of the manuscript. Eventually a final manuscript was delivered in March 1973, but it was subpar with a short page count. It also required heavy editing and an additional chapter by Tidyman before Bantam accepted it for U.S. paperback publication. As a result of the quality issues and Bantam seemingly growing tired of the series, publication was delayed by more than a year until September 2, 1974.

Shaft's Carnival of Killers is undoubtedly the weakest book of the series and the most formulaic. Despite this, there are still moments for fans to treasure. The book was written as a mystery and although it retains the third person approach Tidyman favored, the story is told through Shaft's eyes as he attempts to unravel the assassination plot. The Jamaican characters are colorful and interesting, and even if the plot becomes increasingly absurd, there is an escapist element to it that retains the reader's interest. The mystery is solved in an action-packed finale at a costume party to which Shaft dresses as a matador. A far cry from the tough streets of Harlem.

It was following this book that Bantam severed ties with the series. They had sensed the quality had dropped, and the Shaft phenomenon, which had arrived overnight in mid-1971, was fizzling out just three years later.

Tidyman had meanwhile become dissatisfied with the treatment of his creation on screen. *Shaft in Africa* had received his blessing, if not approval. The film did not match the box-office success of its predecessors. John Shaft's screen adventures moved to TV on October 9, 1973, for a short-lived series of relatively tame TV movies (as part of a rotating movie-of-the-week format on CBS), which while returning Shaft to his New York roots, was cancelled after just seven episodes had aired, the last of which was aired on February 19, 1974.

Tidyman had become so weary of his creation he resolved to kill him off in the final book in the series, *The Last Shaft*.

★

Phillip Rock commenced work on Tidyman's final Shaft story outline on October 22, 1973, and completed his manuscript for *The Last Shaft* on January 11, 1974, which Tidyman turned into a final edit by January 22.

The Last Shaft returns John Shaft to the streets of Manhattan after his excursions in London and Jamaica. The story sees Shaft avenging the murder of his friend Captain Vic Anderozzi, who had arrested the Mafia's bookkeeper and was looking to turn him and the books over to the DA. Shaft, having become embroiled in Anderozzi's folly, goes on the run and systematically looks to wipe out the Mafia families responsible for his friend's death. He enlists the help of a hotel porter, Willie, who happens to be studying to be a detective and keeps an arsenal of weapons in a converted bread van. The pair take on the Mafia at various bases in a series of explosive attacks before a final confrontation with the family boss. Shaft is then seemingly killed off in a random mugging as a coda to the book that had no link to the story itself.

The Last Shaft starts strongly with an excellent opening chapter, which is basically a two-hander between Shaft and Anderozzi as the police captain brings Mafia bookkeeper Morris Mickelberg and his ledgers to Shaft's apartment. Shaft does not disguise his anger as he realizes they have been pinned down by Mafia hit men. He makes an escape to the rooftop where he kills two of the men and then has to get Anderozzi to let him back into his own apartment. Thinking it safe, the police captain and his witness head for the DA's office, but the hit men have planted a bomb in Anderozzi's car, and Anderozzi and Mickelberg go up in the explosion.

This powerful opening sets up the premise for Shaft to go into hiding and, with the help of Willie, seek out the Mafia bosses and deliver maximum destructive mayhem. The convenience of Shaft and Willie's meeting and the nature of Willie's interests in detection and his arsenal of weapons is hard to swallow and

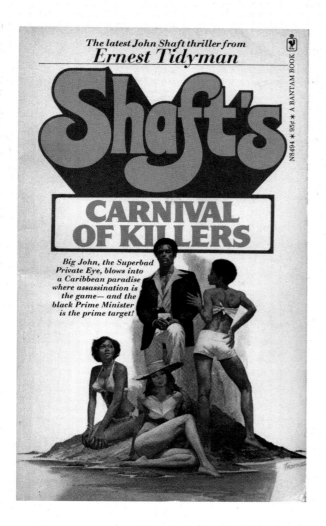

can be put down to lazy plotting. If you can swallow this, then the rest of the book is basically Shaft exacting his revenge by blowing up various mob headquarters before his final showdown with the family boss at a disused warehouse.

There are moments of introspection where Shaft looks back on his life and lack of any real close friends. Indeed, the book as a whole sees him at odds with New York and himself, maybe reflecting Tidyman's own weariness with his creation. That Shaft should be triumphant in his mission but ultimately apparently killed by a random mugger provides a disappointing, if ironic, conclusion to the book, which is at odds with the rest of the series. Tidyman was clear in correspondence with his publishing partners that this was the end for Shaft on the printed page. While Bantam passed on manuscript in the U.S., the book was finally published in hardback in the UK by Weidenfeld & Nicolson on March 27, 1975, with a paperback publication following on January 28, 1977.

The blaxploitation genre of films *Shaft* had largely spawned in 1971 had all but run its course by the mid-1970s and interest in John Shaft had waned. Tidyman, forever the businessman, had even tried to relaunch the film series in the late 1970s but could not garner studio interest. The world had moved on. Summer blockbusters like *Jaws* and *Star Wars* redefined the box office, and Shaft's death on the printed page was symbolic of these changes.

Ernest Tidyman's Shaft books are a product of a time when men's adventure novels and film novelizations dominated the paperback racks. The first three were the strongest in the series. The later books still carried Tidyman's personal style, due to his heavy editorial input and story outlines, but they became more formulaic with an increasing level of absurdity, failing to hide the production line approach to the writing and plotting. Throughout, though, Tidyman heavily protected his creation, and, despite the tough exterior presented by John Shaft, the character remained real because both his strengths and his weaknesses had consequences. He is a hero of his time but also a hero who can transcend time, in the same way Mike Hammer and Philip Marlowe have done, due to his iconic status. The books remain eminently readable and well worth revisiting.

While *Shaft* had a huge influence on the big screen and popular culture, it was much less so on the written page. Blaxploitation was a heavily stylized visual and

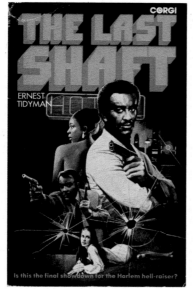

Shaft's Carnival of Killers (Bantam, 1974)
The Last Shaft (Corgi, 1977)

sonic experience that demanded the cinema as a medium. John Shaft on the written page was merely another detective, partly having his roots in the pulp fiction of the 1940s and '50s but also partly tapping into the social changes happening in America the 1960s and '70s. Tidyman, however, was not into making heavy political statements. Instead he wanted to tell traditional crime stories through the perspective of a black hero.

While big-screen John Shaft became an icon for young black Americans, literary John Shaft faded into the background. No tidal wave of black detectives/heroes followed in Shaft's coattails on the printed page as they had on the big screen with *Slaughter* (1972), *Trouble Man* (1972), and *Truck Turner* (1974) among others. What pulp fiction did emerge was riding the crest of the political changes, such as Donald Goines's Kenyatta series in 1974–75 under the pseudonym of Al C. Clark, and the more outlandish creations the blaxploitation genre created. B.B. Johnson (who had offered a script for *Shaft's Big Score!*) was early on the scene and came up with Richard Abraham Spade in his Superspade series of six books (1970–71). Mark Olden's Black Samurai series of 1974 tapped into the mixture of blaxploitation and martial arts genres. James D. Lawrence (co-creator of the *Friday Foster* comic strip) came up with Angela "Angie" Harpe, a sort of female version of Shaft, in his Dark Angel series of four books in 1975, which coasted on Pam Grier's presence in films like *Coffy* (1973) and *Foxy Brown* (1974). These books vanished almost as quickly as they were created as public tastes changed through the mid-1970s. The Shaft series itself disappeared from bookshelves after the final UK paperback print of *The Last Shaft* in 1977. The world had moved on, and Shaft was seemingly being consigned to history.

★

After lying dormant for many years, John Shaft has seen something of a rebirth in recent years. David F. Walker encouraged Dynamite Entertainment to purchase the literary rights to the character, resulting in a well-received six-part comic book prequel being launched in December 2014 and later published as the trade paperback *Shaft: A Complicated Man* in October 2015. Walker also wrote the novel *Shaft's Revenge*, released in paperback in February 2016 alongside a second comic book series entitled *Shaft: Imitation of Life*. Dynamite has also promised to reprint all the original Tidyman novels for the first time outside of Germany since the 1970s.

As the present book was going to press, a new Shaft film starring Samuel L. Jackson was just about to be released in June 2019. In 2000, John Singleton's ill-conceived reboot of the Shaft film franchise, with Jackson playing Shaft's same-named nephew, had been a modest box-office success. But it was not until February 2015 that New Line Cinema and producer John Davis announced that they were to produce a new Shaft film. When a later announcement named the writers as Kenya Barris, the creator of the sitcom *Black-ish*, and Alex Barnow, stating that the film would have a "comedic tone," there was uproar from fans in general and Walker in particular. He wrote an open letter to Davis and New Line, pleading: "Don't make this a comedy. It will suck. It won't make money. And in doing so, it will ruin the chances of there ever being a decent Shaft movie in the remainder of my lifetime."

John Shaft's place in popular culture history has never been doubted, but the recent resurgence in interest in the character demonstrates his longevity and continuing relevance. Who knows, maybe this will even spark a new series of novels featuring the tough detective. One thing is for sure—Shaft is here to stay.

Steve Aldous

Lithe, Lusty, and Liberated

"Pulp Feminism"

SO TIMELY, SO FRIGHTENINGLY POSSIBLE...
—The Feminists (1971)

For readers of Parley J. Cooper's 1971 novel *The Feminists*, the sexual politics of the not-too-distant future were a disconcerting prospect. A dark, dystopic sci-fi tale, *The Feminists* envisaged an America of 1992 in which the battle of the sexes was over, and women stood supreme. Economic crisis and global pollution had sent society reeling and, as the world staggered in chaos, a junta of determined dames—the Feminists—seized the reins of power. Reduced to mere chattel, men were now a subjugated species—submissive slaves in a regime of tyrannical matriarchy where order was enforced by buxom, jackbooted security guards. It was a forecast that, for the book's publishers at least, did not stretch the bounds of credulity. As the paperback's back-cover blurb breathlessly intoned, *The Feminists* was a novel of biting social relevance. It was, the hype proclaimed: "THE STORY THAT HAD TO BE WRITTEN—SO TIMELY, SO FRIGHTENINGLY POSSIBLE, YOU WON'T BELIEVE IT'S FICTION!"

Nor was *The Feminists* a voice in the wilderness. Throughout the late 1960s and '70s a welter of cheap, lurid paperbacks spiced-up their "sex 'n' violence" recipes with a vision of femininity that was as ruthless, as hard-hitting, and as downright coldblooded as the most hard-boiled of tough guys. Alongside the fantasies of female domination conjured up in sci-fi yarns such as *The Feminists*, an array of war stories, spy adventures, and lascivious spiels offered audiences an image of womanhood whose hard-bitten grit and libertine libido were more than a match for any man.

Pulp fiction, of course, was no stranger to women with attitude. From the 1940s through the 1960s a procession of sultry femme fatales, pistol-packing gun molls, and switchblade-toting gang girls had paraded through the pages of gutsy paperbacks. But during the late '60s, the "raunch factor" of the pulp heroine was hiked discernibly higher, while her seductive mystique was complemented by an edge of stridence,

even a touch of militancy. Her change in character was indebted to a combination of factors. A steady relaxation of censorship controls played an obvious role, but so too did broad shifts in society and culture and—especially—the febrile debates that surrounded issues of gender and sexuality.

Pulp fiction has always ransacked contemporary culture for themes and stereotypes guaranteed to draw in readers. Part of the pulp writer's stock-in-trade is to plunder from the hot topics of the day, boiling down the headlines into larger-than-life tales of startling sensation. And by the late 1960s, women's liberation was a big story of the moment.

Challenges to the existing gender landscape had begun twenty years earlier. During the 1940s the wartime economy brought many women into the workforce and, as their employment opportunities widened, expectations grew for social and economic parity with men. Books such as Simone de Beauvoir's *The Second Sex* (1949) and Betty Friedan's *The Feminine Mystique* (1963) popularized the growing challenge to the de facto sexual inequalities that characterized family life, the workplace, reproductive rights, and a host of legal statutes. Beginning in 1961, JFK's administration made women's rights a key aspect of its "New Frontier" initiatives, and the Presidential Commission on the Status of Women brought reforms in the Equal Pay Act of 1963 and the Civil Rights Act of 1964. But there was still a long way to go, and throughout the 1960s women's groups struggled for social justice. Established in 1966, the National Organization for Women (NOW) lobbied tirelessly for women's rights, and by the end of the decade the campaign for change was underway nationwide.

Activism and publicity stunts pushed the women's liberation movement into the social spotlight. In 1968, for example, members of the protest group New York Radical Women led a demonstration against the Miss America beauty pageant. Gathered outside the Atlantic City Convention Hall, where the event was being staged, four hundred activists decried what they called "The Degrading Mindless-Boob-Girlie Symbol" and threw tokens of patriarchal domination—mops, pots and pans, high-heeled shoes, corsets, copies of *Playboy* magazine—into a symbolic "freedom trash can." A cadre of protesters, meanwhile, sneaked into the pageant itself and from the balcony unfurled a giant banner proclaiming "Women's Liberation" before ushers manhandled them out of the arena. A huge publicity coup, the protest not only catapulted the women's liberation movement into the American national consciousness but also helped galvanize the cause of gender equality around the world.

On the other side of the Atlantic the women's movement was also mobilizing. In 1970, women's groups from across Britain met in Oxford for the first National Women's Liberation Conference, and the following year four thousand marchers demonstrated through London to mark the movement's First International Women's Day. The highest-profile protest, however, came in November 1970 when the Miss World beauty competition at London's Royal Albert Hall was brought to a standstill as demonstrators held up placards, shouted, blew whistles, and threw leaflets onto the stage as the event's host—veteran comedian Bob Hope—cowered from a fusillade of flour bombs. Another publicity masterstroke, it garnered global newspaper and TV coverage.

Social and economic equality were key concerns of the women's movement. But so too was sexual independence. Despite moral crusaders' howls of complaint, attitudes toward sex and sexuality were steadily liberalizing, and feminists struggled to ensure women had a fair place in the "sexual revolution." Licensed in America in 1960 and used by over a million women in 1962, oral contraception—"the pill"—had delivered a degree of sexual autonomy, and many women sought to capitalize on (and extend) the new freedoms.

A benchmark of the changes was the success of Helen Gurley Brown's handbook for the modern woman, *Sex and the Single Girl*. First published in 1962, it offered readers step-by-step guidance on personal appearance, home budgeting, and work life. But what sparked the public's greatest interest was Brown's insistence that young, single women should relish their sexual independence—a stance that ensured her book sold two million copies within three weeks of its launch. Transformed into a figure of popular fascination, Brown was appointed editor of the ailing American women's magazine *Cosmopolitan*. Originally

The Feminists (Pinnacle, 1971)

pitched to folksy housewives, under Brown's aegis the magazine was revamped to appeal to sassy and independent eighteen to thirty-four-year-olds. It was an inspired strategy, and *Cosmopolitan*'s circulation figures rocketed from under eight hundred thousand copies a month in 1965 to more than one million by 1970. Readers lapped up *Cosmopolitan*'s cocktail of stylish consumerism and bubbly joie de vivre, but sexual freedom was also part of the pizzazz. *Cosmopolitan* had regular features on birth control, female orgasm, and sexual experimentation, and even began including male centerfolds. The first of these, in the April 1972 edition, saw Burt Reynolds sprawled on a bearskin rug that discreetly covered the rugged actor's manhood.

On American newsstands, 1973 saw *Cosmopolitan* joined by the first softcore porn magazines aimed at women—*Playgirl* and *Viva*. But female sexuality let loose was also a hit at the bookshops. Jostling for space on the shelves were nonfiction best sellers like *The Sensuous Woman* by "J" (1969)—touted as "THE FIRST HOW-TO BOOK FOR THE FEMALE WHO YEARNS TO BE ALL WOMAN"—and Nancy Friday's taxonomy of women's sexual fantasies, *My Secret Garden* (1973), along with Shere Hite's survey of female sexuality, *The Hite Report* (1976). They were joined by blockbuster novels such as Erica Jong's *Fear of Flying* (1973)—the tale of a young woman's search for sexual independence through an anonymous "zipless fuck," which sold over 3.5 million copies within two years of its release. Such sales successes were testament to the way issues of gender and sexuality were convulsing American society.

As the 1960s gave way to the '70s, the book business was riding high. Paperbacks, especially, were booming. The days when paperback books were regarded as a tawdry, second-rate medium were long gone. During the early '60s, paperback books began outselling their hardcover counterparts, and by the end of the decade they dominated the market. Indeed, a high-water mark was reached in 1970 as New American Library set a record initial print run of 4,350,000 for Eric Segal's tearjerker, *Love Story*; while Mario Puzo's *The Godfather* became the fastest-selling paperback in history, publisher Fawcett notching up a figure of more than five million copies sold within a year of the book's release. Such coups were rooted in effective marketing and a general rise in consumer spending; but a steady relaxation of censorship was also a major factor.

During the early 1950s, Cold War fears of radicalism and subversion had cast a puritanical chill over the American book business. A spate of local campaigns by conservative and religious groups against bookstores selling material they deemed "immoral" was followed, in 1952, by the appointment of a government inquiry—the House Select Committee on Current Pornographic Materials—tasked with probing the extent of obscenity in the publishing industry. Headed by Arkansas congressman Ezekiel C. Gathings, the committee pilloried popular paperbacks from the outset. Few publishing voices received a hearing. Instead, a procession of padres, policemen, judges, and teachers testified to the perils of paperback books.

Treska Torres's *Women's Barracks* (1950) triggered particular ire. Published by Gold Medal Books, the tome is a fictionalized account of the author's wartime

service in London with the women's division of the Free French forces. Isolated from the norms of civilian life, passionate attachments soon form in the all-female dormitories—between the older, experienced women and young innocents; between the butch officers and their femme subordinates. By modern standards the sex scenes in *Women's Barracks* are hardly depraved ("Claude unbuttoned the jacket of her pyjamas and enclosed one of Ursula's little breasts in her hand . . ."), yet the committee members couldn't bring themselves to read the offending passages aloud for the Congressional Record. When complete, the committee's report pulled no punches, arguing for much tougher obscenity laws and stricter regulation of the publishing industry. The calls, however, had little impact. Instead, citing First Amendment freedoms, publishers successfully lobbied against strengthened controls, and a series of landmark legal decisions steadily slackened censorship restraints.

In the war against censorship the first key beachhead was taken in 1959 when a ban on D.H. Lawrence's *Lady Chatterley's Lover* was successfully overturned and America's first unexpurgated edition was published by Grove Press. The next victory came in 1964 when the Supreme Court halted the ban on Henry Miller's bawdy fictional memoir *Tropic of Cancer*; and the liberalizing trend crested two years later when the Supreme Court revoked a ban on John Cleland's erotic eighteenth-century novel *Memoirs of a Woman of Pleasure*—more popularly known by the name of its wayward protagonist, Fanny Hill. The more liberal publishing climate that resulted was an asset to the literature emanating from the burgeoning women's movement, much of which dealt with issues of sex and sexuality with straight-talking candor. But it was also a benefit to pulp authors, whose take on sexual liberation was altogether more prurient.

By the late 1960s the pulp fiction business was facing some tough commercial realities. The market for books was buoyant, but competition was intense and, beginning with Random House's purchase of Alfred A. Knopf in 1960, the decade saw countless mergers and acquisitions among both publishing firms and retail outlets. As a consequence, many smaller, independent firms were squeezed out of business. Additionally, during the 1950s, pulp publishers had cornered the market for brash exploitation, and their fare leered out in newsstands and drugstores, enticing readers with a taste for the thrilling and the taboo. But by the end of the 1960s, sizzling prose, torrid covers, and brazen sensation had all become the standard fare of glossy best sellers in the most respectable bookshops. Indeed, many of the sales-topping authors of the day—Harold Robbins, Jacqueline Susann, Jackie Collins—had a writing style and a promotional ballyhoo that owed more than a little to the pulps' salacious heritage.

Compared to their 1950s glory days, then, times were harder for the pulps. But there was still plenty of market space for publishers who could plumb the depths of popular taste. Publisher David Zentner, for example, was wonderfully adept. Starting out in the world of softcore porn magazines, Zentner had helmed titles such as *Escapade* (an ersatz version of *Playboy*) before branching into paperback publishing with Bee-Line Books in 1964. Specializing in seedy erotica, Bee-Line proved a huge success and lasted well into the 1980s. It also spawned a number of profitable offshoots. Carlyle Books, for instance, did a brisk trade in sleazy fiction and nonfiction throughout the 1970s, while Pinnacle Books, launched in 1969, was geared more toward punchy action and adventure.

Good opportunities also remained for writers who could knock out cheap and juicy potboilers that capitalized on topical furors. Parley J. Cooper was exemplary. Throughout the 1970s and '80s, under a variety of pseudonyms, Cooper authored scores of popular paperbacks and specialized in a blend of steamy romance and Gothic horror—for instance, *The Devil Child* (published by Pocket Books in 1972; "LILLITH WAS YOUNG, STRANGELY PRETTY, AND DIFFERENT. THE TOWNS-PEOPLE CALLED HER A WITCH...") and *My Lady Evil* (published by Star in 1974; "A NOVEL OF DEMONIACAL POS-SESSION, TREACHERY AND ROMANTIC INTRIGUE"). But the author's hand could turn to any number of genres and themes. In 1977, for example, *Wreck* (published by Ace) saw Cooper cash in on Hollywood's spate of disaster movies with a tale of railroad catastrophe. Meanwhile, in 1975's *Reverend Mama* (published by Pocket Books) Cooper took the era's fascination for Charles Manson-*esque* hippie cults and combined it with the chills of the contemporary movie hit, *The Exorcist*—"DO YOU KNOW WHERE YOUR TEEN-AGERS ARE? IF THEY'RE WITH REVEREND MAMA, GOD HELP THEM..." And in 1971 Cooper was enlisted by Pinnacle to cash in on the newsworthiness of gender politics by considering the possibilities of female despotism in *The Feminists*.

The future envisioned in *The Feminists* is not without good points. The new, feminine order has brought the global population explosion to heel, crime rates have been halved, and the world's bitterest conflicts have been swiftly resolved:

Since the first year of the women, the war in Vietnam had been ended. Both the President and the Communist premier had met for tea in Switzerland, and before either of the ladies had finished their last crumpet, the order for troop withdrawal had been agreed upon. Women were not natural warriors as men were. They might indulge in a bit of gossip, but they were seldom reduced to physical violence. Violence strong enough to fight wars had been crushed with the men.

Indeed, for men, the world of the future holds little promise. Subdued and enslaved, they have become docile livestock controlled by fascistic matriarchs. Beaten down and strictly disciplined, they even face execution for having sex without a government permit. The only hope for salvation lies in young heroes like Keith Montalvo. After succumbing to temptations of the flesh without the requisite paperwork, Keith goes on the run. Finding sanctuary with "the Subterraneans"—a resistance army hiding out in Manhattan's disused subway tunnels—he joins the group's armed struggle for sexual equality but also finds time for romance after falling for Angela, a pretty guerrilla leader disaffected with her gender's totalitarian rule. Keith and the Subterraneans fight a hit-and-run insurgency against the authorities, until Keith is captured as the security forces battle to stem the insurrectionary tide.

New York's ruthless mayor, Verna Fredricks, nurses a consuming hatred for Keith—"to her, he represented all the evils of the masculine gender she had spent most of her life fighting"—and the plucky rebel is sentenced to death by guillotine. But when Fredricks discovers Keith is, in fact, the child she committed to a state children's home years previously, she is overcome by maternal instinct. Speeding to her son's rescue, Fredricks secures Keith's release in the nick of time—but by now nothing can stop the revolution. Fredricks is grabbed by an angry mob and marched to execution. Facing anarchy, the president admits to her lieutenants, "We must face the fact that Feminist control has failed. Unless we return rights to males and make them equals, our country will be torn apart." And as the chimes of freedom begin to ring, Keith and Angela are reunited. Putting a masculine arm around Angela's shoulders, Keith pulls her "protectively into the curve of his body," and—as the novel draws to a close—readers are reassured that "the battle of the sexes was coming to an end."

Similar themes of dominant women lording over male inferiors cropped up across popular culture of the early '70s. But in the pulps they were especially common. They surfaced, for example, in a number of the vigilante series that proliferated following the huge success of Don Pendleton's Executioner books, launched by Pinnacle in 1969. A publishing phenomenon throughout the '70s, the various vigilante series saw resourceful tough guys enforce justice by operating beyond the pussyfooting niceties of the law. And it was a vocation that regularly pitted the heroes against a phalanx of formidable females.

Andrew Sugar's Enforcer series is a good example. Beginning with *The Enforcer* (1973), the six-volume collection follows the exploits of daring agent Alex Jason who is saved from cancer by the mysterious John Anryn Institute and recruited (in a succession of cloned bodies) to their struggle against evil, invariably in the form of a criminal mastermind named Lochner. The series' sixth installment, *Bio Blitz* (1975), sees Lochner develop mutant insects in his war against the Institute, but he is also in league with a deranged army of feminist radicals, CLAW (Complete Liberation for All Women). Based at their New Jersey training camp, Fort Lesbos, and led by archetypal bull-dyke Wilma Bannertz, CLAW is "an organization dedicated to removing the yoke of the male establishment from the necks of all women," and its members are presented as a motley assortment of misfits and losers:

> There were about a dozen or so, all shapes and sizes. There were the dumpy ones who craved a look from a man, any man, while they complained about being thought of as sexual objects. There were also the fairly attractive but cold women who couldn't warm up to another human being, no matter what sex, and who blamed it on society. The fat, the skinny, the shapely, the strange and the lonely all filed out… some with their arms still waving in heated arguments while others placidly listened without challenging a word. As they filed past . . . Jason

Bio Blitz (Manor Books, 1976)
Reverend Mama (Pocket Books, 1975)
Amazons (Signet, 1976)

heard bits and pieces of their complaints. All standard militant gripes, a few with legitimate bases and the rest too absurd to be considered by any one [sic] with half an intellect.

The portrayal reflects the underlying conservatism of many pulp narratives, especially in the "vigilante" genre. The CLAW membership is rendered in terms of stock misogynistic stereotypes of feminists—either ugly, frigid, inadequate man-haters or bovine dupes easily led astray by militant nonsense. Different but equally chauvinistic representations of defiant women also surfaced in pulp paperbacks. Pandering to male erotic fantasies, powerful female characters could also be presented as sexually voracious viragos—voluptuous vixens eager to impose their lascivious desires on hapless victims. An installment from *The Mind Masters* book series is an apt illustration.

The Mind Masters, another entry in the vigilante genre, is a five-volume collection penned by John Rossman (though he wrote the last two episodes under the pseudonym "Ian Ross"). Beginning with *The Mind Masters* (1974), the series chronicles the adventures of Vietnam veteran Britt St. Vincent, whose latent psychic abilities are triggered by the trauma of combat. Leaving the military, St. Vincent joins the Mero Parapsychological Institute, a clandestine agency determined to fight malevolent exploitation of the paranormal. St. Vincent's day job as a playboy race driver is an ideal cover story, and the novels follow his globe-trotting adventures as he hunts psychic cyborgs, mad Nazi scientists, and a resurrected Jack the Ripper. The fourth book in the series, *Amazons* (1976), finds St. Vincent in Brazil, fighting Dr. Sin, a North Korean "hermaphrodite" who plots to give the "Far Eastern Axis" a foothold in South America. Dr. Sin is also in cahoots with a clan of beautiful but ferocious cannibal women from the Mato Grosso Plateau.

The Amazonian tribe is dominated by its females. Its men are divided into two categories—"breeders," saddled with "tending the huts, raising the children, satisfying the Amazons' sexual appetites and their need to give birth to worthy daughters"; and "workers," who are "inferior types who would only pollute the breed with their sperm. Naturally, they were castrated." Captured by the tribe, St. Vincent becomes the sexual plaything of Txuka, the blonde chieftess, who flaunts "her beautifully shaped legs, her perfect pink-nippled breasts, her full wealth of golden hair."

As St. Vincent beholds the torchlight coming-of-age ceremony for the jungle warrior-women, the author (writing in the third person and the present tense—an unusual style for a pulp writer) makes full use of the titillating opportunities created by the relaxation of censorship:

> The strong hands of the warriors reach out and begin to massage forcefully the taut thighs of the virgins lying helpless before them. Battle-strong adults' thumbs dig deeply into the tender inner flesh of the virgins as they work their way up toward, and into, the blonde pubic hair. The girls react to this touch with deep breaths and straining thigh muscles. Moans of hungry pleasure blend with the drums, and each lovely warrior slowly leans forward . . . their hands slipping beneath the buttocks of the girls and lifting these initiates slightly so that their glistening vaginal lips rise to meet softly the hungry lips that descend to devour them. And the drums grow louder!

Rossman's fervid prose was fairly typical fare in American pulps of the 1970s. And in Europe too, paperback publishers steadily exploited the opportunities for titillating thrills offered by the liberalization of censorship. Not least in Britain, where New English Library were the undisputed kings of paperback prurience.

★

New English Library (NEL) had been created in 1961 following the takeover and merger of two of Britain's many small paperback firms, Ace and Four Square, by the U.S. publishing giant Times Mirror Company. In the United States Times Mirror had hit pay dirt with its subsidiary, New American Library, publishing paperback reprints of classics, along with popular, pulp, and hard-boiled fiction. With NEL, Times Mirror sought to repeat the success by tapping into Britain's growing paperback market. Business was slow during the 1960s, but by the early 1970s NEL was towering over the competition. As in America, a relaxation of censorship laws enabled British publishers to explore widening horizons of sex and violence, and NEL became masters at exploiting the new possibilities, pumping out a heady stream of horror, action, and erotica.

The firm was especially adroit at tapping into a new, lucrative readership of teenagers and young

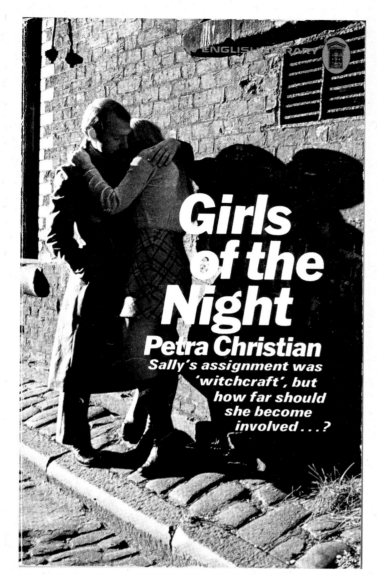

Girls of the Night (New English Library, 1973)
In the Club (New English Library, 1975)
Bed and Bawd (New English Library, 1974)
The Bust-Up (New English Library, 1974)
Free Wheeler (New English Library, 1975)
The Sexploiters (New English Library, 1973)

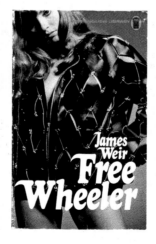

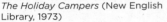

The Holiday Campers (New English Library, 1973)

Hitch-hiker (New English Library, 1971)

The New Drifters (New English Library, 1972)

adults. Hungry for a walk on the wild side, they were hooked in by NEL's promise of illicit kicks. A particular money-spinner was NEL's line of titles capitalizing on the sensationalism of '70s youth subcultures—skinheads, hippies, biker gangs, and soccer hooligans. But NEL's skill at trading on hot issues of the day also generated a succession of books that exploited themes of sexual revolution and women's liberation in tales of feisty young girls out for freedom and fun, chiefly of the carnal variety.

NEL's main foray into this field were the Sally Deenes novels, penned by "Petra Christian," in actuality Peter Cave, NEL's prolific staff writer, who had already written NEL's *Chopper* trilogy of biker novels. At the time, author Christopher Wood was riding high with his Confessions of... series of erotic comedies. Beginning with *Confessions of a Window Cleaner* in 1971, Wood's books were (ostensibly) the first-person chronicle of the sexual escapades of lad about town Timothy Lea. A hit with readers, the series ran to scores of episodes published by Sphere and, subsequently, Futura. To cash in on Lea's popularity, Wood also created a female counterpart, Rosie Dixon, who related her own series of nine bawdy romps, beginning with *Confessions of a Night Nurse* in 1974 (adapted into a film in 1978) and concluding with *Rosie Dixon, Barmaid* in 1977. NEL's Sally Deenes books attempted

to do something similar; and Peter Cave (with input from Christopher Priest—later to become an award-winning sci-fi writer) chalked-up a total of nine saucy adventures for the free-spirited heroine of the series: *Hitch-hiker* (1971), *The New Drifters* (1972), *The Holiday Campers* (1973), *Girls of the Night* (1973), *The Sexploiters* (1973), *Bed and Bawd* (1974), *The Bust-Up* (1974), *Hello Sailor!* (1975), and *In the Club* (1975).

The first in the series, *Hitch-hiker*, introduces Sally Deenes as a prim, young secretary working in a London insurance firm. Life takes an impulsive turn, however, as Sally and her new friend—the really wild Joan—resolve to cut their ties with home and embark on a hitchhiking odyssey across Europe. Recounted in the fervid first-person, the narrative follows the duo's venturesome trek as they contend with the likes of leering French motorists ("I know English girls... They like to make ze fun, eh?") and Arabian white-slavers ("Now my little ones... you find yourself in a butcher's shop for human flesh"). And throughout the directionless travelogue, rampant sex is nearly always on the cards as Sally abandons her inhibitions and delights in having her eyes opened to the ways of the world:

> Dominique's fondling of my body was becoming more insistent... I ran my hands over his skin, bringing him to sudden arousal that made

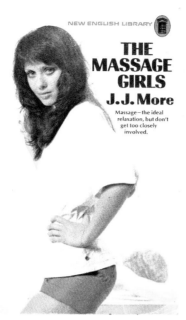

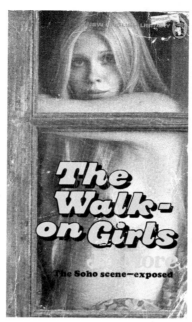

The Massage Girls (New English Library, 1973)

The Walk-On Girls (New English Library, 1975)

The Set-Up Girls (New English Library, 1975)

him shake with passion. His strong, gentle hands massaged my breasts and thighs, and the yearning in my body made my back arch with anticipation. Finally, he entered me once more and the climax, if anything, was greater and more satisfying than before.

The New Drifters sees Sally back in London, but her wanderlust soon returns and she hits the road for Sweden. After sampling Nordic hospitality ("Borje was inside me! I relaxed completely, opened my eyes . . . gasped with the incredible sensation of it"), Sally works as an obliging masseuse in a health spa before starring in a porn movie for the dark, brooding Scandinavian film director Gunnar Olsson. Returning to Britain, Sally heads straight to a rock festival on Salisbury Plain, where she hooks up with the concert promoter ("I let the cool magic of the hash and the sensual thrill of Pete's naked body steal over me"), narrowly escapes gang-rape by Hells Angels, and then heads to Tangiers, where she immerses herself in drug-fueled orgies with a commune of expatriate hippies.

Sally's next adventure sees her working at a Devonshire holiday camp, the Priest's Cave Holiday Centre, where she does her best to entertain the guests ("I felt his fingers, and then his tongue, slip expertly across my breasts, teasing the nipples, then on down,

across my belly, and then further down . . ."), before being whisked away by a macho greaser, "Slippery Hick," and his gang of Hells Angels (clearly a favorite plot device for Peter Cave). The subsequent novels pick up Sally's story after she has become a trendy author (a trio of best sellers having related her freewheeling antics) and has secured a job in journalism. Tapping into the zeitgeist of popular feminism, the book series sees Sally recruited as an investigative reporter for *Freedom Girl*, a zesty new women's liberation magazine that, as Sally explains, treads a wary line between hardcore and softcore fem-lib:

> *Freedom Girl* doesn't advocate banner-carrying, political demonstrations, or the striking of male-oriented words from the Oxford Dictionary. What it *does* support is women treating themselves like human beings, asserting their basic equal human rights in everything from the sexual act to wage-earning. Bra-burning and chanting slogans isn't where it's at.

Thus, in the cause of women's basic equal human rights, Sally embarks on a variety of intrepid assignments for *Freedom Girl*. In *Girls of the Night* she infiltrates a devil-worshipping cult to expose its Satanic rituals ("He put his hands behind my shoulders, and kissed each of my breasts, sucking the nipple into his mouth, and teasing it with his tongue"); while in *The Sexploiters* she uncovers an industrial espionage scam after braving the demands of a perverse nudist colony and the ardors of a sleazy sex show ("The sensations between our oiled and greasy skins were magnified a hundred times, and it wasn't long before I felt the first churning waves of orgasm building up inside me"). By the seventh novel, Sally has tired of journalism and quits *Freedom Girl*. But her career as a popular author continues, and Sally finds plenty of source material in her free-and-easy exploits running a seaside guest house with a casual disregard for normal morality (in *Bed and Bawd*); hanging out with hippie sex therapists in Tijuana (in *The Bust-Up*); making waves with the crew of HMS Thruster (*Hello Sailor!*); and, finally, managing a frenzy of orgiastic activity at a country club for swingers (the premise of *In the Club*).

Always bright and breezy, Sally Deenes was an upbeat and often tongue-in-cheek take on contemporary themes of women's new independence. But a grittier variant appeared in other NEL output. For instance, credited to James Weir, *Free Wheeler* (1975) is tinged with pronounced shades of kitchen-sink realism. The novel's protagonist, Doreen, is portrayed as a dowdy and downtrodden young woman, disillusioned with those men who had "all that power to move and turn a woman's heart, yet . . . walked over tenderness with hobnailed boots." Turning her back on a broken marriage and her job as a London traffic warden, Doreen heads off for a "more freewheeling life" in Leeds, a blue-collar northern town. Working as a dominatrix in the local sadomasochist scene, she casts off the frustrations and boredom of her old life as she is transformed from, as Doreen herself puts it, "a flat-footed traffic warden earning barely enough to live on, to a high-priced kink-furnisher making a bundle by just trampling on somebody for a few minutes."

For premier NEL grit, however, readers always turned to the work of James Moffatt. A hard-drinking, chain-smoking, and cantankerously right-wing hack from Canada, Moffatt had lived in the United States during the 1950s and early '60s where he relentlessly churned out stories for pulp magazines. By the mid-1960s Moffatt had moved to Britain, and was rattling off a profusion of paperback westerns, thrillers and romances under an array of pseudonyms. Working with NEL in the early 1970s he became most famous for his "Richard Allen" books; a series of knuckle-bruising novels such as *Skinhead* (1970), *Boot Boys* (1972), and *Terrace Terrors* (1974), which cashed in on Britain's headline-grabbing subcultures of the day. By the mid-70s however, the Richard Allen series was running out of steam, and Moffatt was exploring new directions. One turn he took was into London's burgeoning sex trade. Under the moniker "J. J. More" he wrote a trilogy of books that rooted through the capital's seamy underside: *The Massage Girls* (1973), *The Walk-On Girls* (1975), and *The Set-Up Girls* (1975).

Kicking off the J. J. More series, *The Massage Girls* follows valiant reporter Anthony Morgan as he goes undercover to penetrate Soho's seediest vice rackets ("'You'll like this, sir,' she murmured and pressed her naked breasts against his stomach as her moist lips moved across his chest . . ."). The theme of probing media exposés continued in *The Walk-On Girls*, which sees Jeanne Woodleigh, editor of *Star-Struck* magazine, reveal the sordid secrets of the film business and the casting couch.

But the premise of investigative journalism got its most over-the-top treatment in *The Set-Up Girls*, where Moffatt plundered freely from the period's most attention-grabbing news stories. The book sees Bill White, leading reporter for the small but influential newspaper *Post Intelligencer*, investigate the kidnap of the Mexican contestant in the famous Miss Beautiful beauty pageant. As the plot unfolds, White uncovers an international conspiracy of subversion perpetrated by an unholy alliance of student radicals and fanatical feminists. The scheming radicals (a recurring bugbear in Moffatt's books) are the Students for a Democratic Equality, denounced by White as thugs whose "aim is the establishment of a no-law, no-restriction permissive society with all those against eliminated." Leading the feminists is power-crazed cosmetics mogul, Luana Ferris. In a final showdown with White, the fanatical Ferris reveals her movement's ambition for a new era of social justice, personal freedom and—somewhat more prosaically—equal rights in consumer credit:

> I'm one of many women who believe that men have dominated for too many centuries. . . . We're not just receptacles for sperm. Not just housewives and bearers of unlimited brats. We're indispensable beings. Without us the cycle would cease. We have rights—equal pay, equal pensions, equality in housing and mortgages, in the purchase of credit goods.

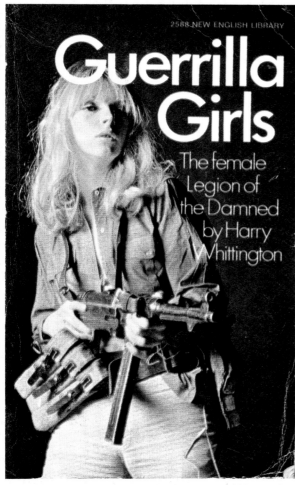

Alongside the belligerent harridan and the libidinous sexpot, the kickass action girl was another trope of "liberated femininity" beloved of pulp authors during the late 1960s and early '70s. Predictably, it was a genre NEL quickly jumped aboard, with a nifty 1970 rerelease of *Guerrilla Girls*, written by Harry Whittington. From the early 1950s to the mid-1980s Whittington was one of America's most prolific pulp authors (purportedly turning out as many as seven novels in a single month). He was a dab hand at westerns and hard-boiled noir, but he also turned out taut adventure stories that were juiced up with gunslinging hellcats and lesbian love interest. *Rebel Woman* (1960), for example, saw American hero Jim Patterson washed ashore on Cuba, where he discovers that his fiancée has not only become a communist commando but has also fallen for her lovely lieutenant, Dolores. In *Guerrilla Girls*, originally published in the U.S. by Pyramid Books in 1961, Whittington's attention turned to the Algerian Civil War where, according to the novel's back-cover blurb, "SOME WOMEN FOUGHT LIKE WILD ANIMALS FOR THEIR MEN—AND OTHERS TURNED TO STRANGE, DANGEROUS RELATIONSHIPS WITH EACH OTHER." Written as the first-person reminiscence of Ilya Mossi, a young French woman whose love for freedom and liberty compels her to join the struggle for Algerian independence, the book is a tense account of insurgent firefights and tough life in the rebels' mountain hideouts. But it was probably the book's lesbian subplot that most whetted editorial appetites at NEL, who capitalized on the vogue for "revolutionary women" by reissuing *Guerrilla Girls* with a new, eye-catching photo cover, which was always something of an NEL trademark.

But tales of tough, dangerous and irresistibly sexy young women was a field where James Moffatt was also quite at home. Indeed, one of the author's earliest books for NEL was 1971's *Jackboot Girls*. Written under the pseudonym "Leslie McManus," the novel is a particularly sleazy World War II story that concocts the Wolverines, a special, all-female battalion of the Nazi SS who are assigned to the interrogation of captured female resistance fighters. Decked out in black uniforms, "knee-high jackboots and standard issue silk, black underwear which Himmler had decreed was a trade mark of his female interrogators," the Wolverines are commanded by the cold-blooded Obersturmbannfuehrer Helga Schwartz. Both a diehard National Socialist and a predatory lesbian,

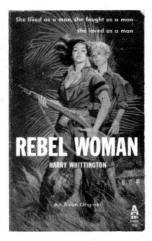

Guerrilla Girls (New English Library, 1970)
Rebel Woman (Avon, 1960)
Jackboot Girls (New English Library, 1971)

Schwartz leads her squad in breaking the spirit of helpless female prisoners by making them submit to the intimacies of sex with another woman:

> With a throaty cry, Helga descended on Erica, wrapping the woman in her perfumed flesh, gnawing and kissing until Erica was unable to resist the final accolade to Venus. Like snakes, they entwined—searching, seeking, taking, giving those pleasures men thought repulsive.

Hot and heavy assignations were, of course, standard pulp fare. There is a difference, however, between the lesbian liaisons in Moffatt's books and those that appear in the likes of Harry Whittington's *Guerrilla Girls* and Treska Torres's *Women's Barracks*. The tone of the latter is frank rather than lurid, allowing readers space to co-opt the stories as pieces of lesbian erotica. Indeed, *Women's Barracks* has become enshrined as a lesbian literary landmark—much to the chagrin of Torres herself, who later bemoaned the public's fascination with her book's lesbian elements. Moffatt's lesbian scenes, in contrast, revel in their salacious excess. Lecherous and lewd, they are calculatedly written as softcore fodder for male sexual fantasies.

By the end of *Jackboot Girls*, however, the war is over for Helga Schwartz. In 1945, amid the shattered ruins of the Third Reich, the arrogant Nazi meets an ignominious end as she is gang-raped by a platoon of battle-worn GIs. But Moffatt could not resist the lure of battle and during the late 1970s he dusted off his "Leslie McManus" byline for a series of rugged wartime adventures. *Operation Backlash* (1977) is a fairly predictable action yarn, but in his *Churchill's Vixens* quartet Moffatt aimed at something more distinctive by spotlighting the daring deeds of the allies' most deadly (and nubile) weapons: "Young beautiful and destructive secret agents as much at home on a midnight mission as in the bed of friend or foe."

Published under NEL's Mews imprint, the four books—*The Breton Butcher* (1976), *The Belgian Fox* (1976), *The Leaning Maiden* (1976), and *The Viking Maiden* (1977)—are self-contained tales, but they share a common theme of lithe young heroines dealing out death and devastation (and a fair degree of moral dissipation) to the German war effort. That said, the *Churchill's Vixens* books are hardly vintage Moffatt. By the late 1970s the years of booze had taken their toll, and the storylines of the *Vixens* books seem strained and plodding.

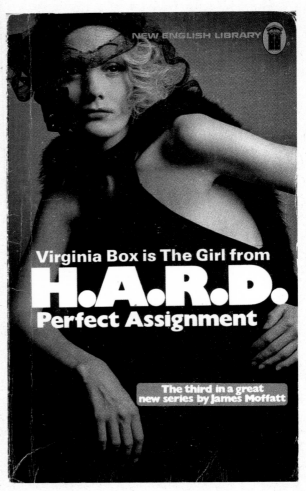

Perfect Assignment (New English Library, 1975)
The Big Snatch (Belmont Tower, 1969)
The Lady from L.U.S.T. (Tower, 1967)

Moffatt's bouncier spin on the "action girl" theme came in the earlier Virginia Box spy spoof series, which was a late entry into the craze for spies and secret agents that had begun during the mid-1960s with the likes of James Bond and *The Man from U.N.C.L.E.* The fad spawned a number of Bond-esque heroines in books, films and TV shows, characters such as Modesty Blaise and April Dancer (from *The Girl from U.N.C.L.E.* TV series). In the Virginia Box books, Moffatt attempted something similar. The author had already ventured into the world of espionage, penning two novels featuring a British intelligence agent, Silas Manners: *The Cambri Plot* (1970) and *Justice for a Dead Spy* (1971). But whereas the Silas Manners books played things straight, the Virginia Box novels struck a lighter note. They retain Moffatt's familiar qualities of downmarket sleaze and belligerent, right-wing bigotry, but the series swathes these in a jokey mix of high camp and smutty innuendo.

The protagonist, Virginia Box, is a top agent for a clandestine organization dedicated to the security of the free world, H.A.R.D. (Hemisphere Administration for Regional Defence). Sending up the spy genre's obsession with plots for world domination, pushbutton gadgetry and quirky acronyms, the novels see Box contend with a succession of enemy agents and cunning master-criminals, not to mention the wandering hands of her lecherous boss, Baird Rodd. In the first caper, *Virginia Box Is the Girl from H.A.R.D.* (1973), Box is dispatched to rescue the abducted wife of a nuclear physicist, the fetish-obsessed Sir Ian Whipps; a mission that brings the redoubtable Virginia up against both the East German sadist Willi Kumm and the villainous Soviet lesbian Ima Kissoff (marked by "a Slavic butchness that slightly detracted from her good looks").

In the sequel, *Virginia Box and the "Unsatisfied"* (1974), Box faces another nefarious line-up. After an initial run-in with mad scientist Dr. Spill and his ingenious sex computer, Box wrestles with a devious conspiracy hatched by the global terror group T.R.U.S.S. (Terrorism, Revolution, and Underground Specialists in Sabotage). Behind the doors of the Red Tiger, a leftie nightclub managed by smug hipster Dick Long, T.R.U.S.S. is fomenting a plot for world revolution that unites the likes of psychedelic rock band the Unsatisfied and their lesbian songstress Connie Linquistam, high-society liberationists Dolores Gamm and Magda Hott (a "leading exponent of female do-it-yourself-sex") and a treacherous CIA turncoat, Divine

Beddin. Needless to say, however, they are no match for the courageous Box.

The final book, *Perfect Assignment* (1975), is in similar vein. But this time the innuendo levels were switched to overload as Box squares up to the fiendish trio of London underworld queen Perfect Laye, KGB bully boy Yura Kraksmann, and Chinese zealot Lo Hung Dong. Of course, the dimension of a Soviet/Chinese alliance was at variance with the global politics of the day. But it was neatly explained by Moffatt, as the author grinded his personal political axe:

> Whatever the West wanted to write-in on the Sino-Soviet confrontation they had to be totally wrong. There existed differences of a two nation conflict on how to go about spreading communism but not on how to subvert Britain. The oldest democracy had to be subjugated. Had to be immersed in a dual conglomerate of Marxist-Maoist militancy. Until, eventually, the shop floor brigade ruled the roost and handed over the reins of power to those who really pulled on the bit—Moscow and Peking. With a little help from Cuba and East Germany.

Moffatt's Virginia Box novels were just one of many "sexpionage" spy spoofs appearing throughout the late 1960s and the '70s. In the United States especially, the line-up was legion: Theodore Mark Gottfried (writing as "Ted Mark") produced The Man from O.R.G.Y., a fifteen-book series published by Lancer between 1965 and 1981; between 1968 and 1971 The Man from S.T.U.D., another Lancer series, spawned ten novels by Paul W. Fairman (writing under his "F.W. Paul" pseudonym); for Ember Library, William Knoles (as "Clyde Allison") knocked out twenty books between 1965 and 1968 for the Man from S.A.D.I.S.T.O. series; Award books hired Bernhardt Jackson Hurwood (as "Mallory T. Knight") to pen the Man from T.O.M.C.A.T. series of nine books between 1967 and 1971; and Paperback Library released thirty-four Coxeman books between 1967 and 1973, written by multiple authors including Michael Avallone (dubbed "The Fastest Typewriter in the East").

But the "sexpionage" genre also included a bevy of "action girls" who were every bit as lethal and licentious as the guys. From 1974 to 1975, for instance, Pocket Books released The Baroness, an eight-book series credited to "Paul Kenyon" (a pseudonym for author Donald Moffitt). It recounts the adventures of voluptuous international playgirl, Baroness Penelope St.

John-Orsini, a former cover model for *Vogue* and *Elle* who runs her modeling agency as a cover for daring forays into the world of superspies.

Leisure Books, meanwhile, offered Cherry Delight, a top agent for N.Y.M.P.H.O. (New York Mafia Prosecution and Harassment Organization), who starred in the twenty-four-book series Cherry Delight: The Sexecutioner between 1972 and 1975, before returning for five more escapades in 1977. Several authors were drafted in for tours of duty with the delightful Cherry, including Gardner F. Fox, who, writing as "Rod Gray," also penned a proliferation of paperbacks under the series title The Lady from L.U.S.T.

Published by Midwood-Tower, the initial Lady from L.U.S.T. series comprised eighteen books released between 1968 and 1974. The novels were reprinted by Belmont Tower (with some title changes) in 1973 and were followed in 1975 by the release of a seven-volume New Lady from L.U.S.T. series. All featured Eve Drum, "Agent Oh Oh Sex" of L.U.S.T. (League of Undercover Spies and Terrorists), a covert branch of the U.S. secret service responsible for deadly missions around the world. Always the coquettish minx, Drum boasts she is the "sexiest spy in the business." As the death-dealing operative herself explains:

> My name is Eve Drum—The lady from L.U.S.T.—the sexiest spy in the world. Anything you can do I can do better. They call me Oh Oh Sex, because sex is my favorite weapon, but I'm just as good at Karate, safe-cracking, knife throwing, scuba diving—you name it. Don't tangle with me: I have a license to kill and I don't care if I use my body—or a Beretta.

Often up against the evil machinations of H.A.T.E. (Humanitarian Alliance for Total Espionage), Drum wrestled her way through novels whose titles increasingly ached with suggestive puns and double-entendres: *The Big Snatch* (1969), *The 69 Pleasures* (1970), *Blow My Mind* (1970), *The Copulation Explosion* (1974). Over the years the novels also became steadily more explicit, though author Fox always gave a certain lyricism to the "bump-and-grind":

> Usually I am the one who sets the pace in matters sexual. I have read all the old masters of making love, studied the tomes of Elephantis and Paxamus, Ovid and Suetonius, plus others, until I consider myself a walking encyclopaedia of erotica. But right now I was content to writhe and twist under male lips that suckled my nipples and beneath female lips that wandered from my belly to my mons veneris.

Popular fiction is always a time capsule of attitudes, issues and controversies. And the pulp paperbacks featuring freewheeling femininity and kickass action girls are a revealing litmus of changing attitudes to sexuality and gender during the late 1960s and the 1970s. The books not only testify to the social impact of the women's movement and campaigns for women's rights but also demonstrate the way responses to these crusades were often rooted in conservative chauvinism. Indeed, "pulp feminists" invariably appeared as either deranged harridans or manipulated dupes; frigid puritans or rapacious bull-dykes. Sexually independent women, meanwhile, are habitually portrayed as easy and available hussies—willing and wanton sex objects served up for men's erotic fantasies.

At the same time, however, the pulp paperbacks were forever shot through with tensions, contradictions, and spaces where different constituencies of readers could find a variety of meanings. And some of these could go against the grain of the conservative mainstream. A handful of titles, for instance, could be appropriated as lesbian erotica. The pulps' visions of a free and independent sexuality—albeit one geared to male desires—may have offered a tantalizing taste of autonomous possibilities at a time when conventional representations of femininity were still rooted in the suffocating confines of family, marriage, and domesticity. At the same time, pulp fiction's elements of misogyny were often acute. Moreover, the pulps' trademark was their passion for the outrageous, the shocking and the lewd, and this flew in the face of conformist tastes and ideals. The prurient paperback was always a provocative presence on the bookshelf, and its uncompromising enthusiasm for the outré stood as a brazen challenge to straitlaced moralism.

Bill Osgerby

City on the Brink

Wally Ferris's *Across 110th*

Released in 1972, *Across 110th Street* is rightly viewed as one of the grittiest and hardest hitting of the many New York crime movies that appeared in the seventies. On a hot summer night, three black men rob a mob-run counting house in Harlem for $300,000. In the space of a few minutes seven people are dead, including two cops, and forces are unleashed that threaten to ignite the tinder-dry city.

The film is based on a little-known and long-out-of-print novel, *Across 110th*, by Wally Ferris, a television news cameraman who passed away in July 2014. Ferris enjoyed phenomenal success with this one book, published in hardcover and paperback in 1970 (it also appeared the same year in the UK, titled *The Hunt*) but never had anything published again. The book recounts the aftermath of the bloody heist from multiple points of view: the doomed men who pull the heist, the mob enforcers ordered to make an example of the thieves, and the two cops, one black, the other white, given the job of apprehending the robbers before more people are killed.

The titular street is New York's symbolic class boundary between Harlem and the wealthy neighborhoods around Central Park, and the title is emblematic of the racial and class politics that permeate the story. These aspects are portrayed in an in-depth and sophisticated way unusual for much of the hard-boiled crime fiction written at the time.

The book moves quickly after the heist. The police are on the scene, headed up by the two men in charge of the investigation. Lieutenant Bill Pope is smooth, educated and ambitious, one of a number of smart black cops moving into positions of seniority in the city's police force. "Pope had the brain and ambition that could capitalize on the new interest New York's liberal politicians had in such men as he. Now more than ever they needed to showcase ebony talent to the city's million blacks."

His partner, Sergeant Frank Sullivan is a grizzled, old-fashioned Irish cop, not averse to cracking heads to get things done. Not so much anti-black as

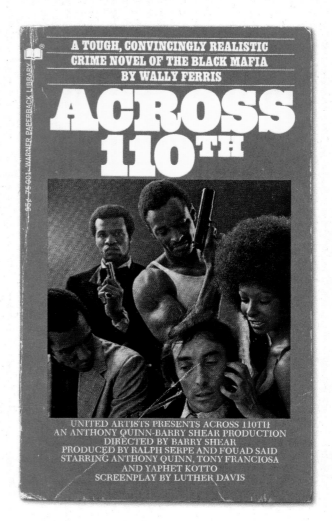

Across 110th (Warner Paperback Library, 1972)

anti-everyone, Sullivan has always been a wild card, but his behavior has become increasingly erratic since the deaths of his wife and child. As the police sift through the post-robbery carnage, Sullivan's senior officer and protector from numerous excessive force charges, Captain Matthews, takes him aside to tell him he is resigning. Sullivan knows his days as a cop are numbered.

The counting house belonged to the Giaccano crime family and its aging Godfather views the robbery as a major challenge to his foothold in Harlem. He assigns an ambitious enforcer, Nick Difalco, to track down those responsible and make a very public example of them. This means going over the head of the mob's sub-boss in Harlem—the man the Godfather holds responsible for his financial loss—a tough black gangster called Doc Johnson. Arriving at Johnson's office in a twenty-four-hours-a-day limousine service, Difalco accuses him of negligence, then starts questioning him about who is responsible for the heist. Difalco suspects it might be the work of corrupt cops but Johnson disagrees. He believes it was

> strictly a black man's gig. I got that straight from the scene, but didn't need to be told 'cause no white man outside the organization would know how I operate up here. And even you people downtown don't know all about the guys and collectin' styles I use. No, it couldn't be cased by no Charlies, 'cause even if they had the guts to nose around, they would have stood out like a white hooker at a black revival.

Johnson gets angry with Difalco for telling him how to do his job.

> Difalco smashed his fist down onto the desk, jarring everybody in the room into immobility. "Your business is running our business," he shouted in a voice that ripped up at Johnson. "You may be somethin' up here, but below a Hundred and Tenth Street you're just another fat nigger." His face constricted, the eyes vanishing behind vitriolic slits. "Giaccano pulled you out of the stink of the back alley and put you up front to represent the Organization; he calls the shots, and if he tells you to shit, you better start squattin', fat man. And that's just what he's tellin' you now. He put you in and he can put you out, and you better believe it. Because anybody that

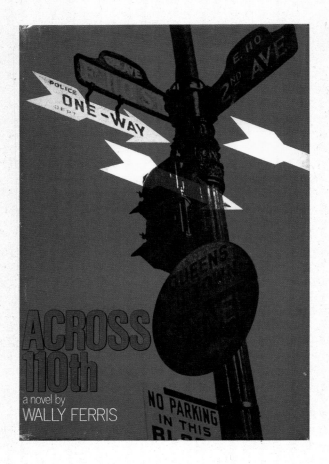

Across 110th (Harper & Row, 1970)

loses money is a bad risk and tonight you lost a bundle."

The black and white Mafia enter into an uneasy alliance to track down the robbers, with the law a few steps behind them. Subsequent events take place in seedy after-hours clubs, brothels, and slum tenement apartments in Harlem. It's a world pulsating with poverty and criminality, in which both the mob and the police are occupying forces.

The men responsible for the robbery are Henry Jackson, Joe Logart, and Jim Harris. Harris is ex-army, fresh out of prison, and the mastermind of the job. He warns his partners to lie low, not flash their recently acquired wealth around and keep their mouths shut. Logart heeds the advice but Jackson goes out to a club-*cum*-brothel where he proceeds to throw money around, drawing the attention of one of Johnson's informers and ultimately Difalco and his men. Jackson is brutally murdered and his body crucified as an example to anyone else thinking of robbing from the mob.

With information obviously supplied by Jackson before his death, Difalco intercepts Logart, who is about to flee the city, and kills him. The book culminates in Difalco's men and the police cornering a heavily armed Harrison in a tenement apartment. The resulting firefight results in the death of several of Difalco's men, Harris, his girlfriend, a dancer in a local after-hours bar, Ivy, and Sullivan.

Barry Shear, who had honed his craft in television directing episodes of *Mod Squad*, *Julia*, and *Hawaii Five-O*, directed the film version, *Across 110th Street*. His only previous feature credit was *Wild in the Streets*, a 1968 movie about a mysterious twenty-four-year-old rock star millionaire who teams up with an ambitious Californian politician to get the voting age lowered to fourteen. Once elected president he ushers in a youth-controlled authoritarian state in which older people are interred in camps, permanently dosed up on psychedelic drugs.

Across 110th Street, which opens with a mobster's black Cadillac cruising through Harlem toward New York's uptown areas to the tune of the iconic Bobby Womack theme song, is one of the least glamorous and most violent examples of American cop noir to emerge from the seventies. It is also one among a crop of movies from the era, including *Panic in Needle Park* (1971), *Death Wish* (1974), *Dog Day Afternoon* (1975),

Taxi Driver (1976), *The Warriors* (1979), and numerous blaxploitation features, that depict New York as on the brink of being completely ungovernable. With one exception, an early scene in the Godfather's penthouse apartment overlooking Central Park, there is no relief from the poverty and squalor of the film's Harlem locations. The plot moves quickly and relentlessly forward to its tragic conclusion. There is a palpable sense of desperation within a city on the edge of chaos.

Not surprisingly given the film's look and tone, it was not particularly well received upon release. It was probably a little too close to the bone given New York's perilous state in the early seventies. It featured numerous black actors and incorporated elements of the blaxploitation aesthetic with a hard-boiled crime sensibility that was no doubt confusing to much of the white audiences it was mainly aimed at.

Yaphet Kotto is particularly good as Pope. Deep-voiced character actor Richard Ward is excellent as Johnson, based on the real-life Harlem gang lord, Ellsworth "Bumpy" Johnson, as is Paul Benjamin as the head of the heist gang, known as Harrison in the film. The exception is Anthony Quinn, who feels like he is hamming it up as Sullivan's character, called Sgt. Mattelli in the film. Quinn was originally on board as executive producer and, according to various stories, stepped into the role only when John Wayne, Kirk Douglas, and Burt Lancaster turned it down.

The film largely mirrors the structure of the novel, with a few exceptions. At the end of the book, Harrison shoots Sullivan, moments before police gun him down. In the film Mattelli is killed by one of the black enforcers who have been assigned by Johnson to help the mob track the men responsible for the heist, a sort of revenge for humiliation and racial abuse they have suffered at the hands of Nick D'Salvio (as Difalco is called in the film), played by Anthony Franciosa. Difalco dies in the film, whereas in the book he is taken into police custody. "And he knew, even as they twisted the handcuffs about his wrists and pulled him down the stairs, that an old man in a palatial house high on the cliffs of New Jersey would take a lock off the treasury and buy him the best legal brains in the country."

Another key difference is the relationship between the two cop characters. The film portrays Mattelli as overtly racist and corrupt, and the conflict between he and Pope is much starker. The book provides far greater insight into their relationship and both are more nuanced characters.

Ferris describes Pope as having been "nurtured by Northern Apartheid and bias, and driven by anger and the hardships his family had endured to ensure that the first male in their family tree was able to jump down clutching a college diploma." He joined the police almost by accident and found that he had a taste for it. His motivations for staying in the force are mixed. He craves "personal equality, the same kind of security the white man seeks in civil service." But this has another side:

> Something he had not realized had existed in him until his promotion from uniform and disarming a holdup man in a crowded street in Bedford-Stuyvesant, and his subsequent assignment to Harlem. He found an expanding ego; now he walked among his own but with a heady authority, feeling the gun on his hip and the badge of entrance in his pocket, and experiencing the ambivalent respect and fear this black community had to offer. The equality he had been searching for had paradoxically transformed itself into the guise of superiority.

Sullivan is also from a disadvantaged background, the product of poor upbringing and an abusive stevedore father. As a cop he is street smart, known for causing trouble but also for getting results. He is cynical and happy to break the rules, rather than financially corrupt, capable of great kindness, as well as ferocious violence.

They have been partners for some time when the book opens. At first, Pope considered Sullivan little more than "northern Honkie cracker, but their tours in the seamy jungle of whores and pimps, pushers and wasted junkies, petty assaults and hysterical murders passed quickly and solidified them into a team." While tensions that remain between them, Pope is realistic, and to some degree even accepting, regarding his partner's faults.

> Pope wondered if this violent man could ever retire. He realized Sullivan was an unconscious seeker of trouble and excitement, and he would be out of step in a world of middle-class calm. He was a boat rocker, born a hundred years too late, a marshal in a frontier town who should have been locking up drunken cowboys or shooting

red men instead of punching contemporary black ones. The ideological chasm rooted in the color of their skin and their backgrounds dictated their approach to life and the job.

While Difalco is fairly one-dimensional, a vicious thug keen to prove himself to his mob superiors, the other criminal characters are given greater depth and texture. Doc Johnson is a brutal gangster, but his hold on power in Harlem is described thus:

> In a ghetto that respected few, Doc Johnson was a revered living legend. To many downtrodden Negroes he was truly an American success story, which had started twenty-five years before when he arrived in New York with just the clothes on his back, one jump removed from a Georgia chain gang.

The book also contains an interesting subplot involving Johnson doing a deal with a rich, amoral black real estate developer who wants to team up with the gangster to muscle the mob out of Harlem.

Harris is poor and uneducated but ambitious in his own way. He mocks his girlfriend's attempts to make him go straight, believing a choice between robbing the counting house and spending his life working in a series of menial and degrading jobs is no real choice at all.

> His voice was a harsh grating sound that barreled frustratingly up from deep within his chest. "Doin' what? Like workin' in a car wash, or maybe deliverin' coffee for a downtown restaurant to one of them big office buildings?" He raised his arms as he took a step further into the light. "Look at me, Ivy. Just look at me. A thirty-four-year-old nigger with no schoolin', no trade, and an ex-convict. Who the hell would want me for anything other than swinging a pick? Get out of your white-woman dream world, baby. It's about time you grew up, because your life was never goin' ta change by me goin' straight. It would be one shit job after another and you'd still be workin' in that club, still being propositioned every night and, baby, when we get up tight with money, and that would be like from the start, I'm going to tell you to bed down with some of them cats because I'm goin' to have you out whorin'."

He turned from her and began to pace the shadowed kitchen. "Or maybe I'd start dealin' drugs on some street corner. Yeah, it would be either that or me back with a gun lookin' for a small quick buck 'cause I'd be tryin' to hold on to some kinda manhood."

Despite being a little overwritten at points, Ferris's book flows well. New York is vividly portrayed and, as previously noted, infused with a sense of the city's class and racial divide. Racial inequality is particularly ubiquitous: the ingrained structural poverty, the constant racial abuse, the cynicism of the news media that uses racial violence and black deaths to sell papers but does nothing about it. So too is the pushback, the "rallies of black nationalists and militants, their marches and picketing and the black power cries of the activists." These details elevate what is a relatively simple plot—a heist and its aftermath—help build tension and give a sense of a city where the power dynamic between the black population, the mob, and the cops is complex and constantly in motion.

The sense of New York City on the brink of some great disorder, while perhaps overmythologized today, was not without basis. The sixties saw the beginning of a widespread social and economic deterioration. In 1964 the shooting of a black teenager, James Powell, by a policeman in front of numerous witnesses resulted in six nights of rioting in Harlem. It was the first of a wave of racial protests that swept major U.S. cities as the sixties progressed. The homicide rate spiraled from 681 in 1965 to 1,690 in 1975.

Manufacturing declined during this period, and the shipping industry, for decades a mainstay of the local economy, moved to New Jersey. Blue-collar neighborhoods fell into disrepair and became centers of crime and drug use. The second half of the decade saw a wave of industrial unrest against the city's Republican mayor, John Lindsay, including a nine-day sanitation strike in 1968 that left the city awash in garbage. By 1975, the city's fiscal crisis had become so serious that it threatened the administration with insolvency. Rather than working to fix the problem, President Gerald Ford, egged on by his young chief of staff, Donald Rumsfeld, used the crisis as an opportunity to shame the New York and its liberal establishment, insisting that the city institute draconian spending cuts that worsened the situation.

"It is difficult to convey just how precarious, and paranoid, life in New York felt around that time," wrote New York novelist and historian Kevin Baker in the *Guardian* in May 2015.

Signs everywhere warned you to mind your valuables, and to keep neck chains or other jewellery tucked away while on the subway. You became alert to where anyone else might be in relation to you, augmented by quick looks over your shoulder that came to seem entirely natural. I knew a few people who had been mugged or worse, but *everyone* I knew had suffered the violation of a home break-in.... There was a pervasive sense that social order was breaking down.

★

The fact that *Across 110th* is such an interesting book and a vivid depiction of New York at the time it was written is in no small part due to its author, Wally Ferris. Ferris was a union cameraman and stage manager for WNEW-TV in New York for almost forty years. He worked on the *10 O'clock News* and most of their other regular programming. He was also a lifelong New Yorker, born and raised in Brooklyn by parents descended from immigrants who had left Ireland during the Great Famine. He grew up during the Depression, brought up by his mother after his father, a policeman, had died at an early age.

"At that time, there was no widows' pension or government assistance," says his daughter, Elizabeth Ferris. "It was just the beginning of Roosevelt's New Deal, and those benefits were not yet available. The Police Department engaged my grandmother to clean firehouses and precincts as a way of ensuring the family's financial survival. At least, that was the official word. But actually she ran numbers [collecting illegal bets] for the cops. It wasn't until my father was an adult that he knew his mom was a bookie."

Ferris had an in-depth knowledge of greater New York, used to good effect in the book. As Elizabeth Ferris explains:

My dad's relationship with this city was so ingrained with who and what he was: "The thing that makes this city so unbearable is there are too many people with different backgrounds, views, cultures. And, the thing that makes this city so great is there are so many people with different backgrounds, views, cultures." He loved this place and, at times, hated it too. Too loud, too crowded, too aggressive, too noisy. "But, where else can I live?" It was home.

He was also fiercely political. "Wally loved politics. He always said politics was the greatest blood sport. Most of our dinner conversations when Dad was home were about what happened in the world today and politics." This included supporting the struggle of the civil rights movement and being empathetic with the situation of much of the city's black population.

Wally was working camera as Malcolm X sat round table with black leaders of the Human Rights Movement. The others were ripping into Malcolm X for his extreme views. When they went to commercial break, Malcolm X addressed each one individually with his grievances about their less than stellar behavior. When the cameras rolled again, the tenor of the table had radically changed with a constructive exchange about the topic of racial equality. Daddy had great respect and was so impressed with Malcolm X. I was very young but still remember when Malcolm X was murdered. My Dad was upset.

Ferris started writing the manuscript that would become *Across 110th* in the sixties.

Wally worked the late news and would get home around midnight. While the house slept, he sat at the kitchen table with all the lights out except for a small goose-necked lamp with a bright intense light and write on yellow legal pads. Every morning the table would be cleared of any of Dad's things and piled on the side cupboard. I once asked my mother what he was writing. She told me love letters to himself.

Elizabeth Ferris is unsure where the exact inspiration for the novel came from.

I do remember my father having a hardcover copy of *The Pawnbroker* [1961] by Edward Lewis Wallant. It was full of Dad's notes written in the margins and pieces of paper sticking out from the pages. He had a notebook where he was recording his thoughts about this novel. I asked him about this and he told me he used this book as a guide and reference. Wally also had a collection of newspaper articles. They were mostly little pieces that would be found deeper in the paper and not headline news. I thought this was curious [as a child] and asked him why. I remember him telling me they were ideas for stories.

Ferris had no publishing industry experience or contacts to get his book into print. In lieu of these he used the opportunities that arose in his day job. In 1969 he was working as a cameraman on a local WNEW-TV show called *Maurice Woodruff Predicts*. Woodruff was a famous British clairvoyant and astrologer who had achieved considerable fame in his native country, mainly due to his celebrity clients, including actor Peter Sellers. According to New Jersey crime writer Wallace Stroby, who met Ferris and kept in contact with him until his death, Ferris asked Woodruff if he could help him get an agent for *Across 110th*. "Woodruff asked his own agent to take it on, but the agent was reluctant, so he asked Woodruff to predict whether the book would be a success of not. Woodruff said it would, so the agent then agreed to represent it. It sold almost immediately, I think a $40,000 advance, astronomical for those days, and was optioned for film before it was even published."

Barry Shear, the director of *Across 110th Street*, and Ferris had worked together in television in the fifties. According to Elizabeth, "Barry moved his family to LA during the 1960s. They were on good terms but had a common friend and co-worker, Arnie Knox, the news director. It was Arnie that put Barry and Daddy together again. So the story goes, Arnie gave Barry an advance copy of the book to read on his way back to LA. By the time Barry got off the plane, he called New York and contacted Daddy through Arnie."

Ferris's family moved to Los Angeles for a short period in the early seventies while he worked on a draft of the script. Luther Davis, whose credits included the 1955 musical adventure, *Kismet* and the thriller *Lady in a Cage* (1964), wrote the final version. Shear offered television scriptwriting to Ferris but, according to his daughter, he turned it down and returned to New York because he disliked LA.

Although Ferris never had another book published, Elizabeth states: "My father wrote almost every day and was working on a project up until the last days of his life. There are a few completed manuscripts." One of these was a thriller called *The Extradition*.

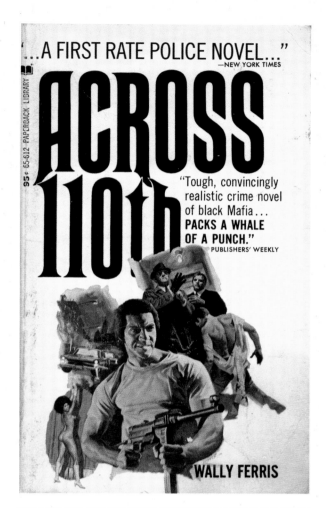

Wallace Stroby, who has seen the manuscript, explains:

The Extradition was about a New York prosecutor and a tough cop who go to Brazil to extradite a Bernie Madoff–like character.* By its nature it was a little dated. Not sure what the history of it was, but Ferris hadn't had an agent since the early seventies, so I doubt it got around much. I think for Wally, the book and the movie were a fluke. He had a good-paying union job at WNEW and was raising a family, and I don't think he wanted to upset all that to chase down some vague literary goal. At least that what I'm guessing.

For Ferris, "It was never about the 'success'; it was about the writing—the journey and not the destination," insists his daughter. "He took a few small stabs at seeking publication but not any real effort. He was okay with that. . . . Wally was forever telling Kevin and me to keep our mouths shut about the book and movie. We weren't to tell anyone. Was Daddy a private person? Did he not want his children to be braggadocios? I guess to both questions the answer is yes."

Andrew Nette

Across 110th (Paperback Library, 1970)
Theatrical poster for Barry Shear's 1972 film adaption of the novel, *Across 110th Street*

* Madoff was a former stockbroker, investment advisor, and financier convicted of fraud in 2009.

The Radical

Donald Goines in the Wake of Civil Rights

Donald Goines was shot to death in his Detroit home on October 21, 1974. The prolific writer was only thirty-nine. His common-law wife Shirley Sailor was also brutally gunned down. In covering the tragedy, the black press noted that "the bloody, suspicious circumstances of his death" could have been a scene out of one of Goines's many novels.

Mourners paid their respects at an open-casket funeral. In recognition of his status as the undisputed king of black pulp, the family placed one of his bestselling books in his hands, which formed a cross in front of his body. The press observed that "a cultish following had built up around the successful Black author," and that his death, while tragic, only seemed to enhance his reputation. Is it any wonder, then, that the book "was stolen out of his lifeless hands"? Goines had practically become a figure of worship: the patron saint of inner-city life.

Donald Joseph Goines was born in Detroit on December 15, 1937, to Joseph and Myrtle (née Baugh) Goines. The Goineses ran a successful dry-cleaning business, which afforded their three children—Donald, his older sister Marie, and his younger sister Joan—a solid, middle-class upbringing. As a boy, Goines attended Sacred Heart, a Catholic school, and helped at the store in his spare time. But he started to drift away from the family in 1946, when he transferred to Detroit Public Schools. Goines fell in with a rough crowd and started to engage in petty crime. His rebellious streak came to a head when, at the age of fifteen, he doctored Marie's birth certificate and enlisted in the U.S. Air Force. He was shipped overseas and did a stint in Japan during the Korean War. Although he eventually became a military police officer, the service introduced Goines to the self-destructive pleasures of vice: he picked up a nasty heroin habit in Asia.

Goines was only seventeen when the war ended in 1953. He came back to Detroit and resumed living with his family. But Goines's addiction followed him, and chasing the next fix soon took over his life. Goines was unable to hold down a steady job, so he turned to the one thing that did pay: crime. Over the next fifteen years, he became a fixture in Detroit's black underworld—and, predictably, the region's penitentiaries. He racked up sentences for, among other things, attempted larceny, armed robbery, and bootlegging. During his final stint as an inmate, in Michigan's Jackson State Prison, he resolved to do something different with his life. He wanted to try his hand at writing.

Goines's inspiration was a black author whose paperback books were in high demand among the incarcerated. Iceberg Slim had parlayed his time as a player in "The Game," or underworld hustle, into a literary career. His fictional autobiography *Pimp: The Story of My Life* (1967) struck a chord with inmates, who felt validated seeing their lives represented so faithfully on the page. The book opened Goines's eyes to the possibility that the ghetto experience—*his* ghetto experience—could be adapted to fiction. He embraced Slim as a literary model and began writing in earnest.

Goines completed the manuscript that would become *Whoreson* (1972) before he got out of prison. The coming-of-age story focuses on the son of a black prostitute and a long-forgotten white john. Early in the story, the narrator explains how he got his rather unusual name. When the doctor attending to his birth asked his mother, Jessie, to name him, she "laughed suddenly, a cold, nerve-tingling sound." For her, the newborn was an unwelcome reminder that she had been "badly misused by some man." Almost out of spite, she marked her baby as the bearer of that shame: "I've got just the name for the little sonofabitch—Whoreson, Whoreson Jones. . . . I'm naming my son just what he is. I'm a whore and he's my son. If he grows up ashamed of me, to hell with him. That's what I'm wantin' to name him, and that's what it's goin to be." Jessie had no qualms about yoking her baby to the condition of his birth.

Far from withering under the stigma of his name, Whoreson embraces it as a birthright. The brazenness of his mother's act accords him a certain degree of street-level respect. Indeed Jessie's defiant

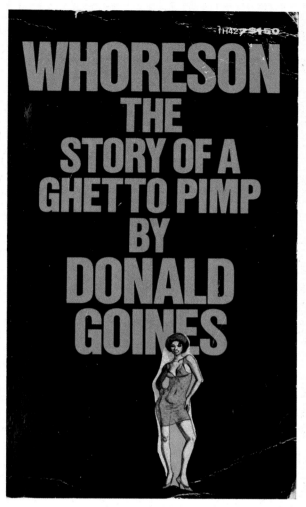

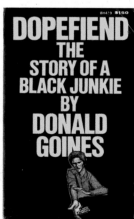

Whoreson (Holloway House, 1972)
Donald Goines
Dopefiend (Holloway House, 1971)

identification as a prostitute leads other ghetto denizens to hold her in some esteem: "Jessie had a way of walking that made people think a queen was going past." Seeing her as role model of sorts, Whoreson notes, "To carry myself with such pride was my desire." Jessie helps him achieve this kind of respect by training him, from a young age, to become her "little pimp." She teaches Whoreson how to collect "trap money" from every night's take, and she cultivates his sense of entitlement to the bodies and earning potential of other women. By essentially becoming her son's first whore, Jessie promotes an ideal of ghetto survival that turns the shameful condition of one's birth into the pretext for an enterprise that affirms one's manhood.

By the time Goines was released from prison, in December 1970, he had already secured a contract for *Whoreson* from Slim's publisher, Holloway House. But while that book was held up in production, the company brought out his more autobiographical work *Dopefiend* (1971). Mirroring the author's own descent into the Detroit underworld, the book concerns two young people from good homes, Teddy and Terry, who turn to a life of crime in order to support their heroin habits. As the couple and their fellow addicts become increasingly desperate for cash, they subject themselves to ever more degrading acts for pay. The local pusher, a portly pervert named Porky, is the one to take advantage of the situation. In a particularly unbearable scene, he forces an addict named Minnie to perform fellatio on his dog. Goines's bitterly ironic citation of cartoon animal names—Porky and Minnie—underscores the profound dehumanization of black bodies in the drug subculture. Minnie is left so traumatized by the abuse that she hangs herself shortly thereafter. Terry comes upon the body, and the already-grisly sight is made even more horrific when she sees "a child's head protruding from between Minnie's naked legs."

Two books in, Goines already had a reputation for writing novels that were more graphic and more harrowing than anything Slim had done. It was a case of the apprentice superseding the master. Though the two never met, Goines may have seen Slim as a rival in a contest of pulp one-upmanship. Yet their stylistic differences could equally be explained by a profound generational shift. Goines was nearly twenty years Slim's junior. That meant he was in his hustling prime when the dream of integration and the promise of civil rights came crashing down around him. Slim had already retired from the streets by the mid-1960s. But

Goines was still on the prowl when Detroit went up in flames, first during the long, hot summer of 1967 and then again in April 1968, after the assassination of Dr. Martin Luther King Jr. Goines experienced the decimation of the inner city up close and in real time. As such, he was more inclined than Slim to question the very possibility of social change in the post-civil-rights era.

Goines's pessimism was so thoroughgoing that he even took a sledgehammer to Black Power, the movement that had replaced civil rights as the primary site of black activism in the late 1960s. His third novel, *Black Gangster* (1972), relates the story of Melvin "Prince" Walker, a twenty-two-year-old ex-convict who uses Black Power as a tool to seize control of the ghetto underworld. Prince's gang, the Rulers, attracts new members through something called the Freedom Now Liberation Movement. By manipulating urban youth's sincere desire for revolutionary action, Prince manages to build a criminal operation with a grassroots following. With no real concern for the people he claims to represent, Prince oversees a destructive crime wave that claims the lives of supporters, policemen, and bystanders alike. Violence begets more violence, effectively plunging the city into a state of emergency. Prince receives his comeuppance by the end of the novel, but not before Goines has emptied meaning out of political struggle, subordinating Black Power idealism to the more concrete laws of the street.

With three titles under his belt and Holloway House clamoring for more, Goines decided to move to Los Angeles. The hope was that extricating himself from the toxic environment of his old haunts would give him the motivation to succeed as a professional writer. Besides, the thinking went, being close to his publisher might help him stay on top of assignments. And with Hollywood around the corner, who knows? He might catch a lucky break with a movie deal. With their daughter Donna (named after Dad), Goines and Sailor set out for La-La Land.

The hopefulness instilled in him by the move out west impacted Goines's output. Though still committed to writing stories about the ghetto experience, he incorporated melodramatic elements into his work to balance out the unremitting bleakness of his aesthetic. *Street Players* (1973), for example, tells the story of a pimp, Earl "the Black Pearl" Williams, who succumbs to the one thing any player worth his salt knows he must avoid: falling in love with one of his prostitutes. Slim, of course, would have sneered at such a notion.

In his calculus, a pimp who falls in love with his prostitute is no longer a pimp; he is a john like the rest of them. But Goines seemed to be writing from his soft spot. Earl dies at the end of the novel, but his having loved at all is held up as a virtue.

For his next book, Goines revisited the interpersonal dynamics he had witnessed in prison. The majority of *White Man's Justice, Black Man's Grief* (1973) takes place in a Detroit county jail cell. The protagonist is Chester Hines—a nod to the hard-boiled writer Chester Himes, whose prison novel *Cast the First Stone* (1952) was an inspiration for this book. Chester is charged with carrying a concealed weapon, and thanks to the inequalities of the criminal justice system—a white judge sets his bond at a prohibitively high $10,000 plus two securities—he is forced to remain behind bars as he awaits trial. Goines takes exception to the fact that black men are imprisoned for long stretches simply because they cannot make bond. He denounces this practice in the novel's "Angry Preface," declaring, "Make no mistake about it, there's big money in the bail bond business, and most of it is being made at the expense of poor blacks." For Goines, setting high bonds permits the "white man's justice" to come at the expense of the "black man's grief."

The book itself is something of a homosocial love story. The jail's resident bully, Tommy, controls other inmates by terrorizing them with spectacular displays of male-on-male rape. In one instance, he shows off his "long black penis" by forcing a young white inmate to perform oral sex on him. Goines observes that the boy "choked and gagged, but it didn't do any good. Tommy held on for dear life." In order to counter this literal and symbolic threat to his masculinity, Chester befriends two younger men, Willie and Tony, one black, the other white. Together the friends affirm their sense of manhood in ways that are both humanizing and openly adoring. Indeed Goines describes their admiration for each other in explicitly sexualized terms. Chester sees Tony, for example, as "a nice looking kid, Italian, with dark hair, a small nose, and lips that a woman would love to kiss." Willie, meanwhile, is flattered when he is complimented for the very thing we are supposed to find grotesque on Tommy: "it made him happy that Chester had referred to how large he was hung in front of the other men." By cultivating a safe homosocial space among themselves, Chester, Willie, and Tony are able to forge a bond that helps them survive the perils of sexual violation in prison.

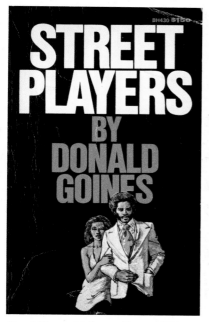

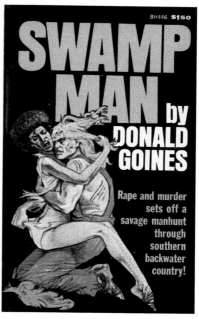

Street Players (Holloway House, 1973)

Street Players back cover

Swamp Man (Holloway House, 1974)

Chester's story, like Earl's, does not end on a happy note—the bond ultimately dissolves, to his detriment— yet Goines is still compelled to romanticize the interracial solidarity that defined their relationship for a time.

Black Girl Lost is a more melodramatic version of Dopefiend, where a young couple's romance is dashed by their involvement in the ghetto underworld. It was a revealing storyline to come back to insofar as it reflected Goines and Sailor's own struggles in Los Angeles. Goines could not kick the habit after all—he simply found new suppliers for his addiction. He also struggled to make enough money from royalties and advances to pay for the next fix. As for any long-shot dreams of making a deal with Hollywood, Goines and Sailor did no better in California than they had in Michigan, so they packed up their family and returned to Detroit.

Back home, Goines was able to embark on the most productive phase of his career. Aside from Black Girl Lost, which Goines completed in 1973 but was copyrighted in 1974, he published an astonishing eight books in 1974 alone. That he and Sailor were gunned down in October made this feat all the more incredible. Naturally, the quality of Goines's writing suffered, but that probably mattered little to him. Goines was a best-selling author, and his new titles were almost guaranteed to be hits, so he recycled formulas that he

had used in his earlier work and devised new ways of telling familiar stories. The result was five standalone novels of widely varying content and the first three parts of a series that reimagined the black revolution as a conspiracy thriller.

Eldorado Red, the first of his standalone books, is based on the numbers game, also known as the policy racket—an illegal lottery that was immensely popular in poor and working-class urban neighborhoods for much of the twentieth century. The narrative pivots on a rebellious son who robs his father's profitable numbers house, where the daily take is counted. Goines knew of that which he wrote: he had served time for attempting to rob a numbers house in Detroit. His representation of the robbery and its violent fallout show the lengths to which people are willing to go to claim their stake in the ghetto's most lucrative underground venture.

Swamp Man is the only Goines novel to be set outside of an urban milieu. By situating the novel in the deepest recesses of the Deep South—namely, the swamplands of Mississippi—Goines may have felt emboldened to advance the strongest indictment of white racism to appear in his work. The protagonist is George Jackson—a homage to the Black Panther prison activist killed by guards in San Quentin during his escape attempt in 1971. As children, George and his sister Henrietta witnessed the brutal lynching of their father by a group of white men. They felt help-less to do anything about it. Now grown up, George largely keeps to himself, while Henrietta has found a way out of the backwoods by going off to college. But on one of her return trips to visit George, Henrietta is kidnapped and brutally raped by the same men who had killed their father. Recognizing that crimes against black people will receive no measure of justice in the Deep South, George takes matters into his own hands and decides to avenge both his father's murder and his sister's assault.

Swamp Man is essentially a revenge fantasy. As such, it is replete with graphic depictions of bloodlust—some of the most disturbing in all of Goines's oeuvre. George's life in the swamp has trained him to become an expert hunter of animals. Now all he has to do is train his sights on human prey. Upon ambushing one of the attackers, George exacts his revenge in the only way he knows how: "He raised his knife and stabbed upward into Jamie's gut. When he pulled the knife out, half the man's intestines came with it. Blood spilled onto his hand, mixing with the blood that was already there." With the white man reduced to a kill, Jackson can now claim a more symbolic victory: "George flipped the wounded man onto his back. He bent over Jamie's bloody body and hacked off the man's penis and testi-cles. Jamie screamed and screamed again, until finally his voice began to fade out." For castrating George's father and tacitly believing George was not a threat himself, the white man must pay the ultimate price.

Never Die Alone returns to the city and to the theme of the crime boss whose hubris brings about his demise. Struggling writer Paul Pawlowski discovers the diary of King David, a recently assassinated gangster. The diary offers an unvarnished look into the machinations of David's criminal enterprise. It makes for grim reading: driven by greed, David muscles his way to the top of the underworld hierarchy, leaving a trail of dead bodies in his wake. He is such an unlikeable figure that even Paul admits David "needed killing" in the end. Goines treads familiar ground with this part of the story. But what makes *Never Die Alone* distinctive is its frame nar-rative. Paul's interest in David's diary is hardly free of self-interest. The writer recognizes that the gangster's confessions present a unique opportunity to jumpstart his own career. What Paul represents—white interest in black criminality—lends itself allegorically to the idea that the white-owned Holloway House was relentlessly capitalizing on Goines's own tales of inner-city crime.

Cry Revenge! (Holloway House, 1974)

Daddy Cool recycles another of Goines's favorite themes: black youth rebelling against their parents. In the novel Goines creates his most sympathetic protagonist. Larry Jackson is a middle-class family man struggling to keep his daughter Janet off the streets. To be sure, Larry is not above reproach. He is a professional assassin—a line of work that, while able to support a middle-class livelihood, still has one foot firmly planted in the underworld. But that is the strength of this novel: Goines explores the contradictory motivations of his characters in ways that are mostly absent in his other works. Janet too is complexly rendered— openly rebellious of her father yet always searching for fatherly protection, desirous of a better life yet drawn to the underworld herself. *Daddy Cool* plays on these contradictions to great effect, setting up a final showdown between Larry and Janet that is at once cruel and bittersweet.

Goines attached the pseudonym Al C. Clark—the name of a friend from Detroit—to the four other novels he published in 1974. Holloway House recommended this to avoid exhausting readers' taste for his writing. But the publisher stood to benefit as well: the hack's trick would mute the impression that it was saturating the pulp market with Goines's fiction. *Cry Revenge!* was the lone standalone novel that Goines published under the pseudonym. The book's front cover summarized its plot as: "CRAP GAMES AND SMACK PITS THE BLACKS AND THE CHICANOS AGAINST EACH OTHER IN A BLOODBATH OF VENGEANCE!" Goines had attempted to write about a cross-racial gangland war, but the novel was largely unsuccessful. Like Slim's Mafia fiction, *Cry Revenge!* faltered in transposing the author's firsthand knowledge of criminal life across racial and ethnic divides. There was nothing about Goines's "Mexican" characters that was culturally specific to the Chicano experience. As a result, this book was his least-read effort.

The other books he published as Al C. Clark were far more successful. Under the pseudonym, Goines created a four-part series featuring his most memorable protagonist: Kenyatta, a ghetto revolutionary crime boss. *Crime Partners*, *Death List*, and *Kenyatta's Escape* appeared in 1974; the final entry, *Kenyatta's Last Hit*, came out posthumously, in 1975. Though the series has strong echoes of *Black Gangster*, it departs from that Black Power novel by representing Kenyatta's desire to help his people as sincere, if ultimately misguided. Over the four books, Kenyatta goes from heading a small militant group in Detroit to leading a two-thousand-strong following in Los Angeles. His rallying cry throughout the series is clear: exploited by pushers and oppressed by law enforcement, ghetto denizens must take matters into their own hands and police the streets themselves.

An important component of Kenyatta's persona is the set of details Goines ascribes to his appearance. Like Huey P. Newton, the charismatic leader of the Black Panthers, Kenyatta seems to understand that a genuine radical movement requires an iconic leader. Goines gives him a grand entrance in *Crime Partners*:

> A tall black man came out, dressed in a pair of old Levis that had seen better days. The white T-shirt he wore was spotlessly clean. He was completely bald, and his head had been greased until it had a shine to it. The only hair he possessed was his beard and mustache. The beard was heavy, running around his cheeks until it would have met his sideburns if he had had any. The most remarkable thing about him was the jet black eyes that stared out without blinking, giving him a hawkish look that went well with the long, keen nose he had.

Kenyatta is described as an imposing yet desirable black man. His appearance evokes ruggedness (Levi jeans) and fastidiousness ("spotlessly clean"), traditional manhood ("beard was heavy") and modern urban flair ("greased head"). Above all, his eyes disclose the heart of a hunter. Without question, it is the most attention Goines ever paid to one of his characters. He clearly wanted Kenyatta to stand out from the rest.

Kenyatta's organization is committed to preserving black manhood by any means necessary. That entails not only cleaning up the streets but also confronting racist law enforcement with force. Reflecting the sentiment of black radical groups at the time, Kenyatta recoils at the sight of "white pigs that ride around our neighborhoods acting like white gods." But Kenyatta's response to that intrusion is where he departs from actual groups like the Panthers (whose full name, it should be recalled, was the Black Panther Party for Self-Defense). Rather than take a defensive posture, Kenyatta follows a policy of actively neutralizing individual officers. When two initiates into the organization, career hit men named Billy and Jackie, balk at Kenyatta's invitation to help him kill two policemen, the leader counters, "Some white-ass pigs are going to meet their fuckin' maker tonight, whether or not you

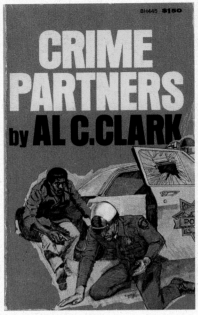

Crime Partners (Holloway House, 1974)

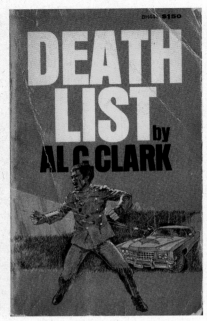

Death List (Holloway House, 1974)

Kenyatta's Escape (Holloway House, 1974)

two guys go along with the program or not." But that program sounds more like a campaign of violence, and Kenyatta begins showing signs that he is a megalomaniac. "It can be done!" he intones, "It can be done, and it will be done."

Action-packed episodes propel the series. The first three books conclude with dramatic scenes of death and destruction, which then serve as the launching-off point for books two through four. *Crime Partners* ends with Billy and Jackie's shooting deaths, which are ordered by a drug boss, King Fisher, as retaliation for their hit against one of his dealers. *Death List* then commences with Benson and Ryan, the Detroit detectives tasked with tracking down Kenyatta and his associates, arriving at the double murder scene moments too late. King Fisher is himself assassinated in the course of the novel, which closes with Kenyatta and a handful of his followers escaping a police raid on their commune just outside of the city. *Kenyatta's Escape* then follows the group literally in flight as they hijack a plane with the aim of transporting themselves to a country "where a Black man is treated like a man." The plane does not make it to Algiers. Instead, it crash-lands in the Nevada desert, where Kenyatta recalibrates and decides to go to Los Angeles. Benson and Ryan spend the entire novel chasing shadows, trying to help local and federal authorities bring Kenyatta to justice. *Kenyatta's Escape* closes with the leader and

four followers again narrowly eluding the law after an explosive gas station shoot-out. Finally, *Kenyatta's Last Hit* commences about a year after the second escape. Benson and Ryan are still smarting after their failed mission, but they return to Los Angeles to make one final grab at Kenyatta. There they discover he now commands a veritable army of foot soldiers.

At this point, Goines holds out a sliver of hope that the leader can reestablish his revolutionary program in California. With a following bigger and stronger than ever, Kenyatta decides to go after the prime mover behind the ghetto's drug economy—a mysterious figure named Clement Jenkins. Finally training his sights on the structural conditions of urban poverty, Kenyatta comes to recognize that white profiteers "were the controlling powers, the fat honkies who sat back in their leather office chairs dealing out death and corruption with one flick of their pudgy pink fingers." In a rare moment of introspection, Kenyatta realizes that men like Jenkins had always been his target, yet he had never really seen them. This rather belated insight suggests that his previous attempts at cleaning up the streets missed the point that the ghetto's real exploiters are men who profit from the drug economy at a distance. Kenyatta's "last hit" promises to take out Jenkins because he is one of these men.

Despite this narrative breakthrough, Goines concludes the series on a despairing note. Kenyatta tracks

Jenkins to a Las Vegas hotel, where there is a climactic showdown between the former's followers and the latter's guards. Kenyatta gains the upper hand when he wounds Jenkins in the shoulder, dropping him to the floor. But then, in an inexplicable seizure of action, Kenyatta simply waits. He waits for what seems like an eternity "to see the white man crawl, the white millionaire who dealt in death." He "would wait all night to see it, to see a man whom he had hated in the abstract for so many years beg him for his life." But in that decisive moment of stasis, Kenyatta is cleanly eliminated with a single bullet to the head fired by one of the guards. In the melee that follows, Jenkins manages to escape via a waiting helicopter.

Violence begets more violence while the white man gets away: Goines could not have wrapped up the series with a more pessimistic takeaway. Yet that message was perfectly in keeping with his aesthetic. From the very beginning, Goines envisioned the ghetto as a world devoid of hope. By the end, even his strongest protagonist, Kenyatta, ultimately failed to pave the way to salvation. Goines, then, was an artistic radical—a black Nietzschean whose pessimistic view of human nature destroyed all illusions of equality and all ideals of brotherhood. The demise of the civil rights movement and the symbolic death of Dr. King's dream made Goines's work possible.

The self-consuming violence that haunts Goines's fiction caught up with him in real life. Theories about his death centered on the ghetto underworld from which he could not divorce himself, even at the peak of his best-selling fame. Detroit police speculated that the slayings were drug-related. Friends and family members thought it was a botched robbery that intended to go after his royalties. And Bentley Morriss, Holloway House's owner, offered that Goines was assassinated as retaliation for writing a bit too close to experience. In interviews conducted for Eddie B. Allen's 2004 biography *Low Road*, Morriss alleged that criminals who had recognized themselves in Goines's fiction set out to silence him once and for all. Unfortunately, none of these theories has borne fruit. The murders remain unsolved.

Appearing almost immediately after Goines's death was Eddie Stone's *Donald Writes No More* (1974), an in-house biography that flattered the publisher for offering the heroin addict an opportunity to pursue his dreams of becoming a writer. Stone was the pseudonym of a white Hollywood screenwriter, Carlton

Hollander, who did a fair amount of hack work for Holloway House—including, as it happens, completing the manuscript for Goines's final novel, *Inner City Hoodlum* (1975). It was no surprise, then, that he cast the publisher in a flattering light.

Journalist Eddie B. Allen Jr.'s *Low Road* is a more evenhanded account of Goines's life and literary career. Drawing on unpublished notes and correspondence that the Goines family entrusted to him, Allen reconstructs the intense editorial pressure under which the author was obligated to work. Far from leading him away from drugs, Goines's fraught relationship with Holloway House, and Bentley Morriss in particular, seems to have exacerbated his need for them. Underneath all the writing he managed to produce for the company was Goines's desperation and anxiety—the need to bankroll his next fix.

Despite his untimely death, Goines has enjoyed a remarkably fruitful afterlife. On the literary side, the hack work he did for Holloway House helped the company build its catalogue of black pulp fiction. Through his oeuvre, Goines left behind a master code for writing black crime and adventure stories. A number of writers—including Odie Hawkins, Joseph Nazel, and James-Howard Readus—took their cues from his templates. Charlie Avery Harris went so far as to copy Goines outright, as evidenced by his 1976 novel *Whoredaughter*. But that, of course, was the name of the game: pulp valued repeatability, not originality, and on those grounds Goines was no less committed to the tried-and-true formula than his literary successors.

More broadly, Goines's influence has been felt in the rise and spread of hip hop culture. Many of the key artists and producers of the past quarter century have made it known that they grew up reading Goines. Characters from his novels and the author himself have been referenced in raps by 2Pac, Jay-Z, Nas, and Ludacris, among others. Indeed one could understand these rappers' body of work as an extension of the post-civil-rights pessimism to which Goines's fiction gave voice so powerfully in the 1970s. That his work resonates with so many people even today should give pause in our assessment of how much has really changed since then.

Kinohi Nishikawa

The Last Refuge, Edward Lindall (Gold Star, 1972)

This at times incoherent thriller revolves around Australian Security Intelligence Organisation agent Jay Landon and his attempt to successfully infiltrate and destabilize a group of Maoist revolutionaries. Led by Chinese puppet Clyde Mansell, the radicals have left their student enclaves and taken to Australia's remote Northern Territory to carry out a guerrilla war against encroaching U.S. multinationals.

Edward Lindall was the pseudonym of Adelaide-based journalist Edward Ernest Smith who based his nom de plume on the names of his two eldest children. He began writing fiction in the UK in 1948, and his first novel *Stranger amongst Friends* was published in 1956. According to a 1960 interview with oral historian Hazel de Berg, short stories became a key source of income during the 1950s, with numerous pieces published in Australian magazines as well as overseas journals such as the *Saturday Evening Post*. The majority of these were in the adventure-romance mold and set in then-exotic locales. With his creativity stifled by the demands of magazine editors, Lindall initially preferred working on full-length works. Possibly reflecting the declining market for short stories, his production of novels increased in the 1960s and '70s, and he completed eighteen before his death in 1978.

Considering that Gold Star had connections to Maoism, it is surprising that *The Last Refuge* is fairly sympathetic to American capital and makes its hero a member of Australia's notoriously conservative internal spy agency. The novel's plot is fairly silly stuff and, considering that Chinese-based multinationals are now Australia's biggest customer for minerals, hardly prescient. Yet it did have some vague basis in the radical politics and rhetoric of the time. As with their peers in other countries, a subsection of Australia's young Left looked to Maoism, particularly in the context of China's Cultural Revolution, as a revolutionary standard bearer for the world. Fusing with older comrades who had split from the pro-Soviet Communist Party of Australia earlier in the decade, their main base was in Melbourne, where they formed the Workers-Students Alliance (WSA). Despite their pretensions, and the later career of many as union officials, virtually all of this group were students at the time.

Though they never approached the stage of liquidating their enemies and blowing up foreign-owned mines, members of Melbourne's Maoist scene

The Last Refuge (Gold Star, 1972)

nevertheless outdid their rivals in terms of bombast and aggression. Raising money for the Viet Cong and leading occupations of university buildings, a section of that milieu also did basic training with guns and directed violence against anarchists and Trotskyists, some of whom were forced to form a self-defense pact at one university. Lacking a peasantry of their own, the Maoists led rowdy demonstrations outside the U.S. embassy and the offices of multinationals and mixed hardline Marxism of the Chinese variation with an Aussie nationalism that harked back to the republicanism of earlier eras. Although some WSA members later admitted to having inhaled, the group officially rejected drug use as decadent and sought to create a Left culture based on Australian traditions by holding bush dances and waving the Eureka flag (originally carried by rebel miners who staged an armed uprising demanding suffrage that was quickly snuffed out in 1854). This included producing political posters featuring Blinky Bill the Koala—a popular children's character created by New Zealand–born Australian author Dorothy Wall in the 1930s—carrying the Eureka flag.

Much of these radicals' political activity, as in this novel, was based on anti-American sentiment, but after Mao's handshake with U.S. president Richard Nixon in 1972 (presumably after *The Last Refuge* was written), his Australian disciples took an increasingly unpredictable and at times incoherent path. Some split off to hail Albania as the new pinnacle of world socialism while others advocated pacts with Australian capitalists and welcomed U.S. military bases as a bulwark against Soviet revisionism. Although some of these radicals retained influence among Australia's more militant unions, most notably the Builders Labourers Federation, most quietly slipped into the mainstream during the 1980s.

Iain McIntyre

"Three hours ago," Mansell said, "we blew an ore railroad bridge to hell and Peta showed these bastards that from now on we're gonna be really tough." He clicked the fingers of his right hand and thrust his head forward. "We're gonna hit harder and more often. And we're gonna shoot any Yankee bastard who tries to stop us. We're gonna drive 'em all back to their own goddam country. They've robbed it of its wealth, fucked up its grazing and farming lands through being so bloody greedy for the almighty dollar. And now they want to plunder Australia . . . take our iron ore and bauxite, nickel and lead and silver, our oil, bash down our scrub and plough up our land . . . they want to take it over and the Right-wing, money-grubbing fascist Australian government is selling out to them. There's even talk, as you probably know, of our entire north becoming their fifty-first blasted State. A sodding business deal, like Alaska."

Mansell snapped his right forefinger against the thumb again, and then the finger stabbed around and the thin lips flattened. "All this bullshit about China being a danger to Australia," he said. His voice had risen, and some of the words cracked in the middle, the syllables flying off as fiery particles. "China's no danger. America is. The Chinese don't want to colonise us. I know, and you know I know. I've got friends in Peking. They just want us to live in peace with them . . . Socialism, Marxism . . . call it what you like. They just want us to get away from the black beast of American capitalism, from the war profiteers, the exploiters . . . the mother-fucking bastards who are moving in with their troops and police."

Pulp Fiction and *The Little Red Schoolbook*

The Brief Life of Gold Star Publications

Gold Star Publications was a short-lived, Melbourne-based publisher of pulp and popular books in the early 1970s. Geoffrey Gold started it with funds from his father's successful business selling remainder books and magazines, including material considered adult and sexually explicit for its time. In addition to original fiction and nonfiction, Gold Star reprinted numerous titles originally published by members of the Communist Party–affiliated Australasian Book Society, which had fallen out of print, often giving them a risqué pulp makeover to ensure better sales. Its most famous book was *The Little Red School Book*. Written by two Danish schoolteachers and originally published in Denmark in 1969, it was subsequently translated into several languages, including English, and published in other countries. The book became the target of controversy, and there were attempts to ban it, including in Australia, for attempting to educate school children on topics such as sex and alcohol, as well as encouraging them to question dominant practices around school discipline and parental authority. The following is an edited interview with Gold.

Gerry Gold

Can you tell us about the origins of Gold Star Publications? I believe it began out of your father's distribution business, is that right?

Gerald Gold, my father, was an importer and distributor, not a publisher. He immigrated to Australia from the UK in 1954. He worked in a number of jobs, eventually got into sales, and did that until the late 1960s. In 1968, I think it was, he went back to visit England and his brother, David Gold, a wholesaler for a number of paperback book imprints in the UK. David said, "Can you sell books?" That's how he started. My father bought books on remainder and out of circulation from his brother and resold them here.

He'd buy a lot of remaindered book for forty cents and sell them for sixty cents to milk bars. He'd have a sales representative go in once a month, count the books and the milk bar owner would pay for what he'd sold. It was a simple operation but it made him a lot of money. Of course this upset the Victorian Newsagency Association because it was outside of their control.

They were standard paperbacks from big name authors, anything that had not sold in the southern UK. There were quite a variety of books. I think Sphere was a major imprint that they used to get in those days, as well as New English Library. Belmont books from the U.S. were another. Dad would look for job lots of books to sell. You know, when a wholesaler has been buying a bit of this and a bit of that, puts them all together, and you go in and just buy it, you don't really know what's there. Dad would buy them by the containerful and relied on the person he was buying them from to have a reasonable mix of titles so it wasn't just all one particular book.

At that stage there was censorship, and a copy of every imported book had to go to the censor. Dad would be putting in hundreds of books a month for censorship. In 1969, [then Australian federal minister for Customs] Don Chipp was liberalizing censorship, and my father noticed a few different sorts of books

Geoff Gold, 1972

were being cleared for general importation, more adult-oriented books. He ordered them, and they sold like wildfire, so he organized to have them reprinted in Australia. It was a period of changing mores. You can't imagine how much money Dad made. He suddenly had a lot of money in his pocket and started looking for other products that could be sold in the market while it was hot. He got introduced to some American magazine publishers and started importing remainders from the States, including Marvel comics.

In 1972, I convinced my father to use some of his money to do a legitimate line of publishing, which was the start of Gold Star Publications. He had the money and he wanted something a bit more respectable.

Gold Star Publications was only around for a short time, about two years maximum. We did some hardcover publications and a book on Aboriginal myths. We did a reprint of Sir Lawrence Hartnet's *Big Wheels and Little Wheels* [first published in Australia in 1964], which was a history of General Motors, some children's books. The rest of it was paperback stuff. I started off by going around and speaking to Australasian Books Society (ABS) people, whose work had been out of print for some time. The ABS had been a Communist Party [of Australia] front, a sort of progressive book club that published popular Australian fiction in hardcover by progressive authors and fellow travelers like Donald Crick, Alan Marshall, Judah Waten, Frank Hardy, all big names I used to read at school. They [the ABS] did a lot of good stuff in the 1950s and '60s, when publishing in Australia was pretty much completely dominated by British books.

I was given a budget to produce books. It was very small, so I basically went around and picked up

paperback rights, which was very economical, and the writers were very grateful for a couple of hundred dollars in the hand—this was 1972—and to have their books out in the marketplace again. I was able to get, as I said, some of the ABS people. I knew a guy over in South Australian, Wal Watkins, who'd written a whole lot of books that had been published in hardback by library publishers in the UK, but hadn't been done in Australia, so I picked up quite a lot of them and put them into the Gold Star catalogue, some of which got really big sales. A book he wrote about homosexuality in the navy called *Wayward Warriors* (1972), it was a really big seller because we had a gay front cover—very unusual in those days—that we did to spice it up for newsagent sales. I think we published eight of his novels.

With the original stuff, we did about twenty of them. *The Last Refuge* (1972) was one. *The Pope and the President* (1972) was another, as was Alan Marshall's *Aboriginal Myths* (1972). We also did quite a bit of politics and history. I picked up [then leading Opposition Labour figure and later treasurer who turned countercultural radical] Jim Cairn's *Quiet Revolution* and Stewart Harris's *Political Football*, about the [1971 protests against the South African] Springbok rugby tour of Australia, both of which were published in 1972.

I'd be interested to know more about how the business ended.

The main money was from the girlie magazines. It had became very competitive and in 1972, around the end of the year, the state secretary in Victoria, Arthur Riley, decided to close down all of these risqué magazines. In his own words any publication that would offend his teenage daughter—and it took the media a while to

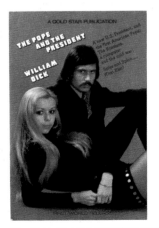
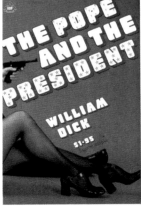

The Pope and the President (Gold Star Publications, 1972)

wake up to the fact that he didn't have a teenage daughter—would be closed down. He then sent the police out, and they went around to newsagencies and seized any of these magazines they found there. They then went to my father's warehouse and cleared the whole thing out, about thirty tonnes, everything. They had to bring semi trailers down one after another to be loaded up with forklifts. There were no writs issued. It was really an illegal seizure. The goods were seized and put it in an old Philip Morris warehouse in Collingwood. No charges ever eventuated, but Dad never got his magazines back. I think in the end rats ate them.

There was another level to what was going on, which was that the Victorian Newsagency Association had sussed out the link between Dad's Knight Books [the name under which David Gold's remainder books were sold] and Gold Star Publications, and they black-banned our books. The reason they gave for the ban was that we were producing sex books, but the real reason was Knight Books selling product to milk bars and breaking their monopoly. It was not stated, but that was the real reason. We were breaking their stranglehold on things.

The whole business started off as a distribution company. It grew and was sustained on cash flow. So when it stopped, it was like being hit by the proverbial truck, and it just died and the receivers came in. Gold Star, all the original publishing was stopped. We tried to recover by getting into harder and harder imports of anything legally allowed to be imported, but they were getting harder to sell because the state government was getting tougher on them. Then it just died.

I was always curious to know whether Gold Star had some sort of vague Labor Party or Maoist affiliation, as the politics of some of the titles was quite left nationalist.

I was a Monash [University] Labour Club graduate. I was heavily into the Monash Labour Club and the Worker-Student Alliance [both of which were Maoist-dominated]. I was always very interested in the Australian story, the Australian narrative. The Maoist thing about promoting national culture coincided with my own views, anyway. And, you know, it was one of the things that were part of the Whitlam era [the period of Australian politics named after the reforming social-democratic government led by Prime Minister Gough Whitlam], rediscovering Australian cultural identity and asserting it for the first time since the Second World War.

So the ethos of Gold Star Publications was in tune with the Left nationalist feel of the time plus what was commercially viable?

Yeah. Even Wal Watkins's books, which were packaged up like pulp fiction, were all middle-of-the-road library novels. In England there were so many libraries that there were specialist publishers that used to produce a stream of novels that would be automatically acquired by the libraries. Wal did that. But when you take him out of that and look at some of his books, he touched upon some very interesting topics, and when you put them in a ritzy cover, it drew them out more. It was very much a potpourri of what was available with the resources we had.

I'm interested to know about your involvement in the various censorship battles that were going on at the time in Australia.

The distribution business was all about censorship. So was that entire erotica product, which my father described as "sexology." It's the type of stuff you wouldn't even put out in a women's magazine these days and try and sell. It wouldn't even be called "erotica" these days. It's very tame stuff, but it was hot in those days. It all happened because Don Chipp relaxed the important rules in 1969–70. And then it became a conflict with the conservative states that didn't like all these girlie magazines appearing in newsagents. State laws controlled retailing, and that's where the censorship issue came up, because it was state police jurisdiction. And this was all before the Commonwealth, with the cooperation of most of the states, brought in the classification system, which gave clear guidelines.

Before, the way censorship worked was that if a person was upset, say a member of the public, they would make a claim that this is offensive. Then the police would go and seize it, charge everyone involved, and it would go to a magistrate to determine the case. There were no guidelines. The English system kept going on like that forever, whereas in Australia they introduced classifications, which at least told everyone the rules. If it's banned, it's banned. If it's restricted, it's got to be in a plastic bag on the top shelf or in a restricted area on the top shelf, etc.

The only time I got directly involved was with *The Little Red School Book*. We acquired the Australian rights from this New Zealand guy, Alistair Taylor, who was a New Zealand publishing entrepreneur, who'd acquired them from a British publisher, who'd

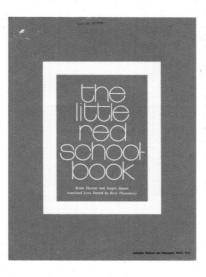

The Little Red Schoolbook (Gold Star Publications, 1972)
Wayward Warriors (Gold Star Publications, 1972)

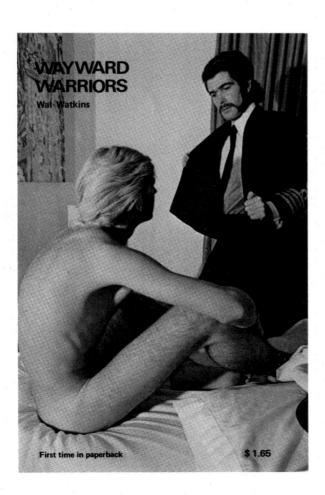

acquired them from a Danish publisher. We then localized the content. The original content had been written for schoolchildren in Denmark. The English edition was localized for kids in Britain, same with the New Zealand edition. So we sort of updated the stuff—where you could get a legal abortion, information about students' rights, etc. We had to get all that stuff up to date and properly reflecting the Australian situation.

It was controversial because it had been banned in the UK. When we bought out an Australian version, we weren't sure what would happen. The book itself was a very matter-of-fact publication; it used profanities in their context. It wasn't a sexually titillating book. In fact, if you read it, it was very boring. It was an educational book about rights and responsibilities, including sexual rights. But the serious conservatives in the states, particularly Queensland, decided to use it as a dividing line. So it was banned in Queensland, banned in New South Wales, and I think it was banned under state legislation in Victoria too. But Chipp refused to ban it for importation into the country, so it could be imported legitimately. We brought it in and published it. The fact was, the majority of adults thought banning it was a ridiculous move. It actually broke the back of censorship, that book. They picked the wrong fight.

With the *Little Red School Book*, we were going for it. My father didn't have a clue about that book, even though he was financing it. That was a battle I was happy to play. It was straight politics.

Did you make some money out of it?
With the number of copies sold, we should have. But all the books were seized and newsagents charged around the country. Everyone forgot to pay. But it was a great cause. The original reprint publishing I was doing was marginal and the girlie stuff was the cash flow machine.

You mentioned a writer called Wal Watkins, several of whose books you published. Can you tell us a bit more about him?
Wal was actually a janitor at the teachers' college in Torrensville, where my fiancée in Adelaide was studying. He used to write novels, and none of them were published in Australia. All except two of the books had only been published in the UK and distributed in the Australian public library system. Wal would sit in his office at the college and type out his novels. *Suddenly of Age* and *Don't Wait for Me, I'm Already Gone* [both 1972] were originals. *Don't Wait* was a *Catch-22*-style parody

of navy life. Wal covered so many issues: race relations in *Race the Lazy River* and *Andamouka* [both originally published in 1967], sex and homosexuality in *Wayward Warriors*. That last book was a huge seller. That might have even been our biggest paperback seller. The book was about homosexuality in the navy. Wal had been in the navy. I simply did not realize there was a market for that stuff. The gay market was totally unsupplied. I can't remember whether the book was sympathetic to gay men or not.

I'd been at Flinders University in 1970–71. I'd been involved in the East Wind Bookshop, a Maoist bookshop. I think it was in Rundle Street, Adelaide. I knew the guy who ran it, Charlie McCaffrey. He was head of the Communist Party of Australia (Marxist-Leninist) [the pro-Chinese faction of the mainstream Communist Party that broke away in 1964 over the Sino-Soviet split] in Adelaide, such as it was. They controlled the Builders Labourers Federation (BLF) union in Adelaide at the time. The BLF was upstairs, and the East Wind bookshop was downstairs. I mentioned I was looking for Australian authors, and he put me onto Wal. It was only when I was reading through Australian Security Intelligence Organisation files much later that I realized Wal was a member of the CPA (M-L), or at least ASIO said he was.

Political Football (Gold Star Publications, 1972)
A Different Drummer (Gold Star Publications, 1972)

Who did the covers for your books?
We had a couple of commercial guys, but I think a lot of the photographs were stock photographs we bought rights to. We were purposely doing pulp covers. We wanted stuff that stood out.

I'm interested in another book you published, *The Last Refuge* by Edward Lindall (1972). That's certainly one of the more pulpy books you published.
The Last Refuge was an original book we did. I remember that cover. The thinking was, there were pictures of a lot of angry demonstrations in the papers, and we thought this was something that could actually happen. It looked dramatic. We wanted something that was recognizable but had a significant dystopian vibe. Notice the Maoist badge.

Another Goldstar cover that's interesting is *A Different Drummer* by Don Crick.
Crick came to me with *A Different Drummer* (1972). It was an antiwar book that no one would publish. I didn't think it was that good. It was pretty turgid, but I

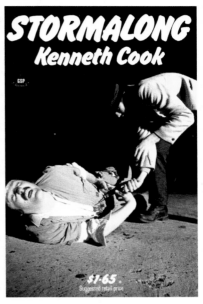

Cry of a Man Running (Gold Star Publications, 1972)

The Sun Is Not Enough (Gold Star Publications, 1972)

Stormalong (Gold Star Publications, 1972)

had a machine I had to fill, so I took it and also his other books, including *Period of Adjustment* and *Martin Place* [originally published in 1966 and 1963, respectively]. I think these were ABS books. Crick was an old [Communist] fellow traveler.

We also published quite a few books by Judah Waten. He was an old Jewish communist. He was pro-Soviet, when the Communist Party split [for the second time, with the main organization adopting a more independent line], he went with the Socialist Party of Australia [which retained its full allegiance to the USSR]. Nice guy, but we had our political disagreements about the Soviet Union, things like the Soviet invasion of Czechoslovakia. He would always take the pro-Soviet point of view. He really did understand ethnic life. You can see that in books like *So Far So Further* [first published in 1971 and republished by Gold Star in 1972], which was a cross-ethnic story about a Jewish Melbourne girl and an Italian Melbourne boy. It was great, but he still couldn't get it published. *The Unbending* [originally published 1954] was about the Wobblies [Industrial Workers of the World] in Australia, who were a very militant and very powerful in the first two decades of the last century. There was a lot of ethnic stuff in that as well. Don't forget that in 1972 these kinds of books were much bigger stuff than they are now. There were not a lot of books out like them.

As you mentioned earlier, you also published *The Quiet Revolution*, by Labor politician Jim Cairns.

The Quiet Revolution was a real coup for us. I'd known Cairns when I was a student. He would sit in the front parlor of his house in Hawthorn on a Saturday morning when parliament wasn't sitting and entertain people. I used to attend, and it was a real who's-who of the labor movement and politics. This book was pre-1972, before Gough Whitlam won the general election that year. *The Quiet Revolution* was his personal manifesto and he was one of the few politicians that actually had a personal manifesto. Politicians would do memoirs when they retired, but no one did manifestos. He was a serious force, had only lost the leadership ballot to Gough by one vote. People took him very seriously.

There were a lot of books like that, political, that couldn't get a publisher. *Political Football* (1972), about the Springbok tour, was another, so was *Why Isn't She Dead!* (1972) [a book about police corruption related to illegal abortions]. The main author of that book, Peggy Berman, was the secretary to Dr. Bertram Wainer, who ran the largest abortion clinic in Melbourne [abortion was not fully decriminalized in Victoria until 2008]. She did it with Kevin Childs, a leading newspaper investigative journalist at the time.

Andrew Nette

All Our Heroes Are Dead

Fictional Vigilantes of the Seventies

After the Second World War, crime rates in the United States steadily increased year after year. The reasons for this were varied, but by the early seventies many people had come to blame what was labeled the "revolving door legal system." The 1964 *Escobedo v. Illinois* U.S. Supreme Court decision held that criminal suspects had a right to counsel during police interrogations under the Sixth Amendment. In 1966, Miranda rights, or the "Miranda warning," as the spiel that U.S. police read suspects is known, became a part of the legal framework police officers had to work within. If these rights were violated, evidence obtained was inadmissible in court, and the alleged perpetrators would go free. To the political Right, it was a system more concerned about the rights of the accused than the victims. A backlash was about to begin. From the perspective of conservatives, it was time to claw back what was lost, and leading the charge were pulp fiction vigilantes.

One of the best-known fictional vigilantes of the seventies was a New York accountant called Paul Benjamin, who first appeared in Brian Garfield's 1972 novel *Death Wish*. Benjamin embarks on a one-man war against street crime after a gang of ruthless street thugs attack his wife and daughter. But he wasn't the only vigilante on the prowl.

★

While the notorious serial murderer known as the Zodiac Killer may have eluded the police, his fictional stand-in, the Scorpio Killer did not. He was brought to justice by San Francisco police inspector Harry Francis Callahan, unleashed on the public in the film *Dirty Harry*, directed by Don Siegel and starring Clint Eastwood in the title role. Callahan would go on to feature in another four films and at least sixteen books and inspire a raft of celluloid imitators. He was one of the defining characters of the vigilante era.

What separated Harry Callahan from the cops who had preceded him was his choice of weapon. He cleaned up the streets with a veritable cannon, a .44

Magnum, the "most powerful handgun in the world," as Callahan put it in the 1971 movie. In a climate of escalating crime, and the belief the police were powerless to stop it, the magnum gave Callahan the power to deliver one-shot justice. With one shot, the criminal was blown away, never to bother peaceful citizens again. There was no judge or jury, and certainly no opportunity to appeal the sentence. Callahan's justice was final.

When *Dirty Harry* was first released, rental video, DVD, Blu-ray discs, and downloads did not exist. One of the only ways to relive the experience of a movie was to read the book. If a successful film wasn't based on an already-published property, a novelization would be released based on the script. Most of the time, the novelizations followed the film scene for scene. On some occasions, though, there were minor differences as authors added their own creative flourishes or diverged from how the film had been conceived, with scenes deleted or altered. The novelization of *Dirty Harry* (1971) by Phillip Rock is different in some respects to the movie. While the meat of the story remains the same, the characters and their motivations are somewhat different. Even Callahan's famous "Do you feel lucky" speech, so familiar to cinephiles, is different from how it appeared in the movie.

Harry's lips curled into a harsh smile. "You been counting?"

The gunman stared at him, eyes glazed with hate. Harry took a step closer, the magnum not wavering.

"Well?" Harry asked softly. "Was it five or was it six? Regulations say five . . . hammer down on an empty . . . only not all of us go by the book."

The gunman's face was waxy and sheened with sweat. His fingers still touched the handle of the automatic but they were as stiff as claws.

"What you have to do," Harry said, "is think about it. I mean, this is a .44 Magnum and it'll turn your head into hash. Now, do you think I

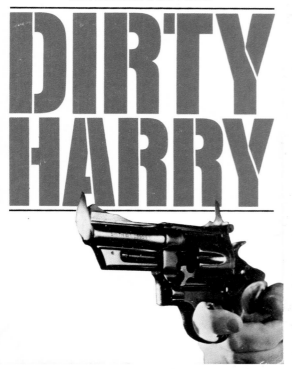

novelisation by PHILLIP ROCK
based on a screenplay by
HARRY JULIAN FINK and RITA M. FINK and
DEAN REISNER
A Malpaso Company Production,
directed by Don Siegel for Warner Bros. release
CLINT EASTWOOD is DIRTY HARRY

DIRTY HARRY

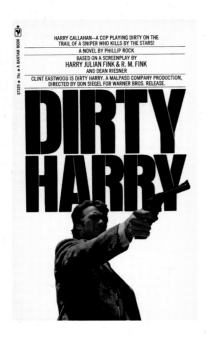

HARRY CALLAHAN—A COP PLAYING DIRTY ON THE
TRAIL OF A SNIPER WHO KILLS BY THE STARS!
A NOVEL BY PHILLIP ROCK
BASED ON A SCREENPLAY BY
HARRY JULIAN FINK & R. M. FINK
AND DEAN RIESNER
CLINT EASTWOOD IS DIRTY HARRY. A MALPASO COMPANY PRODUCTION,
DIRECTED BY DON SIEGEL FOR WARNER BROS. RELEASE.

DIRTY HARRY

Dirty Harry (Star Books, 1972)
Dirty Harry (Bantam, 1972)

fired five or six? And if five, do I keep a live one under the hammer?"

The man licked his lips, eyes riveted on the awesome weapon in Harry's fist.

Harry grinned, almost pleasantly. "It's all up to you. Are you feeling lucky, punk?"

The novel begins in San Francisco, with Sandra Benson taking a swim in a rooftop pool. On an adjacent rooftop, which overlooks the first, a psychopath named Scorpio takes aim at Benson with a sniper's rifle. He fires and she dies. It is not a revenge killing or the result of a relationship gone bad. Scorpio is a psychopath and has killed her because he was going to kill someone that day; she simply happened to be the best target. Inspector Harry Callahan arrives at the crime scene and spies the only vantage point from which the sniper could have fired. It is the top three floors of the Carlton Towers opposite. Callahan puts through a call to his superior to arrange warrants to search the apartments and roof. This contrasts with the movie, which followed no such procedure. On the rooftop, attached to a television antenna is a note from Scorpio addressed to the Mayor of San Francisco. It says:

TO THE CITY OF SAN FRANSISCO.

I WILL ENJOY KILLING ONE PERSON EVERY DAY UNTIL YOU PAY ME ONE HUNDRED THOUSAND DOLLARS. IF YOU AGREE SAY SO WITHIN 48 HOURS IN PERSONAL COLUMN SAN FRANCISCO CHRONICLE AND I WILL SET UP A MEETING. IF I DO NOT HEAR FROM YOU IT WILL BE MY NEXT PLEASURE TO KILL A CATHOLIC PRIEST OR A NIGGER.

SCORPIO

After a meeting with the mayor, a message is put in the newspaper agreeing to pay Scorpio, but it is merely a ploy to gain time. Scorpio never really appears interested in the money. Even though he goes through the motions of trying to collect it, for him it's more about the killing. And he plans to kill again. Soon after, Scorpio kidnaps a young girl, Mary Anne Deacon, and demands a ransom. Callahan agrees to take the money to Scorpio, but this only begins a cat-and-mouse game between the two protagonists, which results in a violent showdown.

One of the most telling moments in both the film and the novelization is when Callahan has apprehended Scorpio and tortures him to learn where he has hidden the Deacon girl, whom Callahan believes to be still alive. It turns out she is dead. Callahan is too late, but that is only the beginning of his problems. He is called before District Attorney Rothko to explain his actions:

Rothko sat back in his chair and shuffled through a document lying open on his desk.

"I've been looking over your arrest report, Callahan. A very unusual piece of police work. Really amazing."

"I had some luck."

Rothko looked up sharply. "Is that what you call it, luck? The only *luck*, Callahan, is that this office isn't indicting you for assault with intent to commit murder!"

Harry stiffened as though slapped in the face. "What are you talking about?"

Rothko picked up the document and waved it at Harry. "*This*. Who the hell gave you the right to kick down doors, torture suspects, deny medical attention and legal counsel? Where have you been for the past five years? Doesn't Escobedo ring a bell? Miranda? Surely you must have heard of the Fourth Amendment? What I am saying to you is that man had rights."

"Yeah. I'm all broken up about his rights." Harry's tone was defensive. He felt confused, unsure of his position or why he was being attacked.

"You should be broken up," Rothko said sharply. "I've got a little news for you. As soon as the suspect's well enough to leave the hospital, he *walks*."

Anger rose in Harry. "What are you handing me, Rothko?"

"The facts of life, Callahan. He goes free. We can't go before the grand jury because we don't have one shred of evidence."

Harry jumped to his feet. "Evidence? What the hell do you need? Have you seen the rifle? The machine pistol?"

"I've seen them," Rothko replied dryly. "They're nice looking weapons, but they aren't worth a damn to me."

"Are you trying to tell me Ballistics can't match up the bullets we dug out of Sandra Benson and the Russell kid with that hunting rifle?"

"No, I'm not saying that at all. The bullets do match, but the rifle is inadmissible as evidence and there are no prints on the machine pistol ... nothing to tie it in with the suspect. There were two nine millimeter bullets in the bottom of the suitcase, but that's inadmissible too. I don't have a case, Callahan, I have a house of cards. I don't have one scrap of real evidence against this man. *Nothing*."

"Who the hell says so?" Harry was shouting now and his face was the color of weathered brick.

"The law," Rothko shouted back.

"Then the law's crazy!"

Callahan's frustration is palpable. He has caught the killer. The district attorney knows the man is guilty but cannot try him, so Scorpio goes free, and ultimately as revenge he kidnaps a busload of school children. Harry's not going to let him kill anyone else. And he's prepared to do what the law courts can't—put the killer away for good.

When the film was released, it received a huge amount of criticism for being extremely right-wing, most notably from film critic Pauline Kael. She said:

This right-wing fantasy about the San Francisco police force as a helpless group (emasculated by the unrealistic liberals) propagandizes for paralegal police power and vigilante justice. The only way that the courageous cop Dirty Harry Callahan (Clint Eastwood) can protect the city against the mad hippie killer (Andy Robinson) who terrorizes women and children is by taking the law into his own hands.

It's also a remarkably single-minded attack on liberal values, with each prejudicial detail in place—a kind of hardhat *The Fountainhead*. Harry's hippie adversary is pure evil: sniper, rapist, kidnapper, torturer, defiler of all human values. This monster—who wears a peace symbol—stands for everything the audience fears and loathes. The action genre has always had a fascist potential, and it surfaces in this movie.

One of the key differences between film and novel is the depiction of the killer, Scorpio. In the novel, Scorpio is not a hippie. He does not represent the counterculture. It is suggested he has escaped from

CLINT EASTWOOD is Dirty Harry in MAGNUM FORCE
novelisation by MEL VALLEY
based on an original screenplay by
JOHN MILIUS and MICHAEL CIMINO
from a story by JOHN MILIUS,
based on characters created by
HARRY JULIAN FINK and RITA M. FINK

Magnum Force (Star Books, 1978)

a mental institution. As he scans the city for his first victim, talking to himself, he states: "Goddam it, yes! No fuckin' bums! No long-haired creeps!"

Scorpio certainly doesn't see himself as a member of the dispossessed or the hippie movement. Yet in the film, as played by Andrew Robinson, he is somewhat of a long-haired freak. He clearly represents the counterculture, with a belt buckle that is a peace symbol. Interviewed for the 2001 documentary *Dirty Harry: The Original*, Robinson said that in the script Scorpio was described as "a balding guy in a T-shirt with a paunch, who hangs around bus stations." This clearly did not match Robinson's physique. Instead, he chose to play him as a deranged Vietnam veteran. It could be argued that Robinson's portrayal of the character twists the film into a different direction. It is not simply a story about a police officer that is frustrated with the system but also a story of competing generations, where the older generation take back their country after they believe it has gone to hell in a handbasket as a result of the cultural shifts of the sixties.

The next film in the Dirty Harry series, *Magnum Force* (1974), expanded on the theme of vigilantism. The novelization, written by Mel Valley, follows the film almost word for word, with minimal attempt at fleshing out the subsidiary characters. It should also be noted, in this novelization, Harry's surname is Calahan—not Callahan as in the other books. As the story begins, San Francisco's leading underworld figures are being systematically executed, and it looks to be the work of a serial vigilante. You'd think Harry Calahan would approve. You'd be wrong. Calahan may hate the system, but until a better one comes along, he'll stick by it. Lieutenant Briggs reluctantly assigns Calahan to investigate the murders. Briggs thinks the killings are part of an underworld turf war, but Calahan has other ideas. He thinks it's a fellow police officer named Charlie McCoy who has been on the force for too long. The bureaucracy and public's attitude to the police have got to him and he is about to crack. During an exchange with Calahan, McCoy expresses his frustration with the system:

> "Harry, we should have put our twenty in the Marines," Charlie interrupted, shaking his head regretfully. "With the way things are these days, a cop kills a hoodlum on the street, he's better off dumping the body in a river than he is reporting it. Those snot-nosed young bastards in the

D.A.'s office crucify you one way or the other. Only the criminals got rights, not us. What's this fucking country coming to? Do you ever think about that, Harry? I think about it all the time. They got this idea here where a hood can kill a cop and get off without so much as a night in the can, but let a cop go and kill a hood and the whole world's crying 'police brutality.' Am I right, Harry?"

But Calahan's suspicions are wrong. McCoy is proven not to be a mad-dog vigilante cop when he is gunned down at the scene of another underworld execution. As the story plays out, it is revealed that a quartet of rookie cops have formed their own death squad and are wiping out the mobsters and pimps. Nearing the climax, the rookies confront Calahan to see if he is for or against them.

Suddenly, from behind, he heard a familiar voice address him sharply.

It said, "Do you have any idea how hard it is to prosecute a cop?"

Harry turned on his heels and saw Davis, Grimes and Astrachan walking out from between two parked cars. Their motorcycles were parked a few feet away.

The voice belonged to Davis, who stared at Harry for a long uncomfortable moment and then repeated himself, more to the point, "Do you have any *idea* how hard it would be to prosecute us?"

Harry straightened up and sneered. "You heroes killed a dozen men last week. What are you figuring on doing next week?"

Davis replied flatly, "Maybe kill another dozen."

"So that's what you guys are about, huh? Being heroes?" Harry tightened his jaw.

Astrachan fielded the question, replying, without a trace of humor, "All our heroes are dead."

"Ha, ha, Astrachan. Very funny," Harry replied facetiously.

"We're the first generation on the force that knows how to fight," Davis said, righteously jutting his chest forward. He and the others were all dressed in their uniforms. "We're only ridding society of killers that would be caught and executed anyway if the courts worked the way they're supposed to work. We've started with criminals like Ricca and Guzman, the big shots, so that people will understand our action. There's enough of a criminal element in this town to keep us busy for a long time to come. We can't tolerate any interference. It's not just a question whether to use violence or not, either. There's just no other way, Harry."

Calahan is against them. Although continually frustrated with the system, he believes the vigilantes are too extreme even for his beliefs. But he knows they will be coming for him, and he'll have to fight back. The story concludes on board a decommissioned aircraft carrier where Calahan confronts the vigilantes one last time.

The Enforcer (Warner, 1976)

The third film, *The Enforcer* (1976), was also novelized, by Wesley Morgan. The story shifts away from the vigilante angle which was prevalent in *Dirty Harry* and *Magnum Force*, although Callahan's actions can still be called vigilante. When Callahan's friend and partner, Frank DiGiorgio, is killed by a terrorist group, he makes it clear that he is willing to go beyond the law to bring the perpetrators to justice.

A militant group calling themselves the People's Revolutionary Strike Force, led by an ex-con named Bobby Maxwell, is on the warpath. They steal a van and raid a military supply warehouse to acquire weapons for use in their campaign of terror. During the robbery, two police officers stumble onto the scene. One is Callahan's partner, Detective Frank DiGiorgio, who is stabbed by Maxwell and left for dead. In the aftermath, DiGiorgio is rushed to hospital and on his death bed tells Callahan who stabbed him. It appears Callahan and DiGiorgio had a run-in with Maxwell several years previously. Despite this lead, Callahan's superior, Bradford McKay, believes black militants are behind the raid. Callahan is assigned a new partner, Kate Moore, and tasked to bring in black leader Big Ed Mohamid. Meanwhile, Bobby Maxwell carries out his next terrorist act, kidnapping the mayor of San Francisco and demanding a $2 million ransom. What makes *The Enforcer* not just a rehash of what has gone before is its exploration of equality and feminism. In this tale, Callahan is given a female partner, Kate Moore. As you'd expect from a dinosaur like Callahan, he is not pleased by the prospect.

★

While Dirty Harry cleaned up the streets of San Francisco, on the other side of the country, the police were losing their battle against the criminal element. In New York, if the citizens wanted justice and to rid the streets of crime, they had to take the law into their own hands—at least that was the message put forth in Brian Garfield's *Death Wish* (1972), about an accountant, Paul Benjamin, who is drawn to extralegal activity after his wife and daughter are attacked. The novel begins with Benjamin returning to his office after a liquid lunch with clients. Not long after he takes a phone call from his son-in-law, Jack Tobey. Tobey explains he just received a call from the police, saying Tobey's wife, Carol, and Benjamin's wife, Esther, have been brutally assaulted in Benjamin's home. Tobey says to meet him at the hospital. There the news is grim,

but Benjamin is not one to fly into a blind rage. Even as the brutality of the attack is revealed in the waiting room, Benjamin, who is somewhat of a bleeding-heart liberal, looks for an answer, or a cure for the problem of street violence. Talking to Tobey, as they wait, he says:

> Christ, I don't know. There ought to be some way to get these animals off the streets before they can have a chance to do things like this. With all the technology we've developed you'd think there'd be some way to test them psychologically. Weed out the dangerous ones and treat them.

Benjamin's views change when the doctor comes out of surgery and informs him that while Tobey's wife Carol will be okay, Esther has died. Her death hits Benjamin hard, slowly eating away at him. When it is suggested that Esther's killers may never be brought to justice he turns against his son-in-law, who works as a defense attorney. He sees him as another cog in a system that cares more about criminals than their victims. During a heated exchange, Tobey tries to calm Benjamin down:

> Pop, you're just working yourself up. It's not doing anybody any good. I feel the same way you do. I understand exactly what you're going through. But they haven't even caught these bastards yet and you're already jumping to the conclusion that some smart lawyer is going to get them off the hook. What's the use of aggravating things with useless speculations? They haven't got these kids, for all we know they never will get them. Why get so upset about miscarriages of justice that haven't even happened yet?

"Because I've seen the way these things work," Benjamin replies. "Even if the police catch them they just go right out again through the revolving door— right back out onto the streets. And largely because of well-meaning bastards like you! Hasn't any of this even made you stop and think about what you're doing?"

Benjamin's journey toward vigilantism is not a fast one. It starts out as a paranoid act of self-defense, keeping a roll of coins in a sock, for use as a cosh. One night, as he makes his way home from a bar, a young street punk accosts him. Without thinking, he swings the cosh down on his attacker and the perpetrator flees. In the aftermath, Benjamin is conflicted. Part of him is disgusted at the violent act he has committed. But

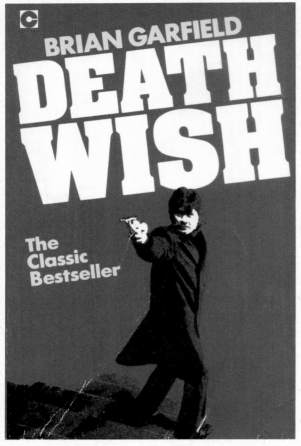

another part feels alive, exhilarated at having been able to fight back and relieve his bottled-up anger and frustration. Benjamin decides to up the ante, acquiring a gun while working in Arizona. Upon his return to New York he begins his campaign to clean up the streets, imposing his own justice on wrongdoers. As the story draws to its conclusion, Benjamin is observed by a police officer, during an act of vigilantism. But the officer involved chooses to turn a blind eye to the crime, allowing Benjamin to go free.

When interviewed in on the Pulp Serenade website in 2011, Garfield had this to say about the inspiration for *Death Wish* and the Benjamin character:

> The Paul Benjamin character was a sort of everyman to me. Impetus for the *Death Wish* story came one night in late 1971. At the time, I lived out along the Delaware River, near Lambertville NJ, and I'd driven into New York to go to a party at a publisher friend's. I parked on the street. When I came down I found that somebody had slashed the convertible top of the car to ribbons. It was about a two-hour drive home, and really cold, and I thought about finding the guy who'd slashed the roof. I never did find him, but the novel came out of it so I think I got the better of him.

While Garfield's novel was well received, it truly came to prominence when it was adapted into a controversial film, directed by Michael Winner, and starring Charles Bronson. Bronson was hardly the balding, middle-aged protagonist of the novel. The character's name was changed from Benjamin to Kersey, and this was not the only difference. A prologue was added, and the rape of Kersey's daughter was shown in graphic detail. The ending also deviated from the source material. On July 25, 1974, *New York Times* film critic Vincent Canby wrote:

> *Death Wish* . . . is a movie that takes a very dim view of New York City, particularly of its muggers who, according to this film, could be easily eliminated if every upright, middle-class, middle-aged citizen got himself a gun and used it at least three times a week.
>
> This is pretty much the plot of *Death Wish*, a bird-brained movie to cheer the hearts of the far-right wing, as well as the hearts of those who don't think much about politics but just like to

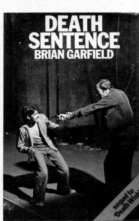

Death Wish (Coronet, 1982)
Death Wish (Bantam, 1989)
Death Sentence (Macmillan, 1976)

see people get zapped, without regard to color or creed.

Garfield also was unhappy with the film, mainly due to the casting of Charles Bronson as the protagonist. In *Bronson's Loose: The Making of the Death Wish Films* (2006), written by Paul Talbot, Garfield is quoted as saying:

> My problem with Bronson is not that I disliked him—he was excellent in some roles—but that he was wrong for the part. As soon as you saw him on the screen, you knew he was going to start blowing people away. If the film had been done with an actor capable of showing the change the character undergoes, I think it would have been a better movie.

Nevertheless, the film did big business at the box office and established Garfield's novel as the father of the countless imitators that followed in its wake.

Garfield reclaimed the vigilante from Hollywood, penning *Death Sentence* (1975), which saw Paul Benjamin stalking the mean streets of Chicago. Although Benjamin has relocated from New York, from the outset it is clear he has not moved to rebuild his shattered life and start afresh, but to continue his vendetta against the criminals and the underworld "because the job was no longer the center of his life; now it was merely a source of income and a camouflage for the appeasement of his private demons."

The story begins in an energetic fashion, with Paul Benjamin purchasing two new guns. After the purchase he doesn't even bother to go home but instead drives around looking for trouble. Naturally enough he finds it: two punks staking out a bar, waiting for a drunk to stagger out into the night. Benjamin becomes that drunk, although he is sober as a pope. When the hoods strike, he blows them away. Benjamin is quick to follow up with several more killings, eager for the press to learn a vigilante is on the loose. But his outlook begins to change when he goes to see a court in session, figuring that courts not only send criminals to jail but also set them free. It seems to be a place where he can find more targets deserving of his attention. There he meets Irene Evans, a woman working for the district attorney's office—and one who appears to be as frustrated with the legal system as he is. She intrigues him, and after he introduces himself, she agrees to meet him for lunch.

As Benjamin's relationship with Irene develops, he begins to question his way of life, to the point that upon catching two young punks in the act of raping two schoolgirls, he chooses to shoot them in the leg, rather than kill them. Justice is served, the crime prevented, but without the irreversible finality of his past actions. While Benjamin is maybe softening his stance, another killer isn't. The vigilante's notoriety has grown to such an extent that a copycat has emerged. Armed with a .45 Luger, he is making a larger dent in the underworld population than Benjamin. As the story moves toward its conclusion, Benjamin confronts the copycat.

Death Sentence was not just a rehash of *Death Wish* but a response to the film and an exploration of society's attitude to violence. Emphasizing this, in the novel, once the newspapers get wind of the vigilante, after each killing, the individual chapters present the media's response to the murder, editorializing the differing opinions of society at large. As admirable as this may be—and it elevates *Death Sentence* from being merely another right-wing revenge fantasy—it makes for a fractured and at times repetitive narrative. Talking about the novel on the Novel Rocket website in 2007, Garfield said: "The novel, which I wrote years ago as a sort of penance for the movie version of *Death Wish*, attempts to demonstrate in dramatic form that vigilantism is not a solution—it's a problem, and tends to destroy those who attempt it."

It was inevitable that Hollywood would come calling again. In 1980, Cannon Films announced plans to make *Death Sentence*, once again starring Charles Bronson in the lead. The film was delayed, allegedly because Bronson refused to work with director Menahem Golan. Eventually Michael Winner, director of the first film, was brought on board, and the movie hit the cinemas in 1982, titled *Death Wish 2*. It was little more than a rehash of the first film. Another three films followed in the series, which like *Dirty Harry*, became a violent cartoon, with little point beyond making money for the producers.

★

While Dirty Harry and Paul Benjamin cleaned up the streets for what they considered the betterment of society, another character was also waging his own war. His reasons were not so altruistic. He was confused, disillusioned, and filled with anger. He was also a highly trained Vietnam veteran, with a knowledge of guerrilla warfare that your average countercultural protester or student radical did not possess. The character was Rambo, and he initially appeared in David Morrell's 1972 novel *First Blood*.

Rambo is one of the most recognizable characters in popular culture, due to the successful film series starring Sylvester Stallone, but the film of *First Blood*, released in 1982, is very different from the novel. One of the biggest differences is the depiction of Rambo himself. In the novel, Rambo did not have a first name; it was added in the film. In the movie, Rambo is portrayed as an older (Stallone was thirty-six) and more sympathetic character, who kills only three people. The novel has a much larger body count, and Rambo is nowhere near as innocent. Also, in the novel the story is told from two points of view, in alternating chapters. One point of view is that of Rambo, the other is of Korean War veteran and police chief Wilfred Teasle. Neither one comes across as a hero.

The novel begins in the small middle American town of Madison, where returned vet Rambo, because he looks like a hippie, is escorted out of town by Teasle. Rambo is somewhat of a contradiction. His outward appearance does not match the man within. As Morrell explained in the introduction to the 2006 Headline Review edition of *First Blood* (portions of which appeared in *Playboy* in 1988):

> Haunted by nightmares about what he had done in the war, embittered by civilian indifference and sometimes hostility toward the sacrifice he had made for his country, he would drop out of society to wander the backroads of the nation he loved. He would let his hair grow long, stop shaving, carry his few possessions in a rolled up sleeping bag slung over his shoulder, and look like what we then called a hippie.

Morrell expands further in his essay "Rambo and Me: The Story Behind the Story" (2008), in which he discusses the genesis of the novel, how hippies were treated at the time:

> I recalled a newspaper item about a group of hippies who'd been arrested in a southwestern town. Their beards and hair had been forcibly shaved off, after which they'd been driven out of town, left among the sun-baked yucca plants at the side of the road, and told to keep going. What if one of them had been my imaginary Special Forces veteran, whose experiences in Vietnam

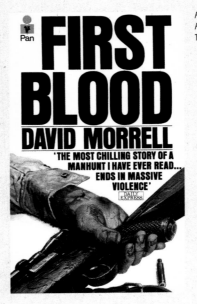

First Blood (Pan, 1975)
First Blood (Fawcett, 1973)

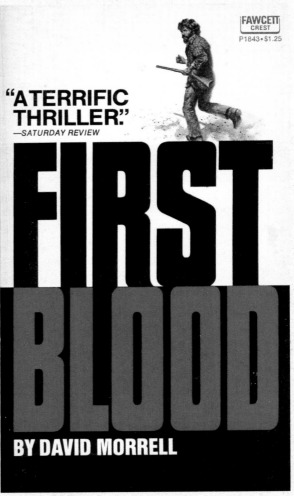

had so disturbed him that he'd dropped out of society?

When Rambo turns around and walks back into Madison, Teasle is notified and picks him up in a diner, and once again drives him to the town limits. Rambo refuses to be bullied and, as Teasle drives away, he enters town for a third time. Teasle believes he has no recourse but to take action. Rambo is taken into custody and brought before a justice of the peace, a man named Dobzyn. Once again, Rambo is treated as a dirty hippie.

"Well, I'll be," he said and rolled his swivel chair squeaking back from the desk. "When you phoned, Will, you should have told me the circus was in town."

Always it came, some remark. Always. This whole business was getting out of hand, and he knew that he had better give in soon, that they could make a lot of trouble for him if he did not. But here the crap was coming his way again, they would not let up, and Jesus, he was just not going to take it.

"Listen, son," Dobzyn was saying. "I really have to ask you a question." His face was very round. When he spoke, he slipped his chewing tobacco against one cheek, and that side of his face bulged out. "I see kids on the TV demonstrating and rioting and all, and—"

"I'm no demonstrator."

"What I have to know, doesn't that hair get itchy down the back of your neck?"

Always they asked the same.

The conversation hints at Rambo's recent history, after Vietnam. Every town he goes to, the reception is the same. Everybody is against him simply because of the way he looks. Therein lies the heart of the contradiction. Rambo is not truly a part of the counterculture. He is not a hippie or a protester and does not want to change the world. He wants to be left alone. It could be argued, as an ex-serviceman, he is a broken part of the establishment. But to those who cannot see beyond the "long heavy beard, and his hair hanging down over his ears to his neck," such as Will Teasle, he is a part of the rebellious sixties generation, a troublemaker who must be taught to obey the rules, to fit into society.

Finally Rambo reaches breaking point and busts out of the police station, killing one of the officers in the process. He steals a motorbike and heads for the mountains, sparking a manhunt. But soon, in the rugged hilltop terrain, the hunters become the hunted. Rambo turns the tables on his pursuers. Ten men go after Rambo, of which he kills nine—and destroys a helicopter. Only Teasle survives the ordeal.

The state police and the National Guard are sent into the mountains after Rambo, and as the cordon tightens, he is trapped in an old mine. Rambo finds a way out and his private war reaches its climax on the streets of Madison. On hand to assist in Rambo's apprehension is Samuel Trautman, the man responsible for his training. It's no coincidence his name is "Sam," as in Uncle Sam. Trautman represents the United States and if his creation has gone haywire, it's his job to fix it. The novel ends very differently from the movie.

The novel *First Blood* is a fascinating time capsule of the era in which it was written. The core of the story is about a cultural clash. The mid to late sixties was a time of great social change, and laws and attitudes changed throughout the land. But by the seventies, the pendulum began to swing back the other way. The old guard was fighting back and trying to reclaim the "lost America" of the 1950s. *First Blood* sits right in the middle of these two movements, and what makes it such an exceptional book is that it does not take sides. Instead it looks at characters from both sides of the cultural gap and presents their conflicting attitudes.

While Rambo may not have truly represented the counterculture, his unkempt appearance and the abuse leveled at him make him a surrogate hippie. Teasle clearly represents the old guard. Their clash represents America tearing itself apart. Author David Morrell was not a stranger to the conflict. He had witnessed campus riots during the late sixties and had taught returned veterans and was aware of their traumas. He distilled these experiences into a fast-moving tale, which continues to be a template for action-adventure novels to this day.

David James Foster

Lone Wolf

The Vigilante Novels of Barry N. Malzberg

In a June 2012 interview with U.S. crime writer Ed Gorman, prominent science fiction writer Barry N. Malzberg said that his career, "like that of most commercial writers, is little more than a function of what I could write and where I could sell it." In 1973, Malzberg was writing *Guernica Night*, a sci-fi novel that would go on to win a Nebula Award for best novel, when he was contacted by New York pulp paperback publisher Berkley, looking for someone who could write a ten-book series in less than a year. He was offered a $27,500 advance, 25 percent payable on receipt of contract.

Malzberg began his writing career as an agent for the Scott Meredith Literary Agency in New York in 1965, started publishing short stories in 1967, novels in 1970, and was known as a prolific writer. In response to Berkley's request he came up with the idea for a series featuring the character, Burt Wulff, an ex–New York policeman turned murderous vigilante against a drug-dealing criminal organization known as "the network." The first of what would be a fourteen-book series, *Night Raider*, appeared under the pseudonym of Mike Barry. Captioned on the front cover "#1 IN THE BLOODY ADVENTURES OF THE LONE WOLF," it ushered in the most bizarre of the vigilante characters that were a mainstay of seventies men's action-adventure pulp.

There were many potential influences behind Burt Wulff. The film *Dirty Harry* appeared in 1971, featuring "Dirty" Harry Callahan, played by Clint Eastwood. Callahan was a renegade, Magnum-pistol-wielding San Francisco police detective, not afraid to bend the rules and up the body count to bring criminals to justice. In 1972, Brian Garfield's hugely successful novel *Death Wish* appeared. The book's story, immortalized on the screen by Charles Bronson in the 1974 film of the same name, follows a liberal New York City accountant who transforms into a cold-blooded vigilante when his wife is murdered by a bunch of street thugs.

But the most obvious influence was Don Pendleton's Executioner series featuring the character of Mack Bolan. Originally conceived as a stand-alone for Pinnacle Books, the first Bolan book, *War against the Mafia*, was published in 1969. It became a men's publishing phenomenon that has so far resulted in over four hundred books and sold an estimated two hundred million plus copies. Bolan is a U.S. Army sergeant called home from the war in Vietnam to look after his brother, Johnny, after the mysterious death of the rest of his family. He discovers that his father, Sam, had gotten into debt to the Mafia and his sister, Cindy, in an effort to help pay off the debt, had been lured in prostitution. Sam, upon learning of his daughter's fate, shot and killed both her and his wife, wounded Johnny, and then took his own life. Armed with this information, Bolan decides his talents would be better suited to fighting the Mafia at home rather than battling communism in Southeast Asia, and he begins a one-man crusade against organized crime.

A former aeronautical engineer who got his start in fiction writing sex paperbacks, Pendleton penned the first thirty-eight books. He then franchised the series to Gold Eagle, an imprint of Harlequin Books, who contracted a stable of ghostwriters to keep the series going. Bolan's target changed over the course of series, from the Mafia to communism to global terrorism after 9/11. The series resulted in numerous spinoffs, including Able Team and Phoenix Force, to cite a couple of the better-known ones.

Upon signing the contract with Berkley, Malzberg bought a copy of one of the Executioner books (no. 9 in the series, *Nightmare in New York*) from a local store and was unimpressed. "Absolutely terrible," he told Gorman, but he added "in the spirit of Schmeling viewing clips of Joe Louis before their first fight, 'I see something.'"

Just how out there the Burt Wulff series would be is signaled in the inside cover page of *Night Raider*, which quotes from Irish poet William Butler Yeats and Wulff. Wulff's words nicely sum up the feel of the entire series:

> Nobody cares. America is one monstrous vein
> and it's being filled with poison. The best and
> the worst are being murdered by drugs and

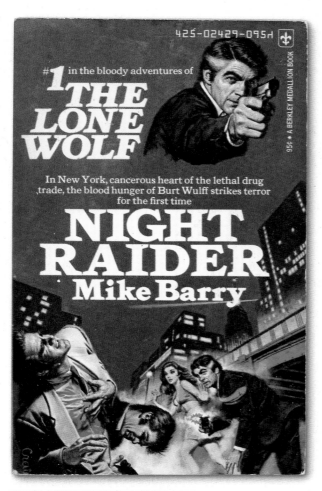

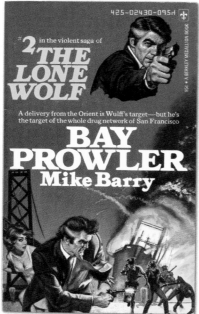

Night Raider
(Berkley
Medallion, 1973)
Bay Prowler
(Berkley
Medallion, 1973)

everyone, even the murdered, profit because it's part of the system. But I'm going to break it. I'm the last man who cares and I'm going to smash them. Their lives will be smashed the way they have smashed millions. And I'll get joy from it and laugh or I won't even start.

As *Night Raider* opens, Wulff is thirty-two years old. Ten of these have been spent in the NYPD, including time out for two tours of duty in Vietnam in the late sixties. Returning to work in 1967, he was assigned to the narcotics division. His superiors conceive the post as a reward for his Vietnam service due to its opportunities for graft, but "something had happened to Wulff overseas it seemed: he had gone crazy. He had become a man of integrity." Instead of giving into the temptation of corruption, Wulff actually tries to do his job and arrest drug dealers. He angers the criminals and his superiors and is busted back to radio patrol duty. The first night on his new job he gets an anonymous tip that a girl has OD'd on the top floor of an old brownstone. The girl's name is Marie Calvante and she is Burt Wulff's fiancée. "They killed her," says Wulff. "Who killed her?" replies his black partner, David Williams. "The filthy drug-pushing sons of bitches."

Wulff goes straight home. "He didn't bother calling in his resignation. They would get the idea soon enough." He moves out of his apartment into a cheap rooming house, thinks about life for a couple of weeks, and then hits the street "to kill a lot of people."

And that's after just four pages.

Wulff captures a low-level criminal operative, a driver for "the network." The driver gives him the name of a street dealer called Richard Jessup. Jessup reveals details of a more senior dealer, Jack Scottis, and so it goes. With each encounter, Wulff extracts just enough information from his victim to move to the next level, collect their weapons and money, and dispatch them. He eventually gets a lead on a senior operative, Albert Marasco. Wulff allows himself to be caught and imprisoned in the basement of Marasco's suburban house. While Marasco is ruminating on the poor state of his marriage and how best to dispose of his captive, Wulff sets fire to the house and kills him and his bodyguards.

Things go on more or less like this for fourteen books. Wulff crosses the country, destroying the network's operation in each city he visits. The network, alarmed by the disruption in their narcotics distribution, stages numerous attempts to eliminate him. Wulff's activities

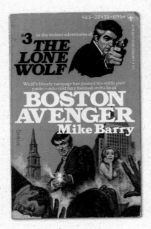

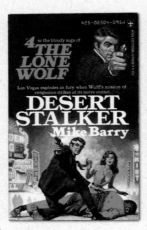

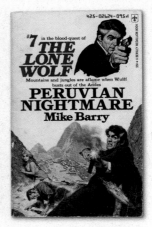

Boston Avenger (Berkley Medallion, 1973)

Desert Stalker (Berkley Medallion, 1974)

Chicago Slaughter (Berkley Medallion, 1974)

Peruvian Nightmare (Berkley Medallion, 1974)

also come to the attention of the police, who nickname him "the Wolf." Book five, *Havana Hit* (1974)—the only time in the series Wulff travels outside the U.S.—begins with a fictitious memo to the New York police commissioner about Wulff and his campaign to destroy the drug trade. He is reported to have traveled to San Francisco, Boston, and Las Vegas within a period of four weeks and "appears to have been responsible for the deaths of several hundred operatives involved in all levels of the national and international drug trade," including senior officers.

"He is, in the bargain, apparently marked for execution at all levels of the network and despite the apparent success of his initial shock tactics, cannot go on for much longer," reads the memo. "It is sincerely hoped that legitimate law-enforcement personnel will apprehend him before employees of the network, since only in that way are we able to interview him and obtain specific details."

Malzberg wrote the first ten of the novels between January and October 1973. Given the pace at which he was working, the books are not exactly quality literature. They have an almost stream-of-consciousness feel to them, replicate many of the same basic plot strands, and are littered with continuity errors.

Despite this, the series stands out from the numerous pulp vigilante works published the seventies. Wulff is not some misanthrope with a gun who kills criminals in order to rid the streets of danger and protect ordinary civilians, as is the case with characters such as "Dirty" Harry Callahan and Paul Benjamin. As Malzberg portrays him, he is quite literally insane and gets more and more violent as the series progressed.

"He sees that he is trapped in two hells—himself and what America has become," Malzberg said in the Gorman interview. "Nothing like this would ever occur in the avenger series by other writers."

Not surprisingly, Berkley was unhappy with the first three books and wanted to stop the series. According to Malzberg, his editor thought that Wulff's murders "were depicted too vividly and sympathetically . . . and their deaths went beyond cartoon deaths." But for some reason the publisher relented, gave him the green light for number four, and never bothered him again.

"Wulff became crazier and crazier," Malzberg wrote in his 2007 autobiography *Breakfast in the Ruins: Science Fiction in the Last Millennium*. "By #13 [*The Killing Run*, 1975] he was driving cross-country and killing anyone on suspicion of drug dealing; by #14 [*Philadelphia Blow Up*, 1975] he was staggering from bar to bar in the City of Brotherly Love and killing everyone because they obviously had to be drug dealers. Finally gunned down for the public safety by his onetime black sidekick, Wulff died far less bloodily than many of his victims."

The genius of the Burt Wulff books is that Malzberg took what was apparent but more latently so in other works of vigilante fiction—the angry, out-of-control white man who has descended into psychosis and had access to massive firepower—and made it the central focus of each story. "It is evident to me now as it was then that Mack Bolan was insane and Pendleton's novels were a rationalization of vigilantism. It was my intent, then, to show what the real (as opposed to mass market) enactment of madness and vigilantism

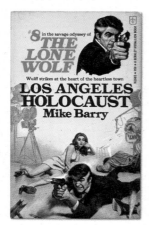

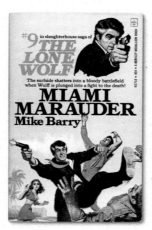

Los Angeles Holocaust (Berkley Medallion, 1974)

Miami Marauder (Berkley Medallion, 1974)

Harlem Showdown (Berkley Medallion, 1975)

Philadelphia Blowup (Berkley Medallion, 1975)

might be if death were perceived as something beyond catharsis or an escape route for bad guys."

As a result, as bad as the books are, they contain a degree of realism not present in other vigilante pulp. No matter how venal they were, his victims are depicted as real people, with real viewpoints, who undergo real pain. Wulff vacillates in terms of his reactions, as if vaguely aware he has lost his grip on reality, from reticence about what he is doing, to an almost sadistic pleasure, mixed with more prosaic concerns that he might get blood or other liquids from his victims on his suit.

There is an almost dystopian vibe to Malzberg's depiction of the drug trade. It is all-encompassing, a grim, nihilistic world from which there is no escape that blurs all sense of right and wrong:

> Sure he knew this: he knew that the police narcotics room downtown was nothing more than another stash for the stuff, he knew that the quiet men who came in their Cadillacs from Teaneck or Rego Park or Scarsdale to do their official business in the city before going back to the wife and kids at five like every other commuter, these quiet men were as deep into it as the police who wandered in and out of the stash room twelve hours a day; he knew that everything in the city had broken down to the point where drugs were the secret out of control; he who sold the drugs administered the territory. He knew all this and a good deal more.

Another unique aspect of the books is the direct parallel between the war in Vietnam and the war against organized crime at home. For example, this passage from *Night Raider*:

> It [New York] looked, Wulff thought, something like the way Saigon had in 1966 with an importance difference: Saigon had been backed up right against it, the civilians in that town could *see* the enemy, knew exactly what they were dealing with, could see their future plain.
>
> But that was the front lines, a healthier situation. New York was tucked back of the combat zone: the civilians here did not know what was actually doing it to them. They could see the effects upon their landscape, upon their lives, lived like hunters and hunted in this place but the enemy was far afield and there was almost no point at which they could get hold of him and break the situation through reality.

New York is an occupied city, like Saigon, barely kept under control by brute force.

> He walked back to the rooming house, digging the scene on West 97th which was pretty much like the scene all over town these days except for the residential East Side and parts of the business district, and those two sections were being kept clear only through a massive influx of cops and private security. As long as the business district and one or two upper-class residential sections held out the city could avoid the appearance of total collapse but Wulff knew, the cops knew, the city knew that they were losing ground. It was only a matter of time now: two

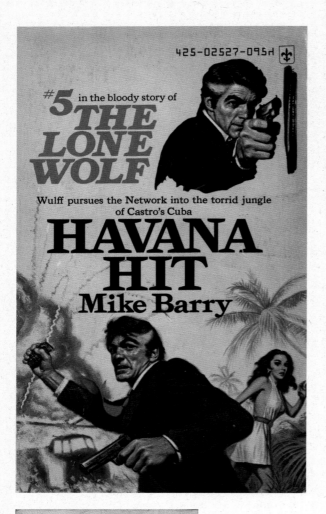

years, maybe three and the last vestiges of safety and wealth would collapse and New York City, the cities all over the country, would collapse into pools of hell that surrounded them.

"Yes, I was quite serious," Malzberg told Gorman. "I had at the time what I took to be a Social Vision. Synchronous to the composition of those first ten novels was the passage of the insane and insanely punitive Rockefeller drug laws in NY State which more or less mandated life sentences without probation or appeal for those convicted of selling drugs in any amount [the law was named after New York State governor Nelson Rockefeller, who had presidential ambitions and wanted to raise his profile by viewed as tough on crime]. Millions of lives were destroyed."

"The Lone Wolf was my own raised fist to a purity and a past already obliterated as they were written, rolled over by tanks and battery of Bolan's ordinance (Operating under Bolan's pseudonym: 'U.S. Government')," he wrote in *Breakfast*. "Bolan killed to kill: I think Wulff killed to be free. It all works out the same, of course."

Andrew Nette

Havana Hit (Berkley Medallion, 1974)
Havana Hit back cover

Rubyfruit Jungle, Rita Mae Brown (Daughters Inc., 1973)

The sexism of the New Left and antiwar movements was a major spur for the emergence of women's liberation in the late 1960s. In turn, the homophobia of many in the women's movement, and the marginalization of lesbians within some gay liberation organizations, gave rise to lesbian feminism. This and other radical strands of second-wave feminism saw new groups and milieus sprout up across the U.S. at a time otherwise viewed as a downturn for putatively left-wing movements.

As within other scenes and causes of the era there was much to take part in. Lesbian, radical feminist, and feminist separatist activists launched campaigns around a host of issues, ranging from workplace and legal rights to providing solidarity to imprisoned black liberation and anti-imperialist political prisoners. Consciousness-raising meetings were held, and new bars, bookstores, and storefront meeting places opened. Many attended or ran workshops and courses in car repair and home improvement, self-defense, and other skills previously denied to women. Treatises, manifestoes, and broadsides were published, debated, and distributed. And there was a new woman-centered culture to be made, including music, poetry, murals, and novels.

The majority of radical feminist, lesbian, and gay works during the first half of the 1970s were released by fiercely independent, recently founded small presses. Amid this ferment the Vermont-based (and later New York–based) Daughters Publishing Company was founded in 1972 by wealthy couple June Davis Arnold and Parke Patricia Bowman. According to novelist and onetime Daughters Inc. editor and factotum Bertha Harris, there was deep-seated conflict within the venture from its inception. Arnold reputedly saw Daughters Inc. as an extension of the radical publishing ventures then run by lesbian feminists, one which was in a financial position to publish full-length, professionally edited and produced books. In her view the company would rise to prominence as the patriarchy crumbled. The more conservative Bowman's focus was on investing in a for-profit business that could take on mainstream publishing houses on their own terms and publish quality women's writing regardless of political content. Despite their differing goals, the pair ultimately eschewed the collectivist and do-it-yourself approach of most lesbian and radical feminist efforts, maintaining tight control of the company and sinking their capital into authors' advances and design work, rather than setting up and running their own printing press.

The company released a slew of paperback books from 1973 onward. The majority of these were sold via gay and lesbian bookshops and mail order, and they were primarily reviewed in movement publications. Yet the company scored major success in its first year of operation with Rita Mae Brown's debut *Rubyfruit Jungle*, a novel that plugged directly into the zeitgeist of early 1970s America.

The coming-of-age tale begins by exploring narrator Molly Bolt's fraught relationship with her adopted mother, the family's semiforced relocation to Florida, and her first sexual relationships. Scoring a scholarship to a Gainesville college, she gets acquainted with the bar scene and fellow lesbian students before being kicked out for defiantly refusing to submit to psychiatric treatment for the supposed malady of same-sex desire. Hitchhiking to New York, she spends the night in an abandoned car with the homeless Calvin, who hips to her to the butch/femme divide. She finds an apartment and various menial jobs, one of which she livens up by literally filling a bully's desk drawers with dog feces. Despite having to deal with pretentious sophisticates in her social life and sexist jerks at film school, Molly keeps on slugging, and loving.

Although Brown claims she was nowhere near as brash, bold, or bawdy as Bolt, she certainly based some of the ups and downs of her character's life on her own. Having been adopted into a conservative family in Pennsylvania as a baby, she lost her scholarship to the segregated University of Florida in 1964, both for being lesbian and for supporting civil rights. A move to New York, where she experienced homelessness, eventually led to further study and work for the National Organization for Women as an editor and administrative coordinator. She quit the group in 1970 after leader Betty Friedan infamously derided "mannish" and "man-hating" lesbians for presenting what she saw as a "lavender menace" to the ability of second-wave feminism to gain widespread appeal. Brown subsequently cofounded the pioneering Washington DC lesbian separatist collective the Furies in 1971. The group developed a number of positions that would be influential within lesbian feminist circles,

$4.00

Rubyfruit Jungle

RITA MAE BROWN

Rubyfruit Jungle (Daughters Inc., 1973)

including that "Lesbians must become feminists and fight against woman oppression, just as feminists must become Lesbians if they hope to end male supremacy." At the same time their goal was, according to cofounder Charlotte Bunch, to "have fun so we do not go mad in male supremacist, heterosexual Amerika." A key contributor to the group's publications, Brown's charisma and popularity saw her unceremoniously booted out of the collective, only months after its formation, for "star-tripping."

All of this could've been channeled into an overly earnest, didactic, and bitter volume, but Brown instead infused her debut with vitality, hilarity, and hope. *Rubyfruit Jungle*'s plot not only distilled the rapid social changes of recent years but featured the kind of plucky and vivacious character a variety of audiences could relate to, cheer on, and want to emulate. The reality of social exclusion is present, but Bolt's irrepressible, audacious, and bolshy attitude and picaresque adventures capture the joy and raw excitement of a new generation of women refusing to be browbeaten and circumscribed any longer.

Rubyfruit Jungle sold around seventy thousand copies in the first few years following its release, rapidly outstripping all other Daughters Inc. releases. Rather than producing a sequel, Brown next opted to write a different kind of novel, the somewhat more sober *In Her Day* (1976), which explored generational issues between women. Having retained the rights to the books, Daughters Inc. sold the rights to *Rubyfruit Jungle* to Bantam in 1977 for $250,000. Some feminists at the time widely criticized this as selling out. For Brown's part, she recalled, in her 1997 autobiography *Rita Will*, "standing on the corner of Seventh Avenue near Bleecker Street, outside the Daughters office, with a check for $125,000 in my hand. It seemed like a dream: Poverty that grinds you to dust, and suddenly a mess of money."

With the Bantam deal, sales of *Rubyfruit Jungle* leapt into the millions, allowing Brown to establish a full-time career as a writer. Eventually moving into the crime genre, most famously with her Mrs. Murphy series, she now has more than fifty books to her name.

Over a six-year period Daughters Inc. published twenty-three titles, including further coming of age tales, such as Elana Dykewomon's *Riverfinger Women* (published as Elana Nachman), and a children's book by science fiction writer Joanna Russ. In 1977, they released M.F. Beal's *Angel Dance*, now widely acknowledged as the first lesbian detective novel. *Angel Dance*'s story concerns a left-wing Hispanic journalist hired to protect a best-selling feminist author from potentially deadly enemies that were politically both on the left and the right. Although not sharing the commercial sales of *Rubyfruit Jungle,* it similarly captured the atmosphere of its time, in this case the post-boom hardships of left-wing and women's movements during the mid to late 1970s.

By 1977, according to Harris, Daughters Inc. had become an "armed camp," with Bowman obsessed by the belief that she and the company were being targeted by FBI. Although government monitoring and interference with radical activities certainly continued during the period and since, little evidence exists beyond Bowman's certainty that the company was the focus of intensive activity. To ward off infiltration and the planting of fake evidence, she had surveillance and security equipment installed in her office and home. Arnold and Bowman apparently initially resisted publishing *Angel Dance.* Once convinced of its worth, they subsequently ordered Harris to undertake cloak-and-dagger means to correspond with the author, requiring that all editing work be done over public phones.

Despite Bowman's paranoia, Arnold organized the first Women in Print Conference in 1977, bringing together over a hundred publishers and writers. By 1979 however health issues and disillusionment at their inability to repeat *Rubyfruit Jungle*'s early success, despite or perhaps because of the mainstreaming of feminist and lesbian writers, led the couple to wind up the firm. Numerous titles were remaindered and rapidly became unavailable, but the quality and historical value of the work has since been acknowledged. A number were rereleased in the 1980s and '90s and remain in print today.

Iain McIntyre

The wine went directly to Polina's tongue and she told me how freaked out she was and how secretly she thought lesbianism attracted and frightened every woman, because every woman could be a lesbian, but it was all hidden and unknown. Did I get into it because of the allure of the forbidden? She then went on to say what a wonderful relationship she had with her husband. They had an understanding about Paul, and wasn't heterosexuality just grand?

"It bores me, Polina."

"Bores you—what do you mean?"

"I mean men bore me. If one of them behaves like an adult it's cause for celebration, and even when they do act human, they still aren't as good in bed as women."

"Maybe you haven't met the right man?"

"Maybe you haven't met the right woman. And I bet I've slept with more men than you have, and they all work the same show. Some are better at it than others but it's boring once you know what women are like."

"You can't sit there and say a thing like that about men."

"Okay, then I won't say anything. Better to shut my mouth than lie about it."

A disturbed pause. "What's so different about sleeping with women? I mean, exactly what is the difference?"

"For one thing, it's more intense."

"You don't think things between men and women get intense?"

"Of course they do but it's not the same, that's all."

"How?"

"Oh, lady, there aren't words for it. I don't know—it's the difference between a pair of roller skates and a Ferrari—ah, there aren't words."

"I think the lady doth protest too much. You wouldn't promote such blatant lesbian propaganda if you were sure of yourself and your sexual identity."

"Propaganda? I took a few minutes to try to answer a question you asked me. If you want to see blatant propaganda then look at the ads in the subways, magazines, t.v., everywhere. The big pigs use heterosexuality and women's bodies to sell everything in this country—even violence. Damn, you people are so bad off you got to have computers to match you up these days."

Incident at La Junta, **Oliver Lange** (Stein & Day, 1973)

The back cover of the 1974 Pocket Books edition of *Incident at La Junta*, first published in 1973, describes it as a tale of two young American revolutionaries on the lam from the authorities who became embroiled in the goings-on of a small, isolated little Mexican town, La Junta. This is indeed part of the story, but a lot more happens.

Jocelyn and Keith are the two insurgents. She is a wild child, ex-junkie, and sexual hustler. He comes across as a good-looking all-American surfer type. Together they head up a small Los Angeles–based revolutionary group called "the Gesture." The politics of the Gesture are a sensationalized knockoff of the European avant-garde revolutionary group, the Situationist International. The Gesture has a manifesto, written by Keith, which they send out anonymously in large numbers. Their basic tenet, according to Jocelyn, is that "random violence in its purest sense will in time disintegrate any social structure."

The Gesture revels in "the spectacle," activities designed to sow discontent with capitalism. Members of the Gesture pour battery acid over phone cables, knocking out a large section of LA's telecommunications. They also firebomb a van carrying costumes belonging to a theater group "dedicated to presenting primitivistic social drama italicizing the criminal injustices committed upon the working class," the FBI investigation into which blames the incident on wealthy land owners.

But the Gesture's most celebrated activity involves throwing buckets of nails over a stretch of freeway, resulting in a massive traffic jam in which a young man is killed. Jocelyn asks Keith who the man was.

> "Maybe a budding research chemist or something who would have isolated some compound that would have eradicated wheat blight all over the world. Or he could have been a murderer."
> "Like us?" she inquired mildly.

When Keith and Jocelyn suspect there is a police informer in the Gesture, they abandon the group, load up a camper van, and flee to Mexico. Jocelyn gets a serious case of dysentery as a result of drinking local bottled water, which she believes has been purified but is really just from a tap. Their camper van breaks down in remote desert in a poor part of Mexico. Unaware that Jocelyn is dangerously dehydrated, Keith leaves her and goes in search of help.

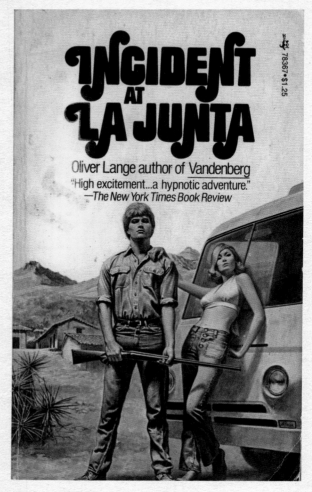

Incident at La Junta
(Pocket Books, 1974)
Incident at La Junta
(P Davies, 1974)

She wakes up in a bed in La Junta to the news that Keith is dead, having fallen victim to a heart attack while walking through the desert. Jocelyn is looked after by Montenegro, a doctor who used to work in Mexico City but now plies his trade in the small town. The other main Mexican character is Jimenez, a fearsome local police chief who has discovered the stash of marijuana she and Keith kept in the camper van and is keen to press drugs charges on her.

As Jocelyn recovers, an unknown virus starts killing people in the town and its surrounds. Even if she can somehow negotiate with Jimenez not to press drugs charges, La Junta and the surrounding district are quarantined for an indeterminate period of time and she cannot leave.

The sixties radical politics component of *Incident at La Junta* is over fairly quickly, and the majority of the novel examines Montenegro's efforts to fight the mysterious virus and Jocelyn's slow acculturation to small town rural life. Most pulp and popular novels in the late sixties and early seventies set in Mexico focused on similar themes: violence, the hippie trail, drug running, corrupt cops and subservient peasants. *Incident at La Junta* touches on all these, but the author's obvious knowledge of the country means his treatment is much deeper and sophisticated. It contains acute, well-written observations on the Mexico's rural/urban divide, the nature of law enforcement, class politics, and masculinity.

The book's relatively sophisticated take on Mexico is explained by the identity of the author, Oliver Lange, a pseudonym for John Wadleigh. Born in a tenement in New York's Hell's Kitchen in 1927, Wadleigh served in the army during World War II, attended Columbia University on GI Bill financing, and moved to New Mexico. An artist and critic, according to his October 2, 2013, obituary in the *Santa Fe New Mexican*, he wrote fifty-five novels, of which thirteen were published. His most famous work, *Vandenberg* (1971), about a group of middle-aged New Mexican misfits who resist a communist takeover of America, bears a striking resemblance to the 1984 film *Red Dawn*, in which teenagers defend their Colorado town again invading Soviet and Cuban forces. It is unclear whether the similarities were intentional, and Wadleigh never contested the matter in court.

Andrew Nette

By midnight six more members of the Gesture had put in an appearance. But it was Jocelyn who gently voiced a doubt that may have existed in the minds of others.

The doubt had to do with one Ivan Goldman, who at the age of twenty-two turned out to be the only casualty of their freeway foray. His name came over the nightcap news. Almost deferentially, hands embracing a sphere of air, she searched. "But we'll never know. I mean, about him."

Keith shot her that wry grin of his, teasing yet affectionately tolerant. The grin told her enough: that he was still riding a euphoric-high. That he was still not sane, let along sensible. It clearly told her to go carefully.

Not that she had much choice. For Keith was already quoting from his thesis. A bound transcript in his lap, opened to the preface. The basic idea from which, she couldn't deny, she herself had given him over a year ago. Keith read in the manner of an enthusiastic Episcopal minister: "The argument is as irrefutable as it is obvious. If mankind has been able to reach its present state of manic behavior through ostensibly 'good' intentions—when it is clear that the evilest of times is upon us—then who can deny, paradoxically, that true, unmotivated *random violence*, at first inspection seemingly the epitome of 'bad' or 'evil' action, may not in the long run prove meritorious, or that it may even bring about or at least contribute to an improvement in our appalling human condition?"

They'd heard it a dozen times, but the demonstration on the freeway tonight lent size and dimension to the notion. Keith clapped the covers of the typescript shut, grinned, and glanced around the others. "How about that shit! Thank old Jocey for that nugget."

Get Radcliff!

The 1970s saw a spate of vigilantes, troubleshooters, and the like, loosely referred to as denizens of the men's adventure subset of publishing—descendants of their Depression-era pulp forebears. These paperback original series most often populated spinner racks and shelves in bus stations, newsstands, drug and grocery stores, and some independent bookstores. These characters, mostly men and in some cases women, were tough, resourceful, often Vietnam vets or ex-spies. Loss and revenge were recurring themes among them—the Batman syndrome, if you will—where in the aftermath of a devastating incident, often a murder of a loved one or close friend, they took up their one-person war on crime and evildoers.

Joining in the mayhem was the likes of Remo Williams, the Destroyer; Baroness Penelope St. John-Orsini a.k.a. the Baroness; Angela Harpe, a rich, kick-ass sister called the Dark Angel ("she owned the most lethal weapons a black chick ever packed, including her luscious, highly-trained body"); a rugged Native American private investigator who went by his last name, Dakota; and Robert Sand, international man of action, sword and martial arts master, the Black Samurai—realized on screen by karate champ turned actor Jim Kelly.

Then there was Joe Radcliff by Roosevelt Mallory.

The driver felt the impact and heard the deadening thud. He saw the woman's body fly into the air, land on the hood, then roll up over the windshield and across the roof of the car. . . . He decided to head for home, in the Santa Cruz mountains. Good fresh air, beaches, Monterrey, San Francisco. It would be good to get home.

This is from an early passage of the first book in the Radcliff the "Hit-Master" series, *Harlem Hit* (1973). Mallory wasted little time establishing the character, a cold, amoral, ruthless killer for hire, with a specialty of not overtly warring against the mob but working for them and other shady types. Before he does this, the reader is informed the woman he whacked with his car was plotting the murder of her current husband, who

helped her take out the previous one. The dangerous husband acts first, paying Radcliff's tab to whack her.

Though Radcliff was also a Vietnam vet (in keeping with the trope of the times) and could dispatch his fellow human beings with little or no inner reflection, there the similarity ended with those hundreds of other paperback original series characters. Radcliff came on the scene before Lawrence Block's affable, stamp-collecting hit man John Keller and Barry Eisler's taciturn contract killer, Vietnam vet John Rain, who, like Charles Bronson's *The Mechanic* (1972), makes his hits look like accidents. Radcliff, and we learn this is a code name, even showed up before his fellow Holloway House scribe's Larry Jackson was unveiled in *Daddy Cool* (1974) by Donald Goines. Jackson, a.k.a. "Daddy Cool," is a middle-aged hit man who specialized in dispatching his victims with his handmade knives. He found himself in a Shakespearean dilemma as he tried to save his wayward teenage daughter from falling for a jive pimp and slipping into "the Life," as Iceberg Slim might have put it.

Radcliff had no family and no qualms about his chosen line of work. He is not motivated to get even after the murder of a wife or child, for his motivation, as espoused by 50 Cent, was "Get Rich or Die Tryin.'" In his second outing, *San Francisco Vendetta* (1974), Radcliff observed, "he calculated that he was knocking off VC for only fifty bucks a head. He figured that the underworld would pay him more for knocking off their own kind than the good guys would pay him for doing so." As Justin Gifford observed in his book *Pimping Fictions: African American Crime Literature and the Untold Story of Black Pulp Publishing* (2014), Radcliff personified an aspect of the fruits obtained in fantastical utopian black crime novels.

Gifford specifically singled out another Holloway House unsung star, Joe Nazel, whose Iceman series portrayed Henry Highland West, a players' version of Doc Savage crossed with Robert "Iceberg Slim" Beck. West was a cat who made ducats in the flesh trade and built his mega-casino-brothel in the Nevada desert, fifty

Roosevelt Mallory
Harlem Hit
(Holloway House, 1973)

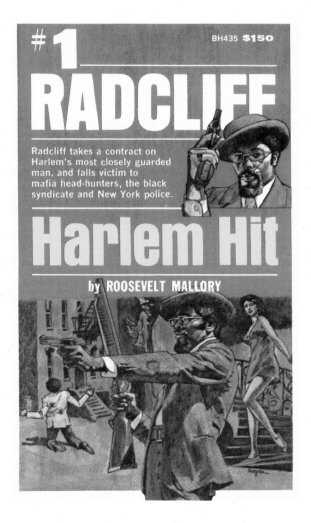

#1
RADCLIFF

BH435 **$150**

Radcliff takes a contract on Harlem's most closely guarded man, and falls victim to mafia head-hunters, the black syndicate and New York police.

Harlem Hit

by ROOSEVELT MALLORY

miles in from Las Vegas. Quadaffi-like, he had a guard of kung fu'ing women (his top security being Kim, an Asian chick with serious martial arts skills, and the black Solema, a weapons specialist), patrolling armed helicopters, and a computer in his "Brain Center" worthy of the Machine in the television show *Person of Interest*.

Iceman and Radcliff become hyper-aspirational pulpish expressions of the masculine end of the Black Power and civil rights movements, with healthy doses of comic book sensibilities. Unlike their antecedents, the adventurer-millionaires of the 1930s—the aforementioned Clark Savage Jr., Richard Wentworth (the kill-crazy Spider), and Richard Henry Benson (the Avenger), to name three—we saw how they got their hands dirty, making their stacks. Surely Wentworth and company, well-off in the depths of the Depression, must have squelched a strike or two by some dirty reds at one of the factories where they were stockholders. Or imagine Doc getting on his experimental visi-phone phone to some hapless flunky in Hidalgo, mentioning calmly that the last shipment of gold from his private mine, in their country mind you, was light and this best not be repeated next time lest the Bronze Devil have to come down there and show them how to count.

The headhunting Hit-Master had a swank, fortified pad in the Santa Cruz Mountains, traveled by Lear jet to his jobs and was aware that as in the first novel, taking a contract by the mob to wipe out a would-be black nationalist leader, he can't trust anybody, including his employer. In *Harlem Hit*, Radcliff is being set up for a double cross by the Syndicate, who intend to bump him off after he takes care of one Leroy Johnson. The killer is brought in to take out this firebrand who is putting black folks in charge of the action uptown. Like a grander thinking Deke O'Malley, the slick hustler in Chester Himes's *Cotton Comes to Harlem* (1964), Johnson is not out to take over the local rackets for the betterment of his people but to solidify his position as the uptown Godfather.

The plan is to use two other imported black killers to make it seem like it was a black-on-black affair and distract the Feds from the mob having a hand in the deadly machinations. The first book sets in motion events that will play out over the course of the subsequent three other Hit-Master novels. While obsessive, Radcliff wasn't out to take down the Mafia like the Executioner, the Butcher, and so on, but that's what he winds up doing. While Mallory doesn't flinch in portraying the ice-in-his-veins nature of his main character, we the reader root for him as he takes on qualities of the anti-hero in his bloody run-ins with La Cosa Nostra.

Curiously, but in keeping with his white paperback-tough-guy contemporaries, Radcliff isn't about upsetting the status quo. In *San Francisco Vendetta*, Radcliff is lured to San Francisco to take a hit job, but this is actually a trap set by the syndicate to pay him back for what he did to their members in the previous novel. In the Bay Area, surviving a shoot-out in Chinatown and realizing he's been set up, Radcliff pays a visit on a white ex-G.I. buddy to obtain the more serious firepower he'll need.

The friend, Barry, is some kind of activist who espouses violence as a way to make change. His stance infuriates the stone-cold killer who reflects, "Radcliff did not like Barry's philosophy nor his organization—an organization of terrorists with the primary mission of making the world just by killing the affluent."

Interesting that Radcliff should see himself as part of or at least have an affinity for the elite . . . or maybe he was just being pragmatic. Unlike the protagonist of Sam Greenlee's 1969 novel *The Spook Who Sat by the Door* or Goines's radicalized gangster Kenyatta, Radcliff knew where his bread was buttered. Did Radcliff hope that as the syndicate sought to legitimize itself by buying into mainstream capitalist pursuits with its ill-gotten gains there'd still be a place for him at their table?

That hope must have been dashed in book three, *Double Trouble* (1975). In this outing, the mob brings in a ringer, a double for Radcliff, who kills a cop in Los Angeles. This compels Radcliff to come to town to straighten this shit out and to change his appearance. He shaves off his short beard and medium-long afro, eschewing his usual gold-rimmed, rose-colored shades.

In book four, the final in the series and, as far as can be determined, the last book ever published by Roosevelt Mallory, *New Jersey Showdown* (1976), Radcliff may not be ready to join his friend Barry's band, but he is looking to retire. The book opens with Radcliff in his fortified pad with the blonde Angie Redman, who was his steady companion in the series. Like Clare Carroll in Donald Westlake's Parker novels, where Parker maintains a humbler abode than does Radcliff on a lake among similar vacation-type homes in the woods, she's a civilian but a constant in his life. The two enjoy the Hit-Master's getting out, but of course a man like Radcliff, can never get out. The grown sons of the Mafia chieftain he iced in book two strike back.

Angie is hospitalized after acid is thrown on her face, and a contrite Radcliff visits her there. Later, she's thrown out the window of her room and killed. Her murder shakes Radcliff, the brutal act breaking though his hard shell and for once it *is* personal. At her burial he swears: "Now he could turn his attention to who was responsible for this. A promise of vengeance was not necessary in Radcliff's world. It was automatic."

The book ends enigmatically after the antihero wipes out the scum responsible for killing his main woman. Was Radcliff out of the business or not?

Hoping to know why he didn't write more Radcliffs or other books, I decided that the hunt for Mr. Mallory was on. There were a few dead ends, including former Holloway House editor Emory Holmes not knowing what had happened to him. But thanks to the gumshoe work of Kevin Burton Smith of the Thrilling Detective website, a lead developed. In the March 1974 issue of *Measure*, an internal publication of Hewlett-Packard whose subtitle read: "For the man and woman of Hewlett-Packard," damned if there wasn't a profile of the author. In an unaccredited piece titled "Get Mallory!" it's revealed that Mallory, a TV director in their Data Systems department, had been a high school dropout, though a top student and football player. He joined the army, then the coast guard, where he became an electronics technician and then an instructor in electronics. When he was discharged, he entered the growing field of computers and in 1966 joined Hewlett-Packard as their first computer instructor.

Mallory said he started writing the first Radcliff novel after seeing a blaxploitation flick about a hit man. "There were all these tough things going on—but no continuity. Bad Writing!" he's quoted saying in the

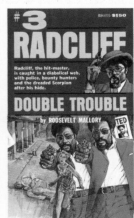

Double Trouble (Holloway House, 1975)

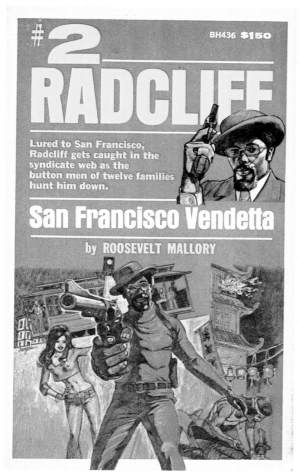

San Francisco Vendetta (Holloway House, 1974)

article. Though he doesn't name the film, it might have been the 1974 movie *Hit Man* with Bernie Casey that he was referring to. He goes on to state that he went to work and wrote the first draft of *Harlem Hit*. Eventually it landed on an editor's desk at Holloway House. In this version Radcliff doesn't survive. But as with what occurred to Parker in his first novel, *The Hunter* (1962), when Westlake killed him off as well, both men took their respective editor's advice and had their protagonists live.

In the piece it's stated that fifty thousand copies of *Harlem Hit* had been sold and that Mallory had enjoyed some sweet royalties and advances for that book and the upcoming *San Francisco Vendetta*. The money has "enabled Mallory to expand his life style somewhat along the lines of the hit master—at least in such material manifestations as custom clothes and favored wines."

It also appears that Radcliff paved the way for two other contract killer efforts from Holloway, *The Big Hit* (1975) by James-Howard Readus and *Black Hit Woman* (1980) by Laurie Miles, as told to Leo Guild.

Yet given the shaky accounting Holloway House was known for, the assertion concerning money definitely suggests a deeper examination. For instance, Dan Roberts, in his article "Holloway House: The World's Largest Publisher of Black Experience Paperbacks," stated that the combined sales of Iceberg Slim's books were more than six million copies (*Paperback Parade*, no. 78, July 2011). But as recounted in the 2012 documentary *Iceberg Slim: Portrait of a Pimp* by Jorge Hinojosa, Robert Beck mostly didn't see that kind of money, even given that one of Beck's books was made into the 1972 movie *Trick Baby* and he got $25,000 in option fees. Beck, like a character wrought from a William Burroughs novel, found himself in his later years, this once smooth pimp and hustler, going bald, taking on the role of an exterminator, a rat and roach killer who had to make ends meet. Despite his infamy and apparent plentiful sales with Holloway House, Beck died at seventy-four from various ailments in hospital in Culver City, a small municipality next door to LA, a day after the 1992 Rodney King riots erupted.

Getting in touch with the Hewlett-Packard Alumni Association, the word back was that though Mallory wasn't a member of the group, the individual who corresponded remembered "Rosey," as he referred to him in an email. He said he'd heard the writer was deceased and, according to some information he passed along, was pretty certain Roosevelt Mallory had died in 2007 in Elk Grove, California.

"Yes, I met him when I started the four books that I did," Monte Rogers said in an e-mail. Rogers was the artist who rendered the dynamic montage-type first edition covers of the four Radcliff books. "Nice guy, very soft-spoken," Rogers also noted. He said the Holloway House editor and Mallory provided photos to him for references, and it's evident as the Rogers covers have tucked under the Radcliff logo a depiction of the Hit-Master in a homburg and tinted glasses, his preferred .38 at the ready, an illustration that looks a lot like Mr. Mallory.

Go on with your bad self, sir.

Gary Phillips

No Ordinary Joe

Joe Nazel and the Pursuit of Black History

When the editor of *Players* magazine, Joseph Gober Nazel Jr. (then thirty years old), walked into the lobby of his Melrose Boulevard offices to greet me, he wasn't happy. Roz, the company's humorless office manager had summoned him out to confront "some crazy guy"—that's me—demanding to see him. Ten minutes later in stormed Joe. Handsome fella—tall, intense, Dash Hammett thin. He'd trimmed his pom-pom Afro round as a halo. He wore nerd glasses, although the remorseless scowl on his brooding face marked him as a sho-nuff brawler. A withering half-spent cigarette slumped forlornly in the coils of his right fist. In his left hand he carried several magazines. He thrust them at me and barked, "Here."

I was flummoxed.

He'd placed in my hands three copies of the latest *Players* magazine, February 1975 edition. The cover featured a full headshot of a cinnamon-skinned babe, her face so close to the lens you could almost taste the musky sweetness of her breath, her lips wide open, her naughty little tongue darting out of the welcoming depths of her mouth.

"What's this?" I had to ask.

"The magazine," Joe said. "Just came out. How did you know?"

How did I know what? I was clueless.

"You're not here to get your copies of the magazine?"

"No sir," I told him, "no sir."

I explained that I'd come because I'd sent him a short story a few weeks after he promised to publish my first story. I was there to demand he publish the new work instantly. My pitch was desperate, tumbling out in a single breath: "I hadn't heard back from you so I figured you must have lost it because it's brilliant and I think it's as good as the other piece you bought even though it's fiction and that first piece is nonfiction but I need the money and if you would let me help you find it I'm sure you're gonna like it and you can write me a check so I can put some gas in my car and get me something to eat."

Roz just glared at me.

I opened the magazine and saw my byline for the first time. It was like staring at a talking bush. I was such a rube it never occurred to me that published writers not only get paid, they also get their names and works beautifully laid out, printed, and distributed across the country for all the world to see.

Joe could see I was a hick.

He pondered me a moment, took a drag from his cigarette, and smiled, "Follow me," he said. He led me down a brightly lit corridor between rows of cubicles. The offices were buzzing. In the larger cubicles were accountants, circulation staff, et cetera, and in the smaller cubicles sat harried editors, singlehandedly turning out one of a dozen or more magazines bearing the imprimatur of Holloway House, the parent company's brand.

The magazine division of the firm specialized in jack-off books with names like *Adam* and *Knight*. Except for the covers, they were printed on cheap paper and featured lily-white seminude pinups photographed in an array of cornball 1950s-era poses. The company also had a homespun line of titles featuring snapshots and contact info of lonely housewives and amateur nudes with black tape covering their faces. *Players* magazine was the company's prize "one-hander," as we soon learned to call this kind of book. *Players* was the first in the catalogue to feature black female nudes. And it sought to capture the then-emerging market for black-themed literature and subjects: black beauty, black music, black personalities, black culture. It aspired to be the "black *Playboy*" and accordingly was Holloway House's first "slick" magazine, printed on expensive paper.

When Joe ushered me into his cluttered office at the end of the corridor, I looked around at the chaos and gave him a sharp, reproving look. No wonder he hadn't read my story and sent me a check. John Shaft couldn't find a pack of rampant elephants in that mess.

Joe grinned, flopped in his chair, and lit a cigarette. He gestured to the stacks of books and paper cluttering every surface, and said, "OK, get at it."

As I began searching the stacks nearest me, Joe started to quiz me. What was my name again? What was my new story about? Who were my favorite writers? Where was I born? Have I traveled—where? Education—what?

I answered his questions and interposed a few of my own: When had he started writing? How many works had he published? What did he consider the great masterpieces of world literature? What were his critical assessments of Richard Wright, James Baldwin, Ralph Ellison? Which great city did he prefer, New York or LA?

In the ninety minutes or so of our mutual interrogations, I learned quite a bit about Mr. Joseph Gober Nazel Jr. He was born in Berkeley but raised in Watts. Considered himself a Los Angeleno to the bone. Began writing early on. Was steeped in classical literature, taking special interest in the works of neglected black authors, like poet Henry Dumas and novelist Chester Himes.

Like me, he'd attended Catholic schools all his life. Even took it one step further: he attended St. Augustine's Seminary in Mississippi, an institution founded specifically to train African Americans for the priesthood. His insatiable curiosity and nagging inquiries into the nature of man and God vexed the faculty so relentlessly that he was politely asked to leave. He joined the Air Force and did a perilous tour in Vietnam from 1964 to 1968. He was wounded in battle, shot in the throat. He'd knocked around a bit when he got out, attending college, working odd jobs, and served a stint as a social worker, walking the meanest streets in the hood. He graduated from the University of Southern California with a degree in ethnic studies in 1972 and was promptly hired as a lecturer. He'd begun writing novels for Holloway House, the notorious white-owned firm that specialized in black "novels of the street" around that time. At the time of our meeting, he had more than a dozen published books to his credit, including six in his Iceman series of crime novels, along with biographies, and a couple of attempts at sappy romance (written under one of his numerous nom-de-plumes Joyce Lezan—Nazel spelled backward).

I continued searching as he talked, and at the end of his long inquisition he said: "Hey . . . um . . . what was your name again? Emory? Emory . . . you wanna take my job?"

The question sent chills up my spine. What could this mean? Was it some kind of sick Hollywood trick? I kept on searching.

Joe Nazel at work in his apartment in an area called "The Jungle," just west of Crenshaw Boulevard, in the Crenshaw District

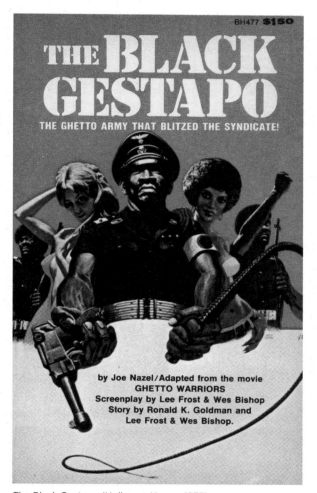

The Black Gestapo (Holloway House, 1975)

"Did you hear what I said?" Joe asked again.

"I'm not quite sure," I told him.

"Listen here," he pressed on. "I hate this fuckin' job. I'm leaving this very day . . . and I want you to take my place."

Naturally, this remarkable turn of events left me dumbfounded. I was twenty-six. Less than four months earlier, I had quit my job as a truck driver for the Salvation Army downtown on skid row to become a writer. The first piece I'd written to launch my new career was an essay on a local black painter whose work celebrated black lives and history. I didn't know how much writers got paid for their work, and hoped I'd get at least a hundred bucks to defray the time and effort it took to write my story. A friend of mine had told me about *Players* magazine and suggested I send my article there. A few days after I mailed it to the magazine's West Hollywood address, I got a note from the editor, Joseph Nazel, informing me that he loved my piece and planned on running it in the magazine. He was prepared to pay me $350 for my effort. Hot damn, I'm a writer!

For the next few weeks everything I sent out received an acceptance letter. It was like I was printing money. I switched from essays to fiction. Then, after a month or so, the rejection letters started rolling in. In a panic, I decided I had made a cosmic blunder. I was probably not a writer at all—perhaps I was . . . a painter. Yes, that's it: a painter! As the money in my bank account dwindled and my Volkswagen crept along on fumes, I did a series of watercolors to reestablish myself as an emerging master of the arts. I drove out to LA's art district. It was arrayed just south of Hollywood along a tony strip of La Cienega Boulevard. I rushed into a half dozen galleries with my paintings under my arm, imploring the owners to look at my work. Surely they would recognize my genius and extend me a loan for gas and a lifesaving respite at Fatburgers.

Naturally, they threw me out on my ear.

Crestfallen, I sputtered grimly home to my flat in the hood. There I would await the judgment of Fate and my inevitable demise from starvation and grief. That's when I realized that I was driving down Melrose Boulevard, a few blocks from the *Players* magazine address. I found the building and took the elevator upstairs to plead my case with the editor who'd purchased my first story. Now, less than two hours later, he was offering me his job.

As I stood in mute astonishment, Joe began cheerfully introducing me as "the new editor of *Players*," to

anyone who passed his cubicle. Presently, he got on the phone and rang up Ralph Weinstock, one of the founding partners of Holloway House. The switchboard lady informed him that Weinstock was out of the office and should be back in an hour or two. "Well, tell him I'm out to lunch," Joseph snapped, "with the new editor of *Players*. And before I leave, I want to introduce him." He slammed down the phone and dialed again. "We're going to lunch," he said, "on the company dime. But first I'm calling my buddy to see if he'll join us."

Twenty minutes later, in walked Joe's best friend, twenty-nine-year-old Stanley Crouch. I'd never heard of him. I soon learned that Stanley was among the brightest in the constellation of stars then rising in the African American cultural firmament. He was a jazz drummer and a spoken-word poet of candescent inventiveness and intellect. And although he possessed no degree, he was then a respected professor at Claremont College.

We knocked off for lunch. Fine restaurant. Top-shelf booze and haute cuisine. Our table talk was like a trip to the Forum. As we spoke these were some topics rattling through my brain:

Following rebellions in Birmingham (1963), in Harlem (1964), in Los Angeles (1965)—and in Nashville, Newark, Chicago, Cleveland, and DC in the five years that followed—America's urban centers seemed ringed with indelible fire. Whites fled the cities, and black neighborhoods sparkled in the vacuum. Properties, once legally denied to black buyers by racist city covenants, now became available. Black youth rose up in the colleges, extolling principles of social justice and espousing the rhetoric of black nationalism. In coffee houses and on the evening news, militant firebrands raised their fists in outrage over white privilege and racial injustice.

Articulate, highly political young writers like Joseph and Stanley were part of this movement and embodied a self-affirmation and pride not witnessed in American public life since the so-called Harlem Renaissance of the 1920s and '30s. They had read Hemingway, Faulkner, and Fitzgerald but were now inspired by the high-minded poetics and political sagacity of Richard Wright, Ralph Ellison, and James Baldwin. And whereas Harlem's cultural awakening was confined to a single proscribed district of Manhattan, the Black Arts Movement, as it was called, was national in scope.

The East Coast saw the emergence of playwrights LeRoi Jones (Amiri Baraka) and Ed Bullins; novelists

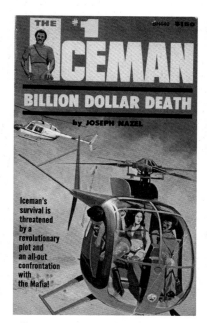

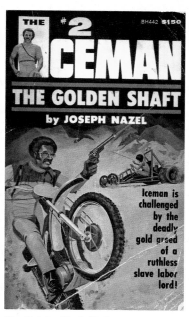

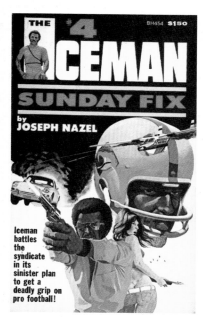

Billion Dollar Death (Holloway House, 1973)

The Golden Shaft (Holloway House, 1974)

Sunday Fix (Holloway House, 1974)

Ishmael Reed and Toni Morrison; and poets David Henderson, Lorenzo Thomas, Sonia Sanchez, and Nikki Giovanni. Ground Zero of the movement on the West Coast centered on the Watts Writers Workshop, founded by white screenwriter Budd Schulberg after the LA rebellion of '65. The workshop attracted a formidable collective of poets and writers, among them Quincy Troupe, Jayne Cortez, Eric Priestley, Curtis Lyles, Ojenke, the Watts Prophets, Kamau Daàood, Wanda Coleman (the first editor of *Players*), Odie Hawkins, and Crouch. In the works of these artists, the destructive fires and rage that had savaged black communities across the U.S. were reset to a different purpose: expression, indictment, affirmation, and the illumination of moral purpose and identity.

Joseph was not part of the Watts Writers' Group. He was a loner—a hostile naysayer and an outsider to all formal collectives.

He was a man of faith; but his faith, like that of Malcolm X and Martin Luther King Jr., was focused on revolution, on the liberating power of education, and on his personal mission to uplift that debased cohort of unregarded and unappreciated Americans whom he loved and lived among. Yet he did not seem to have faith in himself. He did not like or respect many writers, sometimes, it seemed to me, for petty reasons. But when he encountered an author he did respect, he

took a long step back to give them room to shine. This uncanny aspect of his personality was revelatory of his native humility and generosity.

For writers like Joseph, the social and political upheavals of the 1960s sparked a personal metamorphosis. He had absorbed the entirety of the American literary canon. All the bright, transformative white guys and gals. But his special strength and passion lay in his discernment of the works of black writers and poets.

For the five hundred years of their existence, the American authors that he championed had been legally debased, alienated, and made invisible by the doctrine of white supremacy. And now, following the liberating traumas of World War II, the civil rights era, and the social unrest of the 1960s, they were rising en masse out of the urban coffins that confined them, their monumental characters and actions illuminated for the first time in the American narrative by the light of ten thousand burning buildings. For the racists of American culture this was a holocaust fomented by the Other—a holocaust of counterrevolution, of affirmation, of retribution, of fury and deferred dreams whose advent every self-respecting white supremacist had been fearing since the birth of the Republic.

Now, it was here.

Just as Thomas Mann and James Joyce appropriated iconic plotlines and heroes from their mythic

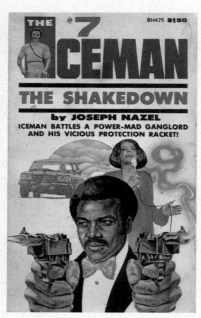

Spinning Target (Holloway House, 1974)

The Shakedown (Holloway House, 1975)

Black Cop (Holloway House, 1974). Dom Gober was a pseudonym for Joe Nazel

European pasts, seminal authors like W.E.B. Du Bois, Richard Wright, and those that followed—Baldwin, Himes, and Morrison, the darlings of high culture; and Melvin Van Peebles, Beck, Goines, Hawkins, and Nazel himself, the bad boys of pulp and pop—purloined the equally treasured icons of seductive, signifying, fearsome and indomitable bad men, double-crossing floozies, and tricksters archived in American Negro lore: Brer Rabbit, the Signifying Monkey, Frankie and Johnny, John Henry, and Stagolee.

Writers like Joe saw themselves as centurions of the people, intellectual Robin Hoods in the service of justice and freedom. And just as the heroes of old had been inspired to serve and protect the societies of antiquity and provide standards for engagement against which any serious hero must be measured, Joseph and his contemporaries took up their pens with the righteous zeal of the warrior hero. The job of the hero, his entire reason for coming into existence is to do battle with monsters, to slay them and extract from them a tribute—a boon—to benefit the societies held under the thrall of mortal terror.

We touched on these themes and many others during our raucous three-hour lunch. Finally, we drained our glasses and said our farewells to Stanley. Then Joe took me back to *Players* to deliver his ultimatum to Weinstock. When we walked into his office, the

publisher was seated at his desk with his face twisted into a spiteful scowl. The February edition of the magazine was lying open before him. The article that I had written on black art had put him in a sour mood. Before Joe could speak, Weinstock demanded to know why he had ignored his directive never to run features in the magazine on subjects he'd decided black folk had no abiding interest in, like art, politics, history, and the struggle for racial justice.

Weinstock was still smarting over his experience with the first editor of *Players*, the strident, supremely gifted and uncompromising Wanda Coleman, a writer-poet of the first order. Wanda's tenure with the magazine had been tempestuous and brief. Her subversive intent had been to transform Weinstock's titty book into a journal of literary quality and aspiration. Weinstock made it clear that lit did not sell smut, tits did. Wanda stormed out after a year on the job. Weinstock selected Joe to take her place, assuming the taciturn, hyper-prolific novel-writing phenomenon would be more pliant.

He was—to a point.

He abhorred doing anything that prevented him from writing, and this exposed him to myriad indignities and humiliations that he seemed to believe were the cost of continuing his labors. And though he loved filling up the magazine with his copious bylines and texts, after a year in the editor's chair, he buckled under the weight of quotidian duties every editor is required to perform. He had threatened to quit if he was not given help, and now he was here to tell his miserly, embittered, meanspirited boss-man that his quitting day had come.

Weinstock was in full-blown rant mode. "Black people don't give a shit about art!" he exclaimed. "I told you never to run stories like this. It's a waste of space."

"Well then," Joe responded calmly, "you need to take that up with the man who wrote it. Emory Holmes, the new editor of *Players*."

Weinstock seemed not to have noticed that I'd entered the room. He snapped his head around and appraised me with sneering contempt. Brusquely, he demanded I wait outside while Joe and he settled their dispute. The thick wooden door did little to blunt the sharpness of the debate that followed. After ten minutes or so, Joe emerged with a conspiratorial grin on his face.

"Let's go find you a desk and a chair," he said triumphantly.

I worked as the first associate editor of *Players* magazine that very day.

Joe never quit.

He had used the threat of leaving the book as a ploy to get some help. He handed over all the editorial duties (which he saw as drudgery) to me. He arrived at work each day at 6:00 or 7:00 a.m. and left the office a few minutes after I arrived at 9:00 a.m. He spent his days prowling the streets developing articles, interviews, reviews, poems, photography, and commentary for the magazine—stuffing our pages with works created exclusively by him under a host of pseudonyms. At night he continued to churn out novels at the rate of one every two months or so. Meanwhile, I was in Negro heaven: answering the mails, the phones, editing text, learning magazine layout, interviewing writers, models, photographers, illustrators. I may have been walking on cloud nine during my tumultuous stay at *Players*, but my experience might best be characterized as that of a writer on scholarship, attending Harvard in Hell.

Weinstock was determined to make my stint on the job both miserable and short-lived. He moved me into the cramped office of Sid Smith, the ultraconservative black man credited with bringing the idea of *Players* to Holloway House. I guess he figured I'd last there less than a week in the company of my ever-suspicious, truculent, boorish, and intolerant office mate. But I've got a gift for dealing with assholes, and within a week or two Sid Smith and I were as cozy as frat brothers.

Nevertheless, I lasted in the job less than a year. Joe, who had become more of a big brother than a benefactor, began to disappoint me. I grew increasingly upset that he routinely pulled articles and stories of new writers I'd discovered out of the book to replace them with works of his own. I had thought our job was to lift unpublished black artists out of obscurity and give them a chance at publication. For Joe, he had taken care of that mandate by hiring me. We began to feud. Meanwhile, my disputes with Weinstock continued unabated. And they were always searing and bitter.

My last day came when Joe and I were summoned into Weinstock's office. He sat at his desk, sallow as a lemon, an unwelcoming smile creeping across his lips. In front of him were two tall stacks of girlie sets. Weinstock informed us that one stack was of models I'd slated for inclusion in the magazine—and he was rejecting them. The other represented models I'd rejected—which he had decided to use.

Then the sour old man made this remarkable claim: "I've looked over these sets and realized that Emory has no clue of how to pick out a beautiful black girl," he said. Ah yes, this shriveled old white man who probably hasn't been laid since Moses was in knee pants will now enlighten us black boys on what constitutes black beauty.

Joe and I stared blankly at the cretinous little shit.

"And what constitutes a beautiful black woman?" I finally had to ask.

Weinstock delivered his punch line with magisterial aplomb, "A beautiful black girl has three qualities," the old boy opined, "She looks like she's eighteen years old, she has European features, and she has big tits," he concluded with pride.

I knew I was a goner before the toxic final phrases escaped his lips. Strangely, Weinstock didn't want me to leave, only to give up the duties I had demonstrated I lacked the talent for: understanding the foundations of African American beauty. I left the meeting, gathered up my gear, said my goodbyes to Sid and Joe, and left. I have never been fired.

Five years later—for reasons too complicated to recount here—I returned. Miraculously, Weinstock, who despised me, hired me again—this time as editor in chief. Holloway House had a policy of hiring even those they despised as long as they made them money. After a few days on the job, I learned that they had treated Joe shabbily in the years after I left. He had been fired several times and rehired every time a new editor left in disgust, which was often. Like the line in *Invisible Man*, they knew how to "keep this nigger running" and coaxed him back into the fold again and again to suffer abuse and work for a pittance. I learned that he was barely making a living on the paltry commissions Holloway House paid its writers. And Holloway House had a well-earned rep for cheating its authors, including its most bankable talents, Robert Beck (a.k.a. Iceberg Slim), Donald Goines, and Joe.

Joe had inculcated in himself what might be termed an "aggressive solipsism." His powers of introspection allowed him to dismiss the niggling intrusions of all external phenomena, even the mechanics of his own body. Eating and sleeping were inconvenient sources of fuel, tasks that he dutifully enslaved to the fevered agencies of his mind. And his mind was ever fixed on the abstract pursuits that obsessed him: the plot point, the construction of believable characters and action, the necessities of hitting the deadline, earning the paycheck. He was a brooding island amid violently buffeting winds. He was utterly alone, a Ghetto Daedalus, forever at work untangling some moral conundrum deep inside his brain, in the midst of riots, concerts, markets, meetings, the distracting swirl of the urban labyrinth, and other preoccupations of the hapless rabble.

My first act as editor in chief was to hire my spiritual big brother, Joe Nazel, just as he had hired me—off the street, sight-unseen—all those years ago. I gave him two pages in every edition to fill to his heart's content, plus any interview or thought piece he could bring me. I lasted in that job for four years until I once again left in utter disgust. For the record, I walked out again. They never fired me. When I left, Joe was named editor in chief once again. I was sad that he took the gig, and Weinstock and his partner, Bentley Morriss, the head honcho at Holloway House, wasted no time in treating their most prolific author disgracefully again.

At the time of his death from brain cancer at the age of sixty-two, on August 30, 2006, Joe had become Holloway House's most prolific writer by far, with fifty-nine books to his credit, including biographies and novels on sports, adventure, crime, and romance.

Although he was a journeyman writer and an editor of historical merit, he was never interested in crossing over into the white literary marketplace, where presumably he might have made a decent living. He knew that white folk already had a substantial literary pantheon to uplift and inspire them. Black folk did

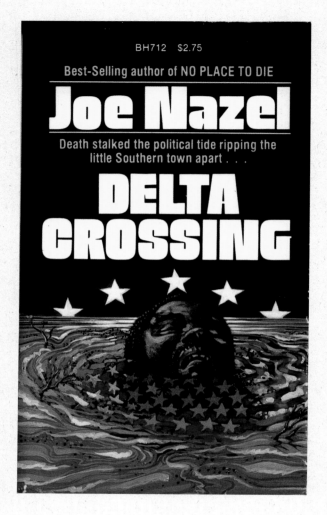

BH712 $2.75

Best-Selling author of NO PLACE TO DIE

Joe Nazel

Death stalked the political tide ripping the little Southern town apart . . .

DELTA CROSSING

Delta Crossing (Holloway House, 1984)

not. So he surrendered his incisive mind and skills to people of color, to students, and to that vast, neglected audience of outsiders that Frantz Fanon called "the wretched of the earth."

Across his thirty-five-year career, he worked as an editor and reporter for every major black publication in LA, including the *Los Angeles Sentinel*, the Wave Community Newspapers, the *LA Watts Times*, *Black Radio Exclusive*, and *Turning Point* magazine. He was a scriptwriter and producer for The Urban Network and the producer-host of a chat show for KACE radio, scripting more than a hundred programs for its black history series. If that wasn't enough, he found time to be a features editor for the *West Palm Beach Gazette* in Florida.

I suspect many of you have never heard of Joe Nazel. If you want to meet Joe, you can find him within the covers of his books. You must force yourself to look past the errata and misspellings that are typical of Holloway House pulp, and you will encounter him gliding up in his metallic blue Rolls-Royce in the guise of Henry Highland West, redoubtable hero of his Iceman series of crime novels. In *Spinning Target* (no. 5 in the series, published in 1983), Joe could be speaking of himself when he writes: "Ice made few public appearances. There's no need to. He was not out to build a fan club. He was not trying to become the most popular man in the world. That wasn't his schtick. His thing was living. Living like no man, Black or white, had ever lived. That's what it was all about."

In *Delta Crossing* (1984), one of his most ambitious works, Joe creates a flawed and fragile, if outraged, hero, along the lines of the flawed and fragile, if outraged hero that Ralph Ellison concocted for his masterpiece, *Invisible Man*. Like Ellison's unnamed hero, the hero of Delta Crossing is never named. Like Joe he is a journalist and a university lecturer, unappreciated and disrespected by the idiots who employ him. Like Joe, he is a chronicler of black lives and culture and he journeys, as did Joe in his seminary years, to the Mississippi delta, the birthplace of the blues, to search out his roots in, as his buddy Stanley Crouch put it, "the profound emotion of America's first truly adult secular music," the blues.

Again, Joe could be describing himself when the battered hero of Delta Crossing mutters:

I wore the uniform, for a time wore it proudly,
but I never believed, could never see that my life

was really going anywhere, or that I was leaving meaningful tracks behind me. Maybe that was the mark of my greatest vanity, my greatest sin, wanting to leave something behind, something that would shine throughout history. It was important to me to be remembered as having contributed something to mankind, to the future, to my race. I began questioning what I owed to life, to myself and to history, when I discovered what I was becoming and could become, etched into history by an engraver who worked from fiction rather than fact.

In all of his endeavors, Joseph was pursuing history—black history—retrieving the great chunks of it that had been lost, uncovering its buried chapters, its debased heroes and heroines, and reinterpreting those inspired passages that had been mangled or obscured by the lies of countless political con men, thieves, and the agents of race supremacy, whether white or black. He followed this course obsessively, past the point of exhaustion.

Joseph Gober Nazel Jr. was a hell of a man: enigmatic, brilliant, reserved. And I am both lucky and proud to have known him. Luckier still to have had him as my mentor, my big brother, and my friend. He aspired to be a man whose life and work counted in the world. His voice in harmony with the grand themes of the national voice and character, themes embodied in the Constitution, the civil rights movement, and the witty pessimism of the blues. His abiding belief was that through the reflections of our profoundest artists, the raw material of everyday life and struggle could be shaped into what we know as civilization: a thing inspiring, confident, and comprehensive in its fecundity and radiance. The boon that resulted from one's ceaseless efforts to reclaim this lost patrimony represented the distillation of countless millennia, countless minds, countless hands—and voices borne aloft on rivers of tears, sweat, and blood.

Emory Holmes II

Black Samurai, Marc Olden (Signet 1974)

At some point in his career, prolific African American pulp author Marc Olden, took a big swig from the swirling waters of early 1970s American popular culture and came up with what would be his best-remembered series, Black Samurai.

The first installment, *Black Samurai*, opens with a raid on a secretive Japanese samurai training school by men under the command of a disgruntled, homicidal army colonel, Leo Dimitri Tolstoy. Nearly all the samurai are killed, including their chief, Master Konuma. The only survivor is orphan and former U.S. marine Robert Sand. Vowing revenge on the men who murdered "the only family he had known" and armed with a "two-hundred-year-old Tanto, a short twenty-seven-inch Japanese sword, his prize for physical and mental excellence, his award for being the best Samurai in a group of men who knew only excellence," Sand sets off in pursuit of Tolstoy.

Sand's presence at the samurai school originated several years earlier. While on leave in Tokyo during his tour of duty in Vietnam, Sand came across a group of white soldiers menacing an elderly local man (unbeknownst to him, Master Konuma). Intervening, Sand received two bullets in the stomach from the attackers and then watched as the old man dispatched his assailants with lightning-fast martial arts skills. Released from hospital, Sand was discharged from the army and became a student at Konuma's school. Cue scenes of Sand trying to master the grueling samurai training regime and Japanese language and culture, in the process learning humility and discipline and turning his body into a lethal weapon.

William Baron Clarke, the Texan ex-president of the United States, helps Sand. Clarke has intelligence that Tolstoy, embittered over the public humiliation he suffered for his role in a series of My Lai–style massacres in Vietnam, is buying weapons, "flame throwers, automatic weapons—rifles, light machine guns, plastic explosives, dynamite, grenades, radios," which he plans to use on an unknown American town, thus bringing home the carnage of the Indochina war. Clarke also wants to prevent a scheme to kidnap his young daughter, living in Paris, which is somehow connected to Tolstoy's scheme.

Clarke pulls every piece of paper, anything that can identify Sand, and makes him disappear. He also puts at his disposal an international network of contacts in

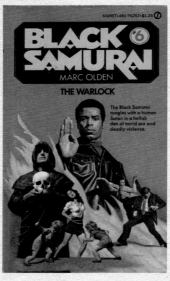

The Warlock
(Signet, 1975)
The Golden Kill
(Signet, 1974)

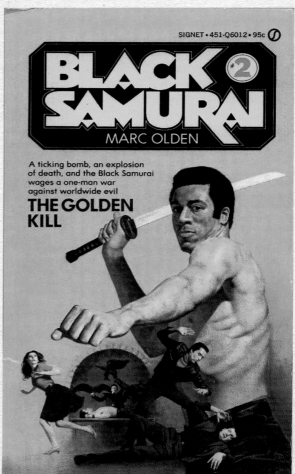

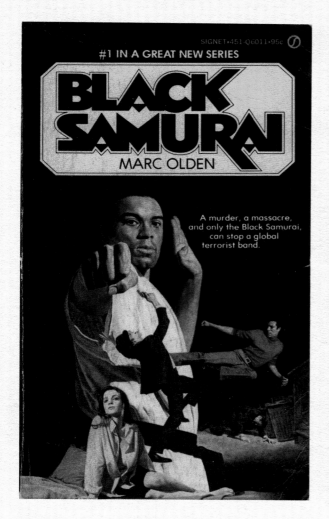

#1 IN A GREAT NEW SERIES

SIGNET•451-Q6011•95c

BLACK SAMURAI
MARC OLDEN

A murder, a massacre, and only the Black Samurai, can stop a global terrorist band.

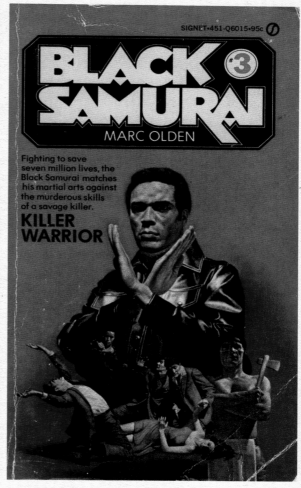

SIGNET•451-Q6015•95c

BLACK SAMURAI #3
MARC OLDEN

Fighting to save seven million lives, the Black Samurai matches his martial arts against the murderous skills of a savage killer.

KILLER WARRIOR

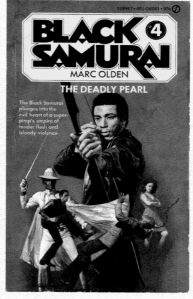

SIGNET•451-Q6061•95c

BLACK SAMURAI #4
MARC OLDEN
THE DEADLY PEARL

The Black Samurai plunges into the evil heart of a super-pimp's empire of tender flesh and bloody violence.

an effort to thwart Tolstoy. Sand chases Tolstoy and his killers through Saigon and Paris, dishing out numerous painful deaths with his superior fighting skills.

Black Samurai manifests many trends in American popular culture in the early 1970s, including blaxploitation cinema, and the turn a lot of pulp fiction took toward men's adventure style tales of secret agents, disgruntled cops, and vigilantes battling various global menaces. No doubt, Olden was also influenced by the martial arts craze sweeping the U.S., which really took off with the success of *Billy Jack* (1971). The film, which spawned two sequels, depicted an enigmatic and nature-loving "half-breed" American Navajo Indian, and ex–Green Beret Vietnam veteran, Billy Jack, who is drawn into defending a rural hippie school from hostile rednecks from a nearby town. On the small screen, David Carradine played an ex–Shaolin priest wandering the Old West in the successful series *Kung*

Black Samurai
(Signet, 1974)
Killer Warrior
(Signet, 1974)
The Deadly Pearl
(Signet, 1974)

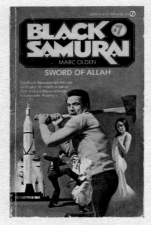

Katana (Signet, 1975)   *Sword of Allah* (Signet, 1975)

Fu (1972–75). And of course there was the 1973 Hong Kong–American coproduction *Enter the Dragon*, Bruce Lee's last film, which blasted him into American consciousness before his untimely death a few months after its release. It costarred Jim Kelly, who would go on to play Sand in a rather lackluster 1976 film adaption of the paperback series. Notably, Olden, who died in 2003, had a keen interest in martial arts, with a black belt in karate and aikido.

The novel's politics display a similar mix of influences. There's a strong antiracist streak as Sand repeatedly has to deal with bigotry on the part of Clarke and those working for him, some of whom consider Sand just an "uppity" black man. At the same time Tolstoy's minions comprise a multinational who's-who of trained killers, including former members of the South Vietnamese army, two South Korean martial arts experts, a member of the Arab Black September movement, and a former IRA assassin.

Olden's writing skills makes *Black Samurai* a superior entry in the canon of men's adventure pulp fiction. Seven further novels followed, featuring a range of deranged global menaces, including "the king of the pimps" and his army of assassins in *The Deadly Pearl* (1974), a global occult empire in *The Warlock* (1975), and fanatical Arab terrorists in *The Sword of Allah* (1975).

Andrew Nette

"**G**oddam it!" yelled the white man, "I demand to know what's going on here! It's my life you're talking about, you hear that, *nigger*?"

Nigger. Sand smiled. It had been a long time since he had been called that to his face. Oh, there were a couple of racial incidents in Japan, nothing he or his brother Samurai couldn't handle, but "nigger" was something American, and even on his few brief trips to America over the past few years, Sand hadn't personally run into it. He'd seen the word there, read it, heard other people saying it, but not to him. It was moments like this that made him realize he had been living in another world for a long time, but that world had been a unique one, preparing him for almost anything.

It had given him strength, knowledge of many kinds along with incredible skills.

Slowly he said to the white man, "I killed a man a few minutes ago and he said no less to me than you just did. I killed him and he never once called me nigger. If *you* ever call me that again, I won't kill you but I will give you enough pain to last you for the rest of your life. Do you understand me?"

Ives stiffened and remained silent. There was no sound in the room.

"I said," repeated Sand, "do you understand me?"

Dropping his gaze to the floor, he said softly, "Yes."

The Jones Men

Born in 1946, Vern E. Smith has only ever had one novel published. Yet that lone title, *The Jones Men* (1974), is a classic of inner-city street literature and a significant item within the canon of black pulp. Smith, a career journalist, penned an acclaimed *Newsweek* magazine story on heroin culture in Detroit and later used that research and the connections he made to author a work of fiction based on his findings.

"I had spent a couple of weeks reporting what became the *Newsweek* article entitled 'Detroit's Heroin Subculture,'" Smith explains.

> The article drew quite a bit of attention in Detroit. One of the columnists for the *Free Press* wrote a column about the *Newsweek* piece. There was a hearing before the city council with various police officials, which concluded that the *Newsweek* story had accurately described the drug problem ravaging the city. I developed other sources and was doing further reporting with plans to turn the story into a nonfiction book, when I received a call from an editor at Warner Books. He said how much they had liked the story and was interested in having me do a novel on the subject.

The Jones Men, which reads like a cross between an Iceberg Slim novel and George V. Higgins's *The Friends of Eddie Coyle* (1970), covers a whole swath of characters involved in Motor City's heroin trade of the early seventies: high-end dealers and midlevel pushers, common users and their partners, sleazy narcotics cops and their informants, women who work for or date the dealers, and so on. A "jones man" is somebody who effectively uses the drug dealing business to become a heavy moneymaker and player on the scene. Lots of dudes would like to be the top jones man, but there's only room for one kingpin.

The story, which takes place over a three-week span of a Detroit winter, basically involves two drug gangs. At the tale's beginning, Willis McDaniel is in control of the heroin trade within a roughly twenty-five-mile stretch

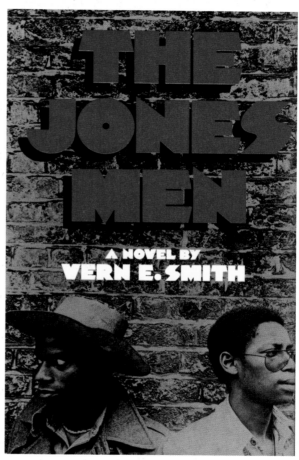

The Jones Men (Weidenfeld & Nicolson, 1974)

of the city's turf. He's got a fleet of flash cars, personal bodyguards, dealers, girls, and other people working for him, an empire he's been running for over a decade. The other outfit is led by a twenty-six-year-old Vietnam vet named Lennie Jack. Jack wants to move in on McDaniel's trade and is given a possible opening when a conniving user named Foxy Newton hears about a big shipment of heroin coming to McDaniel from New York. Newton tells Jack's crew about this, prompting Jack and a team of his men to hijack the transaction and steal the dope. After this, Jack looks to use the large stash and the money he can make from selling it, to set himself up as the new top jones man in the area. McDaniel, meanwhile, sets his fiercest henchmen to the streets in search of the people who stole his stuff, as well as the rat who tipped them off. The local cops catch wind of the escalating tensions within the factions, and they start using informants and undercover agents to try to get a handle on what exactly is going down. The taut story shifts from one set of memorable characters to the next over a succession of brief chapters, all the while hurtling in the direction of a full-on gang war.

Smith, who was a relative newcomer to Detroit while doing research for *Newsweek* and was gone again by the time the novel was published, shares some of his initial perceptions of the city:

> I had been living in Detroit maybe six or eight months when I began to realize that something very different was happening in the city. I noticed it the first time I entered a small neighborhood store in the inner city and saw that the clerk was enclosed in a plexiglass cage with a little revolving window that you put your money in. Coming from California where I had been a newspaper reporter, I'd never seen that before, and as I got to know the city, I discovered this glass cage was a standard thing. I began to notice the big, chromed-up cars cruising the Detroit streets, and the news reports of trussed up bodies found in a "dope house," the first time I had heard that term. Subsequently, I realized that it was all connected to the burgeoning heroin trade. The street term "jones" had come into use to describe the craving for the drug.

In the *Newsweek* article, Smith reported:

> The national blight of heroin addiction is nowhere more acute than in Detroit. The fine white powder is a pall over the city's black ghetto, producing, by conservative estimates, a $350 million take and at least 30,000 addicts—making probably the highest per-capita addiction rate in the U.S.... The heroin boom stems, in large part, from economic blight. In the brief prosperity that that followed the 1967 riots, blacks from the South flocked to Detroit auto plants for work. But good times were short-lived. Nowadays, unemployment is staggering: in the 16-to-22 age group, where most of the city's heroin addicts fall, the jobless rate currently runs 45 to 50 percent. And as the Vietnam war winds down, more and more returning black veterans are being dumped onto the city's streets—where Jones, not jobs, awaits them.

The book opens in startling fashion. The first scene is at a wake for a mid-level heroin dealer who took some liberties with his boss and wound up dead. Players are at the wake in flash clothing and some of them sprinkle cocaine onto the dead man's corpse. And there's this quote from one of the guests at the service: "'We oughta drink a toast to Bennie Lee,' Mack Lee said, 'and ask the Lord how come he made him so stupid.'"

And this from Smith's omniscient narrator:

> The early Sunday morning joggers had found him floating on his back, grotesquely half-smiling from the murky waters at Beckman Pier, his belly bloated and the .357 Magnum bullets in his forehead.
>
> Bennie Lee Sims was gone, so tonight they'd see him off and wish him well; tomorrow they'd compete for his dope bag.

Smith does an excellent job of creating a heavy urban atmosphere in the novel, by way of rich city characters and their vividly described hangouts. People with names like Foxy, Crow, T.C., St. Louis, and Lennie Jack wear floppy hats and furs and cruise around Detroit in conspicuous El Dorados and Fleetwoods. They listen to Aretha Franklin, Al Green, and Miles Davis. Everybody talks in a kind of hard-edged soulful style. The happenings occur in places like projects units, shabby motel rooms, rib joints, and out on the streets. There are all manner of players from the drug-dealing scene, from the high-end jones men to their street dealers to everyday users. There's also hit men, seedy narcotics cops, and the double-dealing creeps they use to get their inside information, and the women who are the lovers of and/or work for the heroin dealers. The story, which takes place over a short span of time, occurs during one of Michigan's bitter winters. Here's a typical passage:

> The last remnants of yesterday's snowstorm had melted into icy puddles that sloshed along the narrow curb and into the foul street sewers. A full moon shining through the rows of oak saplings along the sidewalk bathed the blocks of brick-finished flats on Elmworth Street in eerie shadows.

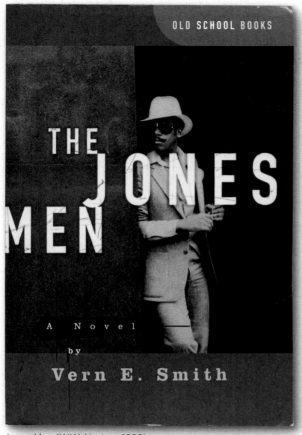

Jones Men (W.W. Norton, 1998)

Lennie Jack maneuvered the Fleetwood slowly up Elmworth, looking for No. 2316.

"That's it there," Joe Red said from the passenger seat. "The house with the sheet or something over the window. Over here on the right. See it?"

Lennie Jack slowed the car in the middle of the block and stared at the row of flats on the right.

"Yeah, that looks like the one."

He drove down the next intersection and waited for the traffic to clear, then made a U-turn and headed back up Elmworth.

Lennie Jack pulled the car over to the curb across from the row of flats in the 2300 block. He cut the lights and they waited in the darkness.

Asked how authoring this work of fiction differed from his experiences in the writing of journalism, Smith reflects:

On one level, the writing in the novel was very different in that it sprang from my imagination, whereas in journalism everything has to be attributed to facts. At the same time, the way I developed as a writer—journalism, novels, screenplays, it's all the same thing to me, trying to get clarity on the page. I wrote for my high school newspaper, and also TV scripts and fiction because it was enjoyable. In college I was a sports columnist and later sports editor of the campus daily at San Francisco State University. My minor was Radio, TV, Film, and I studied screenwriting. The first thing I ever sold outside journalism was a story I wrote for the television series Mannix, about a private eye. I was working as a newspaper reporter in Long Beach, right outside Los Angeles and taking screenwriting classes in a program run by the Writer's Guild. My instructor liked a sample script I had written and arranged a pitch meeting with the show's producers. They liked one of my ideas and signed me to write a full story treatment. The story was never produced, but I did earn a fee nearly half my year's salary as a first-year reporter. Right after that I got an offer from *Newsweek* and moved to Detroit.

As mentioned above, the novel reads as much like one of George V. Higgins's early books as it does any other work of black pulp. Queried as to whether he read any crime fiction in preparation of penning *The Jones Men*, Smith explains: "I read *The Friends of Eddie Coyle* by George V. Higgins, at the suggestion of my editor, and *The Godfather* (1969) by Mario Puzo, which had been published a few years earlier. I had read the Chester Himes detective novels set in Harlem, and was familiar with the Iceberg Slim books from my college days."

This bit of talk from one narcotics cop to another could come from the mouth one of Higgins's characters:

"I realized something unusual was going on when I came in this morning," Boone said. "I drove through that Oak Grove area we passed through the other day and got all those license numbers. You know how they were parked all over the sidewalk the other day, up and down the street? Well, I didn't see one car when I drove through this morning. No Lincolns, no Broughams, El Dorados. Nothing. I figured something had happened to upset everybody. You know dope pushers don't get out of bed before twelve o'clock."

The Jones Men is so well done, a reader would naturally assume its author would go on to craft more works of fiction. The book was nominated for an Edgar Award and was applauded by the *New York Times*. Yet Smith has never published another novel. Why?

My calling was reporting, and it didn't really change after the book. I came into journalism at a time when the country was in crisis, on the heels of a wave of urban riots, and major media being excoriated by a Presidential Commission for its failure to provide coverage on the causes and consequences of these civil disorders. I saw being a journalist as a way to have impact, plus I really enjoyed the challenge of the work. I chose not to try and be both a hotshot novelist and a hotshot journalist at the same time, but I've written other novels, and I will publish them.

There has been talk through the years of a film adaptation of *The Jones Men*. It hasn't happened yet, however, and this is a shame as the story is perfectly ripe for the conversion to a big screen feature. Smith:

The movie and television rights to *The Jones Men* are available at the time of this writing. The book was actually first optioned when it was still in galleys. When that option period ended, I got the rights back. Some years later, I worked with a producer who loved the book and convinced me to write a screenplay, and we were close to a deal with a production company, but it didn't happen.

One of the interesting things about the current revival of the novel is that a new generation of readers are drawn to it because they were fans of the HBO series *The Wire* and see parallels in that show and the book published 30 years earlier. I tell people if you liked *The Wire*, then give *The Jones Men* a look. It has some things in there that aren't in *The Wire*. In addition to the gritty realism and lack of sentimentality in the story, I think the thing some people are surprised and drawn in by is the large, diverse cast of characters from all walks of life, and how they interact with each other in *The Jones Men*. It's still something that you rarely find in books and almost never found on television before *The Wire*. The dealers, the police, the big money men and the junkies operate on a near-equal footing in the novel, which provides an air of uncertainty and suspense for the reader in the same way it did for viewers of *The Wire*.

A scene such as the following could be effectively transposed to celluloid:

The Casa Del Grato had two landings with stairs at opposite ends of the place. Lennie Jack and Joe Red hurried across the concrete parking lot to the steps to the far end. They went up the stairs and down the second landing to room 208. Lennie Jack rapped his knuckles on the worn wooden door.

A voice on the other side said, "Who is it?"

"Jack."

… The room was aged and had a faint musty odor. Lennie Jack nodded to the young man seated in a chair near the door with a carbine resting across his knee. Beyond him, a black and white television set and a ragged vinyl chair had been shoved to the far side of the room and jammed against the wall next to the bad. A small table in the middle of the floor took up the vacant space. A young man in a purple wide-brimmed hat, no shirt, and a .38 holster across his bare back was seated at the table with a marble square in front of him and a sifter in his hand. There were several hexes of aluminum foil on the table, bottles of lactose and quinine and a half-filled plastic bag of heroin. The man in the purple hat was carefully sifting handfuls of a mixture of quinine and heroin and scraping the filtering off the slab into strips of tin foil.

Several tin foil bricks were stacked against the wall; there was a shotgun resting in the corner near the bricks; there were two handguns lying atop the small dresser. J.J. came back to his chair at the table with Lennie Jack and Joe Red at his heels.

"How's it goin'?" Lennie Jack said. "You get a pretty good start on it?"

Whether or not Vern E. Smith ever has another novel published, he is an important author in the world of black pulp because of *The Jones Men*. It is a classic of inner-city street lit.

Brian Greene

The Front Runner, **Patricia Nell Warren** (William Morrow, 1974)

By the mid-1970s there were clear signs that lesbian and gay liberation movements were having a deep impact on American society. The more staid campaigning of the 1950s had overturned the use of obscenity laws to prevent the distribution of gay and lesbian publications via the mail, and in 1961 Illinois became the first state to decriminalize homosexuality. But it was in the context of the new mood of cultural pride of the 1970s that other forms of legal and informal persecution were significantly challenged. As local counties began to enact antidiscrimination ordnances, the Religious Right coalesced, in some cases rolling back gains. In turn those under attack were further politicized, and their support base broadened, leading to the defeat by popular vote of California's Proposal 6 in 1978. If passed, this would have banned the hiring of lesbians and gays in schools across the state. Major breakthroughs regarding immigration, healthcare, work, and other rights would be decades in the making, and homophobia persists to this day. Nevertheless, the fact that religious conservatives felt compelled to countermobilize was proof enough that change was afoot.

A more modest indicator was the immense popularity of gay romance novel *The Front Runner*. Released by William Morrow and Company in 1974, with a paperback via Bantam following shortly after, it would go on to sell more than ten million copies. Not only did its success demonstrate that an audience for gay-positive stories existed, but the book's plot and leading characters challenged prevailing stereotypes. Through this and its exposure of the damages of homophobia, the novel played its own part in pushing back prejudice.

The Front Runner opens with athletics coach Harlan Brown quietly working at New York State's Prescott College. Six years earlier the former marine had been training the cream of the crop at prestigious Penn State, until rumors regarding his sexuality saw him forced out of the job. Despite the existence of a gay lib group at Prescott and the college's general ethos of "tough and virile liberalism" he remains in the closet, discontented but accepting his lot in life.

All this is rapidly upended when three top athletes, Billy Sives, Vince Matti, and Jacques La Font, show up at his office. Sives reveals that Matti and La Font had recently been caught by head coach Gus Lindquist "fooling around in the locker room. . . . They were being very sexy and Vince was taking off

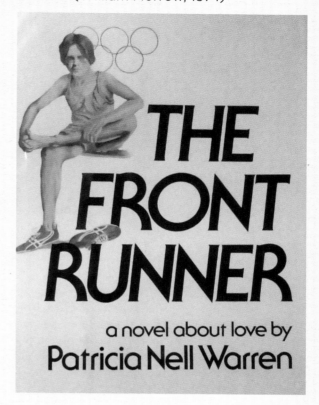

The Front Runner (William Morrow, 1974)

Jacques's belt. . . . They sassed him and said that gay lib had come to Oregon U and a lot of other crap." Vince explains, "Lindquist was fucking livid, man. He put Jacques on the rack and Billy's name came out. And Lindquist is a big straight fascist, so there went our scholarships." Having been hipped to Brown's past by Sives's father, a leading gay rights activist, the trio have hitchhiked across the country in the hope he'll let them join Prescott's track team. This immediately presents Brown with a double quandary. Given the trio's openness about their sexuality, not only is the task likely to fully push him out of the closet, but upon meeting Sives he's experienced love at first sight. Indeed love for the first time at all.

The backstory of Brown's life that follows provides readers with a rapid-fire, single chapter summary of gay life for many in the 1950s and '60s. We learn of a youthful crush that was only requited at the last minute and later dalliances at beats, saunas and movie theaters while building a career as a track coach and maintaining a respectable heterosexual front. With his marriage crumbling after the Penn State sacking, and alimony and child support payments due, Brown reinvents himself as a male model. Due to his "martyr/celebrity" status he soon progresses, in his words, to being "a very expensive, exclusive hustler" with "more business than I could handle" due to a "small, but solid market for meat like mine . . . a hard, angry, bitter, mature beauty." Having taken part in the Stonewall riots, the former conservative feared "growing anger at the gay sufferings would have led me—unwillingly but inevitably—into violent gay activism." But with philanthropist Joe Prescott seeking him out to fill a vacancy at Prescott, he instead resumed his coaching career, joining a faculty "full of brilliant cast-offs."

It doesn't take the narrator/protagonist long to throw his lot in with the elite young sportsmen and over the next three hundred pages we're not only treated to a love story but also an education regarding the politics, pitfalls, and practices of American athletics. Dogged by hostility and underhanded moves from the sports press and establishment, as well as injuries and blandishments from supposed allies for moving too fast, the group suffer immense pressure. Matti and La Font fall by the wayside, but Brown and Sives push all the way through to the Montreal Olympics, gaining respect and getting married along the way. Due to a growing homophobic backlash, tragedy awaits, but the story's tone and eventual outcome is a world away from the suicides and nervous breakdowns with which many writers, often at the behest of their editors, had concluded gay novels during earlier decades.

Although many initially believed the name Patricia Nell Warden was, in keeping with many gay novelists of the time, a pseudonym, the author had decided to go with her own name, something she recalled in a 2010 interview "would also mean that I myself was coming out, so the entire endeavor was a bit scary." Warden received criticism from "some in the gay community who felt that I had somehow broken the rules, being a woman and writing about men." At the same time, the book was widely embraced by gay and lesbian audiences, and numerous anecdotes and tributes can be found online in which people fondly describe it as a formative influence. During the 1970s the first LGBTIQ jogging, walking, and track group emerged in San Francisco, named the Front Runners, and more than a hundred chapters formed thereafter.

The Front Runner largely drew on the author's experiences as a long-distance runner. During the late 1960s and the 1970s she had been involved in forcing the powerful Amateur Athletics Union to change its rules regarding women, both through illegally participating in marathons as well as via intensive campaigning and lobbying. Writing in a 2013 column, she disclosed that while grappling with her own sexuality she had "been running into other people like myself at the races, and we acknowledged each other quietly, subtly." In 1972 at a party she met a young athlete who "came out to me, just like that, over two styrofoam cups of carrot juice, told me that he'd decided to give up his shot at the Olympic 1,500 meter because he was tired of lying . . . at the open amateur races, he could be out and himself. He was happy." Realizing that this could make for a powerful follow up to her 1971 debut *The Last Centennial*, her original idea involved a lesbian coach and runner. "There weren't any women Olympic track coaches," however. "Consequently, for the story to be real, it had to be about men."

Warren would return to the characters from *The Front Runner* with *Harlan's Race* in 1994 and *Billy's Boy* in 1997. She also produced a nonfiction sports collection entitled *The Lavender Locker Room* in 2006. Meanwhile, *The Front Runner* has been issued in various languages and has never gone out of print.

Iain McIntyre

The Front Runner (Bantam, 1975)

THE FRONT RUNNER

The night the Stonewall was busted, I was in the neighborhood on business. Someone had called my client and we got out of bed and ran over there to see, because we hadn't been able to believe our ears.

The street was full of cops and flashing red lights. But what was more amazing, the street was full of hundreds of gays, and they were fighting the cops. For years they had run, let themselves be shoved to the wall, submitted to harassments and arrest, because they felt in their hearts that it was their fate. But the night of Stonewall, they made the instant visceral decision that they had had enough. They were throwing rocks and bottles, your "powderpuff pansies" were. They were fighting New York's Finest with their bare hands. They were daring the nightsticks to crunch on their bodies.

I watched with growing anger and sorrow. I didn't drink, but those bars were about the only public places where gays could be themselves. No straight could understand how precious they were to us. I had always believed in law and order, supported the police. But the cops were busting me, busting my entire lifetime of anguish. They were riding over me with their big horses, and shoving me into vans handcuffed.

Then an amazing thing happened. I had a rock in my hand, and I threw it with all the deadly accuracy of a Marine throwing a grenade. Me, Harlan Brown, the pride of the Marines, I threw a rock at the cops. I punched a cop. I completely forgot I might wind up in jail. I found myself against a wall, being beaten by two big cops. Then I was on the ground in the crush, being kicked and stomped. Somebody rode a horse over me.

Somehow, in the confusion, I managed to get away, bleeding and battered, with three cracked ribs and a broken nose and a few hoofprints on me.

Something cracked in my head that night, and in the heads of the gays. That night saw the coming out of the militant gay. After that they were fighting everybody in sight, demanding human rights and fairer laws. I was not exactly ready for radical activism. But it had dawned on me that I was now a citizen of a nation where straight Americans did not permit the flag to fly.

The Dark Angel Series, James D. Lawrence (Pyramid, 1975)

Author James D. Lawrence was most prolific as one of the Stratemeyer Syndicate's army of ghost writers. Pseudonymously, he wrote various titles for children's mystery company in the Hardy Boys, Nancy Drew, Tom Swift, and Christopher Cool series.

In the late 1960s he took over writing the James Bond comic strip for Britain's *Daily Express*, which was also syndicated internationally. In 1969 he partnered with artist Jorge Longaron for a new comic strip for the *Chicago Tribune. Friday Foster,* which followed the globetrotting adventures of a model turned photographer, was the first nationally syndicated strip to feature a black woman as the main character. Pam Grier appeared in a film adaptation of the comic strip late in the blaxploitation phase of her career, but Lawrence was not involved in the adaptation.

Contemporary to the film version of *Friday Foster* is Lawrence's four-volume Dark Angel series, which at first blush sounds like a vehicle tailor-made for Grier's screen persona. The series, all of which was published in 1975, contains pulp fiction's first black female private eye, a girl who came up the hard way and now devotes herself to the mercenary (and lucrative) work of solving the toughest cases on the mean streets of 1970s New York, armed with a purse full of Bond-like gadgets, an Ivy League degree, all of the wisdom of the Mysterious East and, when necessary, heavy artillery. Unfortunately, the series doesn't live up to its promise, instead offering a truly weird look into the kinky fantasies of its white, male audience.

Angela Harpe's (a.k.a. The Dark Angel) early years are quickly glossed over in the first volume. Born to a junkie mother in Detroit, she suffers a childhood of neglect and abuse before landing at Radcliffe College, graduating *summa cum laude*, and going on to a career as an international model and call girl (the two went hand in hand in the world of seventies men's pulp fiction), before joining the NYPD (from which she resigned after a year, after being repeatedly cited for brutality) and then setting up shop as a private investigator.

Now at the age of twenty-five, Angie is at the top of her game, commanding huge fees from the insurance companies that retain her services without asking too many questions about the underworld criminals who turn up beaten half to death, affixed with a decal bearing the silhouette of a harp-playing angel as a trademark and a warning.

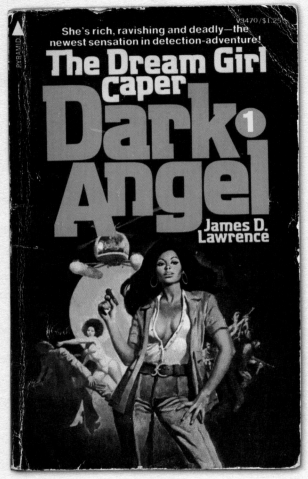

The Dream Girl Caper (Pyramid, 1975)

Angie is the "Exceptional Woman" personified: having overcome the hardships of her childhood on strength of character alone, her luxury apartment in midtown Manhattan is furnished by Eames, the paintings are by Picasso, and all of her books are first editions. She easily moves between the street and high society, shaking down a junkie informant in a Tenth Avenue dive bar and discussing Rothko with a billionaire oil tycoon without pausing for breath.

For the most part, the plots are extremely repetitive: a white Establishment type attempts to retain the services of the notorious Dark Angel, and Angie's curiosity is piqued enough to take on the case, immediately throwing her into highly sexualized situations involving the kinky secrets of New York's rich and famous. Titillation is the order of the day: at the first sign of trouble, Angie is required to either seduce the enemy or yield to rapists, and the plot mechanics conspire to keep her helpless until the moment she can bust out the judo moves or her custom Baby Browning revolver. The nominal plots quickly deteriorate into a tiresome cycle of debasement and revenge.

The biggest tip-off about the intended readership for the series is Angie's assigned love interests: in each book she is paired off with a square white dude, including a stuffy Madison Avenue executive, a dull preppy type, and the sexually puritanical scion of Big Oil. Black men are regulated to the role of platonic pals, ex–Green Berets, or Delta Force operatives, always ready with a helicopter to get Angie and her boyfriend of the week out of a jam.

Angie also has the occasional lesbian interlude in the series. While the lesbian characters are by and large crude caricatures, dykes and deviants, Angie gets a pass as a bisexual, keeping in touch with her former colleagues from her call girl days, who prove themselves useful for both information and an afternoon romp between the sheets. She is nothing if not efficient.

The plots are slight, although several take a stab at then-topical issues, including the ongoing oil crisis (*The Emerald Oil Caper*) and the Patty Hearst kidnapping (*The Gilded Snatch Caper*). The focus remains on sex and violence, using a rapid influx of minor characters that are positioned for importance and then promptly never heard from again.

The violence that climaxes each of these plots is large in scale and cartoonish in tone, always involving bombs and explosions, as Angie and her comrades take up guns of increasing magnitude to rush into the final firefight, Uzis and bazookas blazing away. In this respect the series could be almost prescient: the cinematic finales are less the lone avenger of the *Dirty Harry*–and–*Death Wish* '70s and more *Rambo*-like in both degree and mood.

In addition to the sex and violence, the other notable aspect of the series is its use of language, which like the sex and violence manages to be vulgar and colorful without being creative. In the world of the Dark Angel, a woman is a "fox," a good-looking man is a "dude," and everyone else is a "wop," "dyke," "whore," "hymie," "gash," "lez," "faggot," "dinge," "spade," "suede," or "corn-holing, bog-trotting mick." As such, the series features minor characters such as an informant named Moonshit and a pimp called Long Dong Strong. Lawrence *does* do slightly better with his *femmes fatales*,

Angela Harpe had grown up in the festering Harlem slums—had plied her trade as a call girl in the deadly world of black pimps and white vice lords—had dealt with thieves, perverts, pushers, killers and equally deadly rogue cops during her stint on the NYPD—and had faced death a score of times since embarking on her career as a private eye.

But when the elderly dude in the black executioner's mask chuckled, her blood ran cold.

He smelled her blue bikini panties again, like a French courtier sniffing a pomander ball, and eyed her expectantly. "Well, Miss Harpe? Have you reached a decision yet on whether or not you will take the assignment?"

"I'll think it over and let you know in twenty-four hours."

"I'm afraid that won't do, Miss Harpe. I must know now."

From *The Emerald Oil Caper*

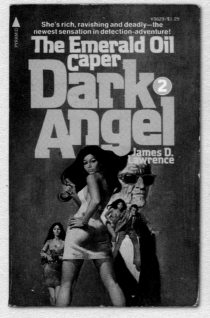

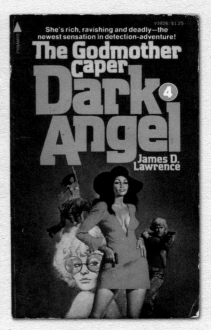

The Emerald Oil Caper (Pyramid, 1975)   *The Gilded Snatch Caper* (Pyramid, 1975)   *The Godmother Caper* (Pyramid, 1975)

whose names recall his roots in the Bond comic strip. Throughout the series the reader is too-briefly introduced to the likes of Vale Trent, Konya Cargill, Dove Glade, and Star Kenning, "the she-wolf of Wall Street."

And any humor regarding the language is strictly single-entendre: *The Gilded Snatch Caper* refers to a missing woman's dyed-blonde pubic hair.

While the first three volumes, which also included *The Dream Girl Caper* are monotonously similar, the fourth, *The Godmother Caper*, can be singled out both for slightly higher writing quality and for the possible intent of the author to take the series in a new direction.

Godmother is notable for finally bringing some real New York City color to the writing: while the prior books name-checked various locations, this one has more of a feel for the various neighborhoods in which the story unfolds. At one point, Angie explicitly references Mayor John Lindsay's infamous 1966 comment about New York being a "fun city" (which came to combine both affection and distress at the city's declining fortunes), as she forms an uneasy alliance with a Mafia-backed vigilante group called WOMAR—Wipe Out Muggers And Rapists—possibly the most noble sentiment heard of in any of the series.

This volume also reveals Angie's past as a CIA operative, involved in various missions around the world with names like Operation Ding Dong and Operation Hot Twat. Late in the book she gets an unwelcome visit

from a new domestic intelligence agency code-named ALICE, "set up after Watergate, to pick up the pieces following the Nixon debacle." This is a twist that attempts to recast Angie as a distaff James Bond, again returning to Lawrence's comic strip roots. Whether this new direction could have made for a more engaging series remains unknown, as this was the final book published.

The impression that remains of the series for the modern reader is a dreary one. The depressing treatment of blacks and women (and specifically the black woman given star billing) sucks any of the campy fun out of the fantasy, leaving behind a depraved, demoralizing fantasy for its intended white, male readership.

Molly Grattan

The Monkey Wrench Gang, Edward Abbey (J.B. Lippincott, 1975)

Born in 1927 and raised in Pennsylvania, pioneering environmental author Edward Abbey was exposed to radical influences from an early age by his anarchist, atheist father. A trip across the U.S. in 1944 saw his life-long passion for Western desertscapes catalyzed, later leading to fifteen years' part-time work as a ranger as well as the composition of his classic nonfiction work, *Desert Solitaire* (1968). Providing an immediate contrast, a two-year stint in the army that followed his initial wanderings solidified the budding writer's antiauthoritarian impulses. His open opposition to conscription in the 1940s and '50s would subsequently draw the attention of the FBI. Having scored a prestigious Fulbright academic scholarship in 1952, Abbey saw his first novel, the semiautobiographical *Jonathon Troy*, published two years later, beginning a writing career that would result in dozens of essays and non-fiction works as well as a further seven novels.

In 1975's *The Monkey Wrench Gang*, fury at the industrial desecration of the West leads a small group of misfits to carry out an unremitting and epic campaign of counterdestruction. Named after their favorite instrument for dismantling bulldozers, trains, and other tools of ecological devastation, the team is made up of Vietnam veteran and former Green Beret George Hayduke, polygamous renegade Mormon river guide "Seldom Seen" Smith, eccentric surgeon Doc Sarvis, and New Ager Bonnie Abbzug. Keeping one step ahead of the law and never causing physical harm to humans, the band range across Utah and Arizona lopping down billboards and disrupting the activities of miners, road construction companies and developers before homing in on the Glen Canyon Dam. The dam's construction during the 1950s and '60s had flooded the surrounding area earning it and its builders Abbey's lifelong enmity.

Combining the influence of American nature writers such as Henry David Thoreau and Aldo Leopold with the cartoonish rambunctiousness of cowboy novels, as well as its author's sardonic and at times corny humor, *The Monkey Wrench Gang* received rave reviews upon its release. Despite valid criticisms regarding the sexist portrayal of female characters and occasionally offensive language, the novel had right-fully come to be regarded as a classic by the time of Abbey's death in 1989. A tenth-anniversary edition, illustrated by noted comix artist Robert Crumb was

The Monkey Wrench Gang (J.B. Lippincott, 1975)

produced in 1985, with another in 1990 adding further images and a previously deleted chapter.

Although there were plenty of radical novels in the 1970s riffing off current events, *The Monkey Wrench Gang* was a rare beast in that it not only tapped into the zeitgeist of the times, in this case by addressing ecological concerns, but also presaged and inspired a political movement. When the Earth First! network kicked off in 1980 in reaction to the faltering efforts of mainstream environmentalists long captive to insider politics, it not only counted Abbey as a mentor but popularized the real-life practice of "monkeywrenching," committing sabotage in defense of nature. As with Abbey's 1975 novel these new activists took cues from Michigan's "Billboard Bandits," Illinois's "The Fox," and Florida's "Eco-Commandoes," as well as other troublemakers who targeted corporate polluters through pranks and actions such as sealing up waste pipes and chimneys. Unlike their early-1970s forebears, Earth First! rapidly grew into a movement, carrying out hundreds of protests and actions from 1980 onward and sprouting chapters across the globe.

The movement not only embraced Abbey's love of wild places and disdain for industrial society but also his derisive humor; applying it to both their opponents and themselves via song and theatrical protest. Paying tribute to both the author and *The Monkey Wrench Gang*, Earth First! used the monkey wrench, alongside a stone-age hammer, as its key symbol, and one of the network's first iconic actions involved rolling a giant "crack" made of black plastic down the Glen Canyon Dam. A group of anonymous activists who later spiked a grove of ancient trees in 1985, driving nails into their trunks and publicizing their act with the aim of making logging uneconomical, chose to do so under the name of "The Bonnie Abbzug Feminist Garden Party."

For his part Abbey attended some of the network's early protests and gatherings, with the latter, to his approval, combining wilderness forays with campfire sing-a-longs, hard drinking and partying. A posthumously published sequel to *The Monkey Wrench Gang* entitled *Hayduke Lives* (1989) saw the original crew team up with Earth Firsters to combat Goliath, an immense excavator that walks on mechanical legs. The novel and various missives saw Abbey, not entirely convincingly, address criticisms regarding his anti-immigration opinions and one-dimensional, often sexist depictions of women. Some of these complaints came from a faction within Earth First! whose feminism and commitment to economic and social egalitarianism would see most of the author's acolytes leave the network in the late 1980s.

Despite growing opposition toward the more misanthropic side of his philosophies, many within the ecology movement mourned Abbey's passing. Enigmatic and unrepentant to the end, Abbey blew off accepting an award from the American Academy of Arts and Letters in 1987 to go rafting. His body was wrapped in a sleeping bag two years later and laid to rest in an unmarked and illegal desert grave.

Iain McIntyre

For diversion she joined the good doctor on his nighttime highway beautification projects, assisting him in the beginning as driver and lookout. When they tired of fire she learned to hold her own at one end of the crosscut saw. She learned how to swing an ax and how to notch the upright posts of a billboard so as to fell it in any desired direction.

When the doctor acquired a lightweight McCulloch chain saw she learned how to operate that too, how to oil and refuel it, how to adjust the chain when it became too tight or too loose. With this handy tool they were able to accomplish much more work in limited time although it did raise the ecological question, whatever that meant, of noise and air pollution, the excessive consumption of metal and energy. Endless ramifications . . .

"No," the doctor said. "Forget all that. Our duty is to destroy billboards."

Looking for Mr. Goodbar, Judith Rossner (Simon & Schuster, 1975)

Theresa Dunn is an intelligent, single woman living in Manhattan, unremarkable in every respect, except one: she likes to trawl seedy singles bars and pick up men for casual sex. A number-one best seller when it first appeared in 1975, *Looking for Mr. Goodbar*, was billed as an examination of the downside of the sexual liberation of the sixties, which resulted, among other things, from the rise of the counterculture and the easy availability of birth control. According to a quote from Rossner in one of her newspaper obituaries in 2005, its key theme was "Is it okay for women to go screwing around in big cities just because the new morality says it's okay?" The book and the subsequent 1977 film adaption also touched on the widely prevalent perception in the seventies of New York being a dangerous city where violent crime was out of control.

The novel is based on the January 2, 1973, murder of Roseann Quinn, a twenty-eight-year-old New York schoolteacher, who led a so-called double life frequenting singles bars where she picked up men. Quinn's assailant, John Wayne Wilson, was a white Vietnam veteran who had a pregnant young wife and a warrant out for his arrest on charges of armed robbery. Police quickly located and arrested Wilson via information supplied by a man he had met in a Greenwich Village gay bar upon his arrival in New York and with whom he had been staying and having sex with in lieu of paying rent.

Unsurprisingly, much of the media and public reaction to Quinn's murder at the time involved claims she had brought on her own death. The trigger for White killing Quinn was her attempts to throw him out of her apartment after sex. Rossner writes at the beginning of the novel, the most notable aspect of his confession was "a very clear sense of himself as the victim of the women he had murdered."

The actual murder is recounted in the killer's words at the beginning of the novel and, again, at the end of the book from Theresa's point of view. The rest of the story deals with the key events of Theresa's life leading up to her death. The youngest of three sisters, she is brought up in a middle-class family in suburban Bronx, a bookish and polite child. After school, she attends teacher-training college in Manhattan where she has a lengthy affair with one of her teachers, who is married. After her graduation she gets a teaching job in Manhattan and moves into the city.

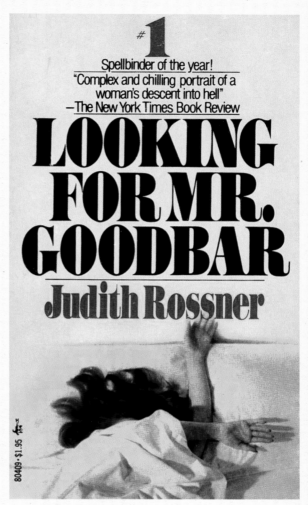

Looking for Mr. Goodbar (Pocket Books, 1976)

Rossner details Theresa's burgeoning post-college sex life. She also details Theresa's relationship with her sisters; Brigid, who lives in the suburbs and is married with children, and Katherine, a sophisticated woman who, like Theresa, has eschewed marriage and lives in Manhattan with her male partner. In the process, Rossner checks off the main signifiers of changing America in the sixties: the Kennedy assassination, Vietnam, the sexual revolution, and the gradual emergence of women's lib (which Theresa is not really into).

The way sexual mores shifted in the second half of the sixties has been the subject of numerous books and films. Often, its portrayal is clichéd, references to "swinging" or "turning on." A great strength of *Looking for Mr. Goodbar* book is how it captures the enormity

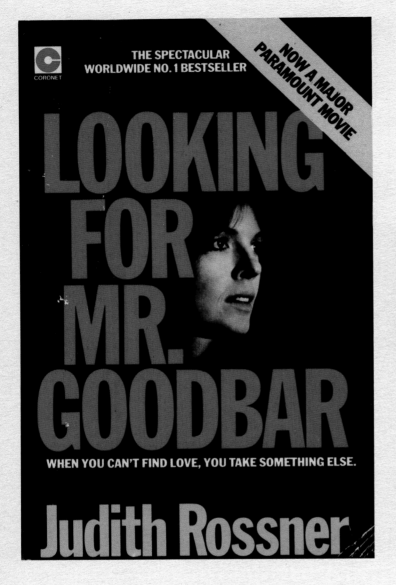

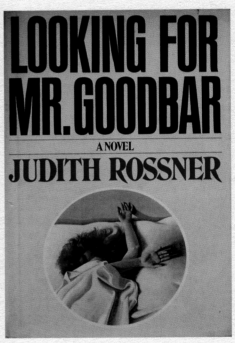

Looking for Mr. Goodbar (Coronet, 1978)
Looking for Mr. Goodbar (Simon & Schuster, 1975)

of the cultural change sweeping America in the sixties and its impact on previously held notions of sex, commitment, drugs, and gender roles. For example, when Katherine tells Theresa she and her partner have started swinging:

> Then we got married and for a while everything was fine. Not that it isn't now, but I mean everything was very regular. Normal. We slept together and we were faithful to each other.... Anyhow, I don't even know how all this—I mean, I sort of know. Not just that there was more grass around all of a sudden, people talking about it,

doing it in the open instead of waiting for the last two or three couples to be left at a party. It was kind of nice, really. It felt like you were in on this really beautiful secret thing. You'd found this way to like your husband, not to be doing anything sneaky but have the extra... you, the stuff that goes away when you're married for a while.

Theresa's first forays into the world of bars and picking up men, too, are not without a sense of how the world is changing. "Theresa felt strange being there. However much she might have read in recent years about women in bars, they were still very much a male preserve, an almost magical kind of place where men went to get away from women."

After a number of anonymous bar pickups, Theresa settles into a routine of sorts with two men. On weeknights she has rough but enjoyable sex with Tony, a hot-tempered working-class Italian garage mechanic, with a shady past. On weekends she sees James, a caring, earnest lawyer who lives in the suburbs with his mother who has been paralyzed by a stroke. James wants a serious relationship with Theresa, including marriage and kids. He is even sympathetic to her flirtation with feminism—anathema to most middle-class white men.

"I may join a women's group," she said to James the next time she saw him.

"Oh?" James said. "That sounds interesting."

"Why?"

"Well," he said, "because they seem to be trying to come to grips with a lot of real problems women have."

The stress of maintaining two relationships, particularly with the unstable, hot-tempered Tony, combined with picking up men in bars, puts a strain on Theresa and leads to her decision to pick up Wilson.

Looking for Mr. Goodbar was based on an article Rossner wrote for *Esquire* magazine on Quinn's murder, which was axed by the magazine's lawyers due to fears it would prejudice Wilson's pending trial. The murder was also the subject of a 1977 book by Lacey Fosburgh entitled *Closing Time: The True Story of the "Goodbar" Murder.* Rossner was incredibly unhappy with the 1977 film version starring Diane Keaton, telling a *Washington Post* reporter: "I feel like the mother who delivered her thirteen-year-old daughter to the door of Roman Polanski and didn't know what was going to happen."

Theresa embodies the one-sided nature of "freedom" experienced by many women in the West in the late sixties and seventies, sex without equality. She appears to be in charge sexually but her control is fragile and one-dimensional. A *New York Times* review in June 1975 said the novel "speaks to a larger question, how much control do women have over their own lives." Theresa lacks the language to discuss her own pleasure let alone wider equality.

Andrew Nette

They left Corners and began walking downtown. He said wait a minute, he'd find a cab, but she didn't want to wait. She wanted to walk. He gave in but she knew that he was giving in because he knew that she had already given in. She sang Beatles songs. She sang "Day Tripper" and "I Want to Hold Your Hand" and "Norwegian Wood" and then she began all over again. He put his arm around her because she was shivering in the cold.

At her apartment she fumbled with the keys until finally he took them and opened the door. The light was on as she'd left it when she . . . a hundred years ago.

He closed the door, locked it and took her in his arms. He smelled of beer. He kissed her for a long time. She moved back away from him—toward the bed. He smiled but he looked like a beast of prey. She sat on the edge of the bed and kicked off her shoes and turned off the light. In the darkness she could just see him taking off his jacket, then his tie, then his shoes.

"Well doctor," she said giggling, "*now* what are you going to do for my own good?"

"Only what you want, teach," he said. "I'm only going to give you what you want for your own good."

He lay down on top of her. He was heavy but she didn't mind. It didn't matter, any more than it mattered that she didn't like him. His body was there and felt good. They made love. He wasn't tender but he was competent and when they finished she fell asleep.

Hatchett, Lee McGraw (Ballantine Suspense, 1976)

Despite the novel's sultry cover promising "A PRIVATE EYE WHO'S NO LADY!," Chicago PI Madge Hatchett is more focused on action than she is on sex, and this novel reads like a sly satire of Mickey Spillane with a gender-reversal twist.

Like Mike Hammer, Madge Hatchett is an ex-cop, and maintains a close working relationship with her former captain. Like Hammer, Hatchett also has a preoccupation with cases involving drugs and pornography; she is supported by a colorful cast of ethnic "types," miscreants, and those living on the margins of society; and like her male counterpart, she tends to use violence as a first resort. It is typical of the hard-boiled humor employed by McGraw that it isn't revealed until halfway through the second chapter that "Hatchett" is female.

The action starts with the murder of Danny O'Brien, the doorman at Hatchett's Lincoln Park high-rise apartment, an ex-junkie that she had arrested during her policewoman days and helped to go straight after his release from prison. After exchanging some crime-scene banter with Captain Pete Connolly, she vows to find his killer. The publicity surrounding the murder brings another case to her door, this one involving a young U.S. Army medic named Mark Flynn, freshly back from Vietnam who had plans to stay with his brother, a neighbor of Hatchett's, upon his discharge. When his brother fails to meet him and hasn't shown at his apartment two days later, Mark calls on Hatchett after seeing her mentioned in a newspaper story about Danny's murder.

As she digs further into each of these cases, Hatchett begins to suspect they are related. All roads lead to the shadowy Mr. Big, a brutal new boss in gangland Chicago with connections ranging from the lowlifes hanging around a decaying Wrigley Field to the high-living lowlifes at the Playboy Mansion.

McGraw's storytelling is generally apolitical, limited to Hatchett commenting on the misogyny directed at her from the men she encounters. This includes noting the fact that most aren't creative enough to come up with an epithet other than "bitch" and protesting her "Bloody Madge" nickname within the Chicago PD, based on her violent reputation as a cop and the body count in her PI career, pointing out that if she were a man they'd be calling her "a goddam hero." Unlike many crime novels written by men, a rape scene midway through the novel is vicious, unsexy and clearly not intended to titillate the reader.

As with Mike Hammer, Hatchett's appearance is left largely up to the imagination of the reader, although in passing she is compared to both Sophia Loren and Raquel Welch in the looks department. Still, McGraw makes Hatchett as tough as any male detective, using her fists in a fight rather than Judo or other martial arts typical of women in the genre. She also shares an appealing solidarity with women across all social strata. In place of Hammer's network of bookies and shoeshines, Hatchett's informants are manicurists and cocktail waitresses.

There are a few nods to mid-1970s milieus. While she fights racketeers trafficking in heroin and coke by day, Hatchett is not opposed to unwinding with a joint at night, and the crime at the core of the story involves a "blue box" phone phreaking scam. Regardless, it is constantly pointed out that Hatchett and her methods are considered unhip and outmoded: she's spiritually closer to the 1940s versions of Philip Marlowe than she is she to the contemporary crop of TV detectives.

Finally, there is the mystery of authorship: while the ambiguous pseudonym "Lee McGraw" is the pen name of Paul Zakaras, to date he has not published another novel. Which is a shame, because (if I may coin a phrase) *Hatchett* is a knockout.

Molly Grattan

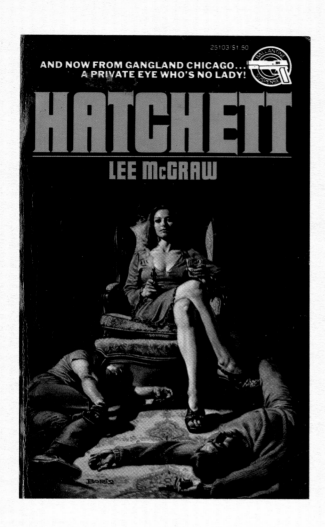

25103 / $1.50

**AND NOW FROM GANGLAND CHICAGO...
A PRIVATE EYE WHO'S NO LADY!**

HATCHETT

LEE McGRAW

Hatchett (Ballantine Suspense, 1976)

The door opened and the prospective client walked in. It turned out to be a he. A tall, well-muscled guy in his early thirties, wearing a canary yellow shirt and matching tie with a shiny peacock-blue blazer and double-knit burgundy pants. His shoes and belt were white. As he looked me over, he flashed a big Tony Franciosa grin.

"Your boss in?" he asked.

I didn't say a word. I put down the phone and stared at him. For a few seconds his bright expression didn't change. Then the grin was replaced by a puzzled frown. He turned from me to the door and back to me again. His eyebrows went up.

"This the detective agency?"

"What does it say on the door, bud?"

"Uh M.L. Hatchett. Investigations."

And then it dawned on him. "Of course!" he grimaced theatrically and snapped his fingers. "You must be—"

"Miz Hatchett."

Meridian, Alice Walker (Harcourt Brace Jovanovich, 1976)

Having grown up in an impoverished sharecropping family in Georgia during the 1940s and '50s, novelist, poet, and essayist Alice Walker became involved in the civil rights movement while studying at Spelman College in Atlanta in 1961 and subsequently took part in voter registration and other campaigns in Mississippi. In 1967 she penned her first published essay, "The Civil Rights Movement: What Good Was It?," which reflected on the proclamation of the death of the civil rights movement by white liberals and radicals and emphatically argued that the movement had broken "the pattern of black servitude in this country."

This essay and Walker's further writings on the state of black activism that followed, were written in the context of calls for nonviolence and integration being superseded by those for self-determination, revolution, and separatism. These changes reflected not only growing self-confidence on the part of oppressed communities but also the resistance the civil rights movement had met from dominant institutions and groups, particularly when campaigning began to tackle deep-seated inequalities. Some southern black communities had long, and for the most part quietly, armed themselves to prevent attacks on campaigners and others. As the rate of change slowed and the movement broadened to tackle police violence and discrimination in northern ghettos, open calls for defensive, and then increasingly offensive, violence arose.

While most of the work of black activists continued to focus on everyday needs and grievances, with far more involved in feeding and educating kids than carrying guns, African American communities increasingly took part in uprisings. Major urban riots—usually sparked by police attacks on black community members but also reflecting frustration at ghetto conditions—numbered in their hundreds, peaking with the "long, hot summer of 1967," during which more than 150 conflagrations occurred. By the time this wave of uprisings wound down in the 1970s hundreds had been killed by the police and national guardsmen, and tens of thousands arrested.

Although civil rights leaders such as Lawrence Guyot acknowledged that within the civil rights movement "it was no secret that young people and women led organizationally," at a public level older men had overwhelmingly dominated. As younger men came

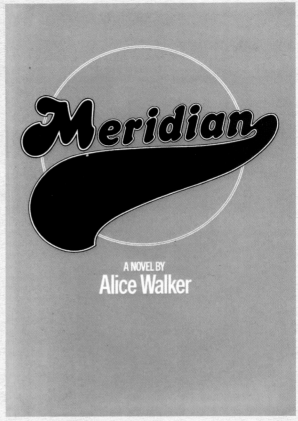

Meridian (Harcourt Brace Jovanovich, 1976)

to the fore in the latter half of the 1960s, the shift to militancy further incorporated patriarchal dominance as an assertion of black pride and masculinity. Both white psychologists and black nationalists pathologized and criticized African American women. The historian Stephanie Coontz notes in her book *A Strange Stirring* that "Psychologist John Dollard, sociologist E. Franklin Frazier, and psychoanalyst/anthropologist Abram Kardiner insisted that black men had been doubly emasculated—first by slavery and later by the economic independence of their women." According to activist and scholar Angela Davis, this meant that for some, "male dominance was considered a necessary prerequisite for black liberation." Radical publications, graphics and statements increasingly erased or denigrated women's role in centuries of struggle while harking back to a mythical Africa in which only men had acted as warriors and protectors. In some cases, as explored in *Meridian,* rape was

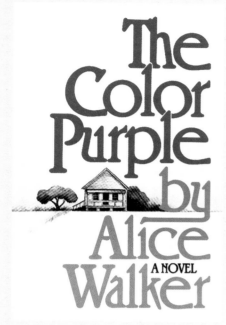

The Color Purple (Harcourt Brace Jovanovich, 1982)

Meridian (Washington Square Press, 1977)

As soon as this line was out of sight, the troopers turned on them, beating and swinging with their bludgeons. One blow knocked Meridian to the ground, where she was trampled by people running back and forth over her. But there was nowhere to run. Only the jail door was open and unobstructed. Within minutes they had been beaten inside, where the sheriff and his deputies waited to finish them. And she realized why Truman was limping. When the sheriff grabbed her by the hair and someone else began punching her and kicking her in the back, she did not even scream, except very intensely in her own mind, and the scream was Truman's name. And what she meant by it was not even that she was in love with him: What she meant by it was that they were at a time and a place in History that forced the trivial to fall away—and they were absolutely together.

Later that summer, after another demonstration, she saw him going down a street that did not lead back to the black part of town. His eyes were swollen and red, his body trembling, and he did not recognize her or even see her. She knew his blankness was battle fatigue. They all had it. She was as weary as anyone, so that she spent a good part of her time in tears. At first she had burst into tears whenever something went wrong or someone spoke unkindly or even sometimes if they spoke, period. But now she was always in a state of constant tears, so that she could do whatever she was doing—canvassing, talking at rallies, tying her sneakers, laughing—while tears rolled slowly and ceaselessly down her cheeks. This might go on for days, or even weeks. Then, suddenly, it would stop, and some other symptom would appear. The shaking of her hands, or the twitch in her left eye. Or the way she would sometimes be sure she'd heard a shot and feel the impact of the bullet against her back; then she stood absolutely still, waiting to feel herself fall.

She went up to a yard with an outdoor spigot and soaked the bottom of her blouse in water. when she came back down to the street to wipe the tear gas from Truman's eyes, he was gone. A police car was careening down the street. She stood in the street feeling the cool wet spot on her side, wondering what to do.

also promoted as a legitimate weapon against white dominance.

As with their white leftist counterparts, some black radicals alternatively or additionally argued that the influence of feminism in the late 1960s was divisive and that struggles regarding sexism needed to be placed on hold until racial oppression had been fully dealt with. Activists such as Frances M. Beal asserted that the subordination of women was already harming and limiting the movement and that it would remain divided until gender inequalities were also addressed.

Many black feminists were in turn critical of white feminist practice and ideology for blindness regarding racial privilege and the way in which white supremacy, and resistance to it, had distinctively shaped African American gender and social relations. Rejecting feminist separatism, the black feminist Combahee River Collective stated in 1977, "Our situation as Black people necessitates that we have solidarity around the fact of race, which white women of course do not need to have with white men, unless it is their negative solidarity as racial oppressors." At the same time the group argued "We struggle together with Black men against racism, while we also struggle with Black men about sexism.... We reject pedestals, queenhood, and walking ten paces behind."

Uniquely affected by racial, gender, and class oppression, black female activists found themselves in an extremely difficult place. And this difficult place is what Walker—and others, such as Toni Morrison, Kristin Hunter, and Toni Cade Bambara—attempted to capture and address in a series of works from the 1970s onward. African American women's activism, and their contrasting experiences and priorities vis-à-vis white, middle-class women in terms of paid and unpaid work, reproductive rights, and gender relations were primarily explored in essays, poetry, and other forms. Novels increasingly emerged that articulated the complexities associated with black and Left movements as they existed, as well as suggested new ways forward. These would have a major political and cultural impact, particularly as books such as *The Color Purple* and *Beloved* came to enjoy mainstream success in the 1980s.

Alice Walker's 1977 novel *Meridian* squarely and directly engages with the experiences of women and men in civil rights and Black Power movements. Critic Roberta M. Hendrickson describes it as "a novel that affirms the Movement's vision of freedom and nonviolence, affirms blackness and African American heritage in a racist society that failed to value and continued to destroy black lives, and focuses on black women and their participation in the Movement, refusing to make them less than they had been."

In doing so, the novel formed part of Walker's evolving articulation of a "womanist" perspective. Elements of this, as outlined in her 1983 book *In Search of Our Mothers' Gardens: Womanist Prose*, include defining "womanist" as:

> A black feminist or feminist of color.... A woman who loves other women, sexually and/or non-sexually. Appreciates and prefers women's culture, women's emotional flexibility (values tears as natural counterbalance of laughter), and women's strength. Sometimes loves individual men, sexually and/or non-sexually. Committed to survival and wholeness of entire people, male and female. Not a separatist, except periodically, for health. . . . Loves music. Loves dance. Loves the moon. *Loves* the Spirit. Loves love and food and roundness. Loves struggle. *Loves* the Folk. Loves herself. *Regardless*.

Written in an at times fractured style, and using a number of short vignettes, *Meridian* reflects this approach by tracing the journey of Meridian Hill, who leaves behind a child and early marriage to enter a life of activism that ultimately damages and fulfills her. Other standpoints come via her severe religious mother Mrs. Hill, Meridian's partner, artist Truman Held, and Lynne Rabinowitz, a white student whom Truman leaves Meridian for and later becomes estranged from in the context of hardening racial divides and the killing of their daughter. Walker brings together these character's experiences and perspectives, along with those of their contemporaries, while also weaving in those of predecessors and ancestors.

Far from a protest novel flicking through a "tick list" of contemporary issues, Walker provides us with intimate insights into the consequences, and working through, of challenges regarding emotional and physical burn out, sexual violence, guilt, ostracism, privilege, trauma, and grief. And all of this is addressed in what feminist author Marge Piercy described in a 1976 *New York Times* review as "a lean book that finishes in 228 pages and goes down like clean water."

Iain McIntyre

The Real Noir

Dambudzo Marechera's Journey from Rhodesia to Britain to Zimbabwe

"I got my things and left. The sun was coming up. I couldn't think where to go."
— *House of Hunger*, 1978

Some years back, a friend pulled a half dozen orange-covered paperbacks from his shelves and said, half-jokingly, "This is the real noir fiction." Of course, I knew what he was talking about. They were all books from Heinemann's African Writers Series, just a few of the over two hundred titles dating back to 1961 when the imprint began, a large proportion of which were tales of corruption, murder, jealousy, and battles with fate. In other words, the very stuff of noir fiction. Mostly set in Africa, the books ran the gamut, from the tribal to the urban, contexts that made the stories, at least for a non-African reader such as myself, as intriguing as they were strange.

The imprint was meant to counter the colonial bias of literature in African classrooms. Produced in various African cities and distributed at an affordable price, its authors spanned the continent. Devoted, for the most part, to black writers, whose work originally appeared in English as well as French, Portuguese, Zulu, Swahili, Acoli, Sesotho, Afrikaans, Luganda, and Arabic, the series exposed readers, in the UK and elsewhere, to a range of African writers, both known and unknown. Heinemann hired the renowned Chinua Achebe as the imprint's initial editor. Half a decade later, Achebe handed over the reins to James Currey, who held down that post until the mid-1980s. By that time the imprint was able to boast such writers as Achebe, Peter Abrahams, Thiong'o Ngugi, Alex La Guna, Buchi Emecheta, Wole Soyinka, Doris Lessing, Naguib Mahfouz, Nadine Gordimer, and Ama Ata Aidoo, not to mention political figures like Steve Biko, Nelson Mandela, Kwame Nkrumah, and Kenneth Kaunda. Purchased in 2010 by the Pearson (owner of the Penguin Group), the series, though still a veritable who's-who of twentieth-century African authors, has recently been criticized by the likes of the Israel-based

The 2009 Heinemann edition of *The House of Hunger*, with the author on the cover

Nigerian Akin Ajayi, for not representing the newer trends and writers of the continent.

I remember saying to my friend that, of the books I'd read in that series, the most memorable was a collection of stories by a young writer, Dambudzo Marechera, entitled *The House of Hunger* (1978). Set in his native Zimbabwe—then Rhodesia—and in Britain, the nine stories and a novella from which the book's title derives, also seemed, when I first read them, to be firmly in the tradition of outsider fiction. These were dark and haunting tales of madness, exile, violence, and despair written in a style reminiscent of Charles Bukowski or French writer Louis-Ferdinand Céline, with a dash of Jim Thompson's doom-ridden brutality thrown in for good measure. Add to that Marechera's take on his home and adopted countries, as well as the era's Black Power and pan-African movements, and the result was something as original as it was unforgettable.

As suggested in the quote that opens this piece, hitting the road would become, thanks to Marechera's peripatetic lifestyle, a favorite theme in his fiction, as it has been for an assortment of protagonists populating the pages of noir-influenced novels. Not quite a rootless cosmopolitan, Marechera arrived in Britain in the mid-1970s, having come from an impoverished background in what would be the dog days of Ian Smith's white-ruled Rhodesia. Thrown out of the University of Rhodesia for his political activities, the author arrived toting a scholarship to study at New College, Oxford, and an attitude a mile long. This was at a time when various smart and industrious Africans were arriving on Britain's shores. This brain-drain allowed them to escape dictatorships and the last vestiges of colonialism, only to find themselves stranded in the dreary oppressiveness of 1970s Britain, with its industrial unrest, a Labour government that, to maintain its hold on power, formed a pact with the Liberal Party, leading to a dilution of its policies, a loan from the International Monetary Fund, and Britain's initial dalliance with monetarism. For Marechera, it was no doubt a relief to be out of Rhodesia, no matter how unsettling it must have been to be estranged in a strange, and perhaps inhospitable, land.

★

Charles William Dambudzo Marechera was born on June 4, 1952, in Rusape, Southern Rhodesia, in the Vhengere Township. In those pre-independence days, his father, Isaac worked as a mortuary attendant and truck driver, only to be killed by a hit-and-run driver when Marechera was still a young boy. As Marechera would later write in *The House of Hunger's* title story: "The old man died beneath the wheels of the twentieth century. There was nothing left but stains, bloodstains and fragments of flesh."

The wheels of the twentieth century were also responsible for grinding down Marechera's mother. Masvotwa Venezia was a nanny for white families who, after the death of her husband, was left to raise nine children. Evicted for not paying her rent, she took up residence in a downtrodden neighborhood where prostitutes, pimps, and criminals were commonplace. Eventually Marechera's mother took to drinking and, finally, prostitution. It was at this time, age thirteen, that Marechera must have decided that in order to escape his family and the chaos and pain of poverty he would have to strike out on his own. A situation he would later describe in the pages of *The House of Hunger*.

> Life stretched out like a series of hunger-scoured hovels stretching endlessly towards the horizon. One's mind became the grimy rooms, the dusty cobwebs in which the minute skeletons of one's childhood were forever in the spidery grip that stretched out to included not only the very stones upon which one walked but also the stars which glittered vaguely upon the stench of our lives. Gut-rot, that was what one steadily became. And whatever insects of thought buzzed about inside the tin-can of one's head as one squatted astride the pit-latrine of it, the sun still climbed as swiftly as ever and darkness fell upon the land as quickly as in the years that had gone.

Bright and inquisitive, Marechera, over the years, managed to win three scholarships: to St. Augustine's Secondary School, the University of Rhodesia, and then Oxford. One imagines him jumping at the opportunity to study abroad. And New College probably never thought for a moment that this young man would do anything other than play the role of grateful and gracious colonial subject. But Britain, with its long history of exiled students and writers, whether Samuel Selvon, Wole Soyinka or Buchi Emecheta, can be an unforgiving place, even for the resilient anglophile.

Adapting to his new surroundings would be no less difficult for Marechera. Not surprising when one considers not only where he was coming from, but the class distinctions and racism endemic to his new university. Of course, he also had to contend with the cultural climate of the time. This was, after all, only a few years after the controversial Conservative member of parliament Enoch Powell delivered his "rivers of blood" speech, which, by criticizing proposed immigration and antidiscrimination legislation, helped feed the flames of racism. It was the era in which *The Black and White Minstrels* and racist comedians appeared regularly on TV and "Paki-bashing" was a favorite skinhead

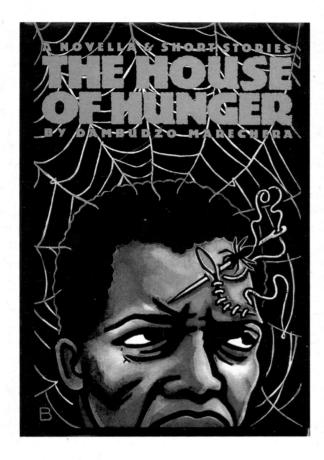

pastime. As a reaction to his immediate environment, Marechera embraced his status as an outsider to the point of parody, adopting a fake Oxford academician accent and unconventional style of dress. In all, his behavior could be interpreted as anarchic, antisocial, or just wickedly funny. With little if any desire to conform to either the academic or social standards of the university, he must have cut an interesting and eccentric figure as he traipsed beneath Oxford's dreaming spires.

Seeking solace where he could find it, Marechera gravitated toward the city's Afro-Caribbean community, most of whom, for economic reasons, lived in East Oxford or a bit further afield in Blackbird Leys, the site of their main source of employment, British Leyland's Cowley car plant. Marechera made frequent visits, drinking in pubs and working men's clubs. Although Afro-rock bands Osibisa and Assagai could be heard on jukeboxes, the predominantly West Indian community in Oxford weren't particularly welcoming when it came to this particular young African. Not only was he odd, he was a student in a city where the long-held separation between "town and gown" still existed, particularly among the city's working class. Not surprising, then, that Marechera, when visiting that part of Oxford, would be ridiculed or, worse, face physical hostility.

Unable to fit into the local black community or the student community, Marechera became increasingly marginalized. Soon he was drinking heavily—hardly an unusual student activity—and getting into pub brawls. He also gravitated toward the city's drug culture. This was at a time when the infamous Oxford-based drug dealer Howard Marks and his minions were supplying Oxonians with an assortment of recreational highs. No doubt the drugs did nothing to tone down his behavior, which became increasingly erratic. It reached its apogee when he threatened to kill certain individuals at the university and then said he would set fire to his six-hundred-year-old college. Sent to the university doctor, he was diagnosed as schizophrenic. Of course, the environment could have partly contributed to Marechera's unease and sense of marginality. On the other hand, it wasn't the first time he'd been an outsider in a predominantly white educational establishment. But at least at school and university in Rhodesia he'd been on familiar terms with the culture, however odious that culture might have been. Now he was given the choice: submit to a psychiatric examination, which would have probably led to his institutionalization, or leave the university. Faced with this no-win situation,

Marechera once again "got my things and left." Now he had the dubious distinction of having been thrown out of every educational institution to which he'd been granted a scholarship.

Fearing deportation, Marechera drifted around the country, including a three-month stint in a Welsh jail for possession of marijuana, prolonged by his now illegal alien status. From jail, he wrote to his eventual publisher:

> I believe I am in a mess, and this time I don't think I know enough to beg myself out of it. I have been in custody/remand and have been remanded in custody for another week. . . . They are threatening me left and right with deportation and I believe that they may just want to throw me out of the country through the quiet back door of Cardiff. All this is, of course, soup in which even a fly could not hope to backstroke it to the shore.

Back in the general population, Marechera joined rootless communities in Oxford and elsewhere, sleeping rough or on friends' sofas. Despite his circumstances, he continued to write short fiction and poetry, much of it composed on park benches, interrupted only by the weather, muggers, and the police. Eventually he joined a group of squatters in north London's Tolmers Square, where he was able to put the finishing touches to *The House of Hunger*. Yet his life was more chaotic than ever. It was around that time, perhaps to stay in the country, that he got married. Whatever the circumstances, the liaison ended not long after it began. Around that time the author was thrown the first of several lifelines when Sheffield University hired him as a writer-in-residence. But the appointment wasn't to last. Without work, Marechera was drinking heavily and rarely eating. Surviving by selling books borrowed from his friends and with nowhere else to go, he ended up at the YMCA. But after firing a fire extinguisher at a night watchman, he was made to pack his bags yet again.

★

> I couldn't have stayed on in that House of Hunger where every morsel of sanity was snatched from you the way some kinds of birds snatch food from the very mouths of babes.

The House of Hunger appears to be, for the most part, autobiographical, written in a style close to aforementioned Bukowski, Céline, and perhaps Jim Thompson in *Savage Night* (1953) or *King Blood* (1954) mode. While it's unlikely that Marechera was familiar with Thompson, James Hadley Chase's *No Orchids for Miss Blandish* (1939) and Raymond Chandler are mentioned in Marechera's *Black Sunlight* (1980) and the posthumously published *The Black Insider* (1990). And he most certainly had read Céline and Bukowski, particularly the latter, whose stories, novels, and poems were a major influence. Moving between these literary approaches, *The House of Hunger* never fully embraces any of them, and the book fails to achieve the level of verbal onslaught associated with Céline or the outrageous grittiness found in Bukowski's prose and poetry. Yet by moving between styles and landscapes, Marechera in his first book was forging a voice, one whittled from its many parts capable of detailing the anxieties, fears and loathing across two continents. The result can be read in the following:

> We were whores; eaten to the core by the syphilis of the white man's coming. Masturbating onto a *Playboy* centrefold; screaming abuse at a solitary but defiant racist; baring our arse to the yawning pit-latrine; writing angry "black" poetry; screwing pussy to prove that white men in reality don't exist—that was all contained within the circumvention of our gut-rot.

This was Marechera's predicament: caught between worlds, unable to feel at home in either. Maybe it was that which made *The House of Hunger* not only Marechera's most celebrated, but, in some ways, his most conservative, book, that is if "conservative" can be applied to anything Marechera would write. At the same time, it's a book that, on the one hand, speaks to colonization as it affects one personally, and, on the other hand, it's in the tradition of books about exile in the United Kingdom, such as Barbadian George Lamming's *The Pleasures of Exile* (1960) or Samuel Selvon's *Lonely Londoners* (1956).

One can see how Marechera's nightmarish articulation of anxiety and powerlessness might be disquieting, even when he returned to post-independence homeland. As he writes in *The House of Hunger*:

> A doorway yawned blankly into me: it led to a smaller room: numb, dark and also utterly empty. I could not bring myself to touch the walls to prove that they were really there. . . . For

some reason I began to wonder if I was really in there; perhaps I was a mere creation of the rooms themselves. Another doorway brooded just ahead of me.

Marechera's book is filled with such visions, as in the hellish story "The Slow Sound of His Feet," which combines "I dreamt last night that the Prussian surgeon Johann Friedrich Dieffenbach had decided that I stuttered because my tongue was too large; and he cut my large organ down to size by snipping off chunks from the tip and the sides" with the horrors of everyday reality, as the narrator-artist struggles to come to terms with the violent deaths of his parents. Often reminiscent of the final section of Thompson's *The Getaway* (1958), Marechera blurs the boundaries between memory, dream and reality, deploying, in the process, references to waking, the eyes opening and closing, as the narrator tries and fails "to paint the feeling of the silent but desperate voices inside me."

A common motif, mirroring *The House of Hunger's* stylistic inconsistency is the inability of Marechera's unsettled narrator—a more or less constant presence throughout the book—to find his voice. When the narrator's mother is killed in "The Slow Sound of His Feet," his sister's hand, "coming up to touch my face, flew to her opening mouth and I could feel her straining her vocal muscles to scream through my mouth." And when the children bury their mother the sun is "screaming soundlessly." And perhaps Marechera's own voice can be located within this stylistic uncertainty. In his story "The Writer's Grain," the narrator, attacked by the ghost of a drowned boy, cries out, "but I could not hear my own voice." While "The Transformation of Harry" ends with "something shrill" tearing into the narrator's ears:

> Startled, I looked up. Philip and Ada were also staring.
> The maddening high-pitched needles were coming from Harry.
> But he was not making any sound.

Uninterested in depicting beauty as such, Marechera's images are frequently violent and set against a bleak or scarred landscape. "Life," as he puts it in the title story, is like "a series of hunger-scoured hovels stretching endlessly towards the horizon." In fact, some African critics have attacked him for his bleak outlook, as well as for his attitude toward, and

depiction of, sex. Juliet Okonkwo writing in 1981 commented that his "excessive interest in sex activity, his tireless attempt to rake up filth, is alien to Africa—a continent of hope and realizable dreams." But the author, pursuing his own brand of freedom, was, according to Marechera authority Flora Veit-Wild, blunt and to the point in his reaction: "If you are a writer for a specific nation or a specific race, then fuck you."

★

Moving from place to place, it's a miracle that Marechera managed to write, much less publish, *The House of Hunger*. Certainly the African Writers' Series must have seemed the logical place for him to submit the manuscript. Though Heinemann was extremely interested in publishing it, Currey believed it needed a fair amount of revision. True to form, Marechera balked at the suggestion, believing that any changes would compromise what the book was about and perhaps result in a different writing style. Moreover, he was worried that Heinemann wanted a more overtly political book, more in keeping with the era's Black Power and pan-African movements. But Marechera never considered himself a political writer, maintaining in a letter to James Currey regarding the author's *The Black Insider* (which appeared in Zimbabwe 1990 and the UK in 1992): "I no longer in my private life indulge in anything remotely political; it nauseates me now because I know it is blood and brains spattered over grit." Not that he didn't feel guilty about taking up such a position, writing in *Black Sunlight* (1980): "Steve Biko died while I was blind drunk in London. Soweto burned while I was sunk in deep thought about an editor's rejection slip."

Not being overtly political—though no one could deny that his writing has always had a political dimension—was just one way in which Marechera challenged the prevailing orthodoxy. Yet no matter how challenging or mercurial he was as a person or as a writer, he always had his share of advocates, Currey not least among them. John Wylie, a reader for Heinemann and later to be a major UK literary agent, considered Marechera "a sort of African Dylan Thomas only much more intelligent." Like Currey, Wylie was enthusiastic about *The House of Hunger*, but he also thought the manuscript needed work. Both Currey and Wylie realized getting Marechera to make revisions was not going to be easy. What they saw as obstreperousness was, for Marechera, a matter of principle. Asking him to alter his writing was akin to asking him to change how he viewed the world. Still, his editors were insistent, and, at some point, Marechera relented. Yet the stories in *The House of Hunger* and elsewhere make it clear that Marechera wrote as though every word mattered and that his life depended on its accuracy. Attesting to that quality, and his fearlessness in the face of upheaval, Marechera's alter ego in *Black Sunlight* says, "To write as though only one kind of reality subsists in the world is to act out a mentally retarded mime, for a mentally deficient audience."

Keeping their young and temperamental writer on a short lead, Heinemann paid him in installments of approximately fifty dollars per month. Not a situation with which Marechera could have been happy. In fact, he must have regarded it as somewhat patronizing, as though they were treating him like a literary field hand. At the very least it harkened back to the work-till-you-die days of pulp fiction when some paperback

The Black Insider (Lawrence and Wishart, 1992)

publishing houses paid writers by the month as an incentive to help them meet their deadlines. If it was a case of making sure that Marechera kept writing, they needn't have worried. Because there wasn't much that could have kept Marechera from *not* writing. Fortunately his economic situation improved slightly when, in 1979, he received an Arts Council grant for a thousand pounds, also to be paid in monthly installments. The following year the Arts Council awarded him a further grant of £1,200. Meanwhile, Pantheon in the U.S. expressed interest in publishing *The House of Hunger*. Though they would ultimately decide against doing so, the book finally came out as part of the African Writers' Series in 1979.

Something of an overnight success, *The House of Hunger* won the Guardian Fiction Prize. And deservedly so, even though the award and the author's short-lived notoriety in London literary circles might have had something to do with Marechera's status as an African exiled in Britain and his growing reputation as a literary *maudit*. Despite his success, Marechera's finger rarely strayed from the self-destruct button. Seemingly unable to not cause some kind of outrage at the *Guardian* dinner where he was meant to receive his award, the author imbibed a little more than he should have and ended up throwing plates at the room's chandeliers. Even so, his performance at the dinner did not deter another university, this time Leeds, from offering him a position as writer-in-residence. True to form, this too would end badly.

Growing increasingly paranoid regarding the London literary establishment, and convinced he was being cheated by his publisher, Marechera initiated a series of raids at curious times of the day on Heinemann's office to demand the money he claimed they owed him. Understandable, perhaps, since, at the time, Marechera was living in abject poverty, not eating, drinking more than ever, and making more phone calls to Currey, asking to be bailed out of trouble. On top of that, he had fallen into the habit of barging into literary events where he invariably made a spectacle of himself. His disruptive behavior even caused him to be thrown out of the Africa Centre, at the time the major cultural meeting place for African and Afrocentric scholars and students. Marechera also became paranoid, believing that his friends, including fellow UK-based Zimbabweans, were conspiring against him, when, for the most part, they were attempting to look out for his interests. To make matters worse, some of his compatriots felt Marechera's tendency to put on airs, including his adoption of an upper-class accent and eccentric sartorial style, was not helping his cause, or theirs.

Then there was the ill-fated incident in Germany. Invited to participate in a celebration of African writers at Berlin's International Literature Days, Marechera neglected to bring the proper travel documents. Fortunately, thanks to the conference organizers, he was allowed into the country, by which time news had spread that Marechera had been detained by the authorities for political reasons. When he finally arrived at the festival hall, Marechera—at twenty-seven, the youngest writer there—was the de facto star of the show and asked to read on the night of his arrival even though he had not been scheduled to appear. His impassioned reading from *The House of Hunger* drew a standing ovation. Suddenly the audience thought it had discovered a new political writer-hero. Though some had no doubt come across African writers before, it's probably true that none had encountered anyone quite like Marechera, someone who, with his keen sense of the dramatic, courted chaos and seemed to be living on the edge, and for whom there was no clear separation between the world he created in his writing and the world in which he lived. Then, before anyone realized it, Marechera was whisked away by a left-wing revolutionary group who had organized an alternative conference. The group wanted Marechera to give a press conference where his ordeal at the hands of the German police would be given a public airing. Of course, Marechera obliged, declaring himself a political refugee, linking his arrival in England on a scholarship to his political stance against Ian Smith's white minority regime. "I am a Communist Party member in England," he declared, probably for the first time, going on to say, "I support Robert Mugabe. I know that any time I am back in Zimbabwe ... I will be arrested."

★

Two years after *The House of Hunger* came the publication of Marechera's more experimental *Black Sunlight*. It's a book that, as Marechera said in his 1986 Harare address, "The African Writer's Experience of European Literature," combines "fantasy and symbolism with low-life naturalism. Odd vantage points offer changes of scale. Heaven and hell are close and may be visited. Madness, dreams and daydreams, abnormal states of mind, and all kinds of erratic inclinations

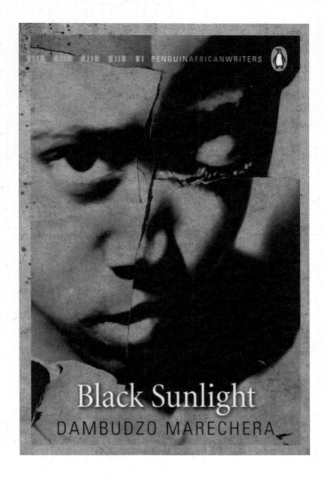

Black Sunlight (Penguin, 2012)

are explored. Scandalous and eccentric behavior disrupts "the seemly course of human affairs.... Society is unpredictable."

Hallucinatory in nature, *Black Sunlight*, which, like his previous book, only appeared after extensive revision, takes place during an unnamed war. Part stream-of-consciousness novel and part poetic diatribe, *Black Sunlight* centers on a group of anarchists who rise up in revolt against a fascist-capitalist opposition. In doing so the novel explores such themes as illusion and reality, as well as the implications of artistic freedom. Given its subject matter and tone, it shouldn't have come as a surprise that Marechera's London-set novel was not well-received, particularly in the author's home country, where it was deemed offensive and subsequently banned. It could be that Zimbabwean censors got no further than the novel's opening pages that portray a corrupt African tribal leader with a giant erection enthroned on a stack of human skulls. Others in Africa viewed the book as evidence that Marechera had sold out to European literary values. The year of *Black Sunlight*'s publication, 1980, would represent another difficult period for Marechera. Thatcher was in power and Britain was less accommodating than ever. "I was terribly lonely," says a character in *The Black Insider*, "especially in England where every day the newspapers carried the most hysterical nonsense about blacks and Asians. I had never really come to terms, I suppose, with my blackness . . . and it was something of a shock suddenly to realize that my skin for the English was a natural label that read Mugger, Rapist, Amin, Inferior." Confirming the extent to which exile can take its toll, not least when there is a liberation struggle going on back home, Marechera would write in *The Black Insider*: "We were talking in English, feeling like hippopotami that have been doped with injections of English culture, and we were quite conscious of how we knew no useful skills besides blasé comments about the book world. Indeed, a new kind of decadence has caught up with us."

It was writer David Caute who, in 1984, found the manuscript to Marechera's *The Black Insider* while sifting through his friend's papers in Heinemann's office, where it had languished for some five years. Like *Black Sunlight*, it takes place during an unnamed war fought by unnamed participants and unnamed factions. Though it weighed in at just over a hundred pages, Marechera considered it a novel. Wylie had liked it but, as usual, thought it needed work. Eventually it

appeared, along with five short stories which recount Marechera days as a student in Britain, summed up in his short story "Oxford, Black Oxford," which, as the title of the collection suggests, reflects his feelings of unease and uselessness as an exiled African, not to mention the absurdity of being a "black insider," that is, inside the culture of his adopted country, but condemned, through race, class and country of origin, to remain on the outside.

Due to his profession and perspective, he would soon discover that he was even an outsider in his home country. Having returned to Zimbabwe in 1982, initially to assist filmmaker Chris Austin in the filming of a Channel 4 adaption of *The House of Hunger*, a disillusioned Marechera would write, "I have been an outsider in my own biography, in my country's history, in the world's terrifying possibilities." Nevertheless, back in his home country, he threw himself into his writing, producing short stories, plays, and poems, much of which comprise collections like *Mindblast* or *The Definitive Buddy* (1984), as it is also known, which criticized the new government for its corruption and intolerance.

Marechera, his anarchism and bohemianism a constant problem for the authorities, would fall foul of the law on various occasions, resulting in short prison sentences, police beatings, and periodic homelessness. Once again out of place, he might have packed his bags and moved elsewhere—in fact, he had wanted to do so as early as 1982 following his "farewell lecture" at the University of Zimbabwe but was prevented from leaving the country by the authorities—had he not become ill. This "one-man civil war," by which Heinemann publisher James Currey meant he was forever at war with himself as well as with society, was only thirty-five years old when, in 1987, he died of an AIDS-related pulmonary disorder. A danger to himself as well as to any society unable to tolerate the chaos he represented, Dambudzo Marechera, with a small stretch of the imagination, really was as noir as it gets.

Woody Haut

The Love Bombers, Gloria D. Miklowitz (Delacorte, 1980)

Eighteen-year-old Jenna Gordon and her brother Jeremy have lived a comfortable, upper-middle-class existence in the suburbs of San Diego. Less than a year apart in age, they have always been exceptionally close, planning out their lives together: Jenna taking extra classes in high school so they could graduate together, to be followed by law school and eventual partnerships in their father's firm.

Jenna only begins to realize that in reality they've drifted apart when, after their freshman year of college, Jeremy elects to spend the summer in San Francisco instead of returning home. Jenna is further baffled by his insistence that he wants to stay and study "Eastern-Western philosophy," because while they were nominally raised Jewish, Jeremy had always held an irreverent attitude toward any religious practices. After a strange phone conversation with her brother, her parents notice some mysterious charges on their credit card, and Jenna decides to take matters into her own hands. Sharing her concerns with Jeremy's best friend, Rick, they decide to take a road trip to northern California and see what has really become of him.

The first part of the book is told from Jenna's point of view, as she and Rick arrive in San Francisco and encounter the Help Our World Project (HOWP) group, also called the Church of the World, and the Family. Ever-knowledgeable Rick also knows the group as the Adamites, a controversial Jewish schism group led by a mysterious Middle Eastern multimillionaire.

The members Jenna and Rick initially meet in San Francisco are anything but Manson-like: clean-cut, with short hair and modest dress, they seem eager to help them locate Jeremy. Jenna finds herself being won over by their outgoing friendliness, and emphasis on helping the poor and elderly around the world. Rick remains suspicious, especially as they are taken under the wing of Werner, the local group leader who is eager to have them learn more about HOWP but won't be pinned down on exactly where Jeremy is or when they can see him. Finally, they agree to accompany Werner to a HOWP meeting in Berkeley, and then a weekend "camp" in the mountains, where he says Jeremy is living.

The second part of the book is told from Jeremy's point of view, and largely deals with the disillusionment he feels after attending his first year of college at Berkeley, feeling that his parents' comfortable, bourgeois lifestyle is completely disconnected from the problems he sees

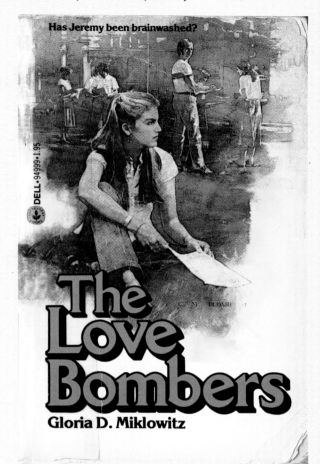

The Love Bombers (Dell, 1980)

in society. It is also revealed that his parents favored the conservative, overachieving Jenna growing up and now he is struggling to establish his own identity.

After flaking out on an important final exam, Jeremy meets Mary Ellen, a cute girl who shares his interest in literature and is working with what she describes as an international aid program to fight Third World famine. Jeremy agrees to accompany Mary Ellen to a meeting of the organization and is taken aback when he learns that it is a part of the Church of the World. When he questions Mary Ellen, she merely dimples and replies that it was "a heavenly deception," the ends justifying the means. Initially skeptical, Jeremy feels more and more at home with the group and their values of friendship and mutual support. It seems a great many young members had similar problems fitting in with their families' value systems.

HOWP is so successful in their "love bombing" of the vulnerable Jeremy, that he doesn't question the late hours members are expected to work on the charity projects or fund raising by selling flowers at the airport. As the months pass, he willingly shares his worldly possessions, including his savings account and credit card, with the group. It is not until group leaders fear that he and Mary Ellen are growing too close and send her to a "special project" in New York City that he questions if he has gotten in over his head, but fatigue from late hours and too little food keeps him from taking any action.

The third part of the book, entitled "The Confrontation," finally brings Jenna and Rick face to face with Jeremy. Surprisingly, Miklowitz lets Jeremy voice a number of salient points about the hypocrisy of their parents' lifestyle, the repression of his personality, and the favoritism they showed toward Jenna, no matter how hard he worked to try to live up to their standards. Jeremy decides to stay with the group, and Jenna respects his right to make that choice, worrying only that if he ever decides to leave, he'll never find a place in conventional society. The ending is tantalizingly ambiguous: although for the time being Jeremy will stay with the Family, he helps another young man escape, and seems to maintain some level of critical thinking. Strangely for a Young Adult novel of the period, running away to join a cult seems to be a viable alternative to the square and uptight world of one's parents.

In a decade bookended by Charles Manson and Jim Jones, California had become a hotbed of cult activity in the public's imagination. The rise of the counterculture movement and professional "deprogrammers" would keep the subject in the public eye through the so-called Satanic Panic of the following decade. The Church of the World itself is a composite of many different cults based on the west coast in the 1970s, taking various aspects from groups like the Brethren, the Children of God, the Unification Church (Moonies) and even a touch of Mormonism, with their clean-cut demeanor and love of cheesy pop songs. ("You Are My Sunshine" and "The Impossible Dream" are two particular favorites.)

The lack of a pat ending is typical of Miklowitz's work, which frequently dealt with such "problem" issues as rape, teen pregnancy, and drugs, without a happy (or moralistic) outcome.

Molly Grattan

She had an uncomfortable feeling that she was somehow being manipulated. But it was all done so smoothly and with such good grace that it would be insulting to protest. She could not do more than grin across Werner at her brother and hope that later they would have time together.

"Are you okay, Jer?" You've lost so much weight," she said.

"Of course he's well. He's fine," Werner responded.

"Sure, I'm fine," Jeremy echoed, glancing first at Werner, as if for approval. A Brother in the row behind leaned forward and began kneading Jeremy's shoulders. Jeremy grinned back at him warmly. She felt she had been forgotten already.

Jenna trembled, but when Werner held out the songbook as the musicians struck up the opening chords of "Gonna Build a Kingdom," she forced herself to smile. As long as Jeremy was surrounded by this throbbing human chain, this hand-holding, swaying, singing brotherhood, he was not Jeremy but part of a huge, pulsating body that had nothing to do with her. The few seconds when they first hugged were real, that was the Jeremy she knew. But now, as she watched him without appearing to, he sang with his entire soul. Eyes closed, face alight, body moving as if truly part of the Family.

It Can't Happen to Me, Arnold Madison (Scholastic, 1981)

As far as Young Adult fiction titles cashing in on the headlines go, the "teen-romance-and-nuclear-power-plant-meltdown" doesn't even qualify as a sub-sub-subgenre. Yet Arnold Madison, a YA and juvenile author specializing in both fiction and nonfiction on topics including drug use, suicide and teenage runaways, used the fear of peacetime nuclear destruction as a backdrop for his minor coming-of-age novel.

Madison's timing couldn't have been better. By the early 1980s the antinuclear movement had come to encompass more than just weapons disarmament. In the wake of the partial meltdown of the nuclear reactor at Pennsylvania's Three Mile Island, the mysterious death of union activist and nuclear plant whistleblower Karen Silkwood, the contamination from nuclear waste in Rocky Flats, Colorado, and the release of the acclaimed "worst-case scenario" film *The China Syndrome*, Madison seems to have been tuned in to the popular imagination. But the plot becomes bogged down in the details of the heroine's familial and romantic troubles, side trips that take the reader away from those looming cooling towers pictured on the cover.

High school junior Sandy Farrell is awakened in the middle of the night by strange noises at the nearby Rocky Falls Nuclear Power Plant. But she quickly shrugs off any worries to focus on her more pressing teenage concerns, including a "bitter divorced mom" and a sensitive eight-year-old brother who is having problems in school. Her overly possessive boyfriend, Bryan, is pressuring her to "go steady," *and* they are scheduled to compete in the big canoe race first thing in the morning!

When Sandy arrives at the river the next morning for the combination race, regatta, and chili cook-off, she hears rumors from her friends that something has happened at the nuclear plant, but brushes it off as nothing serious, as surely the authorities would notify them if there was danger.

After a tense dinner with her family, Sandy escapes to her friend Marta's house, where she shares the discussion that she must have with Bryan over his insistence that she be his "number one girl" and complains of the general pressure to conform to small-town life. Sandy envies Marta's self-confidence and the support she receives from her parents to follow her dream to become an architect. Marta warns Sandy that people take advantage of her being so nice, especially Bryan and her mother.

Monday morning the hippie-ish "Problems in Democracy" teacher, Mr. Wood, treats his class by rolling in the Audio-Visual cart so they can watch the press conference from the Governor concerning the incident at the nuclear plant. The PR flack from the plant intimates that perhaps the incident of two days prior was more serious than they initially let on but assures the public that it has been fully contained. The governor muddies the message, however, suggesting that people who live within five miles of the plant "stay indoors as much as possible."

Mr. Wood leads the class in a spirited discussion about the advantages and drawbacks of relying on nuclear power, and by the time Sandy gets to her lunch period, more rumors are circulating that the plant has experienced a partial meltdown and is orchestrating a cover up. When these rumors are confirmed by the next morning, Mr. Wood's students are incensed that the power plant has been holding back information from the community. With the righteous fury that can only accumulate in an eleventh-grade classroom, the students compose a group letter to the editor of the local paper criticizing the nuclear plant and demanding full disclosure of the details of the incident. Bryan refuses to sign and tells Sandy that she is getting worked up over nothing.

Now the situation in Rocky Falls has attracted the attention of the national media, even causing Sandy's estranged father to call from California and offer plane tickets. Their mother turns him down, assuring him that he's needlessly worried. Three days after Sandy first heard the suspicious noises, school is abruptly dismissed in the middle of the morning, and the town briefly devolves into an apocalyptic panic. Making her way through streets full of stalled traffic, Sandy arrives at her brother's school. Her mother meets them there, and they head home to spend the day locked in the house watching the afternoon soaps and frequent news bulletins that offer no real information. When the afternoon paper is delivered, Sandy's mother is horrified to see Sandy's name attached to the student editorial and orders her daughter to call the editor and have a retraction published. When Sandy refuses her mother announces that she will have Mr. Wood fired but is thwarted by an ominous "all circuits are busy, please try your call again later" message from the phone company.

This familial meltdown is interrupted by the arrival of Marta who has ventured out in a homemade radiation suit to deliver the news that her father has accepted a professorship at the University of Maine, effective immediately, because Maine only has one nuclear plant in the entire state. Her family will be leaving first thing in the morning. After Marta leaves, her mother cheerfully suggests making some hot chocolate for the family, but it is all a trick to convince Sandy to disavow the editorial. They go to bed furious at one another, but by the next morning they've got bigger problems to deal with.

At 7:00 a.m. the army shows up on their doorstep to inform them that they have forty-five minutes to pack their things before being forcibly evacuated. Madison chillingly captures the alarm and panic of having uniformed, M16-toting soldiers showing up in your town during peacetime. Sandy and four hundred of her neighbors are evacuated to a school gymnasium forty minutes down the New York State Thruway, where she and her family are each issued a sleeping bag and mess kit and given instructions to snitch out any looters to the MPs. While Sandy searches for her friends in the crowd, the displaced residents of Rocky Falls do what they do best: walk down to the local strip mall and go shopping.

Sandy and her brother get full body-scans and find out that they are not going to die of radiation poisoning; Sandy finds Bryan and they have a mumbly conversation about "trying to find answers" (about life, not the nuclear cover-up), and the next morning the town is given an anticlimactic all-clear to return home.

Molly Grattan

It Can't Happen to Me (Scholastic, 1981)

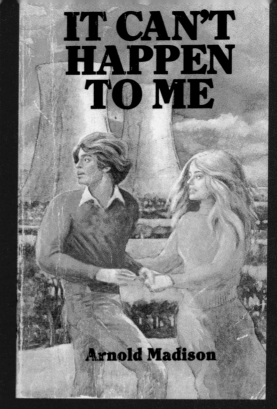

IT CAN'T HAPPEN TO ME

Arnold Madison

Confusion and chaos seized the rooms of Rocky Falls High School. Sandy fought her way through packed hallways, being jostled and crushed by stampeding students. She clutched her books to her chest. If the texts were knocked from her hands, she would never retrieve them from under the trampling feet.

The town was doing anything but remaining calm. Car horns honked, and a distant church bell tolled ominously. Eleven vans, automobiles, and trucks blocked the intersection of Court and Main Streets, waiting for Larabee's Service Station to supply them with enough fuel for the emergency. An unintelligible drone crystalized into a voice addressing the silent rows of watchful houses as a pickup, bearing the blue and gold seal of the Civil Defense unit, turned onto Court Street. The driver clutched a microphone to his mouth like a lonely CBer trying to establish contact with another nighttime driver.

As the truck turned the corner, the sound was muffled by two-story houses and double garages. An unseen gap in the blockage permitted three final words to sneak through to Sandy. "Please remain calm."

Acknowledgments

This book would not have been possible without the assistance of many people.

Tadhg Taylor, Rallou Lubitz, Bruce Milne, Adele Daniele, Simon Strong, David Hyman, Alan Stewart, Nick Jones, Adam Firth, Tim Hewitt, Justin Marriot, Keith Jacobi, Tom Tesarek, Toby Hasley, Thomas Wickersham, Wallace Stroby, and Bill Cunningham, as well as our contributors, assisted with sourcing and scanning a number of covers and images that appear in this book.

The editors would particularly like to thank Kevin Burton Smith, Wallace Stroby and Elizabeth Ferris for their assistance in the preparation of the piece "City on the Brink: Wally Ferris's Across 110th."

The editors would like to acknowledge the following images:
  The image of Nathan Heard was off the back of the 1974 Simon and Schuster edition of *A Cold Fire Burning* and was uncredited.
  The image of author Joe Nazel working in his apartment was generously supplied by the Joseph Nazel Jr. family archive.
  The image of Chester Himes originally appeared on the back cover of the 1959 Ace edition of *If He Hollers Let Him Go* and is uncredited.
  The image of Ernest Tidyman is by Sheedy and Ling, Ernest Tidyman Collection, American Heritage Center, University of Wyoming.

The following material is being reprinted (in edited form) with permission:

"Adolescent Homosexuality: A Novel Problem" originally appeared in *Gay Information*, no 6, Winter 1981.

"Cold Fire Burning: The Nathan Heard Interviews" originally appeared in *African American Review* 28, no. 3 (Autumn 1994): 395–410.

"Emotions Doesn't Change Facts: Remembering Joseph Hansen" originally appeared as an article for lareviewofbooks.org in 2014.

"Fictions about Pulp" originally appeared in *The Gay & Lesbian Review* 8, no. 6, (November/December 2001): 18–20.

"Fifty Shades of Gay" originally appeared as the introduction to a two-in-one edition of *Man Eater* by Dick Jones and *Night of The Sadist* by Paul Laurie (120 Days Books, 2012; reissued by Riverdale Avenue Books, 2018), riverdaleavebooks.com

"Shafted: On Ernest R. Tidyman and the Makings of *Shaft*" originally appeared as an article for www. mulhollandbooks.com in 2011.

"The Cool, the Square and the Tough: The Archetypes of Black Male Characters in Mystery and Crime Novels" originally appeared in *The Black Scholar* 28, no. 1 (Spring 1998): 27–32.

"*To Sir, with Love*: Race and the Unreal City of the Colonial Imagination" originally appeared as an article for www.londonfictions.com in 2013.

"What Men Fear: An Interview with M.F. Beal" is an edited version of an article that originally ran in *The Sixties: A Journal of History, Politics and Culture* 3, no. 2 (December 2010): 269–83.

Iain would like to thank his family for their encouragement and support during the writing and editing of this book. Andrew would like to thank Angela Savage and his daughter, Natasha, for their support throughout the process of putting this book together.

Contributors

Scott Adlerberg grew up in the Bronx and a wooded suburb just outside New York City. He's written *Spiders and Flies*, a crime novel set in Martinique, and the noir/fantasy novella *Jungle Horses*. These were followed by *Graveyard Love*, a psychological thriller that takes place in the dead of winter in a rural part of New York State. His short fiction has appeared in *Thuglit*, *Spinetingler*, and *Beat to a Pulp*, and he contributes pieces to *Criminal Element*, the *LA Review of Books*, and *Literary Hub*. Each summer, he hosts the Word for Word Reel Talks film commentary series in Manhattan. His most recent novel, from Broken River Books, is *Jack Waters*, a story of revenge and revolution on a Caribbean island in the early twentieth century. He lives in Brooklyn with his wife and two sons.

Steve Aldous has a lifelong interest in crime fiction and cinema. He started writing in 2011 and is the author of *The World of Shaft: A Complete Guide to the Novels, Comic Strip, Films and Television Series* (published by McFarland in 2015). He is also a keen writer of fiction and has twice been shortlisted in the Writer's Forum Magazine Short Story Competition. One of these stories, an affectionate parody of pulp PI novels of the 1940s entitled "Lightning Never Strikes Twice," was published by Worldreader. He is currently seeking publishing interest in his first crime novel, *Poisoned Veins*, which is set in Manchester and features black private investigator Joe Gibbs. Steve lives with his wife Kathleen in Bury, Lancashire, and together they have three children and two grandchildren.

Eric Beaumont is a musician, DJ, paralegal, and writer living in Milwaukee. His literary criticism has appeared in the Cleveland *Plain Dealer*, *African American Review*, Milwaukee *Journal Sentinel*, and *Shepherd Express*. As Eric Blowtorch, he has written, performed, and arranged five albums, seven singles, and numerous songs on compilations and soundtracks, frequently collaborating with Jamaican musicians. As a solo singer/guitarist and bandleader, he has played across America and in England, Canada, and Jamaica, where he performed with the Alpha Boys Band. Beaumont has lectured on Jamaican music and history at the University of Wisconsin–Milwaukee, where he received a bachelor of arts degree in history. His published interviews include those with George McGovern, Brian Wilson, Elvis Costello, KRS-ONE, Wayne Kramer, Linton Kwesi Johnson, De La Soul, Manic Street Preachers, Heather Ann Thompson, and filmmaker Karyn Kusama. Beaumont's historical research was recently cited in the *New York Times*.

Danae Bosler is a writer based in Melbourne. She has been published in *Overland*, *Guardian Online*, *National Times*, and *The Conversation*. Her master's thesis at Melbourne University, shortlisted for the Melbourne University Prize, was a fictional account of the New South Wales teachers' union dispute in the mid-1990s. Danae is a union campaigner and councilor for Yarra City in Melbourne.

Michael Bronski is an author, professor, and independent scholar. He has been involved in gay liberation as a political organizer, journalist, writer, editor, publisher, and theorist since 1969. His *Queer History of the United States* won the Lambda Literary Award for Best Non-Fiction as well as the American Library Association's Stonewall Book Award–Israel Fishman Non-Fiction Award. In 2003 his *Pulp Friction: Uncovering the Golden Age of Gay Male Pulps* won the Lambda Literary Award for "Best Anthology." In 2017 he was awarded the Publishing Triangle's Bill Whitehead Award for Lifetime Achievement. He is Professor of the Practice in Activism and Media at Harvard University.

Brian Coffey is a Melbourne-based collector of pulp fiction, with a particular interest in Australian pulp. He's been collecting for about fifteen years or so, after picking up a trashy secondhand novel to read while on a bushwalking trip. As it turned out, the author of the book was Carter Brown, and Brian's been hooked ever since. Rather than achieving great deeds on a sporting field, Brian's ideal Saturday would involve finding some pulp gold in an op shop, and then browsing through his collection of books, while listening to DJ Emma Peel on Melbourne community radio station 3PBS. His all-time favorite book is James Holledge's "pulp faction" classic *The Flower People*, published in 1967 by Horowitz press offshoot Scripts. He also collects secondhand Hawaiian records and loves the soundtrack to the documentary on Erich von Daniken's *Chariots of the Gods* by the Peter Thomas Sound Orchestra.

David James Foster writes under the pen name James Hopwood. He is the author of the retro spy thrillers *The Librio Defection, The Danakil Deception,* and *The Ambrosia Kill*. His short fiction has been published by Sempre Vigil Press, Airship 27, Crime Factory, Clan Destine Press, and Pro Se Publications. Writing as Jack Tunney, he also scribed several books in the popular Fight Card series: *King of the Outback, Rumble in the Jungle,* and *The Iron Fists of Ned Kelly,* .

Harlem native **Michael A. Gonzales** is the coauthor of *Bring the Noise: A Guide to Rap Music and Hip-Hop Culture*. He has been a senior writer for *The Source*, writer-at-large for *Vibe* and a regular contributor to the *Village Voice, Ebony, Essence, Wax Poetics,* and *Stop Smiling*. His essays have appeared in *Pitchfork, Catapult, Best Sex Writing 2005, Cuepoint, Baltimore City Paper,* and both volumes of *Best African-American Essays,* edited by Gerald Early. His fiction has appeared in *Trace, Uptown,* Russell Simmons's *Oneworld, Crime Factory,* and in anthologies including *Black Pulp,* edited by Gary Phillips; *The Darker Mask,* edited by Gary Phillips and Christopher Chambers; *Hood 2 Hood,* edited by Shannon Holmes; *The Global Village: Tell Tales Volume 4,* edited by Courttia Newland; and the Brown Sugar erotica series, edited by Carol Taylor. Gonzales has published fiction and cultural criticism in Africa, England, France, and Japan.

Molly Grattan has turned a longtime fascination with the minutiae of teenage social-problem novels into the long-running YA fiction and pop culture blog mondomolly.com. Her nonfiction work has recently appeared in the collections *Spaceout: Memory* and *Gang Girls, Biker Boys, and Real Cool Cats*. She holds a degree in film and media studies from the City University of New York, Hunter College. She teaches film studies, video production, and journalism to middle school students in New York City and lives in Queens.

Brian Greene's short stories and writings on books, music, and film have appeared in twenty-five publications since 2008. His writing blog can be found at http://briangreenewriter.blogspot.com/.

Woody Haut is the author of *Pulp Culture: Hardboiled Fiction and the Cold War; Neon Noir: Contemporary American Crime Fiction;* and *Heartbreak and Vine: The Fate of Hardboiled Writers in Hollywood,* as well as two novels: *Cry for a Nickel, Die for a Dime* and *Days of Smoke*. As a freelance journalist and noir historian, he's contributed to the likes of *Rolling Stone,* the *Observer, Sight and Sound,* the *Financial Times, Uncut, Crime Time, Noir City Sentinel, Black Mask,* and the *Los Angeles Review of Books*. In the 1980s he was also Labor Editor of *Rolling Stock* magazine. Born in Detroit, raised in Pasadena, and educated at San Francisco State University, Haut has worked as a college lecturer, taxi driver, record shop assistant, post office clerk, and cinema programmer. He moved to the UK in the 1970s, currently lives in London, and maintains a blog dedicated to noir fiction and film (woodyhaut.blogspot.com).

Alley Hector is a queer writer and web developer based in Portland, Oregon, where she has lived since her 1980s childhood. She is currently working on a novel about local life as a teenager in the 1990s. Past projects have included editing *Just Out* magazine, founding and editing local LGBT news and events publication qPDX.com, and freelancing for numerous others including Autostraddle, Nylon, and the Daily Dot. She also maintains an adventure blog called *Out & About* at http://outandabout.space.

Emory Holmes II is a Los Angeles–based novelist, short-story writer, and journalist. His news stories on American crime, schools, and the arts have appeared in the *San Francisco Chronicle,* the *Los Angeles Times,* the *Los Angeles Sentinel,* the *Los Angeles Daily News,* the *New York Amsterdam News, Los Angeles* magazine, *Essence, CODE,* the *R&B Report, Written By* magazine, the *Los Angeles Review of Books,* the *New York Times* wire service, and other publications. He was twice editor of the African-American men's monthly *Players* magazine, during the 1970s and '80s, for whose parent company, Holloway House, he wrote two novels, *Black Rage* (1975) and *Sunday Hell* (1982). His crime stories have been anthologized in *The Cocaine Chronicles* (2005), *The Best American Mystery Stories 2006, Los Angeles Noir* (2007), and *.44 Caliber Funk* (2016). His 2007 story "Dangerous Days" was translated into French and republished in Paris by Asphalte éditions in 2010. This story and his short story "aka Moises Rockafella" were dramatized and published as Audible books in 2014.

Writer, editor, and publisher **Maitland McDonagh**, a film critic and longtime collector of vintage gay adult novels, founded 120 Days Books in 2012 to republish forgotten gay erotic titles of the 1970s. Now partnered with Riverdale Avenue Books, the 120 Days imprint represents novels whose bold depiction of the realities, aspirations, and fantasies of gay men anticipated decades of political and social change and remain strikingly relevant today.

Iain McIntyre is a Melbourne-based author, musician, and community radio broadcaster who has written a variety of books on activism, history and music. Recent publications include *On the Fly! Hobo Literature and Songs, 1879–1941* (2018), *Girl Gangs, Biker Boys, and Real Cool Cats: Pulp Fiction and Youth Culture, 1950 to 1980* (2017) and *How to Make Trouble and Influence People: Pranks, Protest, Graffiti and Political Mischief-Making from across Australia* (2009/2013).

Bill Mohr's poems, prose poems, creative prose, and book reviews have appeared in numerous magazines, and his writing has been featured in over a dozen anthologies. In addition to a spoken-word collection, *Vehemence*, issued by New Alliance Records in 1993, individual collections of his poetry include *Hidden Proofs* (1982) and *Bittersweet Kaleidoscope* (2006). In 2015, Bonobos Editores in Mexico published a bilingual edition of his poems, *Pruebas Ocultas*. From 1974 to 1988, he worked as editor and publisher of Momentum Press, the archives of which are in Special Collections and Archives at the University of California, San Diego. His account of the Los Angeles poetry scene, *Hold-outs: The Los Angeles Poetry Renaissance, 1948–1992*, was published by the University of Iowa Press in 2011. Mohr has a PhD in literature from the University of California, San Diego, and is currently a professor in the Department of English at California

State University, Long Beach, where he has taught both literature and creative writing since 2006. His honors include a visiting scholar award at the Getty Research Institute in Los Angeles and grants to do research at the Huntington Library in San Marino.

Andrew Nette is a writer and pulp scholar based in Melbourne, Australia. He is the author of two crime novels, *Ghost Money* and *Gunshine State*. His short fiction has appeared in numerous print and online publications, most recently, *The Obama Inheritance: Fifteen Stories of Conspiracy Noir*. He is coeditor of *Girl Gangs, Biker Boys, and Real Cool Cats: Pulp Fiction and Youth Culture, 1950 to 1980*. His online home is www.pulpcurry.com

Kinohi Nishikawa is assistant professor of English and African American Studies at Princeton University. He is the author of *Black Pulp Fiction and the Making of a Literary Underground*, a history of the racial and sexual politics of the pulp industry in the age of Black Power. His writing on race and modern print culture has appeared in Chicago Review, Book History, and PMLA, and in the collections *The Blacker the Ink* and *The Centrality of Crime Fiction in American Literary Culture*. Kinohi's next monograph, *Blueprints for Black Writing*, considers book design's role in shaping our perception of modern African American literature.

Bill Osgerby is professor of Media, Culture and Communications at London Metropolitan University. He has published widely on twentieth-century British and American cultural history. His books include *Youth in Britain since 1945*; *Playboys in Paradise: Youth, Masculinity and Leisure-Style in Modern America*; and *Youth Media* and *Biker: Style and Subculture on Hell's Highway*. He has also coedited numerous anthologies, including *Action TV: "Tough Guys, Smooth Operators and Foxy Chicks"*; *Subcultures, Popular Music and Social Change*; and *Fight Back: Punk, Politics and Resistance*.

Jenny Pausacker worked as a writer of children's and young adult fiction from 1975 to 2007. During that time, she published seventy-two books, from picture books to educational kits. Her young adult novel *What Are Ya?*, which won the Angus and Robertson Junior Writers Fellowship in 1985 and was shortlisted for two state awards, was the first Australian children's book with a gay main character. She is currently living in a fifth-floor flat by the sea with her partner and experimenting with other kinds of writing.

Born under a bad sign with family roots in one of the oldest towns in Texas and the Mississippi Delta, South Central LA native **Gary Phillips** must keep writing to forestall his appointment at the crossroads. He has written novels such as *The Jook*, a hardcore tale set in the world of pro football; two books featuring Martha Chainey, a former Vegas showgirl turned cold cash courier; and *The Underbelly*, about a sometimes-homeless Vietnam vet, Magrady. With Christa Faust, he cowrote the recent *Peepland*, a gritty crime graphic novel set in the last bad old days of 1980s Times Square; and he has short stories in anthologies such as *Jewish Noir*, *Asian Pulp*, *The Highway Kind*, and *Echoes of Sherlock Holmes*. One reviewer said of his prose superhero short-story collection *Astonishing Heroes*, "It's a book for anyone who remains nostalgic for the golden age of Toei films, blaxploitation movies, and lusty grindhouse cinema." Phillips coedited the well-received *Cocaine Chronicles* and *Black Pulp* anthologies and solo edited the best-selling *Orange County Noir* and *The Obama Inheritance: Fifteen Stories of Conspiracy Noir*.

J. Kingston Pierce is a longtime journalist and magazine editor living in Seattle, Washington. In 2006 he launched a crime fiction blog titled *The Rap Sheet* (http://therapsheet.blogspot.com/), which in the years since has won the Spinetingler Award for Special Services to the Industry and been nominated twice for Anthony Awards. He also writes the book design blog *Killer Covers* (http://killercoversoftheweek. blogspot.com/), serves as the senior editor of *January Magazine* (http://januarymagazine.com/wp/), and for almost six years was the lead crime fiction blogger for *Kirkus Reviews*. Recently, he signed on as a regular columnist with *Down & Out: The Magazine*, a crime-fiction-oriented periodical available in both print and digital formats. Pierce has published more than half a dozen nonfiction books, among them *San Francisco: Yesterday and Today*, *Seattle: Yesterday and Today*, *Eccentric Seattle*, and *America's Historic Trails with Tom Bodett*. He's currently at work (oh so slowly) on his first novel.

Susie Thomas is a freelance lecturer in London. She has written about British literature from Aphra Behn to Martin Amis. Her *Reader's Guide to Hanif Kureishi*

was published by Macmillan in 2005. She contributes to the London Fictions website and is the reviews editor of the *Literary London Journal*.

Nicolas Tredell has published twenty books and over three hundred essays and articles on writers ranging from Shakespeare and Dickens to Scott Fitzgerald and Martin Amis, and on key topics in literary, cultural, and film theory. He taught English and American literature, international film, and cultural studies at Sussex University and gives frequent talks to conferences, schools, and societies. He is currently consultant editor for Palgrave Macmillan's Essential Criticism series and on the committee of the Literary London Society. His recent books include, in the Analysing Texts series, *F. Scott Fitzgerald: The Great Gatsby/Tender is the Night* and *Shakespeare: The Tragedies*; as well as a revised and expanded edition of his well-received interviews with leading literary figures, *Conversations with Critics*.

Linda S. Watts is professor of American Studies and director of the Project for Interdisciplinary Pedagogy within the School of Interdisciplinary Arts and Sciences at the University of Washington, Bothell. Her published works include *Rapture Untold: Gender, Mysticism, and "The Moment of Recognition" in the Writings of Gertrude Stein* (1996); *Gertrude Stein: A Study of the Short Fiction* (1999); with Brian Greenberg, *Social History of the United States: The 1900s* (2008); with Alice George and Scott Beekman, *Social History of the United States: The 1920s* (2008); and, with Patrick Blessinger, *Creative Learning in Higher Education: International Perspectives and Approaches* (2016).

David Whish-Wilson is the author of five crime novels and three nonfiction books on the social history of Perth, Western Australia. He coordinates the creative writing program at Curtin University.

Index

Page numbers in *italic* refer to illustrations. "Passim" (literally "scattered") indicates intermittent discussion of a topic over a cluster of pages.

ABOUT PM PRESS

PM Press was founded at the end of 2007 by a small collection of folks with decades of publishing, media, and organizing experience. PM Press co-conspirators have published and distributed hundreds of books, pamphlets, CDs, and DVDs. Members of PM have founded enduring book fairs, spearheaded victorious tenant organizing campaigns, and worked closely with bookstores, academic conferences, and even rock bands to deliver political and challenging ideas to all walks of life. We're old enough to know what we're doing and young enough to know what's at stake.

We seek to create radical and stimulating fiction and non-fiction books, pamphlets, T-shirts, visual and audio materials to entertain, educate, and inspire you. We aim to distribute these through every available channel with every available technology— whether that means you are seeing anarchist classics at our bookfair stalls, reading our latest vegan cookbook at the café, downloading geeky fiction e-books, or digging new music and timely videos from our website.

PM Press is always on the lookout for talented and skilled volunteers, artists, activists, and writers to work with. If you have a great idea for a project or can contribute in some way, please get in touch.

PM Press
PO Box 23912
Oakland, CA 94623
www.pmpress.org

FRIENDS OF PM PRESS

Friends of PM allows you to directly help impact, amplify, and revitalize the discourse and actions of radical writers, filmmakers, and artists. It provides us with a stable foundation from which we can build upon our early successes and provides a much-needed subsidy for the materials that can't necessarily pay their own way. You can help make that happen—and receive every new title automatically delivered to your door once a month—by joining as a Friend of PM Press. And, we'll throw in a free T-shirt when you sign up.

- **$30 a month** Get all books and pamphlets plus 50% discount on all webstore purchases

- **$40 a month** Get all PM Press releases (including CDs and DVDs) plus 50% discount on all webstore purchases

- **$100 a month** Superstar—Everything plus PM merchandise, free downloads, and 50% discount on all webstore purchases

For those who can't afford $30 or more a month, we're introducing **Sustainer Rates** at $15, $10 and $5. Sustainers get a free PM Press T-shirt and a 50% discount on all purchases from our website.

Your Visa or Mastercard will be billed once a month, until you tell us to stop. Or until our efforts succeed in bringing the revolution around. Or the financial meltdown of Capital makes plastic redundant. Whichever comes first.

Girl Gangs, Biker Boys, and Real Cool Cats: Pulp Fiction and Youth Culture, 1950 to 1980

Edited by Iain McIntyre and Andrew Nette
with a Foreword by Peter Doyle

ISBN: 978-1-62963-438-8
$29.95   336 pages

Girl Gangs, Biker Boys, and Real Cool Cats is the first comprehensive account of how the rise of postwar youth culture was depicted in mass-market pulp fiction. As the young created new styles in music, fashion, and culture, pulp fiction shadowed their every move, hyping and exploiting their behaviour, dress, and language for mass consumption and cheap thrills. From the juvenile delinquent gangs of the early 1950s through the beats and hippies, on to bikers, skinheads, and punks, pulp fiction left no trend untouched. With their lurid covers and wild, action-packed plots, these books reveal as much about society's deepest desires and fears as they do about the subcultures themselves.

Girl Gangs features approximately 400 full-color covers, many of them never reprinted before. With 70 in-depth author interviews, illustrated biographies, and previously unpublished articles from more than 20 popular culture critics and scholars from the US, UK, and Australia, the book goes behind the scenes to look at the authors and publishers, how they worked, where they drew their inspiration and—often overlooked—the actual words they wrote. Books by well-known authors such as Harlan Ellison and Lawrence Block are discussed alongside neglected obscurities and former bestsellers ripe for rediscovery. It is a must read for anyone interested in pulp fiction, lost literary history, retro and subcultural style, and the history of postwar youth culture.

Contributors include Nicolas Tredell, Alwyn W. Turner, Mike Stax, Clinton Walker, Bill Osgerby, David Rife, J.F. Norris, Stewart Home, James Cockington, Joe Blevins, Brian Coffey, James Doig, David James Foster, Matthew Asprey Gear, Molly Grattan, Brian Greene, John Harrison, David Kiersh, Austin Matthews, and Robert Baker.

"*Girl Gangs, Biker Boys, and Real Cool Cats is populated by the bad boys and girls of mid-twentieth-century pulp fiction. Rumblers and rebels, beats and bikers, hepcats and hippies—pretty much everybody your mother used to warn you about. Nette and McIntyre have curated a riotous party that you won't want to leave, even though you might get your wallet stolen or your teeth kicked in at any given moment.*"
—Duane Swierczynski, two-time Edgar nominee, author of *Canary* and *Revolver*

"*The underbelly of literature has been ignored for too long. This book redresses that imbalance, as over twenty authors explore low-life fiction in Australia, the UK, and the USA. Thoughtfully written and delightfully accessible, this is a book for all seasoned readers.*"
—Toni Johnson-Woods, author of *Pulp: A Collector's Book of Australian Pulp Fiction Covers*

On the Fly! Hobo Literature and Songs, 1879–1941

Edited by Iain McIntyre

ISBN: 978-1-62963-518-7
$27.95   544 pages

From the 1870s until the Second World War, millions of Americans left their homes to board freight trains that would carry them vast distances, sometimes to waiting work, often to points unknown. Congregating in skid rows, socializing around campfires, and bringing in the nation's crops, these drifters were set apart from conformist America by a lifestyle possessing its own haunts, vocabulary, and cultural, sexual, and ethical standards. Alternately derided and lionized for their footloose ways and nonconformity, hoboes played a crucial and largely neglected role in the creation of not only America's infrastructure, industry, and agriculture but also its culture, politics, and music.

The first anthology of its kind, *On the Fly!* brings forth the lost voices of Hobohemia. Dozens of stories, poems, songs, stories, and articles produced by hoboes are brought together to create an insider history of the subculture's rise and fall. Adrenaline-charged tales of train hopping, scams, and political agitation are combined with humorous and satirical songs, razor sharp reportage and unique insights into the lives of the women and men who crisscrossed America in search of survival and adventure.

From iconic figures such as labor martyr Joe Hill and socialist novelist Jack London through to pioneering blues and country musicians, and little-known correspondents for the likes of the Hobo News, the authors and songwriters contained in *On the Fly!* run the full gamut of Hobohemia's wide cultural and geographical embrace. With little of the original memoirs, literature, and verse remaining in print, this collection, aided by a glossary of hobo vernacular and numerous illustrations and photos, provides a comprehensive and entertaining guide to the life and times of a uniquely American icon. Read on to enter a world where hoboes, tramps, radicals, and bums gather in jungles, flop houses, and boxcars; where gandy dancers, bindlestiffs, and timber beasts roam the rails once more.

"This book is a tantalizing boxcar ride back through the history of the hobo, all told from the hobo's point of view. What more could anyone ask?"
—Paul Garon, coeditor of *What's the Use of Walking If There's a Freight Train Going Your Way? Black Hoboes & Their Songs* and author of *Blues and the Poetic Spirit*

*"*On the Fly! *gathers and reassembles forgotten fragments of a lost counterculture that was once so vast it practically defined the working-class experience in the United States. Its call was so alluring to young men of all classes that the hobo became the most commonly depicted character in American popular culture between 1900 and 1920. This collection represents the view from within, the stories and perspectives of those who lived the life of The Road, carrying its burdens and glorying in its freedoms.* On the Fly! *is indispensable for understanding not only the hobo life but also the on-the-ground history of our urban industrial order."*
—Todd DePastino, author of *Citizen Hobo: How a Century of Homelessness Shaped America*

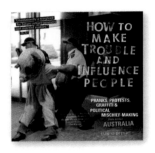

How to Make Trouble and Influence People: Pranks, Protests, Graffiti & Political Mischief-Making from across Australia

Iain McIntyre with Forewords by Andrew Hansen and Josh MacPhee

ISBN: 978-1-60486-595-0
$24.95   320 pages

This book reveals Australia's radical past through more than 500 tales of Indigenous resistance, convict revolts and escapes, picket line hijinks, student occupations, creative direct action, street art, media pranks, urban interventions, squatting, blockades, banner drops, guerilla theater, and billboard liberation. Twelve key Australian activists and pranksters are interviewed regarding their opposition to racism, nuclear power, war, economic exploitation, and religious conservatism via humor and creativity. Featuring more than 300 spectacular images *How to Make Trouble and Influence People* is an inspiring, and at times hilarious, record of resistance that will appeal to readers everywhere.

"I noticed clear back on my first visit in '83 that radical Aussies fighting back seem to be far more tenacious and creative than most Americans—Roxby Downs, that damned Franklin dam in Tasmania, Operation Titstorm, etc. A far better way to heat up the planet than your lovely mining companies. So keep up the good work! A prank a day keeps the dog leash away."
—Jello Biafra

"A fascinating recovery of Australia's neglected past and a worthy inspiration to today's would-be troublemakers."
—Sean Scalmer, author of *Dissent Events: Protest, The Media and the Political Gimmick in Australia*

"The perfect book for enlightened coffee tables."
—Rachel Evans, *Green Left Weekly*

"If you've ever thought of speaking out about an issue or have idly wondered what you could do to make the world a better place, this is the book for you! Fascinating interviews, quirky historical snippets and stunning photos chronicling all the Australians who have made a difference and who have done so with courage, audacity and a lot of humour! Keep it on your desk at work for all those moments when you need some inspiration, a bit of hope or just a good laugh."
—Jill Sparrow, co-author *Radical Melbourne* 1 & 2

"Fascinating interviews with Australia's best troublemakers make for a riotous scrapbook covering our radical history of revolts and resistance."
—Rachel Power, *Australian Education Union News*

"McIntyre has amassed hundreds of tales alongside dramatic photographs in what is unashamedly a songbook for Australia's future culture-jammers and mischief makers."
—Katherine Wilson, *The Age*

The Jook

Gary Phillips

ISBN: 978-1-60486-040-5
$15.95   256 pages

Zelmont Raines has slid a long way since his ability to jook, to outmaneuver his opponents on the field, made him a Super Bowl–winning wide receiver, earning him lucrative endorsement deals and more than his share of female attention. But Zee hasn't always been good at saying no, so a series of missteps involving drugs, a paternity suit or two, legal entanglements, shaky investments, and recurring injuries have virtually sidelined his career.

That is until Los Angeles gets a new pro franchise, the Barons, and Zelmont has one last chance at the big time he dearly misses. Just as it seems he might be getting back in the flow, he's enraptured by Wilma Wells, the leggy and brainy lawyer for the team—who has a ruthless game plan all her own. And it's Zelmont who might get jooked.

"Phillips, author of the acclaimed Ivan Monk *series, takes elements of Jim Thompson (the ending), black-exploitation flicks (the profanity-fueled dialogue), and* Penthouse *magazine (the sex is anatomically correct) to create an over-the-top violent caper in which there is no honor, no respect, no love, and plenty of money. Anyone who liked George Pelecanos'* King Suckerman *is going to love this even-grittier take on many of the same themes."*
—Wes Lukowsky, *Booklist*

"Enough gritty gossip, blistering action and trash talk to make real life L.A. seem comparatively wholesome."
—Kirkus Reviews

"Gary Phillips writes tough and gritty parables about life and death on the mean streets—a place where sometimes just surviving is a noble enough cause. His is a voice that should be heard and celebrated. It rings true once again in The Jook, *a story where all of Phillips' talents are on display."*
—Michael Connelly, author of the *Harry Bosch* books

The Underbelly

Gary Phillips

ISBN: 978-1-60486-206-5
$14.00   160 pages

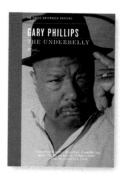

Having grown up in late-sixties South Central Los Angeles, Gary Phillips vividly recalls stories of what happened to brothers who ran afoul of the "polices" of the 77th Division. Small wonder that in his teens he organized against police abuse, later became active in the antiapartheid movement, was down against the contras, did duty as a labor rep, worked for a political action committee, and taught incarcerated youth. So of course matters of race, class, and the social fabric, along with influences of blaxploitation films and Jack Kirby comic books, permeate his crime and mystery stories. *The Underbelly* is a novella about a semi-homeless Vietnam vet searching for a disabled friend gone missing from Skid Row. It's a solo sortie where the flashback-prone protagonist must deal with gentrification, kick-ass community organizers, an elderly sexpot, a magical skull, chronic-lovin' knuckleheads, and the perils of chili-cheese fries at midnight. *The Underbelly* is illustrated with photos and drawings.

Plus . . . A rollicking interview wherein Phillips riffs on Ghetto Lit, politics, noir and the proletariat, the good negroes and bad knee-grows of pop culture, Redd Foxx and Lord Buckley, and wrestles with the future of books in the age of want.

"Honesty, distinctive characters, absurdity and good writing are here in Phillips's work."
—Washington Post

"Magrady's adventures, with a distinctive noir feeling and appreciation for comic books, started as an online, serialized mystery. Drawings and an interview with Phillips enhance the package, offering a compelling perspective on race and class issues in South Central L.A."
—Booklist

"Phillips writes some of the most earnest and engaging crime noir currently being written.
—Spinetingler

Sisters of the Revolution: A Feminist Speculative Fiction Anthology

Edited by Ann VanderMeer and Jeff VanderMeer

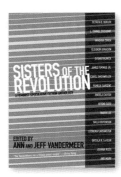

ISBN: 978-1-62963-035-9
$15.95   352 pages

Sisters of the Revolution gathers a highly curated selection of feminist speculative fiction (science fiction, fantasy, horror, and more) chosen by one of the most respected editorial teams in speculative literature today, the award-winning Ann and Jeff VanderMeer. Including stories from the 1970s to the present day, the collection seeks to expand the conversation about feminism while engaging the reader in a wealth of imaginative ideas.

From the literary heft of Angela Carter to the searing power of Octavia Butler, *Sisters of the Revolution* gathers daring examples of speculative fiction's engagement with feminism. Dark, satirical stories such as Eileen Gunn's "Stable Strategies for Middle Management" and the disturbing horror of James Tiptree Jr.'s "The Screwfly Solution" reveal the charged intensity at work in the field. Including new, emerging voices like Nnedi Okorafor and featuring international contributions from Angelica Gorodischer and many more, *Sisters of the Revolution* seeks to expand the ideas of both contemporary fiction and feminism to new fronts. Moving from the fantastic to the futuristic, the subtle to the surreal, these stories will provoke thoughts and emotions about feminism like no other book available today.

Contributors include: Angela Carter, Angelica Gorodischer, Anne Richter, Carol Emshwiller, Catherynne M. Valente, Eileen Gunn, Eleanor Arnason, Elizabeth Vonarburg, Hiromi Goto, James Tiptree Jr., Joanna Russ, Karin Tidbeck, Kelley Eskridge, Kelly Barnhill, Kit Reed, L. Timmel Duchamp, Leena Krohn, Leonora Carrington, Nalo Hopkinson, Nnedi Okorafor, Octavia Butler, Pamela Sargent, Pat Murphy, Rachel Swirsky, Rose Lemberg, Susan Palwick, Tanith Lee, Ursula K. Le Guin, and Vandana Singh.

Jewish Noir

Edited by Kenneth Wishnia

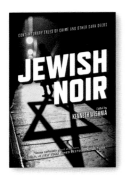

ISBN: 978-1-62963-111-0
$17.95   432 pages

Jewish Noir is a unique collection of new stories by Jewish and non-Jewish literary and genre writers, including numerous award-winning authors such as Marge Piercy, Harlan Ellison, S.J. Rozan, Nancy Richler, Moe Prager (Reed Farrel Coleman), Wendy Hornsby, Charles Ardai, and Kenneth Wishnia. The stories explore such issues as the Holocaust and its long-term effects on subsequent generations, anti-Semitism in the mid- and late-twentieth-century United States, and the dark side of the Diaspora (the decline of revolutionary fervor, the passing of generations, the Golden Ghetto, etc.). The stories in this collection also include many "teachable moments" about the history of prejudice, and the contradictions of ethnic identity and assimilation into American society.

"Stirring. Evocative. Penetrating."
—Elie Wiesel (on Stephen Jay Schwartz's "Yahrzeit Candle")

"Wishnia presents the world of Ashkenazi Jewry with a keen eye for detail. Wishnia never judges his characters, but creates three-dimensional people who live in a very dangerous world."
—*The Jewish Press* on "The Fifth Servant"

"[Wishnia writes for] a diverse audience of intelligent readers. I predict a bright future for Kenneth Wishnia, filled with loyal readers who enjoy a serious and entertaining story. I eagerly await his next venture into any period of Jewish history."
—*Jewish Book World*, on "The Fifth Servant"

"Wishnia's works are addictive, thought provoking page-turners."
—*Impulsive Reviews*

Fire on the Mountain

Terry Bisson with an Introduction by Mumia Abu-Jamal

ISBN: 978-1-60486-087-0
$15.95   208 pages

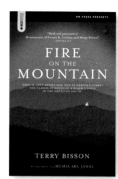

It's 1959 in socialist Virginia. The Deep South is an independent Black nation called Nova Africa. The second Mars expedition is about to touch down on the red planet. And a pregnant scientist is climbing the Blue Ridge in search of her great-great grandfather, a teenage slave who fought with John Brown and Harriet Tubman's guerrilla army.

Long unavailable in the U.S., published in France as *Nova Africa*, *Fire on the Mountain* is the story of what might have happened if John Brown's raid on Harper's Ferry had succeeded—and the Civil War had been started not by the slave owners but the abolitionists.

"History revisioned, turned inside out . . . Bisson's wild and wonderful imagination has taken some strange turns to arrive at such a destination."
—Madison Smartt Bell, Anisfield-Wolf Award winner and author of *Devil's Dream*

"You don't forget Bisson's characters, even well after you've finished his books. His Fire on the Mountain *does for the Civil War what Philip K. Dick's* The Man in the High Castle *did for World War Two."*
—George Alec Effinger, winner of the Hugo and Nebula awards for *Schrödinger's Kitten*, and author of the *Marîd Audran* trilogy.

"A talent for evoking the joyful, vertiginous experiences of a world at fundamental turning points."
—*Publishers Weekly*

"Few works have moved me as deeply, as thoroughly, as Terry Bisson's Fire on the Mountain . . . *With this single poignant story, Bisson molds a world as sweet as banana cream pies, and as briny as hot tears."*
—Mumia Abu-Jamal, death row prisoner and author of *Live From Death Row*, from the Introduction.

Dance the Eagle to Sleep: A Novel

Marge Piercy

ISBN: 978-1-60486-456-4
$17.95   208 pages

Originally published in 1970, Marge Piercy's second novel follows the lives of four teenagers, in a near-future society, as they rebel against a military draft and "the system." The occupation of Franklin High School begins, and with it, the open rebellion of America's youth against their channeled, unrewarding lives and the self-serving, plastic society that directs them.

From the disillusionment and alienation of the young at the center of the revolt, to their attempts to build a visionary new society, the nationwide following they gain and the brutally complete repression that inevitably follows, this is a future fiction without a drop of fantasy. As driving, violent, and nuanced today as it was 40 years ago, this anniversary edition includes a new introduction by the author reflecting unapologetically on the novel and the times from which it emerged.

*"*Dance the Eagle to Sleep *bears a strong family resemblance, in kind and quality, to William Golding's* Lord of the Flies *and to Anthony Burgess'* A Clockwork Orange. *It would be no surprise to see it become, like these others, a totem and legend of the young."*
—*Time*

*"*Dance the Eagle to Sleep *is a vision, not an argument . . . It is brilliant. Miss Piercy was a published poet before she resorted to the novel, exploiting its didactic aspect, and her prose crackles, depolarizes, sends shivers leaping across the synaptic cleft. The 'eagle' is America, bald and all but extinct. The 'dance' is performed by the tribal young, the self-designated 'Indians,' after their council meetings, to celebrate their bodies and their escape from the cannibalizing 'system.' The eagle isn't danced to sleep; it sends bombers to devastate the communes of the young . . . What a frightening, marvelous book!"*
—*New York Times*

The Explosion of Deferred Dreams: Musical Renaissance and Social Revolution in San Francisco, 1965–1975

Mat Callahan

ISBN: 978-1-62963-231-5
$22.95   352 pages

As the fiftieth anniversary of the Summer of Love floods the media with debates and celebrations of music, political movements, "flower power," "acid rock," and "hippies," *The Explosion of Deferred Dreams* offers a critical reexamination of the interwoven political and musical happenings in San Francisco in the Sixties. Author, musician, and native San Franciscan Mat Callahan explores the dynamic links between the Black Panthers and Sly and the Family Stone, the United Farm Workers and Santana, the Indian Occupation of Alcatraz and the San Francisco Mime Troupe, and the New Left and the counterculture.

Callahan's meticulous, impassioned arguments both expose and reframe the political and social context for the San Francisco Sound and the vibrant subcultural uprisings with which it is associated. Using dozens of original interviews, primary sources, and personal experiences, the author shows how the intense interplay of artistic and political movements put San Francisco, briefly, in the forefront of a worldwide revolutionary upsurge.

A must-read for any musician, historian, or person who "was there" (or longed to have been), *The Explosion of Deferred Dreams* is substantive and provocative, inviting us to reinvigorate our historical sense-making of an era that assumes a mythic role in the contemporary American zeitgeist.

"All too often, people talk about the '60s without mentioning our music and the fun we had trying to smash the state and create a culture based upon love. Mat Callahan's book is a necessary corrective."
—George Katsiaficas, author of *The Imagination of the New Left: A Global Analysis of 1968*

Patty Hearst & The Twinkie Murders: A Tale of Two Trials

Paul Krassner

ISBN: 978-1-629630-38-0
$12.00   128 pages

Patty Hearst & The Twinkie Murders is a darkly satiric take on two of the most famous cases of our era: the kidnapping of heiress Patty Hearst, and the shocking assassination of San Francisco Mayor George Moscone and gay leader Harvey Milk. As a reporter for the *Berkeley Barb*, Paul Krassner was ringside at the spectacular California trials. Krassner's deadpan, hilarious style captures the nightmare reality behind the absurdities of the courtroom circus.

Using his infamous satiric pen and investigative chops, Krassner gets to the truth behind the events: the role of the police and FBI, the real deal with Patty and the SLA, and what really happened in Patty's infamous closet.

Plus . . . A merciless exposé of the "Taliban" wing of the gay movement and their scandalous attacks on alt-rock star Michelle Shocked.

Also featured is our Outspoken Interview, an irreverent and fascinating romp through the secret history of America's radical underground. Names will be named.

"Krassner is an expert at ferreting out hypocrisy and absurdism from the more solemn crannies of American culture."
—*New York Times*

"Krassner has the uncanny ability to alter your perceptions permanently."
—*Los Angeles Times*

"Krassner not only attacks establishment values; he attacks decency in general."
—Harry Reasoner, ABC News

"The FBI was right—this man is dangerous—and funny, and necessary."
—George Carlin